LEARNING JAVA™

THROUGH APPLICATIONS

A GRAPHICAL APPROACH

LEARNING JAVA™ THROUGH APPLICATIONS
A GRAPHICAL APPROACH

Duane J. Jarc

CHARLES RIVER MEDIA, INC.
Hingham, Massachusetts

Acquisitions Editor: James Walsh
Cover Design: Tyler Creative

CHARLES RIVER MEDIA, INC.
10 Downer Avenue
Hingham, Massachusetts 02043
781-740-0400
781-740-8816 (FAX)
info@charlesriver.com
www.charlesriver.com

This book is printed on acid-free paper.

Duane J. Jarc. *Learning Java Through Applications: A Graphical Approach*
ISBN: 1-58450-376-9

All brand names and product names mentioned in this book are trademarks or service marks of their respective companies. Any omission or misuse (of any kind) of service marks or trademarks should not be regarded as intent to infringe on the property of others. The publisher recognizes and respects all marks used by companies, manufacturers, and developers as a means to distinguish their products.

Library of Congress Cataloging-in-Publication Data
Jarc, Duane J.
  Learning Java through applications : a graphical approach / Duane J. Jarc.
     p. cm.
  Includes index.
  ISBN 1-58450-376-9 (pbk. with cd-rom : alk. paper)
1. Java (Computer program language) I. Title.
  QA76.73.J38J356 2005
  005.13'3—dc22

                    2005004789

Printed in the United States of America
05 7 6 5 4 3 2 First Edition

CHARLES RIVER MEDIA titles are available for site license or bulk purchase by institutions, user groups, corporations, etc. For additional information, please contact the Special Sales Department at 781-740-0400.

Requests for replacement of a defective CD-ROM must be accompanied by the original disc, your mailing address, telephone number, date of purchase, and purchase price. Please state the nature of the problem, and send the information to CHARLES RIVER MEDIA, INC., 10 Downer Avenue, Hingham, Massachusetts 02043. CRM's sole obligation to the purchaser is to replace the disc, based on defective materials or faulty workmanship, but not on the operation or functionality of the product.

In memory of my mother, my first teacher

Contents

Acknowledgments

I would like to thank Stephen Mosberg of Charles River Media, who first approached me with an inquiry regarding whether I would be interested in writing a book. I also would like to thank Jim Walsh of Charles River for his influence in shaping the approach taken in this book. It was because of his suggestions that what started as a more traditional C++ book evolved into this current book on Java with a strong emphasis on graphics, using pictures, puzzles, and games for many of the examples.

Duane J. Jarc

Preface

WHY JAVA?

Java has become the predominate language used for teaching beginning programming, which is the primary reason for its choice as the language used in this book. Java offers some important advantages compared to the language that it has most often replaced—C++. Among the most important advantages for beginners is the fact that Java generates run-time errors rather than allowing the operating system to catch errors or, worse, letting them go undetected. Furthermore, Java is a simplification of C++, which has in many ways become a complicated language. That simplification involved the elimination of some features like the separation of class specifications from their bodies, explicit call by reference, explicit pointers, operator overloading, the ability to pass methods as parameters, enumerated types and generics. Recognizing that some important and necessary features had been lost, the latest version of Java, originally called version 1.5, but now referred to as version 5.0, which we use in this book, has reintroduced the last two features—enumerated types and generics. A minor improvement is the fact that Java standardized the size of primitive data types, eliminated problematic unsigned types, and required type casts on narrowing assignments.

As an introductory language, we should note that Java is not without its problems. Foremost among them is the fact that "one must know a lot, just to do a little." Even simple programs require the understanding of many language features. The alternative, of course, is to just accept some things as given without much explanation. Simple input and output is an example of something that is not simple in Java. Although the introduction of the Scanner class permits a simplified form of input, the standard approach to input requires explicit parsing and catching input format errors, or at least acknowledging they will be propagated. Another example of needing to understand complex ideas early results from the fact that all data but primitive variables are dynamically allocated. Beginners must confront the issues related to shallow versus deep copying of objects much earlier than would be true using a language like C++ that allows the programmer to decide whether static or dynamic allocation is used. Because the programmer is not free to make that decision in Java, the importance of this distinction is often lost. The lack of explicit pointers with the dynamically allocated object compounds this problem. Furthermore, its implications with the use of parameters can easily be glossed over.

Java has also presented some new opportunities, missing from most of its predecessor languages, including C++. The most important among them is the inclusion of standard classes in Java for graphics and graphical user interfaces and the ability to write applets that can be embedded in Web pages. Also the requirement that all Java methods be included in a class encourages an earlier introduction of object-oriented concepts.

APPROACH

The decision of how to present Java to beginning programmers, capitalizing on its advantages and the opportunities it presents, while minimizing some of the associated problems, can be a challenge. Most current introductory Java books emphasize an objects-first approach capitalizing on the fact that every Java program must contain a class—an important difference compared to C++. We certainly endorse the objects-first approach, but also recognize that many attempts at presenting objects-first results in an everything-first approach, which can easily overwhelm anyone new to the language. Many introductory Java books present the entire control structure of the language in the third chapter using a single class with a single method main, then in the guise of doing objects-first jump to multi-class, multi-method programs by the fourth chapter. Such a transition is difficult for most beginners.

We noted that Java incorporates graphics into its standard libraries, offering the opportunity to create interesting programs that are event driven and to use graphics and graphical user interfaces. Furthermore, Java permits the creation of applets. Consequently, many introductory texts include all of these language features in addition to more traditional command-line interactive programs and batch style programs that accept file input and produce file output. These additional topics add to a number of new ideas that any beginner must master.

Having discussed the approach that many other authors have taken, let's consider the approach taken in this book. Although we have already indicated that we endorse the objects-first approach, we believe it must be done gradually. Furthermore, we believe that taking advantage of the graphics and graphical interfaces possible in Java is important. It too, must be done gradually and should be done in place of more traditional command-line applications initially.

We begin with applets first. All the programs in the first four chapters are applets. Using this approach we can explore many important object-oriented concepts using a single applet object. In Chapter 3, for example, we present a detailed look at scope and lifetime, considering local and class-wide scope and the effects of the access modifiers public and private. Furthermore, we examine the reasons for deciding what level of scope a particular data element requires. This approach also allows a careful discussion of method calls early—distinguishing instance method calls from class method calls, and calls to void methods from those that return values. It also allows the beginner to fully grasp both public and private methods in a program consisting of a single class with several methods. Issues of memory allocation can be avoided at this point because, although we are working with objects, there is only one and the browser creates it. Consequently, explicit dynamic allocation with new is not required in any program in the first four chapters.

Programs that produce graphical output are easier for many new to programming because it is easy to "see" what the program is doing. The final advantage of doing applets first is that it allows us to take advantage of Java graphics without having to deal with all the details associated with creating windows. The Web browser handles those details for us.

Because of the fact that performing simple input involves a number of complexities, we have deferred all real input until Chapter 4, using randomly generated input in the first three chapters. When we introduce input in Chapter 4, we use a custom package InputOutput to avoid a discussion of parsing and catching exceptions. One important difference is that to preserve the use of a graphical user interface, our package uses JOptionPane exclusively and does not permit command-line input. We defer any discussion of command-line input or output until Chapter 11, when files are introduced. This decision is a conscious effort to avoid doing everything first. Since our focus is using graphical-user interfaces, we begin with programs that use such interfaces instead of ones that use command-line interfaces.

Because we have elected to present many object-oriented concepts early, we defer discussing the control structures. Furthermore, to emphasize a gradual approach, we have separated them into two chapters. Our separation is not the customary one chapter on selection and the second on iteration. Instead we have introduced the discrete control statements—the switch and for—first in Chapter 4 and defer the more general control statements until Chapter 6. This order is not customary either. Most books begin with the if and while because they are syntactically simpler. We believe that semantic simplicity is more important. Unlike the general control statements, the discrete control statements do not involve logical expressions. We capitalize on the *for-each* style for statement that was added to Java 5.0, introducing it first, then we discuss the more general for statement with a highly constrained syntax.

Another feature of Java 5.0 that we fully exploit is the type-safe enumerated types. We first introduce them in their simplest form in Chapter 4 to facilitate the discussion of the *for-each* style `for` statement. We return to them in Chapter 5 and illustrate how enumerated types can have associated data and methods. We discuss them again in Chapter 14, at which time we present polymorphic enumerated types as an introduction to abstract classes.

We have already noted that because all objects are dynamically allocated in Java, the issues related to shallow and deep copying and comparing objects needs to be addressed early. With our approach of applets first, we avoid any use of explicit dynamic allocation using `new` until Chapter 5. Although strings are introduced in Chapter 4, their dynamic allocation can initially be hidden by the use of string literals. Furthermore, being immutable, they side-step the problems of shallow copies. Chapter 5 is also our first need for constructors. We introduce class constructors together with the explicit dynamic allocation of objects. At the same time dynamic allocation is introduced, all its related issues are discussed in detail, including its implications with parameters. The significance of immutable objects is introduced in this context. In addition, we revisit enumerated types in Chapter 5, illustrating how constructors can be defined for enumerated types.

As another example of our effort to introduce ideas gradually, we distribute the introduction of the primitive data types across the first six chapters, introducing the integer types in the first chapter, floating point types in the second chapter, and characters in the fourth chapter. Because we discuss general control structures in Chapter 6, the discussion of logical expressions and the primitive type `boolean` are deferred until then as well.

We believe that it is important to introduce not only the syntax of object-oriented programming but also the principles that underlie its design. To achieve that goal, we introduce important object-oriented principles such as class invariants early, in Chapter 7 in conjunction with our discussion of arrays. The importance of class relationships is also emphasized, with two chapters on class relationships: Chapter 10, which discusses composition, and Chapter 12, which explains aggregation and generalization relationships. The *Unified Modeling Language* (UML) symbolism for expressing such relationships is presented along with the design concepts. The more complicated notion of inheritance hierarchies and abstract classes is deferred until Chapter 14.

The new features of Java are fully utilized in our presentation and integrated into the overall approach. As we noted earlier, we take advantage of the *for-each* statement to allow us to introduce iteration before logical expressions and continue to explore the benefits of that statement in Chapter 8. In that chapter we demonstrate how a collection class can be written that allows the *for-each* statement to be used to iterate across it. To facilitate the construction of that collection class, we introduce generics, a version 5.0 addition. Having generics allows us to introduce collection classes before fully explaining inheritance, the associated hierarchies and the role of the class Object at their root.

For simplicity, throughout the first ten chapters, all input and output is done using the class InputOutput mentioned earlier that relies on the standard Java class JOptionPane and a class called InputFile that provides an abstraction of an input file. In Chapter 11, we discuss exceptions and then discuss the details of the class InputOutput. We then proceed to explore other kinds of input/output, such as file input/output and input/output from the command-line.

The idea of programs being triggered by more than one event is presented early, starting with the idea in Chapter 3—using an example containing the paint and init methods, which are both called from the browser. Although mouse event handling is introduced in Chapter 8 as a way to introduce interfaces, the broader idea of event driven programs that use nonmodal input is deferred until Chapter 13.

Although graphical output is used starting with the very first chapter, constructing graphical user interfaces, although not complicated, is laden with detail. Consequently, its details are not presented until Chapters 13 and 14.

One final important characteristic of the approach taken in this book is the use of a large example as the final example in each chapter to illustrate the important concepts presented in that chapter. Those examples use graphics and eventually graphical user interfaces. These examples increase in size as the chapters progress. Many of the examples involve geometric patterns, puzzles, or games—examples chosen that capitalize on the use of graphics and allow the presentation of the examples that should be interesting to the reader. The title "Learning Java through Applications" refers to applications in the generic sense rather than the Java specific meaning, and highlights the fact that we emphasize whole programs including the capstone project in each chapter. Nonetheless, beginning in Chapter 5, we do make exclusive use of Java applications.

AUDIENCE

This book is written in the style of a textbook that is suitable for students who are new to programming and to Java. For those new to both programming and Java, we believe that this book contains far more material than is suitable for a one semester course. Each chapter contains a variety of exercises, including review questions covering the major concepts of the chapter, together with short programming exercises and more complete programming projects.

ON THE CD

Although we occasionally include short program fragments, we favor complete programs, which include both applets and applications. All programs contained in the program listings are included on the CD-ROM that accompanies this book. This approach makes this book useful for those who are engaged in self-study of the Java programming language.

Despite the fact that this book is suitable for beginners, we believe that more advanced students, who have some previous experience with Java will find this book beneficial, particularly those who may be interested in learning some of the features of version 5.0 of Java.

One final note concerns the level of mathematical knowledge expected of the reader. Because this book makes extensive use of graphics, some familiarly with trigonometry will be helpful to understand the algorithms for drawing regular polygons, which is used in a number of examples. Other examples concern some topics from number theory that, although not difficult, require some mathematical skill to fully appreciate. We make no apology for some mathematical expectations since many studies have shown math skills as one of the best predictors of success in learning programming.

PROGRAM STYLE

As we indicated earlier, complete programs are provided wherever possible. Every program has been compiled and executed with Java's new version 5.0 compiler and interpreter.

We have elected the approach of avoiding the use of comments in programs. In place of comments, explanatory identifiers have been used, together with a narrative description of the program. These narrative descriptions could become comments in working versions of these programs. We have chosen to number the lines of all program listings to make it easier to identify the line under discussion.

The lexical conventions followed are the standard ones for Java programs. As has become customary, a constant-width font has been used for programs because it is nonproportional spaced.

1 An Overview of Programming Languages and an Introduction to Java

In this chapter

- Introduction
- Programs, Programming Languages, and Programmers
- Syntax and Semantics
- Constant Declarations and Method Calls
- Graphical Output
- Our First Java Applet
- Program Development

INTRODUCTION

Our approach to presenting Java is to focus on programs that have a graphical component, an ability that using Java easily affords us, unlike most earlier programming languages. As such, this book does not begin with the customary "Hello World" program that displays a message on the screen. In fact, *textual output*—outputting a sequence of characters to a DOS window, is something we defer to a later chapter. Because of the visual nature of programs that draw images, they make better examples with which to learn programming and allow us to write some interesting programs involving geometric patterns initially, then puzzles and games once the fundamentals have been established.

Another important characteristic of the approach taken is to present objects first, as is customary with Java, but incrementally—slowly increasing the size and

1

complexity of the programs from one chapter to the next. Beginning with applets, rather than applications, in the first several chapters, we are able to achieve this goal.

Java and the Web

In addition to Java's ability to develop programs that present a graphical-user interface (GUI), Java has had an intimate connection with the Web from the beginning. Three kinds of programs can be written in Java: *applets, servlets,* and *applications.* An applet is a program run with a Web browser, which runs on the *client side*—the user's computer. A servlet runs on the *server side*—the computer from which the Web page was downloaded. Although applications can be downloaded from the Web, they are less intimately connected with it than the other two kinds of programs. In this book we discuss only applets and applications. In the next four chapters we confine our examples to applets. In the subsequent chapters, the programs are exclusively applications.

Our reason for beginning with an applet is that it is easier to write a simple applet that produces graphical output than to write application. The reason that such applets are simpler is that they are not really whole programs like applications. They are instead an extension of the Web browser. Web browsers contain an interpreter that runs applets that are embedded in Web pages. Programs that have a graphical user interface must create a window and embed some objects in that window. With applets, the Web browser already has created a window that we can use, and it creates the applet object for us and embeds it in the window.

In general, Java programs consist of a collection of *classes*; classes contain a collection of *methods*. The simplest applets consist of a single class containing a single method named `paint`. Before the development of operating systems containing windows, all programs ran in a *command-line interface*. Such programs, which can still be written today, have a single initiating event, which is starting the program. It then runs from start to finish. Programs that contain a GUI might respond to a variety of events, such as clicking the mouse, pressing a button, and so on. The part of the operating system that manages the windows triggers other events that such programs must also respond to. The `paint` method of a simple Java applet is initiated whenever something is done to the window in which it is embedded that requires the repainting of the window. Painting is initiated when a Web page containing an applet is first loaded, but it is performed again whenever the window containing the applet is resized, for example.

PROGRAMS, PROGRAMMING LANGUAGES, AND PROGRAMMERS

Before beginning with the details of the Java programming language, it is important to understand something about what a program is, what a programming language is, and how a programmer uses programming languages to create programs.

Anyone who has used a computer has used many programs. The operating system itself is a program. A Web browser, a word processor, and a spreadsheet are all programs. A program consists of a set of instructions that tell a computer how to perform a particular task. Every program must be written in some programming language that the computer is able to understand. Java is, of course, one such language.

Categories of Programming Languages

Let's consider the various categories of programming languages and see where Java fits. Although there are many different ways we might categorize programming languages, we will categorize them by how close they are to the native language of the machine—a term we use synonymously with computer. In fact there is only one language that a machine understands directly, which is *machine language*—a language consisting of zeros and ones that represent specific machine instructions or data values. Using such a primitive language is too difficult, so no one programs in machine language today. A closely related language is *assembly language*. What is distinctive about assembly language is the fact that there is a one-to-one correspondence between every assembly language instruction and the machine language instruction it corresponds to. The advantage of assembly language is the fact that it is a symbolic language and is therefore easier to read and write than machine language. Assembly languages are machine dependent, which means that a program written in assembly language will only run on one specific kind of computer. Assembly language is still used today when programs need to be very fast or need direct access to features of the machine hardware. Usually, some portion of every operating system is written in assembly language for those reasons.

Java belongs to a family of languages known as *high-level languages*. Languages such as C++, Ada, and Basic are also high-level languages. High-level languages differ from assembly language in a number of important ways. First, they are machine independent, meaning that a Java program can run on many different computers. Second, one line of a program written in a high-level language corresponds to many machine language instructions. Consequently a program written in Java is much shorter than the equivalent program written in assembly language. Third, modern high-level languages are structured, which means that they use *nested statements*— statements that can have other statements embedded within them—to define the *control flow* of the program—the order in which the statements of the program are executed. Unstructured languages, which predate structured languages, use *go-to* statements instead. A *go-to* statement instructs the computer to perform some statement, other than the next statement, next. Programs containing *go-to* statements can be difficult to follow because they can produce programs with a very complicated control flow. Java is one of the first languages to remove *go-to* statements from the language. We will have much more to say about nested statements as we explore the details of the Java language. Another important characteristic of all recently developed high-level languages is that they are object-oriented. We will begin exploring the significance of object-orientation in this chapter and continue examining its features throughout the book.

Before leaving our general discussion of programming languages, we should note that there is one more important category of languages that are more abstract than high-level languages. These languages are declarative languages, in contrast to the high-level languages that we have been discussing that are considered imperative. Functional languages like ML and logic languages like Prolog are considered declarative. These languages are closer to mathematics than imperative languages, and programs written in such languages are usually shorter than the equivalent program written in an imperative language. The drawback to the use of such languages is that programs written in them can be very inefficient.

The Role of the Programmer

If learning Java is your first introduction to programming, it is also important to understand your role as programmer—or software developer. What you will be learning to do is to take a specification for a problem, typically written in English, and design a solution, which is then translated into a programming language, which in our case is Java. Programming languages require much more precision than English does. English often contains ambiguity that listeners can resolve by context. To be able to design a solution given an English specification and translate that design into a programming language requires an ability to think both logically and precisely without making any assumptions.

SYNTAX AND SEMANTICS

We are now ready to discuss two important characteristics of languages—both natural languages and programming languages. All languages have *syntax*, or grammar, and *semantics*, or meaning.

Comparing English Syntax with Programming Language Syntax

An important part of learning any language involves learning the syntax for that language. Languages have syntax rules at both the *lexical level*, the level where letters form words, and at the *textual level*, where words form sentences, sentences form paragraphs, and so on. Before examining any syntax rules in Java, let's begin with English, because it has a very similar set of rules that you are familiar with, although you have probably never given them much thought.

English words, excluding acronyms, cannot be formed from any arbitrary sequence of letters. New words are coined in English periodically, and when they are, they must follow a well-defined set of syntactic rules. As an example, "zwqtj" would be an unacceptable English word. An inherent requirement is a word's ability to be pronounced. That requirement imposes rules governing the use of vowels and consonants. To be able to be pronounced, words must alternatively contain consonants and vowels. But that does not mean that they must strictly alternate between the two. Some sequences of consonants are acceptable. The sequence "str" can begin a word. By comparison, the consonant sequence "jpt" is not acceptable. If we were attempting to describe the lexical syntax of English, we could enumerate all such sequences. Furthermore, English has some other particular rules about letter order, such as the rule that a "q" must always be followed by a "u." Describing English syntax is not our intent, but what is important to understand is that programming languages have similar rules.

In English, words are categorized into various parts of speech, such as nouns, verbs, and adjectives. Although there are rules for forming words in general, there are only minor differences in the spelling of words that belong to the different parts of speech. In most cases one cannot tell from the spelling of a word whether it is noun or a verb. In some cases, the same word can be a noun in one context and a verb in another. Such potential ambiguity, incidentally, makes it more difficult for word processors to perform effective grammar checking. There are a few cases in which we can determine the part of speech of a word from its spelling. For example, we know that words ending with the suffix "ly" are usually adverbs. Words ending with the suffixes "ed" or "ing" are usually verbs.

Just as the words of English are grouped into different parts of speech, the "words" of programming languages, called *lexemes*, are grouped into different *tokens*. In programming languages, unlike English, we can always determine what kind of a token a lexeme is, based on how it is spelled. There is a definite rule for how the lexemes of each token are formed. Later in this chapter we will discuss the rule for forming one particular token, an *identifier*—one of the most frequently used tokens in programs. We will see that the lexeme number2 satisfies the rule for forming an identifier, but the lexeme 2numbers does not.

Next, we consider the textual syntax rules of English. In much the same way that the order of letters is important in forming correct words, word order is important in forming correct sentences. As an example, consider the sequence of words "in of at to by." Clearly, that would be an unacceptable, a very unacceptable, English sentence. The problem is that it contains a sequence of five consecutive prepositions. In much the same way that order of vowels and consonants is important in correctly forming words, the order of nouns, verbs, adjectives, and so on, are important in determining correct syntax of English sentences. One other important observation is that English has different kinds of sentences—declarative, interrogative, imperative, and exclamatory. Each has a different syntax rule and, in some cases, different punctuation. Declarative and imperative sentences end with periods, while an interrogative sentence ends with a question mark, and an exclamatory sentence ends with an exclamation point. In a similar way, each kind of statement in a programming language has a rule that describes the correct order of tokens and also punctuation symbols.

There are two categories of statements in every imperative programming language—declarative statements that specify the data and executable statements that determine what is to be done, often referred to as an *algorithm*. In this way, a program is much like a recipe, the ingredients corresponding to the data and the instructions corresponding to the algorithm. Whenever we encounter a new statement in the remainder of this book, we will always begin by describing its syntax. Later in this chapter, we introduce the first two such statements, one declarative statement, the constant declaration, and one executable statement, the method call statement.

The Syntax Levels of Languages

We have been drawing many comparisons between programming languages and natural languages, so let's summarize some of what has already been said and expand upon it by comparing the syntactic structure of the two kinds of languages. In Table 1.1, we compare the levels of both kinds of languages

Let's consider each level. Sequences of letters form words in natural languages, just as sequences of characters form lexemes in programming languages. Although consonants and vowels govern the correct letter order of words, it is whether characters are alphabetic, numeric, or symbolic that determines the correct character order of lexemes.

We have added one new level between words and sentences—phrases. Word sequences form phrases, and phrase sequences form sentences. In the programming language column we matched expression with phrase. It is a less than perfect analogy compared to most of the others, but it is true that expressions are a part of many different kinds of statements.

TABLE 1.1 Comparing the Levels of Natural Languages with Programming Languages

English	Java
letter	character
word	lexeme
phrase	expression
sentence	statement
paragraph	method
chapter	class
book	package

A sequence of sentences forms a paragraph in English, just like a sequence of statements forms a method in Java. Finally, paragraphs combine to form chapters, which in turn combine to form a book. In Java, a collection of methods is contained in a class and a collection of classes is contained in a package.

We have considered the similarities, but we also need to consider one important difference. Notice that we did not compare a book to a program. In fact, program was not in the list at all. Although it is true to say that a program is comprised of a collection of packages, a particular program does not "own" its component packages. It may share those packages with many other programs and it may use only some of the classes in a particular package. All of our examples will use some of the predefined Java packages, and most will use one package we have written named common, which contains code shared by many of the programs in the book.

This distinction of whether something "owns" its components or just "uses" them is an important one. When we discuss the relationships between classes later in this book, we will encounter a very similar distinction.

Semantics

Now we consider the role of semantics in natural languages and compare it to programming languages. Semantics is involved in languages in two ways—in distinguishing between what is meaningful and meaningless, and in determining the significance of meaningful language constructs.

First, let's consider the rules that languages have to determine whether something is meaningful. Like the syntax rules, the semantic rules are present at both the lexical and textual levels of the language. At the lexical level, in English, a word is meaningful if it is in the dictionary. At the textual level, whether a sentence is meaningful depends upon the relationship between certain characteristics of the words it contains. An example will help illustrate this point. Consider the sentence, "The car ate the window." First, let's observe that it is a syntactically correct declarative sentence. It contains a noun phrase, a transitive verb, and a direct object. But there are two aspects of this sentence that are problematic regarding its meaning. The first problem is that a car is an inanimate object, and the verb "to eat" applies to animate objects only. The second is that a window is an inedible object. What determines whether English sentences are meaningful has to do with a type correspondence between words. Similar rules apply in programming languages. A failure of type correspondence will result in a meaningless program, one that cannot be run.

Now let's consider the second role of semantics—referring to the meaning of a sentence in English or the meaning of a program. Because we know English, we can determine whether two sentences have the same meaning, but how about two programs? Without becoming too formal in our description, let's say that two programs that behave exactly the same from the standpoint of the external observer have the same meaning. One important thing to realize about programming is that for any given problem, there are many programs that can solve the problem—that is, many programs with the same meaning.

CONSTANT DECLARATIONS AND METHOD CALLS

We have been discussing syntax and semantics in a very general way, but now we are ready to investigate some specific syntactic and semantic aspects of Java. In this chapter, we begin with two fundamental statements necessary for creating even the simplest programs, the constant declaration statement and the method call.

Constant Declarations

Constant data is the simplest kind of data. It is the kind that does not change. Constant data, like all data, is divided into different types. In Java, there are several major categories of types—primitive types, class types, enumerated types, and array types. In this chapter we will consider only one kind of the primitive type, the integer types, which are whole number numeric values. Java actually contains several primitive types for integer values, byte, short, int, and long. The only difference between them is the amount of memory they require and, consequently, the range of values that they can contain. In Table 1.2, the memory requirements and value range of each type are shown.

Unless there is good reason to know we are dealing with smaller or larger ranges of data, we nominally will choose one of the middle choices, int.

Primitive data can be expressed in two different ways in programs. We can use the *literal constants*, which in the case of integers consist of the actual numeric val-

TABLE 1.2 The Four Different Sizes of Integers

Type	Memory	Value Range
byte	8 bits	−128 to 127
short	16 bits	−32,768 to 32,767
int	32 bits	−2,147,483,648 to 2,147,483,647
long	64 bits	−9,223,372,036,854,775,808 to 9,223,372,036,854,775,807

ues. An integer literal constant is a kind of token. Syntactically it consists of a sequence of numeric digits that does not contain a decimal point—one that represents a whole number. Negative integers must have a prefix of a minus sign, while positive integers can begin with a plus sign, but it is not required. Integer literals are of type int. If we wish to create integer literals that are so large that they need to be of type long, we must add a suffix of either l or L. So to write the integer literal for the integer ten billion, we would write 10000000000L.

Another alternative is to name constants, assigning to them their literal values once, and thereafter referring to them only by name. Even in programs that involve graphics, which typically require many numeric constants, naming them is a good idea for two reasons. First, if we ever change their value, only a single change is required. This is our first encounter with a more general principle of good software development, which is the avoidance of code duplication. The duplication that we are avoiding is the duplicate use of the literal values. All code duplication presents the same difficulty during code maintenance, which is the need to change the same thing more than once. The second advantage to naming constants is that well chosen names can make programs more readable. Writing code that is clear and easy to read is better than using many comments in the program.

The syntax for declaring integer constants is shown in Syntax Definition 1.1.

Syntax Definition 1.1 Syntax of a Constant Declaration.

```
constant_declaration
    final int  CONSTANT_1  = value_1, ..., CONSTANT_N  = value_n ;
```

The word final signifies that the names of constants follow it. Like int and the other integer type names, final is a *reserved word*, which means it cannot be used for the name of a constant or the name of anything else. Its meaning in Java is fixed. We have italicized *CONSTANT_1* to indicate that you can substitute a name of your choosing, within the allowable rules for names. The ... is not part of the Java syntax but signifies that you can have one or more such names. If more than one is present, they must be separated by commas. The semicolon in Java, like many programming languages, has the same role as a period at the end of a declarative English sentence.

In our discussion comparing English with programming languages like Java, we gave an example of an English sentence that was syntactically correct, but violated certain semantic rules of the language. Here is an example of such a statement in Java:

```
final int NUMBER = 10L;
```

Although this declaration satisfies the syntax rule for a constant declaration, there is a problem with the types. The declaration specifies an int but the constant value to which it is initialized is a literal constant of type long. In Chapter 2, we will discuss the semantic rules that govern types in much greater detail.

We mentioned that programmers are free to name constants whatever they like, within the rules of the language, so let's return to what those rules are. Eventually we will see that in Java programs, names, or what are more formally referred to as *identifiers*, are needed to name not only constants, but also variables, methods, classes, and so on. The rules for naming all identifiers are the same. They must begin with a letter or underscore followed by any additional letters, digits, or underscores. The $ is also permitted but, like leading underscores, is not recommended. In addition to these rules, there are some widely adhered-to conventions regarding names. Among them is that constant names are always written in all upper case and underscores are used to separate words in names consisting of multiple words. Being a convention, it is not enforced by the compiler.

In our first program, we will also have occasion to use some constants that are predefined in other Java classes. These constants are ones that refer to various colors. When using constants that belong to another class, we must prepend the constant name by the name of the class to which it belongs, as shown by the syntax in Syntax Definition 1.2.

Syntax Definition 1.2 Syntax of a Class Constant.

```
class_qualified_constant

    ClassName .CONSTANT_NAME
```

The dot or period punctuation that separates the class name from the constant name is punctuation that we will encounter frequently in the next section when we discuss method calls. We refer to the process of prepending the constant name with the class name as *qualifying the name*.

Method Calls

In this chapter, the only executable statement that we discuss is the method call statement. Recall that Java programs consist of packages that are made up of classes that in turn are made up of methods. The ability to reuse both classes and methods, and therefore avoid duplication, is one important reason for decomposing programs into these parts. Returning to our analogy of recipes, a cookbook for breads might contain a section on preparing the dough that would be common to many kinds of breads. Rather than duplicating these instructions in every recipe, it would make sense to include it once in the book and refer to it when recipes require it. The idea is the same with Java methods. The Java language contains many predefined classes containing predefined methods that allow Java programs to accomplish complex tasks without having to specify all the details involved.

Java contains two kinds of methods, instance and class methods. We will discuss the difference between them in a later chapter. For now, we focus exclusively on *instance methods* and how to call them. The syntax for an instance method call is shown in Syntax Definition 1.3.

Syntax Definition 1.3 Syntax of an Instance Method Call.

```
instance_method_call

    objectName .methodName (argument_1 , ... , argument_n );
```

As before, actual names must be substituted for the italicized names and the ... specifies a list, in this case of zero or more arguments separated by commas. The syntax for a method call contains two terms we have not yet discussed, *objects* and *arguments*. The idea of objects is a central one in an object-oriented language like Java, so it is one we will return to often. For now, we begin with a simple explanation of what an object is. An *object* is an instance of a class in much the same way that the number 73 is an instance of the primitive type int.

Initially we can think of the list of *arguments* as a list of constant values supplied to a method. They are input to the method in much the same way that input is supplied to a program. The input allows it to behave differently based on what values are supplied. Eventually we will see that arguments can be more general than just constants.

Every method has a *signature* that specifies how many arguments must be passed to it, what type they must be, and what they represent. In the next section we will examine some of the predefined graphics methods and their signatures, and discuss the relationship between a method's signature and the corresponding calls to that method.

GRAPHICAL OUTPUT

The concept of a user interface is familiar to anyone who has used a computer. It is the way in which the user interacts with the computer. The general characteristic of user interfaces changed when operating systems changed from command-line interfaces, such as MS-DOS, to the more graphical user interfaces associated with operating systems such as Windows. Java, like any programming language, provides the ability to write programs that run in a command-line environment. Unlike many earlier programming languages, Java also contains built-in classes that allow us to write programs that present a graphical interface to the user. Because these programs are more commonly used today, almost all the programs in this book will be of this type.

Understanding how graphical output is generated in Java requires an understanding of Cartesian (*x-y*) coordinates that one generally first encounters in algebra. The nature of this output differs from the mathematical approach in several ways. First, graphical output on all monitors consists of a discrete number of *pixels*—picture elements. Consequently, the *x-y* coordinates are a pair of integers. In mathematics, the *x-y* plane is viewed as continuous, each point consisting of a pair of real numbers. The distinction between discrete and continuous values will be encountered again.

The other important difference is that in mathematics we view the *x-y* plane as having four quadrants with the origin set in the center. In Java, we use only one quadrant, which is somewhat different than any of the four quadrants of the Cartesian plane. It is like quadrant IV of the Cartesian plane in that the origin is at its upper left corner, but it is like quadrant I in that both the *x* and *y* coordinates are positive. Figure 1.1 illustrates the differences between the two approaches.

Several Simple Graphics Methods

The Java programming language has many predefined classes, more with each new version, and more than most other programming languages. No beginning Java programmer can or should try to master them all initially, but, instead begin with a selected few. Because the focus of this book is on programs that involve graphics, we begin with a few of those predefined methods that enable us to draw some simple graphic images. The first method we consider is `fillRect`, which allows us to draw solid rectangles. Its signature is shown below:

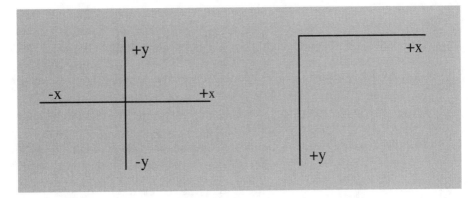

FIGURE 1.1 The Cartesian plane (left) and Java's graphics (right).

```
fillRect(int x, int y, int width, int height)
```

The signature tells us that we must supply four arguments when we call this method. Each of the four arguments must be of type int. The names in the signature—referred to as *parameters*—help us understand what information is being supplied. The first two parameters specify the coordinates of the upper left-hand corner of the rectangle. Although the parameter names x and y suggest that these values are the coordinates of a point, it is necessary to consult some reference to know that they are the coordinates of the upper left-hand corner. The last two parameters width and height need no further explanation.

The second method fillOval is quite similar to the previous one, except it draws solid ovals instead of rectangles. Its signature is shown below:

```
fillOval(int x, int y, int width, int height)
```

Without consulting a reference, we might guess the *x-y* coordinate specified by the first two parameters represents the center, but it does not. It represents the point to the upper left that is the intersection of a horizontal line tangent to the top of the oval and a vertical line tangent to the left side of the oval. Figure 1.2 illustrates what was just described.

The final method that we introduce in this first chapter is setColor whose signature is shown below:

```
setColor(Color c)
```

This method sets the color that will be used when methods like fillRect and fillOval are called. Once a color is set, it stays set until the method is called again with a different color.

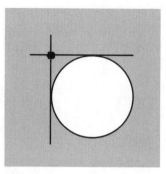

FIGURE 1.2   The coordinates
required by the drawOval method.

All three of these methods belong to the predefined class Graphics that is a part of the package java.awt. To perform any drawing by calling any of these methods, we need an object of type Graphics. In the example presented in the next section, we see how these methods are called.

OUR FIRST JAVA APPLET

Our first Java applet will draw a white circle inside of a black square. The diameter of the circle is 50 pixels and the upper-left hand coordinate is at *x-y* position 50, 50. Because this applet has no input, it will always produce the same output. Figure 1.3 illustrates its output.

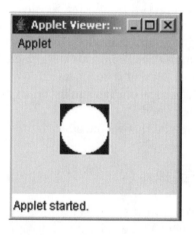

FIGURE 1.3 White circle inside a black square.

The Java code for this applet is shown in Listing 1.1.

LISTING 1.1   An applet that draws a circle inscribed in a square (found on the CD-ROM at chapter1/CircleInSquare.java).

```
 1 // A Java applet displaying a white circle in a black square
 2
 3 package chapter1;
 4
 5 import java.awt.*;
 6 import javax.swing.*;
 7
 8 public class CircleInSquare extends JApplet
 9 {
10     public void paint(Graphics graphics)
11     {
12         final int X = 50, Y = 50, SIZE = 50;
13
14         graphics.setColor(Color.BLACK);
15         graphics.fillRect(X, Y, SIZE, SIZE);
16         graphics.setColor(Color.WHITE);
17         graphics.fillOval(X, Y, SIZE, SIZE);
18     }
19 }
```

Line 1 contains a comment. Comments begin with the characters // and end with the end of the line. Comments in no way affect the behavior of the program, but instead provide information to the reader. Striving to write programs that are easy to read by using descriptive names should be the goal. Some comments are helpful, nonetheless. One per class is a bare minimum. Because we will provide a line-by-line description of each program presented, our discussion will replace what otherwise would be comments.

Line 3 indicates that the class contained in this file belongs to a package named chapter1. Recall that Java provides packages as a way to group together related classes. We have used this mechanism to group together the classes that belong to the programs in each chapter of this book. All the classes belonging to every program in a given chapter are defined in a separate package. General purpose classes that are used by programs in more than one chapter are placed in a package named common.

Lines 5 and 6 are import statements. These statements must be placed before the class definition. One statement is required for each package that is imported. The word import, like final and int, is a reserved word. import statements are not essential, but including them allows us to avoid having to qualify each class name by prepending it with the name of the package to which it belongs. Without the first `import` statement, we would need to write `java.awt.Graphics` and `java.awt. Color` rather than simply `Graphics` and `Color`, respectively. The reason we must either fully qualify the class names or use the `import` statement is that the classes `Graphics` and `Color` belong to the package `awt`, which is nested inside the package `java`. Similarly, the second import statement enables us to write `JApplet` rather than `javax.swing.JApplet`.

Line 8 contains the class heading. As we have already noted, every program, even an applet, is composed of at least one class. Java, unlike some earlier object-oriented programming languages, requires every method to be inside a class. This class is designated `public` because it is referred to from outside this program by the Web browser. The word `class` is a reserved word indicating that a class is being defined and `CircleInSquare` is its name. Previously we explained the lexical convention for constant names, using all upper-case letters. By convention, class names are written in title case, capitalizing the first letter of each word. The final clause in line 8 indicates that the class we are defining is derived from a predefined class named `JApplet`. This is an example of inheritance, an advanced topic that we will not fully explain until much later in the book. The matching braces on lines 9 and 19 are the *delimiters*, markers that indicate the beginning and end of the class. The same delimiters are used for marking method boundaries and boundaries of compound statements, which we discuss later. The alignment of the braces makes it clear that the right brace on line 19 matches the left brace on line 9. Proper indentation, although ignored by the compiler, helps the reader see how all the braces in a program are paired. Proper use of indentation for this purpose is essential in any well-written program.

Line 10 contains the signature for the paint method. Method names, by convention, always begin with a lower case letter. The first letter of each subsequent word, if there are any, is capitalized. This method must be `public` because it is being called from outside the applet. It is a void method, as are the predefined methods `fillRect`, `fillOval` and `setColor`. We will defer an explanation of the meaning of void until the next chapter. As we have already explained, what follows the method name is the list of parameters. This method has one parameter, `graphics`, which is the graphics object of type `Graphics`, onto which we perform the painting. Notice that parameter names use the same lexical convention as method names. This object is being passed to us by the Web browser, which calls paint. The method `paint` is actually a method already defined in the class `JApplet` that we are extending. The only freedom that we have regarding its signature is in the choice of the parameter name. The braces on lines 10 and 18 delimit the beginning and end of the method.

Line 12 contains the declaration of the three constants used in this applet. `X` and `Y` are coordinates of the upper left-hand corner of the square, and `SIZE` is the diameter of the circle and height and width of the square. The use of named constants is very important in this program, as in all programs. By naming these constants we are specifying their values once, but referring to them by name several times. By doing so, we clarify the fact that this program is intended to display the circle atop the square. If we change the coordinate values, we will move both the circle and the square. If we change the size of the diameter, we will change the size of both the square and the circle. If we *hard-coded* the constants, specified the numeric values as arguments to the methods that draw the shapes, it would be less clear that the size and position of the two objects are intended to be the same. Naming the constants, of course, also enhances the readability of the program. Normally one-letter names would be undesirable, but x and y have well-established meanings as the coordinates of a point in mathematics, consequently their use in this case is appropriate.

Lines 14 and 16 contain calls to the method setColor that establish the color for subsequent calls to methods that perform painting. Notice that method calls must be invoked on an object, as we discussed earlier, which is why we need the object graphics to be given to us by the browser. The arguments passed to that method in both cases are predefined constants defined in the class Color, which is why they must be qualified with the class name.

Lines 15 and 17 call the methods to paint the square and the circle, respectively. When the height and width are the same, fillRect produces a square and fillOval a circle.

One important issue to consider in programs is whether the order of statements matters. In many early programming languages, all declarations were required to precede all executable statements. Java allows the two to be interspersed, but there is one requirement that remains. Every identifier that is referenced must have its declaration precede it. Like most programming languages, Java forbids *forward references*. Although interspersing declarations and executable statements is permitted, we adopt the convention of listing all declarations before all the executable statements.

In most cases, the order of declarations does not matter, unless one contains a reference to a name in another, but with executable statements, order is much more important. In our first applet, the four executable statements must be in exactly the order written to produce the proper output. The setColor calls must precede their respective drawing operations and the circle must be drawn after the square. Done in the opposite order, the circle would not be visible. If we were drawing hollow objects of the same color rather than solid objects of different colors, the order would be unimportant.

PROGRAM DEVELOPMENT

Now that we have seen our first Java program that will produce an applet, we will discuss the steps that are required to turn it into a working program and what software tools we must use to accomplish this task.

Editors, Compilers, and Interpreters

We begin with a discussion of the software tools that are needed. The very first step is to take our program and enter it into computer. The file that contains a Java program, also known the *source code*, is just a text file, so any text editor, such as Notepad that is provided in every Windows environment, can be used to accomplish this task.

The next step is to translate our Java program into a language that the computer will understand. As mentioned before, the Java programming language is considered a high-level programming language, which means, in part, that it is written at a higher level than the computer can understand. Consequently it must be translated to machine language, the language the machine—our computer—understands. Before we go into the details of how this process works for Java in particular, let's consider what kinds of tools are available for translating high-level languages in general. There are two fundamental kinds of language translators, *compilers* and *interpreters*. Some languages are fully translated by the compiler. The input to such compilers is the source code and the output produced is called *object code*, which must then be linked with standard language libraries using another software tool called a *linker*, to produce an *executable file*—machine code, which can be run. The program can then be executed, or run, repeatedly without having to perform the translation each time. Other languages are fully interpreted. An interpreter performs both the translation and execution of the program. So the program must be translated each time it is run. The translation process for Java is a hybrid of these two. Java is partially compiled and partially interpreted. Unlike the compiler for a fully compiled language, the output is not object code but *intermediate code*. Java's intermediate code is called *bytecode*. There are several advantages to the approach that Java takes. First, this approach clearly separates the part of the process that is machine independent from the part that is machine dependent. The compiler is machine independent, which means that the bytecode it generates is the same whether the program is to be run on a PC or a Macintosh® computer. Because the interpreter is machine dependent, a different interpreter would be needed for different machines. Next we consider the other advantage of this two-step process. Recall that there are several different kinds of Java programs and that in this book we focus on two of them—applets and applications. The same compiler is used to translate applets and applications into bytecode, but a different program is needed to perform the final translation to machine code and execution. Because applets are intended to be embedded in Web pages, Web browsers contain the interpreter— the *Java Virtual Machine* (JVM)—that is needed to interpret the Java bytecode for the applet contained in that page. Another program called *appletviewer* can be used in place of a browser. It contains only the interpreter needed to execute the applet and ignores any other part of a Web page. The translation and execution process for Java applets using the appletviewer is shown in Figure 1.4.

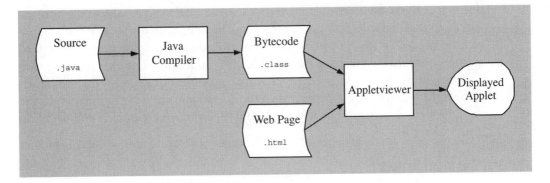

FIGURE 1.4 The Java compiler and appletviewer.

For applications, the JVM is contained in a standalone program. Because we will be considering only applets for the first four chapters, we will defer further discussion of the standalone JVM until Chapter 5, when we encounter our first application.

Command-line or Integrated Development Environments

As a software developer, there is one decision that you must make, which is whether you work at the command-line of an operating system like MS-DOS or UNIX, or whether you work in a graphical Windows-like environment. The basic Java Software Development Kit (SDK), freely available from Sun Microsystems, the creator of Java, contains a compiler and interpreter that are command-line programs. If you wish to work in a Windows-like environment, you will need additional software, called an *integrated development environment (IDE)*. There are several freely available IDEs, such as Sun ONE Studio, NetBeans, Eclipse, or JGrasp. There are also commercially available IDEs, such as JBuilder, Microsoft J++, VisualCafe, and others. Some developers prefer command-line development; others prefer the use of an IDE. To choose between these two approaches, you must understand the advantages of each. Perhaps the main advantage of the command-line approach is that you do not need to invest the time to learn to use an IDE. Some are easier to use than others. Typically the simpler the IDE and the less it does, the easier it is to learn. The name "integrated development environment" describes the fact that the editor and compiler are integrated into a single program. The primary advantage to this approach, present since the creation of such tools, is the ability to easily fix compilation errors. In every IDE, you are able to click on a compilation error and be taken to the line of code that caused the error. A command-line compiler produces a list of error messages with line numbers. Developing programs in this environment requires that you alternately switch between the compiler and editor and that you find the line that corresponds to each error yourself. Newer IDEs offer many other features. Although these additional features offer some benefits, they also add to the amount of time needed to learn to work in that environment. At some point, every programmer should be able to work in either environment. Because there is so much variation from one IDE to another, we will confine our discussion of the mechanics of compiling and running programs to the command-line environment and refer you to the documentation provided with the IDE that you choose, if you decide to pursue that route.

The Development Process

Now that we have discussed the necessary software tools for developing programs, we return to process itself. We have already mentioned that the process begins with entering the program using an editor. Next we compile the program. What comes next depends upon whether any errors were generated during the compilation process. Such errors are called *compilation errors*. These errors are due to violating either the syntactic or semantic rules of the language. For now, let's assume that no compilation errors were generated. In that case, we can proceed to the next step and run the program using the appropriate interpreter. Although the compiler identifies as many errors as possible, some errors cannot be identified until run time. These errors are called *run-time errors*. Let's suppose that no run-time errors occur. There is still one remaining kind of error that can exist. It is called a *logic error*. Unlike compilation and run-time errors, there is no message that tells us that one has occurred. The presence of a logic error can only be determined by comparing the behavior of the program with the specification or requirement that describes what the program is supposed to do. When a program fails to do what the specification states it is supposed to do, a logic error exists.

Next let's consider what must be done if any of the aforementioned errors do exist, beginning with the compilation errors. Before continuing with our description of the process, let's explore the possible causes of compilation errors. A compilation error occurs when the program submitted to the compiler is not a correct program. This can occur for one of two major reasons. Either the program has violated one of the syntax rules or one of the semantic rules of the language. Regardless of the cause, the error must be fixed before attempting to compile the program again. If you are a novice in the use of compilers, there are some important things you should know about fixing these errors. You must understand that the number of errors displayed by the compiler is not always an accurate measure of how many are really there. Sometimes one actual error can generate more than one error message. Other times one actual error can mask many other errors. For this reason, you should not focus on the number of errors, assuming that if some change greatly reduces the number of error messages, it was necessarily a correct change. Instead always attempt to fix the first error. If your change has eliminated that error, you are making progress. It is even possible that properly correcting the first error can cause more errors that had been previously masked. Always fix the first error first. Until you have fixed all the errors, there is no way to be certain exactly how many remain.

Once all the compilation errors have been fixed, you can now run the program. Now, let's consider the possibility that a run-time error occurs. Its cause must be identified and the program must be modified, recompiled, and rerun. Don't forget, though, that every time you change the program, you must recompile it. Every time you compile it, you can get compilation errors, so trying to fix a run-time error can cause a compilation error. Similarly, trying to fix a logic error could cause a compilation error or a run-time error. The process of developing programs is certainly an iterative one. Let's try to formalize what we have been describing by carefully stating an *algorithm* for the program development process. An algorithm is a step-by-step procedure for accomplishing a particular task. To state this algorithm, we will use *pseudocode*, a combination of English and some of the reserved words of Java, which are shown in boldface.

```
type in the program
do
    compile it
    while compilation errors remain
        fix the errors
        recompile the program
    run the program
    if run-time or logic errors exist
        fix them
while there were any run-time or logic errors
```

The logic that underlies every program contains one or more algorithms, so this design technique of using pseudocode can be helpful in describing complicated algorithms before translating them to Java. Of course, in this case we are using the pseudocode to describe the program design process. Writing a Java program to accomplish this task is not our goal.

The Mechanics of Compiling and Running Applets

Because there is such variation in how IDEs work, we conclude our discussion of the program development process with the details of how to compile and run a Java applet from the command line only. There are two environment variables that must be set properly before running the Java compiler. The first is the path that directs the operating system to which directories to search when looking for the Java compiler and interpreter. The path setting depends upon what directory you specified when you installed the compiler. A typical DOS directory might be *c:\"program files"\jdk1.5\bin*. The second is the classpath, which specifies the root directory of the default package of your program. The details on setting environment variables are operating system dependent, so we refer you to your reference manual for whatever particular operating system you are using.

Another important detail that you need to know is how the files are named. By convention, every class is contained in a file of the same name with the file extension .java. In the example from this chapter, the CircleInSquare class should be in a file called CircleInSquare.java. Once your compiler has been installed, your environment variables are set, and you have entered your program with some text editor, you are ready to run the compiler. Let's say you have written a program containing a class MyFirstApplet, which is in MyFirstApplet.java. Unless you have designated this class as belonging to some package, this file must be placed in the directory that has been designated as the class path. To compile that program, you type the following at the command line:

```
javac MyFirstApplet.java
```

If the program compiles without any errors, it will create a file named MyFirstApplet.class. This file contains the bytecode for this applet. To run an applet, you need a Web page, which means that you need an .html file—a file that defines the page with the hypertext mark-up language, HTML. If you are using an IDE, this file is often created for you. If you are working from the command line, you must create it yourself. Like a .java source file, it is also a text file and can be created using any text editor. Listing 1.2 shows the necessary code for the applet MyFirstApplet that we have been discussing.

LISTING 1.2 HTML code for MyFirstApplet applet. (Found on the CD-ROM at **ON THE CD** chapter1/MyFirstApplet.html.)

```
1    <HTML>
2      <HEAD>
3      </HEAD>
4      <BODY>
```

```
5        <APPLET CODE="MyFirstApplet.class"
6          WIDTH=400 HEIGHT=300>
7        </APPLET>
8      </BODY>
9    </HTML>
```

It is not our intent to explain HTML in any great detail. Instead we will only explain enough so that you can create the necessary HTML files for your applets. HTML files mark up the text using tags. One example of a tag is <HTML> on line 1. Each tag is enclosed in corner brackets. Tag names are case insensitive, so we could use <html> in place of <HTML>. Most tags have a corresponding ending tag. The tag </HTML> is the ending tag that corresponds to <HTML>. Every ending tag contains the same name preceded by the / character. The portion of the text that is between the opening and closing tags is the portion affected by that tag. Notice that tags can be and often are nested. For ease of reading, we have placed each tag on a separate line and indented the tags to illustrate the nesting. Neither the use of separate lines nor the indentation is required.

An HTML file generally begins with <HTML> and ends with </HTML>. This pair of tags indicates that all text in between is HTML. An HTML file consists of a head and a body delimited by tag pairs of those names. In our example, lines 2 to 3 constitute the head and lines 4 to 8 constitute the body. Both the head and body tag pairs are nested inside the HTML tag pair. The most common thing to put in the head is the title that will appear on the Web page. In our case, the head is empty. The body contains the tag that is of greatest interest to us—the applet tag. It indicates that this Web page contains an applet. Tags can contain attributes. Attributes usually have an associated value. In our case, the applet tag contains three attributes: CODE, WIDTH, and HEIGHT. In each case, the attribute has a value. The = symbol must be placed between each attribute and its value. The attribute CODE specifies the name of the .class file that contains the bytecode for the applet. The next two attributes, WIDTH and HEIGHT, specify the width and height of the applet in pixels, respectively.

Once you have compiled your applet into bytecode and created an HTML file, you are ready to run your applet. Before we discuss the command for running the applet, there are two points that need to be made about your HTML file—the first being how to name it. Unlike Java source files, whose names must match the classes they contain, there is no such requirement for the names of the HTML file that contains a Java applet. Nonetheless, we have adopted a convention with the HTML files provided for each applet on the CD-ROM that accompanies this book. The convention is to name the HTML file with the same name as that of the applet class. So adhering to that convention, the HTML file contained in Listing 1.2 would be named MyFirstApplet.html. Next we need to consider where to put this file. It is simplest to put it in the same directory as the Java source file and the bytecode, which is in the class path directory. Assuming the file has been named `MyFirstApplet.html` and placed in the class path directory, to run your applet, you would type the following command:

```
appletviewer MyFirstApplet.html
```

The appletviewer is a program that can be used to execute applets. It contains a Java interpreter that executes the applets defined in the Web pages and ignores any other HTML that the page might contain. Using the appletviewer is not the only way to run an applet. The HTML file could be opened with any Web browser, such as Netscape or Internet Explorer.

One other important issue that you need to understand is the relationship between the directory structure used to store Java source and bytecode files and the package structure of Java programs. Any class that is defined without a package designation is considered to be in the default package. The files containing such classes must be placed in the directory defined as the class path directory. Let's consider the case when classes are specifically designated as belonging to a package, which is the approach we have taken with all the examples in this book. Our example in this chapter is defined in a package called `chapter1`; consequently its file must be placed in a subdirectory named chapter 1 of the directory defined as the class path directory. Although we never do so in this book, packages can be nested. In that case, the nested structure of the packages must correspond to the directory hierarchy. For example, if we had a Java class in a package `chapter1.projects`, the file containing that class would be placed in the subdirectory `chapter1\projects` of the class path directory.

Next let's consider how the placement of applet classes in packages affects the HTML files that contain them. Let's consider the applet tag that would be needed for the applet that we discussed earlier in this chapter, `CircleInSquare`. The necessary applet tag is shown below:

```
<APPLET CODE="chapter1\CircleInSquare.class" CODEBASE=".."
    WIDTH=400 HEIGHT=300>
```

Because the files belonging to packages are placed in subdirectories of the class path directory, we must include a path with the name of the `.class` file. Note that the path specified is relative to the class path. Because our applet is in the package `chapter1`, the class file will be in the subdirectory `chapter1` of the directory that is the class path. Assuming the HTML file containing this applet tag is placed in the same subdirectory, it is necessary to specify the location of the class path. Its location is specified using the `CODEBASE` attribute. In this case, the class path is the parent directory of the directory containing this file, which we specify using the relative path designation "`..`".

If you have chosen to use an IDE, many of the issues related to the placement of files into directories and the creation of HTML files may be done for you. Nonetheless, understanding these ideas is important.

SUMMARY

In this chapter, we introduced programming languages in general and explained the significance of Java being a high-level language. We discussed two important characteristics of all languages, syntax and semantics, and then discussed the syntax and semantics of two Java statements—the declaration statement necessary for naming constants and the method call statement needed to draw simple graphic output. Finally, we discussed the process of program development and the mechanics of running Java programs. The key points to remember from this chapter are as follows:

- Java allows three kinds of programs to be written, traditional applications, side applets, and server side servlets.
- Like natural languages, programming languages have syntax rules that define the correct grammar and semantic rules that determine whether a program is meaningful.
- The Java coordinate system consists of just one quadrant of the mathematical Cartesian coordinate system.
- Constant declarations allow the programmer to give names to particular values.
- Method calls allow the programmer to call methods—the ones we studied in this chapter allowed us to set colors and draw solid ovals and rectangles.
- Program development is an iterative process that requires repetition of the compilation and execution steps until all errors have been corrected.
- The Java compiler can be used from the command line or together with an IDE.

Review Questions

Answers to odd numbered review questions are provided in Appendix A. Answers to even numbered questions are available to professors upon request.

1. What is an applet? How does it differ from more traditional applications?
2. Give an example of an English sentence that is syntactically correct but not correct semantically.
3. Explain why it is a good practice to name constants.
4. In choosing constant names, why are single letter names usually a bad practice? Are there any exceptions?

5. Explain the difference between a lexical convention and a syntax rule.
6. What is the difference between a declarative statement and an executable statement in Java?
7. Who calls the method `paint`? When is it called?
8. Give an example of a syntax error in a method call statement.
9. How are logic errors detected? When fixing a logic error, why is possible to generate new compilation errors?
10. What are the advantages and disadvantages of using an IDE to develop your Java programs?

Programming Exercises

11. Indicate whether each of the following character sequences is a valid Java identifier.
    a. `someValue`
    b. `100Times`
    c. `number#13`
    d. `THIS_SIZE`
    e. `Title`
12. Among the syntactically correct identifiers in the previous exercise, identify those that follow the lexical convention for constant names.
13. Which of the following are valid integer literal constants?
    a. `1,000`
    b. `15.35`
    c. `−200000`
    d. `20000000000`
    e. `221`

14. For each of the invalid integer literal constants in the previous exercise, modify them so that they are valid.
15. Write a constant declaration to declare an integer constant named *height* that has the value of 350. Use the proper lexical convention when naming it.
16. Write a constant declaration for an integer constant to represent the number of milliseconds in a year. Be sure to choose the proper size integer.
17. Write a method call that draws a solid rectangle of height 20 and width 30. Its lower right corner should be at *x-y* coordinate 50, 80.
18. Write the method calls necessary to draw a solid blue circle with a radius of 50 that is centered at *x-y* coordinate 75, 75.
19. Write an applet tag for an HTML file to display the applet `AnApplet`. Assume the applet is in the default package. Make the width of the applet 300 pixels and its height 200 pixels.

20. Repeat the previous exercise, assuming that the applet is contained in a package named `aPackage`.

Programming Projects

21. Write an applet that draws two concentric solid circles. The outer circle should be black and have a diameter of 50 pixels. The inner circle should be white and have a diameter of 25 pixels. Figure 1.5 illustrates how the output of this applet should look.
    You are free to choose the position of the circles. Name all the constants.

FIGURE 1.5   Output of Chapter 1, Project 21.

22. Write an applet that draws two solid black rectangles. The first one should have a height of 50 pixels and a width of 25. The second one should have a height of 25 pixels and a width of 50. The output of this applet is shown in Figure 1.6.

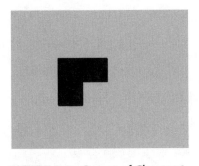

FIGURE 1.6   Output of Chapter 1, Project 22.

The upper left-hand corners of both rectangles should be the same, but you are free to choose their location. Be sure to name all your constants.

23. Write an applet that draws two solid black squares with sides that are 50 pixels wide. The upper left-hand corner of the second one should be in the center of the first one as illustrated in Figure 1.7.

FIGURE 1.7   Output of Chapter 1, Project 23.

24. Modify the applet example CircleInSquare from this chapter so that it becomes an oval in a rectangle instead. Keep the height at 50 pixels, but make the width 100 pixels.

25. Modify the applet example CircleInSquare from this chapter to change the colors. Make the square red and the circle yellow.

2 Variable Declarations, Assignments, and Expressions

In this chapter

- Random Input
- Simple Computation in Java
- More on Methods
- Assignments
- An Applet that Draws a Square Inside a Circle

RANDOM INPUT

Although programs do not require input, a program without input behaves in a way that is rather uninteresting. Each time it is run, it produces the same output. That was the case with the example presented in Chapter 1. Throughout this book, we will explore a variety of different ways to get input into a program. In this chapter, we will use one of the simplest kinds of input: random input. Random input is really a kind of pseudo-input because it does not come from the program user, but is instead generated by the program itself. Nonetheless, it gives a program more interesting behavior because its output will vary depending upon the values that are randomly generated.

Random input will continue to be important in many of the program examples that we encounter in the remainder of the book, particularly the ones that involve games and puzzles.

Most programming languages provide predefined methods for generating random numbers. We will explore one that Java provides later in this chapter.

SIMPLE COMPUTATION IN JAVA

In addition to the need for input to make programs interesting, they must also be able to perform computation—the very task that gives computers their name. In this section, we discuss a second group of numeric data types and then proceed to explain how mathematical formulas are expressed in programming languages like Java.

Real Number Data Types

In the first chapter, we introduced one of the two categories of primitive numeric data types—those that are used to store integers. In this chapter, we will be using several methods that require numeric values that are not integral. Just as there are more than one size of integer types, so too are there multiple sizes for storing real numbers. Java provides two primitive data types, `float` and `double`, which are short for floating point and double precision floating point, respectively. In Table 2.1, the memory requirements and the approximate value range and number of significant digits of both types are shown.

TABLE 2.1 The Two Different Sizes of Floating-point Numbers

Type	Memory	Value Range	Significant Digits
float	32 bits	-3.4×10^{38} to 3.4×10^{38}	7
double	64 bits	-1.8×10^{308} to 1.8×10^{308}	15

The names suggest how these numbers are stored—using what is called floating-point representation. This representation is similar to scientific notation. Some of the bits are used to store the mantissa—others are used for the exponent. The more bits allocated to the mantissa, the greater the precision, so data values of type, `double` have approximately twice as many bits used for the mantissa, hence doubling the precision. The number of bits allocated to the exponent influences the range of numbers that can be represented.

Because floating-point numbers are stored in a binary representation, inherent errors can arise as a result of the conversion from decimal, base 10, to binary, base 2. In much the same way that the fraction 1/3 becomes a repeating decimal, base 10 values such as $.1_{10}$ also repeat when converted from decimal to binary. Consequently no amount of bits allocated to the precision is sufficient to represent such numbers exactly. Such errors are referred to as *representation errors*. For this reason, floating point values must sometimes be treated differently from integers. We will return to this issue when we discuss comparing values in a later chapter.

Variables and Constants

In the example in the first chapter, because it had no input of any kind, we only needed constants since the values that we were dealing with were fixed. In this chapter, we will be using randomly generated values as input to our program, so the values used will differ on different runs of the program; consequently, constants are not enough.

Variable declarations, like constant declarations, cause memory to be reserved of the appropriate size depending on the type. Declaring variables also allows us to subsequently refer to the values in those memory locations by name. The syntax for declaring variables is shown in Syntax Definition 2.1.

Syntax Definition 2.1 Syntax of a Variable Declaration.

```
variable_declaration

    type variable_1 = value_1, ..., variable_n = value_n;
```

The syntax for variable declarations is similar to that of constant declarations ,but there are two differences. First, we omit the reserved word final. Second, the initialization, which is required for constants, is optional for variables. To signify optional syntax in the syntax definitions, we show those parts in gray. There is one additional difference between the syntax shown here and what we saw in Chapter 1. Where we now have type, we had written int before. The reason for this difference is the only types we used in Chapter 1 were integers. In place of type, we can substitute any of the integer types discussed in Chapter 1 or any of the floating-point types we have just encountered. Actually, there are many more possible types that can be used, but for now we confine ourselves to the integer and floating-point primitives.

Arithmetic Operators

Arithmetic operators are a key component of the arithmetic expressions that we introduce in this chapter. Java has five arithmetic operators. The first two, addition and subtraction, use the standard mathematical symbols: the + for addition and the − for subtraction. Because the standard symbol for multiplication, ×, and the standard symbol for division, ÷, are not on a typical computer keyboard, the character * is used for multiplication, and the character / for division. The fifth operator is the %, for remainder of division. This operator is one that is likely to be the least familiar since there is no mathematical symbol that corresponds to it. It is most useful with integer operands. It represents the remainder while / is the integer quotient when integer values are divided. As an example:

$$5 / 2 = 2 \text{ and } 5 \% 2 = 1$$

In Chapter 4, we will encounter an example that makes use of the remainder operator.

There are some mathematical operations, such as exponentiation and roots, for which there are no Java operators. To perform these computations, we need to call predefined methods that Java provides. We will discuss these methods later in this chapter.

Translating Mathematical Formulas to Java Expressions

The first programming language to include mathematical formulas, FORTRAN, a contraction of formula translator, was named for its ability to translate and evaluate these formulas. All subsequent programming languages have adopted a similar style.

Let's begin our discussion of the relationship between these mathematical formulas and the Java expressions that represent them with the simple formula in Equation 2.1:

$$(x + 1) \bullet (y + 1) \tag{2.1}$$

Mathematical formulas have certain characteristics that you are no doubt familiar with, but may have never thought about. The above formula contains three operations, two additions and one multiplication. These operations are nested with the addition operations being innermost. That nesting is conveyed by the parentheses. When formulas are fully parenthesized—one pair of parentheses for each operation—the evaluation proceeds from the innermost operations to the outermost. Expression evaluation in Java is done in exactly the same way when the expression is parenthesized.

When mathematical formulas omit parentheses, there are other rules that apply. Consider the formula in Equation 2.2.

$$xy + ab \tag{2.2}$$

This formula contains two multiplications and one addition. In such a formula, it is understood that the multiplications are done first because multiplication has higher *precedence* than addition. Programming languages have adopted this concept of precedence. The five Java arithmetic operators are divided into two levels of precedence as shown in Table 2.2.

TABLE 2.2 Precedence of Arithmetic Operators

Precedence	*Operators*
Higher precedence	* / %
Lower precedence	+−

Precedence is often described as the order of operations, but that phrase is often misinterpreted. The best way to understand precedence is that it specifies where the location of the missing parentheses would be. In our previous formula, the precedence rules implicitly define the position of the missing parentheses as shown in the formula in Equation 2.3.

$$((xy) + (ab)) \tag{2.3}$$

Because it is possible to have an unparenthesized formula containing two or more operators of equal precedence, some rule must define where the missing parentheses would be placed in such cases. Consider the formula in Equation 2.4.

$$a + b + c \tag{2.4}$$

In such a formula, the understood parentheses are grouped from left to right, so it is interpreted as shown in Equation 2.5.

$$((a + b) + c) \tag{2.5}$$

Java has adopted the same rule for interpreting such expressions. You may be wondering why it matters how such a formula is grouped. In fact, if both operators are addition, it does not matter, because addition is an associative operation. Subtraction is not, however, as illustrated by Equation 2.6.

$$((5 - 1) - 1) \neq (5 - (1 - 1)) \tag{2.6}$$

This rule is referred to as the *associativity* rule. In Java, all five arithmetic operators are *left associative*, meaning that they associate from left to right. In a later chapter, we will encounter other operators that are right associative.

Thus far we have seen that Java expressions have adopted three features of mathematical formulas: the role of parentheses, the precedence rules, and the associativity rules. Next, we examine several ways in which Java expressions differ from the mathematical formulas that they express. Consider the formula shown in Equation 2.7.

$$\frac{xy + 1}{2} \tag{2.7}$$

In mathematics, we typically use single letter variables, so in the above formula, it is understood that x is a single variable, y is another and xy represents the product of the two. This implied multiplication must become explicit when we translate this mathematical formula to a Java expression because Java variables are not restricted to single letters. In fact, use of single letter variables is generally considered to be a poor practice.

Mathematical formulas also contain implied parentheses beyond what are implied by the precedence and associativity rules. Compare the formula in Equation 2.7 with the one in Equation 2.8.

$$\frac{xy}{2} + 1 \tag{2.8}$$

The meanings of the two formulas are different. The length of the division line implies parentheses that must become explicit when translating the formula to Java. The formula in Equation 2.7 translated to Java would be written as follows:

```
(x * y + 1) / 2
```

The implied multiplication must become explicit, and so must the parentheses implied by the division line. The length of the line that is a part of the square root symbol is another example of implied parentheses.

Type Coercion and Type Casting

Another important issue that you need to understand to properly write Java expressions is what happens when an expression contains operands of different types. We have so far discussed two categories of numeric types, the four sizes of integers and the two sizes of floating-point numbers. Unlike some programming languages, Java allows expressions to contain operands of mixed types. When such mixing occurs, the operand of the "smaller" type is *coerced* or promoted to the "larger" type. The primitive types that we have studied thus far are shown below—ordered from "smaller" to "larger."

```
byte → short → int → long → float → double
```

Coercion in this direction never produces any unexpected results because every value that can be stored in an int can be stored in a long and so on.

Java actually performs more coercion than is absolutely necessary to match types. Integer literals are considered to be of type int, which is also the smallest size of integers on which arithmetic can be performed. Consequently, in any arithmetic expression, variables of type `byte` and `short` are always coerced to type `int`—even when the types are not mixed.

Floating point literal constants are taken to be of type `double`, so when a variable of type `float` is mixed with a floating point literal, the variable is coerced to type `double`. As an example, consider the following expression in which `f1` is assumed to be of type `float`:

```
f1 + 1.0
```

The variable `f1` will be coerced to type `double` in the above expression before the addition is performed.

It is also important to understand that coercion is done on an operator-by-operator basis. To illustrate the importance of understanding this issue, consider the following Java expression:

```
i1 / i2 * d1
```

Assume that `i1` and `i2` are of type `int` and `d1` is of type `double`. Because both `i1` and `i2` are integers, the division performed will be integer division, losing any remainder. That integer quotient will then be coerced to a `double` before the multiplication with `d1` is performed but by then it is too late. The fractional part of the quotient has already been lost. One way to solve this problem would be to rearrange the operands so that the multiplication would be done first as follows:

```
i1 * d1 / i2
```

Another alternative is to use *type casting*. The syntax for type casting requires placing the name of the type inside parentheses before the operand as follows:

```
(double)i1 / i2 * d1
```

Note that it suffices to cast only `i1` to be a `double` because the rules involving coercion will cause `i2` to be coerced to a `double`. An important thing to understand about type casting is that it does not change the type of a variable, it makes a copy of the value of the variable and stores it in a temporary memory location large enough to accommodate the new type.

MORE ON METHODS

Although the method call statement is one that we have already encountered, there are several different kinds of methods that must be called in slightly different ways. In this section we examine some of those variations together with a collection of new predefined methods that we will need for the example presented later in this chapter.

Calling Class versus Instance Methods

In the first chapter, each of the methods calls that we encountered were calls to instance methods. In this chapter, we introduce the syntax for calling class methods. The primary difference between these two kinds of methods is that instance methods are associated with a particular object. When we called the graphics methods in Chapter 1, we always invoked them on the graphics object that we were given by the browser. In each case, we were asking that the painting be performed on that graphics object.

Not all methods are associated with objects. In this chapter we will be using several methods from the Math class. All the methods in that class are class methods; they are associated with the class to which they belong, but not with a particular object. The syntax that is needed to call class methods is slightly different from calls to instance methods and is shown in Syntax Definition 2.2.

Syntax Definition 2.2 Syntax of a Qualified Class Method Call.

```
class_method_call

        ClassName.methodName(argument_1, ..., argument_n);
```

The only difference is that what precedes the method name is a class name, not an object name. By adhering to the well-established lexical conventions of Java, it is easy to see which calls are calls to class methods and which calls are calls to instance methods. When the name preceding the method name begins with an upper case letter, the call is a call to a class method, otherwise it is an instance method call.

All of the methods that we have written thus far have been instance methods. In a later chapter, we will introduce class methods and, at that time, discuss how we decide whether a method should be an instance or a class method.

Calling Void versus Value-Returning Methods

All the method calls that we encountered in Chapter 1 were calls to void methods. When we call a void method, we supply it information by sending in arguments. It performs some action, but it does not return any information to us. A value-returning method returns a single value. Because void methods return nothing, calls to them appear alone as a statement. Calls to value-returning methods are usually embedded in a statement. In most of the cases we encounter in this chapter, the calls to these methods will be on the right hand side of assignment—the statement that we introduce later in this chapter. But we will see that they can appear in other contexts as well.

Although we will be calling some value-returning methods in this chapter, we are not yet ready to write our own, something that we will do in the next chapter.

You might notice that each value-returning method that we use in this chapter is a class method and each void method is an instance method. Do not conclude that such is always the case. The two properties of methods are independent, so four combinations are possible. Class methods can be void or value returning, as can instance methods.

The `Math` Class

To help us with some of the calculations that we need to do in our example for this chapter, we need more than just the five built-in arithmetic operators. As we have already mentioned, for one standard arithmetic operation, exponentiation, no arithmetic operator is provided in Java, although some programming languages do provide such an operator. The `Math` class provides us with a method to accomplish this task. Its signature is shown below:

```
static double pow(double a, double b)
```

There are several things about the signature of the method `pow` that we should note. It is a class method, which is signified by the fact that its signature begins with the reserved word `static`. So when we call it, we prepend the method name with the name of the class `Math`. The next feature to notice, in place of `void`, which has preceded each method name in every signature we have studied thus far, is the primitive type `double`. That tells us that this method returns a value of type `double`. What the signature does not make clear, but could have with better chosen names, is the role of the two parameters. We would need to consult a reference to know that the first is the base and the second the exponent.

Although the `pow` method can be used to compute roots, by passing .5 as the exponent for a square root, and .3333 for the exponent for a cube root, for convenience another method is provided for square root. It signature is shown below:

```
static double sqrt(double a)
```

At the beginning of this chapter we discussed how generating random numbers is one simple way to supply input to a program. The program example in this chapter will have such random input. A method from the Math class is needed to generate such random numbers. Its signature is shown below:

```
static double random()
```

The number returned by this method is a number in the interval from 0 to 1—including 0 but excluding 1. This method is the first one that we have encountered that has no parameters. When calling a method with no parameters, we must still include the parentheses after the method name, but the list of arguments will be empty.

We conclude with one final comment about the roles played by classes. Syntactically Math is a class, but not all classes in Java programs serve the same purpose. In an effort to make Java more object-oriented, all methods must belong to some class. But this language design choice makes some things appear more similar than they are. The role of the Math class is different from the role played by the classes that we have been writing. Its role is that of a utility class. A utility class has several characteristics. First, all of its methods are class methods. Second, we never create any objects of this class. For this reason, the Math class and the Graphics classes play very different roles.

Two Additional Graphics Methods

In this chapter, we use two new methods from the Graphics class that we had not used in the first chapter. Their signatures are shown below:

```
void drawRect(int x, int y, int width, int height);
void drawOval(int x, int y, int width, int height);
```

They are very similar to fillRect and fillOval, which we already used. The only difference is that they draw hollow, rather than solid, rectangles and ovals, respectively.

ASSIGNMENTS

In Chapter 1, we encountered one kind of executable statement, the method call statement, which enabled us to call several predefined methods to draw graphical output. In this chapter, we introduce a second executable statement, the assignment statement.

The Syntax and Semantics of Assignments

Assignment statements allow us to store the result of some calculation defined by an expression into the memory location that has been reserved for some variable. The syntax of an assignment statement is shown in Syntax Definition 2.3.

Syntax Definition 2.3 Syntax of an assignment statement.

```
assignment_statement

    variableName  = expression ;
```

The syntax makes clear a few important points. First what appears on the left-hand side of the assignment must be the name of a variable. That means it cannot be a constant, named or literal. Because assignments change the value of what is being assigned to, it makes sense that constants, whose values are unchangeable, would be inappropriate on the left side of an assignment.

The right-hand side of an assignment is quite different. Expressions in their simplest form can be single variables, single named constants or calls to value-returning methods. From our discussion of the difference between void and value-returning methods, it should be clear that a call to a void method could not be a part of an expression. These three simple components—constants, variables, and value-returning method calls—can then be built up into more complex expressions containing one or more operators.

One final point is that, although we have shown the symbol = as a part of the syntax of the assignment statement, it is actually an operator. In the next chapter, we will see that it is really one of many assignment operators. Although we will refrain from such usage for some time, assignments themselves can be expressions nested inside of other expressions. Consequently, like the arithmetic operators, the assignments operators also have precedence, which we will discuss in Chapter 6.

Type Coercion and Casting in Assignments

We have already discussed what occurs when an expression contains operands of different types, so now we consider this issue for assignment statements. In the case of an assignment statement, mixed types arise when the type of the expression on the right-hand side of the assignment is different from the variable on the left-hand side. What occurs in this situation is somewhat different, however, because the variable on left-hand side of the assignment cannot be coerced to a different type. Only the expression on the right-hand side can be coerced. When the expres-

sion on the right-hand side is a "smaller" type than the variable on the right, the coercion is safe. Such conversions are referred to as *widening conversions*. Such conversions are safe and are therefore permitted. The reverse situation—known as
narrowing conversions—is potentially unsafe. To make such assignments, Java requires an explicit type cast. These two kinds of assignments are illustrated in the
code fragment shown below:

```
int i = 1;
double d = 2.5;

d = i;   // Widening conversion, no type cast required
i = (int)d;  // Narrowing conversion, a type cast is needed
```

Let's now investigate what is meant by the fact that narrowing conversions are
potentially unsafe. The extent of the problem depends upon the relative types
and the values involved. There are three different cases to consider. The first is
when a double value is type cast to a float. In this situation, there is a loss of precision. Because double precision values allocate more bits to precision, some of them
will be lost in such a type cast. The ones lost are the least significant bits, so generally such a loss is not too serious. The second case is when either of the floating-
point types is converting to any integer type. What occurs in this case is that the
decimal number will be truncated to an integer. When performing such a conversion, we often will add .5 to cause rounding rather than truncation, as we will see
in the example later in this chapter. The third case is when a larger integer type is
converted to a smaller integer type. In such situations, the highest order bits are
lost. If these bits are zero, there is no problem. If they are anything other than zero,
the conversion becomes highly erroneous. A similar problem can occur in converting from a floating-point type to an integer type when the integral part of the
value exceeds what can be stored in an integer of that size.

The preceding discussion is important because when such erroneous conversions
occur, no run-time error is generated. Consequently, care must be taken when performing narrowing assignments to ensure that such erroneous conversions do not
occur.

Before leaving this topic, let's consider two other cases in which narrowing assignments occur. Recall that variables of type byte and short are always coerced to
int, even when all types match. Consequently the following assignment will not
compile:

```
short s1, s2, s3;
s1 = s2 + s3;
```

Type casting is required in this case as follows:

```
s1 = (short)(s2 + s3);
```

Finally, remember that floating-point literals are considered to be of type double. As a result, the following declaration will not compile:

```
float f = 1.0
```

It requires an explicit type cast as follows:

```
float f = (float)1.0
```

In a later chapter, we will discuss an alternate syntax for designating numeric literals to be other than the default type. To avoid these type correspondence problems, we adopt the practice of declaring integer variables to be type int and floating point variables to be type double unless we have a compelling reason to do otherwise.

AN APPLET THAT DRAWS A SQUARE INSIDE A CIRCLE

Our next Java program is another applet, and it is a variation on the one that we studied in the first chapter. It will produce a square and circle, but there are several differences. First, these objects will be hollow, not solid. That difference is really a minor one. Second, the square will be inside the circle rather than the reverse. Having the circle inside the square was a much simpler program because the x-y coordinates that specified the upper left-hand corner were the same for both the circle and the square. Now the two will be different. An additional complexity this time is that the radius of the circle will be generated randomly, so we cannot hard-code the coordinates as constant values, but we must compute the upper left-hand corner of the square from the radius of the circle. Figure 2.1 shows what the output of this applet will look like.

Before we present the actual Java code for this example, we need to investigate how to compute the x-y coordinates of the upper left-hand corner of the square given the radius of the circle. Figure 2.2 helps us understand the necessary calculation. It requires using the Pythagorean Theorem.

From Figure 2.2, we see that the shaded triangle is a right triangle, so we can apply the Pythagorean Theorem shown in Equation 2.9.

$$c^2 = a^2 + b^2 \qquad (2.9)$$

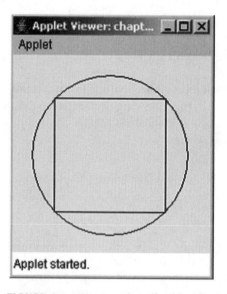

FIGURE 2.1 A square inscribed inside a circle.

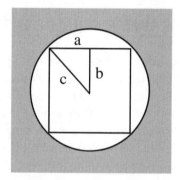

FIGURE 2.2 Computing the square size given the radius.

The hypotenuse of the right triangle c is also the radius of the circle. The two sides of the right triangle a and b are both half of the side of the square. Because a and b are equal, we can substitute a for b giving Equation 2.10.

$$c^2 = 2\,a^2 \qquad\qquad (2.10)$$

Solving the equation for a gives us Equation 2.11.

$$a = \sqrt{\frac{c^2}{2}} \qquad\qquad (2.11)$$

Now that we have the critical formula for solving this problem, we are ready to present our example program for this chapter, which is shown in Listing 2.1.

LISTING 2.1 An Applet that Draws a Square Inscribed in a Circle (found on the CD-ROM at `chapter2/SquareInCircle.java`).

```
 1 package chapter2;
 2
 3 import java.awt.*;
 4 import javax.swing.*;
 5
 6 public class SquareInCircle extends JApplet
 7 {
 8     public void paint(Graphics graphics)
 9     {
10         final int X_CENTER = 100, Y_CENTER = 100;
11         int radius, diameter, halfSide, side;
12
13         radius = (int)(Math.random() * Y_CENTER);
14         halfSide = (int)(Math.sqrt(Math.pow(radius, 2) / 2) + .5);
15         diameter = radius * 2;
16         side = halfSide * 2;
17         graphics.drawOval(X_CENTER – radius, Y_CENTER –
18             radius, diameter, diameter);
19         graphics.drawRect(X_CENTER – halfSide, Y_CENTER –
20             halfSide, side, side);
21     }
22 }
```

As before, we explain this program line-by-line. In this case, however, much of the outer portion of this program is identical to the one from the first chapter, so we begin our explanation with the declarations on lines 10 and 11. On line 10 is the declaration of the only constants in this program, X_CENTER and Y_CENTER. They represent the x and y coordinates of the center of the circle. Line 11 contains the declaration of four integer variables. The variable names radius and diameter are self-explanatory, as variable names should be. The variable side represents the length of a side of the square and halfSide half that amount.

Because this program is our first containing both constant and variable declarations, a comment about the order of declarations is appropriate. Java allows us to place constant and variable declarations in any relative order, but our practice will be to always declare the constants before the variables. Adopting a uniform style enhances the readability of programs, so it is something to strive for. Remember that the only requirement imposed by Java on the order of declarations is that there be no forward references. Our reason for choosing to declare constants first is that it is possible for a variable declaration to contain the name of a constant as a part of its initialized value, but the opposite is never allowed. Initializing a constant using a variable violates the meaning of being constant.

Line 13 contains our first example of an assignment statement. It involves a call to the method random that we introduced earlier in this chapter. To understand this statement, we must reexamine the signature of that method. Recall that it returns a value of type double in the range from 0.0 to 1.0, specifically a value v such that $0.0 \leq v < 1.0$. Multiplying the return value by the constant Y_CENTER, which has the value 100, we have a value v' of type double such that that $0.0 \leq v' < 100.0$. This subexpression is an example of one that contains mixed types. Y_CENTER is an integer and the value returned by the call to random is a floating-point type. Before the actual multiplication takes place, Y_CENTER is first coerced to type double. Recall also that coercion can only occur in an assignment when a widening assignment is being performed. In this statement, the assignment is a narrowing one. The variable on the left side is of type int and the expression on the right is of type double. For this statement to be valid, an explicit type cast is required. Recall also that type casting from a floating-point type to an integer type involves truncation and not rounding. In this case, truncation is acceptable. Consequently this statement will generate random values between 0 and 99.

In line 14 we perform the computation that calculates the length of half the side of the square that we inscribe inside the circle. This statement reflects the translation of the mathematical formula in Equation 2.11 to Java. Recall that the variable radius corresponds to c in Equation 2.11. The variable halfSide corresponds to a. As was the case in the assignment on the previous line, the expression on the right side is of type double, whereas the variable on the left is of type int. For the same reasons as before, an explicit type cast is needed. There is one difference is this case, however. Truncating the value is not acceptable—instead we need to round the result, which is why .5 is added to the result prior to the type cast on line 14.

There are some other type-related issues that warrant discussion in line 14. Recall that the signature of the pow method, which we introduced earlier in this chapter, shows that the type of both its parameters is double. The arguments that we are supplying it are integer values, both the variable radius and the constant 2. At the point of a method call, what occurs is an operation similar to an assignment. The arguments passed into the method call are copied to the parameters declared in the method signature. Consequently, the same rules regarding when coercion occurs and when type casting is required apply in this situation as they do in assignments.

Since the arguments are of type int and the parameters are double, a widening conversion occurs and the arguments are coerced to double automatically. In the reverse situation, an explicit type cast would be required.

Lines 15 and 16 perform assignments to the variables diameter and side each being twice radius and halfSide respectively. Finally, on lines 17–20, the necessary method calls are made to draw the circle and square. In our example in the last chapter, all the arguments to method calls were constants. One thing to notice about arguments in method calls on lines 17–20 is that the first two arguments are expressions, not just simple constants or variables. Another way to think about it is that whatever is permitted on the right-hand side of an assignment can also be an argument to a method call. If you look back to the method calls on line 14, you will notice that a call to the value-returning method pow is a part of the argument passed to another method sqrt. This is an example of a *nested method call*. Only calls to value-returning methods can be nested inside calls to other methods.

One characteristic of programs that you no doubt have already observed is that there are many different programs that can solve the same problem, so many of the decisions we make when we write programs are influenced by making programs easy to read and easy to maintain. One decision that needed to be made in this program was determining which values to make variables. Let's consider two other possibilities. First let's see how we might have used fewer variables. We could have omitted diameter and side as variables and instead written the method calls as follows:

```
graphics.drawOval(X_CENTER -- radius, Y_CENTER -- radius,
    radius * 2, radius * 2);
graphics.drawRect(X_CENTER -- halfSide, Y_CENTER -- halfSide,
    halfSide * 2, halfSide * 2);
```

Let's now consider the other extreme and use more variables. Let's create variables for the *x-y* coordinates needed to draw the circle and for the *x-y* coordinates needed to draw the square. Our code might now look as follows:

```
xCircle = X_CENTER - radius;
yCircle = Y_CENTER - radius;
xSquare = X_CENTER - halfSide;
ySquare = Y_CENTER - halfSide;
graphics.drawOval(xCircle, yCircle, diameter, diameter);
graphics.drawRect(xSquare, ySquare, side, side);
```

If all three versions accomplish the same task, then you might wonder what difference it makes. As we indicated earlier, the difference lies in the readability of the program and ease of making changes. Adding more names and, therefore, more assignments tends to make the program longer, but short programs should not necessarily be our goal. What is more important is that using more variables can enhance the readability, provided that the names are meaningful. There is no one correct answer to this question. In our first solution, we chose a middle ground. We chose to name `side` and `diameter` because they are subsequently referred to more than once. The variable `side` is referred to twice in the call to `drawRect` and `diameter` is referred to twice in the call to `drawOval`. Failing to name them results in a duplication of their computations, which is what occurs in the second version of the program. We have already noted that avoiding code duplication is one of the cardinal rules of good program style. Although we cannot provide an exact rule on how to proceed with such design choices, this issue is important and one that you should think about when writing programs.

ON THE CD   The CD-ROM that accompanies this book contains all three versions in their entirety. The version with the fewest local variables is located at `chapter2\SquareInCircle2.java`. The version with the most variables is located at `chapter2\SquareInCircle3.java`.

SUMMARY

In this chapter, we encountered programs whose behavior varies based on randomly generated input. We learned about the floating-point primitive types used to represent real numbers. We explored how to write mathematical formulas in Java and how calculations can be performed using a new kind of data, variable data, and a new executable statement, the assignment statement. The key points to remember from this chapter are as follows:

- Using the `random` method in the `Math` class, it is possible to write programs that behave differently on each run of the program.
- Unlike constant data, variable data can be changed as the program executes.
- Java provides two primitive types, `float` and `double`, for storing numbers that are not whole numbers. They are stored in floating-point representation.
- Floating-point representation may produce inherent representation errors because fractional decimal numbers cannot always be converted to binary exactly.
- Java expressions adopt the significance of parentheses, precedence, and associativity of mathematical formulas.
- The implied multiplication and implied parentheses of mathematical formulas must become explicit when translating such formulas to Java.
- Because of type coercion, mixed types are permitted in Java expressions. Type coercion is automatic on widening assignments, but type casting is required for narrowing assignments.

- Calls to class methods must be invoked on the class name itself. Calls to instance methods are invoked on objects.
- Calls to void functions are statements, but calls to value-returning functions are expressions.

Review Questions

1. Explain how using randomly generated values can make the behavior of programs more interesting.
2. When fractional decimal numbers are converted to binary, representation errors can occur. Would such errors occur if fractional octal (base 8) numbers were converted to binary? Explain.
3. Why must the implied parentheses in mathematical formulas become explicit in Java expressions? What features of mathematical formulas can imply parentheses?
4. Explain the benefit of the type coercion permitted in Java expressions.
5. Provide an example of an expression where type casting is needed to produce a reasonable result.
6. How can you determine when a method call is calling an instance or class method?
7. Explain why calls to void methods cannot be placed inside compound expressions like calls to value returning methods can.
8. Why is it necessary to know the signature of a method to be able to properly write calls to that method?
9. Explain why Java requires explicit type casting on narrowing conversions.
10. Why does Java prohibit placing a constant on the left-hand side of an assignment?

Programming Exercises

11. Write an expression that generates a random number with the following characteristics:
    a. A random number between 0 and 10, inclusive.
    b. An even random number between 10 and 20.

12. Declare a constant or variable of the appropriate type:
    a. A 64 bit integer variable named hours.
    b. A short integer constant containing the number of days in a year.
    c. A floating point variable with maximum precision to store the slope of a line.
    d. A single precision floating point constant initialized to zero.

e. A long integer constant to store the number of milliseconds since the beginning of the year.

13. Fully parenthesize each of the following arithmetic expressions according to the rules of precedence and associativity and then evaluate the expression. Indicate whether the type of the result is an integer type or floating-point type.

a. ```3 + 4 * 6 - 7 / 2```

b. ```4 - 6 + 6 % 1 - 3```

c. ```3.5 * 3 + 2 - 1.4```

d. ```5 % 6 - 2 % 2```

e. ```4.1 + 3.2 * .5 + 3.3```

14. Identify whether parentheses in each of the following expressions are redundant—removing them would not change the value of the expression:

a. ```x + (y + z)```

b. ```a + b * (c - 3)```

c. ```a - (b - 2)```

d. ```(x / 2) * y```

e. ```a + (b * 4)```

15. Translate the following mathematical formulas into Java expressions:

a. $\dfrac{(x+y)(a-b)}{2a}$

b. $2(xy - ab)$

c. $\dfrac{2x+1}{(x-y)(a+b)}$

d. $\dfrac{\dfrac{(x+1)(y-2)}{(a-b)}}{x+1}$

e. $6(xy - 2a)(2a + 5y)$

16. Using calls to methods in Java's Math class, translate the following mathematical formulas to Java expressions:

a. $x^2 + y^3 - a^4$

b. $\sqrt{2x^2 + 1}$

c. $|x^2 - y^2|$

d. $\sqrt{\dfrac{x^3 + y^3}{3}}$

e. $2(x^2 + y^3) + a + b$

17. Categorize each of the following method calls as calls to instance or class methods:
    a. `Math.random() * 2`
    b. `graphics.drawRect(0, 0, 10, 10);`

18. Given the following declarations, explain whether each of the following assignments is a narrowing assignment and not valid as written:

    ```
    byte b, c;
    int i, j;
    long l;
    float f, g;
    double d;
    ```

    a. `d = f + g`
    b. `b = b + c;`
    c. `l = (int)f + i;`
    d. `i = (double)j + (int)g`
    e. `f = g + 3.5 - i + j;`

19. Given the following declaration

    ```
    int value;
    final int ONE = 1;
    double triple = 3.0;
    ```

    examine the following assignment statements and indicate whether they contain any errors. If so, identify the errors:
    a. `ONE = 2;`
    b. `triple = ONE;`
    c. `triple + 1 = 0;`
    d. `value = triple + 1;`
    e. `triple = (double)value;`

20. Write a method call to accomplish each of the following:
    a. Paint a hollow circle centered at point 20, 20 with a radius of 10.

b. Paint a solid rectangle of width 20, height 10 with its upper right-hand corner at point 40, 10.

Programming Projects

21. Write an applet that draws four squares arranged as shown in Figure 2.3.

All four squares should be the same size. The upper-left and lower-right squares should be filled and the other two should be hollow as shown. The size should be randomly generated and should be between 0 and 99, inclu-

FIGURE 2.3 Output of Chapter 2, Project 21.

sive. The upper left-hand corner of the upper-left square should be located at point 20, 20.

22. Write an applet that draws three squares as shown in Figure 2.4. All three should have the same upper left-hand corner, but the second should be twice the size of the first and the third should be three time the size of the first.

The first should be solid and the second two hollow as shown. The size of the first square should be randomly generated and should be between 50 and 99, inclusive. The upper left-hand corner of the upper-left square should be located at point 50, 50.

23. Write an applet that draws five circles and one oval that surrounds the inner three circles as shown in Figure 2.5. All the circles should have the same diameter. The circumference of each successive circle should pass through the center of the previous one as the drawing illustrates. The height of the oval should be twice the diameter of the circles. The width of the oval should be 4/3 the diameter of the circle. The circle diameter should be randomly generated. You may select the maximum diameter and location of the circles.

24. Write an applet that draws a circle with two ovals inside of it as shown in Figure 2.6. The narrower oval should have a width 1/3 its height. Its height should be the same as the diameter of the circle. The wider oval should have

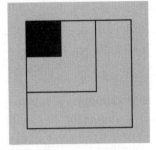

FIGURE 2.4 Output of Chapter 2, Project 21.

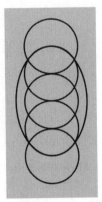

FIGURE 2.5 Output of Chapter 2, Project 23.

height 1/4 its width. Its width should be the same as the diameter of the circle.

The circle diameter should be randomly generated. You may select the maximum diameter and location of circle.

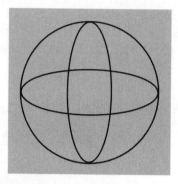

FIGURE 2.6 Output of Chapter 2, Project 24.

25. Modify the program example from this chapter so that it draws a rectangle inside of an oval as shown in Figure 2.7.

   The height and the width of the oval should both be randomly generated independently.

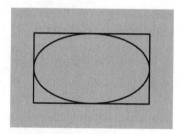

FIGURE 2.7 Output of Chapter 2, Project 25.

3

Methods, Instance Variables, Scope, and Lifetime

In this chapter

- Comparing Instance Data with Local Data
- More on Methods
- More Details on Operators and Statements
- An Applet that Draws a Triangle Inside a Circle

COMPARING INSTANCE DATA WITH LOCAL DATA

The program examples in the first two chapters contained a single class with a single method. The constants and variables that those two programs contained are called *local constants* and *variables*. What makes them local is that they are declared inside a method. Our program example in this chapter still only contains one class, but that class contains several methods. Furthermore, it also contains *instance variables* and *constants*, which are characterized by the fact that they are declared inside a class but outside any method.

One of the important goals of this chapter is to help you understand how to decide whether variables should be instance variables or local variables. To understand how to make that decision, it is necessary to understand scope and lifetime. If you are new to programming, do not be discouraged if you do not fully grasp the details of this discussion initially. The example at the end of the chapter provides a concrete example that should help you understand how to apply these concepts to an actual program. Nonetheless, this chapter is one that you may wish to reread after you have studied some of the larger program examples in later chapters.

Scope Rules

Programming languages as early as ALGOL, first developed in the late 1950s, have had a well defined set of rules regarding the *scope* of names defined by declarations. The reason for these rules is to avoid needing to worry about conflicting names in a large program. If all names were to have *global scope*—program-wide scope, a programmer would have to be sure every selected name did not conflict with every other name in the program. Given that programs have only become larger as time has progressed, the problem is even more important today than it was when this issue was originally recognized. Given that Java has so many predefined packages, the problem would be compounded further. Without scope rules, every programmer would need to ensure that every name chosen for every constant, variable method, and so on, did not conflict with any name in all of the predefined packages that might potentially be used by the program.

A similar naming scheme is used by the file system of most every operating system today. It is possible to have many files on the same computer with the same name, provided they are in different directories. The complete name of every file must include its path, but files within the current directory can be referred to by name, without specifying their path.

The scope rules of programming languages operate in a similar fashion. Like the structure of file systems, the structure of programs is also hierarchical. We first made this observation in Chapter 1. Programs are made up of packages. Packages contain a group of classes. Classes contain a collection of methods. Moreover, we have already seen that packages can be nested. The package `java.awt` is the package `awt` nested in the package `java`. In Chapter 8, we will see that classes, too, can be nested. Method nesting is not permitted, however. The full name of a method like `drawRect` is `java.awt.Graphics.drawRect`. It is the `drawRect` method in the class `Graphics` contained in the subpackage `awt` contained in the package `java`.

Let's now consider the scope rules of Java. A name can only be accessed without qualification—meaning without specifying what it is contained in, within its scope. For simplicity, we will set aside the nesting of packages and classes to explain the scope of names as follows. Package names have global—program-wide—scope. Class names have package-wide scope and, finally, method names have class-wide scope. So, for example, within the class `java.awt.Graphics` we could refer to the method `drawRect` without qualification. Another rule of scope is that duplicate names are generally prohibited at the same level of scope. For example, we cannot have two classes with the same name in the same package. There is an exception to this rule regarding method names, but we postpone discussing that exception until Chapter 5.

Not all names can be accessed outside their scope. We will address the rules governing when they can shortly. If they can be accessed outside their scope, they must be qualified, either explicitly or implicitly using an import statement, as we discussed in Chapter 1.

What we have yet to mention are the scope rules for data, which are really our main reason for discussing scope. Java prohibits any global or package-wide data, which incidentally is not true of all programming languages. Data declarations must have either class-wide or method-wide scope. Recall our primary reason for this discussion of scope is to help you understand which of these two choices is appropriate.

We begin by discussing the method-wide scope. We used the adjective *method-wide* for consistency but it is a bit misleading with regard to data, so we will instead refer to such declarations as local declarations, which is the term used more often. These declarations include constants, variables, and parameters declared inside a method. The scope of local declarations is from their declaration to the end of the method in which they are declared. As long as we confine the placement of our declarations to the beginning of the method, a practice we have adhered to, then this statement is an accurate one. The actual rules are a bit more complicated, but to keep this discussion simple, we postpone those details until we introduce the for statement in Chapter 4. In Figure 3.1, we illustrate this rule. The boxes illustrate the scope of the declarations—the outer-most box defines the scope of ONE, the next inner box the scope of x and the innermost box the scope of d.

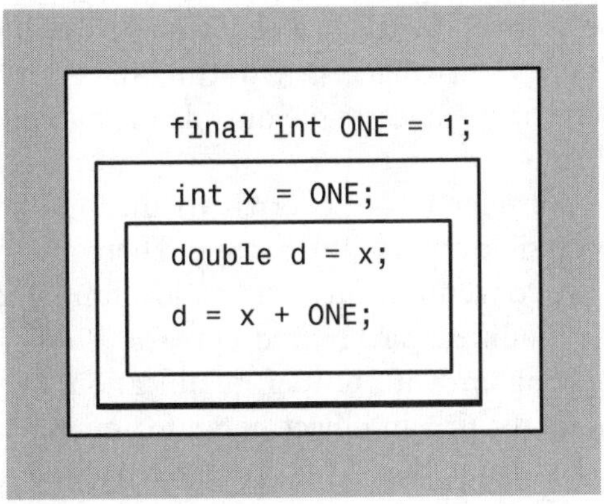

```
final int ONE = 1;

    int x = ONE;

        double d = x;

        d = x + ONE;
```

FIGURE 3.1 Local scope.

In Chapter 1, we discussed the prohibition of forward references—that a local constant or variable must be declared before it can be referenced. This prohibition is really just a direct result of the scope rule for local declarations. As an example, note that in Figure 3.1, x can be referenced in the declaration of d, but the reverse would be an error. This example illustrates why referring to the scope of local declarations as method-wide is not completely accurate, even when the declarations are at the beginning of the method. We should note that this issue of forward references does not apply to package, class, and method names.

Next we consider data that has class-wide scope—instance data, which includes both constants and variables. The scope of instance data includes all methods of the class and all other instance data declarations that follow it. The restriction about forward references does not apply in quite the same way at the class level as it does at the method level. The relative order of methods and instance data is unimportant, but forward references among instance data declarations are still prohibited. It is common practice, and therefore a style we adopt, to always declare the instance data of a class before all the methods. Moreover, we will declare all instance constants before instance variables for the same reason we adopted this practice with local data.

Access Modifiers

Next we consider a related issue, which is what determines whether a name can be accessed outside its scope. We consider the rules at the package, class, and method levels.

We begin with the class names inside a package. Whether a class name can be accessed from another package, qualifying with its package name, depends upon whether the access modifier public, precedes the class name. In both of our programs in the first two chapters, we labeled our classes as public, because they needed to be accessed by the Web browser. We will eventually write some classes that do not need external access. Omitting the reserved word public before class makes the class name inaccessible outside the package, even when qualified by the class name.

Next we consider what governs whether method names and instance data names are accessible outside their scope. There are several accessibility categories. At this time, we concentrate on the two most fundamental ones that are designated by the access modifiers public and private. Public names can be accessed anywhere in the program with proper qualification. We have already noted that instance methods require an object name for qualification, whereas class methods require the class name. Used outside their package, the package name would be needed also. Private names can never be accessed outside their scope.

Finally we consider local data. Local data is never accessible outside its scope. No access modifiers could alter that fact, so none are permitted on local declarations.

Loose Coupling

Now that we have explained how access modifiers can make some names visible outside their scope if properly qualified, we want to address what constitutes good software engineering practice regarding the use of these access modifiers. We begin discussing their proper use on instance data, and will discuss their use on methods at a later time. In this discussion, it is important to distinguish between constants and variables. Because the values of variables can change, they can create what is called *coupling* between any two methods that access them. By coupling we mean interdependence.

One measure of well-designed software is the degree to which it is *loosely coupled*. To understand the meaning of loosely coupled software, an analogy might be helpful. Consider audio systems as they were designed in the 1950s compared to the way they are designed today. Today's systems are loosely coupled. One can replace one set of speakers with another provided that they meet some interface requirements. The earlier systems were quite tightly coupled—sometimes to extent that the controls for one component were on another. Replacing a single component in such a system was difficult and often impossible. With software, the ability to easily replace one class with another class with a different representation—meaning different instance variables—but the same specification is a desirable goal. Such loosely coupled software is easier to maintain. The Y2K problem some years ago is an example of the kind of high cost problem that results when software is tightly coupled.

The importance of this characteristic of software will become clearer once you encounter some larger programs. For now, we simply adopt the practice of only allowing private instance variables, thereby eliminating all instance-variable coupling between classes. Because constants cannot be changed, they do not create the same degree of coupling, hence when we need to access constants from several classes within a program; we will label them with the modifier `public`. In this chapter, we are dealing with a program consisting of only a single class, so there is no reason to label any of the instance data with anything other than the modifier `private`.

Data Lifetime

Next we turn to a related concept, which is data *lifetime*. The lifetime of a constant, variable, or parameter is the time period during the execution of the program that the data exists. When we analyze our program example for this chapter, we will see how both scope and lifetime influence whether variables should be local or instance variables.

Because the issues related to the lifetime of nonprimitive data are somewhat more complicated, we confine our discussion only to primitive data in this chapter, data of the integer and floating-point types. The lifetime of local primitive data—constants, variables, and parameters—is the lifetime of the method in which they are declared. Such data is created when the method is called and destroyed when the method completes. We cannot assume that the value contained in a local variable when leaving one call to a method will still be there when we reenter it on a subsequent call. Another way to think about this issue is that local variables can have many lifetimes during the execution of a program.

By contrast, the lifetime of primitive instance variables and constants is the lifetime of the object to which they belong. To fully appreciate this idea, you need to examine programs with multiple classes that contain multiple objects. In this chapter, we are dealing with a single class and a single applet object of that class. So for now, we can view the lifetime of instance data as the lifetime of the program. Such data is created once and exists through the life of the program.

MORE ON METHODS

The programs that we have seen until now have been so small that there was little that could be meaningfully said about the design process. Although we are still dealing with relatively small programs in this chapter, the issue of design is so important that we want to introduce some fundamental design concepts now. Because Java is an object-oriented language, the kind of design done before writing Java programs is object-oriented design, which involves breaking the problem into its component classes first. Before object-oriented programming languages were developed, the design process used involved breaking a problem into its component methods. Despite this change, one thing remains constant in the design process— it is a process that involves decomposition of a large problem into the smaller components that are required to solve it.

We have chosen to avoid introducing very large programs containing multiple classes too soon because such programs require that you understand too many features of Java. Instead we are beginning with a program that still involves a single class—but one that has multiple methods.

Let's explore the rationale behind decomposition, which is the same for classes as for methods. Breaking a problem into smaller components has several benefits. The first is reuse and, therefore, the avoidance of code duplication. This reuse includes reusing the component both within a single program and among programs. The second reason for decomposition is for the purpose of simplification. Although a problem may be complex, if we can properly decompose it, its components will be simpler, and therefore easier to understand, develop, and test.

Choosing Between Public and Private Methods

In the last section, we discussed the access modifiers when applied to instance data, but these modifiers apply to methods as well. When a method is declared `public`, it is accessible with qualification throughout the entire program, so it can be potentially called by any other method in the program. When it is labeled with the modifier `private`, it is not accessible outside its scope. So a private method can only be called by other methods, both public and private, of the same class.

Although it is important to understand the difference between the scope of the name of a public method compared to a private one, it is equally, if not more, important to understand when a method should be made public and when it is best made private. Until we encounter programs containing multiple classes, it will be difficult to fully understand this design decision. For now, we confine ourselves to how to make the decision in an applet consisting of a single class. When we first introduced the `paint` method in the first chapter, we explained that it needed to be declared `public` because it is called from the Web browser, which is external to the program. At this point, we let that consideration determine our choice. Methods that are called from the Web browser must be public, but we will make the others private.

We have addressed the importance of order in a number of contexts thus far. Another to consider is the relative order of methods within class. Because the scope of all methods includes the entire class, the order in which methods are listed is unimportant. As a matter of style, we adopt the practice of declaring all public methods before all private ones and enumerating the public methods in alphabetical order by name.

Before concluding this discussion, there is one term that is appropriate to define—*specification*. The specification of a class consists of the signatures of the public methods of that class. The specification defines how those outside the class can communicate with the methods of the class. The notion of specification is something that also requires the examination of programs with multiple classes to fully appreciate, so it is a term that we will reexamine in a later chapter.

Determining the Signature of a Method

In the previous two chapters, the only method that we wrote was `paint`, which is a method whose signature is already defined in the class `JApplet`, so we had no role in determining its signature. In this chapter, for the first time, we will be writing some methods that are entirely our creation; hence the decision about the signatures of these methods will be ours.

Before we come to the main example for this chapter, it would be useful to discuss the general issues that must be considered when determining the signature of a new method. Recall that the signature of a method specifies several important things: the number and type of the parameters and the return type of the method. Let's review the role of parameters and the return type of methods. A method is supplied information, it performs some kind of computation or action and it sometimes returns information to the method that called it. For now, for the sake of simplicity, we confine our discussion to parameters that are primitive types. The only role of such parameters is to send information into the method. We are free to have as many such parameters as we need. With the return mechanism, we are restricted to returning a single value to the caller. In deciding the signature of a method, we need to think about these issues. Another factor to consider is whether it is appropriate for a method to access any of the instance variables. Because instance variables have class-wide scope, methods are free to access or change the values of these variables. It is difficult to provide any exact rules about how to decide what a proper method signature is. Instead, like most design issues, these are best learned by example. When we come to our example program for this chapter, we will explain in some detail the reasons for the choices we make regarding the signature of the methods that we have chosen.

Some Additional Predefined Methods

In the last chapter, we introduced the Math class and two methods that it contains, pow and sqrt. There are many more methods provided by the Math class, but as it is our intent not to be exhaustive, we introduce only two more in this chapter—ones that we will need for the example contained in this chapter. They are the methods for computing two of the trigonometric functions, sine and cosine. Their signatures are the following:

```
static double sin(double a)
static double cos(double a)
```

The parameter that is sent into each of these two methods is the angle in radians, not degrees. The correspondence between degrees and radians is that 360° is equivalent to 2π radians, which leads us to the one constant from the Math class that we will need in this chapter, the value of π, whose name is the rather obvious Math.PI.

In case your familiarity with trigonometry is a bit rusty, let's review the trigonometric functions sine and cosine. They apply to a right triangle as illustrated in Figure 3.2. The sine function maps the angle Θ to the ratio of the opposite side a and the hypotenuse c. With the cosine function, the ratio involved is that of the adjacent side b to the hypotenuse c.

In this chapter, we will use one new method from the Graphics class that we had not used in the first two chapters. Its signature is shown below:

```
void drawLine(int x1, int y1, int x2, int y2)
```

The drawLine method draws a line connecting the two points specified by the two pairs of x and y coordinates.

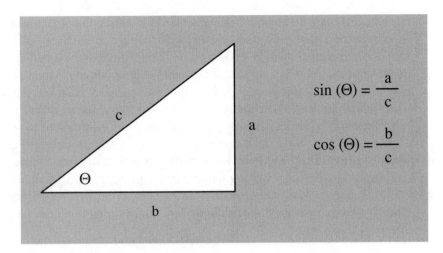

$$\sin(\Theta) = \frac{a}{c}$$

$$\cos(\Theta) = \frac{b}{c}$$

FIGURE 3.2 The sine and cosine functions.

MORE DETAILS ON OPERATORS AND STATEMENTS

We have been using only two types of statements in our programs so far—the method call statement and the assignment. In this chapter, we discuss some variations on those two statements and introduce a third statement—the return statement.

The Shortcut Assignment Operators

We begin with some variations on the assignment statement that use a new collection of assignment operators. The assignment operator that we have used until now is the simple assignment operator =, which simply indicates that the value specified on the right-hand side of the assignment is to be stored in the variable on the left. Now we introduce a collection of new shortcut assignment operators that can be used in special situations. They are +=, -=, *=, /=, and %=. Although we only plan to use the first of these in the example later in this chapter, we introduce them all now because they are so similar. They can only be used when the variable on the left-hand side of the assignment and the left operand of the arithmetic operator on the right-hand side are the same. So for example, the following two statements are equivalent:

    x = x + y   is equivalent to   x += y

Whenever a programming language provides a redundant set of syntaxes for accomplishing the same task, it enhances the readability of a program written in that language, if programmers adopt a particular style regarding when to use which syntax. In this case, the shortcut assignment operators can be used only in more restrictive contexts than the normal assignment and the arithmetic operator of which they are composed. Specifically, if we can use +=, we could also use the regular assignment with the arithmetic operator +. The reverse is not true, however. When redundancy exists, but one syntax is more restrictive than another, we adopt the style rule to use the more restrictive one whenever we can. In the case of +=, what we are saying is that when it is applies to a particular situation, we will always use it rather than +.

When writing an English essay, students are often encouraged to use variety, to choose a synonym for a word rather than using the same word repeatedly. Such a writing style makes the written work more interesting to read. Although we often cite similarities between writing natural language and writing programs in a program language, in this case there is a difference. When writing programs, consistency is much more important than variety. To do otherwise adds confusion, not interest, to programs.

Calling Another Method in the Same Class

We first introduced the syntax for method calls in Chapter 1 and provided additional details in Chapter 2 distinguishing between calls to instance versus class methods and void versus value-returning methods. There is one remaining variation on the syntax for methods calls. It is when we call another method in the same class. The syntax of such a method call is shown in Syntax Definition 3.1.

Syntax Definition 3.1 Syntax of an Unqualified Class Method Call.

```
same_class_method_call

    methodName ( argument_1 , ..., argument_n );
```

When a method of the same class is called, the method name does not need to be qualified by either an object or class name because the scope of method being called includes the method that is calling it. We will have occasion to use such method calls in the example later in this chapter. The syntax is the same regardless of whether the method being called is an instance method or class method. We should note, however, that although we have had occasion to call class methods, those in the Math class, we have not yet written any such methods. All the methods in the previous chapters and those in the current one are instance methods.

The `return` Statement

Because we will be writing some value-returning methods of our own in this chapter, there is one more statement that we need to use—the `return` statement. The syntax of the `return` statement is shown in Syntax Definition 3.2.

Syntax Definition 3.2 Syntax of a `return` statement.

```
return_statement

    return expression ;
```

Syntactically it is a simple statement consisting of the reserved word `return` followed by an expression. This syntax applies when a `return` statement is used inside a value-returning method. A `return` statement can be used in a void method, although we have never yet had the need to do so, but in that context its syntax is slightly different. When we have need of a `return` statement in that context in Chapter 7, we will explain the difference.

The last line of a value-returning method must be a `return` statement, although we will see in later chapters that they can appear elsewhere also. The `return` statement has two functions—the first is to specify the value to be returned, the second is to direct control back to the calling method. In its first capacity, the `return` statement acts like an assignment copying the value back to the calling method, most often to the variable to which the method call is assigned. Consequently type correspondence rules similar to those of an assignment apply to a `return` statement. There is a required correspondence between the type of the expression in the `return` statement and the type specified in the method signature. The type of the expression must either be the same type or a type that can be coerced to the return type specified in the signature. The second function of the `return` statement, which is returning to the calling method, is of no significance when that statement is the last statement of the method. In that case, control would return to the calling method anyway. That function will become important once we encounter methods that contain a `return` statement whose position is something other than the last line.

AN APPLET THAT DRAWS A TRIANGLE INSIDE A CIRCLE

Our program example for this chapter is an applet that draws an equilateral triangle inside of a circle. This example will require a more complex program than those we have studied thus far.

The examples in the first two chapters contained applets that consisted of a single class with a single method, `paint`. Our example for this chapter is more complex in several ways. Although it still involves only a single class, that class consists of four methods, two public and two private, and some private instance constants and variables.

Before we begin our line-by-line discussion of this program, we explain an additional requirement that mandates the use of another public method, `init`, and several instance variables. The applet that we studied in the previous chapter randomly generates the radius of the circle, but it generates the random value each time the method `paint` is called. So, if the browser window is resized, when the applet is repainted, a circle of a different size will be created. The additional requirement that we impose on our new applet is that the random generation of the radius of the circle must only be done when the applet is first created, not each time it is repainted. What is required is a method that will be called only when the applet is first created. The `JApplet` class defines such a method, which is the `init` method that we referred to earlier. Because this method is already specified in the `JApplet` class, we must use the same signature, which is shown below:

```
public void init()
```

From the signature it is clear that nothing is supplied to it, nor does it return anything. Its role is to do those things that need to be done when the applet object is first created.

The next important thing to understand in this program is that the `init` method will generate the radius and compute the coordinates of the vertices of the triangle, but it is the `paint` method that needs to refer to those values. One technique for sending information from one method to another is by having the first method call the second and pass the necessary information using parameters. We have used that technique repeatedly in calls to many of the predefined methods. The situation we are faced with here is different, however. Although methods within the same class can call one another, it would be inappropriate for the `init` method to call `paint`. Both are called externally by the browser and at different times. The solution to that problem is to use private instance variables, whose scope includes all methods of the class. Figure 3.3 shows what the output of this applet will look like.

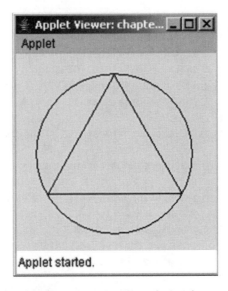

FIGURE 3.3 An equilateral triangle inscribed in a circle.

Let's now consider the complete program line-by-line as shown in Listing 3.1.

LISTING 3.1 An Applet that Draws an Equilateral Triangle Inscribed in a Circle (found on the CD-ROM at `chapter3\TriangleInCircle.java`.)

```
1   package chapter3;
2
3   import java.awt.*;
4   import javax.swing.*;
5
6   public class TriangleInCircle extends JApplet
7   {
8       private final int X_CENTER = 100, Y_CENTER = 100;
9       private int x1, y1, x2, y2, x3, y3, radius;
10
11      public void init()
12      {
13          final double ONE_THIRD_CIRCLE = 2 * Math.PI / 3;
14          double theta;
15
16          radius = (int)(Math.random() * Y_CENTER);
17          theta = - (Math.PI / 2);
18          x1 = computeX(theta);
19          y1 = computeY(theta);
```

```
20              theta += ONE_THIRD_CIRCLE;
21              x2 = computeX(theta);
22              y2 = computeY(theta);
23              theta += ONE_THIRD_CIRCLE;
24              x3 = computeX(theta);
25              y3 = computeY(theta);
26          }
27      public void paint(Graphics graphics)
28          {
29              int diameter = radius * 2;
30
31              graphics.drawLine(x1, y1, x2, y2);
32              graphics.drawLine(x2, y2, x3, y3);
33              graphics.drawLine(x3, y3, x1, y1);
34              graphics.drawOval(X_CENTER - radius, Y_CENTER - radius,
35                  diameter, diameter);
36          }
37      private int computeX(double theta)
38          {
39              return X_CENTER + (int)(Math.cos(theta) * radius + .5);
40          }
41      private int computeY(double theta)
42          {
43              return Y_CENTER + (int)(Math.sin(theta) * radius + .5);
44          }
45  }
```

We begin with the instance constant declarations on line 8. It is essential that the two constants X_CENTER and Y_CENTER, which represent the coordinates of the center of the circle, be instance constants because each is referred to in more than one method. The constant X_CENTER, for example, is referred to in the method paint and the method computeX. If we chose to declare this constant locally, we would be required to repeat the declaration in both methods, resulting in code duplication, a practice that we have repeatedly cautioned against. Adhering to good style in determining the scope level of constants allows us more freedom than the same decision with variables. Broadening the accessibility of constants to the widest scope causes no harm. The same is not true of variables. As a matter of style, we adopt the practice of declaring constants as private instance constants as the default—a middle ground approach. When we feel certain that a constant will only be used within a method, we may still opt to declare it locally. When necessary—when they are needed outside the class—we will declare them as public instance constants.

Line 9 contains the instance variables needed by this class. They include the six variables that represent the *x-y* coordinates of the three vertices of the triangle, and the radius of the circle. The instance variables of a class represent the state of objects of that class. We have already explained that the triangle coordinates and circle radius must be instance variables for reasons of scope. They are assigned values in the init method, but accessed in paint. Recall that good software engineering style mandates that instance variables, unlike constants, should always be declared as private. Keeping instance variables private is referred to as *information hiding*. We are hiding the representation of objects from other classes, thus insulating all the code outside the class from any representation changes.

Next we discuss each of the four methods of this class, beginning with the init method. We have already discussed the signature of this method, which appears on line 11, so we will begin with the local constant declaration of ONE_THIRD_CIRCLE on line 13. This constant represents one third of a circle in radians, or 120°. We elected to declare it locally because it is only needed inside this method, although choosing to make it an instance constant instead would have also been acceptable. There is one caution about writing this declaration properly that gives us an opportunity to review some of the issues that relate to type coercion—something we discussed in Chapter 2. Suppose we had instead written this declaration as follows:

```
final double ONE_THIRD_CIRCLE = 2 / 3 * Math.PI;
```

At first, it seems that this change should be acceptable because mathematically we know that the Equation 3.1 holds:

$$\frac{2\pi}{3} = \frac{2}{3}\pi \tag{3.1}$$

Before reading on, try substituting the statement above for line 13 and running the program and see whether you can explain what has happened.

If you ran the modified program, what you noticed is that the triangle disappeared altogether. If you suspect that it is parentheses that are now needed because the operands have been rearranged, try running it with the following:

```
final double ONE_THIRD_CIRCLE = (2 / 3) * Math.PI;
```

What you should have noticed in this case is that the triangle is still missing, so it is not a lack of parentheses that accounts for this change. Instead it is the fact that the type coercion is performed on an operator-by-operator basis. In the original statement, the multiplication of 2 times π causes 2 to be coerced to type double because the variable Math.PI is of type double. The constant 3 is then coerced for the same reason. The problem with the other approach, with or without the parentheses is that the division of 2 by 3 is performed first. Since both constants are integers, integer division is performed, giving a quotient of 0. Adding a decimal point to either the 2 or 3 would fix the problem, so using the following line would be correct.

```
final double ONE_THIRD_CIRCLE = 2. / 3 * Math.PI;
```

What makes understanding these issues so important is that using the wrong approach produces no compilation errors, warnings, or run-time errors—just an incorrect result.

Next we consider the local variable declaration of the variable theta that appears on line 14. We have mentioned that it is acceptable to avoid the declaration of local constants altogether, but the same is not true for variables. One might be tempted to declare theta as an instance variable. If we did so, we could avoid passing it to computeX and computeY because they would already have access to it, since it would have class-wide scope. That approach might seem like a good idea, given that the signatures of computeX and computeY would be simpler. There is, however, another consideration that should be made when deciding whether a variable should be an instance variable or not. Benefiting from a wider scope is not reason enough. To qualify as an instance variable, a variable should require an object-long lifetime. The triangle coordinates and circle radius both meet this requirement. Their values must persist throughout the life of the object. Such is not the case with the variable theta. It is used temporarily during the execution of the method init. The value left in this variable is never needed again after the applet initialization is complete. Another way to characterize this idea is to say that theta is not a part of the state of the applet object.

Next let's consider lines 16 and 17 that initialize radius and theta, respectively. We have already dealt with the generation of random numbers, so the fact that line 16 generates numbers in the range from 0 to 99 should be clear. The initialization of theta is to $\pi/2$, which is the angle that corresponds to the point of the vertex at the top of the circle.

In lines 18-25, we compute the coordinates of each of the three vertices of the triangle. Because the formulas used for each of the computations are the same, it is desirable to "factor-out" that common code into methods, thus avoiding code duplication, our oft-mentioned rule of good software design. In our earlier discussion of methods, reuse is one reason for creating methods. Reuse, in this case calling both of those methods three times, is exactly what is being done here. The calls to computeX and computeY are method calls to other methods in the same class. As we explained in an earlier section of this chapter, such method calls do not require prepending the method name with the name of the object.

A few additional comments are appropriate with regard to lines 20 and 23. On both lines we are adding the constant ONE_THIRD_CIRCLE, which is π to the angle Θ. Given that a whole circle is $(2/3)\pi$ radians and that an equilateral triangle is also equiangular, we need to add $(2/3)\pi$ to get to the next vertex. In both of these lines, we are using one of the shortcut assignment operators that we introduced previously in this chapter, the += operator. The proper way to read these statements would be to say "Add ONE_THIRD_CIRCLE to theta." The statement that we have written is equivalent to having written:

```
theta = theta + ONE_THIRD_CIRCLE;
```

Next we consider the paint method, the one method with which we have had some previous experience. The local variable, diameter, declared on line 29 is used only within this method, so there should be no temptation to make it an instance variable. Lines 31-33 draw the three sides of the triangle using the drawLine method that we introduced earlier in this chapter. Finally, lines 34 and 35 draw the circle. The order of these four method calls is unimportant.

Finally, we turn our attention to the remaining two methods in the class—computeX and computeY. We begin with the reason for having created these methods. Recall that it was to avoid repeating the same code three times—once for each vertex. Another important issue is our decision to make these methods private. As we discussed earlier in this chapter, a private method is one that can only be called from another method of the same class. Because our program only contains one class it, would not have made much difference whether they were public or private. Nonetheless, our intent is that these methods be used internally, so making them private conveys that intent.

These are the first methods we have written whose signatures we created, so some discussion on how we decided upon the parameter and return type is appropriate. Parameters define the information passed into the method, information that changes from call to call. The one value that varies on each of the three calls is the angle theta. Although the calculation requires the radius, once determined, it remains constant, so accessing the instance variable that contains it is a proper approach. In another program, passing the radius as a parameter might well be reasonable. A program that drew several triangles inside circles with different radii might be such an example. These methods compute the x and y coordinates of one of the vertices of the triangle, so they have a value that needs to be returned to the calling method; therefore, using a value-returning method is appropriate. The value returned is an ordinate, which is an integral value, hence, the return type of int in both cases.

The final topic that we wish to discuss in regard to this program is to examine the *Unified Modeling Language* (UML) class diagram for the TriangleInCircle class, shown in Figure 3.4.

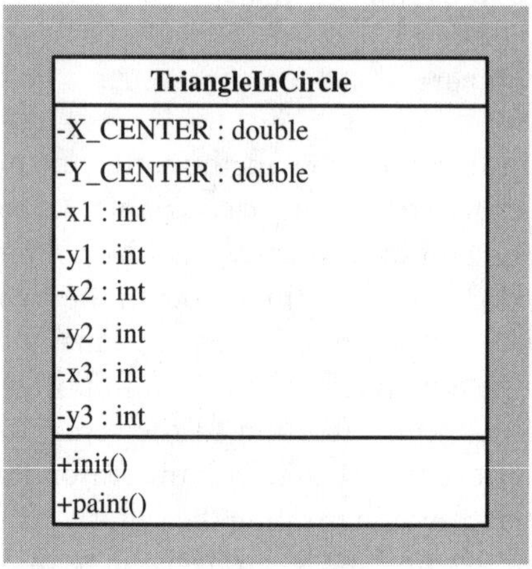

FIGURE 3.4   Class diagram for the TriangleInCircle class.

Although referred to as a language, UML really consists of a variety of different kinds of diagrams. UML has become the standard method for illustrating the design and structure of programs, regardless of the programming language in which they are written. Although we will use other kinds of UML diagrams in this book, the class diagrams are the most important. They are especially important in programs that consist of several classes because they illustrate the interaction between the classes. Nonetheless, we elected to introduce the class diagram in this chapter so that we could explain the individual components of each class diagram. A class diagram has three parts arranged vertically. The top component contains the class name. The middle component contains the instance data of the class, and the bottom part contains the class methods. Notice that the symbol + is used as a prefix for public data or methods and - as a prefix for private data or methods. Finally the type of data is placed after the constant or variable name, not before, as in Java.

SUMMARY

In this chapter, we encountered our first class that contained more than one method. Such classes usually need instance variables that can be accessed by every method of that class. We learned the meaning of scope and lifetime and how the scope and lifetime of instance variables differ from local variables. We also saw how to decide when to make a variable an instance variable. Finally, we learned the difference between private and public methods and why instance variables should always be private. The key points to remember from this chapter are as follows:

■ The public methods of a class define its specification and determine how it can be accessed from outside the class.

■ The instance variables of a class define the representation of objects of that class. By making all instance variables of a class private, we hide the representation of the class and promote the development of loosely coupled programs.

■ Declarations inside a method are local and are accessible only within that method. They are created when the method is called and destroyed when the method completes.

■ Declarations outside all methods but inside a class are accessible to all methods in that class. They are created when objects of that class are created and destroyed when the objects are destroyed.

■ Public methods can be called from outside the class. Private methods can only be called by other methods of that class.

■ The shortcut assignment operators provide an abbreviated syntax for assignments where a variable is being added to, subtracted from, and so on.

Review Questions

1. Explain how you can determine whether a declaration is a local declaration or an instance declaration.
2. What is the scope and lifetime of a local variable?
3. What is the scope and lifetime of a private instance variable?
4. When should a variable be made an instance variable?
5. Under what circumstances should a method of a class be made private?
6. Explain what information is conveyed by a value returning method signature.
7. Explain why it is best to make all instance variables private.
8. Explain why the `init` method cannot call the `paint` method.
9. Explain why, in a value-returning method, the last statement must be a `return` statement.

10. Are the shortcut assignment operators necessary?

Programming Exercises

11. Indicate whether each of the following sequences of local declarations will compile.

    a. `final int SIZE = HALF_SIZE * 2;`

        `final int HALF_SIZE = 10`

    b. `inal int RADIUS =10;`

        `int smallRadius = RADIUS;`

12. Write a value-returning method called `computeDistance` that accepts the *x*-*y* coordinates of two points and returns the distance between the two points.

13. Write a value-returning method that accepts the radius of a circle and returns the area of that circle. The formula for the area of a circle is $A = \pi\, r^2$.

14. Write a value-returning method `degreesToRadians` that converts an angle from degrees to radians. (Note: 360° = 2π radians.)

15. Write a value-returning method computeHeight that returns the height of an equilateral triangle given the length of one of its sides. Use the formula $h = \frac{1}{2}a\sqrt{3}$ to compute the height h, where a is the length of a side.

16. Write a value returning method that returns the area of an equilateral triangle given the length of one of its sides using the formula A = 1/2 a h, where a is the length of one side and h is the height. Call the method computeHeight in Exercise 15 to compute the height.

17. Using two calls to the `drawLine` method, draw two horizontal parallel line segments of length 1 that are 10 pixels apart.

18. Given the following variable declarations:

    ```
    int i = 1, j;
    double d = 0;
    ```

    and the following method signature:

    ```
    int m(double x, int a);
    ```

    indicate whether each of the following method calls will compile:

    a. `j = m(i, i);`

    b. `j = m(d, d);`

    c. `j = m(d, i);`

    d. `d = m(d, d);`

    e. `j = m(d, i, j);`

19. Determine whether each of the following can be rewritten using a shortcut assignment operator. If they can, rewrite the assignment using one.

a.   x = x % y;
b.   a = b + a;
c.   x = y − x;
d.   x = x + y * 5;
e.   x = x * 5 + y;

20. Assuming the x is 1, and y is 2, what is in x after each of the following assignments?

a.   x %= 3 + y;
b.   x *= y − 1;

Programming Projects

21. Write an applet that draws a hollow rectangle with a line connecting the upper-left and lower-right corners and a line connecting the upper-right and lower-left corners as shown in Figure 3.5. The height and the width of the rectangle should both be randomly generated independently once, when the applet is first created.

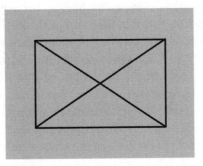

FIGURE 3.5   Output of Chapter 3, Project 21.

22. Modify the program example from this chapter so that it draws three lines connecting each of the vertices of the triangle with the center of the circle as shown in Figure 3.6.

23. Modify the program example from this chapter so that it draws a both an inscribed and circumscribed circle around an equilateral triangle as shown in Figure 3.7. Make use of the fact that the radius of an inscribed circle is half the radius of a circumscribed circle of an equilateral triangle.

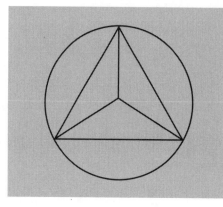

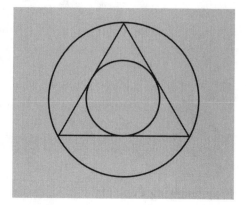

FIGURE 3.6 Output of Chapter 3, Project 22.

FIGURE 3.7 Output of Chapter 3, Project 23.

24. Modify the program example from this chapter so that it draws a diamond inside of a circle as shown in Figure 3.8.

25. Modify the program example for this chapter to test some of the methods written in the programming exercises. Redeclare the local constant ONE_THIRD_CIRCLE to be of type int and initialize it to 120. Redeclare the local variable theta to be of type int also. Modify the methods computeX and computeY so that they accept the angle in integral degrees. Have those methods call the method degreesToRadians written in Programming Exercise 14. Next, use the method computeDistance from Programming Exercise 12 to compute the length of one side of the triangle. Then use the method computeHeight from Programming Exercise 15 to determine the height of the triangle. Use the height to determine the *y* coordinate of the point in the base of the triangle. Draw a vertical line from the top vertex of the triangle to the base of the triangle as shown in Figure 3.9.

NOTE

There are much simpler ways to determine the y coordinate of the bottom vertex of the line perpendicular to the base of the triangle. The suggested technique is to enable some of the methods written in the programming exercises to be used and tested.

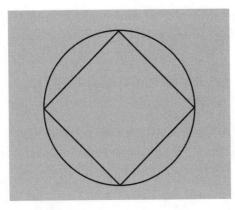

FIGURE 3.8   Output of Chapter 3, Project 24.

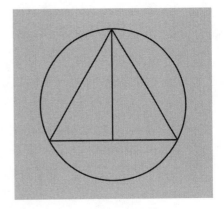

FIGURE 3.9   Output of Chapter 3, Project 25.

4　Discrete Selection and Iteration

In this chapter

- Characters and Strings
- Enumerated Types
- Keyboard Input
- Discrete Selection
- Discrete Iteration
- The Checkerboard Applet

CHARACTERS AND STRINGS

Until now we have been using two groups of predefined types, those for integer and floating-point numbers, and two classes, `Graphics` and `Color`. The example that we have chosen for this chapter requires one new primitive type, `char`, and a related class, `String`.

Single Character Data

The primitive data type `char` is intended for constants and variables that contain single character data. Java uses a 16-bit representation called Unicode to store characters. It is a superset of the predecessor 8-bit representation called ASCII. Unicode is designed to include a more international set of characters.

Like the numeric primitives, the data type char has a predefined syntax for designating *character literal constants*. This syntax is to delimit the character with the single quote character '. As an example, an upper case A would be represented with the character literal 'A'. Although character literals can represent only one *logical character*, there are some characters that must be represented with two *physical characters*—sometimes referred to as *escape sequences*. Some of these characters represent a key on the keyboard that performs an action but does not produce a glyph. The tab key is one such example. Its character literal is '\t'. Another case that requires an escape sequence is when we wish to represent the single quote character itself as a character literal. The problem is that there needs to be a way to distinguish between the single quote as a delimiter—a role often referred to as a *metacharacter*—from the single quote as the character itself. The way to write the single quote as a character literal is the following: '\''. Regardless of the reason for using an escape sequence, a backslash is always the first of its two characters.

Multi-Character Data

As we have just discussed, constants and variables of type char can only contain a single character. Often we need character data that consists of a sequence of characters. To represent such data we need to use the type String. Although it is not a primitive type, it shares some of the characteristics of a primitive type—it has a special syntax for designating its literal values and it has some predefined operators. Neither is true of any other nonprimitive type.

First let's consider the syntax of the literal representation for strings. String literals consist of zero or more characters delimited by the double quote character ". So first of all, the null string, written "", consisting of zero characters, is a valid string literal—in fact, one that is used frequently. It is the string that contains no characters. Another important thing to understand is that a one-character string is different from a character literal that contains the same character. So, for example, the character 'A' is different from the string "A". In most contexts the two are not interchangeable. There is one final issue that is noteworthy regarding string literals. It is a similar situation to the one that we have with character literals—how to write a string that contains the string delimiter ". The backslash character that we used in the escape sequences we discussed earlier is used again in this context. For example, to express the string the language "Java", we would write "the language \"Java\"".

The other characteristic that the type String shares with the primitive types is its predefined operators. Some languages allow programmers to define operators for user-defined types. This feature is called *operator overloading*. Java does not support this feature, which makes the operators defined for String unique among nonprimitive types. Although the only operator defined for strings is +, which means concatenation, this operator is overloaded. In other words, although the left operand of this operator must be a string, the right operand can be a string, but it can also be any of the primitive types. When a primitive type, such as an integer, is concatenated to a string, the representation of the integer is changed to the string that represents it—for example, the number 542 is converted to the string "542". In our example at the end of this chapter, we use two of these overloaded concatenation operators.

Being a nonprimitive type, `String` is a class, which contains many methods that allow manipulation of string objects. In this chapter, we will only use one of those methods—`toUpperCase`—that we will explain when we encounter it. We defer discussing the others to a later chapter.

ENUMERATED TYPES

Java is a language that has undergone many revisions since it was first created. The latest version of Java, version 5.0, has incorporated a feature that was absent from the earlier versions, although present in Java's predecessor, C++, as well as many other programming languages. This feature is the ability to create user-defined types for data that is commonly referred to by names. These types are called *enumerated types*. Programs often involve data that is neither numeric nor character data. Common examples include the days of the week, colors of the rainbow, and suits in a deck of cards, just to name a few that we will have occasion to use in the program examples in the remainder of the book.

The syntax for a simple enumerated type definition is shown in Syntax Definition 4.1.

Syntax Definition 4.1 Syntax of an Enumerated Type Declaration.

```
enumerated_type

    enum type {literal_1 , ... , literal_n }
```

From the syntax definition, we see that it begins with the reserved word `enum`, followed by the name of the enumerated type that we are defining, followed by a list of enumerated literals that represent the possible values of that type. Let's consider some examples:

```
enum Days {SUN, MON, TUE, WED, THU, FRI, SAT}
enum Suits {CLUBS, DIAMONDS, HEARTS, SPADES}
```

Notice the lexical conventions that are used. Like the name of a class, an enumerated type is a type name and it is written in title case—the first letter upper case and the remainder lower case. The convention for the names of the literals is to use all upper case because they are implicitly final objects.

Another important issue is determining where to place these type declarations—determining how broad their scope should be. Although Java allows such declarations to be placed as local declarations inside a method, we discourage such a placement. It is better to broaden the scope of enumerated type names to class-wide scope but limit their accessibility with the modifier `private`, which is the practice we adopt in this chapter. In later chapters, we will broaden their scope further.

Another necessary consideration when defining enumerated types is deciding upon an order for the literal values. The order in which we list them becomes significant in a number of situations. In the examples in this chapter, we iterate across the literal values of an enumerated type. The order in which they are listed determines the order of the iteration. The order is also important in several other situations, another of which we discuss shortly. When the data that we are defining has a well-established order, we should use that order. In the previous examples, days of the week are certainly ordered, although there is some disagreement whether Sunday or Monday is the first day of the week. For the deck of cards, we followed the suit order used in games such as Bridge in our type definition.

With any kind of data type, knowing what operations are permitted is important, which is what we consider next. The most fundamental operation of any kind of data is the ability to assign values to variables of that type. Consider the following declarations and assignments that illustrate the various possibilities:

```
Days weekday, today;

weekday = Days.MON;
today = weekday;
```

Notice first that we can declare variables of an enumerated type in much the same way that we declare variables of any of the primitive types. The preceding code segment illustrates two kinds of assignments. The first assignment assigns a literal value to a variable. Notice that, when we refer to literal values, they must be qualified by prepending them with the name of the type, in much the same way as constants belonging to another class are qualified with their class name. The second assignment assigns one variable to another variable. Such assignments are permitted, provided both variables are of the same type. One kind of an assignment that is prohibited is attempting to assign an integer value to a variable of an enumerated type. Java enumerated types are often referred to as *type-safe*, which means that the language ensures that variables of this type can never contain values other than the literal values defined for that type.

Finally, among the methods that are predefined on all enumerated types, there are two that are important to consider at this time. The first is the method `ordinal`. This method produces an integer value that is the underlying ordinal value that represents a particular literal value. Using the variables from the previous example, `weekday.ordinal()` would be 1. The values of an enumerated type are given ordinal values beginning at 0 in the order in which they are listed. So the literal value `Days.SUN` would have the ordinal value 0 and `Days.MON` the ordinal value 1, which is why `weekday.ordinal()` would be 1. The other method is `name`. It produces a string value that corresponds to the name of the literal. For example, `weekday.name()` would produce the string `"MON"`.

KEYBOARD INPUT

We will examine our first program that allows the user to enter input in this chapter. Such programs are more interesting because they give the user some control over the behavior of the program and its output. In programs that are executed in a command-line environment like MS-DOS, the input is entered on the command-line, which is sometimes referred to as *console input*. Until Chapter 11, all our programs run in a graphics mode, so the input must be entered in some window. Java provides a class called `JOptionPane` that contains numerous methods that allow this kind of input. Rather than using this class directly, we have created an intermediary class `InputOutput`, which in turn uses `JOptionPane`. Our reason for doing this is that there are things needed for certain types of input that require language features, such as exception handling, that we have not yet discussed. The CD-ROM that accompanies this book contains the source code for this class, which can be found at `common\InputOutput.java`, so that you can compile and run the program example presented later in this chapter. The CD-ROM also contains documentation generated by a Java documentation generation tool called `javadoc` for the InputOutput class, among others. We will explain the details of the `InputOutput` class once we have discussed all the language features it requires.

For now, we confine our discussion to how to use the `InputOutput` class, which, like the `Math` class, has the role of a utility class. Recall that a class acting in the role of a utility is one that contains exclusively class methods and never has objects created of that class. Furthermore, it contains no instance variables. In this chapter, we use one method of `InputOutput`, whose signature is shown below:

```
static char getCharacter(String prompt, String validChars)
```

This method allows the user to enter a single character. The character entered is returned by this method. The caller supplies getCharacter with a string containing a prompt that is displayed in the input window explaining to the user what to enter. The second parameter is a string that contains a list of all the valid characters. This method is used for input that allows selection from a short menu of choices. The character entered is how the user specifies which one is chosen. The method does not return to the caller until one of the characters in the list of valid characters is selected.

DISCRETE SELECTION

Although some of the programs that we have studied so far have had multiple entry points, starting with either the init or paint method, once entered, the program execution always followed a single path. Like programs with no input, such programs are of limited interest because there is little variation in their behavior. In this chapter, for the first time we encounter programs that contain multiple paths.

Discrete Types

Before we examine the details of the switch statement, we first need to consider another categorization of types. We have already categorized types into primitive and nonprimitive or class types. Next we subdivide the primitive types into *discrete types* and *nondiscrete types*. Discrete types are sometimes referred to as *ordinal or integral types*. The discrete types include all of the integer types, the character type and any user-defined enumerated type. The key feature of a discrete type is that each value, with the exception of the first and last, has one predecessor and one successor. Notice that the types excluded from this group are the floating-point types that represent real numbers. In mathematics, the real numbers are infinitely dense—between any two real numbers, there is always another real number. In practice, both floating point representations have finite precision, so although a real number may exist between two *model numbers*—those that can be exactly represented—there may not be a model number between them. Nonetheless, we still regard the floating-point types as nondiscrete, because the real numbers that they are intended to represent are not discrete.

Most Java books present the if and while statements before the switch and for statements because they are syntactically simpler. The latter two statements are simpler semantically, which is why we have chosen to begin with them. Both rely on discrete types. A switch statement chooses among a discrete set of values. A for statement, when properly used, iterates across a discrete ranges of values.

The Syntax and Semantics of the `switch` Statement

Both of the executable statements that we have studied so far—the method call and the assignment statement—have been simple statements, meaning that they cannot contain other statements. The `switch` statement that we consider now is the first executable statement that can have other statements nested inside it, which is again expressed by the use of indentation. Let's examine its syntax, which is shown in Syntax Definition 4.2.

Syntax Definition 4.2 Syntax of a `switch` Statement

```
switch_statement

    switch ( expression )
    {
        case  expression_1 :
            statements
            break;
        ...
        case  expression_n :
            statements
            break;
    }
```

Let's consider how a `switch` statement is constructed. The reserved word `switch` is followed by an expression that contains the `switch` selector, whose role we explain shortly. It generally consists of at least two cases. Each case consists of a `case` statement that specifies the `case` value after the reserved word `case`, followed by one or more statements ending with a `break` statement that consists of a single reserved word—`break`. The actual syntax of the `switch` statement is somewhat more general, but we will elaborate on those generalities in a later chapter.

Although the syntax of the `switch` statement may appear somewhat complicated, conceptually its semantics, that is, its behavior, are really quite simple. The `switch` selector expression is evaluated and control is transferred to the case whose `case` value it matches. If it matches no `case` value, the control transfers to the statement following the `switch` statement. So the `case` statement splits the control flow into several paths, which are rejoined after the statements belonging to the selected case are executed.

There are two semantic rules associated with this statement. The first is that the type of the expression that is contained in the `switch` selector must be a discrete type—hence our characterization of the statement as a discrete selection statement. It is selecting among a discrete set of choices. The second semantic rule is that the expression contained in each case value must be a constant expression. A constant expression is one that contains no variables. A similar restriction is imposed on the initializer expression of a constant declaration.

There is one pitfall that is important to avoid, which is failing to include a break statement at the end of each case. Unfortunately, this omission does not create a syntax error. Instead it alters the behavior of the statement in an undesirable way, causing the flow of control to fall from one case into the next.

An enumerated type is an ideal type to use with a switch statement. There is one special syntactic feature of this combination that you should be aware of. When a literal value is listed as the value of a particular case inside a switch statement, the literal value does not need to be qualified by the type name. The type of the case selector has already established its type. The example that follows will illustrate this point.

An Example Using an Enumerated Type and the switch Statement

Our first example is an applet that displays a random shape. The shape displayed is a square, a rectangle, a circle, or an oval. An enumerated type is well suited for this problem specification. The code for this applet is shown in Listing 4.1.

LISTING 4.1 An applet Displaying a Random Shape (found on the CD-ROM at

ON THE CD   chapter4\RandomShape.java.)

```
1   package chapter4;
2
3   import java.awt.*;
4   import javax.swing.*;
5
6   public class RandomShape extends JApplet
7   {
8       private enum Shapes{SQUARE, RECTANGLE, CIRCLE, OVAL}
9
10      private Shapes shape;
11
12      public void init()
13      {
14          int shapeNumber = (int)(Math.random() * 4);
15
16          switch (shapeNumber)
17          {
18              case 0:
19                  shape = Shapes.SQUARE;
20                  break;
21              case 1:
```

```
22                              shape = Shapes.RECTANGLE;
23                              break;
24                          case 2:
25                              shape = Shapes.CIRCLE;
26                              break;
27                          case 3:
28                              shape = Shapes.OVAL;
29                              break;
30                      }
31              }
32              public void paint(Graphics graphics)
33              {
34                  final int XY = 50, WIDTH = 100;
35
36                  switch(shape)
37                  {
38                      case SQUARE:
39                          graphics.drawRect(XY, XY, WIDTH, WIDTH);
40                          break;
41                      case RECTANGLE:
42                          graphics.drawRect(XY, XY, WIDTH, WIDTH / 2);
43                          break;
44                      case CIRCLE:
45                          graphics.drawOval(XY, XY, WIDTH, WIDTH);
46                          break;
47                      case OVAL:
48                          graphics.drawOval(XY, XY, WIDTH, WIDTH / 2);
49                          break;
50                  }
51              }
52      }
```

Let's examine the code. On line 8 is the declaration of the enumerated type Shapes. As we already mentioned, we have elected to give the enumerated type declarations in the examples in this chapter class-wide scope, with accessibility limited to this class by using the access modifier private. This type is visible throughout the class RandomShape. As in previous examples, the random selection is made only once when the applet is first created, so the random selection is done in the method init and the value is saved in the instance variable shape declared on line 10. On line 14, we generate a random number between 0 and 3. Because we cannot assign an integer to an enumerated variable, a switch statement spanning lines 16-30 is required to make the correspondence between the integer value and the enumerated literal. In this statement, the switch selector is an integer, as are the values for each of the four cases.

The `paint` method also contains a `switch` statement that accesses the enumerated type variable `shape`. The type of the `switch` selector in this statement is the enumerated type `Shapes`. It draws the kind of shape specified by that variable. Notice, as mentioned earlier, enumerated literals need not be qualified by the type name in a `case` selector. For example, on line 38 we can refer to `SQUARE` and need not write `Shapes.SQUARE`.

One thing that you may have noticed if you compiled this class is that two `.class` files were generated. Not only is the file `Shapes.class` that you have come to expect created, but also a file named `RandomShape$Shapes.class`. The latter file contains the bytecode for the definition of the enumerated type `Shapes`. Notice the use of the `$` in this name. In Chapter 1, we mentioned that Java allows a `$` to be used in identifiers, but cautioned against their use because the compiler itself generates such names. When we encounter inner classes in a later chapter, we will observe a similar behavior.

Choosing Test Data

Once we begin to write programs that contain more than one path, it becomes important to be sure that we choose adequate test data for the program. Although no amount of test data can guarantee that a program is completely correct, by carefully choosing test data, we increase the likelihood of correctness.

Considering the various paths a program can follow provides one basis for choosing test data. Running the program once with test data that will follow each of the various paths would be desirable, but once we realize how quickly the number of paths grows, we may need to aim for a lesser goal. In a program containing two `switch` statements—each contributing 3 paths—the total number of paths is 9, which is 3 × 3. So you can see how rapidly the number of paths will grow as programs become large. A lesser requirement would be to choose enough different test cases so that each line in the program is executed by at least one of the test cases.

DISCRETE ITERATION

No matter how many `switch` statements a program has, the direction of the flow of control is still always in the forward direction. Consequently this control mechanism is inadequate for a particular class of problems—those that require repetition or iteration. Next we consider a statement that allows us to write programs that are capable of repeating sections of code. Such programs then have a control flow that contains loops—control flow that at some point goes backwards.

The Syntax and Semantics of the `for` Statement

The `for` statement is the ideal choice for iterating over a discrete range of values. Although the `for` statement has been in Java since the first version, we begin with a new variation of the syntax, added in Java 5.0, that is ideally suited for iterating across all the values of an enumerated type. The syntax is shown in Syntax Definition 4.3.

Syntax Definition 4.3 Syntax of a *for_each* Style `for` Statement.

```
for_each_statement

    for ( enumerated_type variable  :  enumerated_type .values())
        statement
```

As you could no doubt predict, `for` is a reserved word. The variable, which is declared in this statement, is referred to as the *loop control variable*. The statement that is nested inside of the `for` statement is known as the *loop body*. This variation of the `for` statement is sometimes referred to as a *for-each* statement because it can be read "for each value of the enumerated type, execute the specified statement." Specifically, the loop control variable takes on each of the possible values of the enumerated type, once for each execution of the loop body. The method `values` returns an object that has what is called an *iterator*. The *for-each* variation of the `for` statement can be used with other types, which we will see in Chapter 7 when we discuss arrays.

Now we turn to the original version of the `for` statement, but we confine our discussion to a restricted usage that behaves much like the new *for-each* variation. The actual syntax of the original `for` statement is more general than we present here, but we postpone the more general discussion until we come to general iteration in Chapter 6. We will consider two kinds of loops, those that count upward and those that count downward. Let's begin with the syntax of the upward counting loops shown in Syntax Definition 4.4.

Syntax Definition 4.4 Syntax of an Upward Counting `for` Statement.

```
upward_for_statement

    for ( type variable = start; variable <= end; variable ++)
        statement
```

The type specified should be a discrete type, an integer, or character type. There is one difference here compared to the `switch` statement discussed earlier. Using a switch selector that is a type other than a discrete type causes a compilation error. Although that result would not occur here, we treat the requirement as though it were a language rule for the sake of good style. Unfortunately, unlike the newer for-each variation, the loop control variable must be repeated in each of the three parts of the loop. The placeholder *start* specifies the initial value of that variable. Syntactically, it can be as general as an expression. In the programs we consider initially, it will always be a constant. The placeholder *end* specifies the last value of the variable. It too can be an expression, but initially will most often be just a constant. The loop body is executed repeatedly for varying values of the loop control variable. One important restriction upon which we insist, but the compiler does not enforce, is that the loop control variable is never modified in the loop body. With that restriction, we are guaranteed that the loop will always stop, which is why we introduce it first. It is conceptually simpler than the while loop that we will encounter in Chapter 6. With this restricted usage, this variation of the for statement behaves much like the newer variation that can be used for enumerated types. Reading a for statement in English properly is helpful in understanding the similarity. The following for statement

```
for(int i = 1; i <= 10; i++)
    ...
```

should be read "for i, taking on each value in the range from 1 to 10, do such and such." So the body of the loop will be executed ten times, with i containing the values 1, 2, 3, ...10.

Next let's consider the syntax of downward counting loops shown in Syntax Definition 4.5.

Syntax Definition 4.5 Syntax of a Downward Counting for Statement.

```
downward_for_statement

    for ( type variable = start; variable >= end; variable --)
        statement.
```

Notice that two things have changed in the syntax: <= and ++ were replaced by >= and --, respectively. Although all four of these symbols are operators, we view them as a fixed part of the statement syntax for the moment. We elaborate on the ++ and == operators shortly and the other two in Chapter 6.

In upward counting loops, the starting value should be less than or equal to the ending value, and the reverse should be true in downward counting loops. Failing to arrange the values in this way is not an error, however. A starting value that is larger than an ending value in an upward loop will result in the body of the loop never executing.

The Standalone Increment and Decrement Operators

Although we have shown the symbol ++ as a fixed part of the upward for statement and the symbol –– as part of the downward counting for statement, these symbols are actually the *increment* and *decrement operators*, respectively. They can be used in contexts other than a for loop. Used independently, they are assignment expressions. The increment operator causes 1 to be added to the specified variable and the decrement operator causes 1 to be subtracted. We specify the syntax of the increment assignment explicitly in Syntax Definition 4.6 to emphasis one important point.

Syntax Definition 4.6 Syntax of an Incrementing Assignment Expression.

```
increment_assignment_expression

    variable ++
```

What is placed before an increment or decrement operator must be a variable, not a constant or an expression. These expressions are assignments, so it is as though the variable is on the left-hand side of an assignment.

In Chapter 3, we encountered other assignment operators. At that point, we observed that those operators introduced redundancy into the language. The increment and decrement operators add additional redundancy. We now have three different ways to increment the variable x:

```
x = x + 1;
x += 1;
x++;
```

We return to the observation that we made in the previous chapter with regard to the operators + and +=. We observed that the latter was less general than the former and could only be used when we are adding some value to a particular variable, but could not be used when we are adding together two variables and storing the result in a third. The increment operator is the least general of all three. So we extend the guidance about good style provided in the previous chapter to include when to use each of them. If you are adding 1 to a variable, use ++. If you are adding a value other than 1 to a variable, use +=, otherwise, use +. In other words, always use the least general of the three that can be used.

There is yet another variation on the use of the increment and decrement operators, but we will postpone the discussion of those variations until Chapter 7.

Compound Statements

There is one more important feature of the syntax of the `for` statement, in each of its forms, that is important to notice. The placeholder for the loop body is *statement*, singular, which means exactly one statement. If you look back at the `switch` statement syntax you will notice that each case consisted of *statements*, plural, meaning one or more statement was permitted. All of the remaining Java statements that we will study that allow other statements nested inside of them will be similar to the `for` statement in this regard. The natural question is: What do we do if we need more than one statement in the body of a `for` loop—something that is frequently required? The answer is to make that one statement a compound statement whose syntax is shown in Syntax Definition 4.7.

Syntax Definition 4.7 Syntax of a Compound Statement

```
compound_statement

    {
        statements
    }
```

A compound statement is a sequence of statements, usually two or more, that are delimited by matching braces. We have already seen the braces used as delimiters for class and method boundaries. This context is yet another instance of their use as delimiters. One comment regarding indentation is warranted. When the body of a loop is a single statement, that statement is indented beyond the reserved word `for`. When the body is a compound statement, its braces are aligned with the `for`, but all the statements inside are indented.

The Scope and Lifetime of the Loop Control Variable

In Chapter 3, we discussed the difference between the scope of local variables and instance variables. Now we consider the scope and lifetime of the loop control variable of a `for` loop. Its scope is the body of the loop. What that means is that a loop control variable cannot be accessed outside the loop. Its lifetime is the time period during which the `for` statement is executing. It is created when the loop begins and destroyed when the loop ends.

It is permitted to have two for loops in the same method in succession that contain loop control variables with the same name, but keep in mind that they are not the same variable. What is not permitted is to have a local variable in a method with the same name as a loop control variable.

More Details on the Scope of Local Variables

For the sake of completeness, at this point we will elaborate on some details of the scope rules for local variables that we omitted in our discussion of the topic in the previous chapter. At that time, we stated that the scope of a local variable was from its declaration to the end of the method in which it is declared, which is true if the declaration is in the outermost *block*—a practice that we have always adhered to. A block is a compound statement that contains declarations. Java not only permits the interspersing of statements and declarations—a practice that we prefer to avoid—but it also permits nested blocks. It is easiest to understand this concept with an example. Consider the following code segment:

```
{
    int outer;
    {
        int inner;
    } // The scope of inner ends here
    inner = 1; // A compilation error be generated
} //The scope of outer ends here
```

The proper way to state the scope of any local variable, or constant, is that its scope is from its declaration to the end of the block in which it is declared. As was true with the for statement, having two variables or constants of the same name in the same method is permitted if their scopes are disjoint. What is not permitted is local variables or constants with the same name declared in different but overlapping blocks.

Because methods in programs written in object-oriented languages tend to be small, we see little advantage to using inner blocks. Consequently, none of the examples in this book contain declarations in inner blocks—aside from the special case of the for statement.

An Example Using an Enumerated Type and switch and for Statements

We are now ready to consider our first example using a for statement. This example involves an enumerated type, so the for statement it contains is the new *for-each* variation. It is an applet that displays a sequence of circles of decreasing diameter—one for each color of the rainbow. The code for this program is shown in Listing 4.2.

ON THE CD **LISTING 4.2** An Applet Displaying Rainbow Colored Circles (found on the CD-ROM at chapter4\ColoredCircles.java.)

```java
1   package chapter4;
2
3   import java.awt.*;
4   import javax.swing.*;
5
6   public class ColoredCircles extends JApplet
7   {
8       private enum RainbowColors{RED, ORANGE, YELLOW, GREEN, BLUE,
9           INDIGO, VIOLET}
10
11      public void paint(Graphics graphics)
12      {
13          final int XY = 50, DECREMENT = 10;
14          int diameter = 100;
15
16          for (RainbowColors color: RainbowColors.values())
17          {
18              graphics.setColor(getColor(color));
19              graphics.fillOval(XY, XY, diameter, diameter);
20              diameter -= DECREMENT;
21          }
22      }
23      private Color getColor(RainbowColors color)
24      {
25          switch(color)
26          {
27              case RED:
28                  return Color.RED;
29              case ORANGE:
30                  return Color.ORANGE;
31              case YELLOW:
32                  return Color.YELLOW;
33              case GREEN:
34                  return Color.GREEN;
35              case BLUE:
36                  return Color.BLUE;
37              case INDIGO:
38                  return Color.MAGENTA;
39              case VIOLET:
40                  return Color.MAGENTA.darker();
41          }
```

```
42          return Color.BLACK;
43      }
44  }
```

We begin on line 8, which contains the enumerated type definition for the colors of the rainbow. Notice that we have arranged the colors in their natural order, which is by wavelength. As we had done in the previous example using an enumerated type, we have given the enumerated type definition in this example class-wide scope, with access limited to the class using the access modifier private.

This applet contains two methods—the method paint that all our applets contain and a private method, getColor. The former contains a for statement, beginning on line 16, that the iterates across all colors of the rainbow. The variable color, declared on that line, is the loop control variable. The loop body is executed seven times, once for each of the rainbow colors. Notice that the body, which spans lines 17-21, contains three statements, so those three statements must be embedded inside a compound statement, which accounts for the braces on lines 17 and 21.

The method getColor, which is called on each iteration to set the proper color, performs the association between the colors that comprise the type RainbowColors and the constants defined in the predefined class Color. A switch statement that forms the body of getColor is ideal for making this association.

Notice that none of the cases of the switch statement that spans lines 25-41 contains a break statement, which contradicts the syntax of the switch statement, as we first presented it, earlier in this chapter. Our initial explanation that a break is required at the end of every case was an oversimplification. Omitting a break statement will never produce a syntax error, but what will happen is that the flow of control will fall into the next case—something that we usually do not want to happen. Using a return statement as the last statement of each case prevents control from falling into the next case because it causes the method to return to its caller. Consequently, in this situation no break statements are needed.

Finally, notice the return statement on line 42. This statement will never be executed, but we must include it to prevent a compilation error. The compiler wants to be sure that we never leave a value-returning method without executing a return statement as the last statement executed. Although we know that the return statement on line 42 will never execute, it is difficult for the compiler to perform a perfect path analysis to reach the same conclusion. As a result, occasionally we need to include a return statement or initialize a variable that should not be necessary.

An Example Using a for Loop Across a Discrete Range of Integers

Our next example makes use of the traditional for loop syntax. It involves one of the most famous sequences of numbers, the *Fibonacci sequence*. This number sequence appears frequently in the description of growth patterns in nature. As an example, the number of seeds in every sunflower is a Fibonacci number. It also appears frequently in computer science—especially in data structures, so it is a number sequence that you should be familiar with, if you are not already. The first fifteen terms of the sequence—the ones that we will compute in this example—are shown below:

0 1 1 2 3 5 8 13 21 35 21 34 55 89 144 233 377

The sequence begins with a 0 followed by a 1, then every subsequent term is the sum of the two previous. Our example draws a Fibonacci spiral, which consists of rectilinear line segments whose lengths are successive Fibonacci numbers. The line segments are drawn in rotating directions. In our example, the directions rotate counter clockwise, first to the right, then up, then to the left, next downward, and then to the right again. The output of this program is shown in Figure 4.1

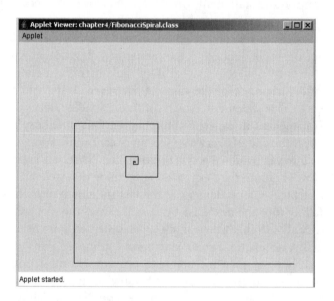

FIGURE 4.1 The Fibonnaci spiral.

Smoothed out, a Fibonacci spiral becomes a logarithmic spiral, which is characteristic of seashells. The code for this applet is shown in Listing 4.3.

LISTING 4.3   The Fibonacci Spiral Applet (found on the CD-ROM at chapter4\FibonacciSpiral.java.)

```
1   package chapter4;
2
3   import java.awt.*;
4   import javax.swing.*;
5
6   public class FibonacciSpiral extends JApplet
7   {
8       private enum Directions {RIGHT, UP, LEFT, DOWN}
9
10      private final int CENTER = 200;
11
12      public void paint(Graphics graphics)
13      {
14          Directions direction = Directions.RIGHT;
15          int secondPrevious = 0, previous = 1, current;
16          int fromX = CENTER, fromY = CENTER, toX = fromX, toY = fromY;
17
18          for (int count = 1; count <= 13; count++)
19          {
20              current = secondPrevious + previous;
21              switch (direction)
22              {
23                  case RIGHT:
24                      toX = fromX + current;
25                      toY = fromY;
26                      direction = Directions.UP;
27                      break;
28                  case UP:
29                      toX = fromX;
30                      toY = fromY − current;
31                      direction = Directions.LEFT;
32                      break;
33                  case LEFT:
34                      toX = fromX − current;
35                      toY = fromY;
36                      direction = Directions.DOWN;
37                      break;
38                  case DOWN:
39                      toX = fromX;
40                      toY = fromY + current;
41                      direction = Directions.RIGHT;
```

```
42                          break;
43                      }
44                  graphics.drawLine(fromX, fromY, toX, toY);
45                  secondPrevious = previous;
46                  previous = current;
47                  fromX = toX;
48                  fromY = toY;
49              }
50          }
51      }
```

This example provides us another opportunity to make use of an enumerated type. On line 8, we declare the enumerated type Directions, which defines the four different directions in which the line segments of the spiral will be drawn. Inside the paint method, on line 14, we declare a local variable of that type, which we arbitrarily initialize to first point in the right direction.

On line 15, we declare three integer variables, secondPrevious, previous, and current, that will contain three successive terms of this sequence. The first two of them must be initialized. These three variables maintain a kind of window across this sequence that always keeps three terms of the sequence in view, which is necessary because to compute each subsequent value we need the previous two. The use of several variables to create this kind of a moving window is a common programming technique that we will encounter again later in the book. When we examine more of the code in this program, we will explain the assignments needed to effectively move this window one position forward.

On line 16, we declare four integer variables: fromX, fromY, toX, and toY. These four variables contain the *x-y* coordinates of the two end points of the line segments of the spiral. The beginning point of the spiral is the center, so the *from* coordinate must be initialized to that point. Notice, however, that we also initialized the *to* coordinate to the same point. The reason for initializing the *to* coordinate is only to satisfy the Java compiler that would otherwise give us an error message on line 44 stating that that these variables may be uninitialized. In fact, it is not possible to reach 44 without having them be initialized in one of the four cases of the switch statement, but the compiler is not "smart" enough to realize that. This situation is similar to the return statement that was required in the previous example. Often, however, when the compiler gives such errors, the variables really are uninitialized. Because using uninitialized variables creates programs that exhibit one of the worst possible behaviors—producing different results on different runs of the program—it is better for the compiler to err on the side of caution. Forcing the programmer to perform unnecessary initializations may be a nuisance, but it causes no harm. Allowing programs that contain uninitialized variables to run, as many languages do, is much more harmful, so we should be thankful that Java prevents this.

In fact, Java ensures that all variables and returned values are initialized. In the case of local variables and values returned by value-returning methods, it prohibits suspected problems by generating compilation errors. In the case of instance variables, the compiler initializes them, which is another way of preventing the possibility of any variable being uninitialized.

This program contains our first use of the traditional `for` loop syntax. Specifically it uses the upward `for` loop syntax, which begins on line 18. It iterates across the range of values from 1 to 13. Although this loop does not use the new *for-each* syntax, we should still read it in a way similar to how we read loops that use the new syntax—"for each integer in the range from 1 to 13." Conceptually we need to specify three things to the syntax skeleton—the name of the loop control variable, the starting value and the ending value. Recall, though, that unlike the newer *for-each* style syntax, the name of the loop control variable must be written three times. Now let's consider the body of the loop. The assignment of line 20 computes the next Fibonacci number as the sum of the two previous. This Fibonacci number will be the length of the next line segment to be drawn. One of the *to* ordinates will be that distance away from the *from* ordinate. The `switch` statement that spans lines 21-43 determines exactly how that distance is achieved. For the right and left direction, the Fibonacci number is added to or subtracted from, respectively, the `fromX` ordinate to produce the `toX` ordinate. A similar calculation is done on the *y* ordinates for the up and down directions. At the end of each case, line 26 being the first such instance, the new direction is updated to be the next direction—moving counterclockwise. Once the *to* coordinate is calculated, the line segment is drawn, which occurs on line 44. The next two lines accomplish moving the "window" that we described earlier to the next triplet of values. Figure 4.2 illustrates the effect of these two lines of code, showing the window before and the window after.

When this technique is used, we always see the same kind of assignments at the end of the loop—regardless of what kind of data we are dealing with. The last two lines in the loop, lines 47 and 48, are accomplishing a similar task. In addition to the sequence of Fibonacci numbers, our program involves a sequence of coordinates of the spiral being drawn. We need to also maintain a window across this sequence; however, it needs only two values of the sequence in view. Lines 47 and 48 are both effectively "assign previous to current" statements. The only difference is that we have used the adjectives *from* and *to*, in place of *previous* and *current*.

There is one final observation about this program that is warranted. Another approach that we could have used to achieve the circular rotation of the directions would have been to perform modular arithmetic using the remainder operator in place of the enumerated type. As a case selector, we could have used `count % 4`, and made the four case values 0, 1, 2, and 3. If we wanted to ensure the direction to the right would be done first, `(count - 1) % 4` would actually be needed. That approach would shorten the program, eliminating all the assignments to the next direction, but we would lose the documentation that the enumerated literals add to the program. In the example at the end of this chapter, we will use modular arithmetic implemented with the remainder operator to create a similar kind of circular behavior.

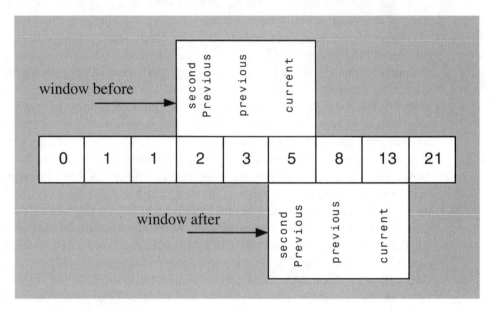

FIGURE 4.2 Moving the window across the Fibonacci number sequence.

Nested `for` Statements

With statements like the `for` and `switch` statements that allow other statements to be nested inside of them, the nested statements themselves cannot only be simple statements, but can also be other `for` or `switch` statements. Such nesting is an essential feature of programs of even modest complexity.

An Example Using an Enumerated Type and Nested `for` Statements

Before we turn to our primary example of this chapter that contains nested `for` statements involving a discrete range of integers, let's consider a simpler example of nested `for` loops. It is an applet that outputs a calendar for the month of February 2009. We chose that month for simplicity because 2009 is not a leap year, so it contains 28 days, and in that year, February 1st is a Sunday. The output of this applet is shown in Figure 4.3.

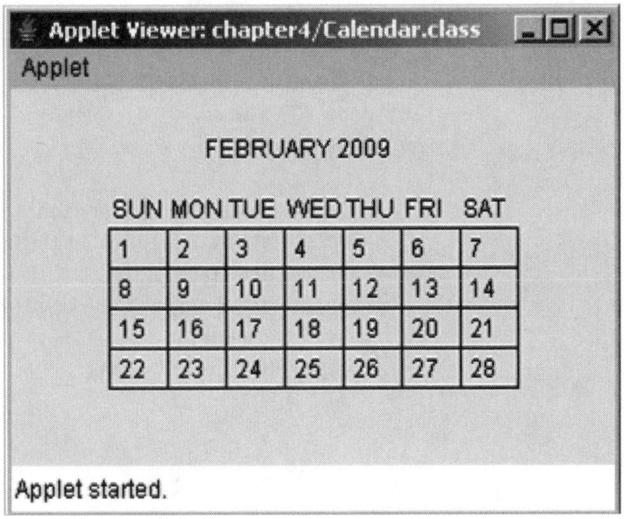

FIGURE 4.3 Output of the applet that displays the calendar for February 2009.

The code for this applet is shown in Listing 4.4.

LISTING 4.4 An Applet Displaying a Calendar for February 2009 (found on the CD-ROM *ON THE CD* at chapter4\Calendar.java.)

```
1   package chapter4;
2
3   import java.awt.*;
4   import javax.swing.*;
5
6   public class Calendar extends JApplet
7   {
8       private enum Days {SUN, MON, TUE, WED, THU, FRI, SAT}
9
10      public void paint(Graphics graphics)
11      {
12          final int WIDTH = 30, HEIGHT = 20, LEFT_MARGIN = 50,
13              TOP_MARGIN = 50, DAY_OFFSET = 2, X_OFFSET = 5,
14              Y_OFFSET = 15, MONTH_INDENT = 50;
15          int x, y, dayOfMonth = 1;
16
17          graphics.drawString("FEBRUARY 2009", LEFT_MARGIN +
18              MONTH_INDENT, TOP_MARGIN - Y_OFFSET);
19          for (Days day: Days.values())
```

```
20                    graphics.drawString(day.name(),
21                        LEFT_MARGIN + DAY_OFFSET + day.ordinal() * WIDTH,
22                        TOP_MARGIN + Y_OFFSET);
23            for (int week = 1; week <= 4; week++)
24                for (Days day: Days.values())
25                {
26                    x = LEFT_MARGIN + day.ordinal() * WIDTH;
27                    y = TOP_MARGIN + week * HEIGHT;
28                    graphics.drawRect(x, y, WIDTH, HEIGHT);
29                    graphics.drawString("" + dayOfMonth, x + X_OFFSET,
30                        y + Y_OFFSET);
31                    dayOfMonth++;
32                }
33        }
34  }
```

This applet uses the enumerated type Days, declared on line 8, that we used earlier as one of the examples of enumerated types. Like many of our simpler applets, this one consists only of the single method paint, which paints the calendar. We have declared numerous constants on lines 12-14, in keeping with the practice that naming constants, especially numeric ones, is a helpful practice, particularly if we ever need to modify the program. These constants are mainly ones to adjust the position of what is being painted, hence, names that involve margins, indents, and offsets. Three local variables, declared on line 15, are needed, the first two, x and y, to keep track of the coordinates of what is being painted, and the third, dayOfMonth, represents the current day to be displayed.

Next, we consider the executable statements that accomplish the actual calendar construction. This is our first example to use the drawString method—another method from the Graphics class. It is first used in this example on lines 17 and 18, to draw the title "FEBRUARY 2009." Let's examine the signature of this method to clarify its use:

```
void drawString(String str, int x, int y)
```

The first parameter is the string to be drawn, the second and third represent the *x-y* coordinates of the upper left-hand corner of the location where it is to be drawn.

After drawing the calendar title, the headings are drawn for the names of each day of the week. The for statement on lines 19-22 draws the names of the days. This for statement is again one that involves an enumerated type—Days. The body of this loop consists of a call to the method drawString as was needed to draw the title. The string that is displayed is the string that corresponds to the day of the week. The method name that we discussed earlier, which is defined for all enumerated types, is used to produce the string that corresponds to the enumerated literal. It converts the literal SUN to the string "SUN". Although the *y* ordinate of all the day names is the same, the *x* ordinate varies. To compute the *x* ordinate, we need to use the ordinal method, another method defined for all enumerated types. Recall that this method produces the underlying ordinal value: 0 for Sunday, 1 for Monday, and so on.

The remaining code consists of nested for loops that span lines 23-32. The outermost loop iterates across the four weeks in February 2009. It uses the traditional for loop syntax for loops that count upward. It is intended to iterate across the range of values from 1 to 4. This loop controls the drawing of the four rows of the calendar that correspond to the four weeks of the month. The innermost loop iterates across the seven days of the week, just as was done with the earlier for loop that began on line 19. This inner loop controls the drawing of the seven columns that correspond to the days of the week. One important thing to realize about nested loops is that the number of times the body of the innermost loop is executed is the product of the number of times the two loops iterate. In this case, the outer loop produces four iterations and the inner loop produces seven, so the total iterations are 28 the product of the two. We will make a similar observation when we examine the nested loops in the primary example of the chapter that follows. Now let's consider this code that is repeated 28 times. First we must compute the position of this day on the calendar. Its *x* position depends upon the ordinal value of the day of the week, as was true for the day labels. This calculation is performed on line 26. It *y* position depends upon the week number. Its value is calculated on line 27. On line 28, a hollow rectangle is drawn at the coordinates that were just calculated. Then on lines 29 and 30, the day of the week is drawn using the drawString method that we used earlier to draw the day names. The expression "" + dayOfMonth, has the effect of converting the day of the month into a string. It does this by concatenating an integer variable, dayOfMonth, to the null string "". Recall that a + operator is defined that performs such concatenations. Finally the variable dayOfMonth is incremented using the increment operator that we introduced previously in this chapter.

THE CHECKERBOARD APPLET

We are now prepared to discuss our main program example for this chapter. It is an applet that draws a checkerboard, which contains the usual 64 squares, arranged 8 by 8. They alternate between red and black, as is customary on a checkerboard. This program performs one task atypical of a standard checkerboard, however, which is to number the squares in one of three different ways, either horizontally, row by row; vertically, column by column; or with row and column number pairs. Understanding these three numbering schemes has an added benefit, which is preparing you for understanding some related ideas concerning two-dimensional arrays that we will encounter in a later chapter. Figure 4.4 shows the output of this applet.

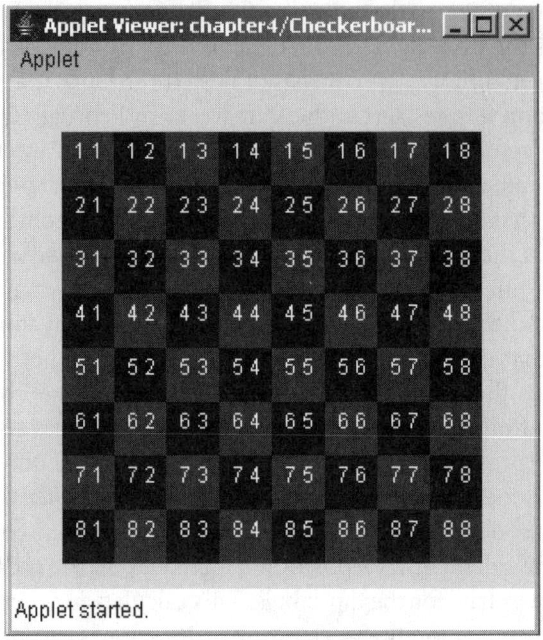

FIGURE 4.4   The output of the checkerboard applet.

This program is structurally similar to the one in the previous chapter. It is an applet that consists of a single class that contains multiple methods and some instance constants and variables. As before, the same two methods, init and paint, are public. The remaining methods are private. One important difference between this program and all that we have studied so far is that this one is the first that allows the user to supply input.

Let's begin our customary analysis of the code for this program shown in Listing 4.5.

LISTING 4.5   An applet that Draws a Numbered Checkerboard (found on the CD-ROM
ON THE CD   at chapter4\Checkerboard.java.)

```
1   package chapter4;
2
3   import java.awt.*;
4   import javax.swing.*;
5   import common.*;
6
7   public class Checkerboard extends JApplet
```

```
8   {
9       private final int SIZE = 8, SQUARES = SIZE * SIZE;
10      private char scheme;
11
12      public void init()
13      {
14          scheme = InputOutput.getCharacter(
15              "Enter (H)orizontal, (V)ertical, (B)oth: ", "HVB");
16      }
17      public void paint(Graphics graphics)
18      {
19          switch (scheme)
20          {
21              case 'H':
22                  paintHorizontal(graphics);
23                  break;
24              case 'V':
25                  paintVertical(graphics);
26                  break;
27              case 'B':
28                  paintTwoDimensions(graphics);
29                  break;
30          }
31      }
32      private void paintHorizontal(Graphics graphics)
33      {
34          int row, col;
35          String horizontalNumber;
36
37          for (int square = 1; square <= SQUARES ; square++)
38          {
39              row = (square - 1) / SIZE + 1;
40              col = (square - 1) % SIZE + 1;
41              horizontalNumber = "" + square;
42              paintSquare(graphics, row, col, horizontalNumber);
43          }
44      }
45      private void paintVertical(Graphics graphics)
46      {
47          int row, col;
48          String verticalNumber;
49
50          for (int square = 1; square <= SQUARES; square++)
51          {
```

```
52                          row = (square - 1) % SIZE + 1;
53                          col = (square - 1) / SIZE + 1;
54                          verticalNumber = "" + square;
55                          paintSquare(graphics, row, col, verticalNumber);
56                      }
57              }
58          private void paintTwoDimensions(Graphics graphics)
59          {
60              String rowColNumber;
61
62              for (int row = 1; row <= SIZE; row++)
63                  for (int col = 1; col <= SIZE; col++)
64                  {
65                      rowColNumber = "" + row + " " + col;
66                      paintSquare(graphics, row, col, rowColNumber);
67                  }
68          }
69          private void paintSquare(Graphics graphics, int row, int col,
70              String label)
71          {
72              final int RED = 0, BLACK = 1;
73              final int SIZE = 30;
74              int x = col * SIZE, y = row * SIZE, diagonal = row + col;
75
76              switch (diagonal % 2)
77              {
78                  case RED:
79                      graphics.setColor(Color.RED);
80                      break;
81                  case BLACK:
82                      graphics.setColor(Color.BLACK);
83                      break;
84              }
85              graphics.fillRect(x, y, SIZE, SIZE);
86              graphics.setColor(Color.white);
87              x += SIZE / 4;
88              y += SIZE / 2;
89              graphics.drawString(label, x, y);
90          }
91  }
```

We begin with the `import` statement on line 5 that imports the package `common`. This is the first `import` statement that imports a package that is not one of the standard Java packages. This program will use the class `InputOutput` that is in the package common. The class InputOutput will be used by many of the programs in the subsequent chapters. We have placed all our general purpose classes in this package.

Next consider the instance constant declaration on line 9. As we have already discussed, when more than one method in the class needs to access a constant, it is essential that it be an instance constant, which is true of both SIZE and SQUARES. Because our program consists of only a single class, there is no reason to make them public constants, so, as before, we have elected to make them private. This constant declaration contains one characteristic that we have not seen before. The value to which SQUARES is initialized is an expression that contains another constant SIZE. The initialization portion of a constant declaration can contain an expression, but it must be a constant expression—one consisting of only other named or literal constants, but no variables. We have often addressed when order is important and when it is not. In this case, the relative order of the declaration of SIZE and SQUARES is important. Reversing the order would create a forward reference and, consequently, a compilation error. One last thing to consider is why we chose to use an expression to initialize SQUARES rather than just initializing it to 64. The constant SIZE represents the number of rows and also the number of columns, so the total number of squares, SQUARES, is a related value. If we ever decided to change the size of the checkerboard—admittedly an unlikely prospect if we really intend for it to be a checkerboard—only one value would need to be changed. Declaring them in this fashion also emphasizes the fact that the two values are related.

Next we consider the instance variable declaration on line 10. This declaration is the first in which we have used a char variable, one additional primitive data type that we introduced earlier in this chapter. The variable scheme contains a character that indicates which of the three numbering schemes the user has selected. It needs to be an instance variable for the same reason we needed instance variables in the example in the previous chapter. Its value will be initialized by the method init and referenced by paint. As we have emphasized before, we will always make instance variables private to hide the representation of the object that they define.

Now we turn to the five methods of the class. Once we begin to study larger programs that contain multiple classes, we will again use UML diagrams that we introduced in Chapter 3 to show the class relationships. Before object-oriented languages became the norm, however, other diagrams were used to help both in designing programs and understanding them. One such diagram is the *structure chart*, which illustrates the relationships between methods. Figure 4.5 contains a structure chart for this program that includes only the methods of the Checkerboard class.

All programs have a control structure—object-oriented or not. A structure chart helps us understand that control structure by understanding the relationships between the methods. At the top of the structure chart are the public methods that are called from outside the class—specifically, from the Web browser. The init method is quite short; it calls no other methods in the class. The paint method is much more complicated. It calls one of three methods, `paintHorizontal`, `paintVertical`, or `paintTwoDimensions`, depending upon the value of `scheme`. That fact is illustrated by the fact that the called methods are connected to but located beneath the calling method. Each of those methods calls `paintSquare`. Those calling relationships are illustrated in a similar fashion. A structure chart that shows the calling relationships between the methods of a single class should never get too deep. If it does, it indicates that the class decomposition has been inadequate. In many cases, all the methods are public—none call any of the others, so we have only one level. The structure chart, in that case, is rather uninteresting.

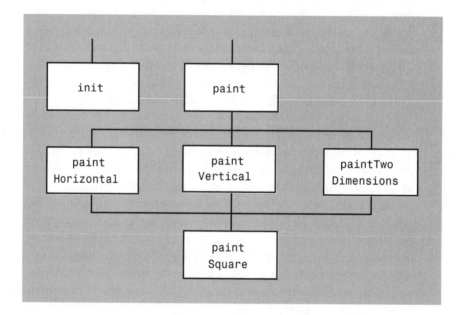

FIGURE 4.5 Structure chart for the checkerboard applet.

Now we consider each of the six methods in turn, beginning with `init`. It is a very simple method consisting of one statement, which is on lines 14 and 15, a call to the method `getCharacter` of the `InputOutput` class that we discussed earlier. In that call, the user is asked to select which of the three numbering schemes to use, and a character, H, V, or B, is stored in the instance variable `scheme` to be accessed whenever `paint` is called.

Next we discuss the `paint` method. It consists of a single `switch` statement, one of the new statements that we introduced in this chapter. It uses the character variable `scheme` as the `switch` selector. Each of the three cases contains a call to the appropriate method to paint the checkerboard using the corresponding numbering scheme.

One comment is appropriate at this juncture regarding some design decisions that we have made. All of the painting could have been done in the method `paint` alone. Instead, we have elected to break it into five separate methods. Let's consider why. First, one factor to consider in the decomposition process that we perform at each level of design is size. We should strive to limit the number of classes in a package, the number of methods in a class, and, finally, the number of lines of code in a method. There is no precise number that represents the maximum in any of these cases. Here the designer must exercise judgement. The fundamental reason for limiting the size is that it is easier to understand small components than larger ones. The three methods, `paintHorizontal`, `paintVertical`, and `paintTwoDimensions`, were introduced primarily to reduce the size of `paint`. There is one added benefit to having made them methods—the introduction of three names, method names that serve to document the program without any added comments. The method `paintSquare` was created for the other main reason we create methods—to be able to reuse them, thus avoiding code duplication. The structure chart makes it clear that `paintSquare` is called by the other three methods.

Now we turn our attention to the first of the three numbering schemes, the horizontal numbering that is done in `paintHorizontal`. Let's begin with the signature of that method, which is on line 32. We have explained the rationale for making this method private—the fact that it is called only by methods inside the class. We have made the return type `void` because there is nothing it needs to return to `paint`. Finally, let's consider the one parameter that is passed to it. Because this method needs to call `paintSquare`, which needs to call some methods to do some painting, it needs the `Graphics` object that came from the browser to be able to pass it to `paintSquare`. Passing it as a parameter is the proper approach. Before we examine the actual code in this method, we will explain the technique that we are using in it. Figure 4.6 illustrates the numbering scheme used.

Notice that the picture shows the otherwise flat checkerboard wrapped into a cylinder in such a way that the last square of each row is adjacent to the first square of the next row. In this way, we are conceptually turning a two-dimensional checkerboard into a one-dimensional sequence of squares. This idea is reflected in the code used for this method. In the core of this method is the `for` statement that spans lines 37-43. Notice that we are using a loop with a loop control variable that repeats 64 times—enumerating the value of `square` from 1 to 64. The variable `square` represents the number that will be painted on that square. The formulas on lines 39 and 40 are important to understand. This is our first example to make use of the remainder operator `%`, so some explanation is appropriate. Choosing an example might help you see how the remainder operator can be used to perform what in mathematics is called modular arithmetic. Consider square number 11, which will be the square on row 2, column 3 when we enumerate the square row by row. Let's apply the formulas used to see that they indeed produce the correct results. The calculations are shown in Equations 4.1 and 4.2.

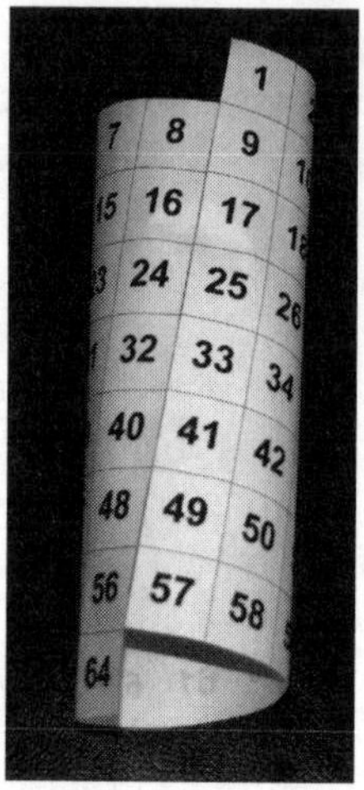

FIGURE 4.6 Horizontal numbering of checkerboard.

$$\text{row} = (11 - 1) / 8 + 1 = 10/8 + 1 = 1 + 1 = 2 \tag{4.1}$$

$$\text{col} = (11 - 1) \% 8 + 1 = 10 \% 8 + 1 = 2 + 1 = 3 \tag{4.2}$$

Study these formulas to be sure you understand them. This is a commonly used technique. Next, notice that we have declared one local variable in this method in addition to the variables row and col that we have just discussed. It is our first use of a variable of the predefined type String. On line 41, we make an assignment to this variable. The assignment has the effect of converting the integer square number into a string by concatenating the integer variable square to the null string "" as we had done in the calendar example. The last line inside the loop calls the method paintSquare to do the actual painting and numbering of the square. Recall that we have "factored-out" this common code into this method because each of the three different numbering methods needs to paint squares. When we discuss paintSquare, we will elaborate on why it needs the four values that are passed to it.

Next, we consider the paintVertical method that begins on line 45. There is little that needs to be said about it because it is so similar to paintHorizontal, but there is one important difference. The formulas to compute row and col are reversed.

The result is a circular effect, as illustrated in Figure 4.7, that shows the last square in a column adjacent to the first square in the next column.

FIGURE 4.7   Vertical numbering of checkerboard.

The method `paintTwoDimensions` is different from the previous two methods. Rather than one `for` statement that enumerates all 64 squares, it contains nested `for` statements. The outer loop contains a loop control variable `row` that ranges from 1 to 8. The inner loop has `col` as its loop control variable with the same range. In this case, no formulas are needed to compute the row and column. Recall from the previous calendar example that the number of times the body of the innermost loop is executed is the product of the number of times each of its components iterates—in this case $8 \times 8 = 64$. With this numbering scheme, each square will be numbered with both its row and column, so on line 65 the variable `rowColNumber` is being assigned a string that will contain both. This line illustrates what we mentioned earlier in this chapter about the + operator being overloaded. The first + and the third + operators concatenate an integer onto a string. The second operator is one that concatenates two strings. One final comment with regard to this method concerns why the inner loop must contain a compound statement, but not the outer loop. The inner loop contains two statements, the assignment to `rowColNumber` and the call to `paintSquare`, but the outer loop contains only one statement—the inner `for` statement.

Now we examine the final method in this class, `paintSquare`. Let's begin with the method signature on lines 69 and 70. First there is nothing the method needs to return, so its return type should be `void`. Next we consider the list of parameters. To paint a square, this method needs the graphics objects onto which it is to paint; it needs the row and column of the square to be painted and the number with which to label the square. If you are tempted to think that they should have been made instance variables, thereby avoiding the need for parameters, remember the guidelines we have given for when it is appropriate to make a variable an instance variable—when it needs class-wide scope and object-long lifetime. Although these variables fulfill the first criterion, they fail on the second. So now let's consider the details of how this method accomplishes its task. The constant SIZE, declared on line 73, represents the height and width of the square, and the variables x and y declared and initialized on line 74, represent its coordinates. Finally the variable diagonal, also declared on line 74, is initialized to the sum of the row and column. Figure 4.8 illustrates why we have chosen the name diagonal for this variable.

2	3	4	5	6	7	8	9
3	4	5	6	7	8	9	10
4	5	6	7	8	9	10	11
5	6	7	8	9	10	11	12
6	7	8	9	10	11	12	13
7	8	9	10	11	12	13	14
8	9	10	11	12	13	14	15
9	10	11	12	13	14	15	16

FIGURE 4.8   The diagonal values.

Notice that along each of the *minor diagonals*—those that extend upward as they move to the right—the variable diagonal has the same value. On a checkerboard, it is true that along any diagonal the color of the squares is the same and the colors of adjacent diagonals are different. We can model that second fact with the observation that if the numbers along any diagonal are odd, the numbers along the adjacent diagonals are even, and vice-versa. Now we turn to another common use of the remainder operator—determining whether a number is odd or even. It is a simple arithmetic fact that when we divide any positive integer by 2, the remainder will either be 0 or 1—0 when the number is even and 1 when it is odd. All the preceding discussion leads us to the switch statement on lines 76-84, which sets the color to red or black depending upon the remainder of this division. Because we have two discrete cases, a switch statement is an ideal statement to use. The solid colored square is then painted on line 85. On lines 86-89, the color is set to white in preparation for painting the number, the *x* and *y* coordinates are adjusted to position the number in the middle of the square and the number is painted using the drawString method we introduced earlier in this chapter.

SUMMARY

In this chapter, we encountered several new kinds of data. They included the primitive data type char, the nonprimitive type String and the enumerated types—user-defined data types that are used to create types for data that is neither numeric nor character data. In addition, two control statements were introduced, the switch statement used for discrete selection and the for statement, which is used for discrete iteration. The key points to remember from this chapter are as follows:

- The primitive type char is used for storing single characters which are stored using the Unicode representation. Character literals are written by enclosing a character inside single quotes.
- The nonprimitive type String is required for storing sequences of characters. String literals are written by enclosing the sequence of characters inside double quotes.
- Enumerated types were a recent addition to Java—added in version 5.0. They provide a type safe method for dealing with data that is commonly referred to by name.
- The class InputOutput defined in package common is a class supplied with this book to simplify handling user input and output.
- The switch statement enables the programmer to write programs that contain multiple paths. The switch statement selects which path to follow when the program runs. The type of the switch selector must be a discrete type.
- The for statement makes it possible to write programs that repeat designated sequences of statements. Java 5.0 contains two different forms of this statement, the original version and a new *for-each* variation that was introduced in Java version 5.0.

Review Questions

1. Give an example of a character, other than a space that has no corresponding glyph. How are such characters written in Java?
2. Explain the problem associated with writing a string that contains a double quote character. How can this problem be solved?

3. What operator symbol is used to specify string concatenation? What kind of data can be concatenated onto a string using this operator?

4. What is the lexical convention used for naming enumerated type names and enumerated literals?

5. Explain how programs that do not allow user input differ from programs that do.

6. What happens if the break statement is omitted at the end of a case inside a switch statement?

7. What restrictions are placed on the case expressions that are contained inside a switch statement?

8. Is it possible to accomplish the kind of iteration done by a for statement using one or more switch statements?

9. When a for statement iterates across all the values of an enumerated type, in what order is the iteration performed?

10. Indicate two other ways to increment a variable other than using the increment operator. Of the three choices, which is the best to use?

Programming Exercises

11. Write an enumerated type definition for coins that includes a penny, a nickel, a dime, and a quarter.

12. Write a value-returning method coinValue that accepts a parameter of the type defined in the previous exercise and returns the integer value of that coin. The method should use a switch statement.

13. Consider the following value-returning method sumSquares:

```
int sumSquares(int n)
{
    int sum = 0;

    for (int i = 1; i <= n; i++)
        sum += i * i;
    return sum;
}
```

What value is returned by the sumSquares method for each of the following method calls?

```
sumSquares(2)
sumSquares(4)
```

14. Write a method `factorial` that accepts an integer value *n* and return *n*!, which is the product of the first *n* integers. Use a `for` loop to perform the computation.

15. Consider the following value-returning method `alternateColors`:

```
Color alternateColors(int n)
{
    Color color = Color.BLACK;

    switch (n % 3)
    {
        case 0:
            color = Color.RED;
            break;
        case 1:
            color = Color.BLUE;
            break;
        case 2:
            color = Color.YELLOW;
            break;
    }
    return color;
}
```

What value is returned by the `alternateColors` method for each of the following method calls?

```
alternateColors(7)
alternateColors(9)
```

16. Consider the following value-returning method `multiply`:

```
int multiply(int n, int m)
{
    int sum = 0;

    for (int i = 1; i <= n; i++)
        for (int j = 1; j <= m; j++)
            sum++;
    return sum;
}
```

What value is returned by the `multiply` method for each of the following method calls?

```
multiply(2, 3)
multiply(4, 11
```

17. Write your own version of the exponentiation method pow using successive multiplication to perform exponentiation using a technique similar to what was used in multiply in the previous exercise.

18. Define an enumerated type definition for shape categories that is either rounded or rectilinear.

19. Write a method that accepts a parameter of type Shapes as defined in Listing 4.1 and returns its shape category—a value of the type defined in the previous exercise. Squares and rectangles are to be considered rectilinear and circles and ovals rounded.

20. Write a method that returns a string consisting of all possible shapes of the enumerated type Shapes as defined in Listing 4.1. For example, it should return "square rectangle circle oval". The method should create this string using a for statement so that it would require no modification if additional shapes were added to the enumerated type.

Programming Projects

21. Modify the RandomShape applet in Listing 4.1 so that it adds a caption above the figure that is drawn. The caption should read "Shape is circle, possibilities are square rectangle circle oval", when a circle is drawn. The appropriate shape name should be displayed for the other shapes. The final clause of the caption should be displayed by making a call to the method that you wrote for Programming Exercise 20.

22. Modify the ColoredCircles applet in Listing 4.2 so that instead of coloring the circles according to the colors of rainbow, it calls the method alternateColors from Programming Exercise 15 to determine the color. The ordinal value of the color should be passed to the alternateColors.

23. Write an applet that randomly generates one of the coins of the enumerated type defined in Programming Exercise 11. Draw a circle of 20 pixels in diameter for a penny, 25 pixels for a nickel, 20 for a dime, and 40 for a quarter. Call the method you wrote in Programming Exercise 12 to determine the denomination of the coin and place that denomination inside the circle. Draw a caption above the coin that gives the name of the coin.

24. Write an applet that draws a multiplication or addition table. Prompt the user to select which kind of table is to be drawn—an A should be input for an addition table and an M for a multiplication table. It should be a table with ten rows and ten columns. The digits 0 to 9 should be the row and column labels. Each square should contain the sum or product of the row and column according to

the type of table that was selected. The output of the applet when multiplication is chosen is shown in Figure 4.9.

25. Modify the `Checkerboard` applet in Listing 4.5 so that it can also number the squares diagonally as illustrated in Figure 4.10.

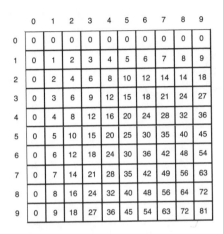

	0	1	2	3	4	5	6	7	8	9
0	0	0	0	0	0	0	0	0	0	0
1	0	1	2	3	4	5	6	7	8	9
2	0	2	4	6	8	10	12	14	14	18
3	0	3	6	9	12	15	18	21	24	27
4	0	4	8	12	16	20	24	28	32	36
5	0	5	10	15	20	25	30	35	40	45
6	0	6	12	18	24	30	36	42	48	54
7	0	7	14	21	28	35	42	49	56	63
8	0	8	16	24	32	40	48	56	64	72
9	0	9	18	27	36	45	54	63	72	81

FIGURE 4.9 Output of Chapter 4, Project 24.

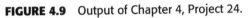

1	3	6	10	15	21	28	36
2	5	9	14	20	27	35	43
4	8	13	19	26	34	42	49
7	12	18	25	33	41	48	54
11	17	24	32	40	47	53	58
16	23	31	39	46	52	57	61
22	30	38	45	51	56	60	63
29	37	44	50	55	59	62	64

FIGURE 4.10 Output of Chapter 4, Project 25.

5 Objects and Primitive Data

COMPARING APPLICATIONS AND APPLETS

Each of the program examples that we have studied in the first four chapters has been an applet. We began with applets because it is simpler to write Java applets that produce graphical output than applications. Recall that an applet is not really a whole program but an extension of the Web browser, so the browser handles the creation of the window in which the applet is displayed and it also handles the creation of the applet object.

By contrast, an application is a complete program, so both of those responsibilities that were handled by the browser must now be done explicitly by the application. So that we can defer discussing the details about creating windows, we have created a class called Application that we will treat like the InputOutput class, which

ON THE CD

we introduced in the previous chapter. Although it is not a predefined Java class, at this point we will treat it as though it were. In Chapter 13, we will discuss it in detail. It is included on the CD-ROM at `common\Application.java`, so that you can compile and run the examples in this chapter.

In much the same way that we extended the `JApplet` class to create the applet classes that we have been writing, we now extend `Application` to create an application class. We need to create a `paintComponent` method in our application class that serves the same purpose that the `paint` method did in our applet classes. One new requirement, however, is that we must explicitly instruct the window in which our application is to be drawn to be displayed. Calling the method `display` that is defined in `Application` accomplishes this task.

A complete Java program must have a main thread of control that is initiated when the program is started. Java applications must have a designated class that contains a method named `main`. That method is the beginning point of the program. When a Java program is started, the main thread of control begins executing with the first statement in `main`. With the applets that we have used until now, this `main` method resided in the browser.

In more traditional programs that run in a command-line environment that accept only text input from the keyboard and display only text output to the screen, this main thread of control follows the program from start to finish. As we have already seen with the applets, when a program contains graphical output, the window system of the operating system initiates events that cause a different thread of control to execute methods like `paint`. The role of the main thread in such programs is often little more than creating the window that will display the graphical output.

CONSTRUCTORS AND OBJECT CREATION

Throughout the previous chapters, we have been careful to make a distinction between variables of a primitive type and objects of a class type—specifically in the discussion of the role of parameters and the discussion of the lifetime of data. There is one other important difference that we have thus far not needed to discuss. It pertains to the creation of these two different types of data. Before we explain the difference, let's look back over how we have used objects so far. We have been using a `Graphics` object as the object onto which we have been painting, but we never needed to create it. It was created by the browser and passed to us in the `paint` method. We have used `Color` objects, but those were constants already defined in the `Color` class. Our program contained an applet object, which was an instance of the applet class that we wrote, but the Web browser created that object for us. Finally, we used some `String` objects, but unlike all other objects, it is possible to create them with an implicit syntax—by merely writing the string literal that corresponded to the string we wish to create.

Comparing Object and Primitive Data Allocation

In this chapter, we begin to explicitly create objects, so we need to first understand the difference between creating primitive variables and objects of a class type. Understanding what occurs as a result of the declaration of each is important. First, when we declare primitive data, the compiler will set aside the necessary amount of memory to hold that data. By contrast, when we declare an object of a class type, the compiler allocates only enough memory for an *object reference*, which contains enough space to hold the memory address of the actual object. It is only when that object is *instantiated*—an instance of the class is created—that memory is allocated for the object itself. Consider the following declarations:

```
int x = 5;
String s = "abc";
```

Figure 5.1 illustrates the difference between the memory allocation that occurs in the above two declarations.

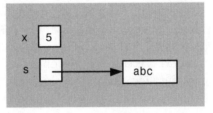

FIGURE 5.1   Comparing primitive and object declarations.

In the case of the primitive integer variables, enough memory is allocated for a single integer value. In the case of the string, memory is allocated for a reference—space enough for an address—and then the memory for the string itself is allocated and its address is stored in the object reference. It is customary to illustrate the fact that one memory location contains the address of another by drawing an arrow that emanates from the location containing the address to the memory location whose address it contains.

We refer to the memory allocation of objects as *dynamic allocation*. Dynamic allocation occurs as the result of an allocator expression, which begins with the reserved word new. String objects are the only ones in Java where the dynamic allocation can be implicit, but it can also be written explicitly using an allocator expression as follows:

```
String s = new String("abc");
```

The above line has the same effect as the one shown earlier.

Following the reserved word new is a call to a *constructor*. A constructor is a method of a class that has the same name as the class name. Calls to constructors must be a part of an allocator expression—meaning they must follow the reserved word new. Allocator expressions need not be done as an initialization of the object reference declaration. They can be done subsequent to the declaration, as illustrated by the following example.

```
Polygon triangle;

triangle = new Polygon();
```

In this case, only the object reference is created when triangle is declared. If triangle is declared local to some method, attempting to invoke any method on it will result in a compilation error, because Java requires that local data be initialized before it can be referenced. If triangle is an instance object, it will be initialized to a null reference. Attempting to invoke any method on it in that case will result in a run-time error. In either case, it is necessary to always instantiate an object before the object reference is used. In the subsequent assignment, a Polygon object is instantiated and its address is stored in the object reference triangle. As with all objects except strings, the allocation of this object can only be done explicitly. Later in this chapter, we will discuss the Polygon class and its methods that will be needed by the main example at the end of this chapter.

Shadowing Instance Variables

In preparation for our discussion of constructors, we digress a bit to discuss an exception to one of the general rules of scope—that a name can be accessed without qualification anywhere in its scope. Although duplicate names are not permitted among local data within the same method when their scopes overlap, what is permitted is having local data and instance data of the same name in the same class. Clearly in any such case, their scopes will overlap. Shown below is an example of what we just described.

```
class aClass
{
    private int aVariable;
```

```
void aMethod()
{
    int aVariable;

    aVariable = 1;
}
}
```

Declaring local data that has the same name as the name of instance data is known as *shadowing*. For obvious reasons, shadowing, although not prohibited, is generally considered a bad practice. We always avoid shadowing instance variables with local variables, but we adopt the practice of shadowing them with parameters in constructors, which we will describe shortly. When referring to a shadowed variable, as in the assignment aVariable = 1, it is unclear whether aVariable refers to the local variable aVariable or to the instance variable of the same name. Such references always refer to the local variable. When shadowing occurs, there is a portion of the program within the scope of an instance variable where the instance variable is not accessible—at least not without qualification. So there needs to be a way to access such shadowed instance variables. Qualifying them with the reserved word this is the technique that must be used. Inside instance methods, this refers to the object upon which the method was invoked.

Constructors

We have discussed how constructors are called; now we need to examine how constructors are written. As we have already noted, a constructor is a method whose name is the same as the name of the class. Constructors differ from other methods in one other important way: constructors have no return types.

Calling a constructor causes sufficient memory to be dynamically allocated to store the object. Generally constructors also initialize the instance data that belongs to the object being created. The degree to which the instance data is initialized depends upon the constructor. Note that constructors can be *overloaded*. Overloading methods means having two methods belonging to the same class with the same name but different signatures. Overloading is an exception to the general rule that duplicate names within the same scope are prohibited. Any method can be overloaded, but constructors are overloaded more often than most methods. The simplest constructor is a *default constructor*. A default constructor is a constructor that has no parameters. It can either leave all the instance variables uninitialized—meaning that they contain the default initial value of 0—or it can initialize some or all of them to some other appropriate default value.

Our custom is to define parameters with the same name as the instance variables for which they are intended to supply initial values. We should note that some feel that shadowing is best avoided even here, but we disagree. To avoid shadowing in this context requires artificially creating a different name for the instance variable and the parameter. We now need the reserved word `this` that we mentioned earlier. Inside a construction, the reserved word `this` is a reference to the object being created. Although `this` can be used inside any instance method, we use it most often inside constructors to access shadowed instance variables. A simple example, shown in Listing 5.1, will help illustrate how constructors are written.

LISTING 5.1 A Class that Illustrates Constructors (found on the CD-ROM at
chapter5\AClass.java.)

```
1   package chapter5;
2
3   class AClass
4   {
5       private int a, b, c = 3;
6
7       public AClass() //default constructor
8       {
9           a = 5;
10      }
11      public AClass(int a, int b)
12      {
13          this.a = a;
14          this.b = b;
15      }
16  }
```

In this example there are two constructors, so the constructors are overloaded. The first one is the default constructor. It initializes the instance variable a to 5. The instance variable b is not explicitly initialized and therefore contains the default value of 0. Finally let's consider the instance variable c. Notice that it is initialized in its declaration. When an instance variable is initialized in its declaration, it is as though the initialization is in each constructor of the class. To express this idea another way, the initialization of instance variables occurs whenever any constructor of that class is called.

The second constructor contains two parameters whose names are the same as the names of two of the instance variables of the class. The values of those parameters represent the initial values for the corresponding instance variables. Recall that because parameters and instance variables are at different levels of scope, duplicate names are permitted. The assignment `this.a = a;` copies the value of the parameter a to the instance variable a. There is one danger associated with the use of shadowing in this context. Misspelling the parameter name, which is only likely with long names, will not cause a compilation error. In that case, the assignment this.a = a; would assign the instance variable to itself.

When methods are overloaded, the compiler must perform *overload resolution*, which means deciding which of the overloaded methods to call. It resolves the overloading by examining the type and number of the arguments and matching them with the type and number of the parameters of each of the overloaded methods. Consider the following calls to the constructors of the class AClass.

```
AClass one = new AClass();
AClass two = new AClass(1, 2);
```

In the first case, it is clear that the default constructor is being called because the call contains no arguments. In the second call, the second constructor is being called because two arguments, both integers, are supplied. Although a matching signature containing the same number of parameters as there are arguments in the call is required, the types do not have to match exactly. The rules of type coercion that we discussed in a previous chapter apply.

In addition to the reserved word this, there is another reserved word that can be used inside instance methods that is often needed in constructors. It is the reserved word super. Although we are still not prepared to discuss inheritance in much detail, we have been writing *derived classes* in each example that we have done. In each of the first four chapters, the class that we wrote extended JApplet, or, we might also say, was derived from it. In this chapter, we will be again writing a derived class—one that is derived from a class called Application. It is often necessary for the constructor of a derived class to call the constructor of the class from which it was derived, known as the *base class*, and also called either the *parent class* or *super class*. The call to the constructor of the base class is done as follows:

```
super();
```

The call to the constructor of the base class must be the first line in the constructor. We will have more to say about the reserved word super when we discuss derived classes more completely in Chapter 12.

CLASS METHODS

Although we have been using calls to predefined class methods beginning in Chapter 2, the example provided in this chapter is the first to contain class methods that we have written. Recall that, syntactically, the only difference between an instance method and a class method is that the signature of a class method contains the reserved word `static`. Syntactically making a method a class method is quite simple. We would like to focus on how to decide when to make a method a class method.

Let's consider the various factors that influence this decision. We begin with the method `main` that we are encountering for the first time in this chapter. As discussed earlier, every Java application must have this method. In the case of `main`, there is no choice to be made; Java requires `main` to be a class method. Any methods subordinate to `main`—methods created to decompose and simplify the main thread of control—must also be class methods. When we create a utility class of methods that are related, but not related to any particular kind of object, they too should be class methods. The predefined `Math` class was such an example. The `InputOutput` class that we have been using is another example. Occasionally a class that is an object class, one that will have objects, may need a class method. Such methods have no need to access the instance variables of the class and do not need to be connected to any particular object. They are nonetheless related to the class in some way and are therefore defined inside the class. Remember that all Java methods must belong to some class.

There is one more important idea to understand about writing class methods. Inside a class method, use of the reserved word `this` is not permitted. Understanding the connection will help you understand the significance of both class methods and the reserved word `this`. Because class methods are not invoked on objects, there is no `this` object inside a class method.

There is one final related idea that is important. Normally a method of the same class can be called by referring to the method name only. It is just the result of the fact that the scope of every method name of a class includes all the methods of that class. But there is one important restriction. A class method can call another class method in this way, but a class method can only call an instance method if it is invoked on some object of the class that would have to be supplied to the method as a parameter. Table 5.1 shows which methods can call other methods of the same class using the method name alone.

TABLE 5.1   Relationship Between Class and Instance Methods

Can Call	Instance Method	Class Method
Instance Method	✓	✓
Class Method	✗	✓

This situation is an exception to the general rule that names can be accessed within their scope without qualification. Your ability to understand why an instance method can call a class method without qualifying the name but not vice versa is a measure of the extent to which the distinction between these two kinds of methods is becoming clear.

CONVERTING AN APPLET TO AN APPLICATION

Now that we have discussed how to write constructors and class methods, we are ready to show how one of the applets that we studied in the previous chapter can be transformed from an applet to an application. The applet that we have selected is the one that draws a random shape. Listing 5.2 contains that applet converted to a class that creates the window for an application.

LISTING 5.2   A Class that Creates a Window for the Random Shape Application (found
ON THE CD   on the CD-ROM at `chapter5\RandomShape.java`.)

```
1   package chapter5;
2
3   import java.awt.*;
4   import common.*;
5
6   class RandomShape extends Application
7   {
8       private enum Shapes{SQUARE, RECTANGLE, CIRCLE, OVAL}
9
10      private Shapes shape;
11
12      public RandomShape()
13      {
14          int shapeNumber = (int)(Math.random() * 4);
15
16          switch (shapeNumber)
17          {
18              case 0:
19                  shape = Shapes.SQUARE;
20                  break;
21              case 1:
22                  shape = Shapes.RECTANGLE;
23                  break;
24              case 2:
25                  shape = Shapes.CIRCLE;
```

```
26                    break;
27                case 3:
28                    shape = Shapes.OVAL;
29                    break;
30            }
31        }
32        public void paintComponent(Graphics graphics)
33        {
34            final int XY = 50, WIDTH = 100;
35
36            super.paintComponent(graphics);
37            switch(shape)
38            {
39                case SQUARE:
40                    graphics.drawRect(XY, XY, WIDTH, WIDTH);
41                    break;
42                case RECTANGLE:
43                    graphics.drawRect(XY, XY, WIDTH, WIDTH / 2);
44                    break;
45                case CIRCLE:
46                    graphics.drawOval(XY, XY, WIDTH, WIDTH);
47                    break;
48                case OVAL:
49                    graphics.drawOval(XY, XY, WIDTH, WIDTH / 2);
50                    break;
51            }
52        }
53  }
```

Let's examine what changes were necessary to make this transformation. First, on line 4, we now import our package common in place of the predefined Java package javax.swing. The reason for this change is that, on line 6, our new class now extends the class Application, which is in the package common, rather than JApplet. One other change on line 6 is that we remove the reserved word public before class. Although this change is not essential, it is no longer necessary to have this class be public.

On line 12, we converted the method init into a constructor. The change involved renaming the method to be the name of the class and removing its return type. The body of this method is unchanged.

The final changes were to the method that draws the shape. As we mentioned at the beginning of this chapter, it was necessary to name this method paintComponent rather than paint, which we have done on line 32. One change needed inside the method was to call the paintComponent method of the class Application, which requires the use of the reserved word super, as discussed earlier. That call is made on line 36.

One brief side note is appropriate at this point regarding our decision to group the code for each chapter in a separate package. There is no need to give this class a different name from the previous one because of being in a different package—it already has one. The full name of this class is chapter5.RandomShape. The name of the first version from the previous chapter is chapter4.RandomShape.

With applets, the Web browser or applet viewer contains the method main, which every program must have. With applications, we must provide this method. The class RandomShapeMain, which contains this method, is shown in Listing 5.3.

LISTING 5.3 The Class Containing main for the Random Shape Application (found on the CD-ROM at chapter5\RandomShapeMain.java.)

ON THE CD

```
1   package chapter5;
2
3   public class RandomShapeMain
4   {
5       public static void main(String[] args)
6       {
7           RandomShape shape = new RandomShape();
8
9           shape.display();
10      }
11  }
```

We begin with a discussion of the signature of the method main on line 5. Like the methods paint and init that we used in our applets, main has an already defined signature. There are two things about its signature that are noteworthy. First, it is a class method. Although we have had occasion to call class methods before, this example contains the first instance of a program containing a class method that, we have written. Having seen the signature of class methods already, we realize that syntactically, the only thing that separates class methods from instance methods is the presence of the reserved word static in their signature. Like the predefined Math class and the class InputOutput that we have been using, the class RandomShapeMain contains only class methods. RandomShapeMain is also like the other two in that we never create objects of this class. To say that the role of the RandomShapeMain class is that of a utility class would be incorrect, however. This class is an example of a third role that classes play in Java. It is neither a class from which objects are created, nor a utility class, but a class defined to execute the main thread of control of an application.

The second aspect of the signature of `main` that warrants a comment is the parameter `args`. This parameter contains what are called *command-line arguments*—data that is supplied to the program when a program is executed from the command-line. We plan to defer the use of this kind of input until Chapter 11, because it is associated with programs that run in a command-line environment.

Next, we consider the body of `main`. On line 7, we instantiate an object `shape` of the `RandomShapes` class by calling its constructor. Recall that, with applets, the instantiation of the applet object was done for us by the Web browser or applet viewer. The final task that `main` must perform is to call the method `display`, which causes the window defined by this object to be displayed. The method `display` is actually defined in the class `Application`, but because `RandomShape` extends `Application`, much like the previous classes extended `JApplet`, it inherits the method `display` defined in `Application`.

ENUMERATED TYPES WITH CONSTRUCTORS

Now that we have discussed class constructors, we return to the new type safe enumerated types that were added in version 5.0 to illustrate the fact that enumerated types, like classes, can have constructors. Although other languages, like C++, contain enumerated types, their syntax is limited to what we used in Chapter 4. Java's implementation of enumerated types has added a number of new features. In the examples in this chapter, we illustrate the use of constructors, methods, and variables with enumerated types. In Chapter 14, we will return to enumerated types one more time and discuss polymorphic enumerated types.

Our first example is a revised version of the `ColoredCircles` example that we discussed in Chapter 4. Recall that in the original version, which you may wish to refer back to in Listing 4.2, the enumerated type `RainbowColors` was defined as a private type inside the applet class. Enumerated types, like classes, can be placed in separate files, which is the approach we use in this new version. In addition to modifying the enumerated type, we also changed the program from an applet to an application, as we did with the random shape example. First, let's consider the new version of the class that defines the window for the application shown in Listing 5.4.

LISTING 5.4 The Colored Circles Example as an Application (found on the CD-ROM at *ON THE CD* chapter5\ColoredCircles.java.)

```
1    package chapter5;
2
3    import java.awt.*;
4    import common.*;
5
```

```
 6  class ColoredCircles extends Application
 7  {
 8      public void paintComponent(Graphics graphics)
 9      {
10          final int XY = 50, DECREMENT = 10;
11          int diameter = 100;
12
13          super.paintComponent(graphics);
14          for (RainbowColors color: RainbowColors.values())
15          {
16              graphics.setColor(color.getColor());
17              graphics.fillOval(XY, XY, diameter, diameter);
18              diameter -= DECREMENT;
19          }
20      }
21  }
```

All the same changes that were necessary to convert the previous example to an application were made in this program. One difference worth noting is that this class does not have a constructor. Java automatically provides a default constructor in such cases—one with an empty body.

The one important difference in this new version that pertains to the change that we have made to the enumerated type is that this class no longer contains the method getColor. On line 16, a getColor method is still being called, but the method now belongs to the enumerated type, so the call is now color.getColor() rather than getColor(color) as it was in the original version.

Next let's consider the modified version of the enumerated type RainbowColors shown in Listing 5.5.

LISTING 5.5 Rainbow Colors Enumerated Type with a Constructor and Private Data
ON THE CD (found on the CD-ROM at chapter5\RainbowColors.java.)

```
 1  package chapter5;
 2
 3  import java.awt.*;
 4
 5  enum RainbowColors
 6      {
 7      RED(Color.RED),
 8      ORANGE(Color.ORANGE),
 9      YELLOW(Color.YELLOW),
10      GREEN(Color.GREEN),
11      BLUE(Color.BLUE),
```

```
12        INDIGO(Color.MAGENTA),
13        VIOLET(Color.MAGENTA.darker());
14
15        private Color color;
16
17        private RainbowColors(Color color)
18        {
19            this.color = color;
20        }
21        public Color getColor()
22        {
23            return color;
24        }
25 }
```

When enumerated type definitions are placed in separate files, the naming convention is the same as the one used for classes, so the code in Listing 5.5 is stored in a file named RainbowColors.java.

Let's begin with the constructor whose signature is on line 17. Constructors for enumerated types are syntactically identical to class constructors. Their name is the name of the enumerated type, and they have no return type. Their role is much the same as well. This constructor copies the value of the supplied parameter to the private variable, declared on line 15, of the same name.

What is different, however, is how the constructors of enumerated types are called. They can only be called inside the type definition as the enumerated literals themselves are being created. Although it is permissible to omit the access modifier private, because it is the only allowable modifier, we adopt the convention of always including it. The next difference is that, unlike calls to class constructors, the reserved word new does not precede the call. Each of the lines 7-13 contains a call to the constructor. In this case, when a RainbowColors literal is created, a java.awt.Color is specified and becomes associated with it. So enumerated literals can have attributes other than just their ordinal values.

The absence of the use of new and the fact that the constructors of enumerated types cannot be called outside the type definition underscore an important difference between such literals and objects of an ordinary class. With an ordinary class, any number of instances—objects—can be instantiated. With an enumerated type, there is only one instance of each literal.

You should also observe that, in addition to variables and constructors, enumerated types can have methods. The method getColor whose signature is on line 21 is an example. Compare this method with the method of the same name in the previous version. Notice that the previous version contained a switch statement, but this one does not. This disappearance of switch statements is a recurring theme of object-oriented programming that we will encounter again when we discuss polymorphism.

As was necessary in transforming the random shape applet to an application, we need a class containing main that instantiates the window object. Listing 5.6 contains that class.

LISTING 5.6 The Class Containing main for the Colored Circles Application (found on *ON THE CD* the CD-ROM at chapter5\ColoredCirclesMain.java.)

```
1   package chapter5;
2
3   public class ColoredCirclesMain
4   {
5       public static void main(String[] args)
6       {
7           ColoredCircles circles = new ColoredCircles();
8
9           circles.display();
10      }
11  }
```

On line 7, the default constructor supplied by the compiler is called when we instantiate the object circles. Notice that for many graphics applications, main contains very little code. In Chapter 7, we will examine a technique which allows us to avoid writing a separate class containing main in such cases. By contrast, main plays a very central role in applications that do not contain a window for graphics, like the one we consider next. Even in some graphic applications, like the final example of this chapter, main can contain more code than what we have seen thus far.

Our final example at the end of this chapter illustrates another use of an enumerated type, with a constructor, a variable, and a method to retrieve the value of that variable.

SHALLOW VERSUS DEEP COPYING

Now that we have explored how to instantiate objects, there is an important difference between primitives and objects that you need to understand to avoid bugs in even very simple programs. When an assignment is made between two primitives, a copy of the value of the primitive is made. When an assignment of two objects is made, only the object reference is copied. Consider the following few lines of code:

```
String s = "abc", t;
int x = 5, y;
t = s;
y = x;
```

Figure 5.2 illustrates the difference between these two assignments.

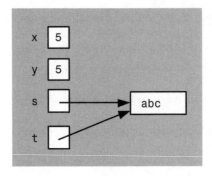

FIGURE 5.2 Assignments of primitives compared to objects.

After the assignment of the integer variable x to y, both contain copies of the value 5, but after the assignment of the string s to t, we have two copies of a reference to a single copy of the actual object.

Mutable and Immutable Objects

The assignment that occurs between objects is referred to as a *shallow copy*—only the reference is copied, not the object itself. There is another important characteristic of objects that is necessary to understand in order to appreciate the significance of the shallow copying of objects. It is whether an object is a *mutable object* or an *immutable object*. The mutability of objects depends upon the methods defined for a particular class. If a class defines methods that allow the actual object to be changed after it is created, then all objects of that class are mutable. If no such methods are defined, all the objects of that class are immutable. Strings are immutable. No string operations modify the objects that they are invoked on directly. There is, however, another predefined class called `StringBuffer`, whose objects are mutable. Consider the following several lines of code that will amplify the importance of object mutability in relation to shallow copying.

```
String s = new String("abc"), t;
StringBuffer u = new StringBuffer("abc"), v;
```

```
t = s;
v = u;
t += 'd';
v.append('d');
```

Both a string and string buffer object are created and initialized to the sequence of characters abc. Each is copied to another object of its respective type and then the letter d is appended to the copies. There is an important difference between the way the += operator of the String class behaves and the way the append method of the StringBuffer class behaves. This difference can best be understood by the illustration provided in Figure 5.3.

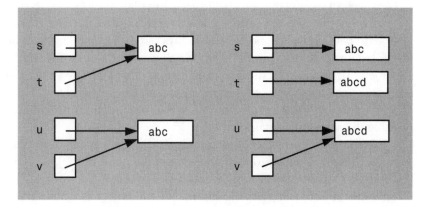

FIGURE 5.3   Appending to strings versus string buffers.

In Figure 5.3, the diagram at the left illustrates what happened after the assignments. In both cases, there are two object references referring to a single object. The diagram at the right illustrates the effect of the appending operations. In the case of the += operator of the String class, a copy of the original object was made before the letter d was appended to it. With the append method of the StringBuffer class, the letter d was appended to the existing object. The results are quite different, as the diagram shows. Because string objects are immutable, it is not especially important that their assignments are shallow, but with mutable objects, the situation is quite different. When the letter d was appended to the string buffer v, it was also appended to u. It is this unexpected behavior that it is important to understand and to guard against. One way to guard against such behavior is to always do an explicit deep copy when assigning mutable objects. In the case of string buffers, a deep copy could be done as follows:

```
v = new StringBuffer(u.toString());
```

The above statement extracts the string from the string buffer and passes it to the constructor of the `StringBuffer` class. Unfortunately there is no universal way to deep copy objects.

This issue is somewhat subtle and you may not fully grasp it at this point. Be assured, however, it is something that must be eventually understood to be able to write correct Java programs. The main example for this chapter will provide you another opportunity to understand the significance of this issue.

Object Parameters

Next we will discuss the role that objects can play when passed as parameters. Let's first review the case of primitive parameters. Primitive parameters can only be used to send data *in* to a method. Because Java passes parameters by value, the value of the argument supplied in the method call is copied to become the value of the parameter defined in the method signature, so changing the value of the parameter does not change the corresponding argument. Consequently, with primitive values, any number of values can be sent into the method, but only one can be returned using the `return` statement.

When objects are used, the situation is different. When objects are parameters, the argument is copied to the parameter at the point of the call as before. The difference is that, like object assignments, a shallow copy is performed. That means that only the object references are copied. If the object is immutable, it cannot be changed, so its role is the same as a primitive parameter. It can only be used to send data into the method. For mutable objects, the situation is different. Mutable object parameters can play the role of *in out* parameters—they can send data in, have it be changed and have the changed data returned to the caller. To understand these issues, it will help to consider a simple example shown in Listing 5.7. This example is also our first example of an application that does not display a graphics window.

LISTING 5.7   An Example that Illustrates Parameter Passing (found on the CD-ROM at **ON THE CD** chapter5\ParameterExample.java.)

```
1   package chapter5;
2
3   import common.*;
4
5   public class ParameterExample
6   {
7       public static void main(String[] args)
```

```
 8        {
 9            StringBuffer a1 = new StringBuffer("abc"),
10                a2 = new StringBuffer("abc");
11            String a3 = new String("abc"), a4;
12
13            a4 = parameters(a1, a2, a3);
14            InputOutput.putString("a1 = " + a1);
15            InputOutput.putString("a2 = " + a2);
16            InputOutput.putString("a3 = " + a3);
17            InputOutput.putString("a4 = " + a4);
18        }
19    private static String parameters(StringBuffer p1,
20            StringBuffer p2, String p3)
21        {
22            String 14 = new String("def");
23
24            p1.append('d');
25            p2 = new StringBuffer("def");
26            p3 += 'd';
27            return 14;
28        }
29  }
```

To test your understanding of these ideas, before reading on, try predicting what values this program will display for the four objects. This program illustrates the various possibilities. Let's examine each of them in turn.

The first argument a1 passed in is a mutable string buffer whose initial value is abc. Inside the method parameters, on line 24, the letter d is appended to it. Because it is a mutable object, changes made to the object itself will be preserved upon return, so the string abcd is displayed for a1.

Next we consider the mutable string buffer a2 that is initialized to abc. On line 25, the object reference of parameter p2 is changed. But because it is a copy of the argument a2's object reference, this change will be lost upon return. When a2 is displayed, it still contains the string abc. Changing the object reference of either a mutable or immutable object inside a method will have no effect once control is returned to the caller.

The third argument passed into the method a3 is a string that is initialized to abc. On line 26, the letter d is appended to the corresponding parameter p3 using the += operator. Recall that strings are immutable objects, so all string operations manipulate copies of the object—not the object itself. Consequently when control is returned to the method main, the string argument a3 is unchanged.

Finally the method parameters creates a local string object 14 on line 22 and returns it to main on line 27. The result of the method call is assigned to string object a4 on line 13. Because the object reference is copied back when a `return` statement is executed, the change is preserved and the string `def` is displayed for the value of `a4`. Both mutable and immutable objects can be returned in this fashion. One final comment is appropriate with regard to the method call on line 13. It is unrelated to the central point of this example, but we make this observation because it is the first time we have encountered a method call to a class method in the same class. Notice that, like a call to an instance method in the same class, the method name needs no qualification.

Again a diagram will help with understanding these issues. Figure 5.4 shows what occurs at two important steps during the execution of this program.

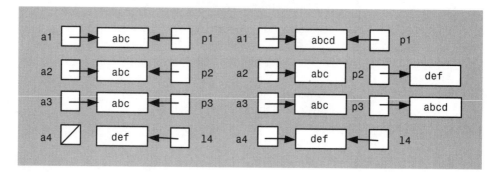

FIGURE 5.4 Object parameters.

The diagram at the left shows the state of the objects after the execution of line 22. The state after the execution of line 27 is shown on the right side. The program example at the end of this chapter will provide another opportunity to ensure that you understand the role of object parameters.

Object Lifetime and Garbage Collection

There is one final issue that must be understood to fully appreciate the differences between primitives and objects—their lifetimes. In Chapter 3, we explained the lifetimes of primitive local data and primitive instance data. Local data is created when the method in which it is defined is called and destroyed when the method completes. The lifetime of instance data is the lifetime of the object to which it belongs. Although object references have the same lifetimes as primitive data, the objects themselves do not.

The best way to understand this idea is by studying an example. The example from the previous section is ideal for this purpose. Consider the three parameters `p1`, `p2`, and `p3` and the object `14` in the method `parameters` in the previous section. Each of them is local and so the lifetime of each of the object references is the lifetime of the method. When the method completes, all four of those object references are destroyed. Let's consider whether the same is true for the objects that they refer to. First consider p1. It refers to the string abcd that was modified by the method. Notice that both a1, the argument in the calling method, and p1 refer to this object. So although the reference p1 is destroyed at the end of the method, the object it refers to is not. Objects are only destroyed when all the references to them are destroyed. An object that no longer contains any references is referred to as *garbage*. In Java, the memory associated with no longer referenced objects is automatically reclaimed. This process is known as *automatic garbage collection*.

Next, let's consider the references p2 and p3. Because the method parameters causes both of those object references to be changed, each of those objects is referred to by only one reference—a reference local to the method that will be destroyed when the method completes. So after parameters is done, both of those objects no longer have any references to them. They have become garbage and consequently their lifetimes end. Their memory is reclaimed by the garbage collector. Finally, let's consider the local object 14. Although the value of that object reference is changed in the method, just like p2 and p3, the object reference is returned by the method, so a copy of that object reference is made. The variable a4 now contains a reference to that object. Consequently that object continues to exist when control is returned to the method main.

MORE ON GRAPHICS

Until now, all of the drawing that we have been doing has been accomplished by using methods in the Graphics class, which is in the java.awt package. That package contains many other classes that are helpful in creating graphics. In the final example for this chapter, we will need one of those other classes, the Polygon class, to draw polygons. As has been customary, we present only the methods from that class that we use in our example and refer you to the Sun Website at http://java.sun.com/2se/1.5.0/docs/api/ for a more complete description of the class.

The first method we need is a constructor. Like most classes, the Polygon class has more than one constructor. The only one that we plan to use is the default constructor whose signature is shown below:

```
Polygon()
```

Like all default constructors, it has no parameters, so it creates an empty polygon initially.

Because we are starting with an empty polygon, we need a method to help us construct the polygon. The method addPoint provides us this ability. Once we have created an empty polygon, we can repeatedly add points to it by invoking this method on that object. Its signature is shown below:

```
void addPoint(int x, int y)
```

As should be evident from the signature of the method, we supply this method with the *x-y* coordinates of the point that we wish to add.

Once the polygon has been constructed, we can draw it using a method in the Graphics class that looks similar to ones that we have used in the past. It is the fillPolygon method whose signature is shown below.

```
void fillPolygon(Polygon p)
```

As you might expect, there is also a drawPolygon method. The difference between the two is the same as the difference between the other draw and fill methods that we have already encountered.

THE MULTIPLE POLYGON APPLICATION

The example for this chapter has been designed to illustrate some of the important characteristics of objects and how they differ from variables. As such, some features of this program do not necessarily reflect ideal design. This program creates four polygon window objects—three containing triangles and one that is intended to contain a quadrilateral. The program then prompts the user for an acknowledgement, after which it attempts to change one of the triangles into a quadrilateral. The output of this program is shown in Figure 5.5.

Like one of the earlier examples in this chapter, this program consists of two classes—excluding those that we take as predefined—and one enumerated type. The first class is PolygonMain. Having seen several examples of applications, you know that Java applications must contain a main method, which is where the main thread of control of the program begins. The code for that class is shown in Listing 5.8.

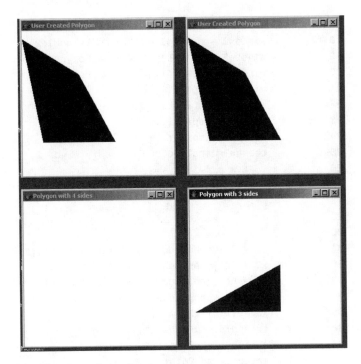

FIGURE 5.5 The polygon window application.

LISTING 5.8 The Main Class for the Polygon Window Application (found on the CD-
ON THE CD ROM at `chapter5\PolygonMain.java`.)

```
1   package chapter5;
2
3   import java.awt.*;
4   import common.*;
5
6   public class PolygonMain
7   {
8       public static void main(String[] args)
9       {
10          Color color;
11          Polygon triangle1 = new Polygon(), triangle2;
12          PolygonWindow window1, window2, window3, window4;
13
14          color = InputOutput.getColor("Select color for polygons");
15          makeIsosceles(triangle1);
16          triangle2 = triangle1;
```

```
17            window1 = new PolygonWindow(triangle1, color);
18            window2 = new PolygonWindow(triangle2, color);
19            window3 = new PolygonWindow(PolygonShapes.QUADRILATERAL);
20            window4 = new PolygonWindow(PolygonShapes.TRIANGLE);
21            window1.display();
22            window2.display();
23            window3.display();
24            window4.display();
25            changeTriangleToQuad(window1, window2, triangle1);
26        }
27        private static void makeIsosceles(Polygon triangle)
28        {
29            int x1, x2, x3, y1, y2;
30
31            x1 = PolygonWindow.randomCoordinate();
32            x2 = PolygonWindow.randomCoordinate();
33            y1 = PolygonWindow.randomCoordinate();
34            y2 = PolygonWindow.randomCoordinate();
35            x3 = (x1 + x2) / 2;
36            triangle.addPoint(x1, y1);
37            triangle.addPoint(x2, y1);
38            triangle.addPoint(x3, y2);
39        }
40        private static void changeTriangleToQuad(
41            PolygonWindow window1, PolygonWindow window2,
42            Polygon triangle1)
43        {
44            int x, y;
45
46            InputOutput.putString("Change Triangle to Quadrilateral");
47            x = PolygonWindow.randomCoordinate();
48            y = PolygonWindow.randomCoordinate();
49            triangle1.addPoint(x, y);
50            window1.repaint();
51            window2.repaint();
52        }
53  }
```

One line 11, we declare two `Polygon` object references. `Polygon` is a class defined in the package `java.awt` that is used to define polygons that can subsequently be drawn. The first object reference `triangle1` is initialized to a polygon created by the default constructor of the `Polygon` class. Such polygons initially contain zero vertices. The second object reference `triangle2` is uninitialized, so recall that at this point it contains a null reference. Line 12 contains the declaration of the four object references for the four `PolygonWindow` objects that will be created in this program.

On line 14, a call is made to another of the methods in `InputOutput`, one that allows the user to select a color for the polygons. Like all the methods in `InputOutput`, it uses a predefined Java class, in this case `JColorChooser`, to perform its task.

On line 15 a call is made to the method `makeIsosceles` to which the empty polygon object `triangle1` is passed. After returning from the call to this method, the object `triangle1` will contain an isosceles triangle. Recall that when parameters of a primitive type are passed to a method, nothing that the method does can affect their values upon return, which is to say that primitive parameters can be used to send data *in* to a method only. Clearly object parameters behave differently. In this case the data flow is *in-out*. An empty polygon is passed in, it is modified and a triangle is passed back out. Be sure you understand the difference in the roles that can be played by object parameters compared to primitive parameters.

On line 16 is an assignment to the object reference `triangle2`. As with any assignment of objects, this assignment performs a shallow copy. We now have two object references referring to the same object. Be sure to reread the discussion on shallow copies earlier in this chapter if its meaning is not yet clear. The implications of this topic will become clearer in the last step of the execution of this program.

On lines 17-20, the four `PolygonWindow` objects are created. The creation of each involves a call to a constructor, so each of the four lines contains the reserved word `new`. There is an important difference between the first two lines and the second two, however. They involve calls to different constructors of the `PolygonWindow` class. Recall that classes can have overloaded constructors. The constructor called for the first two windows requires that we supply the polygon object to be drawn in the window and its color. We supply the references to the isosceles triangle and the color chosen by the user. In the second pair of calls, the constructor must be supplied with an enumerated literal of the enumerated type `PolygonShape`—which can be either a triangle or a quadrilateral. The constructor will create the actual polygon in those cases.

On lines 21-24, the four windows containing the polygons are displayed with a call to the `display` method for each window.

Finally, on line 25 is a call to the method `changeTriangleToQuad`. We separated that code into a separate method simply to avoid allowing `main` to become too large. We will explain its role when we reach the method itself.

Next we turn to the second method in the `PolygonMain` class—`makeIsosceles`, whose signature appears on line 27. We have already explained when we discussed the calls to this method the fact that an empty `Polygon` is passed into it. It then creates an isosceles triangle—one with two equal length sides—using two pairs of randomly generated coordinates. Those coordinates are generated by calls to the class method `randomCoordinate` of the `PolygonWindow` class. On line 35, the midpoint of the *x* ordinates is calculated to ensure the triangle is isosceles. Finally, the `addPoint` method is called four times to add the vertices.

The final method in the `PolygonWindow` class is `changeTriangleToQuad`. It begins by making a call to a method in the `InputOutput` class called `putString`, which outputs a message indicating that the triangle will be changed to a quadrilateral and waits for the OK button to be pressed. Once it is pressed, the method proceeds to add another vertex to `triangle1`. Then both of the first two windows are repainted. It is very important to run this program and watch its behavior to understand what occurs next. What you should have noticed if you ran the program is that the triangles in both of the first two windows were changed to quadrilaterals despite the fact that we added a new point to only `triangle1`. If you understand the behavior of this program, you now appreciate what it means when we say that object assignments are shallow assignments. To deepen your understanding of this point a bit further, we recommend substituting line 16 with the following line and running the program again:

```
triangle2 = new Polygon(triangle1.xpoints, triangle1.ypoints,
    triangle1.npoints);
```

The above line causes a deep copy to be made. When you run the program, having replaced line 16, only the first triangle should change to a quadrilateral. There is one more issue that is noteworthy. Objects of the `Polygon` class must be mutable objects and the `addPoint` method must be changing the polygon on which it is invoked—otherwise we would observe no change to the number of vertices in that polygon.

There is one additional issue that warrants some discussion. On lines 50 and 51, we are calling a method named `repaint` to cause the windows to be repainted. The class `PolygonWindow` inherits this method from `Application`. All classes that can perform painting, including applet classes, have such a method. This method is necessary because we cannot call the `paintComponent` method of the `PolygonWindow` method directly, since we do not have the graphics object it needs on which it does the painting. By calling `repaint`, we are directing the window system to call `paint-Component`.

Now we turn our attention to the second class of this program—`PolygonWindow`, which is shown in Listing 5.9.

LISTING 5.9 A Class that Draws a Polygon in a Window (found on the CD-ROM at `chapter5\PolygonWindow.java`.)

```
1   package chapter5;
2
3   import java.awt.*;
4   import common.*;
```

```
5
6   class PolygonWindow extends Application
7   {
8       private Polygon polygon;
9       private Color color;
10
11      public PolygonWindow(PolygonShapes shape)
12      {
13          super("Polygon with " + shape.getSides() + " sides");
14          polygon = new Polygon();
15          color = Color.BLUE;
16          switch (shape)
17          {
18              case TRIANGLE:
19                  polygon = makeRightTriangle();
20                  break;
21              case QUADRILATERAL:
22                  makeQuadrilateral(polygon);
23                  break;
24          }
25      }
26      public PolygonWindow(Polygon polygon, Color color)
27      {
28          super("User Created Polygon");
29          this.polygon = polygon;
30          this.color = color;
31      }
32      public void paintComponent(Graphics graphics)
33      {
34          super.paintComponent(graphics);
35          setBackground(Color.WHITE);
36          graphics.setColor(color);
37          graphics.fillPolygon(polygon);
38      }
39      public static int randomCoordinate()
40      {
41          final int MAXIMUM = 250;
42
43          return (int) (Math.random() * MAXIMUM);
44      }
45      private void makeQuadrilateral(Polygon quadrilateral)
46      {
```

```
47          final int QUADRILATERAL = 4;
48          int x, y;
49
50          quadrilateral = new Polygon();
51          for (int vertex = 1; vertex <= QUADRILATERAL; vertex++)
52          {
53              x = randomCoordinate();
54              y = randomCoordinate();
55              quadrilateral.addPoint(x, y);
56          }
57      }
58      private Polygon makeRightTriangle()
59      {
60          Polygon triangle = new Polygon();
61          int x1, x2, y1, y2;
62
63          x1 = randomCoordinate();
64          x2 = randomCoordinate();
65          y1 = randomCoordinate();
66          y2 = randomCoordinate();
67          triangle.addPoint(x1, y1);
68          triangle.addPoint(x1, y2);
69          triangle.addPoint(x2, y1);
70          return triangle;
71      }
72  }
```

As we discussed earlier in this chapter, the class we are defining, PolygonWindow, extends the class Application in much the same way that all the applet classes in each of the previous chapters extended JApplet. The only difference is that the class Application is one we created, not a predefined Java class. We will explain its contents in Chapter 13.

The PolygonWindow class contains two instance variables, the Polygon object that is to be drawn in the window and its color. Those instance variables are declared on lines 8 and 9.

As we mentioned earlier, this class has two constructors. The first constructor begins on line 11. It allows the caller to specify the kind of polygon to be created by supplying a value of the enumerated type PolygonShapes. On line 13 is a call to the constructor of the class Application. Recall that invoking the method named super results in calling the constructor in the base class. In this case, the value passed to that constructor is a string that will become the title displayed in the polygon window. This constructor then creates either a right triangle or a quadrilateral of color blue depending upon the value of the parameter.

This class has a second, overloaded constructor whose definition begins on line 26. The caller here is required to supply both the polygon to be drawn and its color. The format of this constructor is typical of many constructors. It copies the value of the parameters to their corresponding instance variables. Notice that, as is our standard practice, the names of the parameters are the same as the instance variables, so the reserved word `this` must precede the instance variables to distinguish them from the parameters of the same name.

Next we consider the method `paintComponent`. Recall that `paintComponent` behaves in the same way that `paint` behaves in applets. Whenever an event occurs that requires the window to be repainted, this method is called. Like the `paint` method, the graphics object to be painted on is supplied. There is one difference, however. Like the constructors, it must call the corresponding method in its base class first. It then proceeds to set the polygon color to whatever color is required and then to draw the polygon.

The next method in this class is the class method `randomCoordinate`. We have already seen the definition of several class methods in the `PolygonMain` class, but this is our first encounter with the definition of a class method inside an object class. This method has no particular association with any object of this class, however. It has no need to access any instance variables of the class. An important question to consider is why to include it in this class. Our decision to include it in the class is based on the fact that it is called by other methods of this class and therefore is closely associated with it. We have encountered such methods before and chosen to make them private methods. The reason we have elected not to do that in this case is that we wish to be able to call this method from outside the class apart from any objects of the class. Look back at lines 31-34 of the `PolygonMain` class and you will recognize this usage.

Finally, we turn our attention to the two private instance methods in this class. The first is `makeQuadrilateral`, which begins on line 45. Before reading on, run this program and then study the `makeQuadrilateral` method and see whether you can explain the behavior that you observed. What you should have noticed is that the third polygon window appeared to be empty—meaning that the quadrilateral that claims to be created by this method appears not to be displayed. We have intentionally written in this way to further amplify some of the ideas that we were discussing earlier in this chapter. We have already established that polygons are mutable objects, so adding points to them should change the objects, so what mistake accounts for the behavior that you should have observed? The problem lies with line 50. Try removing this line and rerunning the program; with that line removed, the program behaves like it should. Let's return to some of the ideas that we have been emphasizing. By allocating a new polygon object on line 50, we are changing the object reference, which is a copy of the original object reference that was passed in. So when we begin adding points, we are adding them to this new object. Once the method ends, the only reference to that method is destroyed and the modified object becomes garbage and is automatically deallocated. The original object that was passed in remains unchanged.

Finally, let's examine the last method in this class—makeRightTriangle. Notice that, like the previous method, it allocates a new polygon object inside the method. There is an important difference, however. It returns the object reference it creates, so that object reference is copied back to the constructor and, although the local reference to the object is destroyed when the method completes, the copy remains and the points added are preserved.

The last file of this program is the one that contains the definition of the enumerated type PolygonShapes. Its code is shown in Listing 5.10.

LISTING 5.10 The Enumerated Type for Different Shaped Polygons (found on the CD-ROM at chapter5\PolygonShapes.java.)

```
1   package chapter5;
2
3   enum PolygonShapes
4   {
5       TRIANGLE(3),
6       QUADRILATERAL(4);
7
8       private int sides;
9
10      private PolygonShapes(int sides)
11      {
12          this.sides = sides;
13      }
14      int getSides()
15      {
16          return sides;
17      }
18  }
```

This enumerated type is similar to the one that we used in the new version of colored circles discussed earlier in this chapter. It contains a private variable, a constructor, and a method for retrieving that variable. The reason for using this approach is so that we can attach an attribute to each PolygonShapes literal that contains the number of sides. Although we have included only two shapes with different numbers of sides, it is conceivable that we might have a variety of shapes, such as a rectangle, parallelogram, rhombus, or square, that all have four sides.

Try drawing some pictures like the ones in Figure 5.4 that illustrate the behavior of this program, so you are certain that you can explain its behavior. We conclude our discussion of this example with a reminder that this example is one of the few that we have designed primarily to illustrate the ideas of shallow copying, parameter passing, and object lifetime. It is not intended to be imitated as an example of good design.

UML Class Relationships

Excluding the classes from external packages, the programs in this chapter have been the first consisting of more than one class. In Chapter 3, we introduced the UML class diagram—one consisting only of a single class. These diagrams are actually most useful for describing the structure of programs that contain more than one class, because they illustrate the kind of relationship that exists between the classes. The one kind of relationship that exists in the program example that we just discussed is the *dependency relationship*. It is a directed relationship that indicates that one class depends on another. There are many different kinds of relationships that can exist between classes, and as we explore progressively larger programs as we proceed through the remainder of the book, we will encounter examples that illustrate some of the other relationships. Let's now consider the UML diagram that describes the polygon window application shown in Figure 5.6.

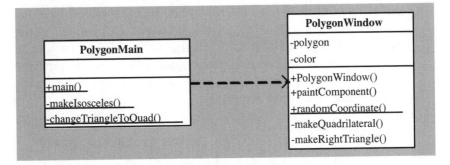

FIGURE 5.6   The UML diagram for the polygon window application.

In this diagram, we have elected to include only the two classes, but not the enumerated type. One thing to realize about UML is that it is a design and documentation tool intended to be independent of the programming language. Although many programming languages have enumerated types, the way enumerated types are implemented in version 5.0 of Java is unique—as the examples in this chapter illustrate. These enumerated types have methods, which makes them seem very much like classes. Consequently, we might choose to use the UML class diagram to illustrate them. UML is flexible enough to give us some latitude. The choice we have elected for this UML diagram is to exclude the enumerated type and illustrate only the relationship between the two classes.

Let's examine this diagram. First, we note that for simplicity the types of the instance data and return types of the methods have been omitted. Some of the symbolism used in this diagram we saw previously in the class diagram encountered in Chapter 3. Recall that the three sections of the box representing a class contain the class name, the data, and the methods. The symbols + and – are the UML symbols for `public` and `private`, respectively. The new symbolism in this diagram includes the underlining of the class methods, which distinguishes them from instance methods. The other new symbol is the dotted line with an open arrowhead that illustrates the dependency relationship. In this case class `PolygonMain` uses, and is therefore dependent upon, the class `PolygonWindow`. When a class contains a method that contains a local variable whose type is the type of another class, as is the case in this program, such a dependency exists. Since this is a directed relationship, the arrow points to the class being depended upon.

More on the Mechanics of Compiling and Running Programs

In Chapter 1, we discussed how to compile applets. Although compiling applications is no different than compiling applets, several examples in this chapter differ from any that we have encountered so far, in that they consist of more than one .java file—excluding any that are in another package. The first of those examples is the colored circles application that consists of three source files: `ColoredCircles-Main.java`, `ColoredCircles.java`, and `RainbowColors.java`. For this program it suffices to specify the first file only—the one containing `main`—when invoking the compiler. The following is required:

```
javac ColoredCircles.java
```

Because the class contained in that file refers to the type name `ColoredCircles`, the compiler will search for a file `ColoredCircles.class` in the same directory. If none exists, it will look for a file `ColoredCircles.java` and if the compiler finds that file, it will be compiled. In fact, even if it finds a `ColoredCircles.class` file, it will verify that it is current by comparing the time stamp of the .java and .class files. If the source file has been modified since it was last compiled, it will be recompiled. Similarly, the file `RainbowColors.java` will also be compiled, if necessary

This discussion presupposes that you are invoking the compiler from the command line. If you are working in an IDE, the perspective may be different. Some IDEs require that you define what is generally called a *project*, which specifies which source files are required for a particular program.

Until this chapter, we have been dealing exclusively with applets. Although the mechanics for compiling applications are no different from compiling applets, the mechanics for running them differ. As you surely know by now, an applet can be run using either the appletviewer program or using a Web browser. Both contain the JVM, which interprets the Java bytecode. Furthermore, an .html file is required containing an applet tag that identifies the applet. For applications, there are some differences. First, no .html file is needed. Second, the JVM that interprets the bytecode is not embedded in another program, but is a standalone program. Invoking the interpreter from the command-line for our polygon window application requires the following command:

```
java PolygonMain
```

Just as we did when compiling the program, we specify only one name—the name of the class that contains main. No file extension is specified. The .class extension is assumed.

With an IDE, how an application is run depends upon the design of the interface for that IDE. Many of them have a single key to initiate both compiling and executing a program.

SUMMARY

In this chapter, we encountered our first examples of Java applications, so our first programs containing the method main. So it was also our first encounter with programs containing class methods—the method main, among others. Other new features included the explicit creation of objects and the dynamic allocation that they require. We studied the important differences in the behavior of primitive data compared to objects when they are copied by assignments and passed as parameters. The key points to remember from this chapter are are as follows:

- Primitive variable declarations allocate space for the value of the object, but object declarations only allocate space for an object reference.
- To allocate space for objects, the constructor of the class must be called after the reserved word new.
- Inside an instance method, the reserved word this refers to the object on which a method was invoked.
- Class methods are denoted by the reserved word static. Class methods cannot call other instance methods in the same class unless the instance methods, names are qualified.

- Immutable objects are objects that have no methods that change any of their instance variables.
- Changes made to mutable object parameters are preserved upon return to the calling method, but changes to the object references themselves are not.
- Assignments of objects perform shallow copies. Only the object reference is copied.
- Garbage is dynamically allocated memory that is no longer accessible. Garbage is created when an object no longer has any references to it.

Review Questions

1. Explain the difference between a Java application and a Java applet.
2. What is an object reference?
3. What reserved word signifies a request for dynamic allocation?
4. What is the role of a constructor? How do constructors differ from other methods?
5. How does the compiler determine which method to call when a method is overloaded?
6. What makes a constructor a default constructor? What does a default constructor do?
7. Explain the difference between shallow and deep copies. Explain the difference between assignments of primitive variables compared to objects.
8. What causes garbage to be created?
9. What is the purpose of automatic garbage collection?
10. Are shallow copies a problem for immutable objects? Explain.

Programming Exercises

Consider the class for the following exercises.

```java
public class NumberObject
{
    private int value;

    public NumberObject()
    {
    }
    public NumberObject(int value)
    {
        this.value = value;
    }
    public int get()
    {
```

```
            return value;
        }
        public void set(int value)
        {
            this.value = value;
        }
    }
```

11. Write a declaration for two object references, number1 and number2, of type Num-berObject. Initialize the first using the default constructor. Initialize the second with an object containing a 5 using the other constructor.

12. Consider the following lines of code using the objects declared in Exercise 11.

```
        number1= number2;
        number1.set(2);
```

What is in the instance variable value of the number2 object?

13. Are NumberObject objects mutable or immutable? Explain.

14. What is the output of the following program?

```
        public class TestParameters
        {
            public static void main(String[] args)
            {
                NumberObject first = new NumberObject(1),
                    second = new NumberObject(1);
                double1(first);
                InputOutput.putString("Value of first = " + first.get());
                double2(second);
                InputOutput.putString("Value of second = " + second.get());
            }
            public static void double1(NumberObject object)
            {
                object.set(object.get() * 2);
            }
            public static void double2(NumberObject object)
            {
                object = new NumberObject(object.get() * 2);
            }
        }
```

15. Identify the overloaded methods in the class NumberObject. Explain why the methods double1 and double2 cannot have the same name in the TestParame-ters class in Exercise 14.

16. Suppose the following method was added to the NumberObject class.

```
public static void setAll(int value)
{
    set(value);
}
```

Would the program compile? Explain.

17. Add a constructor to the NumberObject class that accepts another object of the same type as a parameter. It should create another NumberObject containing the same number as the object supplied as a parameter. The signature of the constructor should look as follows:

```
NumberObject(NumberObject number)
```

18. Consider the following lines of code using the object references declared in Exercise 11 that use the constructor defined in Exercise 17.

```
number2.set(1);
number1= new NumberObject(number2);
number1.set(2);
```

What is in the instance variable value of the number2 object?

19. Is the copy performed in Exercise 18 a shallow copy or a deep copy?

20. Refer back to the lines of code in Exercises 12 and 18. Identify every line of code that generates garbage.

Programming Projects

21. Modify the PolygonShapes class in Listing 5.10 so that it includes all of the following shapes: equilateral triangle, isosceles triangle, right triangle, triangle, square, rhombus, rectangle, parallelogram, and quadrilateral. Add two more attributes to it: the number of equal length sides and the number of right angles. Modify the constructor so all three attributes are initialized for each of the literal values. Provide two additional methods to retrieve each of these values.

22. Write an application that iterates through each of the enumerated literals of the type PolygonShapes as defined in the previous project. For each one, it should display a message like the following one that describes a square: "A square has 4 sides 4 equal length sides and 4 right angles."

23. Modify the final example from this chapter in the following ways:
    a. Replace the PolygonShapes enumerated type with the one defined in Project 21.
    b. Move the method makeIsosceles into the PolygonWindow class. Have it accept no parameters but return a Polygon object.
    c. Eliminate the method changeTriangleToQuad method from PolygonMain. Also eliminate the selection of a color from the main method of that class.

    d. Have it display three windows: one with an isosceles triangle, one with a right triangle, and one with a quadrilateral.

    e. Remove the second constructor from the `PolygonWindow` class.

    f. Modify the `makeQuadilateral` method so that it returns the polygon instead of having it passed as a parameter.

    g. Draw a message at the top of each window that describes the polygon like the one displayed in the previous project.

24. Modify the program in Project 23 so four windows are output containing the four kinds of triangles: equilateral, isosceles, right, and regular. Add methods `makeEquilateralTriangle` and `makeTriangle` to the `PolygonWindow` class.

25. Modify the program in Project 23 so four windows are output containing the following four kinds of quadrilaterals: square, rhombus, rectangle, and parallelogram. Add methods to the `PolygonWindow` class to create each of these four kinds of polygons.

6 General Selection and Iteration

THE BOOLEAN DATA TYPE AND LOGICAL EXPRESSIONS

There is one primitive data type that we have not yet encountered—the `boolean` type that is used to store logical data, data that is either true or false. In fact, the literal values of this type are the reserved words `true` and `false`. Logical expressions—those of type `boolean`—are needed for both the `if` and the `while` statement that we introduce in this chapter.

Relational Operators

The primary way that logical expressions are created is by performing comparisons using a group of operators known as *relational operators*. Java has six relational operators, which are shown in Table 6.1.

TABLE 6.1   Java's Relational Operators

Symbol	Meaning
==	is equal to
!–	is not equal to
>	is greater than
>=	is greater than or equal to
<	is less than
<=	is less than or equal to

The first two operators that compare whether two values are equal or not equal vary among programming languages. The other four are quite standard in most languages.

Next, let's consider the use of these operators with the different kinds of data types that we have studied so far—beginning first with the integer types. Comparing integers is perhaps the most straightforward kind of comparison. When we compare integer variables or constants, the truth of the expression is determined by the well-established ordering of integers.

Like the integers, the ordering of real numbers that are stored in either `float` or `double` types is well-defined. But there is an important issue to consider when we compare such numbers for equality. Recall that there can be an inherent error associated with the conversion of the fractional part of base 10 numbers to base 2. As a result, numbers that should be equal after some simple arithmetic computations may be very close, but not identical. Consider the following two lines of code:

```
float f = .01f, g = .015f;
boolean b = f + g == .025;
```

Note first that we have chosen single precision floating-point numbers rather than double precision in this example because it is easier to illustrate this problem with the less precise representation. Because literal floating-point constants are double precision by default, we must append the letter f to the constants to store them as single precision values. Otherwise, the first line will not compile. Most importantly, the variable b should be true because mathematically .01 + .015 = .025. Nonetheless, the variable b is false due to the inherent errors that we just mentioned. Changing the type to `double` will correct the problem for these particular numbers, but we can still find smaller numbers that will produce the same problem—even when we use double precision. The proper way to compare two numbers for equality is to compare their absolute difference with a very small number as follows:

```
boolean  b = Math.abs(f + g - .025) < .0000001;
```

We must be sure that we do not choose a constant that is so close to 0 that *underflow* occurs. Underflow is when a number is so close to zero that insufficient precision is available to represent it and it is represented as zero.

To understand the truth of character comparisons, it is necessary to recall how character data is represented. Recall that the representation used by Java is Unicode. To know whether the comparison of two characters will evaluate to true or false requires knowing their underlying numeric representation. Some comparisons produce the expected result. For example `'0'` < `'5'` is true and `'c'` > `'w'` is false. Others are perhaps unexpected. For example, we might expect `'A'` > `'a'` to be true, but it is not. The uppercase letters come before the lowercase letters in Unicode. The only way to be certain of the result is to consult the table of Unicode characters to determine the numeric value of each.

Now we will consider comparing data that is not of a primitive type. Unlike some programming languages, as we mentioned in a previous chapter, Java does not support *operator overloading*—the ability to define the meaning of operators for values of nonprimitive types. Recall that objects of these types are stored as object references. If we attempt to use either the `==` or the `!=` operators to compare objects, it is a *shallow comparison*—the references are compared, not the values. The data type that we focus on for our current discussion is `String`. Consider the following two lines of code:

```
String s = "abc", t = "ab";
boolean b = s == t + 'c';
```

If the values were compared, the variable b would be true. But, because the references are compared, the variable b is assigned the value false. To achieve a *deep comparison*—one that compares the values—we must use the method `equals`. The proper way to perform the preceding comparison is as follows:

```
boolean b = s.equals(t + 'c');
```

The `equals` method can be used to compare two strings to determine whether they are equal or unequal. To compare strings to determine their relative ordering, a different method must be used. The required method is `compareTo`. Consider the following two lines of code:

```
String s = "abc", t = "ab";
boolean b = s.compareTo(t) > 0;
```

The above call to `compareTo` determines whether s > t. In this case, b would be true. Strings are compared using *lexicographic ordering*—dictionary ordering. The first character of a string is most significant, the second character is second most significant, and so on.

The method `compareTo` returns one of three results: a negative value to indicate that s < t, a zero to indicate that they are equal and a positive value to indicate that s > t. So if we wanted to determine whether string s was greater than or equal to t, we would write `s.compareTo(t) >= 0`.

Although the `equals` method is defined for all objects, whether it performs a deep comparison depends on the type of the objects. By contrast, some, but not all, have a `compareTo` method.

The final kinds of data types that we need to consider are the user-defined enumerated types. The first important issue is to recall that all enumerated types are ordered, so any pair of values belonging to the same enumerated type can be compared. As we discussed when we first introduced enumerated types in Chapter 4, the order in which they are listed defines the ordering. The technique used for comparing enumerated types is very similar to the one used for strings. The methods `compareTo` and `equals` are defined and used in exactly the same way as strings. There is one slight difference, however, which is that the relational operator `==` can be safely used in place of the `equals` method. The reason for this difference is that, unlike strings, there can never be more than one instance of any enumerated literal. To illustrate their use, let's reconsider one of the enumerated types that we first introduced in Chapter 4, the type `Days` whose definition is shown below:

```
enum Days {SUN, MON, TUE, WED, THU, FRI, SAT}
```

Now let's consider several comparisons, assigning each to a `boolean` variable.

```
Days today = Days.MON, firstWorkDay = Days.MON,
    lastWorkDay = Days.FRI;
boolean isTodayFirst = today == firstWorkDay;
boolean isTodayBeforeLast = today.compareTo(lastWorkDay) < 0;
```

Both `boolean` variables `isTodayFirst` and `isTodayBeforeLast` would evaluate to true.

We conclude our discussion of data comparisons with a brief discussion of the variety of different English words that can be used to express such comparisons. Carefully understanding the meaning of English words is essential to properly translating specifications written in English to Java expressions. As an example, one might use the predicate *at least* to express the relationship between two values. Understanding such correspondences is important if you are to write programs that correctly fulfill their requirements.

Logical Operators

Although the relational operators produce logical values, sometimes they alone are not sufficient to express more complicated conditions that require several separate conditions to be true. To express such compound conditions, we need the *logical operators*. Java has three logical operators: `&&` denoting *and*, `||` denoting *or*, and `!` denoting *not*. Truth tables are the customary way to express the meaning of these operators. Table 6.2 displays the truth tables for the two binary operators `&&` and `||`.

TABLE 6.2 Truth Table for the Logical Operators

	p	*q*	*p && q*	*p || q*
1	T	T	T	T
2	T	F	F	T
3	F	T	F	T
4	F	F	F	F

It is not necessary to memorize the entire table. It is sufficient to remember the following two facts. *Conjunctions*—expressions containing *and*—are true only when both operands are true. *Disjunctions*—expressions containing *or*—are only false if both operands are false. Let's now consider how to apply the truth table to the evaluation of some compound logical expressions. Consider the following conjunction:

$$8 > 6 \;\&\&\; 3 \;!= 5 \equiv T \;\&\&\; T \equiv T$$

We have used the symbol $\equiv$ rather than $=$ to emphasize that what is meant here is logical equivalence and not assignment. The relations are evaluated first, then we choose the appropriate value from the truth table, which in this case comes from line 1. Let's look at one disjunction:

```
9 >= 10 || 7 < 10 ≡ F || T ≡ T
```

In this case, we choose the value in line 3 of the *or* column.

From the truth table we can derive two important logical identities that are shown in Equations 6.1 and 6.2 in which x represents either true or false, $\wedge$ is the mathematical symbol for *and*, and $\vee$ is the mathematical symbol for *or*.

$$F \wedge x \equiv F \tag{6.1}$$

$$T \vee x \equiv T \tag{6.2}$$

These identities tell us that when the left operand in a conjunction is false, the value of the right operand is unimportant because the result will always be false. Similarly, in a disjunction, when the left operand is true, the result will be true regardless of the value of the right operand. For this reason *short circuiting* occurs in these cases, which means the right operands are never evaluated. Knowing that these operators short circuit can be used to our advantage, as illustrated by the following expression:

```
y != 0 && x / y > 1
```

In the above expression, if y is zero, the left operand of the conjunction will be false and the right operand will not be evaluated. Avoiding the evaluation of right operands is highly desirable in this case because otherwise the division by zero would occur, which is a runtime error that will terminate the execution of the program.

A runtime error during the evaluation of an expression is one example of what is called a *side effect*. More generally, a side effect is any change to the program state. Other examples of side effects are the modification of some variable or the execution of input or output. Although runtime errors are undesirable side effects to be guarded against, others, like performing input or output, may be desirable. If we have an expression in which the right operand contains a desirable side effect that we want to ensure occurs, we need to use the nonshort circuiting logical operators. The symbols for these operators are & for *and* and | for *or*. When we use these logical operators, the right operand will always be evaluated.

Certainly you realize that unlike human beings, computers have little tolerance for ambiguity. The word *or* in English is one that can be ambiguous. In English, the ambiguity is resolved based on the context. Consider the following use of the word *or*. To master Java, you need experience programming in another language *or* a strong mathematical background. Focus not on whether you believe this statement to be true, but how *or* is used in it. In particular, suppose both conditions were true. Certainly then the whole condition would be true. This use of *or* is called an *inclusive or*—the result is true when both are true. Based on the truth table we presented earlier, you can see that the logical operator || is an inclusive *or*. Next consider a restaurant menu that lists what is included with a complete dinner. Among the included items is soup *or* salad. In this context, the use of *or* is called an *exclusive or*—one or the other but not both. In programs, like in English, we more often use the inclusive or. Java does, nonetheless have an exclusive *or* operator, but only one that does not short circuit. The symbol for this operator is ^.

There are several other English words whose meanings warrant some discussion. The first two are the words *both* and *all*. If a problem specification lists two conditions and states that both must be true for a third condition to be true, a conjunction is being specified. Consequently, we need to use the logical operator &&. Let's illustrate this point with an example. Suppose we were using a program that was determining voter eligibility. Suppose the requirements read as follows: "There are two eligibility requirements for voters. 1) The person must be at least 18 years of age. 2) The person must be a citizen. To be an eligible voter, one must meet *both* requirements." Such a condition might translate to the following Java expression:

```
age >= 18 && isCitizen
```

The relationship between *both* and *and* should not be very surprising since the two are frequently used together in the same sentence. Next let's consider *all*. Suppose that there is a list of five conditions and the requirements stated that *all* five must be met for some other condition to be satisfied. We would translate those requirements into a compound logical condition containing four *and* operators. Another word that often appears with *all* is the word *necessary*. We might say that all five conditions are *necessary* for another condition to be true. The word *necessary* also conveys a compound conjunction.

In much the same way that the word *both* is often paired with *and*, the word *either* is frequently paired with *or*. When used alone, *either* still conveys a disjunction. Suppose we had a list of five conditions, then stated that at least one was required for some other condition to be met. Such a condition would be a compound disjunction containing four *or* operators. In the same way that the word *necessary* suggests a compound conjunction, the word *sufficient* would frequently be used in the specification of a compound disjunction.

To write correct programs, you must be able to properly translate English requirements. Being able to identify key words, such as the ones that we have been discussing, is useful to ensure that your translation is a correct one. After we introduce the final logical operator, *not*, we will consider one more English word that contains a logical meaning—*unless*. Although the *not* operator is much simpler than the others because it takes only one operand, we have included its truth table in Table 6.3 for completeness.

TABLE 6.3   Truth Table for the not Operator

	P	**!p**
1	T	F
2	F	T

Now that we have included the logical operator *not*, we return to our discussion of translating English words that have a logical content. The final word whose logical meaning we consider is *unless*. We postponed its discussion until now because it contains a hidden *not*. In fact, *unless* should be translated as meaning *and not*. Let's consider the condition that determines whether a student will receive a failing grade in a Java programming course. The English requirement might say that the student will receive a failing grade if the student's average is less than 60 unless the student is auditing the course. Suppose average is an integer variable and isAuditing is a boolean variable. The compound condition would be translated as follows:

```
failingGrade = average < 60 && !isAuditing;
```

Let's consider one more English specification of a logical condition that involves *unless*, which illustrates that the meaning of *unless* is a bit more complicated when used more than once in a specification. Consider the specification of what years are leap years. The specification might read, "Every year divisible by 4 is a leap year *unless* it divisible by 100 *unless* it is divisible by 400." Here is the translation:

```
isLeapYear = (year % 4 == 0 && year % 100 != 0) || year % 400 == 0
```

Notice that the second *unless* is translated to *or*.

There are several important logical identities that involve *not* that are shown in equations 6.3–6.5. In these equations, the mathematical symbol ~ means *not*.

$$\sim \sim p \equiv p \tag{6.3}$$

$$\sim(p \wedge q) \equiv \sim p \vee \sim q \tag{6.4}$$

$$\sim(p \vee q) \equiv \sim p \wedge \sim q \tag{6.5}$$

The identity in Equation 6.3 conveys the meaning of a double negative. Logically a double negative is equivalent to the affirmative. In English, double negatives are cautioned against. In reality, double negatives should be avoided when a single negative is meant. A double negative can properly be used to mean the affirmative. The sentence, "you should not always avoid double negatives" contains a double negative—in the words *not* and *avoid*. It is a perfectly fine sentence, however, and means, "you can sometimes use double negatives."

Equations 6.4 and 6.5 are known as DeMorgan's Laws. They show the effect of distributing *not* across *and* and *or*. These laws can be proven using truth tables, but that is a topic for a book on logic or discrete mathematics. For our purposes, it is sufficient to understand that they are true, particularly because they are often counterintuitive. Although these may seem like abstract properties, understanding them is important when writing logical expressions. Once we have introduced the general iteration statements later in this chapter, we will see an example that illustrates their importance. We will again encounter this when we come to the program example for this chapter.

Operator Precedence

In Chapter 2, we introduced the concept of operator precedence and noted how it originated in mathematical expressions. In addition, you learned how the precedence rules determine the placement of otherwise absent parentheses. Now that we have encountered two more groups of operators, let's consider their relative precedence. Consider the following expression that contains arithmetic, relational, and logical operators:

```
5 + 3 > 8 * 2 && 10 == 5 + 5
```

There is only one meaningful way to parenthesize this expression, which is the following:

```
(((5 + 3) > (8 * 2)) && (10 == (5 + 5)))
```

We have parenthesized this expression by grouping the arithmetic operators first, then the relational operators, and finally the logical operators. Fortunately, the Java precedence rules correspond exactly to that order, so the original unparenthesized expression would be evaluated exactly as the parenthesized one. Let's now consider the precise precedence of all of the operators that we have studied so far. Table 6.4 illustrates the relative precedence of these operators.

In reviewing the table, you should notice that the category of unary operators has highest precedence—those that have a single operand. Included among the unary operators is one of the logical operators—the *not* operator. Although we

TABLE 6.4 Operator Precedence

Operator Categories	Operator Symbols
Unary Operators	+ − !
Arithmetic Operators	* / %
	+ −
Relational Operators	< <= > >=
	== !=
Nonshort Circuit Logical Operators	&
	^
	|
Short Circuit Logical Operators	&&
	||
Assignment Operators	= += −= *= /= %=

have not ever mentioned the unary plus and unary minus operators, they are also included in this category. Because the unary plus has no effect, it is seldom used. The unary minus is useful for negating numeric values.

Although the relative precedence of the arithmetic, relational, and logical operators are defined in such a manner that parentheses are often not needed, the same is not true with the *not* operator. Unless we are dealing with Boolean data, parentheses are almost always required in expressions that have at least one other operator. Fortunately, failing to parenthesize such expressions correctly will produce a compilation error.

Notice that the relational operators have two precedence levels, as do the short circuit logical operators. Although one is rarely concerned about the two levels of the relational operators, the fact that *and* has a higher precedence than *or* is very important because the two are frequently contained in the same expression, as we saw in the expression that defined leap years. The three nonshort circuit logical operators each have a separate precedence level and, collectively, they have higher precedence than the short circuiting operators.

At the lowest precedence level are the assignment operators that include all of the shortcut assignment operators that we introduced in Chapter 3. When assignment expressions are embedded in logical conditions, they most often need explicit parentheses.

Associativity

One final issue we need to mention is the associativity of these operators. Recall that operators can be either left or right associative. Both the relational operators and the binary logical operators are left associative. Just as any difference in precedence of the relational operators is rarely an issue, their associativity is also rarely of concern. Because *and* and *or* have different precedence and separately each is an associative operation, associativity is not especially important with these operators either.

Although we discussed the assignment operators in previous chapters, we never discussed their associativity. These operators are right associative. Understanding this fact and the fact that assignments are expressions in Java explains why the following assignment is valid:

```
x = y = 1;
```

Such an assignment enables two variables to be assigned a single variable in one statement.

GENERAL SELECTION

In Chapter 4 we introduced the `switch` statement that is used to split the control flow of a program into multiple paths. With a `switch` statement, selecting which path to follow depends upon the value of some expression, which is most often just an integer variable. We are now ready to consider a more general technique to decide which path to take based upon the value of a logical expression.

The `if` Statement

This more general selection statement is the `if` statement. As we have done when we introduced new statements before, we begin by examining the syntax of the `if` statement shown in Syntax Definition 6.1.

Syntax Definition 6.1 Syntax of an `if` Statement.

```
if_statement

    if ( expression )
        statement 1
    else
        statement 2
```

Recall that the gray portions of syntax definitions indicate an optional component. So every if statement begins with the reserved word if, followed by an expression inside parentheses, followed by a single statement, followed by an optional else clause. The else clause begins with the reserved word else, followed by a second single statement. There is one semantic rule associated with this statement, which is that the type of the expression must be Boolean. Notice that in both instances only a single statement is permitted, so as with a for statement, a compound statement must be used when we wish to have more than one statement in either context. To describe the behavior of an if statement, it is customary to use a *flowchart*—a diagram that illustrates the flow of control of the program. In such diagram, a diamond is used to illustrate a decision based on the value of some logical expression. The flowchart that shows the behavior of an if statement is shown in Figure 6.1.

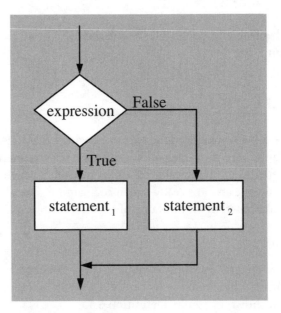

FIGURE 6.1 Flowchart of an if statement.

From the flowchart, it is evident that an if statement splits the flow of control into two paths. If the else clause is absent, there are still two paths—the second path simply bypasses the statement after the if clause. We have described the if statement as a more general selection statement than a switch statement, since an if statement breaks the control flow into only two paths and the switch statement can break it into many different paths. The generality of the if statement lies in its selection mechanism—the logical expression. We will see that by using nested if statements, we can break the flow of control into any number of paths, just as we do with a `switch` statement.

To illustrate the behavior of an `if` statement, consider a simple application that determines the largest of three integers shown in Listing 6.1.

LISTING 6.1 An Application that Determines the Largest of Three Integers (found on the CD-ROM at chapter6\Largest.java.)

```
1 package chapter6;
2
3  import common.*;
4
5  public class Largest
6  {
7      public static void main(String[] args)
8      {
9          int value1, value2, value3, largest;
10
11         value1 = InputOutput.getInteger("Enter first integer: ");
12         value2 = InputOutput.getInteger("Enter second integer: ");
13         value3 = InputOutput.getInteger("Enter third integer: ");
14         if (value1 > value2)
15             largest = value1;
16         else
17             largest = value2;
18         if (value3 > largest)
19             largest = value3;
20         InputOutput.putString("Largest = " + largest);
21     }
22 }
```

This program illustrates an `if` statement with an `else` clause, which is the statement beginning on line 14, and one that has no `else` clause, the statement beginning on line 18. In the second case, none is needed. If the `value3` is not greater than `largest`, `largest` is unchanged, so nothing needs to be done. Whether an `else` clause is needed or not depends entirely on the problem at hand.

There is one final issue related to this program. Think about whether the relational operators that are used must be >, or whether >= would work also. If you concluded that >= would work, you are correct. If the values are equal, it does not matter which one we choose. If you concluded otherwise, you may be confusing this problem with a similar, but more difficult problem. If the problem requires us to find which value was largest, rather than the largest value, it would be necessary to consider the cases when two or more of the values were equal, but that is a different problem. Finally, do not misunderstand this observation to mean that >= and > are always interchangeable. They are not. It just happens to be true in this case.

Nested `if` Statements

We have already encountered nested control statements in Chapter 4 when we examined the nested `for` statements needed to draw the checkerboard. Like `for` statements, `if` statements can also be nested inside other `if` statements. With `if` statements, there is one difference, however; another `if` statement can either be nested in the `if` clause or in the `else` clause. We will consider both possibilities because different issues arise in each case.

We begin with the case when an `if` statement is nested in the `if` clause of another `if` statement. This situation requires greater caution because of potential misinterpretation. Consider the following statement in which the message "Even positive number" is to be displayed when the variable `value` is both even and positive and "Odd number" is intended to be displayed if `value` is odd.

```
if (value % 2 == 0)
    if (value > 0)
        InputOutput.putString("Even positive number");
else
    InputOutput.putString("Odd number");
```

Unfortunately, this statement does not behave as intended. It illustrates a problem known as a *dangling else*—a situation in which an `else` could be matched to one of two `if`s. Our intent is clear from the indentation. We wish the `else` to be paired with the first `if`. The compiler ignores indentation and follows the rule that the `else` is matched with the closest `if` in such cases. Consequently, the message "Odd number" is displayed when the number is even but not positive. There are two ways to rectify this problem. The first is to embed the nested `if` inside a compound statement as follows:

```
if (value % 2 == 0)
{
    if (value > 0)
        InputOutput.putString("Even positive number");
}
else
    InputOutput.putString("Odd number");
```

By placing the nested `if` inside a compound statement, we are forcing the nested `if` to end at the right brace of the compound statement. This arrangement forces the `else` back to be matched with the first `if`. The second alternate is to use two `else` clauses with a null statement in the second one, as follows:

```
if (value % 2 == 0)
    if (value > 0)
        InputOutput.putString("Even positive number");
    else
        ;
else
    InputOutput.putString("Odd number");
```

Although this second method is used less often, if you choose to use it, place the semicolon that constitutes the null statement on a line by itself to emphasize that it was intended to be the null statement and is not a misplaced semicolon.

Next we consider the second possibility—an `if` statement nested in the `else` part of another `if` statement. A simple program, which categorizes the age of the user, illustrates such nesting. That program is shown in Listing 6.2.

LISTING 6.2 An Application to Categorize Ages into Four Groups (found on the CD-ROM *ON THE CD* at chapter6\CategorizeAges.java.)

```
1  package chapter6;
2
3   import common.*;
4
5   public class CategorizeAges
6   {
7       public static void main(String[] args)
8       {
9           final int CHILD = 12, TEENAGER = 19, ADULT = 64
10          int age;
11
12          age = InputOutput.getInteger("Enter your age: ");
13          if (age <= CHILD)
14              InputOutput.putString("You are a child")
15          else if (age <= TEENAGER)
16              InputOutput.putString("You are a teenager")
17          else if (age <= ADULT)
18              InputOutput.putString("You are an adult")
19          else
20              InputOutput.putString("You are a senior");
21      }
22  }
```

The first observation that you should make about this program is that it contains not just one if statement nested in the else part of another if statement, but a succession of such statements. Such nesting accomplishes the separation of the control flow into many paths, not just two. This program will select only one of the four phrases to output. It is important to observe how we chose to indent the statements. Normally, indentation is a reflection of nesting. If we adhere to that approach with such statements, the successive statements move further to the right. More importantly, we convey something other than simply dividing the flow into one of four paths. Successive indenting would suggest that we view this problem as dividing people first into children and nonchildren. The nonchildren are then divided into teenagers and nonteenagers. In fact, we really view this program as dividing people into four age groups, which is what our indentation style conveys. Remember that indentation is ignored by the compiler but serves to inform the reader of our view of the problem being solved. One final observation is that by ordering the selection properly and by using an else on each subsequent check, we only need to check the lower bound each time. So to determine that someone is a teenager, we do not need the compound condition age <= TEENAGER && age > CHILD. The second condition has already been established by the fact that we are in the else clause of the first if statement. Of course, we could have used the opposite order and still avoided compound conditions. Those two orders are the only orders in which the compound conditions could be avoided, however.

The Conditional Expression Operator

Having now introduced the if statement, there is an operator that can play a similar role that you should be familiar with. It is the conditional expression operator—an unusual operator in several ways. It has the distinction of being the only Java operator that is a ternary operator—one that has three operands. It is also unusual in the regard that it contains two symbols that separate the three operands. A conditional expression can be considered the expression level equivalent of an if statement. Our reason behind this characterization will become apparent once we illustrate how one can be transformed into the other. So, let's consider the following assignment, which is a simple use of a conditional expression to determine the maximum of two integers:

```
max = x > y ? x : y
```

This assignment should be read as "max becomes x if x is greater than y else it becomes y." Notice our use of the words *if* and *else* in our English rendering of the Java statement. It suggests that an if statement could accomplish the same task, which is indeed the case. The following if statement illustrates that fact:

```
if (x > y)
    max = x;
else
    max = y;
```

These two possibilities illustrate another case of redundancy in Java. In such instances, we have tried to offer some guidance as to good style. In this case, the use of the conditional expression operator should be avoided altogether. Although its use shortens the code, short is good when "short means simple," but not so good when "short means cryptic." Because conditional expressions are so symbolic, they tend to be very cryptic. If a single conditional expression does not persuade you, then consider the following nested conditional expressions:

```
max = x > y ? x > z ? x : z : y > z ? y : z;
```

This assignment determines the largest of three integers. Notice the absence of parentheses, which, of course, adds to the difficulty in reading it. Understanding how it is parsed requires knowing that the conditional expression is right associative.

If you were able to make sense of this last statement, you might be tempted to use your newfound tricks to ensure your job security, if you are already a programmer, by writing code that no one but you will be able to decipher! It's not a strategy we are recommending, however. The security may be short-lived if, several months later, you cannot figure out your own code. So why mention an operator that we never plan to use again in this book and one that we are discouraging you from using? It is because sometimes you may need to read the code others have written, whose programming style may not be up to your standards. Beginning programmers are often assigned the task of code maintenance, which involves more code reading than writing—not because it is easy, but because no one else wants to do it. To be able read the Java code written by others, you need to know the language completely—even the parts that you may never intend to use.

GENERAL ITERATION

In much the same way that the `if` statement is a generalization of the `switch` statement, the two iteration statements that we will now consider generalize the `for` statement that we studied in Chapter 4. As we used the `for` statement, it allowed iteration across a discrete range of values. The `while` and `do-while` statements use a logical condition to determine when the loop stops.

The `while` Statement

Let's begin by examining the syntax of the `while` statement shown in Syntax Definition 6.2.

Syntax Definition 6.2 Syntax of a `while` Statement.

```
while_statement

    while ( expression )
        statement
```

Syntactically, it looks very similar to the `if` statement, aside from the absence of the `else` clause. One other similarity is that the same semantic rule regarding the expression in the `while` condition applies here, which is that the expression must be a Boolean expression. Despite the similarity of the syntax, the meaning of this statement is very different, as demonstrated by the flowchart in Figure 6.2.

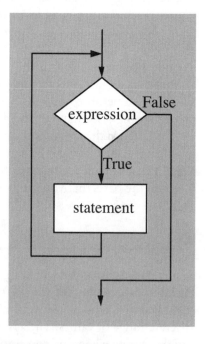

FIGURE 6.2 The flowchart of the `while` statement.

No number of successive if statements could produce the behavior of a while statement, because a while statement causes the flow of control to go backward.

Because we were very restrictive in how we used the for statements, they were very well behaved. They caused the body of the loop to be repeated the specified number of times. Most importantly, they never failed to stop. Because the termination of the while statement depends upon a logical condition, it is possible for the logical condition to be forever true. When that occurs, we have an *infinite loop*. Great care must be taken in designing while loops to ensure that something changes in the body of the loop that will eventually cause the loop to stop.

We mentioned the null statement during our discussion of the dangling else problem. Recall that a null statement consists of just a semicolon. One common mistake when first learning the syntax of Java is inadvertently placing a semicolon after the while condition as follows:

```
while (expression); // misplaced semicolon
        statement
```

Misplacing a semicolon in this fashion will lead to an infinite loop, provided that the expression is initially true. Be careful to avoid this pitfall.

Let's now consider a simple program containing a while loop that uses an algorithm similar to the one contained in the example at the end of this chapter. Studying the algorithm in this simpler example will make it easier to understand when it is embedded in a more complicated context later. This program is to read in integers until the sum of the integers read in exceeds 100. Clearly the loop requires a condition to control its termination. There is no way to know beforehand how many numbers must be read in. The number of repetitions depends upon the values that are input. As they are being read in, the program determines the largest so far, the smallest so far, and the sum. When the loop terminates, the largest, smallest, and average values are displayed. So let's examine this program, shown in Listing 6.3.

LISTING 6.3   An Application to Find the Minimum, Maximum, and Average of a List of *ON THE CD*   Integers (found on the CD-ROM at `chapter6\MinMaxAverage.java`.)

```
1   package chapter6;
2
3   import common.*;
4
5   public class MinMaxAverage
6
7       public static void main(String[] args)
8       {
9           final int LIMIT = 100;
```

```
10          int value, counter = 0, sum = 0
11              smallest = Integer.MAX_VALUE,
12              largest = Integer.MIN_VALUE;
13          double average;
14
15          while (sum <= LIMIT)
16          {
17              value = InputOutput.getInteger("Enter an Integer: ");
18              sum += value;
19              counter++;
20              if (value < smallest)
21                  smallest = value;
22              if (value > largest)
23                  largest = value;
24          }
25          average = (double)sum / counter;
26          InputOutput.putString("Smallest = " + smallest);
27          InputOutput.putString("Largest = " + largest);
28          InputOutput.putString("Average = " + average);
29      }
30  }
```

This program requires several variables to fulfill its task. The variables sum and counter are needed to compute the final average, and largest and smallest are needed to keep track of the largest and smallest values so far. The only remaining variable, value, is used to store each value that is read in.

Typically variables that are to be updated inside a loop require initialization before the loop begins, so let's consider the appropriate way to perform such initialization. Because sums and counters are almost always initialized to zero, you might think that initializing to zero is appropriate whenever any initialization is required, but it is not so. The reason that sums and counters are initialized to zero is because they are added to inside the loop and zero is the additive identity. By that we mean the following algebraic equivalence, shown in Equation 6.6, is true:

$$\forall x, \ x + 0 = x \tag{6.6}$$

As expected, sum and counter are initialized to zero in their declaration on line 10. So, similarly, if we needed to successively multiply some value inside a loop, the proper initial value would be to one. One is the multiplicative identity, as shown in Equation 6.7.

$$\forall x, \ x \times 1 = x \tag{6.7}$$

Now, let's consider the process of finding the smallest and largest value among a sequence of values. The two identities shown in Equation 6.8 and 6.9 apply.

$$\forall\, x,\, \min(x, \infty) = x \tag{6.8}$$

$$\forall\, x,\, \max(x, -\infty) = x \tag{6.9}$$

Infinity is the identity element for the minimum operation, and negative infinity for the maximum. To express these values in a less mathematical way, we might say that every number is smaller than infinity and greater than negative infinity. Unfortunately, infinity is not an integer, but it also true that for each of the integer types, only a limited range of values can be represented. The constant `Integer.MAX_VALUE` is the largest representable value for variables of type `int`. So we use it as the initial value for the variable `smallest` declared on line 11. Similarly, we use `Integer.MIN_VALUE` for the initial value of the variable `largest`, which is declared on line 12. The class `Integer` is a predefined class, known as the *wrapper class* for the primitive type `int`. All the primitive types have a corresponding wrapper class. We will encounter other uses of wrapper classes in later chapters.

Next let's consider the `while` loop itself, which follows the declarations. In the requirements for this program, we stated that the program should read in numbers *until* the sum exceeds 100. We have been emphasizing the importance of understanding the meaning of words in English. Another word that you need to understand is *until*, which was contained in the requirements for this program. In particular, we must understand the difference between meanings of the words *until* and *while*. Consider the following sentence, "You should continue studying the example in each chapter of this book *until* you fully understand it." Although the words *while* and *until* have similar meanings, they are not identical. We could rewrite the previous sentence using *while* instead of *until*—but it is not sufficient to simply replace one with the other. The modified sentence would read, "You should continue studying the example in each chapter *while* there remain aspects of it that you do *not* understand." The key observation to make in this transformation is that it was necessary to include *not*. Specifically, the word *until* means *while not*. In some programming languages *until* is a reserved word, but not in Java. Consequently, requirements that contain the word *until* must be translated in Java code that instead contains `while`. In our case, the transformation from requirements to Java code might proceed as follows:

```
until (sum > LIMIT)
while (!(sum > LIMIT))
while (sum <= LIMIT)
```

Next let's examine the body of the loop itself. The syntax of the while state-ment, like the for and if statements, allows only a single statement in the loop body. In this case, we need several statements so, as before, they must be embedded in a compound statement delimited by the braces on lines 16 and 24. Inside the loop, we read in the value on line 17, add to the sum on line 18, increment the counter on line 19, and then check whether the value is smaller than the smallest so far or larger than the largest so far. The two if statements accomplish that task.

When the loop ends, the average is computed and the smallest, largest, and av-erage values are displayed.

The do-while Statement

Next we consider the other general iteration statement—the do-while statement. Its syntax is shown in Syntax Definition 6.3.

Syntax Definition 6.3 Syntax of a do-while Satement.

```
do_while_statement

    do
          statement
    while ( expression );
```

Syntactically, it looks different from both the if and while statement. It has a pair of reserved words that bracket the body of the loop. The reserved word do marks the beginning and the reserved word while marks the end. Despite this full bracketing, a single statement is all that is permitted in the loop body, so a com-pound statement is still needed when the loop body consists of more than one statement. One other syntactic difference is that since the syntax of the do-while statement does not end with a statement, the semicolon is actually part of its syn-tax. Like the if and while statements, it has the semantic rule that requires the ex-pression to be a Boolean expression.

Despite the differences in syntax, the behavior of the do-while loop is quite sim-ilar to the while loop. Its flowchart is shown in Figure 6.3.

It is noteworthy that the testing of the while condition occurs at the bottom of the loop, which means that the body of every do-while loop is executed at least once. This statement was included in the language for convenience and adds no ad-ditional capability. In fact, some programming languages do not have such an iter-ation statement. One could accomplish the same thing using a simple while loop by duplicating the loop body as follows:

```
statement
while (expression)
    statement
```

We have repeatedly emphasized the undesirable characteristics of code duplication, so we certainly would encourage the use of the do–while when appropriate.

The example at the end of this chapter contains a do–while loop, so we will not present any example as a part of this discussion.

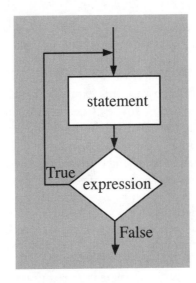

FIGURE 6.3 The flowchart of the do–while statement.

Applying DeMorgan's Laws

In our discussion of the while statement, we explained what is involved in translating a requirement that contains *until* to Java code that contains while. Now we consider such translations when a compound condition is involved. Consider the following example line from the requirements for some programs, "Continually re-prompt the user to enter a response until a *y* or *n* is entered." This requirement mandates iteration using either a while or do–while statement. In either case, a while condition is needed. Many beginners are inclined to translate the previous requirement into the following while condition:

```
while (response != y' || response != 'n')
```

The requirement contained the logical condition *or*, so it may seem natural that the Java code also contains this. But let's examine this compound condition further, evaluating it for several different responses illustrated in Table 6.5.

TABLE 6.5 Evaluating a Compound Condition

response	response != y	response != n	‖
Y	F	T	T
N	T	F	T
Q	T	T	T

Notice that in each case this expression evaluates to *true*. In fact, no matter what character we choose, the expression evaluates to *true*. To be false, we would have to find a character that was both a *y* and *n*. Clearly no such character exists. Earlier in this chapter, during our discussion of the logical operator *not*, we introduced DeMorgan's Laws. Using one of these laws, we can derive the proper result. Consider the following sequence of equivalent expressions:

```
until (response == y' || response == 'n')
while (!(response == 'y' || response == 'n'))
while (response != 'y' && response != 'n')
```

The first expression translates the requirement literally using the word *until*. The second expression replaces the *until* with while *not*, in keeping with our earlier discussion regarding their relative meanings. The third expression transforms the second by applying one of DeMorgan's Laws, shown in Equation 6.10.

$$\sim(p \vee q) \equiv \sim p \wedge \sim q \tag{6.10}$$

In the program example for this chapter, we encounter an application of De-Morgan's other law.

The for Statement Revisited

Although we have been characterizing the for statement as more restrictive than the while and do–while statement, that characterization is only true if it is used as we described its syntax in Chapter 4. Its actual syntax, shown in Syntax Definition 6.4, can be more general.

Syntax Definition 6.4 Syntax of a general `for` Statement.

```
for_statement
    for (expression 1; expression 2; expression 3)
        statement
```

Although the first component can be a declaration, it can also simply be any expression. Furthermore, the second two components can also be any expressions, and it is not required that all three involve the same variable. In the case that the first component is just an expression, the for statement is equivalent to the following while statement.

```
expression1;
while (expression2)
{
    statement
    expression3
}
```

In reality, the `for` and `while` are equally general. Either could be used in place of the other. We mention this fact for the sake of completeness, but continue to recommend that the use of the `for` statement be restricted to how we first introduced it in Chapter 4.

The `break` Statement Inside Loops

There is one kind of loop that we have not yet discussed. It is a loop that uses a *sentinel value* to control its termination. A sentinel value is a value that signals an end to the input. When reading in a sequence of numbers from the user, using a sentinel value can avoid the need to ask whether there are any more values remaining after each value has been input. A sentinel can only be used when there is a value that is outside the range of valid values. Suppose we wish to read in a sequence of nonnegative integers from the user, echo the values that were input, excluding the sentinel, sum them, and display the result. Because we are restricting valid input to be nonnegative integers only, we can designate a -1 as the sentinel—the value that signifies that there is no more input. Consider the following code segment that accomplishes the task that we have just outlined.

```
int sum = 0, value;
value = InputOutput.getInteger
    ("Enter a nonnegative integer, -1 to quit:");
```

```
while (value >= 0)
{
    InputOutput.putString("" + value + " was input");
    sum += value;
    value = InputOutput.getInteger
        ("Enter a nonnegative integer, -1 to quit:");
}
InputOutput.putString("Sum = " + sum);
```

There is one important thing to notice about this code segment, which is that the variable value is part of the while condition, so it must be initialized before the while statement is encountered. As we discussed in Chapter 4, failing to initialize variables before their values are used is something the Java compiler checks. A compilation error results if we fail to perform such initializations. Although we could initialize it to 0 in its declaration, doing so would cause it to be echoed as though it were a value input, which is contrary to the requirements. The other way to initialize it is to read in a value before the loop begins, which is what we have done in the preceding code segment with the first call to getInteger. This kind of input is sometimes referred to as a *priming read*. This approach has one shortcoming, however. A second read as the last statement in the body of the loop produces duplication of the input statement. Admittedly the duplication is minor, but we have frequently decried such duplication, so let's see whether the problem is that we have selected the wrong kind of loop. Perhaps using a do–while loop is really the proper choice for such problems. The loop, rewritten as a do–while loop, is shown below.

```
int sum = 0, value;

do
{
    value = InputOutput.getInteger
        ("Enter a nonnegative integer, -1 to quit:");
    if (value >= 0)
    {
        InputOutput.putString("" + value + " was input");
        sum += value;
    }
} while (value >= 0);

InputOutput.putString("Sum = " + sum);
```

Using a do–while loop did indeed eliminate the duplication of the call to get-Integer. But notice what happened instead. It is now necessary to duplicate the while condition in an if statement to prevent the sentinel value from being displayed and added to the sum. Without overstating the harm of duplicating such a small amount of code, the fact that some duplication is needed with either approach is a clue that this problem really needs another kind of loop. We need one in which the condition for termination is neither checked at the beginning nor at the end, but in the middle. It is possible to create such loops using the break statement. Until now, we have not used the break statement in any context other than as a part of a switch statement. Although a break statement cannot be used wherever any statement is used, it can be used in one other context, which is inside any loop statement, which includes the while, the do–while, and the for loop. Consider yet a third version of the code segment that we have been discussing, shown below:

```
int sum = 0, value;

while (true)
{
    value = InputOutput.getInteger
        ("Enter a nonnegative integer, −1 to quit:");
    if (value < 0)
        break;
    InputOutput.putString("" + value + " was input");
    sum += value;
}
InputOutput.putString("Sum = " + sum);
```

Executing a break statement causes control to be transferred to the statement following the body of the loop. In the preceding code segment, executing the break would cause the putString method call to be executed next. The fact that no duplication exists in this implementation is evidence that the problem itself demands a mid-loop exit. One final thing to notice in the transformation from a while condition to the break condition is that they are logical opposites. A while condition is a continuing condition, but a break condition, like an *until* condition, is a stopping condition.

Although the example we used to illustrate the use of a break involved a sentinel controlled loop, any loop that requires a mid-loop exit can benefit from the use of a break statement. In our main example at the end of this chapter, we will encounter one other such example.

The continue **Statement**

There is another statement similar to the break statement that can be used exclusively inside of loop statements. It is the continue statement. Instead of transferring control to the statement following the loop, the continue statement transfers control to the end of the loop, skipping any remaining statements in the body of the loop. Consider the following program segment that reads in ten integers, sums the positive ones, and displays the sum:

```
int value, sum = 0;

for (int i = 1; i <= 10; i++)
{
    value = InputOutput.getInteger("Enter an integer:");
    if (value <= 0)
        continue;
    sum += value;
}
InputOutput.putString("The sum = " + sum);
```

When negative values are encountered, adding the value to the sum is skipped by using the continue statement. Unlike using a break statement, which can sometimes avoid code duplication, a continue statement really offers no significant benefit. A loop that uses a continue statement can be easily rewritten without it, as the following loop, which is equivalent to the preceding one, illustrates:

```
for (int i = 1; i <= 10; i++)
{
    value = InputOutput.getInteger("Enter an integer:");
    if (value > 0)
        sum += value;
}
```

We mention this statement for the sake of completeness only. Because it offers no real benefit, we will not use it in any of the remaining examples in this book.

STRUCTURED PROGRAMMING

Much is made of the fact that modern programming languages are object-oriented—rightly so, because the development of object-oriented languages was a significant milestone in the history of programming languages. Equally significant, however, was the earlier development of structured languages. In the Chapter 1 discussion of the various kinds of programming languages, we mentioned that high-level languages, like Java, in addition to being object-oriented, are also structured—meaning that nested statements can be used in place of explicit *go-to* statements. Although programming languages, like ALGOL, developed as early as the late 1950s, had a fully nested statement syntax, Java is one of the first popular programming languages that does not contain the *go-to* statement. Now that we have explored the two general control statements, the `if` and `while`, we can elaborate on the significance of a language like Java lacking the *go-to* statement.

Structured Programs Have Simple Flowcharts

Before the development of structured languages, flowcharts were an important design and documentation tool. Although we used flowcharts to illustrate the semantics of the `if` and `while` statements, as it is customary to do, they are no longer either necessary or useful as a tool for algorithm design. The reason that we no longer need them is that the flowchart of structured programs is much simpler than that of unstructured programs. In an unstructured program, because *go-to* statements govern the control flow, the lines of control flow can go in any and every direction. The metaphor of spaghetti code is often used to describe highly convoluted unstructured programs that contain many crossing lines of control flow.

The important thing to understand about any method written in a structured language is that its flowchart has no crossing lines of control flow. Keep in mind that we are excluding the control flow between methods. It is reasonably easy to demonstrate this fact, once we make several observations. First, the atomic flowcharts of the `if` and `while` statement contain no crossing lines. Next, we can compose statements in only two ways, by putting them in sequence and nesting them. Arranging two statements in sequence can introduce no crossing lines because the control flows out of one and into the other. Nesting one statement inside of another creates no crossing lines because the flowchart of the one being nested is wholly within the other.

To see the structure of such programs, we need to be able to distinguish between statements in sequence and statements that are nested. Indentation accomplishes that goal. Statements in sequence are aligned, whereas a nested statement is indented relative to the statement in which it is contained.

One fact that should be obvious, but is so important that it is worth emphasizing, is that removing the *go-to* statement from a structured language does not reduce the expressive power of the language. In other words, it does not reduce the number of problems that can be solved using that language. What it can do in some cases, however, is cause slight inefficiency. This point was often made by its early critics. The minor inefficiencies are greatly offset by the simplicity that structured programs provide.

The Labeled break Statement

One might wonder why it took almost forty years between the time a language was developed that had a fully nested syntax and the time a mainstream language was developed that elected to eliminate the *go-to* statement. The reason was because of a concern that there were still situations where a *go-to* might be useful. We observed that once full statement nesting is provided, *go-to* statements are never needed, but let's consider the remaining situations where they are still helpful. One situation was dealing with error conditions. The introduction of exceptions in programming languages that we will discuss in later chapters eliminated this need.

The other situation was the need to break out of a nested loop. With programs written in C++, a language that also has exceptions, the most frequent use of *go-to* statements is to break out of nested loops. Let's consider a problem of that kind. Suppose we wish to ask the user to enter numbers until the user enters a number that is not a prime number—one that is evenly divisible by some number other than one and itself. Consider the following program segment in Java that implements this algorithm:

```
int number;
boolean isPrime;

do
{
    number = InputOutput.getInteger("Enter an integer: ");
    isPrime = true;
    for (int divisor = 2; divisor <= Math.sqrt(number); divisor++)
        if (number % divisor == 0)
        {
            isPrime = false;
            break;
        }
} while (isPrime);
InputOutput.putString("" + number + " is not prime");
```

The preceding program segment demonstrates that writing such an algorithm without a *go-to* statement is possible, but to do so one needs a *flag-controlled loop*. A flag is just another name for a Boolean variable. In this case, the flag is the variable isPrime. Until now, we have avoided discussing such loops because normally any flag-controlled loop—providing it is not a nested loop—can generally be written without a flag as a while loop containing a break statement. Furthermore using data, such as a flag, to achieve control is usually regarded as a somewhat undesirable practice. To avoid the use of a flag, such situations are often handled with a *go-to* statement—in languages that have one.

To accommodate such problems, and to compensate for having removed the *go-to* statement, Java added the ability to use a labeled break statement. The following code illustrates how the algorithm that we have been discussing can be rewritten using a labeled break statement.

```
        int number;
        boolean isPrime;

        primes: while(true)
        {
            number = InputOutput.getInteger("Enter an integer: ");
            for (int divisor = 2; divisor <= Math.sqrt(number); divisor++)
                if (number % divisor == 0)
                    break primes;
        }
        InputOutput.putString("" + number + " is not prime");
```

Notice that, in this version, the need for a flag has been eliminated. What has been added is the label `primes:` that precedes the `while` condition, which is now simply a `true`. Notice that a label is an identifier followed by a colon. The labeled `break` statement that reads "`break primes;`" specifies that label. It causes control to transfer to the statement following the outer loop, which is the labeled loop. So after the labeled `break` statement is executed, the call to the method `putString` follows.

Labels can be placed on statements other than loops, but that practice should be avoided, as it begins to resemble the *go-to* statement. We recommend that their use be confined to situations where exiting a nested loop is required.

MORE ON GRAPHICS

As we have done in each of the earlier chapters, we will introduce the additional Java graphics capabilities that are needed for the primary example at the end of the chapter. In the previous chapter, we encountered the `Polygon` class that allowed general polygon objects to be defined and drawn. Our example in this chapter uses a similar class, `Rectangle`, that permits drawing rectangle objects.

Although we have been using colors since the very first chapter, we have relied on the predefined colors. In the main example for this chapter, we will use some custom colors that requires us to understand how to custom mix colors.

Rectangle Objects

Although we have been drawing rectangles since our first example, we have been using the methods `drawRect` and `fillRect` to accomplish that task. Until now, we have not needed to save the rectangle objects that we have drawn—a capability that we now need. Among the predefined classes in the package `java.awt`, there is one called `Rectangle` that allows us to maintain objects that represent such rectangles.

Although the Rectangle class has numerous constructors, there are two constructors that we need. Their signatures are shown below:

```
Rectangle(int width, int height)
Rectangle(int x, int y, int width, int height)
```

The constructor that has only two integer parameters allows only the dimensions of the rectangle to be specified. The one with four integer parameters allows both the dimensions and the coordinates of the upper left-hand corner to be initialized.

There is one more feature of this class that we will need. The Rectangle class has four public instance variables: x, y, height, and width. In our discussion of the principle of information hiding, we explained that public instance variables are best avoided because they expose the representation of the object to methods outside the class and can therefore create expensive maintenance costs. The designers of this predefined class did not adhere to that practice, however. We, nonetheless, caution against using public instance variables. Although some designers may find it acceptable when they are absolutely certain that the representation of a class will not change, it is still preferable to use methods to return the value of the instance variables instead.

Color Mixing

Although our example in the last chapter allowed the user to select a custom color using the getColor method from the InputOutput class that we provided, we have yet to create custom colors within our own code. We are about to do that in the example that follows, so let's consider one of the constructors provided by the Color class that allows us to create custom colors. The signature of the one that we plan to use is shown below:

```
Color(int r, int g, int b)
```

The three parameters specify the red, green, and blue components of the custom color. Each of the parameters must be in the range 0-255. The lower the value, the lower the brightness of that color component. Let's consider some examples to help illustrate this point. Black, the darkest color, is created by Color(0, 0, 0); white is created by Color(255, 255, 255). A medium gray is created by Color(127, 127, 127). Finally a red color, darker than the brightest red, is created by Color(127, 0, 0)—half the full brightest in the red component and nothing in the other two.

THE MATCHBOOK APPLICATION

Our primary example in this chapter is a program that draws a horizontal series of rectangles of random height and width. Because most are tall and skinny, they have the appearance of matchsticks. Figure 6.4 illustrates a typical output of this program.

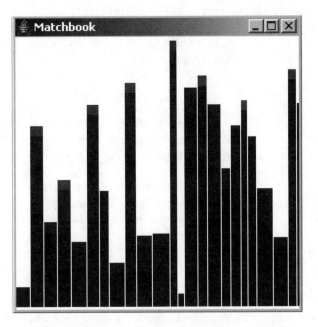

FIGURE 6.4   Output of the matchbook application.

Initially the matchsticks are colored black. Every matchstick that is taller than its immediate neighbors is a local maximum and has a red tip. Every one that is shorter than its immediate neighbors is a local minimum and has a blue tip. If you have studied calculus, you recognize the terms local maximum and minimum as the points in a continuous function where the derivative or slope of the function is zero. This situation is similar, except we are dealing with number sequences and not continuous functions. The tallest match of them all has a dark red tip, and the shortest one has a dark blue tip. The user is allowed to choose the average number of matches that are to be displayed.

Let's now examine the class that contains the method main for this application.

LISTING 6.4   The Main Class for the Matchbook Application (found on the CD-ROM at chapter6\MatchbookMain.java.)

```
1 package chapter6;
```

```
2
3   import java.awt.*;
4   import common.*;
5
6   public class MatchbookMain
7   {
8       public static void main(String[] args)
9       {
10          final int MIN_VALUE = 10, MAX_VALUE = 50;
11          int averageMatches;
12
13          do
14          {
15              averageMatches = InputOutput.getInteger(
16                  "Enter average number of matches " +
17                  MIN_VALUE + "-" + MAX_VALUE + ": ");
18          }
19          while (averageMatches < MIN_VALUE ||
20              averageMatches > MAX_VALUE);
21          Matchbook matchbook = new Matchbook(averageMatches);
22          matchbook.display()
23      }
24  }
```

As is often true, this class contains only the `main` method, which is quite short. Its role is to create a `Matchbook` object. As we will see when we examine the code for that class, its only constructor requires that we supply the average number of matches to be drawn. The user is required to supply this average. On line 10, constants are defined that specify the minimum and maximum values for the average.

The requirements for this method state that the user should be prompted to enter this average and continually reprompted until a value within these bounds is entered. To be somewhat more specific, the user must be prompted to enter this average until a number greater than or equal to 10 and less than or equal to 50 is entered. You should notice that this is another condition where one of DeMorgan's Laws is involved. Consider the following sequence of equivalent expressions as we did earlier.

```
until (averageRectangles >= 10 && averageMatches <= 50)
while (!(averageMatches >= 10 && averageMatches <= 50))
while (averageMatches < 10 || averageMatches > 50))
```

The third expression transforms the second by applying one of DeMorgan's Laws, shown in Equation 6.11.

$$\sim(p \wedge q) \equiv \sim p \vee \sim q \qquad (6.11)$$

One final issue to consider here is our choice of a do–while loop. Clearly the user must enter at least one value before a valid entry is provided, so what we have here is a case where the body of the loop must be executed at least once—the type of loop that is ideally written using a do–while statement.

Once the user enters a valid number of matches, the matchbook object is created and the main thread of control has completed its work.

Next we consider the class that draws the matchbook object, which is shown in Listing 6.5.

LISTING 6.5 The Matchbook Drawing Class (found on the CD-ROM at
ON THE CD chapter6\Matchbook.java.)

```
1   package chapter6;
2
3   import java.awt.*;
4   import common.*;
5
6   class Matchbook extends Application
7   {
8       private enum States {START, INCREASING, DECREASING}
9       private final Color TALLEST_COLOR = new Color(191, 0, 0),
10          SHORTEST_COLOR = new Color(0, 0, 127);
11      private final int MIN_HEIGHT = 10, MAX_HEIGHT = 270, WIDTH = 300,
12          VARIATION = 4;
13      private int minWidth, maxWidth;
14
15      public Matchbook(int averageMatches)
16      {
17          super("Matchbook");
18          minWidth = WIDTH / averageMatches - VARIATION/ 2;
19          maxWidth = minWidth + VARIATION;
20      }
21      public void paintComponent(Graphics graphics)
22      {
23          Rectangle previous, current,
24              shortest = new Rectangle(0, MAX_HEIGHT),
25              tallest = new Rectangle(0, MIN_HEIGHT);
26          States state = States.START;
27          int width, sumOfWidths = 0;
28
```

```
29          super.paintComponent(graphics);
30          setBackground(Color.WHITE);
31          current = randomRectangle(sumOfWidths);
32          while (true)
33          {
34              if (current.height > tallest.height)
35                  tallest = current;
36              else if (current.height < shortest.height)
37                  shortest = current;
38              graphics.setColor(Color.BLACK);
39              graphics.fillRect(current.x, current.y,
40                  current.width, current.height);
41              sumOfWidths += current.width + 1;
42              previous = current;
43              current = randomRectangle(sumOfWidths);
44              if (sumOfWidths + current.width > WIDTH)
45                  break;
46              state = newState(graphics, state, previous,
47                  current);
48          }
48          colorMatchTip(graphics, tallest, TALLEST_COLOR);
50          colorMatchTip(graphics, shortest, SHORTEST_COLOR);
51      }
52      private Rectangle randomRectangle(int sumOfWidths)
53      {
54          int y, width, height;
55
56          width = (int)(Math.random() * (maxWidth - minWidth))
57              + minWidth - 1;
58          height = (int)(Math.random() * (MAX_HEIGHT - MIN_HEIGHT))
58              + MIN_HEIGHT;
60          y = MAX_HEIGHT - height;
61          return new Rectangle(sumOfWidths, y, width, height);
62      }
63      private void colorMatchTip(Graphics graphics, Rectangle
64          rectangle, Color color)
65      {
66          graphics.setColor(color);
67          graphics.fillRect(rectangle.x, rectangle.y,
68              rectangle.width, MIN_HEIGHT);
68      }
70      private States newState(Graphics graphics, States state,
71          Rectangle previous, Rectangle current)
72      {
```

```
73          switch (state)
74          {
75             case START:
76                if (previous.height > current.height)
77                   state = States.DECREASING;
78                else if (previous.height < current.height)
79                   state = States.INCREASING;
80                break;
81             case INCREASING:
82                if (previous.height > current.height)
83                {
84                   state = States.DECREASING;
85                   colorMatchTip(graphics, previous, Color.RED);
86                }
87                break;
88             case DECREASING:
89                if (previous.height < current.height)
90                {
91                   state = States.INCREASING;
92                   colorMatchTip(graphics, previous, Color.BLUE);
93
94                }
95                break;
96          }
97          return state;
97       }
99  }
```

Let's begin on line 8 with the enumerated type States that defines the three states that this application can be in with regard to its search for the local minimums and maximums. This enumerated type is a simple one that requires nothing but the definition of the names of the literal values. We will elaborate on the meaning of these three states shortly, once we come to the method newState.

Next, let's consider the instance data in this class. On lines 9 and 10 are the declarations of two color constants. They are custom colors created by using the constructor of the Color class that we discussed earlier. The constant TALLEST_COLOR, which will be used to color the tallest match, is a red, darker than the predefined Color.RED. The other constant, SHORTEST_COLOR, is a blue, darker than Color.BLUE. The color signifies the shortest match. The constants MIN_HEIGHT and MAX_HEIGHT, declared on line 11, define the minimum and maximum heights of the matches, and the constant WIDTH is the width of the matchbook. The instance variables min-Width and maxWidth, declared on line 13, are computed in the constructor on lines 18 and 19 using the average number of matches requested by the user.

Next, let's consider the method `paintComponent` that is responsible for drawing and properly coloring each of the matches. It contains a `while` loop that continues the creation of new rectangles until no more room is left to draw them. The loop condition is `true` because the termination of this loop is accomplished using a `break` statement. We will elaborate on our reason for using a `break` statement shortly.

On line 23 are the declarations of two local `Rectangle` objects, `previous` and `current`. The practice of using a pair of variables typically containing the names *previous* and *current* is a practice that we first introduced with the Fibonacci spiral example in Chapter 4. Observe that the same code used in that example reappears here, despite the fact that the variables `previous` and `current` represented integers in the earlier example and represent `Rectangle` objects in this one. In this case, maintaining the height of two adjacent rectangles enables us to identify the local minimum and maximum values. We are keeping whole `Rectangle` objects, rather than just their heights, so that we have all the necessary information about each rectangle, including both its size and its position. In this way, it will be easy to recolor the tips of any that qualify as a local minimum or maximum.

Among its responsibilities, the loop that spans lines 32-48 must determine the shortest and the tallest matches, which must be specially colored at the end. There are two local `Rectangle` objects that are used to accomplish these purposes. They are `shortest` and `tallest`, which are declared on lines 24 and 25. Although we have used `Integer.MAX_VALUE` and `Integer.MIN_VALUE` to initialize the miniumum and maximum variables in our earlier example, in this case the ranges of possible values that a match's height can assume are more constrained. Consequently, it suffices to initialize the height component of `shortest` to our instance constant `MAX_HEIGHT` and the height component of `tallest` to `MIN_HEIGHT`. As we did with `previous` and `current`, we have also made them `Rectangle` objects so that we have all the necessary information about each rectangle to recolor its tip when we reach the end of the loop.

The local variable `state`, declared on line 26, is used to keep track of the current state of the sequence of rectangles. This state information keeps track of whether the width of the rectangles is increasing or decreasing, which will help us locate those that are local minimums and local maximums.

The variable `width`, declared on line 27, contains the width of the current rectangle and the variable `sumOfWidths`, declared on the same line, is the sum of the widths of all the matches drawn so far, including the spaces between them. We use this variable to determine when we have filled the matchbook. Like all sums, it is initialized to zero.

Now we are ready to examine the algorithm inside the `paintComponent` method. The `while` loop is at the center of the algorithm, but before the loop can begin, it is necessary to create the first `Rectangle` object, which is done on line 31 by a call to the `randomRectangle` method that we will discuss shortly. This initialization is necessary because we will need both `previous` and `current` to be initialized by the time we reach the end of the loop on the first iteration.

Inside the body of the loop, the determination is made whether the height of the current rectangle is taller than the tallest or shorter than the shortest. The `if` statements spanning lines 34-37 accomplish this task. This code is similar to the code used in the `MinMaxAverage` class presented earlier. On lines 39 and 40 the rectangle is drawn and its width is added to the `sumOfWidths` variable on line 41. One extra pixel is added so there is some space between the matches. On line 42 is the assignment of `previous` to `current`, which is always present when we use this technique to maintain a window across any sequence of objects. A new rectangle is created on line 43. Notice that generating this new rectangle toward the bottom of the loop is appropriate because an initialization is done outside the loop. On line 44, we check to see whether there is room for the rectangle just created. If adding the width of that rectangle to the current sum of the widths exceeds the matchbook width specified by the constant `WIDTH`, the loop must stop. We have used the `break` statement on line 45 to accomplish this task. The last statement in the body of the loop is a call to the method `newState`, which appears on lines 46 and 47. It requires that we supply it an initialized value for both `previous` and `current`, which again is why we needed the initialization before the loop.

One important decision that requires explanation is why we decided that an exit from the middle of the loop was warranted. The reason is that the last rectangle created will never be drawn. If we allow the `newState` method to be called one extra time, it is possible that the last rectangle drawn could mistakenly be labeled as a local minimum or maximum. As we will see shortly, labeling the local extremes—minimums or maximums—is a part of the responsibility of the `newState` method. But because of how we defined the local extremes, neither the first value nor the last value should ever be one of them.

Once the loop stops, the tip of the tallest match is recolored, which happens on lines 49 by a call to the method `colorMatchTip`. Finally the shortest match's tip is recolored on line 50 with a similar method call.

Now we consider the three private methods in the `Matchbook` class. The first of those three methods is `randomRectangle`. There should be no question about whether this sequence of code needs to be factored out into a separate method. The fact that it needs to be done twice in `paintComponent` is reason enough to make it a method. Now, let's consider what this method does. It begins by generating a random width on lines 56 and 57 and a random height on lines 58 and 59. We should note that we might have elected to create a method to compute a random number between a specified lower and upper bound, because the assignments to these two variables do involve some code duplication. Although we have been emphasizing its avoidance, this guidance is never absolute. Because the calculations are so short, we opted to allow that small amount of duplication. In the last assignment in that method, on line 60, the y ordinate of the upper left-hand corner of the rectangle is calculated so that the bottoms of all rectangles will be aligned. The x ordinate is simply the current value of sumOfWidths, which was passed in as a parameter. It generates a rectangle object by a call to the constructor that accepts both the position and size information and returns a rectangle object, which occurs on line 61. Returning a whole Rectangle object is a convenient way to return these four values—remembering, of course, that a method is able to return only one value, but if that value is an object, as it is in this case, it can contain a collection of values.

The second of the private methods in the Matchbook class is the method color-MatchTip, whose signature is defined on lines 63 and 64. It is called four times, twice by paintComponent to recolor the tips of the tallest and shortest matches, and twice by nextState to recolor the local extremes. The Graphics object, the rectangle to be drawn, and its color are the information it requires, so those three are its parameters. It uses all the rectangle's attributes except its height to draw the rectangle that recolors the match's tip. All tips are made the minimum height of a match.

Now we consider the last method in the Matchbook class, nextState. This method determines whether a local minimum or maximum occurs and recolors its tip with the appropriate color. Its signature, on lines 70 and 71, shows that it requires the Graphics object, the current state and a pair of adjacent rectangles. It implements the state transition illustrated in the UML finite state diagram shown in Figure 6.5.

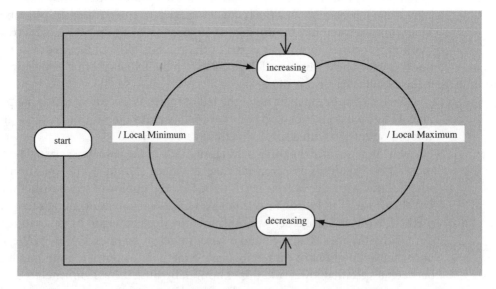

FIGURE 6.5 The UML finite state diagram for the matchbook application.

Before explaining the significance of this diagram, we need to explain why we resorted to using this design tool for this problem. It may seem that this problem could have been easily solved without the diagram by simply maintaining a window of the values across the sequence of rectangles. Let's see why that would not suffice. What we are suggesting is the use of the three variables `secondPrevious`, `previous`, and `current`—just as we had done in the Fibonacci spiral applet in Chapter 4. For simplicity, let's assume that there are three integers containing the heights of three consecutive matches. With three consecutive values, we should be able to identify the local extremes. For example, the following condition would define a local maximum:

```
secondPrevious < previous && previous > current
```

If that condition was true, `previous` would be a local maximum. Let's consider the case that we had two adjacent equal values that were both local maximums. The ability to identify such cases is a necessary skill one must develop to become a good software developer. So let's consider this case, which, if it occurred, would be missed by this condition. One might argue that with randomly generated values it would seldom happen, but if we wish to have a carefully constructed program, we need to consider it. Having identified this case, it becomes necessary to reconsider the requirements because there are two possible ways we might be required to handle such cases—either color the tips of both of them or just the last one. Let's assume the requirements have been refined to specify the latter choice. One might propose modifying the previous condition as follows:

```
secondPrevious <= previous && previous > current
```

In the case that we had a sequence of values such as 10 25 25 15, this condition would identify the second 25 as a local maximum. There's just one problem. It would also generate what we might call a false positive—mistakenly identifying values as local maximums that are not. Consider the following sequence of values: 35 25 25 15. In this case, the second 25 is not a local maximum. It is similar to what, in calculus, would be called a point of inflection, were this a continuous function. So now we might try another approach, skipping consecutive equal values in our window of three values. Done carefully, that approach should work, but it does complicate the assignments that implement the moving of the window of three values. We have explored this line of thought to illustrate the fact that the possibility of consecutive equal values introduces an inherent complexity to the problem, so it is likely to complicate any correct solution to some degree. The fact that we had to keep "patching up" our algorithm using this approach suggests that looking at the problem in another way might help. To arrive at the solution we have used in our program, it would certainly be necessary to be familiar with finite state diagrams and recognize this problem as a candidate for using one. Of course, we chose such a problem as an opportunity to present this technique. But the more such techniques you know, the more tools you have at your disposal to create a simple design.

Let's consider how modeling the problem with a finite state diagram can help. In such a model, we have states and events. Events can cause actions to occur and also cause a transition to a new state. Finite state diagrams capture this behavior. In our case, we need to recognize what the states are. Identifying that a sequence can be in an INCREASING or DECREASING state should not be too difficult, but what might be less apparent is the need for a START state. By starting out in that state, we ensure that we never find a local extreme until we have at least three values. We need the first two, which of course must not be equal to establish which of the other two states we are in. Then only after examining a third value would we ever find a local extreme. The diagram shows that there are two events: previous < current is one and previous > current is the other. Notice that the case of two successive equal values is a nonevent. This first event always takes us to the DECREASING state, but only when we are coming from the INCREASING state does it indicate the presence of a local minimum. A similar situation occurs with the other event.

Finally, once we have the finite state diagram, writing the code for the new-State method is not difficult. That method generates the necessary actions. In this case, it calls colorMatchTip and returns the new state according to what is specified by the diagram.

We have elected to omit the class diagram for this example, since it illustrates no new UML symbolism. Like the one in the previous chapter, it would show the two classes with a dependency relationship between them—the class MatchbookMain depending upon Matchbook.

SUMMARY

In this chapter, we encountered logical expressions for the first time, which were necessary for the general selection and iterations statements. These statements are a generalization of the discrete selection and iteration statements that we studied in Chapter 4. The key points to remember from this chapter are:

- Logical expressions are formed using the relational operators and produce a value of the primitive type boolean.
- The relational operators are defined only for the primitive data types.
- Truth tables define the meaning of the logical operators.
- An if statement separates the flow of control into two paths, but using nested if statements can separate the flow of control into a number of paths.

- The indentation of nested `if` statements should reflect the problem it is designed to solve.
- The `while` statement provides what is needed to solve problems that require repetition until some event occurs.
- Variables that are manipulated inside loops should be initialized to the identity element of operation performed on that variable inside the loop.
- Counter controlled loops should be implemented using `for` statements.

Review Questions

1. What is the difference between an inclusive and an exclusive *or*? Is the logical operator `||` inclusive or exclusive?

2. Explain why care must be taken when comparing floating point values for equality.

3. Why it is incorrect to compare strings for equality using the `==` operator? What should be used instead?

4. What is a truth table? When two variables are involved, how many lines does a truth table contain?

5. Explain what is meant when we say that the logical operators short circuit.

6. Under what circumstances does a dangling `else` occur?

7. Which selection statement is more general, the `if` or `switch`?

8. What is an infinite loop? How do you design loops to ensure that infinite loops do not occur?

9. Explain the difference between the English words *while* and *until*.

10. What is the primary difference between a `while` loop and a `do-while` loop?

Programming Exercises

11. Evaluate each of the following logical expressions, assuming x has the value 2 and y has the value 3. Also indicate whether the logical operation short-circuits.

   a. `x >= 6 && y !=7`
   b. `!(x + 1 > 2) || y == x + 1`
   c. `3 <= x && y == 3`
   d. `!(x != 3 || y <= 4)`

12. Write a logical expression for each of the following conditions.

   a. The variable x is between 10 and 20, inclusive.
   b. A person's age is at least 21 and height is at most 6 feet.

    c.   A rectangle's width is 50 and its height exceeds 20.

    d.   A character is between `'e'` and `'j'`, exclusive.

13. Indicate whether or not the following logical expressions will compile correctly. If they are incorrect, correct them. Assume x and y are integer variables.

    a.   `0 < x < 10`

    b.   `x && y == 0`

    c.   `x == y && !(y ==0)`

    d.   `! x > y`

14. Are the following two logical expressions equivalent? Explain.

    `x > 5 && y == 7     !(x < 5 || y != 7)`

15. Indicate the value of the variable x after each of the following `if` statements execute.

    a.
```
x = 5;
if (x > 1 || x < 10)
    x += 3;
else
    x -= 2;
```

    b.
```
x = 1;
if (x >= 1)
    if (x <= 1)
        x = 7;
```

    c.
```
x = 10;
if (x > 10)
    if (x < 10)
        x = 1;
else
    x = -1;
```

    d.
```
x = 1;
if (x <= 0)
    if (x %= 2 == 0)
        x = 2;
    else
        x = 3;
else
    if (x %= 2 == 0)
        x = 4;
    else
        x = 5;
```

16. What is the value of sum after the following loops execute?

    a.
    ```
    index = 8;
    sum = 0;

    while (index >= 4)
    {
        index -= 2;
        sum += index;
    }
    ```
    b.
    ```
    value = 6;
    sum = 0;

    do
    {
        sum += value;
        value += 3;
    }
    while (value < 8);
    ```

17. Write the necessary if statements to categorize the value in a variable tempera-ture in the following way. Assign the constant COOL to the variable weather if the temperature is less than 60. Assign WARM for 60 up to 90 and HOT for 90 and over.

18. Write a while loop that reads in integers until a negative integer is read in or until ten numbers have been read in. It should compute the sum of all the even numbers input.

19. Translate the following switch statement into if statements.
    ```
    switch (i)
    {
        case 1:
        case 2:
            j = 0;
            break;
        case 3:
            j = 1;
            break;
        case 5:
            j = 2;
            break;
    }
    ```

20. Translate the following do–while loop into a while loop. Add any other statements that are needed.

```
do
{
    x += 2;
}
while (x < 10);
```

Programming Projects

21. Modify the applet example from Chapter 3 to be an application that draws a triangle inscribed in a circle, so that it continues to draw a circle inside of the triangle and then another circle inside the smaller triangle until the radius of the circle becomes one pixel or less. The largest circle should have a radius of 50 pixels. The output that shown be produced by this program is shown in Figure 6.6.

FIGURE 6.6   Output of Chapter 6, Project 21.

Each circle should have a radius half of the previous circle.

22. Create a program that draws a "stair-step" sequence of squares beginning in the upper left-hand corner. The size of the squares should be randomly generated and have size between 0 and 19 pixels. The final square should not go beyond point 200, 200. The color of the square should depend upon the size of the square. Squares less than 5 pixels should be yellow. Squares between 5 and 9 pixels should be green. Squares between 10 and 14 pixels should be red. Larger squares should be blue.

23. Write an application that draws the x and y axes of an x-y plane with the origin at the center of the window. It should then randomly generate points on that

plane. The points should be plotted as filled circles with a diameter of six pixels. A count should be kept of the number of the points in each of the four quadrants. Points on either axis should be plotted, but not counted. It should continue to generate and plot points until all four quadrants have at least a required number of points. The user should be permitted to supply that required number of points when the program begins. Values between 25 and 50 should be accepted.

24. Write an application that repeatedly generates either a circle or square with a random size and location. Once generated, they should be drawn as filled shapes. On average, there should be an equal number of circles and squares. Their maximum size should be 50 pixels. As the shapes are generated and drawn, the area of each should be computed and a total area of all shapes drawn should be maintained. Once that total reaches at least 100,000 square pixels, the drawing should stop.

25. Write an application that draws the logarithmic spiral that was discussed in Chapter 4 when the Fibonacci spiral applet was presented. The spiral should consist of a sequence of straight-line segments. Refer back to the code for the Fibonacci spiral and recall how the coordinates fromX, fromY, toX, and toY were used. You should use a similar scheme. The values of the coordinates of the endpoints must be computed in a different manner, however. The method that you should use follows. You should compute a distance, let's call it r, from the center of the spiral with the formula $r = e^{\Theta}$. The x ordinate relative to the center should be computed as r cos Θ and the y ordinate as r sin Θ just as was done in the example in Chapter 3 that drew the triangle inscribed in a circle. The angle Θ should initially be zero and should be increased in increments of 0.1 radians. Once the spiral goes outside the boundaries of the window, the drawing should stop. The output of this program is shown in Figure 6.7.

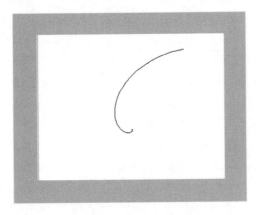

FIGURE 6.7 Output of Chaper 6, Project 25.

7 One Dimensional Arrays and Class Invariants

In this chapter

- Class Constants
- Array Basics
- The Increment and Decrement Operators Revisited
- Array Parameters
- Sorting
- Arrays of Objects
- Class Invariants
- The Cyclic Quadrilateral Application

CLASS CONSTANTS

Our primary topic for this chapter involves arrays, but we will begin with a discussion of class constants, because each of the examples in this chapter will use them. We began distinguishing between calls to class methods from calls to instance methods in Chapter 2 and began writing class methods in Chapter 5. To minimize the number of new concepts, we have avoided any discussion of the distinction between class and instance data until now.

Declaring Class Data

Recall that the way that we designate that a method is a class method is by using the modifier static. The same technique is used for declaring class data—both constants and variables. Because we will not have occasion to use a class variable for several more chapters, for now we focus on constants exclusively.

In much the same way that a class method is associated with the class, but not a particular instance, the same is true of class constants. There is only one copy of the constant for the whole class, not one for each instance. Because there is no benefit to having multiple copies of a constant, instance constants are rarely used. We used them until now for simplicity because nothing compelled us to do otherwise. An optimizing compiler could certainly turn instance constants into class constants for us, provided they are either primitives or immutable objects—the only kind of instance constants that we have used so far. Remember that the final modifier only prevents an object reference from being changed, so there is no way in Java to create a truly constant mutable object.

Accessing Class and Instance Constants

Let's review what we know about how class methods are called. When a public class method is called from a class other that the one to which it belongs, the class method must be qualified by prepending it with the name of its class. A call to Math.sqrt is an example. Similarly, when a public class constant is referred to from another class, its name must also be qualified by prepending it with the name of its class. We have already used such syntax when referring to enumerated literals— Shapes.square is an example.

We know that when a class method is called from another method in the same class, its name can be used unqualified because the method name is being accessed from within its scope. The same is true when we access a class constant from a method in the same class.

In Chapter 5, we discussed some restrictions on the ability of class and instance methods of the same class to call one another without qualification. Table 5.1 summarizes the restriction, indicating that a class method cannot call an instance method in the same class, unqualified. A similar restriction applies to accessing instance constants. An instance constant cannot be referenced unqualified from a class method. The reason is that within a class method, no instance has been selected; in other words, there is no this object. An attempt to refer to an instance constant unqualified is not permitted because we have never specified to which object it belongs. This situation is another exception to the general rule that names can be accessed within their scope without qualification.

This restriction is what has driven our need for one class constant in the final example of this chapter. We need to have some constants with class-wide scope in the class that contains main. Of course, main and all the private methods it calls are class methods and so would be unable to access instance constants.

In Chapter 9, we encounter another situation where a class constant would be required, but for a different reason. From this point forward, we will always use class constants rather than instance constants regardless of whether they are essential, just because there is no benefit to having a separate copy of constants for each object.

Lifetime of Class Constants

One final point about class constants is appropriate. Although instance and class constants have the same scope, they have different lifetimes. The lifetime of an instance constant is the lifetime of the object to which it belongs. It is created when the object is created and is usually destroyed when the object is destroyed. Class constants have the lifetime of the class.

It is the fact that class constants are created when the class is created that motivates our use of them in several of the preliminary examples in this chapter. When we encounter the first such use of a class constant for this reason, we will elaborate further.

ARRAY BASICS

Programming languages since the very earliest high-level language, FORTRAN, have provided a mechanism for defining collections of data elements called arrays. When we create an array, we specify the number of elements that it contains and when we wish to select a particular element, we make the selection by number, using an element's *subscript or index*. Clearly if we have an object that consists of a large number of elements of the same type, say 100 integers, although it would be possible to declare 100 variables, each with a different name, doing so would be awkward at best. Moreover, although we could write code that would allow us to select one variable among the 100 variables, given an index, we would need a switch statement with 100 different cases to do so. So although arrays do not provide us any capability that could not be achieved without them, they make declaring and accessing large collections of data much simpler.

Array Declarations

Because the syntax for declaring an array is very simple, we dispense with a syntax definition and simply illustrate the syntax by example. There are two different ways arrays can be declared. We begin with the syntax that Java introduced.

```
int[] array1, array2;
```

The above declaration declares two arrays whose elements are integers. The presence of the square brackets after the type of the elements signifies that we are declaring an array and not a single integer variable. Notice that the size of the array is not specified. The reason for this is because thus far we have only declared an array reference, but not an array object. This distinction is similar to what occurs when we declare an object of a nonprimitive type. So we must still create, or instantiate, the arrays themselves, as follows:

```
array1 = new int[10];
array2 = new int[20];
```

The reserved word new is used just as it is when we create objects, but instead of the parentheses, what follows are square brackets that contain the size of the array. So in this case, array1 now refers to a collection of 10 integers and array2 refers to a collection of 20. Just as with objects of a class, we can declare the array reference and create the array objects in the declaration as follows:

```
int[] array1 = new int[10], array2 = new int[20];
```

The alternate syntax for declaring arrays is the more traditional syntax that Java inherited from C++. To illustrate this syntax, let's consider declaring the same two array objects with it.

```
int array1[] = new int[10], array2[] = new int[20];
```

As you should notice, the difference is where the square brackets are placed. Using this alternate syntax, the brackets are placed after the array name rather than the type name. Consequently it is necessary to place the square brackets after each array in the declaration. To emphasize this point, consider the following declaration:

```
int intArray[], intVariable;
```

That declaration contains both an integer array and a simple integer variable. In all our examples in this chapter and throughout the remainder of the book, we shall use the former, newer syntax. As we have done in other similar situations, we have mentioned the alternate syntax for completeness so you will recognize it if you encounter programs that use it and understand how it differs from the newer syntax.

Array Subscripts

Next we consider the other important aspect of the syntax associated with arrays, which is how we designate a particular element of an array. We have already mentioned that because array elements do not have individual names, we refer to them by number, using subscripts. The term subscript has its origin in mathematical notation, where a collection of values is referred to using subscripts. Because the syntax is so simple, we illustrate it by example as before. The following statement shows how to assign the value of 10 to subscript 5 of array1, one of the arrays that we declared earlier.

```
array1[5] = 10;
```

Just as was the case in the declaration, the square brackets are again involved, but for a different purpose. In this case, the number inside the brackets refers not to the size of the array but to the array subscript. It is important to know the range of subscripts for an array. For an array containing n elements, the first element is designated by the subscript 0 and the last one is designated by the subscript $n-1$.

The ability to access array elements by their subscript is actually a more powerful selection mechanism than accessing an element of a class by name. The reason that it is more powerful is that an array subscript is not restricted to being a constant. It can be any integer expression. Furthermore, that expression can contain variables, which means that a subscripted array can refer to different array elements at different times during the execution of the program. As is so often true, adding power to a language feature can also bring with it some danger. Recall that the while statement is more general than the *for-each* version of the for statement, so it can solve a wider range of problems. The downside is that the possibility of infinite loops is introduced. The downside of a selection mechanism that can contain variables is that it is now possible for that expression to contain a value outside the bounds of the array. Unfortunately, such problems cannot generally be detected at compile time. When this situation occurs, it manifests as a runtime error. Whether such errors can occur in a particular program is something that we will consider when we write programs that contain arrays.

Arrays and for Loops

One more aspect of the syntax associated with arrays pertains to the close association of the for statement with arrays. Because a for statement is used to iterate across a discrete range of values, it is a natural companion to arrays. Let's consider how both the traditional for statement syntax and the newer *for-each* syntax can be used in connection with arrays, beginning with the former. The following statement computes the sum of all the elements of the array array1, declared earlier.

```
sum = 0;
for (int i = 0; i < array1.length; i++)
    sum += array1[i];
```

The first important aspect of this loop to observe is the use of the name `length`. Every array has this attribute. Although array types are not really classes, the attribute `length` is treated syntactically as though it were an instance variable. Using this attribute rather than hard coding the constant 10 is good style because it avoids code duplication. Next, let's consider using the *for-each* version of the `for` statement with an array. Consider how the *for-each* syntax could be used to accomplish the same purpose.

```
sum = 0;
for (int value: array1)
    sum += value;
```

We last saw this statement used to enumerate across all the values of an enumerated type. Its syntax for enumerating across all the elements of an array is quite similar. If anything, it is somewhat simpler since, after the colon, we only need the array name itself. What is generated for the array by this syntax is an *iterator*, a topic we will discuss again in the next chapter. This statement should be read "for each value in array1." This syntax is preferable because it avoids the need for a subscript entirely. Note, however, that although the *for-each* style is preferable when it can be used, there are instances when it cannot be used. One case is when we need the actual subscript inside the body of the loop. There is an even more important restriction on the use of this syntax. The iterator that is generated by the use of the *for-each* syntax is a *read-only iterator*, which means that this syntax can only be used when we are accessing the elements of the array, never when we are assigning them values. Unfortunately, if we mistakenly attempt to use this syntax to assign values to array elements, no compilation error occurs, but neither do the attempted assignments succeed. Consider the following loop again using the array `array1`:

```
for(int value: array1)
    value = 1;
```

So, the above statement compiles, but none of the array elements are changed to 1.

Array Constants

There is one final bit of special syntax that is associated with arrays that we need to describe. It involves a technique that allows an array to be declared and an instance to be created and initialized at the same time. The declaration

```
int[] array1 = new int[10];
```

declares the array reference, creates the array object, and initializes all the elements of the array to zero. Initializing the array elements to zero may be exactly what we need if they will be subsequently treated as sums or counters. Suppose each element will be used as a product, however. In that case, we would like each element to be initialized to one, not zero. We could use a traditional `for` loop to initialize the array elements, but another alternative is to use an array constant as follows:

```
int[] array1 = {1, 1, 1, 1, 1, 1, 1, 1, 1, 1};
```

This declaration declares the array reference, creates the array object, and initializes each array element to 1. Notice that the array size is not specified because the compiler infers the size based on the number of elements in the *array constant*—the list of values.

One restriction regarding the use of array constants is that they can only be used in the array declaration. Consequently, the following statements will not compile:

```
int[] array1;
array1 = {1, 1, 1, 1, 1, 1, 1, 1, 1, 1};
```

An Application That Draws a Square Spiral

Now that we have presented all of the necessary syntax needed to write programs containing arrays of primitive types, let's consider one such example. This example is an application that draws a rectilinear spiral. The output of this program is shown in Figure 7.1

FIGURE 7.1 The output of the square spiral application.

This application is similar to the Fibonacci spiral applet that we studied in Chapter 4, so you may wish to review the code for that applet, which is shown in Listing 4.3, before studying this one. It uses some of the same techniques, except that it uses an array to store the values and the spiral grows much more slowly. The lengths of the line segments that form this spiral grow arithmetically, not exponentially like the Fibonacci spiral. The code for the class that creates the window for this application is shown in Listing 7.1.

LISTING 7.1   A Class that Creates a Window that Draws a Rectilinear Spiral (found on
ON THE CD   the CD-ROM at chapter7\SquareSpiral.java.)

```
1    package chapter7;
2
3    import java.awt.*;
4    import common.*;
5
6    class SquareSpiral extends GraphicsApplication
7    {
8        private enum Directions {RIGHT, UP, LEFT, DOWN}
9
10       private static final int SIZE = 250, TOP_BORDER = 20,
11           POINTS = 50, SPIRAL = new SquareSpiral().display();
12       private int center, increment;
13       private int[] x = new int[POINTS], y = new int[POINTS];
14
15       public SquareSpiral()
16       {
17           super("Square Spiral", SIZE, SIZE + TOP_BORDER);
18           center = SIZE / 2;
19           increment = SIZE / POINTS - 1;
20           createSpiral();
21       }
22       public void paintComponent(Graphics graphics)
23       {
24               super.paintComponent (graphics);
25           for (int point = 1; point < x.length; point++)
26               graphics.drawLine(x[point - 1], y[point - 1],
27                   x[point], y[point]);
28       }
29       private void createSpiral()
30       {
31           Directions direction = Directions.RIGHT;
32           int length = increment;
33
34           x[0] = y[0] = center;
```

```
35              for (int point = 1; point < x.length; point++)
36              {
37                  switch (direction)
38                  {
39                      case RIGHT:
40                          x[point] = x[point − 1] + length;
41                          y[point] = y[point − 1];
42                          direction = Directions.UP;
43                          break;
44                      case UP:
45                          x[point] = x[point − 1];
46                          y[point] = y[point − 1] + length;
47                          direction = Directions.LEFT;
48                          break;
49                      case LEFT:
50                          x[point] = x[point − 1] − length;
51                          y[point] = y[point − 1];
52                          direction = Directions.DOWN;
53                          break;
54                      case DOWN:
55                          x[point] = x[point − 1];
56                          y[point] = y[point − 1] − length;
57                          direction = Directions.RIGHT;
58                          break;
59                  }
60                  length += increment;
61              }
62          }
63  }
```

In Chapter 5, when we first began using applications, we noticed that many of those programs contained a main that did little more than create a window object and display it. For many of the graphics applications in the remainder of the book, a similar situation exists. Consequently, we have introduced another class named GraphicsApplication, which can be found on the CD-ROM at common\GraphicsApplication.java. This method contains an empty main, which is inherited by classes that are derived from GraphicsApplication. Notice that on line 6, we now extend this new class. We elected this approach to underscore the fact that when all user interaction with a program is in a window, main plays essentially no role. It must be present nonetheless. But one thing that main did was to create the window and display it. Notice that we have accomplished that task inside the declaration of a class constant, which we named SPIRAL, on line 11. We never actually reference the value of the constant itself, but because it is a class constant, it is initialized when the class is created, which is important. Placing it in as a local object of main had a similar purpose. There is one other comment that is warranted regarding the initialization of SPIRAL. In its initialization, we are creating an *anonymous object*—an object that has no name. That object is created by the expression new SquareSpiral(). That object, which is the window object on which we draw the square spiral, will never again be referred to once we display it, which we do within that same initialization. Consequently, there is no compelling reason to name it.

Because the Fibonacci spiral did not use an array, the lengths and coordinates of the line segment of the spiral were computed each time the applet was painted. One advantage to using an array is that the computation of the coordinates needs to be done only once in the createSpiral method. Notice that this class contains *parallel arrays*—two or more arrays of the same length with a correspondence between respective array elements. The parallel arrays are x and y that represent the *x* and *y* coordinates of the endpoints of the line segments that form the spiral. Because of the parallel arrays, we elected to declare a constant POINTS on line 11 that represents the number of points and, consequently, the size of both those arrays. On line 12, the instance variable center is declared. It is both the *x* and *y* coordinates of the center of the spiral. As we mentioned earlier, the lengths of the line segments of this spiral grow arithmetically, each being greater than the previous one by the instance variable increment declared on the same line. On line 13, the parallel array references are declared and the array objects are instantiated.

Next, let's consider the constructor. It computes the values of the instance variables center and increment based on the value of the constant SIZE, which specifies the width of the window that is to be created. The constructor then calls the private method createSpiral that actually computes the endpoints of the line segments that form the spiral.

The next method we discuss is the other public method—paintComponent. Because most of the work is done when the window object is created, all that paint-Component must do is to draw the line segments that form this spiral. Notice that the traditional for statement syntax is used here again. It is important to note that the *for-each* syntax could not be used here for several reasons. First, the loop begins with subscript 1, not 0. Second, we are accessing two parallel arrays, not just one array. Third, we need the subscript, because on each iteration, we must access not only the current element but also the one before it.

Finally, we consider the one private method createSpiral, which is called by the constructor. It uses a switch statement inside a for loop and alternates between the four directions just as the applet that draws the Fibonacci spiral does. What is different in this case is that an array is being filled as the loop iterates. The for loop that begins on line 35 iterates across all the points in the array. For the upper bound, we used x.length, but since we declared the length as a constant, we could have equally well used POINTS here. Notice that the traditional for loop syntax is used here again for the same reasons that required us to use it in `paintComponent`. But there is one additional and perhaps more important reason that the *for-each* syntax cannot be used here, which is that we are attempting to modify the values of the array, which cannot be accomplished with the *for-each* syntax.

Using an array simplifies the code somewhat. We no longer need to maintain a moving window of three elements across the sequences, as we did with the Fibonacci spiral, because with an array we have what constitutes a window as large as the sequence itself. Consider a typical assignment like the one on line 40. In that assignment the *x* ordinate of the current point is being computed using the *x* ordinate of the previous point. Because array subscripts can be expressions containing variables, we can use `point − 1` to refer to the *x* ordinate of the previous point. This illustrates one of the key reasons for using arrays—this ability to select array elements using an expression. One final statement in this method that warrants discussion is the assignment on line 60. It computes the next term of the arithmetic progression that represents the sequence of the lengths of the line segments.

There is one final issue that we should consider regarding this class, which is whether it is possible for it to ever generate a subscript that is out-of-bounds of the array. Recall that generating out-of-bound subscripts is the danger that accompanies the power afforded by subscripts that contain variables, which is exactly what we are using here. You should note, however, that because we are carefully controlling the values of these subscripts with our `for` loops, such a situation cannot occur. Had we improperly coded the program by starting either of the `for` loops at 0 instead of 1, then such an error would occur.

THE INCREMENT AND DECREMENT OPERATORS REVISITED

In Chapter 4, we introduced the increment and decrement operators, first as a part of the `for` statement syntax, and then as standalone operators. There is one aspect of these operators that we have not yet discussed, and that is the difference between using these operators in *prefix* position compared to *postfix* position. We have deferred that discussion until now because this distinction is especially important when these operators are placed on array subscripts, although this distinction can be important in other contexts as well.

Comparing the Meaning of the Prefix and Postfix Operators

Let's begin by explaining the syntactical difference between prefix and postfix. Until now, we have used them exclusively with the postfix syntax—meaning the operator was after the variable that was to be incremented or decremented. Recall that these operators are assignment operators, so they must be attached to variables only—not to constants or to expressions. So, let's now consider how the prefix form looks. To increment a variable x using the prefix increment operator, we would write the following:

```
++x;
```

The operator is placed before the variable, as the name prefix suggests. One reason that we have avoided this discussion until now is that in many contexts, there is no difference in meaning between the two forms. Every time that we have used this operator until now, we have used the postfix form, but we could have used the prefix form as well. That leads us to the discussion of good style and adopting a rule for the consistent use of these two forms. In Chapter 4, we noted that the presence, the +, the +=, and ++ operators introduces redundancy into the language and offered some guidelines on how to deal with that redundancy. We observed that there were three ways to add 1 to a variable. The prefix operator makes four. So we offer another guideline in dealing with this added redundancy, which is wherever the meaning of the prefix and postfix forms are the same, use the postfix form. The rationale for this guideline is less compelling that those we offered earlier. Since neither form is more general than the other, the choice of which one to use is arbitrary. Our choice is based, however, on what is common practice. We continue to adhere to this practice throughout the rest of the book.

What remains unanswered is which to use when the two forms do have different meanings. Before considering these operators on array subscripts, we consider a simpler case, which is when they are embedded in assignments. Consider the following assignments that use the postfix form:

```
n = 4;
m = n++;
```

In this case, the variable n is incremented *after* the assignment because the operator is in postfix—placed *after* the variable. So after these two assignments, m is 4 and n is 5.

Let's now consider the same two assignments with the increment operator in prefix form:

```
n = 4;
m = ++n;
```

In this case, the variable n is incremented *before* the assignment because the operator is in prefix—placed *before* the variable. So after these two assignments, both m and n are 5.

To summarize, the meaning of these two forms differs when the increment or decrement subexpression is embedded in another expression.

The Prefix and Postfix Forms in the `for` Statement

The characterization of when the meaning of these two forms differs is often misunderstood by beginners, who conclude that the prefix and postfix forms have different meanings when used in the `for` statement. That conclusion is incorrect. Consider the following `for` statement using a prefix increment operator:

```
sum = 0;
for (i = 0; i <= 10; ++i)
    sum += i;
```

The above `for` loop is equivalent to the following `while` loop, which should help clarify why there is no difference:

```
sum = 0;
i = 0;
while (i <= 10)
{
    sum += i;
    ++i;
}
```

The update component of a `for` statement—the third expression—is really just a separate statement executed as the last statement inside the loop, as the translation indicates. Because there is no difference between the two forms, postfix is customarily used in `for` statements, as it is in other contexts.

The Prefix and Postfix Forms on Array Subscripts

Now we are ready to discuss the significance of whether the increment or decrement operator is placed on an array subscript in prefix or postfix position. As we noted earlier, we deferred discussion of this distinction until now because their placement on array subscripts is perhaps the most frequent context in which the meaning is different.

Let's assume that we have the following declarations of an integer array and an integer subscript:

```
int[] array = new int[10];
int i = 0;
```

Consider the following assignment of a subscripted array.

```
array[i++] = 5;
```

The meaning in this context is similar to what we discussed previously. Because the increment operator is in postfix—*after* the subscript—the subscript is incremented *after* it is used as a subscript, so the previous assignment is equivalent to the following sequence of statements:

```
array[i] = 5;
i++;
```

Similarly, placing the increment operator in prefix as follows:

```
array[++i] = 5;
```

would be equivalent to the following statements in which the increment statement appears first.

```
i++;
array[i] = 5;
```

An Application to Find the *n*th Prime Number

Now that we have explained the difference between prefix and postfix placement of these operators, we are ready to examine a program that makes use of them. The example that we have chosen is a program that prompts the user for which prime number to display, finds that prime number, and displays it. The code for this program is shown in Listing 7.2.

LISTING 7.2 An Application that Determines the *n*th Prime Number (found on the CD-ROM at `chapter7\Primes.java`.)

```
1   package chapter7;
2
3   import common.*;
4
5   public class Primes
6   {
7       public static void main(String[] args)
8       {
9           int oneToFind, thePrime;
10          oneToFind = InputOutput.getInteger
11              ("Enter which prime to find: ");
```

```
12          thePrime = findPrime(oneToFind);
13          InputOutput.putString("The " + oneToFind +
14              ordinalSuffix(oneToFind) + " prime is " + thePrime);
15      }
16      private static int findPrime(int oneToFind)
17      {
18          int[] primes = new int[oneToFind];
19          boolean isPrime;
20          int numberFound = 1, candidate = 3;
21
22          primes[0] = 2;
23          while (numberFound < oneToFind)
24          {
25              isPrime = true;
26              for (int index = 1; index < numberFound; index++)
27                  if (candidate % primes[index] == 0)
28                  {
29                      isPrime = false;
30                      break;
31                  }
32              if (isPrime)
33                  primes[numberFound++] = candidate;
34              candidate += 2;
35          }
36          return primes[--numberFound];
37      }
38      private static String ordinalSuffix(int number)
39      {
40          int rightMostDigit = number % 10,
41              secondRightMostDigit = number / 10 % 10;
42          if (secondRightMostDigit == 1)
43              return "th";
44          switch (rightMostDigit)
45          {
46              case 1:
47                  return "st";
48              case 2:
49                  return "nd";
50              case 3:
51                  return "rd";
52              default:
53                  return "th";
54          }
55      }
56  }
```

The `main` method gets which prime number to display from the user. Our prompt may lack the clarity that a user-friendly program should demonstrate. In any case, let's clarify what we are asking for. We are not asking the user to enter the prime number itself, but its ordinal position. What we are asking is, "Do you want the first, second, or third and so on, prime number?" You need to understand the difference between cardinal and ordinal numbers, because this distinction is especially germane to the discussion of array subscripts. The numbers one, two, three, and so on are cardinal numbers. The numbers first, second, third, and so on are called ordinal numbers. Once the user inputs the ordinal position of the prime to be found, `main` sends that ordinal number to the method `findPrime`, which finds it and returns it. The `main` method then displays that prime number together with its ordinal position.

Let's now consider the method `findPrime`, which illustrates the use of the increment and decrement operators on array subscripts. A word of explanation is required as to why we need an array in this method at all, since it is only required to return one prime. The reason that we have elected to use it, other than to illustrate our topic at hand, is that by maintaining a list of all the prime numbers found so far, fewer divisors are needed to test whether a number is a prime. It is sufficient to test only the prime numbers less than the candidate to see whether the candidate is a prime. Saving all the primes as we find them enables us to do just that. The size of the array `primes`, declared and instantiated on line 18, needs to be the same size as the ordinal value of the prime we are to find. Next let's consider the integer variable `numberFound` declared and initialized to 1 on line 20. This variable plays a dual role, common to many array applications. It is a count of how many primes we have found so far and, at the same time, it represents the subscript of the *next available* slot in the array `primes` to be filled. We initialized it to 1 because we fill in the first prime number, 2. Doing that initialization enables us to check only odd numbers thereafter, since 2 is the only even prime. It explains why the variable `candidate`, the variable containing the numbers that we will check for prime, also declared on line 20, is initialized to 3. A `while` loop is the right kind of loop for this algorithm because although we know how many primes we must find, we do not know how many candidates we need to test before we find the required number. We forego much explanation of the `for` loop that spans lines 26-31, since we already discussed the workings of finding primes in the previous chapter when we illustrated the labeled `break` statement. The primary difference in this algorithm is that the divisors are coming from the array `primes`, so the loop iterates on the array index. We would have used the *for-each* syntax for this loop were it not for the fact that we want to skip the first prime—2—because we are only testing odd numbers. The fact that we are testing only odd numbers is why, on line 34, we are adding 2 to the candidate, not 1.

Now to one of the most pertinent lines in this program—line 33. Notice that we are using the increment operator on the array subscript in postfix form. When used on array subscripts, the two forms almost always have different meanings, which is certainly true in this case. Because the subscript `numberFound` refers to the next available slot, we want to use it as our subscript first and increment it afterward. In postfix position, the increment operator does just that. Had we initialized `numberFound` to 0 instead of 1, it would always refer to the *last used* slot in the array. In that case, prefix incrementation would be the correct choice. The drawback to the latter approach is that `numberFound` would no longer be an accurate count of the number of primes found, which is why the first approach is the better one. Finally, let's consider line 36. This line illustrates the use of the decrement operator in prefix position. Because `numberFound` is now referring to the next available slot in the array, the prime number that we wish to return is in the previous slot, which explains why we want to decrement it before we use it as a subscript. In fairness, we must confess that our choice of the decrement operator was to illustrate its use. Without that consideration, we would have been more inclined to have written the following:

```
return primes[numberFound - 1];
```

In this case, either approach will work, but using the decrement operator is somewhat misleading because it suggests we care about what remains in the variable `numberFound` after we use it as a subscript, which is not the case. Its lifetime is about to end because it is a local variable in that method, so its value will never again be used.

We conclude our discussion of this program with the final method in the class—`ordinalSuffix`. This method returns the suffix that is placed on ordinal numbers when they are written using numeric digits. For example, first is written 1st, second as 2nd, and so on. Let's review the rules for such suffixes so the logic in this method is clear. Most ordinal numbers except for those that end in 1, 2, or 3 have the suffix *th*. Even some that end in 1, 2, or 3, like 11, 12, and 13, have the suffix *th*. Using this method, the output of this application might read something like "The 11th prime is 31."

Finally, there is something about the `switch` statement used in this method that warrants a comment. When we first introduced the `switch` statement in Chapter 4, we presented a simplified syntax for simplicity. This example contains a variation of that statement we have never before used, which is the inclusion of the `default` statement. Its meaning should be apparent, nonetheless. The `default` is akin to an `else` in an `if` statement. That choice is taken when "none of the above" applies. In this case, that choice would be taken for the digit 0 or the digits 4 through 9. Like the `case` statement, the `default` statement can only be placed inside a `switch` statement. Although it is not required, it is customary to place the default case last when it is present.

The Prefix and Postfix Forms on Subscripted Arrays

Our discussion of the increment and decrement operators in connection with subscripted arrays is not yet complete, because there is the possibility that these operators can be placed on subscripted arrays, but not on the subscripts themselves. For example, we might use the increment operator in either of the following two ways:

```
array[i]++;
++array[i];
```

It is important to understand first that, in both of the preceding cases, the element of the array at that subscript is being incremented, not the array subscript. Because no assignment or other operation is involved in either of these two statements, the prefix and postfix forms have the same meaning. Had their assignment to some variable been included, then the behavior would differ in much the same way that it does when a simple variable with an increment operator attached is being assigned to another variable. Our next program example will illustrate the increment operator used to increment an array element.

ARRAY PARAMETERS

In Chapter 5, we discussed most of the issues regarding the roles that parameters can play in exchanging data between the calling method and the one being called. Recall that there is an important difference between primitive parameters and mutable object parameters in this regard. Because array objects are references, and because arrays are inherently mutable objects, array parameters behave like mutable object parameters. Changes to the array reference made inside a called method are lost upon return to the caller, but changes to the array elements are preserved.

To illustrate the ways in which array parameters can be used, we have selected an example that contains several methods with array parameters. This program allows the user to input a sequence of grades and determines how letter grades should be assigned to the number grades. Grade inflation has become an often-discussed problem in universities today, so some have proposed limiting the number of students that can receive particular grades. In this program, we take this idea to the extreme by determining the thresholds for grades that would assign the lowest fifth of the class an F, the next fifth a D, and so on. In keeping with our preference to use graphical displays for output whenever possible, this program illustrates the range of each of the five grades with a rectangle whose width is proportional to the size of the range. In addition, the numeric threshold for each range is displayed. To avoid the possibility of the numeric thresholds overwriting one another should any of the ranges be very narrow, the rectangles that represent each grade range are arranged in a stair step fashion. The output of the application on a set of grades that has a very even distribution is shown in Figure 7.2.

Based on the thresholds illustrated in Figure 7.2, the exam that produced these grades must have been a very difficult one. For such an exam, such a scheme would actually help students, much like the more traditional idea of "grading on a curve" does. Of course, in this case, it might be called "grading on a straight line" since the distribution of grades would be a uniform distribution rather than the normal distribution of a bell-shaped curve.

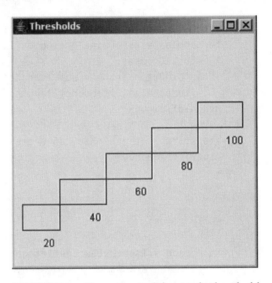

FIGURE 7.2 The output of the grade threshold application.

This program uses two arrays. It first tabulates the frequency of each grade using an array of 101 positions, one for each possible grade in the range from 0 to 100. It then uses the frequency array to generate an array of threshold points. This application consists of two classes—one to tabulate the frequencies and generate the thresholds and a second class to graphically display the output. Graphic applications can perform input and output in the main thread before the window that is used for drawing is created, which is the case in this application. Consequently, this application has a class containing `main`, named `GradeThreshold`, whose code is shown in Listing 7.3.

LISTING 7.3 The Main Class for the Grade Threshold Application (found on the CD-ROM *ON THE CD* at `chapter7\GradeThresholds.java`.)

```
1 package chapter7;
```

```
2
3   import common.*;
4
5   public class GradeThresholds
6   {
7       public static void main(String[] args)
8       {
9           int totalGrades;
10          int[] frequency = new int[101], thresholds;
11
12          totalGrades = getGradeFrequencies(frequency);
13          thresholds = determineThresholds(frequency,
14              totalGrades);
15          ThresholdGraph graph = new ThresholdGraph
16              (thresholds, frequency.length);
17          graph.display();
18      }
19      private static int getGradeFrequencies
20          (int[] frequency)
21      {
22          int grade, count = 0;
23
24          while (true)
25          {
26              grade = InputOutput.getInteger(
27                  "Enter grade, -1 to stop:");
28              if (grade < 0)
29                  break;
30              if (grade < frequency.length)
31              {
32                  frequency[grade]++;
33                  count++;
34              }
35          }
36          return count;
37      }
38      private static int[] determineThresholds
39          (int[] frequency, int totalGrades)
40      {
41          int frequencySum = 0, thresholdNo = 0;
42          int[] thresholds = new int[5];
43
44          for (int grade = 0; grade < frequency.length; grade++)
45          {
```

```
46                frequencySum += frequency[grade];
47                if (frequencySum >= totalGrades *
48                    (thresholdNo + 1.0) / thresholds.length)
49                    thresholds[thresholdNo++] = grade;
50            }
51        return thresholds;
52    }
53 }
```

There is an important difference with the way the array subscripts of the array frequency are used in this program compared to the previous two programs that we have considered in this chapter. The array subscripts in both of those earlier programs represented ordinal values, which was why we previously went into some detail in explaining ordinal numbers. In the program that drew the square spiral, x[0] represented the *x* ordinate of the *first* point in the spiral. In the prime number application, primes[0] represented the *first* prime number. In fact, array subscripts play the role of ordinal values more often than not. Although single letter variable names are usually a bad idea, it is not unusual to use i for an array subscript. In our prime number program, we used index, but, in reality, that name is no more meaningful than i. The fact that it is often difficult to choose a meaningful name for an array subscript is because its role is simply that of an ordinal value. Our reason for emphasizing this point is that sometimes subscripts represent something other than an ordinal value. The array frequency in this program is one such example. The subscript to the array frequency represents one of the possible grades from 0 to 100. We will see how this difference affects our ability to give a meaningful name to the subscript.

So, let's now turn to a more detailed look at the code for this program itself. We begin with the main method. It contains the declarations of both the array that contains the frequencies of each of 101 grades, named frequency and thresholds, which is the array of thresholds. Both are declared on line 10, but only the array frequency is instantiated. On line 12, the first of the two methods containing an array parameter is called. Upon entry, the array contains all zeroes, but upon return from the call to that method, the array will contain the frequency values. Remember that because arrays are mutable objects, array parameters can be used to send information back to the calling methods, which is exactly what is happening in this case. Another value is returned as a result of that call, which is a count of the total number of grades input. It is returned, as any single integer value must be, as the return value of the method call.

On lines 13 and 14, the method determineThresholds is called. The call to that method involves two array objects. The first of them, frequency, is an argument, just as it was in the call to getGradeFrequencies. Although both of these two method calls involve the array parameter frequency, its role in the first case was to receive information from the called method, whereas in this case, it is providing information to the method. The direction of data flow is *out* of the called method in the first case but *in* to the called method in this case. The second array object involved in the call to determineThresholds is the array returned by the call that we assigned to the array object thresholds. As with any returned data, the direction of data flow is *out* of the called method.

The roles that can be played by an array parameter are the same as those of any mutable object parameter. It can be used to send data in either direction. Also, just like any mutable object, array objects can be sent out of the called method by using a parameter as we did in the case of getGradeFrequencies or by returning the array object as we did with determineThresholds. In the first case, we had no choice but to use a parameter, since we were already using the return value for another purpose. Given the choice, however, we recommend the style of returning arrays sent back by method calls.

The final tasks performed by main are to instantiate and display a ThresholdGraph object. It is instantiated on lines 15 and 16. The call to the constructor that accomplishes the instantiation contains an array parameter—the array object thresholds. In this case, the parameter is used to send the threshold data into the constructor.

Next, we consider the method getGradeFrequencies that begins on line 19. Remember that arrays are initialized to zero when they are instantiated, which, in this case, is exactly what we need, because the array frequency is really an array of counters. The loop that spans lines 24-35 reads in grades from the user and updates the frequency array. Notice that this is a sentinel-controlled loop, so the sentinel that signals the end of data is any negative integer; nominally, we suggest a −1 to the user. Like most sentinel-controlled loops, the natural exit point is the middle, which is why we elected to use a break statement to exit the loop. On line 32, the counter that corresponds to the grade that was input is incremented. Recall our earlier discussion about how the subscripts to the array frequency are not simply ordinal values, so the name of the subscript we have chosen is a more meaningful one—grade—because for this array, the subscripts correspond to the 101 possible grades. The other noteworthy aspect of line 32 is that it illustrates the use of the increment operator on a subscripted array element, rather than on the subscript, as we saw in the prime number example. The operator is outside the brackets here because the array element, not the subscript, is being incremented. In this case, we could have used either the prefix or postfix position without altering the meaning, so we have chosen postfix, which is our custom in such cases.

We skipped over the if statement on line 30, so let's return to why it is needed. When we first discussed the fact that array subscripts could be expressions, we observed that it is therefore possible for an array subscript to be outside the bounds of the array. Furthermore, checking for that possibility must happen at runtime and, should it occur, a runtime error is generated. In both of the previous programs in this chapter, it was impossible to have a subscript that was out-of-bounds because we carefully controlled the subscripts in our code. In this case, the subscript is being computed from input provided by the user. Because we are using negative values as the stopping sentinel, they can never cause a problem; but a grade value that exceeds 100 will result in an out-of-bounds condition. Because we do not want the program to terminate in such cases, we must prevent that situation from occurring. The if statement on line 30 does just that.

Now we consider the final method in this class—determineThresholds. This method is the one that determines the threshold point for grades so that the grade distribution will be uniform. Recall that this method not only accepts the array parameter frequency, but also must return an array object. Because an array object needs to be returned, it is necessary to declare and instantiate a local object, which is done on line 42. The for loop, which comprises the bulk of this method, iterates through all the grade frequencies. On line 46, we accumulate a sum of all the frequencies thus far. When the sum meets or exceeds one-fifth of the total students, the first threshold has been found. When the sum meets or exceeds two-fifths, the second one has been found, and so on. The formula, which is in the if condition on lines 47 and 48, makes this comparison. Finally, notice the use of the increment operator in the assignment on line 49. It is being applied to the subscript, as it was in the prime number example, not to the array element, as it was in the previous method.

There is one final observation that we wish to make about array objects as parameters that send data out and array objects that are returned. Our observation is really about a pitfall to avoid. Notice that we instantiated an array object in the method determineThresholds, which involves an array parameter used to send data out, but not in getGradeFrequencies, which involves a returned array object. Suppose that we had instantiated one in the later method. Specifically, suppose the following line were inserted after line 22:

```
frequency = new int[101];
```

The program would still compile, but it would not work properly. What we now have is a copy of an array reference that will be gone when we return to main. If this idea is still not clear to you, you might want to reread the discussion of mutable object parameters in Chapter 5.

At this point, we wish to mention one aspect of Java syntax that relates to parameters that we have not yet discussed. It is the use of the modifier final on parameters. It can be used with any kind of parameter, not just arrays. Had we used that modifier, it would look as follows:

```
private static int getGradeFrequencies (final int[] frequency)
```

Adding the subsequent instantiation of frequency would have caused a compilation error. Although parameters are seldom labeled with the modifier final, we should treat them as though they were—especially when the parameters are objects or arrays. It is seldom beneficial to modify such parameters.

We are now ready to consider the second class of the grade threshold program. It is the class ThresholdGraph. The code for that class is shown in Listing 7.4.

LISTING 7.4   The Class that Draws the Threshold Graph (found on the CD-ROM at chapter7\ThresholdGraph.java.)

```
1  package chapter7;
2
3    import java.awt.*;
4    import common.*;
5
6    class ThresholdGraph extends Application
7    {
8        private final int TEXT_X = 20, TEXT_Y = 50,
9            Y_START = HEIGHT * 2 / 3, GRAPH_HEIGHT = 30, MARGIN = 10;
10       private double multiplier;
11       private int[] thresholds;
12
13       public ThresholdGraph(int[] thresholds, int maxValue)
14       {
15           super("Thresholds");
16           this.thresholds = thresholds;
17           multiplier = (WIDTH - 2. * MARGIN) / maxValue;
18       }
19       public void paintComponent(Graphics graphics)
20       {
21           int thisX = MARGIN, nextX, y = Y_START;
22
23           super.paintComponent(graphics);
24           for(int threshold: thresholds)
25           {
26               nextX = (int)(threshold * multiplier + .5);
27               graphics.drawRect(thisX, y, nextX - thisX,
28                   GRAPH_HEIGHT);
29               graphics.drawString("" + threshold, nextX - TEXT_X,
30                   y + TEXT_Y);
31               thisX = nextX;
32               y - = GRAPH_HEIGHT;
33           }
34       }
35  }
```

Notice that, because we have supplied a class containing `main`, this class is an extension of the `Application` class, rather than `GraphicsApplication`, which we extended in our first example in this chapter. This class contains the minimum of methods for such classes—a constructor and the method to paint the window. The constructor has an array parameter that supplies the array of thresholds, which is copied to a corresponding instance array of the same name on line 16. The second parameter, `maxValue`, contains the maximum value of the data, which is used to compute a multiplier that ensures that the graph fills out the window horizontally. Notice that this class knows nothing about the kind of data involved. It is capable of graphing any kind of data, not just grades. This separation of responsibilities is a feature of good design that we will explore further in subsequent chapters as our programs begin to contain more and more classes.

The method `paintComponent` uses a `for` loop to iterate through all the thresholds in the supplied array to create the stair step graph illustrated in Figure 7.2. None of the code used to accomplish that task should be unfamiliar.

SORTING

Many problems that involve arrays require sorting the elements of those arrays. Two of the examples in the remainder of this chapter involve sorting. So let's consider the problem of sorting in general in preparation for studying those examples. To sort a collection means to put the elements of that collection in order—usually ascending order according to some key. Whatever the sort key is, its type must clearly be an ordered type. Of all algorithms, sorting has been studied perhaps more than any other has. In the first several decades during which computers were available, when the term *data processing* was commonly used, most data processing involved inputting data on punched cards, sorting them and processing them against a master database, often on magnetic tape. During that time, computers were much slower than they are today, so there was a real practical need for developing fast sorting algorithms. It turns out that the fastest sorting algorithms are the least straightforward, making a complete investigation of sorting a topic more advanced than would be appropriate here. Instead, we confine our discussion to two simple algorithms for sorting—the selection sort and the insertion sort.

The Selection Sort

The selection sort is a reasonably intuitive algorithm, one that you might naturally use to sort some collection of physical objects. Like many sorting algorithms, with the selection sort we can think of the values being in two groups—those that have been sorted and those that remain to be sorted. Initially, all the values are in the former group. In practice, all the elements are in the same array; we simply keep track of the "dividing line" between the two groups. The selection sort repeatedly searches through the yet-to-be-sorted group looking for the smallest value. The algorithm for finding the smallest and largest values is one with which you should be very familiar, so that aspect of this algorithm should be relatively easy to understand. Once the smallest value is found, it is appended to the end of the sorted group. In practice, what really occurs is that the smallest value is swapped with the first element of the yet-to-be-sorted group and the dividing line is moved so that it joins the sorted group. To help you understand this algorithm, study Figure 7.3, which illustrates the steps that are involved in sorting an array of five integers. The sort key in this case is the integers themselves.

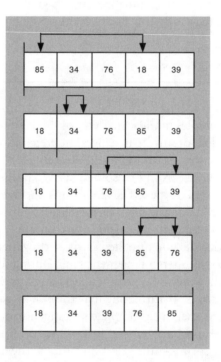

FIGURE 7.3 The steps of the selection sort, sorting an array of five integers.

The Insertion Sort

The other sorting algorithm that we have chosen to discuss is the insertion sort—another quite intuitive algorithm. It is one you have undoubtedly used, perhaps to sort your cancelled checks you receive each month from the bank, or when arranging playing cards in your hand. As with the selection sort, we can think of the array elements being divided into the sorted and yet-to-be-sorted groups. The sorting process in this algorithm works somewhat differently from the selection sort. The first element of the yet-to-be-sorted group is inserted into its proper position among the sorted group. This operation is achieved, not by swapping elements, but by shifting them to the right. Each element in the sorted group is examined, moving from right to left, and shifted one position to the right until one is found that is no greater than the one to be inserted. At that point, the new element is inserted into its proper position. As before, seeing the steps of this algorithm should help you visualize what we just described. In Figure 7.4, the steps of the insertion sort are illustrated using the same array of five integers as before.

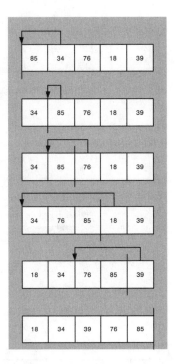

FIGURE 7.4 The steps of the insertion sort, sorting an array of five integers.

Physical and Logical Sorts

The adjectives *physical* and *logical* are commonly used in computer science to distinguish between an actual object or process, the physical one, and one that in some way refers to it, its logical counterpart. These adjectives are often applied to sorting in this way. What we have been describing until now have been physical sorts. A logical sort instead sorts, not the array elements themselves, but a parallel array that refers to them. Typically, the latter array is an array of subscripts. In the early days of computing that we were recounting earlier, when memory was expensive and therefore scarce, it was often impossible to load the entire array to be sorted into memory. So rather than physically sort the data on a disk, which would be very slow, a logical sort was performed with the parallel array in memory being sorted instead. Although scarce memory is hardly an issue today, performing logical sorts is still sometimes useful. In the next example in this chapter, we will have occasion to use one. To help you understand the workings of a logical sort, Figure 7.5 reillustrates a logical selection sort of the same array of five integers shown in Figure 7.3.

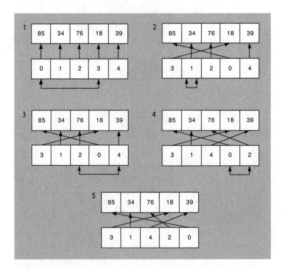

FIGURE 7.5   The steps of the logical selection sort, sorting an array of five integers.

ARRAYS OF OBJECTS

Until now, we have been discussing arrays of primitives exclusively. Next, we will consider arrays that contain objects.

Creating Arrays of Objects

Although the two kinds of arrays are similar in most ways, there is one important difference. With arrays of primitives, we must declare the array and then instantiate the array object. With arrays of objects, those two steps must also be done, but an additional third step is required. Because objects are references, when we instantiate the array we have only created an array of object references, so we must then instantiate the actual objects themselves. Let's consider an example that involves an array of four polygons.

```
Polygon[] polygons = new Polygon[4];
for (int i = 0; i < polygons.length; i++)
    polygons[i] = new Polygon();
```

The first line declares the array reference and instantiates the array object as before. What is new is the `for` loop that follows that instantiates the four actual polygon objects. Because the array elements are being initialized, the traditional `for` statement syntax must be used here.

Object Array Constants

It is possible to initialize object arrays to array constants in their declarations in a fashion similar to what we use for arrays of primitives. Consider the following example of a string array that is so initialized:

```
String[] ordinals = {"first", "second", "third", "fourth"};
```

Because string literals implicitly instantiate string objects, no explicit use of `new` is required. For other object array constants, its explicit use is necessary. Consider how we might initialize the array of polygons that we were discussing earlier:

```
Polygon[] polygons = {new Polygon(), new Polygon(), new Polygon(),
    new Polygon()};
```

As before, the compiler infers the size of the array from the number of elements in the list that defines the array constant.

An Application That Determines the Mean and Median

We are now ready to consider a program that illustrates the use of an array of objects—to be more specific, an array of rectangles. The rectangles represent bars that are drawn as a bar graph. The width of the bars is fixed, but their heights are randomly generated. The program calculates the mean height of the bars and draws a horizontal line at that height. Mean is a synonym for average. It also determines the median of the heights. Although median is often confused with the mean, it is not a synonym for the average. It is the middle value. We have chosen an odd number of bars, 33, so that there will be only one in the middle. The bar whose height is the median height is painted black, while the other bars are painted gray. The output of this program is shown in Figure 7.6.

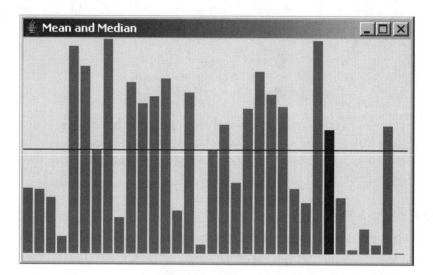

FIGURE 7.6 A bar graph illustrating the mean and median bar heights.

The code for the class that creates the window for this program is contained in Listing 7.5.

LISTING 7.5 A Class that Creates a Window that Illustrates the Mean and Median (found on the CD-ROM at chapter7\MeanMedian.java.)

```
1 package chapter7;
2
3 import java.awt.*;
4 import common.*;
5
6 class MeanMedian extends GraphicsApplication
7 {
8     private final static int BAR_COUNT = 33, WINDOW_HEIGHT = 250,
9         MAX_HEIGHT = WINDOW_HEIGHT - 35, WIDTH = 10,
10         MEAN_MEDIAN = new MeanMedian().display();
11     private int meanHeight;
```

```
12      private Rectangle[] bars;
13      private int[] subscripts;
14
15      public MeanMedian()
16      {
17          super("Mean and Median", (BAR_COUNT + 1) * (WIDTH + 2),
18              WINDOW_HEIGHT);
19          bars = new Rectangle[BAR_COUNT];
20          subscripts = new int[BAR_COUNT];
21          initializeBars();
22      }
23      public void paintComponent(Graphics graphics)
24      {
25          int median = subscripts[bars.length / 2 + 1];
26
27          super.paintComponent(graphics);
28          graphics.setColor(Color.GRAY);
29          for (Rectangle bar: bars)
30              graphics.fillRect(bar.x, bar.y, bar.width, bar.height);
31          graphics.setColor(Color.BLACK);
32          graphics.fillRect(bars[median].x, bars[median].y,
33              bars[median].width, bars[median].height);
34          graphics.drawLine(0, meanHeight,
35              bars.length * (WIDTH + 2), meanHeight);
36      }
37      private void initializeBars()
38      {
39          double heightSum = 0;
40
41          for (int i = 0; i < bars.length; i++)
42          {
43              bars[i] = randomBar(i);
44              subscripts[i] = i;
45              heightSum += bars[i].height;
46          }
47          selectionSort();
48          meanHeight = MAX_HEIGHT -
49              (int)(heightSum / bars.length +.5);
50      }
51      private Rectangle randomBar(int i)
52      {
53          int height = (int)(Math.random() * MAX_HEIGHT);
54          int x = i * (WIDTH + 2);
55          int y = MAX_HEIGHT - height;
```

```
56
57              return new Rectangle(x, y, WIDTH, height);
58      }
59      private void selectionSort()
60      {
61          int minIndex;
62
63          for (int i = 0; i < bars.length - 1; i++)
64          {
65              minIndex = i;
66              for (int j = i + 1; j < bars.length; j++)
67                  if (bars[subscripts[j]].height <
68                          bars[subscripts[minIndex]].height)
69                      minIndex = j;
70              swap(minIndex, i);
71          }
72      }
73      private void swap(int left, int right)
74      {
75          int temp = subscripts[left];
76
77          subscripts[left] = subscripts[right];
78          subscripts[right] = temp;
79      }
80 }
```

We begin examining the data of this class. On line 8, we have declared a number of class constants that define the size of the window and have instantiated the window object and displayed it. On line 11, we have declared an instance variable for the mean height of the bars. The array of rectangles, named bars, which is of primary interest in this example, is declared on line 12, but the array is not instantiated. The final instance variable is the integer array subscripts declared on line 13. These two arrays are parallel arrays—something we encountered in one of our previous examples. We plan to use the array subscripts to perform a logical sort of the bars. Another alternative would have been to make a second copy of the array of rectangles and sort that one but leave the other unsorted, because, in effect, we need both. Using this array of subscripts accomplishes the same goal without having to copy more than what is needed.

Next we consider the role of the constructor. It creates a window whose size is based on the class constants and then instantiates the array bars on line 19 and subscripts on line 20. The constructor then calls initializeBars to actually instantiate the Rectangle objects in the bars array.

As always, the role of the `paintComponent` method is to do the drawing—in this case, to draw the bar graph, a line of mean height and to highlight the bar of median height. On line 25, we declare and initialize the local variable `median` to contain the subscript of the bar whose height is the median height. Because our `selectionSort` sorts the `subscripts` array, not the bar array, the middle element in the `subscripts` array contains the subscript of the bar of median height. If you cannot quite follow the reason behind that statement yet, come back to it after reading about the `selectionSort` method. The `for` loop on lines 29 and 30 draws each of the bars, coloring them gray. Whenever possible, notice that we opt to use the *for-each* syntax. On lines 32 and 33, the bar of median height is repainted black to highlight it, and on lines 34 and 35, a horizontal line is drawn that represents the mean of the heights of all the bars.

Next let's examine `initializeBars`, which is called by the constructor. In the loop that spans lines 41-46, the bars are instantiated by a call to the `randomBar` method, the subscript array is initialized so each element contains its subscript and the total height of the bars is accumulated. The next task performed by this method is to call `selectionSort` to sort the bars—actually their corresponding subscripts—so that we can determine the bar whose height is the median height. Lastly, the mean height is calculated on lines 48 and 49.

The `randomBar` method that begins on line 51 should not contain anything unfamiliar. It is quite similar to the `randomRectangle` method that we used in the matchbook example in Chapter 6, except, in this case, the rectangles all have a fixed width.

Now we examine the `selectionSort` method, which is the most complicated algorithmically of any in this program. We already discussed this algorithm earlier, so you may want to reread that discussion before proceeding to ensure the workings of this algorithm are clear. We begin our explanation with an unusual starting point by considering the inner loop first—the one that spans lines 66-69. This loop should be a familiar loop that finds the smallest element of an array—actually a subarray that begins at subscript `i + 1`. This subarray is what we called the yet-to-be-sorted group during our earlier discussion. What we are saving is the subscript of the smallest value in `minIndex`, not the smallest value itself. The values that we are comparing are the heights of the bars, of course. One other aspect of this loop that warrants explanation is what in this code makes it a logical rather than physical sort. Although this idea may seem complicated, the transformation from a physical sort to a logical order involves a minor change to the code. To help you understand this point, what follows are lines 67 and 68 rewritten as they would need to be if this sort were a physical one.

```
if (bars[j].height < bars[minIndex].height)
```

Notice that the only difference is that, in the physical sort, the subscripts j and minIndex are used directly. In its logical counterpart, j and minIndex are used as subscripts to the array subscripts whose values are then used as the subscripts to the array bars. It sounds more complicated than it really is. This technique and ones like it are used frequently in programming. A technique of this kind is often referred to as *indirection*—we are accessing the array bars indirectly through the array subscripts. Once the smallest element is found, it is swapped with the first element of the yet-to-be-sorted subarray. This swapping is accomplished with a call to the method swap on line 70.

Now that we have explained the operation of the inner loop, let's consider the outer loop that begins on line 63. Its loop control variable, i, defines what we previously called the "dividing line" between the group of sorted elements and those yet-to-be-sorted. As the outer loop proceeds, the former group grows to eventually become the whole array as the latter group shrinks down to nothing.

The last method in this class is swap, which begins on line 73. Swapping or interchanging values is a fundamental operation, one that is used by the majority of sorting algorithms. Swapping is a three-step operation that must involve a temporary location to avoid overwriting one of the values. The steps of a swap are illustrated in Figure 7.7.

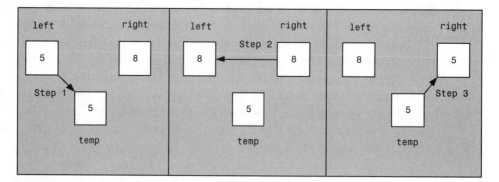

FIGURE 7.7 The three steps of a swap.

One important point to note is that, because parameters can only be passed by value in Java, a swap method cannot be written in which the values to be swapped are themselves passed as parameters. Your ability to fully understand the previous statement should help you gauge your understanding of the significance of passing by value. So what we must do instead is pass the subscripts as parameters instead. The swap method then swaps the array elements at those subscripts. In our case, because we are doing a logical sort, the elements of the array subscripts are swapped. Had this been a physical sort, the elements of the array bars would have been swapped instead.

Arrays of Objects in Place of Parallel Arrays

We have used parallel arrays in two of our examples so far in this chapter—the square spiral example and the mean and median example that we just studied. It is worth noting that the presence of parallel arrays in a design may signal a missed opportunity to create an additional class that might provide a more object-oriented design. Let's return to our first example of this chapter and see how the use of another class and an array of objects might replace the parallel arrays of integers. The other class that we use here is the predefined Java class Point, which defines the *x-y* coordinates of a point. This class has a constructor that allows a point to be created, given its *x-y* coordinates. It also has two public instance variables, x and y, that contain the coordinates. Listing 7.6 contains the modifier version of this program.

LISTING 7.6 The Square Spiral Application Using an Array of Points (found on the CD-ROM at chapter7\AnotherSquareSpiral.java.)

```
1   package chapter7;
2
3   import java.awt.*;
4   import common.*;
5
6   public class AnotherSquareSpiral extends GraphicsApplication
7   {
8       private enum Directions {RIGHT, UP, LEFT, DOWN}
9
10      private static final int SIZE = 250, TOP_BORDER = 20,
11          POINTS = 50, SPIRAL = new AnotherSquareSpiral().display();
12      private int center, increment;
13      private Point[] points = new Point[POINTS];
14
15      public AnotherSquareSpiral()
16      {
17          super("Another Square Spiral", SIZE, SIZE + TOP_BORDER);
18          center = SIZE / 2;
19          increment = SIZE / POINTS - 1;
20          createSpiral();
21      }
22      public void paintComponent(Graphics graphics)
23      {
24          super.paintComponent(graphics);
25          for (int point = 1; point < points.length; point++)
26              graphics.drawLine(points[point - 1].x,
27                  points[point - 1].y, points[point].x,
28                  points[point].y);
```

```
29        }
30        private void createSpiral()
31        {
32            Directions direction = Directions.RIGHT;
33            int length = increment;
34
35            points[0] = new Point(center, center);
36            for (int point = 1; point < points.length; point++)
37            {
38                switch (direction)
39                {
40                    case RIGHT:
41                        points[point] = new Point(points[point - 1].x
42                            + length, points[point - 1].y);
43                        direction = Directions.UP;
44                        break;
45                    case UP:
46                        points[point] = new Point(points[point - 1].x,
47                            points[point - 1].y + length);
48                        direction = Directions.LEFT;
49                        break;
50                    case LEFT:
51                        points[point] = new Point(points[point - 1].x
52                            - length, points[point - 1].y);
53                        direction = Directions.DOWN;
54                        break;
55                    case DOWN:
56                        points[point] = new Point(points[point - 1].x,
57                            points[point - 1].y - length);
58                        direction = Directions.RIGHT;
59                        break;
60                }
61                length += increment;
62            }
63        }
64 }
```

Let's consider how this version differs from the original one. First, we now have one array of objects, points, declared on line 13, instead of the parallel arrays. Because we have an array of objects with public instance variables, we now refer to the x ordinate for the first point, for example, as point[0].x. This modified version makes numerous such references throughout.

We don't mean to suggest by this revision that parallel arrays must always be avoided, simply that, if they are used, one should consider the alternative. We will have occasion to use parallel arrays in some of the remaining examples in the book, but whenever we use them, we will explain why we have considered and rejected the alternative.

CLASS INVARIANTS

Until now, we have not devoted too much discussion to the principles of object-oriented design. All the programs that we have studied so far have been relatively small, consisting of no more than two classes, so there has been little need for explaining how to decide which classes are required for a given program. We have discussed at some length the rationale for methods within a class—particularly private methods that may be useful to avoid code duplication. Before we proceed to larger programs, which we will do within the next few chapters, it is important to discuss some design issues that relate to the design of individual classes—particularly how we should choose the public methods of a class. Recall that the public methods of a class form the specification—the view of the class from outside.

One important principle of object-oriented design that we introduced in Chapter 3 was the idea of information hiding—limiting the visibility of the representation of objects of that class, which we achieve in Java by making the instance variables of the class private. When we introduced this idea, we explained that information hiding made programs easier to maintain by restricting knowledge of the details of the representation of objects of a class to the methods of that class. Equally important in achieving this enhanced maintainability is properly designing the class specification.

Some background on the development of object-oriented languages will help you better understand this issue. Java has its roots in C, a language that is not an object-oriented language. C does not have classes, but has structures instead. A structure can contain data, but not methods, and all the data is public. One could take a nonobject-oriented program and transform it into an object-oriented one by changing to a language like C++ or Java that has classes, changing all the structures to classes, making all the data private, and adding a *get* and *set* method for each data element. Wherever the data was accessed outside the class, calls to one of the two methods could be made—using the *get* method when the value of the data element was being referenced and the *set* when it was being changed. Technically, we would now have an object-oriented program. The problem with such an approach is that although we would be adhering to the letter of object-oriented design, we would be missing an important aspect of its spirit.

Part of that spirit lies in the idea of recognizing *class variants* and designing an interface that preserves those invariants. Rather than trying to give a formal definition of a class variant, we prefer to illustrate this idea and the associated design principle by several examples.

The Invariant for a Grade Record

We begin with the example of a program designed to maintain grade records for students. "Grade record" would be an obvious candidate for one of the classes of such a program. Let's suppose we wish to maintain just enough information to be able to compute a student's grade point average. Internally, we might elect to represent the current state of a student's grade record by keeping track of two pieces of data—the total number of credits earned and the total number of quality points. The latter quantity represents the product of the numeric value of the grade earned for a course multiplied by the number of credit hours. So, for example, an A in a three-credit course earns 12 quality points. Suppose as our specification to this class we blindly create a *get* and *set* method for each instance variable, giving us the following specification:

```java
class GradeRecord
{
    private int credits, qualityPoints;

    public int getCredits()
    {
        return credits;
    }
    public void setCredits(int credits)
    {
        this.credits = credits;
    }
    public int getQualityPoints()
    {
        return qualityPoints;
    }
    public void setQualityPoints(int qualityPoints)
    {
        this.qualityPoints = qualityPoints;
    }
}
```

Having made the instance variables private, we have adhered to the principle of information hiding, but as we indicated earlier, missed the spirit of good object-oriented design. The source of the problem is that we failed to recognize an invariant of this class, which is the following:

```
0 <= qualityPoints / credits <= 4
```

There is a relationship between two instance variables that must be preserved by the specification to this class. The invariant states that a student grade point average must be between 0 and 4. Allowing either of these quantities to be changed independent of the other could cause this invariant to be violated. A more appropriate specification is the following:

```
class GradeRecord
{
    public enum Grades{F, D, C, B, A};

    private int credits = 0, qualityPoints = 0;

    public void addCourseGrade(Grades grade, int courseCredits)
    {
        credits += courseCredits;
        qualityPoints += grade.ordinal() * courseCredits;
    }
    public double gradePoint()
    {
        return (double)credits / qualityPoints;
    }
}
```

Notice that we have taken advantage of the enumerated type feature to define a type for grades. In so doing, we guarantee that an invalid grade can never be supplied. We ordered the grades so that their underlying ordinal values will correspond to the numeric equivalent of the letter grade. The specification to this class now allows only two operations, the ability to supply a grade for a newly completed course and the ability to inquire about the grade point average for all courses completed so far.

The Invariant for a Generalized Rectangle

In keeping with the graphics focus of this book, let's consider an example of a graphics class, its invariants and how choosing an improper specification might violate them. Suppose that we wanted to create a class for a rectangle. Unlike the rectangles defined by the class `java.awt.Rectangle` and the rectangles that can be drawn by the `drawRect` method of `java.awt.Graphics`, this class would allow rectangles to be defined whose sides were not necessarily parallel to the x and y axes. It is, after all, not a requirement for a polygon to be a rectangle. A rectangle is just a four-sided polygon in which each of the angles is a right angle. The invariant property of rectangular objects is contained within this definition. Because the sides need not be parallel to the axes, the internal representation of such objects needs to be more than the coordinates of the upper left-hand corner, the width, and height. For ease of drawing the rectangle, we might reasonably decide to have the coordinates of each of the four vertices as the instance variables. Suppose for our specification we allow each of the eight instance variables to be individually *get* and *set*. It should not be hard to see that individually setting only one ordinate value to a different value will certainly cause the invariant of this class to be violated. Although we choose to forego the formality, we could express the invariants of this class with logical conditions that involve the coordinates of the rectangle's vertices.

Every class invariant must be true for an object before any method of the class acts upon that object, and it must remain true after that method completes its action. So it is imperative to design the specification for every class so that the invariants of the class are preserved in this fashion.

We do not wish to close this discussion without pointing out that it would be wrong to conclude from the foregoing information that using a *get* or a *set* method for an instance variable is always an improper design choice. In fact, C++, a successor language of Java, has formalized the notion of *get* and *set* into a special syntax referred to as *properties*. In some cases, a *set* method can ensure that an invariant is preserved by simply checking the range of the value supplied to it. Such checks are often sufficient when an invariant only involves constraints on the value of one instance variable and not a relationship between two or more variables. A *get* or *set* method is only improper when it allows objects of that class to enter a state that violates any of the invariants. Blindly having a pair of methods for each instance variable is, however, a red flag for a poorly conceived design. It suggests that the designer may have never considered whether there are any invariants for the class.

THE CYCLIC QUADRILATERAL APPLICATION

The final example in this chapter is one that will involve most of the topics that we discussed in this chapter. It contains arrays of both primitives and objects, array parameters, sorting, and the design principle related to preserving class invariants.

The class that we chose to illustrate the principle of class invariants is a graphic object similar to the generalized rectangle that we were just discussing but, admittedly, a bit more exotic. The graphical object that we use in this application is called a cyclic quadrilateral. Like a rectangle, it is a four-sided polygon—a quadrilateral—but rather than requiring that all its angles be right angles, the quadrilateral is required to be inscribed inside a circle. Although it is no doubt possible to describe this invariant with a more formal logical expression, such formality is not essential to be able to ensure that the class preserves it.

We have written the class to illustrate both proper and improper methods. All but one of the methods preserves this invariant. We have intentionally included one that does not, just to amplify the difference. Let's consider the kinds of operations that preserve the class invariant. The ones that we have chosen are contracting the figure, rotating it, and translating it. These same operations would be invariant preserving operations for the generalized rectangle object that we described earlier. To illustrate an operations that could cause the class invariant to be violated, we have included an operation that allows the vertices of the quadrilateral to be returned. We then modify one of the vertices of the quadrilateral independent of the others, performing an operation we characterize as skewing, creating a quadrilateral that is no longer cyclic and so violating the invariant.

Because we need a main, this program does more than just create the window objects. This program consists of two classes—the one that contains the main method and the one that extends Application and does the drawing. The code for the former class is provided in Listing 7.7.

LISTING 7.7 The Main Class for the Cyclic Quadrilateral Application (found on the CD-ROM at chapter7\CyclicQuadMain.java.)

```
1   package chapter7;
2
3   import common.*;
4
5   public class CyclicQuadMain
6   {
7       private enum MenuChoices {CONTRACT, ROTATE, TRANSLATE, SKEW,
8           QUIT};
9       private static final int SIDES = 4, TEN_DEGREES = 10,
10          TWENTY_PIXELS = 20;
11
12      public static void main(String[] args)
13      {
14          CyclicQuadrilateral[] quads = new CyclicQuadrilateral[4];
15          MenuChoices choice;
16          int quadNo;
17
18          for (int quad = 0; quad < quads.length; quad++)
19              quads[quad] = new CyclicQuadrilateral(randomAngles());
20          for (CyclicQuadrilateral cyclicQuad: quads)
21              cyclicQuad.display();
22          while (true)
23          {
24              choice = (MenuChoices)InputOutput.getEnum(
25                  "Select an action: ", MenuChoices.values());
26              if (choice == MenuChoices.QUIT)
```

```
27                          return;
28                      quadNo = InputOutput.getInteger(
29                          "Enter quadrilateral number", 1, quads.length) − 1;
30                      switch(choice)
31                      {
32                          case CONTRACT:
33                              quads[quadNo].doContraction(TWENTY_PIXELS);
34                              break;
35                          case ROTATE:
36                              quads[quadNo].doRotation(TEN_DEGREES);
37                              break;
38                          case TRANSLATE:
39                              quads[quadNo].doTranslation(TWENTY_PIXELS,
40                                  TWENTY_PIXELS);
41                              break;
42                          case SKEW:
43                              skew(quads[quadNo]);
44                              break;
45                      }
46                  }
47              }
48          private static double[] randomAngles()
49          {
50              double[] angles = new double[SIDES];
51
52              for (int angle = 0; angle < SIDES; angle++)
53                  angles[angle] = Math.random() * 2 * Math.PI;
54              return angles;
55          }
56          private static void skew(CyclicQuadrilateral quad)
57          {
58              int[] x = quad.getQuadrilateralX();
59              int[] y = quad.getQuadrilateralY();
60
61              x[1] += TWENTY_PIXELS;
62              y[1] += TWENTY_PIXELS;
63              quad.repaint();
64          }
65  }
```

Let's begin with the enumerated type definition for MenuChoices declared on lines 7 and 8. As its name suggests, this type definition provides the menu of actions from which the user can select. This class also contains several class constants declared on lines 9 and 10. Although only one of them requires class-wide scope, we are always free to widen the scope of constants, so we have elected to give them all class-wide scope. Notice the inclusion of the reserved word static. They are class constants, not instance constants. Making them class constants was essential because they are accessed from the methods of this class, and all the methods are class methods. Furthermore, as is customary with such applications, no objects exist of the class CyclicQuadMain. You may want to reread the discussion earlier in this chapter about class constants if you are still unsure about this issue.

Now let's examine the first of the three methods in this class—main. On line 14 is the declaration of the array of four cyclic quadrilateral objects that are the focus of this application. Figure 7.8 illustrates these four windows displaying the quadrilaterals.

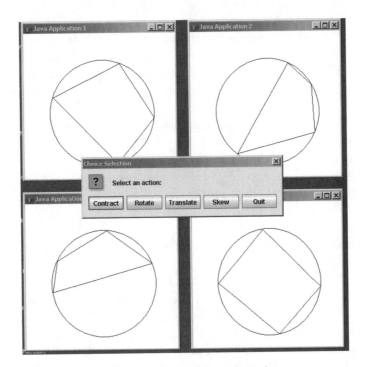

FIGURE 7.8   The four cyclic quadrilateral windows.

On lines 18-21, the four cyclic quadrilateral objects are instantiated and the four windows are displayed. The method randomAngles is used to generate four random angles of a circle that are supplied to the constructor of the CyclicQuadrilateral class. Those four angles specify the location on the circle of the four points that become the four vertices of the quadrilateral. Once the windows are displayed, the user is provided a menu of various transformations that can be performed on a selected quadrilateral. The choices are the operations that we mentioned earlier:

contraction, rotation, translation, or skewing. The user is also permitted to select which of the four quadrilaterals the operation is to be performed upon. This is our first occasion to use the method getEnum from the InputOutput package we created. It allows the user to select among a set of menu choices. It is supplied the prompt and an array of the enumeration literals that is generated by calling the method values, which is defined for every enumerated type. This method values is the same one that we began using in Chapter 4 to iterate across all the elements of an enumerated type. The method getEnum returns the enumeration literal that corresponds to the selected choice. Notice that it is necessary to type cast the value returned to the actual enumerated type. Such type casts are referred to as *downcasts,* and we will elaborate on why they are needed when we discuss inheritance in detail in Chapter 12. After we have read in the choice, on line 26 we check whether the choice to quit has been selected. If it has, we execute the return statement on line 27. Although we have used the return statement many times before, this is our first use of it in a void method. Notice that when it is used in a void method no expression follows the reserved word return because no value is being returned. The only action that results is leaving the method. In this case, because we are leaving main, we are exiting the program. If a choice other than "quit" has been selected, the user is queried to determine which quadrilateral should be the target of the transformation. Although we have used the method getInteger from the InputOutput class before, the call on lines 28 and 29 is our first use of the overloaded version of this method that allows us to specify the bounds of acceptable values.

The second method in this class is randomAngles. As we mentioned when discussing the call to this method, it generates four random angles in radians. The method needs to send this array out of the method. We elected to send the array out by returning it.

The third method of this class is skew. It is the only one of the four operations that violates the class invariant. For that reason, we elected not to make it a method of the CyclicQuadrilateral class like we did the three invariant preserving operations. It uses two methods of the CyclicQuadrilateral class that allow the class invariant to be violated. Those two methods are getQuadrilateralX and getQuadrilateralY, which are called by skew on lines 58 and 59. Those methods return the *x* and *y* ordinates of the vertices of the quadrilateral. We have elected to construct such methods to illustrate a more subtle point about preserving class invariants. The requirement of proper design of a class specification is really more than what we described earlier. It is not sufficient to require that the variants be preserved after every call to the methods to the class. Calling getQuadrilateralX and getQuadrilateralY does not cause the class invariant to be violated, but it does make it possible to subsequently violate it. That subsequent violation occurs on the next two lines—lines 61 and 62—where the value of the second vertex is modified independent of the others, creating a quadrilateral that is no longer cyclic. Figure 7.9 illustrates the quadrilateral after the skewing operation has been selected.

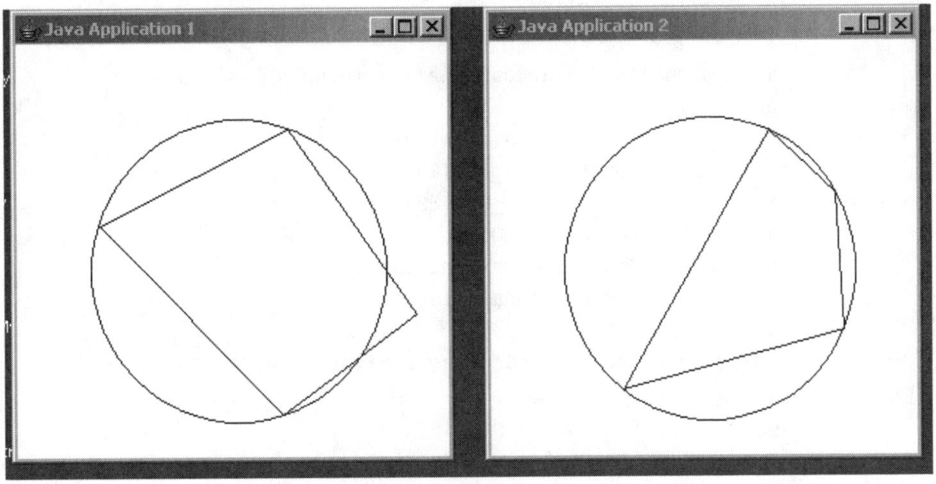

FIGURE 7.9 The first two quadrilateral windows after skewing the first.

The source of the problem is that those two methods returned the actual coordinates of the four vertices, rather than returning copies. We discuss shortly how those methods could be modified so this problem would no longer occur.

One final comment is just a reminder about the method `repaint` called on line 63. Just as the `paint` method of an applet cannot be called directly, so too the `paintComponent` method cannot be called directly because it requires a graphics object to be supplied that only the windowing system can provide. We must call `repaint` to cause `paintComponent` to be called.

Next let's consider the second class of this application—`CyclicQuadrilateral`. The code for this class is provided in Listing 7.8.

LISTING 7.8 The Cyclic Quadrilateral Window Class (found on the CD-ROM at *ON THE CD* chapter7\CyclicQuadrilateral.java.)

```
1   package chapter7;
2
3   import java.awt.*;
4   import common.*;
5
6   class CyclicQuadrilateral extends Application
7   {
8       private static final int X_CENTER = 150, Y_CENTER = 150,
```

```
 9              RADIUS = 100, QUAD = 4;
10         private int radius, xCenter, yCenter;
11         private double[] angles;
12         private Polygon polygon = new Polygon();
13
14         public CyclicQuadrilateral(double[] angles)
15         {
16             this.angles = angles.clone();
17             xCenter = X_CENTER;
18             yCenter = Y_CENTER;
19             radius = RADIUS;
20             insertionSort(this.angles);
21             computeCoordinates();
22         }
23         public void doContraction(int pixels)
24         {
25             radius - = pixels;
26             if (radius < 0)
27                 radius = 0;
28             computeCoordinates();
29             repaint();
30         }
31         public void doRotation(int degrees)
32         {
33             for (int angle = 0; angle < QUAD; angle++)
34                 angles[angle] += Geometry.degreesToRadians(degrees);
35             computeCoordinates();
36             repaint();
37         }
38         public void doTranslation(int x, int y)
39         {
40             xCenter += x;
41             yCenter += y;
42             computeCoordinates();
43             repaint();
44         }
45         public int[] getQuadrilateralX()
46         {
47             return polygon.xpoints;
48         }
49         public int[] getQuadrilateralY()
50         {
51             return polygon.ypoints;
52         }
```

```
53        public void paintComponent(Graphics graphics)
54        {
55            int diameter = radius * 2;
56
57            super.paintComponent(graphics);
58            setBackground(Color.WHITE);
59            graphics.drawPolygon(polygon);
60            graphics.drawOval(xCenter — radius, yCenter — radius,
61                diameter, diameter);
62        }
63        private void insertionSort(double[] array)
64        {
65            for (int i = 1; i < array.length; i++)
66            {
67                double temp = array[i];
68                int j = i — 1;
69
70                while (j >= 0 && temp < array[j])
71                    array[j + 1] = array[j--];
72                array[j + 1] = temp;
73            }
74        }
75        private void computeCoordinates()
76        {
77            int x, y;
78
79            polygon = new Polygon();
80            for (int vertex = 0; vertex <= QUAD; vertex++)
81            {
82                x = Geometry.computeX(xCenter, radius,
83                    angles[vertex % QUAD]);
84                y = Geometry.computeY(yCenter, radius,
85                    angles[vertex % QUAD]);
86                polygon.addPoint(x, y);
87            }
88        }
89    }
```

Let's begin by examining the data requirements for this class. We begin with the class constants declared on lines 8 and 9. Notice that they are class constants, not instance constants. In this case, either would work, but recall that we mentioned earlier we will always use class constants from now on whether they are essential or not because there is little benefit to giving each object its own copy of constants. Because this class not only draws the quadrilateral, but also the circle it is inscribed in, we need to maintain the necessary data for the circle, which are the center and the radius. The instance variables on line 10 are maintained for that purpose. On line 11 is the array of angles and on line 12 the polygon object. We are maintaining a redundant representation here. The angles, radius, and center point can generate the polygon. We are keeping both representations for convenience. By keeping the polygon object, its coordinates do not need to be recomputed each time the window is repainted. It is equally useful to keep the angles, center, and radius, because performing the contraction, rotation, and translation is most easily accomplished by modifying these values.

This class has only one constructor, which begins on line 14. It saves the angles supplied by the caller and initializes the center and radius to their starting values. Notice that when it copies the array `angles` on line 16, it first calls `clone`, which makes a deep copy of the angle. The method `clone` is defined for all arrays. The importance of making deep copies to preserve class invariants will become clear later when we discuss the methods `getQuadrilateralX` and `getQuadrilateralY`, which fail to make deep copies. On line 20, the instance variable `angles` is sorted by a call to the `insertionSort` method. The reason it is necessary to sort these angles is that we want to be sure to generate a convex quadrilateral. Although any random four points on a circle define a convex quadrilateral, if we add these points to a polygon object in the wrong order, a polygon of the kind illustrated in Figure 7.10 can result. Figure 7.10 also shows the corresponding convex quadrilateral that results when the angles that correspond to the vertices are in sorted order.

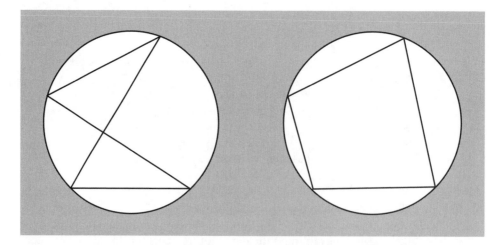

FIGURE 7.10   A nonconvex quadrilateral and its convex counterpart.

The last line of the constructor, line 21, makes a call to computeCoordinates, which is the method that computes the *x-y* coordinates from the center, radius, and angles.

Next, let's consider the three methods that perform invariant preserving transformations of the quadrilateral, beginning with the doContraction method on line 23. The radius of the circle is reduced by the specified number of pixels, ensuring that the radius does not become negative, and then the new coordinates are recomputed and the new circle and quadrilateral are repainted.

The doRotation method that begins on line 31 adds the specified number of degrees, which is supplied as a parameter, to each of the four angles, then recomputes the coordinates and repaints the window. Notice that on line 34 a call is made to a method degreesToRadians in a class Geometry. As the name suggests, it converts an angle from degrees to radians. This is not a standard Java class, but one that we have written that we plan to use in future chapters. Consequently, we have put it in the package common that contains all the classes that are shared by programs in different chapters of this book. Since this is our first encounter with the Geometry class, we will examine its code shortly.

The final of the three transformations is the doTranslation method, which begins on line 38. It adds the *x* and *y* displacements supplied as parameters to the coordinates of the center point of the circle. It then recomputes the coordinates of the translated quadrilateral and repaints the window.

Now we consider the methods getQuadrilateralX and getQuadrilateralY. These are the two methods that, although they do not violate the class invariant directly, allow it to be violated. The source of the problem is that when an array is returned, the array reference is copied, not the array object. In other words, a shallow copy is made. To prevent this problem, a deep copy is needed. As we mentioned earlier when we discussed the constructor, the clone method is provided for that purpose. So replacing line 47 with the following line would solve the problem.

```
return xpoints.clone();
```

Try making this change and a corresponding change to the getQuadrilateralY method and running the program, and you will see that the skew method no longer has any effect. The class invariant is now preserved by all the methods of the class.

The next method, paintComponent, draws the quadrilateral on line 59 and the circle on lines 60 and 61. The insertionSort method, which begins on line 63, is used by the constructor to ensure that the angles, and therefore the vertices, of the quadrilateral are in sorted order so that the quadrilateral will be convex. An insertion sort repeatedly inserts elements of the array into their proper position until the entire array is sorted. Refer back to our earlier discussion of this sort to review the details of this algorithm. The element of the array at position i, the loop control variable of the outer for loop that begins on line 65, is the element that is being inserted on each iteration. Notice that i begins at 1, not 0, because the first element needs no insertion. One line 67, we save the element to be inserted in a temporary local variable named temp. We have used a while loop for the inner loop that begins on line 70 because there is a compound condition that controls how long the loop must run. The loop control variable j begins at position one to the left of i and moves from right to left, searching for the position where the element should be inserted. If the first condition of the while condition on line 70 is false, we have come to the front of the array, and the element must become the new first element. If the second condition is false, the loop stops because we have come to a value smaller than the one to be inserted. The body of the loop consists of the single statement on line 71 that moves the element at position j one position to the left and then decrements j. After the proper position to insert the element has been located, it is inserted. The assignment on line 72 accomplishes that insertion. This loop has a compound condition, and we rely on the value of the loop control variable j to contain a value that specifies where to perform the insertion when the loop terminates. So it is important to verify that our use of j on line 72 is correct, regardless of which condition causes the loop to stop. We leave it to you to convince yourself that j + 1 is the proper place to insert the element in both cases.

Now let's examine the last method of this class—computeCoordinates. We have already mentioned that this method is used by the constructor and each of the three transformation methods to compute the x-y coordinates of the vertices of the quadrilateral from the center point, radius and angles. On lines 82-85, it computes the coordinate of each vertex from each angle using the methods computeX and computeY of the Geometry class we mentioned earlier and will examine shortly. By using the subscript vertex % QUAD, the coordinates of the fifth pair are the same as the first pair. When constructing a polygon, recall that the first and last points must be the same for it to be a closed figure.

Finally, we consider the class Geometry that is used by this program. As we indicated earlier, because it also will be used by other programs in the remaining chapters, we placed it in the package common that we have created for that purpose. Its code is shown in Listing 7.9.

LISTING 7.9 The Utility Class Containing Geometric Operations (found on the CD-ROM ON THE CD at common\Geometry.java.)

```
1    package common;
2
3    public class Geometry
4    {
5        public static final int DEGREES_IN_CIRCLE = 360;
6
7        public static int computeX(int xCenter, double radius, double theta)
```

```
8       {
9            return xCenter + (int)(Math.cos(theta) * radius + .5);
10      }
11      public static int computeY(int yCenter, double radius, double theta)
12      {
13           return yCenter + (int)(Math.sin(theta) * radius + .5);
14      }
15      public static double degreesToRadians(int degrees)
16      {
17           return 2 * Math.PI / DEGREES_IN_CIRCLE * degrees;
18      }
19  }
```

Notice that this class plays the role of a utility class, like the predefined class Math. Like all utility classes, all its methods are class methods, it has no instance variables, it has no defined constructors, and it is pointless to ever create objects of this class.

The first two methods of this class, computeX and computeY, compute the *x* and *y* ordinates, respectively, of a point on a circle given the center point, radius, and angle specified in radians. This computation is one that we first used in Chapter 3, so you may want to refer back to that chapter if you do not recall the basis for these formulas.

The last method converts an angle in degrees to radians using the fact that 2π radians is equal to 360°.

SUMMARY

One-dimensional arrays were the primary topic of this chapter—both arrays of primitives and arrays of objects. We discussed the difference between the prefix and postfix increment and decrement operators and their use on array subscripts and subscripted arrays. One important object-oriented design principle—the preservation of class invariants—was introduced, and an example was provided to illustrate operations that adhere to it and those that do not. The key points to remember from this chapter are as follows:

- An array declaration declares only an array reference; an array object must be instantiated to generate the actual array.
- The subscripts of an array of length *n* range from 0 to *n–1*.
- For arrays of objects, instantiating the array only creates an array of object references. A for loop is required to instantiate the object themselves.
- Array constants can be used to initialize arrays, but cannot be used in array assignments.

- The increment and decrement operators can appear in both prefix and postfix positions. In some instances the meaning differs.
- Changes made to the elements of an array parameter are preserved upon return to the calling method unless the array reference itself is changed.
- Class constants are always preferable to instance constants because it is pointless to provide each object with a separate copy of the constant.
- A class invariant is a condition that must remain true throughout the life of the objects of a class.

Review Questions

1.   Compare using the traditional for statement to iterate across the elements of an array with the new *for-each* syntax. What are the restrictions on using the latter, and what are the advantages?

2.   Describe a situation in which it is necessary to check an array subscript to ensure that it is not out of bounds.

3.   Explain the difference between using the prefix and postfix positions when an increment or decrement operator is placed on a variable that used an array subscript.

4.   What is the difference between the following two for statement that initialize all the elements of an array to 1?

```java
for (int i = 0; i < array.length; i++)
    array[i] = 1;
for (int i = 0; i < array.length; ++i)
    array[i] = 1;
```

5.   What additional step is needed to fully create an array of objects, compared to creating an array of primitives?

6.   What is the effect of labeling an array parameter or an object parameter as final?

7.   Describe the two techniques that can be used to send meaningful data contained in an array out of a method.

8.   What syntax distinguishes a class constant from an instance constant? What is the difference between the two kinds of constants?

9.   Describe a situation where a class constant must be used rather than an instance constant.

10. Describe an indicator of poor specification design in which class invariants have not been carefully considered.

Programming Exercises

11. Given the following array declaration:

    ```
    int[] intArray;
    ```

    Write the necessary statements to accomplish each of the following:
    a. Instantiate an array object that would contain 10 integers.
    b. Set the first element of the array to 25.
    c. Set the last element of the array to 10.
    d. Using a for statement, set all the middle elements to 15.

12. Which of the following array declarations will compile? For those that do not compile, explain why.

    a. float numbers[] = new float[];
    b. int[] gradeThresholds = {90, 80, 70, 60};
    c. int squares = {1, 4, 9, 16, 25, 36};
    d. int values[] = int[20];
    e. double[] diameters = new double[];

13. What will be in the array geometric after the following code segment?

    ```
    int[] geometric = new int[10];
    geometric[0] = 1;
    for (int i = 1; i < geomtric.length; i++)
        geometric[i] = geometric[i - 1] * 3;
    ```

14. Write the necessary code to declare and instantiate an array of 25 Color objects. Then write a for loop that instantiates the 25 color objects so that they contain ever increasingly brighter shades of red.

15. Given the following array declaration:

    ```
    int[] numbers = new int[10];
    ```

    what is the effect of the following for loop?

    ```
    for (int number: numbers)
        number = 10;
    ```

16. Given the following declarations:

    ```
    int[] pair = new int[2];
    int i = 0;
    ```

    what is in the array pair after the following assignment statements?

    ```
    pair[i++] = 1;
    pair[--i] = 2;
    ```

17. Write a void method that reverses the elements of the array supplied as a parameter. For example, the method should transform the array {1, 2, 3, 4, 5} to {5, 4, 3, 2, 1}.

18. Rewrite the method in the previous exercise so that it leaves the array parameter unchanged and returns the reversed array using a `return` statement.

19. Write a method that accepts two integer array parameters. The method should copy the elements of the first array to the second, performing a left rotation. For example, if the first array contains {1, 2, 3, 4, 5} the second array should be contain the values {2, 3, 4, 5, 1} upon return.

20. Write a method that accepts an array of `Rectangle` objects as a parameter. The method should return the average area of all the rectangles in the array.

Programming Projects

21. Write an application that generates ten concentric circles of decreasing diameters. The colors of the circles should be the various shades of red containing an array of colors like the one written for Programming Exercise 14.

22. Write an application to test the three methods in Programing Exercises 17, 18, and 19. Allow the user to enter the five values of the array and display the arrays produced by calls to each of those three methods.

23. Modify the application in Listing 7.2 that computes the nth prime number to instead compute the nth superperfect number. A superperfect number is one that has the property that the sum of its factors, excluding the number, is greater than the number itself. As an example, 12 is the first superperfect number because $1 + 2 + 3 + 4 + 6 = 16 > 12$.

24. Write an application that draws ten rectangles of random heights and widths at random locations. The random selection should be done only once in the constructor. The array of rectangles should be an instance variable of the class. The method that you wrote for Programming Exercise 20 should be used to calculate the average area of the rectangles, and that value should be displayed in the upper left-hand corner of the window.

25. Write an application similar to the final example of this chapter that draws a generalized rectangle—one whose sides are not necessarily perpendicular to the axes. Provide the user the ability to perform the same operations: contraction, rotation, and translation.

8 Generics and Interfaces

In this chapter

- Unbounded Arrays
- Generics
- Wrapper Classes
- Interfaces
- Iterators
- Java Collection Classes
- The Round Spiral Application

UNBOUNDED ARRAYS

In the previous chapter, we introduced arrays. One of the primary limitations of an array is the fact that its size must be specified when the array is instantiated. Java provides a mechanism that lifts this restriction using a class called `ArrayList`. It is one of a group of predefined Java classes known as collection classes. We will use the Java `ArrayList` class for the final example of the chapter, but before making use of that class, we plan to build a simplified version so that you can understand its inner workings. To enable us to build such a class, we introduce two new features of Java, generics and interfaces.

An Unbounded Integer Array

Before introducing those concepts, we wish to illustrate the basic algorithm needed for creating a class of unbounded arrays. For simplicity, we begin with a class whose objects are, specifically, unbounded arrays of integers. The code for that class is shown in Listing 8.1.

LISTING 8.1 A Class for Unbounded Integer Arrays (found on the CD-ROM at

ON THE CD chapter8\IntArray.java.)

```
1    package chapter8;
2
3    class IntArray
4    {
5        private static final int INITIAL_SIZE = 10;
6        private int[] array = new int[INITIAL_SIZE];
7        private int used;
8
9        public void add(int value)
10       {
11           if (used == array.length)
12               expand();
13           array[used++] = value;
14       }
15       public int get(int index)
16       {
17           return array[index];
18       }
19       public void set(int index, int value)
20       {
21           array[index] = value;
22       }
23       public int size()
24       {
25           return used;
26       }
27       private void expand()
28       {
29           int[] newArray;
30
31           newArray = new int[array.length * 2];
32           for (int i = 0 ; i < used; i++)
33               newArray[i] = array[i];
```

```
34          array = newArray;
35      }
36  }
```

The underlying representation for this class is, not surprisingly, an integer array, which is declared and instantiated on line 6 to be an arbitrarily set initial size. On line 7, an instance variable used is declared that maintains how many of the elements of the array are actually used at a given point in time. The default initial value of zero is the initial value we require.

This class provides four public methods. The add method causes the integer value supplied as a parameter to be added to the end of the array. It is this method that enables the length of the array to grow, if necessary. If all the positions in the allocated array are used, which is checked on line 11, the private method expand is invoked, on line 12, to increase the size of the array. Finally, on line 13, the element is placed into the array and the used counter is incremented.

Because Java does not permit the subscripting operation to be overloaded, we must instead provide two methods to access array elements. The first is the get method that is designed to retrieve the value at a specified index supplied as a parameter. The second is the method set that alters the value located at the index supplied as the first parameter to the value supplied as the second parameter. It is the caller's responsibility to perform bounds checking before calling either of these methods, if necessary. The bounds checking can be done by calling the size method, which returns the current number of used positions in the array.

The class has one private method, expand. On line 31, it allocates a new array with twice the capacity as the current array and, using the loop on lines 32 and 33, it copies all the values of the original array into the new one. Finally, on line 34, it sets the new array to be the instance variable array. By doubling the array size each time, we minimize how many times the expansion operation must be performed.

An Integer Reversal Application

To illustrate the use of this class, we have chosen a simple application that reads in integers until a sentinel value is entered and then displays them in reverse order. Because a sentinel value determines when the loop stops, there is no way to know beforehand the maximum number of values that will be input, so an ordinary array could not be used. Furthermore, we need to keep all the values in memory so that they can be displayed in reverse order; consequently, we need to store them in an array-like structure. The code for this application is provided in Listing 8.2.

LISTING 8.2 An Application to Reverse a List of Integers Using the `IntArray` Class (found on the CD-ROM at `chapter8\ReverseInts1.java`.)

```
1   package chapter8;
2
3   import common.*;
4
5   public class ReverseInts1
6   {
7       public static void main(String[] args)
8       {
9           int number;
10          IntArray numbers = new IntArray();
11
12          while (true)
13          {
14              number = InputOutput.getInteger
15                  ("Enter integer, −1 to stop: ");
16              if (number < 0)
17                  break;
18              numbers.add(number);
19          }
20          for (int i = numbers.size() − 1; i >= 0; i−)
21          {
22              number = numbers.get(i);
23              InputOutput.putString("Number " + i + " is "
24                  + number);
25          }
26      }
27  }
```

This application uses three of the four public methods of the class, along with the default constructor, of course. The `IntArray` object `numbers` is declared and instantiated on line 10. It is then filled with the values entered by the user by calling the `add` method on line 18.

After the sentinel-controlled loop terminates because a negative value is entered, the loop that displays the values in reverse order is executed. It uses the `size` method to determine the initial value of the loop control variable `i` on line 20 and the `get` method to retrieve the integer stored at index `i` on line 22.

The details of how the unbounded behavior is achieved are hidden from the client, as is appropriate. There are many variations on the algorithm that we have selected for resizing the array that might alternately be used.

GENERICS

Examining the class IntArray that we have just discussed, you should note that the behavior of this class is really independent of what type of data is contained in the array. If we needed a similar class for values of type double, we would have to copy that class and replace all occurrences of int with double, except where int was used as the type of an index, of course, and presumably rename it DoubleArray. Such copying causes significant code duplication and all the maintenance problems that result, so it is clearly an undesirable practice.

The latest version of Java, version 5.0, provides a new feature that the predefined ArrayList class and all the collection classes use. This new feature is the ability to create what are called *generic classes*. With generic classes, we are permitted to specify the type of the elements that the collection contains when we declare objects of a generic class. Programming languages that provide syntax, such as the new generic syntax in Java, are said to support *type parameterization*. Such classes are referred to as *template classes* in Java's predecessor language, C++.

There is new syntax associated with generic classes that is needed both when writing generic classes and when declaring objects of a generic class type. As a way to illustrate this syntax and to help you better understand how the predefined ArrayList class is written, we modify our class IntArray to be a generic class. The code for the modified class is shown in Listing 8.3.

ON THE CD

LISTING 8.3 A Generic Class for Unbounded Arrays (found on the CD-ROM at chapter8\Array.java.)

```
1   package chapter8;
2
3   class Array<Element>
4   {
5       private static final int INITIAL_SIZE = 10;
6       private Element[] array = (Element[]) new Object [INITIAL_SIZE];
7       private int used;
8
9       public void add(Element value)
10      {
11          if (used == array.length)
12              expand();
13          array[used++] = value;
14      }
15      public Element get(int index)
16      {
17          return array[index];
18      }
```

```
19        public void set(int index, Element value)
20        {
21            array[index] = value;
22        }
23        public int size()
24        {
25            return used;
26        }
27        private void expand()
28        {
29            Element[] newArray;
30
31            newArray = (Element[]) new Object[array.length * 2];
32            for (int i = 0 ; i < array.length; i++)
33                newArray[i] = array[i];
34            array = newArray;
35        }
36  }
```

If you compare this version with our original version, you will see that relatively few changes are required. The first difference is on line 3, where <Element> has been placed after the class name. The presence of the corner brackets is what makes this a generic class. The name, Element, inside those brackets is referred to as a generic type parameter. Like a method parameter acts as a placeholder for the argument supplied in the method call, a generic type parameter acts as a placeholder for the actual type supplied when an object of this class is declared.

Throughout the class, wherever int was used as the type of the array elements, the generic type parameter Element is now used. So, on lines 6 and 29, the arrays that were type int[] become Element[]. The type of the parameter to add on line 9, the return type of get on line 15, and the type of the second parameter to set on line 19 are all Element now instead of int.

There is one more change that was made to create this class that requires some explanation. On lines 6 and 31 where the arrays are instantiated, we were not able to instantiate an array of type Element[] because Element is not a real type, it is just a generic type parameter. What we must do instead is create an array of type Object[] and type cast it to be type Element[]. This is our first occasion to use the predefined type Object. For now, we explain its role by saying that any nonprimitive can be considered to be of type Object. We will more fully explain the role of this important type when we discuss inheritance.

The ArrayList class was in versions of Java prior to the latest version, 5.0. In earlier versions, ArrayList objects were inherently heterogeneous collections. We could not specify the type of the elements like we do when we declare an array. This may, at first, seem like a good thing, because it affords us more flexibility, and when we truly need such flexibility, it is a good thing. But when we don't need it, it is actually a hindrance. It limits the type checking that can be done at compile-time and, consequently introduces the possibility of runtime errors. A more complete explanation of the reasons that underlie the previous statement must wait until we have discussed inheritance, which requires a more thorough understanding of the role of the class `Object`.

To illustrate the other aspect of generic syntax, let's declare an object of this new generic class. There is one important restriction regarding the kind of type that can be used to constrain a generic class, however. That type can be a class type or an enumerated type, but it cannot be a primitive type. In other words, we cannot create objects for an array of type `int`. So for this example we use the class `Rectangle` and create an unbounded array of rectangles called `bars` similar to one we used in one of our examples in the previous chapter.

```
Array<Rectangle> bars = new Array<Rectangle>();
```

Notice that the corner brackets are again needed, but this time they surround the generic type argument `Rectangle` both in the type of the object and in the name of the constructor called to instantiate the object.

You may be wondering about the limitation that prohibits the type of the generic type arguments from being primitive types. It may seem that the limitation restricts the usefulness of generic classes. Next we discover how to overcome that limitation.

WRAPPER CLASSES

We introduced the term wrapper class in Chapter 6 in conjunction with the wrapper class `Integer` that corresponds to the primitive type `int`. Let's reiterate an important point mentioned previously. There is a wrapper class that corresponds to each primitive type. Aside from `Integer` and `Character`, the names of the wrapper classes have the same name as the primitive type name, except written in title case—the first letter in upper case.

We are ready now to discuss the purpose of wrapper classes. Let's begin by reviewing what we have already seen. Because primitive types are not classes, they cannot contain data or methods. The constant `Integer.MIN_VALUE` that we used in Chapter 6 is an example of a constant that is associated with the primitive type `int`, but must be placed inside its corresponding wrapper. In the next chapter, we will need the method `Character.toLowerCase`—a method that converts an alphabetic character to lower case. It is a class method designed to act on `char` variables, but must be placed inside its wrapper class `Character`.

Beyond using constants and methods of wrappers, we sometimes need objects of wrapper classes, so you need to understand what such objects are like. Each wrapper class has an instance variable whose type is the primitive type that corresponds to that wrapper, which explains the origin of the name wrapper. Wrapper classes wrap a class around an instance variable of a primitive type. For example, the wrapper class `Integer` has an instance variable of type `int`. Also every wrapper class has a constructor that allows us to create wrapper objects that initialize that instance variable and have a method that allows us to extract that variable. The signatures of these two methods for the `Integer` class are the following:

```
Integer(int value)
int intValue()
```

Of course, wrapper classes have many more methods, but there are no methods that allow their singular instance variable to be modified once the object is created, which is another way of saying that the wrapper classes and their objects are immutable.

Let's return to generic classes, because they were the motivation for this further explanation of wrapper classes. As we mentioned earlier, generic classes cannot be constrained with primitive types. So if we want an unbounded array of integers, we cannot write the following:

```
Array<int> numbers; // will not compile
```

What we must do instead is to use the wrapper that corresponds to the primitive type. What is needed is the following:

```
Array<Integer> numbers;
```

Autoboxing and Unboxing

In the versions of Java prior to version 5.0, whenever we wanted to convert between a variable of a primitive type and a wrapper object of the corresponding type, explicit conversions were required. Conversions in both directions required something more than simple type casting. Consider the following pair of declarations:

```
int i = 1, j;
Integer iWrapped, jWrapped = new Integer(1);
```

To wrap the primitive `i` into the wrapper object `iWrapped`, an explicit call to the wrapper's constructor was needed. For example:

```
iWrapped = new Integer(i);
```

To unwrap the wrapper object `jWrapped` into the primitive `j`, an explicit call to the method in the wrapper class that returns its value was required, as follows:

```
        j = jWrapped.intValue();
```

Version 5.0 added two new features called *autoboxing* and *autounboxing* that wrap and unwrap automatically. To illustrate the first of these features, consider the following assignment:

```
        iWrapped = i;
```

This assignment compiles because i is autoboxed, or wrapped into an Integer object by an implicit call to the constructor. The following assignment illustrates autounboxing:

```
        j = jWrapped;
```

This assignment is now legal because the object jWrapped is automatically unwrapped by an implicit call to the intValue method.

These features do not add a new capability, but just simplify the conversion between primitive variables and their corresponding wrapped objects.

An Example Using a Wrapper as a Generic Argument

Now that we have explained wrapper classes more fully and the new feature of autoboxing and unboxing, we are ready to illustrate how the generic class that we wrote earlier—Array—can be used to create an array of integers.

For simplicity, we use the same problem as before—reversing a list of integers that has been input by the user. The code for this new version of the program is shown in Listing 8.4.

LISTING 8.4 An Application to Reverse a List of Integers Using the Array Class (found
ON THE CD on the CD-ROM at chapter8\ReverseInts2.java.)

```
1   package chapter8;
2
3   import common.*;
4
5   public class ReverseInts2
6   {
7       public static void main(String[] args)
8       {
9           int number;
10          Array<Integer> numbers = new Array<Integer>();
11
12          while (true)
13          {
```

```
14              number = InputOutput.getInteger
15                  ("Enter integer, -1 to stop: ");
16              if (number < 0)
17                  break;
18              numbers.add(number);
19          }
20          for (int i = numbers.size() - 1; i >= 0; i-)
21          {
22              number = numbers.get(i);
23              InputOutput.putString("Number " + i + " is "
24                  + number);
25          }
26      }
27  }
```

So let's examine the differences between this version and the one that used the IntArray class. On line 10, we declare the object of type Array and constrain it with the wrapper class Integer. On line 18, when the method add is called, autoboxing occurs. The argument that we supply, number, is of type int and it is automatically wrapped into an Integer object. On line 22, when we call get, autounboxing occurs. The get method returns an object of type Integer that is automatically unwrapped to become an int variable.

INTERFACES

The second new aspect of Java syntax that we introduce in this chapter is *interfaces*. Our reason for introducing interfaces in this chapter is that we need that capability to implement an iterator for the unbounded array class that we have been constructing.

Throughout this book, we have observed how the syntax of classes is used to implement classes that play three different roles. The first kind is a class that we use to create objects like all the applet classes we have used. The second kind is a class that contains the main thread of control, and the third kind is a class that implements utilities like Math. In C++, Java's parent language, classes are also used to implement what Java calls interfaces. Java wisely departed from using the class syntax for yet another role and instead elected to introduce a special reserved word, interface, to accommodate such situations. An interface differs from a class in several important ways. First, it cannot have any instance variables. Second, it contains only method signatures, but not their bodies. Finally, interfaces cannot have constructors, nor is any default constructor supplied, so no objects of such types can be instantiated. It might be useful to review the variety of different kinds of types that Java provides. They include the primitive types, class types, enumerated types, array types, and now interface types.

Having described how an interface differs from a class, let's now explain the purpose of defining interfaces. An interface allows us to separate a specification from its implementation. Interfaces can be used for a variety of purposes. In this chapter, we begin with one of the most common uses of an interface, which is to facilitate the handling of events.

Mouse Event Handling

In this chapter, we offer a glimpse of event handling—enough to introduce interfaces, which is our main goal. We will return to a more complete discussion of event handling in Chapter 13, when we discuss creating graphical user interfaces (GUIs).

The events we discuss handling at this time are mouse events, since they can be handled without creating any GUI components. Recall that the `paint` method of an applet is called when a repainting event occurs. If we wish to be able to respond to events associated with the mouse, the event handling mechanism must know what method to call when mouse events occur. An interface named `MouseListener` defines the names of methods that correspond to the various mouse events that can occur. The code for the `MouseListener` interface is shown below:

```
interface MouseListener
{
    void mouseClicked (MouseEvent event);
    void mousePressed (MouseEvent event);
    void mouseReleased (MouseEvent event);
    void mouseEntered (MouseEvent event);
    void mouseExited (MouseEvent event);
}
```

Notice that the method signatures each end with a semicolon. You should also observe that it is customary to omit any access modifier, because it is understood that all such methods are public. Declaring them private would be a syntax error.

Let's consider a simple example of an application that listens for mouse events to see how this interface comes into play. In Listing 8.5 is the class that defines a window that allows the user to click on various points of the window. Each point becomes the next vertex of a polygon that is then drawn. When you run this program, be aware that nothing will become visible until you have clicked the third point, which is the minimum number of points for a polygon.

LISTING 8.5 A Window that Allows the Vertices of a Polygon to be Specified by Mouse Click (found on the CD-ROM at `chapter8\DrawablePolygon1.java`.)

```
1   package chapter8;
2
```

```
3   import java.awt.*;
4   import java.awt.event.*;
5   import common.*;
6
7   class DrawablePolygon1 extends GraphicsApplication
8       implements MouseListener
9   {
10      private static final int SIZE = 400,
11          POLYGON = new DrawablePolygon1().display();
12      private Polygon polygon = new Polygon();
13
14      public DrawablePolygon1()
15      {
16          super("Drawable Polygons 1", SIZE, SIZE);
17          addMouseListener(this);
18      }
19      public void paintComponent(Graphics graphics)
20      {
21          super.paintComponent(graphics);
22          graphics.fillPolygon(polygon);
23      }
24      public void mouseClicked (MouseEvent event)
25      {
26          Point clickPoint = event.getPoint();
27          polygon.addPoint(clickPoint.x, clickPoint.y);
28          repaint();
29        }
30      public void mousePressed(MouseEvent event)
31      {
32      }
33      public void mouseReleased(MouseEvent event)
34      {
35      }
36      public void mouseEntered(MouseEvent event)
37      {
38      }
39      public void mouseExited(MouseEvent event)
40      {
41      }
42  }
```

Let's examine the key aspects of this program. On line 4, we are importing all the classes of a package that we have never imported before. It is java.awt.event, which is a subpackage of `java.awt`. It contains the definition of the interface `MouseListener` and the class `MouseEvent`, which is the type of the parameters of all the mouse event handling methods. Notice that the imports on lines 3 and 4 are not redundant. Importing `java.awt.*` does not import all the classes in its subpackages.

On line 8, notice the clause `implements MouseListener`. As you might suspect, `implements` is a reserved word, one that must always be followed by the name of an interface. Including this clause has two important consequences. First, a compilation error will result if this class does not contain methods whose signatures correspond to the signatures defined in the interface. Second, any object of this class is now type compatible with the type `MouseListener`, so, for example, the following declaration would be valid:

```
MouseListener aWindow = new DrawablePolygon1();
```

Although we do not see such a declaration in this program, a similar type association is made on line 17. The type of the parameter of the method `addMouseListener` is `MouseListener`, but the type of the argument `this` is `DrawablePolygon1`.

What is done on line 17 is usually described as "registering this window object as a listener for mouse events." Its effect is to inform the event handling mechanism to invoke the appropriate method of this class on this window object when any of the mouse events occur. Another term that is often used to describe what is being done is a *callback*—designating what method to call back when an event occurs. You may find this process a bit convoluted, because, frankly, it is. What we really desire here is to supply the `addMouseListener` method the names of methods, but Java does not allow methods to be passed as parameters. C++, a successor to Java, includes syntax called delegates that effectively allow method parameters, so registering listeners is a bit more straightforward. In Chapter 13, we will explain how to compensate for the absence of method parameters, which may help you further understand the technique that is being used here.

One final comment concerns the `addMouseListener` method and where it is defined. This class inherits `addMouseListener` from `Application`, just like it inherits the method `display`. In Chapter 12, we will discuss inheritance in more detail, which should help clarify this idea.

Now let's examine the methods that we were required to supply to implement the `MouseListener` interface. The first of these, and the only one that is nonempty, is `mouseClicked`. It accepts a `MouseEvent` object as a parameter, which has a method `getPoint` that we call on line 26. That method returns an object of type `Point`, a class in `java.awt` that we introduced in Chapter 7. Recall that the class `Point` has two public instance variables, `x` and `y`. The authors of this class have failed to hide the representation—a poor practice to imitate. Keeping all instance variables private is something we have been extolling as a measure of good object-oriented design since Chapter 3. Once the position at which the mouse was clicked is obtained, that point is added to the polygon on line 27, and then the window is repainted.

There are four other methods in this class—all empty. They must be present, however, or this program will not compile because we would not have fulfilled implementing the MouseListener interface.

Inner Classes

There is an alternate way to implement the previous program that uses inner classes—something that we will need later in this chapter. We include the following discussion both as follow-up to the previous example and as an opportunity to introduce some syntax that we require shortly.

The code for the modified version of the window class for the previous program that uses an inner class is provided in Listing 8.6.

LISTING 8.6 A Revised Class for a Window that Allows a Polygon to be Specified by
ON THE CD Mouse Clicks (found on the CD-ROM at chapter8\DrawablePolygon2.java.)

```
1   package chapter8;
2
3   import java.awt.*;
4   import java.awt.event.*;
5   import common.*;
6
7   class DrawablePolygon2 extends GraphicsApplication
8   {
9       private static final int SIZE = 400,
10          POLYGON = new DrawablePolygon2().display();
11      private Polygon polygon = new Polygon();
12
13      private class PolygonMouseAdapter extends MouseAdapter
14      {
15          public void mouseClicked (MouseEvent event)
16          {
17              Point clickPoint = event.getPoint();
18              polygon.addPoint(clickPoint.x, clickPoint.y);
19              repaint();
20          }
21      }
22      public DrawablePolygon2()
23      {
24          super("Drawable Polygons 2", SIZE, SIZE);
25          addMouseListener(new PolygonMouseAdapter());
```

```
26        }
27        public void paintComponent(Graphics graphics)
28        {
29            super.paintComponent(graphics);
30            graphics.fillPolygon(polygon);
31        }
32  }
```

The inner class, which spans lines 13-20, is `PolygonMouseAdapter`. Although we have never before used an inner class, we have used an inner enumerated type. In fact, our first use of an enumerated type was as an inner type. As the name suggests, this class is defined inside another class. Unlike most class names, the scope of its name is not package-wide.

Notice that we are extending a defined class to create this one, which is akin to how we have defined all our application window classes. The advantage to this approach is that the class we are extending already has empty methods to handle the mouse events that we wish to ignore, so we need define only the one that interests us—`mouseClicked`.

Let's examine what is happening on line 25. The object that is now the mouse listener is no longer the window object, as it was previously. It is an object that is instantiated as the argument to the `addMouseListener` method. Notice that the mouse listener object is an anonymous object, which we first encountered in the previous chapter. Because the mouse listener anonymous object will never again be referred to, there is no compelling reason to name it.

One final issue that warrants explanation is why it was appropriate to make this class an inner class. By making it an inner class, its only method, `mouseClicked`, is within the scope of the instance variable `polygon` of the outer class `DrawablePolygon2`, which the method `mouseClicked` needs to access. Because `polygon` is declared private, it is inaccessible outside the class. Had `PolygonMouseAdapter` not been an inner class, it would have been unable to access the instance variable `polygon`.

ITERATORS

Now that we have introduced both interfaces and inner classes with our digression into event handling in the previous section, we return to our primary application of generics and interfaces, which is building an unbounded array class.

Our next goal is to modify the class `Array` that we developed earlier in this chapter to include an iterator. Furthermore, we plan to illustrate how this class can be enhanced so that its objects can be used in *for-each* style `for` statements, like enumerated types and array types. Version 5.0 provides not only the syntax of this new statement, but also the necessary language features to enable programmers to create classes whose objects can be used in the new `for` statement syntax.

The `Iterator` and `Iterable` Interfaces

The key to providing a class with this capability involves implementing a particular interface. Actually, there are two interfaces involved. Both of them are generic interfaces. For simplicity, we introduced interfaces first in the context of event handing where generics were not also required. So let's consider the first of these two—the `Iterator` interface shown below:

```
interface Iterator<E>
{
    boolean hasNext();
    E next();
    void remove();
}
```

To be an iterator, a class must contain three methods. The first, `hasNext`, returns whether there are more elements left in the iteration, the second, `next`, returns the next element in the collection and the third, `remove`, is intended to remove the last element returned by the iterator. Although the `remove` method must be provided, it is optional whether it actually implements the intended operation. Because the concept of iteration is independent of the type of elements of the collection over which the iteration is done, parameterizing the type with the generic type parameter `E` is appropriate.

The second interface, which is the one that our modified `Array` class must implement, is `Iterable`, which is shown below:

```
interface Iterable<T>
{
    Iterator<T> iterator();
}
```

To be iterable, a class must implement a method called `iterator`, whose return type is the generic interface `Iterator` that we just discussed. It may sound a bit complicated, but once you see an example, the mechanics for achieving it should become clear.

The `IterableArray` Class

We are now ready to examine the modified version of the `Array` class that we presented earlier. The new version now implements the interface `Iterable`, so we have renamed the class `IterableArray`. Its code is shown in Listing 8.7.

LISTING 8.7 A Generic Class for Unbounded Arrays that Provides an Iterator (found on the CD-ROM at chapter8\IterableArray.java.)

```
1   package chapter8;
2
3   import java.util.*;
4   import common.*;
5
6   class IterableArray<Element> implements Iterable<Element>
7   {
8       private static final int INITIAL_SIZE = 10;
9       private Element[] array = (Element[]) new Object [INITIAL_SIZE];
10      private int used;
11
12      private class ArrayIterator implements Iterator<Element>
13      {
14          private int index;
15
16          public boolean hasNext()
17          {
18              return index < used;
19          }
20          public Element next()
21          {
22              return array[index++];
23          }
24          public void remove()
25          {
26          }
27      }
28
29      public void add(Element value)
30      {
31          if (used == array.length)
32              expand();
33          array[used++] = value;
34      }
35      public Element get(int index)
36      {
37          return array[index];
38      }
39      public Iterator<Element> iterator()
40      {
41          return new ArrayIterator();
42      }
43      public void set(int index, Element value)
44      {
```

```
45              array[index] = value;
46      }
47      public int size()
48      {
49          return used;
50      }
51      private void expand()
52      {
53          Element[] newArray;
54
55          newArray = (Element[]) new Object[array.length * 2];
56          for (int i = 0 ; i < array.length; i++)
57              newArray[i] = array[i];
58          array = newArray;
59      }
60  }
```

Let's examine the changes that needed to be made to the previous version. First, on line 6, we must state that this class implements `Iterable<Element>`. It is the implementation of this interface that will now allow objects of this class to be used in a *for-each* statement. Adding this clause means that we agree to provide a method called `iterator` that returns an iterator of type `Iterator<Element>`.

To fulfill that promise, we need to define a class that allows us to create such iterator objects. We named that class `ArrayIterator`. It spans lines 12-27. Notice that, on line 12, we must state that the class we are defining implements `Iterator<Element>`. By so doing, when the method `iterator` returns an `ArrayIterator` object, it will be returning an object that supports, and is therefore type compatible with, the `Iterator<Element>` interface.

The `ArrayIterator` class requires one instance variable, `index`, declared on line 14, which maintains the current position of the iteration. The default initialization to zero is required when any iterator object is instantiated.

No explicit constructor is needed, as the default constructor will suffice, but we do need the three required methods for any iterator. The body of the method `hasNext` contains a single statement, on line 18, which determines whether the current position `index` is less than the number of used positions in the array containing the instance variable `used` of the outer `IterableArray` class. The body of the method `next` also contains just one statement, which appears on line 22. It returns the value at position `index` in the array and then increments `index`. We have elected to leave the method `remove`, whose implementation is optional, unimplemented.

Another point that warrants explanation is why `ArrayIterator` needs to be an inner class. Given our discussion of the `MouseAdapter` class earlier, you should probably be able to provide the explanation, since the reasons are the same in both cases. In this case, the methods of the `ArrayIterator` class need to access the private instance variables of the outer class `IterableArray`.

The only other change that we made to the previous version is the addition of the method `iterator`, whose signature is on line 39. It is another method with a one statement body that instantiates and returns an object of type `ArrayIterator`. We have been using the term *anonymous object*. The object created on line 41 is another example of such an object.

An Application for Testing `IterableArray`

To illustrate the use of the class that we just created and to compare the explicit and implicit use of iterators, we have created a simple application that iterates across an iterable array of strings, both implicitly and explicitly, and compares the results. The code for this application is contained in Listing 8.8.

LISTING 8.8 An Application to Compare Implicit and Explicit Iterations (found on the CD-ROM at chapter8\CompareIterations.java.)

```
1   package chapter8;
2
3   import java.util.*;
4   import common.*;
5
6   public class CompareIterations
7   {
8       public static void main(String[] args)
9       {
10          int maxValue;
11          String explicitIteration = "", implicitIteration = "";
12          IterableArray<String> words = new IterableArray<String>();
13
14          maxValue = InputOutput.getInteger("Enter a maximum value: ");
15          for (int i = 0; i < maxValue; i++)
16              words.add(new String("" + i));
17          for (String word: words)
18              implicitIteration += word;
19          Iterator<String> iterator = words.iterator();
20          while (iterator.hasNext())
21              explicitIteration += iterator.next();
22          if (implicitIteration.equals(explicitIteration))
23              InputOutput.putString("The strings match");
24          else
25              InputOutput.putString("The strings don't match");
26      }
27  }
```

On line 12, we declare and instantiate an object, words, whose type is Iter-ableArray<String>. The loop on lines 15 and 16 fills the array with strings containing numbers, using the add method to append the strings to the end of the object words. The implicit iteration of the collection is done on lines 17 and 18. Notice that we can now use the *for-each* loop on objects of the type that we have just created—IterableArray objects—because it implements the interface Iterable. The explicit iteration is done on lines 19-21. It is important to understand that the two are equivalent. The former is a shortcut notation for the latter. The compiler, in effect, replaces every implicit *for-each* iteration with an explicit iteration. Running this program highlights this fact. The output will be the display of the message "The strings match," demonstrating that the results of the two kinds of iterations are the same.

JAVA COLLECTION CLASSES

We have devoted most of this chapter to developing a class, IterableArray, that provides an array of unbounded length that can use the *for-each* statement just like ordinary arrays can. In developing this class, we introduced the language features of generics and interfaces and the concept of an iterator.

Because the need for an unbounded array and other collections like it is common to so many programs, Java provides a set of predefined classes called *collection classes*, as we mentioned at the beginning of this chapter. Although we do not wish to discussion all the predefined collection classes, there is one that is especially relevant to the focus of this chapter. That class is the ArrayList class, which is very similar to the IterableArray class that we have just discussed. It belongs to the package java.util.

Some Methods in the ArrayList Class

Like every predefined class, the ArrayList class has many predefined methods. We will examine the methods in the predefined ArrayList class that correspond to the ones in our IterableArray class.

In most cases, the names and signatures are the same. Let's begin with the most fundamental element extraction method. It is named get. Its signature is shown below:

```
Type get(int index)
```

Since ArrayList is a generic class and we are showing the signatures outside the complete class definition, we adopt the practice of italicizing the types that are generic type parameters. Shown below are the signatures of two methods that allow the elements to be added to the collection:

```
boolean add(Type element)
void add(int index, Type element)
```

The first of these overloaded methods causes an element to be added to the end of the array list. Although the return type is `boolean`, it always returns `true`, so the return value is typically ignored. For this reason, we made the return type of `add` in our `IterableArray` class `void`. The second one causes the element to be inserted at a particular subscript. We provided no such method in our implementation. The final method we discuss is one that sets the value at a specified subscript. Its signature is shown below:

```
Type set(int index, Type element)
```

It corresponds to our method `set`. The one difference is that the predefined method returns the old value of the object being set. In our implementation, nothing is returned.

The `ArrayList` class also has a method, `iterator`, whose signature and behavior is the same as the one we implemented. As we indicated earlier, this predefined class has many additional methods. As always, you can consult the Sun Website at *http://java.sun.com/2se/1.5.0/docs/api/* for a complete list.

THE ROUND SPIRAL APPLICATION

Having now discussed the predefined `ArrayList` class, we are ready to illustrate a program that uses this class. The example we have chosen is a variation on the first program in the previous chapter that drew a square spiral. In that program, we knew beforehand exactly how many line segments we were going to draw, so using an array to contain the endpoints was not a problem. In this program, we draw a round spiral that contains many points—the number of points depends upon a tightness factor that we allow the user to supply. Although it would be possible to development a formula that we could use to determine the required number of points based on the spiral tightness factor, it is simpler to just use an array list to hold the points. In that way, we avoid the possibility of an error in our formula and the problems it might cause. The output of this program is shown in Figure 8.1.

The square spiral application drew four line segments each time around the circle. To achieve a rounder spiral, this application draws 20 line segments each time

FIGURE 8.1 The output of the round spiral application.

around the circle. The code for the class that creates the window for this application is shown in Listing 8.9.

LISTING 8.9 A Class Defining a Window Containing a Round Spiral (found on the CD-ROM at chapter8\RoundSpiral.java.)

```
1    package chapter8;
2
3    import java.awt.*;
4    import java.util.*;
5    import common.*;
6
7    class RoundSpiral extends GraphicsApplication
8    {
9        private static final int TOP_BORDER = 20, TIGHT = 1,
10           LOOSE = 20, SIZE = 250, CENTER = SIZE / 2 - 5,
11           SPIRAL = new RoundSpiral().display();
12       private ArrayList<Integer> xPoints = new ArrayList<Integer>(),
13           yPoints = new ArrayList<Integer>();
14
15       public RoundSpiral()
16       {
17           super("Round Spiral", SIZE, SIZE + TOP_BORDER);
18           createSpiral();
```

```
19          }
20          public void paintComponent(Graphics graphics)
21          {
22              int fromX = CENTER, fromY = CENTER, toY;
23              Iterator<Integer> iterator = yPoints.iterator();
24
25              super.paintComponent(graphics);
26              for (int toX: xPoints)
27              {
28                  toY = iterator.next();
29                  graphics.drawLine(fromX, fromY, toX, toY);
30                  fromX = toX;
31                  fromY = toY;
32              }
33          }
34          private void createSpiral()
35          {
36              final double ANGLE_INCREMENT = Geometry
                        .degreesToRadians(9);
37              int x, y;
38              double angle = 0, radius = 0;
39              int increment = InputOutput.getInteger
40                  ("Enter tightness ", TIGHT, LOOSE);
41
42              do
43              {
44                  x = Geometry.computeX(CENTER, radius, angle);
45                  y = Geometry.computeY(CENTER, radius, angle);
46                  xPoints.add(x);
47                  yPoints.add(y);
48                  radius += increment * .1;
49                  angle += ANGLE_INCREMENT;
50              }
51              while (radius < CENTER);
52          }
53  }
```

As we noted when we introduced the ArrayList class, it is in a package that we have not used previously, java.util. The Iterator interface, which is used in this class, is also in that package. Consequently, we import that package on line 4.

The instance variables needed for this class are the array lists xPoints and yPoints, declared and instantiated on lines 12 and 13, that contain the *x-y* coordinates of the endpoints of the line segments that form the spiral. The important thing to recognize is that no size is required in these declarations, which, of course, is the advantage to using array lists rather than arrays.

The constructor calls the private method createSpiral, which actually computes the coordinates of the line segments that define the spiral.

Next, let's examine the paintComponent method. This method uses both an implicit and explicit iterator because we need to iterate across the parallel array lists xPoints and yPoints at the same time. We use an implicit iterator for xPoints, which should be apparent from the for loop that begins on line 26. We create an explicit iterator for yPoints on line 23 by making a call to the method iterator. Note that because the type of the array list is ArrayList<Integer>, Integer being the generic type argument, the type of the iterator must be Iterator<Integer>. On each iteration, one line segment is drawn, which is accomplished by the call to drawLine on line 29. The assignments on lines 30 and 31 are akin to the "previous becomes current" assignments we have seen so often before.

Finally, we examine the one private method in this class—computeSpiral. On lines 39 and 40, we allow the user to enter a value that must be between 1 and 20 inclusive, which determines the tightness of the loop. It becomes the value that affects how much we increment the radius, so the smaller the number, the tighter the loop. The do-while loop in this method that spans lines 42-51 computes the endpoints of the line segments. The computeX and computeY methods of the Geometry class that we first used in the cyclic quadrilateral example in Chapter 7 are used again here to compute the coordinates of a point given the center, radius, and angle. The add method that appends a value to the end of an array list is called for each of the two array lists on lines 46 and 47. The autoboxing that we discussed earlier occurs here. We are passing in an argument of type int and the method is expecting an object of type Integer. Finally, the variables radius and angle are both increased. The tightness factor influences how much the radius is increased, while the angle is always increased by the constant ANGLE_INCREMENT, which is 9° expressed in radians. It was initialized on line 36 with a call to another of the methods in the Geometry class. Using an increment of 9° creates 40 line segments each time around the circle, giving a reasonably rounded spiral. Notice that we do not use a for loop here because we have never determined how many line segments will be in the spiral. We stop when radius becomes so large that the spiral would begin to go outside the window, which is expressed by the condition on line 51.

In the previous chapter, we mentioned that whenever we elected to use parallel arrays, we would explain why we chose to do. In this example, we did not use parallel arrays, but parallel array lists, but from a design perspective there is little difference. Our reason in this example was so that we would have an opportunity to illustrate both implicit and explicit iteration across an array list. Had that not been an objective of this example, we would have opted to use a single array list of points, as we did in our second version of the square spiral example in the previous chapter.

SUMMARY

In this chapter, we developed a class that generalized an array, removing the requirement that the size of the array-like object be specified when the object is instantiated. We studied two new language features, generics and interfaces, that were required to create this class. Finally, we compared the class that we created to the predefined Java collection class ArrayList. The key points to remember from this chapter are as follows:

■ In a generic class, the type of some of its instance variables and method parameters can be parameterized. The actual type is not specified until objects of that class are declared.

■ An interface contains a collection of method signatures, but not their implementation. It cannot contain any instance variables or have any constructors.

■ To handle an event, an object must be registered as a listener for that event.

■ An inner class is one that is declared inside another class. The methods of the inner class are within the scope of the private instance variables of the outer class.

■ A wrapper class corresponds to some primitive type and contains a single instance variable of that type.

■ Autoboxing is the automatic conversion of a primitive to an object of its corresponding wrapper class. Autounboxing is the conversion in reverse.

■ An iterator is an object that allows the sequential access of every element of a collection.

■ The Java collection classes are generic classes that implement the fundamental data structures. The ArrayList class is among them.

Review Questions

1. Explain in what sense generic classes are reusable. How do they avoid undesirable duplication of code?

2. Explain why it is possible to declare object references of an interface type, but it is not possible to instantiate objects of such a type.

3. Explain how the ability to pass methods as parameters would simplify registering an object as a listener for an event.

4. What is the advantage of using the MouseAdapter class instead of the MouseListener interface when handling mouse events?

5. In what circumstances is it appropriate to use an inner class?

6. What is the characteristic of an anonymous object? When are such objects useful?

7. In what case is a wrapper class needed when declaring an object of a generic class?

8. When do autoboxing and autounboxing occur?

9. Explain the roles of the methods `hasNext` and `next` in an iterator.

10. How can we create a class whose objects can be iterated across using the *for-each* style `for` statement?

Programming Exercises

11. Define a generic class called `Pair` that has two instance variables, whose type is the generic type parameter. The class should have a constructor that creates such objects given a pair of values, and two methods that individually return each of the values.

12. Declare and instantiate an object that creates an integer pair using the generic class defined in the previous exercise.

13. Define an interface called `Hashable` that requires a class to have a method called `hashCode` that returns an integer.

14. Define a generic interface named `KeyedObject` that has an operation `hasKey` that returns a key of the type of generic parameter.

15. Create a class called `PhoneEntry` that implements the interface defined in the previous exercise. The class should contain instance string objects for name, address, and phone number. The `hasKey` method should return the name as the key.

16. Create a class called `Student` that implements the `KeyedObject` interface. It should contain a string that is the student name and an integer student ID. The student ID should be the key.

17. Given the following declarations:

    ```
    int i = 5, j;
    Integer k = new Integer(3), l;
    ```

    explain whether autoboxing, autounboxing, or neither occurs in each of the following:

    a. `j = k;`
    b. `i = j;`
    c. `k = i;`
    d. `l = k;`

18. Which of the following statements contains an anonymous object?

    a. `return new String("name");`
    b. `Point origin = new Point(0, 0);`
    c. `someColorArrayList.add(new Color(127, 255, 0));`
    d. `ArrayList<Color> rainbow = new ArrayList<Color>();`

19. Declare an `ArrayList` object that contains double precision floating point numbers.

20. Write a `for` loop that computes the sum of all the elements in the object declared in the previous exercise in each of the following ways:
    a. Using an implicit iterator.
    b. Using an explicit iterator.
    c. Using a subscript calling the `get` method.

Programming Projects

21. Write an application that draws *x* and *y* axes and allows the user to click on a point. The point clicked on should be drawn and a message should be displayed indicating which quadrant the point lies in or whether the point is on one of the axes or at the origin. Use the `MouseListener` interface to register the mouse event handling.

22. Rewrite the application defined in Project 21 using the `MouseAdapter` class instead.

23. Write an application that allows the user to enter a sequence of nonnegative integers, entering a −1 as the sentinel marking the end of the sequence. It should add these integers to an array list. Once all the numbers have been entered, it should iterate across the list searching for the largest value, which should then be displayed.

24. Write an application that contains two parallel `ArrayList` instance variables, one a list of type `Point` that represents the coordinates of the center of a circle and a second one that contains the diameter of the circle. These lists should be generated in the constructor of the class that creates the window. It should continue to generate circles with random centers and diameters until the sum of the areas of all the circles generated exceeds some constant value.

25. Write an application that allows the user to click on points that represent the endpoints of a sequence of line segments. Maintain these points in an array list of type `Point`. Each time a new point is clicked, add it to the list and repaint the screen. The painting operation should draw a line segment connecting every pair of adjacent points in the list.

9 Strings

In this chapter

- Extracting Characters From Strings
- Subdividing Strings
- Input Files
- Pattern Matching
- Mutable Strings
- Graphics Definition File Application

EXTRACTING CHARACTERS FROM STRINGS

We begin our discussion of strings with an exploration of some of the features of strings that we have not yet encountered, beginning with the technique for extracting individual characters from strings. In some programming languages, like Ada, strings are arrays of characters, so all the behavior of arrays applies to strings. Java is different in that regard. String is a class, so strings themselves are objects. Regardless of whether an array is used inside the String class to represent these objects, the representation is hidden, so clients can use only the public methods of the class. In C++, like Java, strings are objects of the class String, but because C++ allows operator overloading, the [] operator is overloaded, which makes string objects behave exactly like arrays with regard to subscripting. We have already noted that Java does not support operator overloading; nonetheless, it does overload the + operator for string concatenation. The same is not true for subscripting, however.

If the subscript operator were defined for strings in Java and subscripted strings were allowed on the left side of an assignment, string objects would be mutable objects. We have already noted that they are not and explained why that characteristic is so important in Java.

Some Additional String Methods

Although strings do not appear quite as array-like in Java as they do in some other languages, there are still some strong similarities between strings and arrays. Like arrays, Java strings do have subscripts, and the subscript values range from 0 to one less than the length of the string. Instead of using the brackets to extract a character from an array at a specific position, the method charAt is used. Its signature is shown below:

```
char charAt(int index)
```

The parameter index designates the subscript and what is returned is the character in the string at that position. Notice, however, that because method calls can only appear on the right-hand side of an assignment, this method is a read-only technique for accessing a character inside an array preserving the immutability of string objects.

The other array-like feature we require is the ability to determine the length of a string. With an array, we accessed an attribute named length that had the appearance of an instance variable. With strings, we access their length with a method of the same name. Its signature is shown below:

```
int length()
```

Of course, the String class has many more methods. At this point, we want to discuss these two in particular because of their similarity to arrays. As always, we refer you to the Sun Website at *http://java.sun.com/2se/1.5.0/docs/api/* for a complete list of the methods in the String class.

A Character Frequency Application

Now we present a simple application that illustrates the use of these two methods with strings. This application asks the user to input a sentence. It then computes the frequency within that sentence of each letter in the alphabet and displays those frequencies using a bar graph. Figure 9.1 contains the output of this program.

In one of our examples that deals with cryptography in the next chapter, we will discuss how computing such frequencies can help crack a cipher.

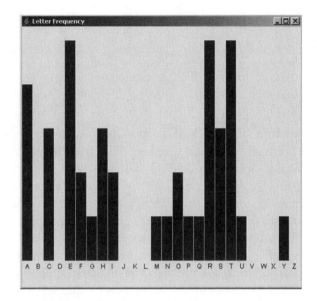

FIGURE 9.1 The output of the frequency application.

This program contains two classes. The first of the two classes is the class that contains the main method whose code is shown in Listing 9.1.

LISTING 9.1 An Application that Determines the Most Frequent Letter in a Supplied
ON THE CD Sentence (found on the CD-ROM at chapter9\LetterFrequency.java.)

```
1   package chapter9;
2
3   import common.*;
4
5   public class LetterFrequency
6   {
7       public static void main(String[] args)
8       {
9           char letter;
10          int[] frequencies = new int[26];
11          String sentence;
12          LetterFrequencyGraph graph;
13
14          sentence = InputOutput.getString("Enter a sentence: ");
15          for (int ch = 0; ch < sentence.length(); ch++)
16          {
17              letter = sentence.charAt(ch);
18              if (Character.isLetter(letter))
```

```
19                         frequencies[Character.toLowerCase(letter) - 'a']++;
20            }
21            graph = new LetterFrequencyGraph(frequencies);
22            graph.display();
23        }
24  }
```

Let's examine the details of the main method, which is the only method in this class. We begin with the local variables. The character variable letter, declared on line 9, is used to hold the individual characters of a sentence. On line 10, we declare the array frequencies and create the array object it refers to, an array consisting of 26 integers—one for each letter of the alphabet. The role of this array is similar to the one we used in the grade frequency example in Chapter 7. This array really represents 26 counters—one for each letter of the alphabet. The string object sentence, declared on line 11, contains the sentence input by the user. Finally, the object graph declared, but not instantiated, on line 12 will contain the bar graph window object that will display the bar graph of the letter frequencies.

Now we consider the algorithm contained in the main method. On line 14, we read in the sentence from the user. Spanning lines 15-20 is a for loop that processes each character of the sentence that was read in. The String class does not provide an iterator that would allow us to use a *for-each* style loop, so a traditional for loop is used instead. The loop control variable is initialized to 0—the subscript of the first character in the string—and the length method is used to specify the upper bound of the loop. On line 17, we use the charAt method that we discussed earlier to extract the next character from the sentence.

On line 19, we use this character to select which element in the frequencies array to update. There are several aspects of this line of code that require further explanation, however. First, we do not want to count upper- and lowercase letters separately, so the first necessary step is to convert all letters to the same case. Which case we choose is unimportant, so we arbitrarily choose lowercase. The Character wrapper class has a class method toLowerCase that accomplishes this task. We cannot use the character itself as a subscript to our array, however. We need to convert the character to a numeric value that will be the subscript that corresponds to that letter. The counter at subscript 0 corresponds to A and the one at 25 to Z. To perform that conversion, it is necessary to subtract 'a' from that letter. Java allows us to subtract characters, because what are really being subtracted are their underlying numeric Unicode representations. The value computed by that subtraction then becomes the array subscript. As was the case in the grade frequency example in Chapter 7, what we want to do here is to increment the array element stored at that subscript, so the ++ operator is placed outside the square brackets.

We skipped over the if statement on line 18, so let's review why such checks are needed. In this case, the subscript is being computed from input provided by the user. If any characters in the sentence are nonalphabetic characters, our formula will produce a value that is either negative or greater than 25, resulting in an out-of-bounds condition. Because we do not want the program to terminate in such cases, we must prevent that situation from occurring. The if statement on line 18 does just that. It uses another class method in the Character class, isLetter, which, as you would expect, returns true if the character is either an upper or lower case letter and false otherwise. Once the frequencies have been determined, the bar graph is instantiated and displayed.

The other class of this program is the class LetterFrequencyGraph that draws the bar graph of the letter frequencies. The code for this class is shown in Listing 9.2.

LISTING 9.2   The Class that Draws a Bar Graph for Letter Frequencies (found on the CD-ROM at chapter9\LetterFrequencyGraph.java.)

```
1   package chapter9;
2
3   import java.awt.*;
4   import common.*;
5
6   public class LetterFrequencyGraph extends Application
7   {
8       private static final int BAR_WIDTH = 20, HEIGHT = 400,
9           WINDOW_HEIGHT = HEIGHT + 100, OFFSET = 25, CAPTION =
10          HEIGHT + 40, CAPTION_OFFSET = 6, MARGIN = 10;
11      private int[] frequencies;
12      private int maxFrequency;
13
14      public LetterFrequencyGraph(int[] frequencies)
15      {
16          super("Letter Frequency", frequencies.length * BAR_WIDTH
17              + MARGIN, WINDOW_HEIGHT);
18          for (int frequency: frequencies)
19              if (frequency > maxFrequency)
20                  maxFrequency = frequency;
21          this.frequencies = frequencies.clone();
22      }
23      public void paintComponent(Graphics graphics)
24      {
25          int x = 0, height, caption = 0;
26
27          super.paintComponent(graphics);
```

```
28            for (int frequency: frequencies)
29            {
30                height = (int) (frequency * HEIGHT / maxFrequency + .5);
31                graphics.fillRect(x, HEIGHT + OFFSET - height,
32                    BAR_WIDTH - 1, height);
33                graphics.drawString("" + (char) (caption++ + 'A'),
34                    x + CAPTION_OFFSET, CAPTION);
35                x += BAR_WIDTH;
36            }
37        }
38  }
```

On lines 8-10 are the declarations for the constants used by this class. Their names describe their roles; in most cases they are intended to control the position of various aspects of the graphic output. There is one thing about this declaration that is noteworthy, however. In Chapter 7, when we introduced class constants, we mentioned that we would always use class rather than instance constants from that point forward. So our use of class constants here should be no surprise. In this case, however, several of the constants had to be class constants. In Chapter 7, we needed to use class constants in an example where constants needed to be shared among several class methods and no object of the class existed. In this case, the reason that class constants are needed for several of the constants is different and a bit subtler. On lines 16 and 17, the constructor of the class Application is called and several of the constants are passed to it. A compilation error will result if those constants are instance constants because they will not have been created yet.

Next let's consider the instance variables. On line 11 is the array of frequency values frequencies that is supplied as a parameter in the constructor. On line 12, maxFrequency is declared. It is used to determine the largest frequency in the frequencies array, which allows us to scale the bars so they better fill out the graph vertically. Because we expect no negative values, the default initial value of 0 for maxFrequency will suffice.

Next we consider the two methods of this class beginning with the constructor. In the call to the constructor of Application on lines 16 and 17, we are specifying the size of the window, whose width will be determined by the length of the array. On lines 18-20 is a for loop that computes the maximum element of the frequencies array—an algorithm that should by now be very familiar.

The other method in the class, paintComponent, draws the bar graph by iterating across the frequencies array. The computation of height on line 30 uses the variable maxFrequency to scale the height of the bars.

SUBDIVIDING STRINGS

In the previous section, we explored the process of extracting individual characters from strings. Another, perhaps even more commonly needed, operation is splitting a string into substrings. Java provides a variety of different techniques to accomplish this task. We explore three different techniques.

Finding Delimiters and Extracting Substrings

The first technique that we explore for splitting strings into words delimited by spaces is a technique that uses two methods of the String class—the indexOf and substring methods. Because these methods are so fundamental, they are ones you need to know. Both methods have several overloaded versions. As is customary, we discuss only those that we plan to use.

First, let's examine the signature of the indexOf method that we need.

```
int indexOf(int ch, int fromIndex)
```

This method searches the string beginning at subscript fromIndex for the first occurrence of the character ch. If the character is found, it returns the subscript at which it was first found; otherwise, it returns a –1. We intend to use the indexOf method to find the delimiting spaces.

Once found, we use two overloaded versions of the substring method to extract the word. The signatures of the two versions of substring that we use are shown below.

```
String substring(int beginIndex)
String substring(int beginIndex, int endIndex)
```

The first of these two methods extracts the substring beginning at subscript beginIndex to the end of the string. The second one extracts the substring beginning at beginIndex and ending at endIndex − 1.

The example that we have chosen to illustrate the use of these methods is an application that prompts the user for a sentence, then breaks the sentence into words, sums the lengths of the words, and computes and displays the average word length.

To review the implementation of iterators, we have elected to divide this program into two classes. The first class contains the main method and the second class implements an iterator that allows its clients to iterate across the substrings of a string, considering single spaces as the substring delimiters. Any collection can have an iterator associated with it. A string can be viewed not only as a collection of characters but also a collection of substrings. In the latter case, we can think of the strings as a sentence consisting of a collection of words. We will describe the implementation of this iterator shortly, but first let's consider the class that contains the `main` method for this application. Its code is shown in Listing 9.3.

LISTING 9.3   An Application that Determines the Average Length of the Words in a
ON THE CD   Sentence (found on the CD-ROM at `chapter9\AverageWordLength1.java`.)

```
1   package chapter9;
2
3   import java.util.*;
4   import common.*;
5
6   public class AverageWordLength1
7   {
8       public static void main(String[] args)
9       {
10          int totalLength = 0, wordCount = 0;
11          double averageLength;
12          String word, sentence =
13              InputOutput.getString("Enter a sentence: ");
14          Iterator<String> iterator =
15              new SubstringIterator(sentence);
16
17          while (iterator.hasNext())
18          {
19              word = iterator.next();
20              totalLength += word.length();
21              wordCount++;
22          }
23          averageLength = (double)totalLength / wordCount;
24          InputOutput.putString("Average word length is "
25              + averageLength);
26      }
27  }
```

The only declaration in the `main` method that requires explanation is the object `iterator` that is declared and instantiated on lines 14 and 15. On that line, we are creating an iterator object whose type is the template interface `Iterator` that we discussed in Chapter 8. We must provide it the string that we wish to iterate across.

The body of `main` consists of a loop spanning lines 17-22 that repeatedly extracts substrings, accumulates their total length, and counts the number of substrings. Once the loop completes, the average length is computed and displayed.

Now we examine the class that defines the iterator that the class Average-WordLength1 uses. It code is shown in Listing 9.4.

LISTING 9.4   The Class that Defines an Iterator for Space-Delimited Substrings of
a String (found on the CD-ROM at chapter9\SubstringIterator.java.)

```
1   package chapter9;
2
3   import java.util.*;
4
5   class SubstringIterator implements Iterator<String>
6   {
7       private String string;
8       private int startIndex, endIndex;
9
10      public SubstringIterator(String string)
11      {
12          this.string = string;
13      }
14      public boolean hasNext()
15      {
16          return endIndex >= 0;
17      }
18      public String next()
19      {
20          String nextString;
21
22          endIndex = string.indexOf(' ', startIndex);
23          if (endIndex < 0)
24              nextString = string.substring(startIndex);
25          else
26              nextString = string.substring(startIndex, endIndex);
27          startIndex = endIndex + 1;
28          return nextString;
29      }
30      public void remove()
31      {
32      }
33  }
```

First, notice that on line 5, we are implementing the template interface Iterator<String>. Next, we examine the instance variables of this class. First, we need a reference to the string that we are to iterate across, which is declared on line 7 and initialized by the constructor on line 12. The other state information is necessary to keep track of where we are in the iteration. The variables startIndex and endIndex maintain that information. The default initialization to 0 is exactly what we require.

Now we consider the hasNext method whose signature is on line 14, which indicates whether there are more substrings left to be extracted. It is used in the while condition of a loop that uses the iterator, as we did on line 17 of Listing 9.3. It becomes false when endIndex becomes −1 due to the indexOf method failing to find any more spaces in the remainder of the string.

Next, let's examine the next method, which begins on line 18. It searches for the next space in the remainder of the string using the indexOf method on line 22. If the space was not found, line 24 is executed, which contains a call to the substring method that is the one that extracts the substring starting from the specified subscript until the end of the string. Otherwise, the substring method that is supplied a pair of subscripts is used to extract the string on line 26. Finally on line 27, the substring startIndex is set to be one beyond endIndex to skip over the space and then the extracted substring is returned on line 28.

Although it has an empty body, we must provide the method remove to fulfill implementing the interface Iterator.

The StringTokenizer Class

The iterator that we created will split a string into substrings properly if the substrings are delimited by a single space. It will not, however, perform as we might want if the substrings are separated by more than one space or if we wish other characters besides spaces to be delimiters. If we wish to split a sentence into words, we would most likely not want punctuation characters to be included as part of the words, which is exactly what will happen with the iterator that we just discussed.

The reason for presenting the previous example was to illustrate the two important methods indexOf and substring and to show how they can be used to construct an iterator. As a practical tool for splitting strings, it is not ideal because, as we mentioned, it has several limitations. Moreover, Java already provides predefined classes that serve this purpose. One such class that has been in Java since the earliest version is the StringTokenizer class. In Chapter 1, in our discussion of the structure of language, we were careful to distinguish between lexemes and tokens—the former being the analog to words, the latter the analog to English parts of speech. In common usage this distinction is sometimes lost, which is true in the name chosen for this class. It breaks a string into lexemes, but does not categorize those lexemes as tokens. By contrast, a related class StreamTokenizer, that we will discuss in Chapter 11, does both.

Let's now consider the same problem of splitting a sentence into words, but this time we use the StringTokenizer class so any punctuation is treated as a delimiter and is removed. The code for this revised version is shown in Listing 9.5.

LISTING 9.5 An Application that Determines Average Word Length Using StringTokenizer (found on the CD-ROM at chapter9\AverageWordLength2.java.)

```
1   package chapter9;
2
3   import java.util.*;
4   import common.*;
5
6   public class AverageWordLength2
7   {
8       public static void main(String[] args)
9       {
10          int totalLength = 0, wordCount = 0;
11          double averageLength;
12          String word, sentence =
13              InputOutput.getString("Enter a sentence: ");
14          StringTokenizer tokenizer =
15              new StringTokenizer(sentence, " .,:;!");
16
17          while (tokenizer.hasMoreTokens())
18          {
19              word = tokenizer.nextToken();
20              totalLength += word.length();
21              wordCount++;
22          }
23          averageLength = (double)totalLength / wordCount;
24          InputOutput.putString("Average word length is "
25              + averageLength);
26      }
27  }
```

This program is very similar to the previous one. One difference is that when the tokenizer object is instantiated on line 15, the constructor is supplied not only the string to be split but also a second string that contains all the characters that should be treated as delimiters. We have included most punctuation characters in this second string together with a space.

The only other differences between this version and the previous one are the names of the methods. The method to check whether there are more substrings is hasMoreTokens rather than hasNext, and the method to get the next substring is nextToken, not next. This class predates the inclusion of the predefined interface It-erator. Actually, StringTokenizer implements an older interface called Enumera-tion, which has no relationship to enumerated types.

The split Method

Next, we examine one final technique for subdividing strings that is the most general of the three, because it permits the most flexibility in how we specify what delimits the strings. It is a much later addition to the language than the StringTokenzier class that we just studied.

This technique uses *regular expressions*—a symbolism for specifying string patterns. Regular expressions are not unique to Java, but are used by interpreted languages, such as Perl, that are well suited for string processing. Many of the utilities of the UNIX operating system also use them. In addition, they are used to define the syntax for the various tokens in a programming language. For example, consider the regular expression for Java identifiers shown below:

[_a–zA–Z]+[_a–zA–Z0–9]*

This regular expression defines the rule for forming identifiers similar to the one that we first encountered in Chapter 1, which is that they must begin with a letter or underscore and can be followed by zero or more underscores, letters, or digits. Let's examine how that regular expression conveys that definition. First, it is important to explain the meaning of a collection of metacharacters—characters that are symbols of the regular expression language and do not represent themselves. There are five metacharacters in the above regular expression. Let's consider what each of them means. First the square brackets enclosed a list of possible choices of characters. For example, the regular expression [aeiou] represents a vowel—exactly one of the five. If we wanted a series of them, we could use the metacharacters + or * that mean one or more and zero or more, respectively. So the regular expression [aeiou]+ means one or more vowels. Lastly, the final metacharacter in the regular expression for identifiers is –. It designates a range. So the regular expression [a–z] is any lower case letter—any character in the range from a to z.

Whenever a language uses metacharacters, such as the double quotes Java uses to delimit string literals, the question of how to differentiate the metacharacter from the character itself arises. The technique used in regular expressions is the same one used with double quotes in string literals. We prepend a backslash onto a metacharacter to turn it into the character itself. So, for example, the regular expression [\+\–*] represents either the addition, subtraction, or multiplication operator.

Having introduced regular expressions, we are now ready to discuss how they are used by the method split, which belongs to the class String. The signature of that method is shown below.

```
String[] split(String regex)
```

This approach to subdividing strings is quite different from the previous two. Rather than providing an iterator, split is invoked on the string that is to be split. It is passed a regular expression that defines the delimiters and returns an array of strings that constitutes the collection of component substrings.

To illustrate this technique for splitting strings, we present a third version of our program to determine the average word length of a sentence. This version is shown in Listing 9.6.

LISTING 9.6 An Application that Determines Average Word Length Using the split
Method (found on the CD-ROM at chapter9\AverageWordLength3.java.)

```
1   package chapter9;
2
3   import java.util.*;
4   import common.*;
5
6   public class AverageWordLength3
7   {
8       public static void main(String[] args)
9       {
10          int totalLength = 0, wordCount = 0;
11          double averageLength;
12          String sentence =
13              InputOutput.getString("Enter a sentence: ");
14          String[] words = sentence.split("[ .,:;!]+");
15
16          for (String word: words)
17          {
18              totalLength += word.length();
19              wordCount++;
20          }
21          averageLength = (double)totalLength / wordCount;
22          InputOutput.putString("Average word length is "
23              + averageLength);
24      }
25  }
```

The statement of greatest interest to our current discussion is the call to split on line 14. The regular expression that is passed to split is [.,:;!]+. It defines the delimiters as one or more of any characters inside the square brackets, so the delimiters defined in this version are identical to what is used by the string tokenizer in the previous example.

When we introduced this technique, we mentioned that it was a more general technique. To illustrate that point, let's suppose that we wanted to split the strings with either one or more spaces or a punctuation mark followed by one or more spaces. In other words, the string some.name should not be subdivided, but some.name should. With the string tokenizer, we cannot specify context; either a period is a delimiter or it is not. With a regular expression, we can specify context. The regular expression we use is [.,:;!]?[ ]+. It contains one additional metacharacter, which is ?, which means optional; another way to express it is either zero or one. In English, we would read that regular expression as an optional punctuation character followed by one or more spaces.

INPUT FILES

Although we plan to discuss the details of Java input and output in Chapter 11, we have elected to preface that discussion by presenting an abstraction of an input file—that is, a view of an input file without any of the underlying details. From this more abstract perspective, we look at an input file as a sequence of strings—each string being one line of the file. We use a class that we have written called InputFile, defined in our package common. We supply the name of the actual file to the constructor when we create an object of this class. To access the file contents, we use a *for-each* style for statement. Given what you learned about implementing a class that supports this statement in Chapter 8, you have no doubt concluded that InputFile must implement the interface Iterable. When we examine the code for this class in Chapter 11, you will see that it is indeed implemented in that fashion.

The example we chose to first demonstrate the use of this class is a variation on the first example of this chapter. It reads through the contents of a file and tabulates the frequency, not of the characters, but individual words. This program consists of two classes. We begin with the one that contains main because it is the one that uses the InputFile. Its code is shown in Listing 9.7.

LISTING 9.7 The Class Containing main for the Word Frequency Application (found on the CD-ROM at chapter9\WordFrequencyMain.java.)

```
1   package chapter9;
2
3   import common.*;
```

```
4
5   public class WordFrequencyMain
6   {
7       public static void main(String[] args)
8       {
9           int frequency;
10          String wordToCheck;
11          String[] words;
12          InputFile file = new InputFile("input.txt");
13          WordFrequency wordFrequency = new WordFrequency();
14
15          for (String line: file)
16          {
17              words = line.split("[.,:;!\\s]+");
18              for (String word: words)
19                  wordFrequency.incrementOccurrence(word);
20          }
21          while (true)
22          {
23              wordToCheck = InputOutput.getString(
24                  "Enter a word, empty string to quit: ");
25              if (wordToCheck.equals(""))
26                  break;
27              frequency = wordFrequency.getFrequency(wordToCheck);
28              InputOutput.putString(wordToCheck + " occurred " +
29                  frequency + " times");
30          }
31      }
32  }
```

On line 12, we declare and instantiate the InputFile object file. Notice, as we mentioned earlier, the physical file name must be passed to the constructor, which in this case is input.txt. The presumption is that this file is in the same directory as the program. Were that not the case, it would be necessary to supply a path along with the file name. On line 13, we create an object of the class WordFrequency, the class that we examine next. The word frequency object will also allow us to update the frequency of words as they are read in and allow us to inquire about the frequency of particular words subsequently.

The for loop that spans lines 15-20 reads in the lines of the file one at a time. The elegance of this abstraction is that, from our perspective, this file is just an iterable sequence of strings. On line 17, we break the individual lines into words, using the method split that we just studied. The regular expression passed into that method contains an aspect of regular expressions that we have not as yet encountered, which is the use of a predefined character collection. The symbol \\s represents any *whitespace* character, which includes not just spaces, but also other delimiting characters, such as tabs and new line characters. Table 9.1 provides a list that includes some other character collection symbols.

TABLE 9.1   The Predefined Character Collection Symbols

Character Collection Symbol	*Meaning*
/d	any numeric digit
/s	any whitespace character
/w	any alphanumeric or underscore
/D	any character except a numeric digit
/S	any character except whitespace
/W	any character except alphanumerics or underscores

The symbols themselves consist of a single backslash, but because the backslash is a metacharacter, another backslash must precede it to designate the backslash character itself. So the regular expression [.,:;!\\s]+ that we pass to split specifies the delimiters as one or more punctuation or whitespace characters. Once the string is split into an array of strings, we use an inner for loop on lines 18 and 19 to iterate across the individual words. Each word is added to the word frequency tabulator object by a call to the method incrementOccurrence on line 19.

The second loop that spans lines 21-30 allows the user to inquire about the frequency of specific words in the file. The inquiry is made by a call to the method getFrequency on line 27, which is provided the word to check and returns the frequency of that word.

Next, we consider the other class of this program—the WordFrequency class. Its code is contained in Listing 9.8.

LISTING 9.8   A Class that Maintains the Frequency of Words (found on the CD-ROM at chapter9\WordFrequency.java.)

```
1   package chapter9;
2
3   import java.util.*;
4
5   class WordFrequency
6   {
7       private ArrayList<String> words = new ArrayList<String>();
8       private ArrayList<Integer> frequencies =
9           new ArrayList<Integer>();
```

```
10
11      public int getFrequency(String word)
12      {
13          int index = words.indexOf(word);
14
15          if (index >= 0)
16              return frequencies.get(index);
17          return 0;
18      }
19      public void incrementOccurrence(String word)
20      {
21          int frequency;
22          int index = words.indexOf(word);
23
24          if (index >= 0)
25          {
26              frequency = frequencies.get(index);
27              frequencies.set(index, frequency + 1);
28          }
29          else
30          {
31              words.add(word);
32              frequencies.add(1);
33          }
34      }
35  }
```

We begin by discussing the representation of the objects of this class, defined by the instance variables words and frequencies defined on lines 7-9. Notice that they are parallel array lists. As we first noted in Chapter 7, the presence of parallel arrays or array lists may suggest that a possible class has been missed in the design process. In this case, we might have created such a class, calling it WordFrequencyPair, that contained a word and its frequency. Using that class, we would then have a single array list of these word-frequency pairs. Let's weigh the pros and cons of using that additional class. In this case, there is one benefit to keeping the parallel lists, which is that we are able to make use of the indexOf method to find the word. There is also, however, one benefit to the creation of a separate class in addition to the general benefit that it provides a more object-oriented design. That is that the frequency value could be represented using an int value, rather than the wrapper Integer, which is now needed for the array list of frequencies. In this case, we opted to stay with the parallel structure so we could avail ourselves of the indexOf method. Certainly when a design requires three or more parallel structures, the case for a new class would become more compelling. In an example in the next chapter that develops a document index, we have such a situation, where we have a word paired with, not one other value, but a whole list of other values. In that example, the case for another class is much more compelling, and it is the approach we take. Remember that with design, there are no absolute rules, just general guidelines. It is only with experience that you develop the judgment needed to make wise design choices.

Let's return to the WordFrequency class and examine its methods. The first method, getFrequency, looks up the frequency for a word that is passed to it as a parameter. On line 13, it calls the method indexOf in ArrayList that we mentioned earlier, but have never used before. This method returns the index or subscript of the first occurrence of the value supplied to it. If the value is not found, it returns −1. So if the return value is not negative, we use that index to access the corresponding frequency in the array list frequencies by calling get on line 16. There is something happening on this line that we discussed in Chapter 8 that also warrants review. The method get returns a value of type Integer, whereas getFrequency returns a value of type int. This code compiles as written because autounboxing is being done for us.

Finally, let's consider the other method in this class incrementOccurence. Like the previous method, it first checks to see whether the word supplied is already in the array of words. If it is, we retrieve the frequency of that word from the array list of frequencies, as we did before. This time, we increment it and save the incremented value back into the array list. Notice that in the call to set on line 27, autoboxing is being done. If the word was not found, we add it to the array list words and add one to the parallel position in the array list frequencies.

PATTERN MATCHING

The inclusion of regular expressions in Java involved more than just their use in the split method of the String class. Two new classes were also added—Pattern and Matcher. Both of these classes are in the package java.util.regex. They provide the capability of performing a frequently needed task known as pattern matching. To illustrate the use of these classes, we present a simple program that extracts all monetary amounts from a sentence input by the user. The code for the only class of that program, named ExtractMoney, is shown in Listing 9.9.

LISTING 9.9   A Simple Program that Extracts Monetary Amounts from a User-Supplied Sentence (found on the CD-ROM at chapter9\ExtractMoney.java.)

```
1  package chapter9;
2
3  import java.util.regex.*;
```

```
4   import common.*;
5
6   public class ExtractMoney
7   {
8       private static final Pattern moneyPattern =
9           Pattern.compile("\\$\\d+.\\d\\d");
10
11      public static void main(String[] args)
12      {
13          String sentence, moneyAmount;
14          Matcher matcher;
15          int count = 0;
16
17          sentence = InputOutput.getString
18              ("Enter a sentence containing money amounts");
19          matcher = moneyPattern.matcher(sentence);
20
21          while (matcher.find())
22          {
23              moneyAmount = matcher.group();
24              InputOutput.putString(moneyAmount);
25              count++;
26          }
27          InputOutput.putString("Sentence contained " + count
28              + " money values");
29      }
30  }
```

The regular expression that defines a monetary amount, supplied to the method `compile` on line 9, requires that the string begin with a dollar sign, followed by one or more digits, then a decimal point, followed by exactly two digits. To understand this code, we need to understand how the methods `find` and `group` behave. From its use on line 21, it should be clear that `find` returns a Boolean value. That returned value indicates whether a match was found. Subsequent calls indicate whether subsequent occurrences are found. The method `group`, called on line 23, returns the string that corresponds to the current occurrence. Together these two methods allow us to extract all occurrences of that pattern in the string. In the next chapter, we present another, larger example that performs such pattern matching.

MUTABLE STRINGS

In Chapter 5, we introduced the StringBuffer class to illustrate the kinds of problems that can occur when mutable objects are copied with a shallow copy. Do not conclude that, because of the problems associated with the shallow copying of mutable objects, such objects should be avoided. In some cases, there is an advantage to using mutable objects. To understand this advantage, let's consider how operations of the String class must be implemented to preserve immutability. Let's focus on the concatenation operation. Whenever two strings are concatenated, both strings must be copied into a new string. If we continually concatenate onto the end of a string, forming an ever-longer string, the beginning portion of that string is being copied many times.

To illustrate this point, we have constructed a simple example that allows the user to enter a sentence delimited in the same fashion as in our average word length example in Listing 9.6. We output the words of the sentence delimited by commas exclusively. This example requires a single class, named DelimitWithCommas1, shown in Listing 9.10.

LISTING 9.10 A Program that Outputs the Words of a Sentence Delimited by Commas (found on the CD-ROM at chapter9\DelimitWithCommas1.java.)

```
1   package chapter9;
2
3   import java.util.*;
4   import common.*;
5
6   public class DelimitWithCommas1
7   {
8       public static void main(String[] args)
9       {
10          int totalLength = 0, wordCount = 0;
11          double averageLength;
12          String originalSentence, modifiedSentence = "";
13          String[] words;
14
15          originalSentence =
16              InputOutput.getString("Enter a sentence: ");
17          words = originalSentence.split("[ .,:;!]+");
18          for (int i = 0; i < words.length; i++)
19          {
20              modifiedSentence += words[i];
21              if (i < words.length − 1)
22                  modifiedSentence += ", ";
```

```
23              }
24              InputOutput.putString(modifiedSentence);
25          }
26  }
```

In this example, every time we concatenate a word in the array words with the string modifiedSentence on line 20, we are making a copy of both originalSentence and words[i]. To avoid all this repetitive copying, we could use a StringBuffer object instead. Listing 9.11 contains a modified version of the previous program, rewritten using a StringBuffer.

LISTING 9.11 A Modified Program that Outputs the Words of a Sentence Delimited by **ON THE CD** Commas (found on the CD-ROM at chapter9\DelimitWithCommas2.java.)

```
1   package chapter9;
2
3   import java.util.*;
4   import common.*;
5
6   public class DelimitWithCommas2
7   {
8       public static void main(String[] args)
9       {
10          int totalLength = 0, wordCount = 0;
11          double averageLength;
12          String originalSentence;
13          String[] words;
14          StringBuffer modifiedSentence = new StringBuffer("");
15
16          originalSentence =
17              InputOutput.getString("Enter a sentence: ");
18          words = originalSentence.split("[ .,:;!]+");
19          for (int i = 0; i < words.length; i++)
20          {
21              modifiedSentence.append(words[i]);
22              if (i < words.length − 1)
23                  modifiedSentence.append(", ");
24          }
25          InputOutput.putString(modifiedSentence.toString());
26      }
27  }
```

There are several noteworthy points about this alternate version. The String-Buffer class has a constructor that allows us to turn a string into a string buffer, which is called on line 14. Most importantly, in place of the concatenation that we did in the original version, in this implementation, we use the method append on line 21 and 23. This method alters the string buffer being appended to. Consequently the repetitive copying is avoided. Also note that to convert a string buffer back to a string, we use the toString method of the StringBuffer class on line 25. There is one final observation that is appropriate regarding the use of the method append. It may occasionally need to reallocate a bigger buffer and copy the existing string into the large buffer, much like the class ArrayList does with the add method. The important difference is that it does not happen each time, as it does with the concatenation operator.

There is one other situation where using a string buffer in place of a string would greatly reduce the amount of necessary copying and therefore make the program more efficient. It is when a single character of a string needs to be changed. Recall that the String class has a method to extract a character at a particular index—the charAt—method but it does not, of course, have a method to set a character a particular index. Let's consider a method that would have the effect of changing a single character of a string. That method is shown below.

```java
String setCharAt(String string, int index, char ch)
{
    if (index < 0 || index >= string.length())
        return string;
    return string.substring(0, index) + ch +
        string.substring(index + 1);
}
```

Notice that to achieve the effect of changing a single character, the entire string must be copied twice. The two halves are copied by the two calls to substring once, and the concatenation operator copies them a second time. For long strings or when individual characters are being frequently changed, you should consider using the StringBuffer class instead. It has a method setCharAt whose signature is shown below.

```java
void setCharAt(int index, char ch)
```

No copying is done. Only the character at the specified position is modified.

Although efficiency should not be the foremost consideration in program design, it is a factor that you sometimes need to consider. Using immutable objects like strings can introduce a considerable amount of unnecessary copying in the two situations that we just discussed.

GRAPHICS DEFINITION FILE APPLICATION

In our final example for this chapter, we have chosen a program that reads in a file that contains a sequence of definitions of graphics objects, which the program then displays. To better understand how this program works, let's consider a sample input file and the corresponding graphic object that it displays. Shown below is the input file.

```
S 50, 50, 100
S 60, 60, 100
S 70, 70, 100
S 80, 80, 100
S 90, 90, 100
S 100, 100, 100
R 100, 50, 100, 200
R 50, 100, 200, 100
```

Each line represents one object to be drawn. The first letter indicates the kind of object, s for a square and R for a rectangle. For squares, three values are required—the coordinates of the upper left-hand corner and the size of a side. For a rectangle, there are four values that must be specified. The first two are the coordinates of the upper-left corner. The second two are the lengths of the width and height. Figure 9.2 contains the output of this program, given the previous input file.

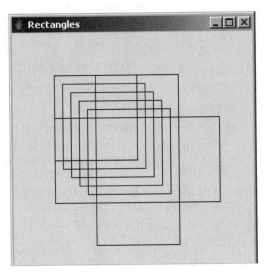

FIGURE 9.2 The output of the graphics definition file program.

This program consists of two classes. The first of the two is the class named GraphicFileMain shown in Listing 9.12, which contains main.

LISTING 9.12 The Class Containing main for the Graphics File Application

ON THE CD (found on the CD-ROM at chapter9\GraphicsFileMain.java.)

```java
1   package chapter9;
2
3   import java.awt.*;
4   import common.*;
5
6   public class GraphicsFileMain
7   {
8       public static void main(String[] args)
9       {
10          char objectType;
11          int[] values;
12          InputFile file = new InputFile("rectangles.txt");
13          RectanglesWindow window = new RectanglesWindow();
14
15          for (String line: file)
16          {
17              objectType = line.charAt(0);
18              switch (objectType)
19              {
20                  case 'S':
21                      values = stringToInts(line.substring(2),
22                          "\\d+(,\\s*\\d+){2}");
23                      window.addSquare(values[0], values[1],
24                          values[2]);
25                      break;
26                  case 'R':
27                      values = stringToInts(line.substring(2),
28                          "\\d+(,\\s*\\d+){3}");
29                      window.addRectangle(values[0], values[1],
30                          values[2], values[3]);
31                      break;
32                  default:
33                      InputOutput.putString("Invalid graphic type");
34                      return;
35              }
```

```
36                }
37                window.display();
38          }
39          private static int[] stringToInts(String numberString,
40               String regularExpression)
41          {
42               String[] splitStrings;
43               int numbers[];
44
45               if (!numberString.matches(regularExpression))
46                    {
47                         InputOutput.putString("Input file format error");
48                         System.exit(1);
49                    }
50               splitStrings = numberString.split(",\\s*");
51               numbers = new int[splitStrings.length];
52               for (int i = 0; i < numbers.length; i++)
53                    numbers[i] = stringToInt(splitStrings[i]);
54               return numbers;
55          }
56          private static int stringToInt(String number)
57          {
58               int result = 0;
59               for (int i = 0; i < number.length(); i++)
60               {
61                    result *= 10;
62                    result += number.charAt(i) - '0';
63               }
64               return result;
65          }
66   }
```

This program uses the `InputFile` class that we used previously in this chapter. It instantiates an object of that class on line 12 and iterates through each line of the file with the `for` loop that spans lines 15-36. Based on the first letter on the line, it determines the type of object. For the two valid objects, squares and rectangles, it calls the method `stringToInts` to convert the remainder of the string to an array of integers. Notice the second argument passed into that method on lines 22 and 28. It is a regular expression that specifies the required format for the rest of the string. These regular expressions use a quantifier that we have not yet encountered. Table 9.2 summarizes the quantifiers that can be used in regular expressions.

The quantifier that we are using in both of these regular expressions is the one that requires an exact number of repetitions. Let's consider the first of these two regular ex-

TABLE 9.2 The Regular Expression Quantifiers

Quantifier	Meaning
?	zero or one—optional
*	zero or more
+	one or more
{n}	exactly n
{n,}	at least n
{n,m}	between n and m, inclusive

pressions—\\d+(,\\s*\\d+){2}. The pattern defined by this regular expression is three numbers separated by commas. The pattern is expressed by specifying one number followed by exactly two comma-number pairs. The {2} is the quantifier that indicates "exactly two". Notice one other feature of this regular expression, which is the use of parentheses. They are metacharacters that define grouping, so the "exactly two" applies to the comma, the optional spaces and the number.

Let's return to the program itself. Notice that the calls to stringToInts return an array of integers, whose values we then pass to the constructor of either the ad- dRectangle or addSquare. The last thing to notice in the method main is the use of a return statement in the default case. A return statement in main ends the program, in this case, after displaying an error message.

Now let's consider the role of the method stringToInts. It uses a method of the String class that we have not used before. That method is matches, called on line 45, which is passed a regular expression and returns whether the string on which the method was invoked matches that regular expression. If it does not, we display an error message and terminate the program with a call to the class method exit, called on line 48. It is customary to pass a nonzero value to exit to indicate that the program exited with an error condition. If it matches the pattern, we split the string into its number components using the split method on line 50. That array of strings—splitStrings—is then converted to an array of integers—numbers—by re- peated calls to the method stringToInt on line 53.

Finally, we need to examine how the remaining method of the class—string- ToInt—performs its task. Whenever we called the method getInteger, a sequence of numeric characters was converted to type int for us. In Chapter 11, we will dis- cuss how getInteger performs that conversion using a predefined Java method, but we believe it is instructive to understand how such methods work. Consequently, we have written the method stringToInt that we intend to use, in this program only, to perform that task. Because of the pattern matching done previously, we know that stringToInt is being passed a string that contains only numeric digits, so we need not make any such checks.

We must convert each numeric character to an int, weigh it by its place value, and sum the resulting values. The for loop that spans lines 59-63 processes each character in the string. On line 62, the character is extracted using the charAt method and then converted to its integer value. Type casting cannot be used to perform this conversion. Subtracting the character literal '0' from the numeric digit is how the conversion is done. We don't really need to know the underlying numeric Unicode representations for the numeric digits; all we need to know is that the Unicode representations for the digits are in sequence. Because they are in sequence, we know the following identities hold: '0' − '0' ≡ 0 and '1' − '0' ≡ 1 and so on. Multiplying the result by 10 on line 61 applies a weight to the digit according to its position. A trace of the steps for converting the string "534" to the integer 534 is shown in Table 9.13.

TABLE 9.3 The Trace of stringToInt for the String "534"

Line	Value of i	charAt(i)	Value of result
61			0
64			0
65	0	'5'	5
64			50
65	1	'3'	53
64			530
65	2	'4'	534

In Chapter 11, we will begin to use the Java method parseInt of the Integer class to perform such conversions. Unlike our method stringToInt, we will see that it must account for the possiblity that the string passed to it does not contain numeric digits.

To complete this program, we need the class that defines the window on which the rectangles and squares are painted. That class, named RectanglesWindow, is in Listing 9.13.

LISTING 9.13 The Class for a Window of Rectangles and Squares (found on the CD-ROM at chapter9\RectanglesWindow.java.)

```
1   package chapter9;
2
```

```
3   import java.awt.*;
4   import java.util.*;
5   import common.*;
6
7   public class RectanglesWindow extends Application
8   {
9       private ArrayList<Rectangle> rectangles =
10          new ArrayList<Rectangle>();
11
12      public RectanglesWindow()
13      {
14          super("Rectangles");
15      }
16      public void addRectangle(int x, int y, int width, int height)
17      {
18          rectangles.add(new Rectangle(x, y, width, height));
19          repaint();
20      }
21      public void addSquare(int x, int y, int size)
22      {
23          rectangles.add(new Rectangle(x, y, size, size));
24          repaint();
25      }
26      public void paintComponent(Graphics graphics)
27      {
28          super.paintComponent(graphics);
29          for (Rectangle rectangle: rectangles)
30              graphics.drawRect(rectangle.x, rectangle.y,
31                  rectangle.width, rectangle.height);
32      }
33  }
```

This class should contain nothing that is unfamiliar.

SUMMARY

In this chapter, we examined some additional aspects of the use of strings. Although we had been using string literals since Chapter 4, there were many features of the String class that we had not yet studied. In this chapter, we also explored some additional methods of the String class. Those methods included one that allows us to extract characters at particular subscript and one that allows us to extract substrings from strings. We also investigated several techniques for breaking strings into a collection of substrings, including one that involves using regular expressions. Because string objects are immutable, Java provides a related class, String-Buffer, for situations when mutable strings are required, which we also examined.

Finally, we introduced a class that is not a standard Java class, but one that we have defined in our package common. It is the InputFile class. It represents a collection of strings stored in a file. Although directly manipulating Java files is a topic that we will explore in Chapter 11, the InputFile class provided us an abstraction of an input file that conceals those details much as the InputOutput class does. Consequently, it provided a graceful introduction to that topic. The key points to remember from this chapter are as follows:

- The String class provides a method, charAt, to extract characters at a particular index, but no method for modifying them.
- The substring method allows a portion of a string to be extracted by making a copy of the designated substring.
- The StringTokenizer class provides an iterator that breaks a string into substrings by specifying which characters are to be considered delimiters.
- Regular expressions allow the syntax of string patterns to be specified using a collection of metacharacters.
- The split method of the String class provides a technique for subdividing strings that uses regular expressions to define the delimiters.
- A generalized string pattern matching facility is provided by the classes Pattern and Matcher.
- When a string is being constructed by repeatedly appending strings to it, the StringBuffer class offers a more efficient alternative that avoids unnecessary copying.
- The InputFile class, an abstraction of an input file, allows us to iterate across the records of a file using the *for-each* style for loop.
- To convert a numeric character to an integer, subtracting the character '0' is required. Type casting does not work.

Review Questions

1. Why does the String class not provide a method for modifying particular characters within a string?

2. Explain the limitations of using the StringTokenizer class for subdividing strings.

3. Why is −1 a reasonable sentinel value for the method indexOf to return when the specified character is not in the string?

4. In regular expressions, how are metacharacters differentiated from the characters themselves?

5. Explain the difference between the role of parentheses and square brackets in regular expressions.

6. Why would using the regular expression \\s* be a poor choice for defining the delimiters for splitting a string?

7. Why can we conclude, without seeing its code, that the class InputFile implements the interface Iterable?

8. Compare the behavior of the append method of the StringBuffer class with the concatenation operator of the String class.

9. In what circumstances is it more efficient to use the StringBuffer class than the String class?

10. Why is it necessary to convert strings of numeric digits to their integer representations?

Programming Exercises

11. Write a method that accepts a string as a parameter and returns a copy of that same string, but in title case—the first letter of every word is upper case and the other letters in lower case.

12. Write a method that accepts a string buffer parameter and modifies the string so that it is in title case.

13. Write a method that tests whether a string is in title case. First break the string into an array of strings delimited by whitespace using the split method, then test each substring with the matches method using a regular expression that defines a word in title case.

14. Write a method that accepts a string parameter and returns a copy of that string with all the whitespace removed.

15. Write a method that accepts a string buffer as a parameter and replaces all whitespace characters with dashes.

16. Write a regular expression to define each of the following patterns:
    a. A sequence of digits preceded by an optional plus or minus sign.
    b. A sequence of alphanumeric characters including underscores, but consecutive and trailing underscores are prohibited.
    c. A sequence of unsigned integers separated by either one space or one comma, but not both.
    d. A sequence of at least ten alphabetic characters.

e.   A hexadecimal number that consists of one or more numeric digits or a letter from A to F, in either lower or upper case.

17. Write a method that accepts a string, splits the string into substrings, and returns the array of substrings. The delimiters should be any combination of spaces or commas. Use the StringTokenizer class to accomplish the subdivision.

18. Write a class that implements the Iterator interface that subdivides a string. The string to be subdivided and a regular expression defining the delimiters should be supplied to the constructor. Internally, the string should use the split method to subdivide the string.

19. Write a method that accepts a string to be subdivided and a string containing the characters that are to be considered as delimiters. It should return an array of the subdivided strings. Internally, it should use the StringTokenizer to perform the subdivision.

20. Write a method that accepts a string that contains a hexadecimal number. Use the regular expression defined in Programming Exercise 16e to verify that it is in the correct format. If so, convert it to a decimal integer and return that integer.

Programming Projects

21. Write an application that searches through a file for the largest number in the file. Extract only the character sequences that consist of possible signed integers using a Matcher object and the regular expression defined in Programming Exercise 16a. Use a modified version of the stringToInt method that allows a leading sign to perform the conversion from strings to integers.

22. Write a version of the average word length application using an object of the class defined in Programming Exercise 18 to subdivide the string.

23. Write a version of the average word length application that uses the method defined in Programming Exercise 19 to subdivide the string.

24. Modify the graphics file example in this chapter so that it also draws circle objects. The file should contain a line beginning with the letter C to designate a circle followed by the coordinates of the upper-left corner and its diameter.

25. Write a program that tests whether a whole file is in title case using the method in Programming Exercise 13 and the InputFile class.

10 Composition Relationships

DETERMINING CLASS RELATIONSHIPS

In each chapter until now, we presented some new feature of Java syntax. In this chapter, we introduce a minimum of new syntax and, instead, focus exclusively on object-oriented design principles. Let's begin by reviewing the design principles that we have discussed already. In Chapter 3, we discussed how to select the instance variables of a class that constitute the representation for objects of that class. We stressed the importance of the principle of information hiding, which requires that all instance variables of a class be declared with the access modifier private. In Chapter 7, we introduced the principle of preserving class invariants and discussed why it is important to design the class specification to contain only methods that preserve such invariants.

Until now, none of our examples involved more than two classes, excluding any predefined classes, inner classes, and classes in our package common that we treated as predefined. We are now ready to begin looking at examples with programs that have more classes. To understand the design of such programs, it is necessary to understand the various kinds of relationships that can exist between classes. Let's begin by characterizing the one type of relationship that we have seen so far. In each of the applications that we studied, there were two classes—the class that contained the method `main` and the class that defined a window that allows us to draw on. In those programs, the `main` method contained one or more objects of the other class. This relationship is generally referred to as a *dependency* relationship. The main class depends upon the window class. The UML symbolism for this class relationship is a dotted line with an open arrowhead, as we saw in Chapter 5. This relationship is also sometimes referred to as a *uses* relationship. The main class uses the window class.

Before we introduce some of the other possible class relationships, let's step back and consider the overall process of object-oriented design. When we began discussing design, we mentioned that there is one common thread of software design, whether it was the structured design that was used before the advent of object-oriented languages or object-oriented design that is now used. That common thread is decomposition—breaking the problem into smaller parts. With object-oriented design, the decomposition involves determining the classes that should be used to solve the problem at hand. Developing skill in choosing the right classes for a particular problem requires practice. There is no precise technique that can be given to help you make the right choices, but there are some general guidelines. Although it is somewhat simplistic, the first step in determining what might be good candidates for classes is to consider all the nouns in the problem requirements. Among those nouns, the ones that are large are more likely to be classes than smaller ones. The ones that have operations associated with them are more often better candidates for classes than are those that do not. Such operations, which often appear as verbs in the requirements, typically become the methods of such classes.

Once the classes and at least some of their methods have been identified, it is important to determine the kind of relationships that exist between those classes. To characterize the relationship, finding a predicate that connects the two classes is helpful. Aside from uses, the other two most common predicates are *has a* and *is a*. To illustrate the difference between these two predicates, consider the following two sentences, which each contain one of them.

- A car *has an* engine.
- A car *is a* vehicle.

Clearly car, engine, and vehicle are all nouns and potentially candidates for classes. The relationship between car and engine is very different, however, from the relationship between car and vehicle. The first relationship is a *compositional re-*

lationship. As evidence of that fact, we could use a slightly different predicate to express the relationship.

■ An engine *is one of the components of* a car.

Because the verb *to have* can have various meanings, it is often best to test the candidate *has a* relationships with this alternate predicate. The second relationship is a *generalization relationship*. Using an alternate predicate is useful in this case because the verb *to be* can also have different meanings. This relationship can be verified using the alternate predicate, as shown below.

■ A car *is a kind of a* vehicle.

In this chapter, we will focus exclusively on compositional relationships. In Chapter 12, we will consider generalization and some other relationships.

COMPOSITIONAL RELATIONSHIPS

Once we know how to establish whether a compositional relationship exists between two classes, we next need to know how such relationships are realized in Java code. The technique for establishing such relationships is one with which we are already familiar. An object of the component class typically becomes an instance variable of the class of which it is a component. Specifically, if we had established that Car and Engine were appropriate classes in our design, the Car class might look as follows:

```
class Car
{
    private Engine engine;
...
}
```

The difference between instance variables such as these compared to those we have used before is that, until now, the type of all our instance variables has been either a primitive type or a predefined class such as String. In this case, we assume that both Car and Engine are classes that we define.

A Window of Rectangles Application

The first example that we use to illustrate compositional relationship is an application that allows the user to add any number of generalized rectangles—rectangles whose sides are not necessarily parallel to the axes—to a window. Let's compare this approach with the approach we took with the cyclic quadrilateral application in Chapter 7. In that program, the class that created the window was the same class that drew the quadrilateral. In fact, we have used that approach in all of our drawing examples so far. In this example, we separate the rectangle objects from the window object on which they are drawn. This design has the advantage that the class that defines the rectangles is usable for other programs that draw such rectangles. Furthermore, by separating the window class from the rectangle class, a window could contain a different number of rectangles in different programs. Moreover, the window could also contain figures other than rectangles. The relationship between the window class and the rectangle class is, of course, compositional. The window contains some number of rectangle objects. We discussed a generalized rectangle class in Chapter 7, but never implemented it. So first, let's examine the code for such a class, which is shown in Listing 10.1.

LISTING 10.1   A Generalized Rectangle Class (found on the CD-ROM at
ON THE CD   chapter10\Rectangle.java.)

```
1   package chapter10;
2
3   import java.awt.*;
4
5   public class Rectangle
6   {
7       public static final int SIDES = 4;
8       public static final double RIGHT_ANGLE = Math.PI / 2;
9       protected int x, y, length1, length2;
10      protected double angle;
11
12      public Rectangle(int x, int y, int length1, int length2,
13          double angle)
14      {
15          this.x = x;
16          this.y = y;
17          this.length1 = length1;
18          this.length2 = length2;
19          this.angle = angle;
20      }
21      public void draw(Graphics graphics)
22      {
23          int previousX = x, previousY = y, currentX, currentY;
24          int [] lengths = {length1, length2, length1};
25          double currentAngle = angle;
26
27          for (int side = 0; side < SIDES - 1; side++)
```

```
28              {
29                      currentX = (int) (previousX + Math.cos(currentAngle) *
30                          lengths[side] + .5);
31                      currentY = (int) (previousY + Math.sin(currentAngle) *
32                          lengths[side] + .5);
33                      graphics.drawLine(previousX, previousY, currentX,
34                          currentY);
35                      previousX = currentX;
36                      previousY = currentY;
37                      currentAngle += RIGHT_ANGLE;
38              }
39              graphics.drawLine(previousX, previousY, x, y);
40          }
41  }
```

One minor point about this and several of the other classes in this chapter, is that we have declared them as public classes because we plan to use them again in future chapters. Remember that to be able to refer to a class outside its own package, it must be declared public.

Now let's examine the representation for these rectangles. We have declared a constant, SIDES, which defines the number of sides in a rectangle, on line 7. On line 8, we declare the constant RIGHT_ANGLE to emphasize the fact that as we compute the coordinates of the vertices, we do so by adding 90° to the previous angle. Recall that the invariant property of a rectangle is that all of its angles are right angles.

The representation that we are using is similar to the representation used by the predefined rectangle class. It involves the coordinates of one vertex and the lengths of two sides, defined by the instance variables x, y, length1, and length2, respectively, defined on line 10. In this case, the vertex defined by the coordinates is a left-most vertex, but not necessarily the upper-left vertex. Because the sides of our generalized rectangle are not necessarily parallel to the axes, naming the lengths of the sides with the names width and height would be misleading. Nonetheless, we only need two lengths, because another invariant property of a rectangle is that the lengths of opposite sides are equal. This property is weaker than the one about right angles, since all parallelograms satisfy this property as well. The final component of this representation is the instance variable angle that defines the angle of the first side as it emanates from the first vertex. Providing this variable allows for the more general rectangles.

There is one more important observation that we need to make about the instance variables declared on lines 9 and 10. We have used an access modifier that we have never used before—protected. The reason for having made that choice is to enable us to reuse this class in an example in Chapter 12, when we discuss generalization relationships that are implemented with inheritance. At that time, we will explain the meaning of the reserved word `protected` and why we need to use it. If we were using the class `Rectangle` in this program only, the access modifier `private` that we have used until now would have sufficed.

The constructor for this class contains nothing new; it copies the parameters to instance variables of the same name.

Finally, we need to consider the method `draw` that draws the rectangle. Unlike the `paint` method in all our applets and `paintComponent` in our applications, we were free to choose the name of this method. We could have named it `paint` if we preferred. This method computes the coordinates of the remaining three vertices and draws the lines that connect them. As we have so often done, we use previous and current pairs for the endpoints of the line segment to be drawn. The array `lengths`, declared on line 24 and initialized to an array constant, is a convenient way to alternate between the two different lengths. The loop that spans lines 27-38 iterates three times and draws the first three sides of the rectangle. The calculations on lines 29-32 calculate the coordinates of the next vertex using the sine and cosine trigonometric functions that we have used before. On line 37, we add 90° to the angle to compute the angle of the next side, in keeping with the invariant property of a rectangle. On line 39, the fourth side is drawn by using the original vertex and the last computed vertex as the endpoints.

Now we are ready to consider the second of the three classes that comprise our example. It is the class that defines the window on which the rectangles will be drawn. The code for that class is contained in Listing 10.2.

LISTING 10.2   A Window Class Containing a Collection of Rectangles (found on the CD-ROM at `chapter10\RectanglesWindow.java`.)

```
1   package chapter10;
2
3   import java.awt.*;
4   import java.util.*;
5   import common.*;
6
7   public class RectanglesWindow extends Application
8   {
9       protected ArrayList<Rectangle> rectangles =
10          new ArrayList<Rectangle>();
11
12      public RectanglesWindow()
13      {
14          super("Rectangles");
15      }
```

```
16      public void addRectangle(Rectangle rectangle)
17      {
18          rectangles.add(rectangle);
19          repaint();
20      }
21      public void paintComponent(Graphics graphics)
22      {
23          super.paintComponent(graphics);
24          for (Rectangle rectangle: rectangles)
25              rectangle.draw(graphics);
26      }
27  }
```

The declaration of the instance variable `rectangles` on lines 9-10 is our first encounter with a compositional relationship between classes that we defined. In this case, the window class is composed of some number of rectangle objects. We used the generic Java collection class `ArrayList` in this declaration because we do not know beforehand how many rectangles will be in the window. We allow the user to add any number of rectangles to the window. An array of rectangles would not have provided us this flexibility. Notice again how we constrain generic classes with the type of their components by placing that type inside corner brackets, so the type of our instance variable is really `ArrayList<Rectangle>`.

Next, let's consider the `addRectangle` method. It allows the caller to supply a rectangle to be added to the window. It calls the `add` method of the `ArrayList` class to accomplish that task. Finally, let's examine the method `paintComponent`. Its task is to draw all the rectangles, which it accomplishes by iterating through the array list and invoking the method `draw` on each of the rectangles.

We are now ready to discuss the third and final class of this program—the one that contains `main`. The code for that class is shown in Listing 10.3.

LISTING 10.3 The Class Containing `main` for the Rectangles in a Window Application
ON THE CD (found on the CD-ROM at `chapter10\RectanglesMain.java`.)

```
1  package chapter10;
2
3  import java.awt.*;
4  import common.*;
5
6  public class RectanglesMain
7  {
8      public static void main(String[] args)
9      {
```

```
10          final int MAX_POS = 250, MAX_LENGTH = 60;
11          int x, y, length1, length2;
12          double angle;
13          char response;
14          RectanglesWindow window = new RectanglesWindow();
15
16          window.display();
17          do
18          {
19              x = (int)(Math.random() * MAX_POS);
20              y = (int)(Math.random() * MAX_POS);
21              length1 = (int)(Math.random() * MAX_LENGTH);
22              length2 = (int)(Math.random() * MAX_LENGTH);
23              angle = Math.random() * Rectangle.RIGHT_ANGLE;
24              window.addRectangle(new Rectangle(x, y, length1,
25                  length2, angle));
26              response = InputOutput.getCharacter("More? y or n: ",
27                  "yn");
28          }
29          while (response == 'y');
30      }
31  }
```

On line 14, the method main declares and instantiates an object of the class Rec-tanglesWindow that we just discussed. It displays that window and then enters a do-while loop, in which random characteristics of a rectangle are generated and used to create a rectangle that is then passed to the method addRectangle of the Rectan-glesWindow class. The user is then allowed to choose between adding another rectangle or not. Typical output of this program is shown in Figure 10.1.

UML Diagrams Depicting Compositional Relationships

As we begin to create programs with many classes, UML diagrams that illustrate the relationship between the classes become increasingly important. We are now ready to examine our first UML diagram containing three classes and our first with a compositional relationship between two classes. The UML diagram for the window of rectangle application that we just discussed is shown in Figure 10.2.

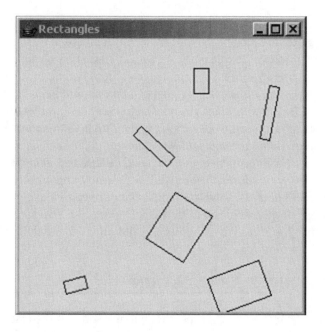

FIGURE 10.1   Output of the window of rectangles application.

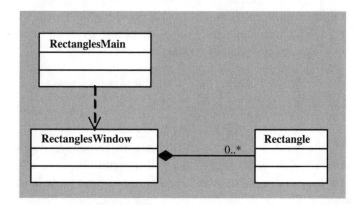

FIGURE 10.2   UML diagram for the window of rectangles application.

There are two features of this diagram that require explanation. The first is the symbol that denotes a compositional relationship. It is a solid diamond symbol. Composition is a directed relationship, so we place the diamond next to the class that is the one that contains objects of the other class. In this case, the diamond is next to RectanglesWindow, because a RectanglesWindow object is composed of objects of the class Rectangle. At the other end, we place what are called multiplicity markers—in this case 0..*. That marker indicates that a rectangle window is composed of zero or more rectangles. One final comment about this relationship is warranted. We are omitting the role of the ArrayList class. Technically, a RectanglesWindow object contains an ArrayList<Rectangle> object, which, in turn, contains some number of Rectangle objects. Our goal of UML should be to capture the essence of the relationships, rather than always illustrating every implementation detail. The fact that we have chosen to use an array list rather than an array is the kind of implementation detail that we prefer to ignore.

The relationship between RectanglesMain and RectanglesWindow is the usual dependency relationship that we have already encountered. Notice that we have omitted all details on the individual class diagrams except their names to keep this diagram simple. Remember that UML is flexible. You can include those design issues that you most wish to illustrate and omit other details, if you wish.

DOCUMENT INDEX APPLICATION

Next, we consider an example that will use some of the features of strings and pattern matching that we discussed in the previous chapter and will also illustrate two levels of compositional relationships—our topic for this chapter. This program builds an index—similar to the index contained in most books of selected words. The input to this program is a text file in which the words that are to be included in the index are highlighted by enclosing them in double corner brackets. Shown below is a sample of what this text file might contain.

```
This is an example of how the annotated <<input>> of the text file
might look. Enclosing them in double corner brackets designates
<<words>> that are to be included in the <<index>>.
```

So the words input, words, and index are to be included in the index. One additional requirement is that we wish to have both the page and line of each word in the index. For simplicity, we have elected to have page boundaries marked by a blank line. This program consists of four classes. The first one that we examine is WordIndex, which maintains the document index. Its code is shown in Listing 10.4.

LISTING 10.4   A Class that Maintains a Document Index (found on the CD-ROM at *ON THE CD* chapter10\WordIndex.java.)

```
1 package chapter10;
2
3 import java.util.*;
```

```
 4  import java.util.regex.*;
 5  import common.*;
 6
 7  class WordIndex
 8  {
 9      private static final Pattern indexableWord =
10          Pattern.compile("<<[a-zA-Z]+>>");
11      private ArrayList<WordLocations> index =
12          new ArrayList<WordLocations>();
13
14      public WordIndex(String fileName)
15      {
16          Location current = new Location();
17          InputFile file = new InputFile(fileName);
18
19          for (String line: file)
20          {
21              if (line.equals(""))
22                  current.nextPage();
23              else
24              {
25                  addLineWords(line, current.clone());
26                  current.nextLine();
27              }
28          }
29      }
30      public WordLocations find(String word)
31      {
32          for (WordLocations wordLocations: index)
33              if (wordLocations.matches(word))
34                  return wordLocations;
35          return null;
36      }
37      private void addLineWords(String line, Location location)
38      {
39          String word;
40          Matcher matcher = indexableWord.matcher(line);
41
42          while (matcher.find())
43          {
44              word = matcher.group();
45              addWord(word.substring(2, word.length() - 2),
46                  location);
47          }
```

```
48        }
49        private void addWord(String word, Location location)
50        {
51            WordLocations wordLocations = find(word);
52            if (wordLocations != null)
53                wordLocations.addLocation(location);
54            else
55                index.add(new WordLocations(word, location));
56        }
57  }
```

First, let's consider the class constant indexableWord that defines the pattern for the words in the document that are to be compiled into the index. From its declaration, it should be clear that objects of the class Pattern correspond to regular expressions. Recall that the class method compile of the class Pattern is used to create patterns from their corresponding regular expressions. The regular expression that we supplied to compile is <<[a–zA–Z]+>>. You may wonder why we did not use the character collection symbol \\w in place of [a–zA–Z], but recall that it allows numeric digits and underscores, which are not appropriate here.

This class contains one instance variable, which is the array list index. Notice that the components of this class are WordLocations objects. These objects consist of a word and a list of locations where that word appears. Incorporating an additional class in this case is clearly preferable to any use of parallel array lists. In Chapter 7 when we first studied arrays, we noted that when a problem requires parallel structures, such as words and their corresponding lists of locations, parallel arrays might be used, but that a more object-oriented design alternative would be to create another class. In Chapter 7, when we transformed the square spiral applet from a design that used parallel arrays to one that used an array of objects, we were able to use a predefined class, Point. For this problem, no such predefined class exists, so we clearly need to create one.

Most constructors until now have done little more than copy parameters to instance variables, but such is not the case with the constructor for this class. It creates the index from the supplied file name that is passed to it. The first local object in the constructor is current, an object of the class Location, which is one of the classes defined for this program. A location consists of a page and line number. The object current contains the current location as the input file is processed. We again use the class InputFile that we introduced in the previous chapter. As before, we use a for loop to read that file line by line. Recall that we said that blank lines would designate page boundaries, which is the check made by the if statement on line 21. When page boundaries occur, a method called nextPage in the Location class is called to advance the current location. Otherwise the private method addLineWords is called to process all the words to be indexed on that line and the line is advanced by a call to the nextLine method of the Location class.

Starting in Chapter 5, we have been emphasizing the importance of understanding whether objects are mutable or immutable. In this program, we have elected to make the Location objects mutable. It should be evident from how they are called that the methods nextPage and nextLine change the objects on which they are invoked. Recall that when we have mutable objects, the shallow copying which occurs as the default can be a problem. This program provides an excellent illustration of this principle. Notice that on line 25, when we pass the current location to the method addLineWords, we do not pass the object current, but instead pass a deep copy of that object by calling the method clone provided by the Location class. If you are unsure of why a deep copy is needed here, we suggest that you remove the call to clone and then run the program, so you can see firsthand what results from such logic errors.

Because the constructor uses two private methods to complete its task, let's discuss them before returning to the only other public method, find. We begin with addLineWords, which is called directly by the constructor. The constructor provides it the line from the file and the location of that line. It creates a local object named matcher of the class Matcher on line 40, supplying it with the string that contains the line from the file. The body of this method consists of a loop that extracts each of the words to be indexed from the line and calls the other private method addWord to actually add them. Once each word is extracted we call addWord on line 45, passing to it the word to be indexed. Notice that we use the method substring to strip off the double corner brackets that define the pattern.

To complete our discussion of the code that builds the index, we need to consider the other private method, addWord. It is provided the word and its location as parameters. It must first determine whether that word is already in the index. It does that by making a call to the method find—the public method of this class, which we have yet to examine. The method find returns the WordLocations object that contains the word that we were attempting to find if it was found. Otherwise, it returns null. Although we have frequently mentioned that uninitialized objects contain null references, this program is our first encounter with a use of the reserved word null that represents a null reference. In this case, we use it as a sentinel value in much the same way that a −1 is used by the find method of ArrayList to indicate that the word was not found. If the word is found, on line 53 we call the addLocation method of the WordLocation class to add the current location to the list of locations where the word appears. If the word is not found, on line 55 we create a new WordLocations object containing the word and its first location, which is then added to the array list index.

Finally, we consider the public method find. It is called both from outside the class and by the method addWord that we just discussed. It iterates through the list of words, repeatedly calling the method matches of the WordLocations class to see whether the word supplied as a parameter matches the word in that element of the array list. If a match is found, on line 34, it returns the object of type WordLocations that contains that word. If after examining each element of the array list, no match is found, on line 35, it returns the sentinel value null that we discussed earlier. Because the array list is not being kept in any order, we are obliged to examine the elements of the array list in sequence.

Now let's consider the second of the four classes that comprise this program—the class WordLocations, which is the type of the elements of the array list index in the class that we just discussed. The code for this class is in Listing 10.5.

LISTING 10.5   A Class Representing a Word and its List of Locations (found on the CD-ON THE CD   ROM at chapter10\WordLocations.java.)

```
 1  package chapter10;
 2
 3  import java.util.*;
 4
 5  class WordLocations
 6  {
 7      private String word;
 8      private ArrayList<Location> locations =
 9          new ArrayList<Location>();
10
11      public WordLocations(String word, Location location)
12      {
13          this.word = word;
14          locations.add(location);
15      }
16      public void addLocation(Location location)
17      {
18          locations.add(location);
19      }
20      public boolean matches(String word)
21      {
22          return word.equals(this.word);
23      }
24      public String toString()
25      {
26          String string = word + " ";
27          Iterator<Location> iterator = locations.iterator();
28
29          while (iterator.hasNext())
30          {
```

```
31                      string += iterator.next();
32                      if (iterator.hasNext())
33                          string += ", ";
34              }
35          return string;
36      }
37  }
```

We begin by examining the representation of a WordLocations object. Not surprisingly, it consists of the string word declared on line 7 and an array list of Location objects declared and instantiated on lines 8 and 9. Notice that this program exhibits two levels of composition—something that, until now, we had not encountered. The class WordIndex is composed of a list of WordLocations objects. A WordLocations object is composed of a list of Location objects. Once we have examined the complete program, we will examine its UML diagram, and should expect these two levels of composition to be apparent in that diagram.

This class has one constructor that creates a new object from a word and its first location. This constructor is called from addWord of WordIndex on line 55 of Listing 10.4 when a word is added to the index for the first time. It copies the parameter word to its corresponding instance variable and adds the supplied location to the array list of locations.

The method addLocation adds a location to an existing object. It is called from addWord of WordIndex on line 53 of Listing 10.4 when subsequent locations are added to the index for a word that the index already contains. The method matches compares the word supplied as a parameter with the word belonging to the object on which this method was invoked. It is called from find of WordIndex on line 33 of Listing 10.4 during its search to see whether the index contains a particular word. Notice that the comparison done on line 22 uses the equals method of the String class, which does a deep comparison. Both addLocation and matches are needed because the instance variables of this class are private, as they should be, so they cannot be directly accessed by the methods of the WordIndex class.

Finally, we consider the last method in this class, the toString method. Although we have called methods named toString before, this is the first time we are writing one. There is a characteristic of this method you need to be aware of. Although it can be called by name, it can also be called implicitly by concatenating it to a string using the concatenation operator +. We will encounter such an example shortly. This method creates a string that consists of the word followed by the list of its locations. Commas separate the locations. On line 26, the string value to be returned is initialized to contain the word. Because we need to treat the last location differently, by not inserting a comma after it, we must use an explicit iterator rather than a for statement. On line 27, we create that iterator. The while loop that spans lines 29-34 forms this list of locations, separated by commas. The assignment statement on line 31 requires some additional explanation. It concatenates the next element of the array list onto the end of the string that is being formed. The method next is returning an object of type Location. The use of the concatenation operator here is really an implicit call to the method toString of the Location class. To be more explicit, the following statement could replace the assignment on line 31.

```
string += iterator.next().toString();
```

When multilevel compositional relationships exist and forming a string representation is needed, it is not unusual for each class to have a toString method and to have each of those toString methods call the toString method of its components. In fact, this same kind of chain of calls among methods of the same name is true for other operations, as well. The fact that the representation is hidden at each level is what requires each class to call upon its component class for assistance in completing its task. We will revisit this issue when we examine the final example in this chapter. Before concluding our discussion of the toString method, let's recall a point from the previous chapter. Because this method uses the concatenation operator, a great deal of unnecessary copying is being done. Think about how that copying could be eliminated by using a string buffer and the method append instead.

Now we examine the Location class, which defines the components of the Word-Locations class that we just examined. Its code is shown in Listing 10.6.

LISTING 10.6 A Class Defining a Location Consisting of a Page and Line Number (found on the CD-ROM at chapter10\Location.java.)

```
1  package chapter10;
2
3  class Location implements Cloneable
4  {
5      private int pageNumber, lineNumber;
6
7      public Location()
8      {
9          pageNumber = 1;
10         lineNumber = 1;
11     }
12     public Location(int pageNumber, int lineNumber)
13     {
14         this.pageNumber = pageNumber;
15         this.lineNumber = lineNumber;
16     }
17     public Location clone()
```

```
18      {
19            return new Location(pageNumber, lineNumber);
20      }
21      public void nextLine()
22      {
23            lineNumber++;
24      }
25      public void nextPage()
26      {
27            pageNumber++;
28            lineNumber = 1;
29      }
30      public String toString()
31      {
32            return "" + pageNumber + ":" + lineNumber;
33      }
34  }
```

Our first observation is that we have stated that this class implements the interface Cloneable, which, as you should expect, means that it must implement the method clone that performs a deep copy. Including this clause is not necessary for this program to compile or run, but we believe that it serves as useful documentation to the reader that this class is mutable. In fact, as a matter of style, we recommend designating mutable classes in this fashion.

Next, we consider the representation for Location objects. Their representation consists of the two instance variables, pageNumber and lineNumber, defined on line 5. These variables are both initialized to 1 by the default constructor, illustrating the fact that a default constructor sometimes does initialize the instance variables to values other than 0.

We have included a second constructor that allows an object to be created given the page and line numbers. We included this constructor primarily for use by the method clone, which calls this constructor on line 19.

Notice our choice of methods in this class. We might have included methods to set the line and page numbers individually, but that design would have unnecessarily exposed the representation and would not have captured the way in which locations are intended to be used. Although objects of this class are mutable objects, there is an invariant behavior to the way they change. When a Location object is changed, it can only refer to the next location in the file. Notice how the methods nextLine and nextPage ensure this restriction. A line can only be advanced by one line, and advancing a page always resets the line number. This class captures the location of elements in a stream—a sequence of objects that can only be accessed one after another. Our abstraction of a file in InputFile also reflects the stream-like characteristic of an input file.

The remaining method in this class toString is one we already referred to. It is the method that is implicitly called by the concatenation assignment operator in the toString method of WordLocations. The string that is created consists of a page and line number separated by a colon.

We are now ready to discuss the fourth and final class of this program—the one that contains main. The code for this class, named IndexMain, is shown in Listing 10.7.

LISTING 10.7 The Class Containing main for the Word Index Application (found on the CD-ROM at chapter10\IndexMain.java.)

```
1   package chapter10;
2
3   import common.*;
4
5   public class IndexMain
6   {
7       public static void main(String[] args)
8       {
9           String word;
10          WordLocations wordLocations;
11          WordIndex index = new WordIndex("input.txt");
12
13          while (true)
14          {
15              word = InputOutput.getString(
16                  "Enter a word, empty string to quit: ");
17              if (word.equals(""))
18                  break;
19              wordLocations = index.find(word);
20              if (wordLocations == null)
21                  InputOutput.putString(word +
22                      " is not in the index");
23              else
24                  InputOutput.putString(wordLocations.toString());
25          }
26      }
27  }
```

The main method contains the WordIndex object index, which is declared and instantiated on line 11. Once the index is created, the user is permitted to make inquires about the locations of any number of words. Once the user supplies a word, it is passed to the method `find` of the `WordIndex` class. If the word is in the index, the word and its locations are displayed on line 24 using a call to the `toString` method of `WordIndex`.

Now that we have examined each of the four classes of this program, let's consider the UML diagram that shows the relationships between the four classes. Figure 10.3 contains that UML diagram.

Notice the two levels of compositional relationships that we discussed earlier.

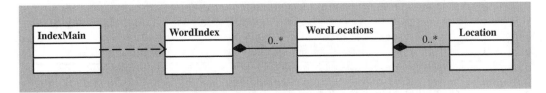

FIGURE 10.3   The UML diagram for the word index program.

CLASS VARIABLES

There is one additional topic we have included in this chapter—class variables. Although not directly related to the central topic for this chapter—compositional relationships—it is a topic that we need for one primary example in this chapter. As early as Chapter 2, we discussed calling class methods. In Chapter 5, when we wrote our first applications, we introduced writing class methods. In Chapter 7, we discussed class constants. Because we have saved the topic of class variables until now, you could properly infer that they are less often necessary. By now the syntax that distinguishes a class variable from an instance variable should come as no surprise. Like class methods and constants, class variables are specified by including the reserved word `static` in their declaration.

Just as with class constants, what makes a class variable different from an instance variable is that there is only one per class—not one per object. Consequently, the lifetime of class variables is the lifetime of the class.

Initializing Class Variables

When we initialize an instance variable in its declaration, that initialization is performed each time any constructor of that class is executed. Similarly, when we initialize any class variables, that initialization occurs when the class is created. There are certain kinds of initialization for objects, however, that must be done in the constructor. A similar need exists for initialization that must be performed when the class is created, but cannot be accomplished through the initialization of class constants. To fulfill that need, Java provides a special syntax known as a *static initializer*. What might be more descriptive would have been to call ordinary constructors object or instance constructors and to call static initializers class constructors. The syntax for a static initializer is shown in Syntax Definition 10.1.

Syntax Definition 10.1 Syntax of a `static` Initializer.

```
static_initializer

    static
        block
```

Recall that a block is a compound statement that can contain declarations. Another way to look at this syntax is that it is like a method without a signature. In place of the signature is the reserved word static. These static initializers are placed inside a class, just like any method. The example that we examine shortly will help clarify the placement of these initializers.

Importing Class Data and Methods

There is one final bit of syntax that we introduce at this juncture, which relates, not to class variables, but to class constants. We have been referring to class constants in the predefined classes, like Math, since Chapter 2, but there is one feature that we have not yet mentioned. It is one of the language features added in the latest version of Java, 5.0. It allows class constants to be imported using a syntax similar to the one used for importing the classes contained in a package. The syntax for this statement is shown in Syntax Definition 10.2.

Syntax Definition 10.2 Syntax of an import `static` Statement.

```
import_static_statement

    import static   name;
```

This statement is placed before the class definition, similar to the regular import statement. There are two differences, however. The first difference is the obvious addition of the reserved word static after import. The other difference is the kind of name that is used. With the regular import statement, the name specified is a qualified class name, possibly using the wildcard symbol (*) —in that case, importing every class in the package. With the static import statement, the name is a qualified name of class constants, variables, or methods—again with possible use of a wildcard—in that case, importing every class data name and method name in the class.

Perfect Squares as the Sum of Consecutive Triangle Numbers

To illustrate the use of class constants, static initializers, and the statement that imports static names, we have chosen an example that illustrates a curious property of number theory. The property is that every perfect square can be computed as the sum of two consecutive triangular numbers.

The sequence of triangular numbers is the sequence whose nth term is the sum of the first n integers. If we represent the nth term as $\Delta(n)$, the sequence can be defined using a summation, as Equation 10.1 illustrates.

$$\Delta(n) = \sum_{i=1}^{n} i \tag{10.1}$$

The reason this sequence of numbers is referred to as the sequence of triangular numbers is because this sequence appears along the right side of the triangle of integers as, illustrated in Figure 10.4. The numbers in bold face, 1 3 6 10 15 21, are the first six terms of the sequence.

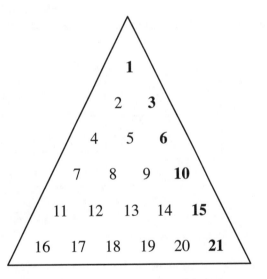

FIGURE 10.4 The triangular number sequence.

The property of number theory illustrated by our program is that every perfect square can be computed as the sum of two consecutive triangular numbers, which is expressed in Equation 10.2.

$$n^2 = \Delta(n-1) + \Delta(n) \qquad (10.2)$$

This property is not difficult to establish algebraically once we know the solution to the summation shown in Equation 10.3.

$$\sum_{i=1}^{n} i = \frac{n(n+1)}{2} \qquad (10.3)$$

The proof of Equation 10.3 is one of the most frequent applications demonstrating the proof technique of mathematical induction. We refer you to any textbook on discrete mathematics if you are unfamiliar with it. Once we have the closed form solution of the summation defining triangular numbers, it is easy to see that Equation 10.2 is true. Equation 10.4 contains the algebraic proof.

$$\Delta(n-1) + \Delta(n) = \frac{(n-1)n}{2} + \frac{n(n+1)}{2} = \frac{n^2 - n + n^2 + n}{2} = \frac{2n^2}{2} = n^2 \qquad (10.4)$$

This fact can also be demonstrated geometrically. In Figure 10.5, we illustrate how 3^2 can be computed as the sum of the second and third triangular numbers.

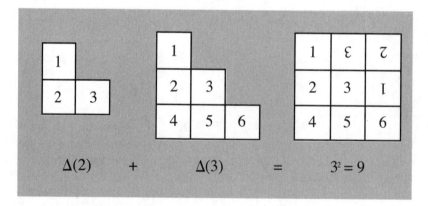

$$\Delta(2) \qquad + \qquad \Delta(3) \qquad = \qquad 3^2 = 9$$

FIGURE 10.5   Geometric illustration that $3^2 = \Delta(2) + \Delta(3)$.

There is one more geometric property that we need to discuss before we present the code for this example. If we draw an n-sided polygon and connect every pair of its vertices with a line segment, the drawing contains $\Delta(n-1)$ line segments. A triangle has three sides, which is $\Delta(3-1) = 3$. A quadrilateral has six sides, which is $\Delta(4-1) = 6$. This property is not hard to see. Starting with the first vertex, there are $n-1$ line segments emanating from it. To avoid counting the same segments twice remove that vertex from consideration and move on to the next. There are $n-2$ line segments emanating from it. Continue until you reach the second to the last vertex, where there is only one segment emanating from it. Clearly the sum of all line segments is the sum of the integers from 1 to $n-1$, which is $\Delta(n-1)$. Figure 10.6 illustrates this fact for a square.

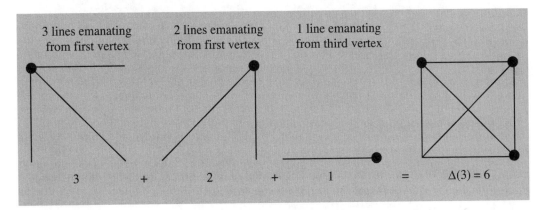

FIGURE 10.6 A square has six line segments connecting every pair of vertices.

We now have everything necessary to explain the behavior of our example program. This program will prompt the user for a number between 2 and 21 and then show how the square of that number can be computed as the sum of two consecutive triangular numbers by illustrating each triangular number as a number of line segments connecting the vertices of regular polygons. We have chosen regular polygons for simplicity and because they generate attractive visual patterns. Figure 10.7 illustrates the output of this program when the number 11 is input.

Notice that the output illustrated in Figure 10.7 shows a 10-sided polygon with 55 connecting line segments and an 11-sided polygon with 66 connecting line segments. The sum $55 + 66 = 121$ is 11^2.

Next, we consider the component classes of this program. The first of those classes, shown in Listing 10.8, is a class named `RegularPolygon`.

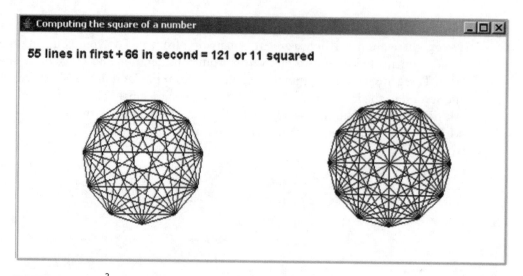

FIGURE 10.7 11^2 computed as the sum of 55 and 66.

LISTING 10.8 A Class that Draws Regular Polygons and their Connecting Lines (found
ON THE CD on the CD-ROM at chapter10\RegularPolygon.java.)

```
1   package chapter10;
2
3   import java.awt.*;
4   import static java.lang.Math.*;
5   import common.*;
6
7   public class RegularPolygon
8   {
9       private static int[] triangular = new int[50];
10      protected int[] x, y;
11      protected int numberOfSides;
12
13      static
14      {
15          int value = 1;
16
17          triangular[1] = value++;
18          for (int i = 2; i < triangular.length; i++)
19              triangular[i] = triangular[i - 1] + value++;
20      }
21      public RegularPolygon(int numberOfSides, int xCenter,
22          int yCenter, int radius)
```

```
23      {
24          double theta = 2 * PI / numberOfSides;
25
26          this.numberOfSides = numberOfSides;
27          x = new int[numberOfSides + 1];
28          y = new int[numberOfSides + 1];
29          for (int vertex = 0; vertex <= numberOfSides; vertex++)
30              {
31                  x[vertex] = Geometry.computeX(xCenter, radius,
32                      PI / 2 + theta * vertex);
33                  y[vertex] = Geometry.computeY(yCenter, radius,
34                      PI / 2 + theta * vertex);
35              }
36      }
37      public static int computeNumberOfLines(int numberOfSides)
38      {
39          if (numberOfSides <= triangular.length)
40              return triangular[numberOfSides - 1];
41          return (numberOfSides * (numberOfSides - 1)) / 2;
42      }
43      public void paintPolygon(Graphics graphics)
44      {
45          graphics.drawPolygon(x, y, numberOfSides);
46      }
47      public void paintStar(Graphics graphics)
48      {
49          int fromX, fromY, toX, toY;
50
51          for (int from = 0; from < numberOfSides; from++)
52              for (int to = from + 2; to < numberOfSides; to++)
53                  if (from != (to + 1) % numberOfSides)
54                      graphics.drawLine(x[from], y[from], x[to],
55                          y[to]);
56      }
57  }
```

Our first observation is about the use of the import static statement on line 4. Notice the name that follows it: java.lang.Math.*. What we are importing here is all the data and method names inside the class Math, not all the classes inside a package, which is what we import with the regular import statement. We can refer to the constant π as PI, rather than Math.PI, which we do on line 24. Although we do not do so in this class, if we needed to call the sine method, we could use sin rather than Math.sin.

Another new Java feature that this example is intended to illustrate is the use of a class variable. The class variable is the array `triangular` declared and instantiated on line 9. Although we can instantiate it in its declaration, aside from using an array constant with 50 values, we cannot initialize it. The other data defined in this class are three instance variables. The arrays x and y, which are declared on line 10, contain the coordinates of the vertices of the polygon. The instance variable `numberOf-Sides` contains exactly what its name suggests. Notice, also, that we have used the access modifier `protected` on all three variables. In Chapter 12, we plan to extend this class and expect to need to be able to access these variables.

Next, let's examine the static initializer contained in this class—another Java feature that we designed this example to illustrate. We have adopted the convention of placing static initializers before the constructors. This is just a convention because it can be placed anywhere in the class. Since we have encouraged you to view it as a "class constructor," it seems reasonable to place it with the "object constructors." The purpose of this static initializer is to initialize the class variable `tri-angular`. It performs this initialization by making use of another feature of triangular numbers, which is that each can be computed using the previous one to avoid having to recalculate the sum each time. The property that we are using is expressed by Equation 10.5.

$$\Delta(n) = \Delta(n - 1) + n, \text{ if } n > 1 \tag{10.5}$$

The assignment on line 19 makes use of this property. Definitions of these kinds are referred to as *recursive* definitions since the definition makes use of itself. We will return to this recursive definition in Chapter 15. Because it refers to the previous value, clearly this equation cannot hold for when n is 1. Consequently, we need to initialize the first element separately on line 17. We leave position 0 of the array unused.

This class has one constructor, whose signature is defined on lines 21 and 22. The client supplies the coordinates of the center point, the radius, and number of sides as parameters. From that information, the coordinates of the vertices are computed using the `computeX` and `computeY` methods of the `Geometry` class that we have used frequently before. For an n-sided regular polygon, the vertices are points on a circle with an angular separation of $\frac{2\pi}{n}$, which the variable `theta`, initialized on line 24, represents.

The class method `computeNumberOfLines` returns the number of connecting line segments in a polygon with the number of sides supplied as a parameter. We have already pointed out that this value is a triangular number, so it accesses the array `triangular`, provided the parameter contains a value that is a valid subscript of the array. Otherwise, on line 41, it computes the triangular number using the formula in Equation 10.3. Saving the values in the array saves us this calculation, which, admittedly, is not very big. Our primary motivation for including the class variable and static initializer was to illustrate these features.

The final two methods in this class, paintPolygon and paintStar, paint the line segments. We have separated them into two methods to enhance the reusability of this class. In Chapter 12, we will want to draw only the polygon itself. The method paintPolygon uses the method in the Graphics class drawPolygon. This overloaded version of drawPolygon accepts the two arrays containing the *x* and *y* coordinates and a third parameter containing the number of sides. The method paintStar draws the line segments individually, using a nested loop to ensure that each vertex is connected to every other one. To avoid drawing each one twice, the inner loop control variable to begins at from + 2 instead of 0. To avoid duplicating the lines that form the polygon, we have included the if statement on line 53 to exclude adjacent vertices. Notice the use of modular arithmetic to make the first and last vertices adjacent.

Now we are ready to consider the second class required for this program. It is a class that defines a window onto which a collection of regular polygons can be drawn. The code for this class, named PolygonNTuple, is shown in Listing 10.9.

LISTING 10.9 A Class Defining a Window Containing a Collection of Regular Polygons (found on the CD-ROM at chapter10\PolygonNTuple.java.)

ON THE CD

```
1  package chapter10;
2
3  import java.awt.*;
4  import common.*;
5
6  public class PolygonNTuple extends Application
7  {
8      private static final int HEIGHT = 300, X_CENTER = WIDTH / 2,
9          MESSAGE_X = 10, MESSAGE_Y = 30, RADIUS = 75;
10     private int numberOfSides;
11     private String message;
12     private RegularPolygon[] polygons;
13
14     public PolygonNTuple(String title, String message,
15         int[] numberOfSides)
16     {
17         super(title, WIDTH * numberOfSides.length, HEIGHT);
18         this.message = message;
19         polygons = new RegularPolygon[numberOfSides.length];
20         for (int polygon = 0; polygon < polygons.length; polygon++)
21             polygons[polygon] = new RegularPolygon(
22                 numberOfSides[polygon], X_CENTER + WIDTH * polygon,
23                 HEIGHT / 2, RADIUS);
24     }
25     public void paintComponent(Graphics graphics)
26     {
```

```
27              super.paintComponent(graphics);
28              setBackground(Color.WHITE);
29              for (RegularPolygon polygon : polygons)
30              {
31                  polygon.paintStar(graphics);
32                  polygon.paintPolygon(graphics);
33              }
34              graphics.setFont(new Font("Sans Serif", Font.BOLD, 14));
35              graphics.drawString(message, MESSAGE_X, MESSAGE_Y);
36          }
37      }
```

You should not find much in this class that is unfamiliar, so we will confine our remarks to a few key points. The constructor for this class creates the polygons specified by the information contained in the parameters. The array numberOfSides contains the number of sides for each polygon that is to be created. The length of that array specifies the number of polygons. These polygons are arranged horizontally in the window and stored in the instance variable polygons of type RegularPolygon.

Finally the method paintComponent paints each of the polygons by making calls to the methods paintStar and paintPolygon of the RegularPolygon class that we just discussed. It also displays the message that was supplied initially to the constructor that is contained in the instance variable message. Also notice the instantiation of the anonymous font object on line 34 that is passed to the setFont method of the Graphics class. This is our first encounter with the predefined class Font, which is defined in the package java.awt. When creating a font object, we must specify the name of the font, whether it is plain, bold, or italic and its point size.

To complete this program, since it is an application, we need a class that contains main. The code for that class, PolygonMain, is shown in Listing 10.10.

LISTING 10.10   The Class Containing main for the Computing Square Application (found on the CD-ROM at chapter10\PolygonMain.java.)

```
1  package chapter10;
2
3  import common.*;
4
5  public class PolygonMain
6  {
7      public static void main(String[] args)
8      {
9          final int MIN_VALUE = 2, MAX_VALUE = 21;
10         int number, totalLines = 0;
```

```
11          int[] sides = new int[2], lines = new int[sides.length];
12          String message;
13          PolygonNTuple polygonNTuple;
14
15          number = InputOutput.getInteger("Enter number to square ",
16              MIN_VALUE, MAX_VALUE);
17          sides[0] = number;
18          sides[1] = number + 1;
19          for (int polygon = 0; polygon < sides.length; polygon++)
20          {
21              lines[polygon] =
22                  RegularPolygon.computeNumberOfLines (sides[polygon]);
23              totalLines += lines[polygon];
24          }
25          message = "" + lines[0] + " lines in first + " + lines[1] +
26              " in second = " + totalLines + " or " + number +
27              " squared";
28          polygonNTuple = new PolygonNTuple(
29              "Computing the square of a number",    message, sides);
30          polygonNTuple.display();
31      }
32  }
```

An overall explanation for this class should suffice, as it contains no new features. It obtains the number to be squared from the user, and the two polygons are created in the for loop that spans lines 19-24. Finally the window polygonNTuple is created and displayed on lines 28-30.

We conclude this example with a UML diagram, shown in Figure 10.8. Notice that there is a compositional relationship between PolygonNTuple and RegularPolygon.

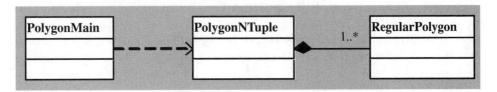

FIGURE 10.8   UML diagram of the program that computes the square of a number.

TILED WINDOW APPLICATION

As always, our final example of this chapter is one that involves drawing some graphic images. The example we have chosen draws a tiled image on a window. The window contains three large tiles, which are composed of four smaller tiles of another kind. Each of those smaller tiles contains four smaller tiles of yet another kind. Clearly, we have designed this example to illustrate several levels of composition. The smallest tiles are numbered consecutively, giving us an opportunity to use the other main topic of this chapter—class variables. Figure 10.9 contains the tiled window drawn by this program.

FIGURE 10.9 Output of the tiled window application.

In presenting the five classes that comprise this program, we have elected to begin with the most elementary class—the one that is not composed of objects of any of the other classes. It is the class named SquareWithDiamond, which creates objects that are the smallest tiles. Listing 10.11 contains the code for this class.

LISTING 10.11 The Class that Draws Numbered Tiles Containing Diamonds Inside
ON THE CD Squares (found on the CD-ROM at chapter10\SquareWithDiamond.java.)

```
1   package chapter10;
2
3   import java.awt.*;
4
5   class SquareWithDiamond
6   {
7       private static int nextSquareNumber = 1;
8       private int left, top, size, squareNumber;
9       private boolean isWhite;
```

```
10      private Polygon diamond = new Polygon();
11
12      public SquareWithDiamond(int left, int top, int size,
13          boolean isWhite)
14      {
15          this.left = left;
16          this.top = top;
17          this.size = size;
18          this.isWhite = isWhite;
19          squareNumber = nextSquareNumber++;
20          diamond.addPoint(left + size / 2, top);
21          diamond.addPoint(left, top + size / 2);
22          diamond.addPoint(left + size /2, top + size);
23          diamond.addPoint(left + size, top + size / 2);
24          diamond.addPoint(left + size / 2, top);
25      }
26      public void draw(Graphics graphics)
27      {
28          Color squareColor = Color.WHITE,
29              diamondColor = Color.BLACK;
30
31          if (!isWhite)
32          {
33              squareColor = Color.BLACK;
34              diamondColor = Color.WHITE;
35          }
36          graphics.setColor(squareColor);
37          graphics.fillRect(left, top, size, size);
38          graphics.setColor(diamondColor);
39          graphics.fillPolygon(diamond);
40          graphics.drawRect(left, top, size, size);
41          graphics.setColor(squareColor);
42          graphics.drawString("" + squareNumber,
43              left + size / 3, top + 2 * size / 3);
44      }
45  }
```

The objects of this class are squares that contain diamonds inside them. The location and size of the squares is provided to the constructor, together with whether the square is black or white. The diamond color is the opposite of the square color. A square number is drawn inside the diamond. The squares are numbered consecutively as they are created. The class variable, named nextSquareNumber, contains the number of the next square to be created. It is initialized in its declaration on line 7 and incremented after it is copied to the instance variable `squareNumber` on line 19.

The next larger tiles are ones that contain a circle pattern. Inscribed inside that circle are four squares containing diamonds, which are objects of the class that we just discussed. The code for the class that creates the circle tiles is named `Circle-WithSquares`. Its code is shown in Listing 10.12.

LISTING 10.12   The Class that Draws Tiles Containing a Circle with Four Inscribed

ON THE CD   Squares (found on the CD-ROM at `chapter10\CircleWithSquares.java`.)

```
1   package chapter10;
2
3   import java.awt.*;
4   import static java.lang.Math.*;
5
6   class CircleWithSquares
7   {
8       private static final int COUNT = 2;
9       private int left,top, diameter;
10      private boolean isWhite;
11      private SquareWithDiamond squares[] =
12          new SquareWithDiamond[COUNT * COUNT];
13
14      public CircleWithSquares(int left, int top, int diameter,
15          boolean isWhite)
16      {
17          int x, y;
18          int newSize = (int)(sqrt(pow(diameter / 2, 2) / 2) + .5);
19          int inset = diameter / 2 - newSize;
20
21          this.left = left;
22          this.top = top;
23          this.diameter = diameter;
24          this.isWhite = isWhite;
25          for (int i = 0; i < squares.length; i++)
26          {
27              x = left + inset + (i / COUNT) * newSize;
28              y = top + inset + (i % COUNT) * newSize;
29              squares[i] = new SquareWithDiamond(x, y, newSize,
30                  i / 2 == i % 2);
31          }
32      }
33      public void draw(Graphics graphics)
34      {
```

```
35          if (isWhite)
36              graphics.setColor(Color.WHITE);
37          else
38              graphics.setColor(Color.BLACK);
39          graphics.fillOval(left, top, diameter, diameter);
40          graphics.drawRect(left, top, diameter, diameter);
41          for (SquareWithDiamond square: squares)
42                  square.draw(graphics);
43      }
44  }
```

In keeping with our desire to illustrate each of the new concepts introduced in each chapter in the final example, we have used the import static statement on line 4. Consequently, the references to the methods sqrt and pow, on line 18, require no qualification.

Now let's consider instance data defined in this class. The four squares inside these tiles are defined by the array squares, declared on line 11. The constructor of this class calculates the size of the inside squares on line 18 and creates these squares in the for loop that spans lines 25-31. Notice that the expression on line 30, which defines the color, alternates between black and white. The draw method of this class calls the draw method of the SquareWithDiamond class for each square on lines 41-42.

Next we consider the largest tiles—ones that draw squares that contain four tiles with circles. Listing 10.13 contains the code for this class, which is named SquareWithCircles.

LISTING 10.13 The Class that Draws Tiles Containing Squares with Four Inscribed
ON THE CD Circles (found on the CD-ROM at chapter10\SquareWithCircles.java.)

```
1  package chapter10;
2
3  import java.awt.*;
4
5  class SquareWithCircles
6  {
7      private static final int COUNT = 2;
8      private CircleWithSquares circles[] =
9          new CircleWithSquares[COUNT * COUNT];
10     private int left, top, size;
11     private boolean isWhite;
12
13     public SquareWithCircles(int left, int top,
14         int size, boolean isWhite)
15     {
```

```
16            int x, y, newSize = size / COUNT;
17
18            this.left = left;
19            this.top = top;
20            this.size = size;
21            this.isWhite = isWhite;
22            for (int i = 0; i < circles.length; i++)
23            {
24                x = left + (i / COUNT) * newSize;
25                y = top + (i % COUNT) * newSize;
26                circles[i] = new CircleWithSquares(x, y, newSize,
27                    !isWhite);
28            }
29        }
30        public void draw(Graphics graphics)
31        {
32            if (isWhite)
33                graphics.setColor(Color.WHITE);
34            else
35                graphics.setColor(Color.BLACK);
36            graphics.fillRect(left, top, size, size);
37            for (CircleWithSquares circle: circles)
38                circle.draw(graphics);
39        }
40  }
```

The instance array `circles` defines these four circles, which are created in the `for` loop in the constructor spanning lines 22-28 and drawn by the loop in the method `draw` on lines 37 and 38.

There is one final level of composition. The window contains three objects of the class `SquareWithCircles` that we just examined. The code for the class that defines the window, named `TiledWindow`, is shown in Listing 10.14.

LISTING 10.14 The Class that Defines the Window Containing Tiles (found on the CD-ROM at `chapter10\TiledWindow.java`.)

```
1  package chapter10;
2
3  import java.awt.*;
4  import common.*;
5
6  class TiledWindow extends GraphicsApplication
7  {
```

```
8        private static final int BORDER = 25,SIZE = 200, TILES = 3,
9            WINDOW = new TiledWindow(SIZE, TILES).display();
10       private SquareWithCircles squares[];
11
12       public TiledWindow(int size, int count)
13       {
14           super("Tiled Window", SIZE * TILES, SIZE + BORDER);
15           squares = new SquareWithCircles[TILES];
16           for (int i = 0; i < squares.length; i++)
17               squares[i] = new SquareWithCircles
18                   (size * i, 0, size, i % 2 == 0);
19       }
20       public void paintComponent(Graphics graphics)
21       {
22           super.paintComponent(graphics);
23           for (SquareWithCircles square: squares)
24               square.draw(graphics);
25       }
26 }
```

As before, the component objects are defined with an instance variable—the array squares—whose elements are created in the constructor on lines 16-18 and drawn in the method paintComponent on lines 23 and 24.

We chose an example with several layers of composition to emphasize the fundamental behavior of the methods of such classes. In this program, the class Tiled-Window contains objects of SquaresWithCircles, which, in turn, contains objects of CircleWithSquares, which, finally, contains objects of the class SquareWithDiamond. So, you should notice that the constructor of the class TiledWindow calls the constructor of SquareWithCircles, which calls the constructor of CircleWithSquares, which, in turn, calls the constructor of SquareWithDiamond. Similarly, the paintComponent method of TiledWindow calls the draw method of SquareWithCircles, which calls the draw method of CircleWithSquares, which, in turn, calls the draw method of SquareWithDiamond. Because the instance variables of each class are private, the methods of each class must rely on the corresponding methods of their component classes to accomplish their task.

Finally, let's examine the UML diagram for this program, which is shown in Figure 10.10.

Notice how the UML diagram illustrates the several layers of composition in this program.

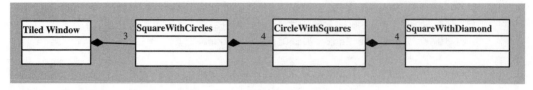

FIGURE 10.10   UML diagram of the tiled window application.

SUMMARY

In this chapter, we examined composition relationships between classes and how to represent such relationships with UML notation. We also discussed class variables and static initializers that can be used to initialize them. The key points to remember from this chapter are as follows:

- Composition relationships exist when one object is a component of another object.
- When the *has a* predicate defines the relationship between objects, a composition relationship is indicated.
- The UML symbol that designates a composition relationship is the solid diamond.
- Multiplicity markers are used in UML diagrams to indicate the number of component objects contained in a class.
- There is only one copy of every class variable for each class.
- Class variables can be initialized in their declarations for simple initializations. Static initializers can be used for more complicated initializations.
- Static imports allow the class names to be omitted from class constants, variables, and methods.

Review Questions

1. How are composition relationships implemented?
2. Is composition a directed or undirected relationship?
3. Describe the behavior of the constructors of two classes when a composition relationship exists between them.
4. What alternate predicate beside *has a* should be used to confirm that a relationship between two objects is composition?
5. What reserved word is used to distinguish class variables from instance variables?
6. In what situations is it appropriate to use a class variable?
7. If a class variable is initialized in its declaration, when is that initialization performed?
8. When are static initializers executed?

9. What is the effect of using static imports?

10. What follows the reserved words `import static`?

Programming Exercises

11. Indicate whether each of the following is an appropriate or inappropriate use of composition:

    a. Car composed of a vehicle

    b. Person composed of hands

    c. Fruit composed of oranges

    d. House composed of windows

12. Define a class called `Sentence` that consists of an array list of strings that represent the words in the sentence. Include a constructor and a method that returns the number of words in the sentence.

13. Define a class called `Paragraph` that consists of an array list of strings of type `Sentence`, defined in the previous exercise, that represent the sentences in the paragraph. Include a constructor and a method that returns the number of words in the paragraph.

14. Define a class called `Chapter` that consists of an array list of type `Paragraph`, defined in the previous exercise. Include a constructor and a method that returns the number of words in the chapter.

15. Define a class called `Point` that contains the integer coordinates of a point. Include a constructor and a method named `draw` that draws the point as a solid circle three pixels in diameter centered at that point.

16. Define a class called `Line` that consists of two objects of type `Point`, defined in the previous exercise. Include a constructor and a method named `draw` that draws the line segment and both of the endpoints.

17. Define a class called `LineDrawing` that consists of an array list of objects of type `Line`, defined in the previous exercise. Include a constructor and a method named `draw` that draws the all of the line segments and their endpoints.

18. Write a class called `NumberedObject` that assigns a consecutive number to each object created. Initialize the class variable that you use to 1 in its declaration.

19. Add an instance method to the class `NumberedObject`, defined in the previous exercise, that returns the number of the object and a class method that returns the number of the last created object.

20. Modify the class `NumberedObject` defined in Programming Exercise 18 so that the class variable is initialized by a static initializer.

Programming Projects

21. Write a program that reads in a file using the InputFile class. It should build a Chapter object from the file, as defined by Programming Exercise 14, by breaking the file into Paragraph and Word objects using the StringTokenizer class. Assume that words are delimited by spaces and sentences by periods. Once the file has been converted to a Chapter object, display the total number of words in the chapter.

22. Write a program that reads in the definition of a LineDrawing object, as defined in Programming Exercise 17, using the InputFile class. Each line of the file should contain the coordinates of the endpoints of a line. After the file is read in, draw the lines in a window.

23. Modify the program for the previous project so that each Point object contains a NumberedObject, as defined in Programming Exercise 18. When the line drawing is drawn, each point should be labeled with its number.

24. Make the following modifications to the document index program:

    a. Modify the Location class so that it is an immutable class.

    b. Include all acronyms in the index.

    c. If the same word appears twice on the same line, include it only once in the index.

25. Modify the tiled window program discussed in this chapter so that the CircleWithSquares objects are numbered, instead of the SquareWithDiamond objects. Place the number at the top of the circle above the square.

11

Exceptions and Input/Output

In this chapter

- Catching Exceptions
- File Input/Output
- Defining and Throwing Exceptions
- Command-line Input/Output
- Other Input/Output Topics
- Graphics Serialization Example

CATCHING EXCEPTIONS

During the execution of any program, error conditions can arise that cannot be detected when the program is compiled. If a program does not handle such error conditions when they occur, the program is often said to *crash*. This issue is of prime importance in so-called embedded software that controls whatever it is embedded in. When such software controls a spacecraft or an aircraft, allowing the program to terminate in such situations with an error message, "System error, please reboot," is unacceptable. Ada, a programming language that was designed specifically for such embedded systems, was one of the first popular languages to include syntax to make recovery from such error conditions easier.

The reason a special language mechanism is helpful is that the place in a program where such an error condition is detected may be far from where the recovery can be done. Without special syntax, it becomes necessary to have each method return an error status and every method call check the error status returned. In programs that have the potential for many such errors, the error checking code can quickly begin to obscure the primary code. The special syntax that Ada introduced, and that Java and many other languages have adopted, is the syntax of exceptions. An *exception* is an error condition that is defined with this special syntax. In Java, classes are used to define exception types. When an exceptional condition occurs, we say that the code that identifies the error condition *throws* an exception. If is possible to recover from this error condition, that recovery is done in another part of the program that *catches* the exception. We begin our discussion with catching predefined exceptions and will address throwing them later in this chapter.

Predefined Exceptions

We have already discussed some situations that can give rise to such exceptions, so let's review some of them. One of the first examples that we encountered was the possibility of an error in arithmetic calculations. Division by zero is the simplest example. Because the compiler cannot determine the value in variables at compile time, such errors can only be detected as the program runs. Arithmetic errors, such as division by zero, cause the exception `ArithmeticException` to be thrown.

Another example involves array subscripts. Because array subscripts can contain variables, it is impossible for the compiler to check whether the value of such subscripts will always be within the bounds of the array. When a subscripted array contains a subscript out-of-bounds, an exception named `ArrayIndexOutOfBounds Exception` occurs.

Another frequent source of errors at runtime occurs if we attempt to dereference a null object reference. This situation occurs when we have neglected to instantiate an object for a declared object reference and then attempt to invoke a method on that reference. In that case, the exception `NullPointerException` is thrown. Notice Java's use of the term *pointer* here. It is being used as a synonym for reference. Although pointers and references are similar, we have been careful to always use the term reference. Some programming languages, like C++, have both pointers and references. In such languages, there is a difference between a pointer and a reference.

One other such exception that we will encounter in Chapter 12 is the `Class- CastException`, which is thrown when an object is cast to an improper class.

Checked and Unchecked Exceptions

Java exceptions fall into two categories—*checked* and *unchecked exceptions*. Checked exceptions are ones for which there is a reasonable expectation that recovery is possible. Unchecked exceptions are generally program errors that are unrecoverable and require a modification to the program to subsequently prevent. Although, in most cases, it is clear to which exception category an error condition should be assigned, there are certainly some cases where the programmer defining the exception must exercise judgment.

All the predefined exceptions that we mentioned in our introduction are unchecked exceptions. Recall that we mentioned that exception types are defined as classes. Specifically, they are classes that extend the predefined class `Throwable`. Unchecked exceptions are those exceptions that extend the predefined classes `Error` or `RuntimeException`. The class `Error` is intended for serious program errors. All the unchecked exceptions that we discussed earlier extend the class `RunTimeException`. Exceptions that extend neither `Error` nor `RuntimeException` are checked.

The significance of making an exception checked is that it must either be caught or designated as thrown by any method in which it may occur. Failure to do either results in a compilation error. We will examine shortly how each of these two possibilities is accomplished. By comparison, the compiler does no checking regarding unchecked exceptions.

The `try` Statement

To catch an exception, we need a statement that we have not yet discussed, which is the `try` statement. The syntax of the `try` statement is shown in Syntax Definition 11.1.

Syntax Definition 11.1 Syntax of a `try` Statement.

```
try_statement

    try
        block
    catch ( ExceptionClass exceptionObject )
        block
    ...
    catch ( ExceptionClass exceptionObject )
        block
    finally
        block
```

The syntax of this statement introduces three new reserved words: try, catch, and finally. The compound statement that follows the reserved word try is executed first. It contains the code that may cause an exception to be thrown. If no exception is thrown during the execution of that block, all the catch blocks are skipped. Notice that a try statement can contain one or more catch blocks.

Each catch block specifies the type of exception it catches and the name of the exception object that is caught. Every catch block catches exception objects of the class specified or objects of any class that extend that class. If an exception is thrown during the execution of the try block, the first catch block that can catch the exception will be executed. If a class and another class that extends it are both specified in catch blocks, the extended class must be listed first. For example, if we had two catch blocks—one for ArithmeticException and one for RunTimeException— the catch block for ArithmeticException would have to appear first. In this case, the first block would catch arithmetic exceptions and the second one would catch any other runtime exceptions. If an exception is thrown that cannot be caught by any of the catch blocks, the exception is propagated. We will discuss exception propagation shortly.

The finally block is optional, which recall is conveyed in the syntax definition by coloring it gray. The finally block is executed regardless of whether an exception is thrown. It is even executed when the last line of try block is a return or break statement or when an exception must be propagated. The finally block is typically used to free any resource acquired in the try block. We will see an example of the use of the finally block later in this chapter when we discuss file I/O.

Converting Strings to Integers

Until now, we have most often relied upon the method getInteger to convert strings containing numbers to their integer values. In Chapter 9, for the first time, we needed to parse the input and perform the conversion ourselves. In that case, we wrote a method stringToInt to perform that conversion. In that program, we checked to be sure that the string we passed to that method contained only numeric digits. Java has a predefined method for converting strings containing integers to their numeric values. That method is parseInt, which is a class method in the wrapper class Integer. Unlike our stringToInt method, it makes no assumptions about what kind of characters the supplied string contains. Consequently, this method throws the exception NumberFormatException if the string provided is not in the proper format for an integer. This exception is a checked exception. Let's consider a simple program that calls parseInt. This program allows the user to repeatedly enter simple formulas that contain two integers separated by an operator. Spaces must separate the operator from the operands. This program is shown in Listing 11.1.

LISTING 11.1 Program to Evaluate Simple Formulas (found on the CD-ROM at *ON THE CD* chapter11\Calculator1.java.)

```
1  package chapter11;
2
```

```
3   import java.util.*;
4   import common.*;
5
6   public class Calculator1
7   {
8       public static void main(String[] args)
9       {
10          Integer result;
11          String formula;
12          StringTokenizer tokenizer;
13
14          while (true)
15          {
16              formula = InputOutput.getString("Enter a formula: ");
17              if (formula.equals(""))
18                  break;
19              tokenizer = new StringTokenizer(formula);
20              if (tokenizer.countTokens() != 3 ||
21                  (result = evaluate(tokenizer)) == null)
22                  InputOutput.putString("Invalid Syntax");
23              else
24                  InputOutput.putString("value = " + result);
25          }
26      }
27      private static Integer evaluate(StringTokenizer tokenizer)
28      {
29          String leftString = tokenizer.nextToken(),
30              operation = tokenizer.nextToken(),
31              rightString = tokenizer.nextToken();
32          int leftValue, rightValue;
33
34          try
35          {
36              leftValue = Integer.parseInt(leftString);
37              rightValue = Integer.parseInt(rightString);
38          }
39          catch (NumberFormatException exception)
40          {
41              return null;
42          }
43          switch (operation.charAt(0))
44          {
45              case '+':
46                  return leftValue + rightValue;
```

```
47              case '-':
48                  return leftValue - rightValue;
49              case '*':
50                  return leftValue * rightValue;
51              case '/':
52                  return leftValue / rightValue;
53              default:
54                  return null;
55          }
56      }
57  }
```

This program repeatedly allows the user to enter formulas until any empty string is entered, which is apparent from the check made on line 17. Once a string is entered, we break it into the three required tokens using the StringTokenizer class. In this case, we specified no delimiters, so whitespace is taken to be the delimiter. Because we require whitespace on both sides of the operator, there must be exactly three tokens, which we verify by calling the method countTokens on line 20. Although we have not used this method before, its name makes clear its purpose, which is to report how many tokens remain. The condition in the if statement on lines 20 and 21 warrants some comment. Remember that the logical operator || short circuits when the first operand is true. Consequently, if the formula does not contain exactly three tokens, the method evaluate is never called. The other noteworthy aspect of the if condition is that we have nested an assignment expression inside a logical condition. When the right operand of the || operator is evaluated, the method evaluate is called first, the value it returns is stored in result, and then result is compared with a sentinel null. Because assignment operators have low precedence, the assignment subexpression must be parenthesized to ensure the assignment is grouped first. The sentinel null returned by evaluate indicates a syntax error. We elected to have evaluate return an Integer rather than an int, so a sentinel value would be available.

Let's consider the method evaluate next, which is of great interest to our current discussion because it contains a try statement. After extracting the three tokens on lines 29-31, this method attempts to convert the first and third tokens to integers by calling parseInt. Because parseInt can throw the checked exception NumberFormat Exception, we nest the calls to parseInt in a try block that spans lines 35-38. If either of the two calls to parseInt throws that exception, the catch block that spans lines 40-42 is executed. Notice that we must specify not only the name of the exception class on line 39, but also the name of the exception object, which in this case we called exception. The scope of the exception object's name is the catch block. Often, as is the case in this catch block, the exception object's name is never referenced.

When the NumberFormatException is thrown, no evaluation is performed and evaluate returns the sentinel null, which indicates that a syntax error has occurred.

Designating Checked Exceptions as Not Caught

Earlier we mentioned that checked exceptions must either be caught or designated as thrown. Now that we have discussed how exceptions can be caught using a try statement, let's consider the alternative. There is a reserved word that we have not yet encountered that is needed to designate that a method does not catch a checked exception. That reserved word is throws. Although we just examined a program that used the parseInt method, we did not explicitly examine its signature. Because parseInt may throw the NumberFormatException and does not catch it, it must indicate that fact in its signature, which is shown below.

```
int parseInt(String s) throws NumberFormatException
```

Notice that the throws clause appears at the end of the method signature. It can consist of a list of exception names separated by commas.

Let's consider a variation on the simple calculator program that we examined earlier. It is not absolutely necessary to catch the number format exception in evaluate, because it must notify main of the error anyway. In the modified version shown in Listing 11.2, main, rather than evaluate, catches the exception.

LISTING 11.2 Modified Program to Evaluate Simple Formulas (found on the CD-ROM at
ON THE CD chapter11\Calculator2.java.)

```
1  package chapter11;
2
3  import java.util.*;
4  import common.*;
5
6  public class Calculator2
7  {
8      public static void main(String[] args)
9      {
10         Integer result;
11         String formula;
12         StringTokenizer tokenizer;
13
14         while (true)
15         {
16             formula = InputOutput.getString("Enter a formula: ");
17             if (formula.equals(""))
```

```
18                    break;
19                try
20                {
21                    tokenizer = new StringTokenizer(formula);
22                    if (tokenizer.countTokens() != 3 ||
23                        (result = evaluate(tokenizer)) == null)
24                        InputOutput.putString("Invalid Syntax");
25                    else
26                        InputOutput.putString("value = " + result);
27                }
28                catch (NumberFormatException exception)
29                {
30                    InputOutput.putString("Invalid Number Format");
31                }
32            }
33        }
34      private static Integer evaluate(StringTokenizer tokenizer)
35          throws NumberFormatException
36      {
37          String leftString = tokenizer.nextToken(),
38              operation = tokenizer.nextToken(),
39              rightString = tokenizer.nextToken();
40          int leftValue, rightValue;
41
42          leftValue = Integer.parseInt(leftString);
43          rightValue = Integer.parseInt(rightString);
44          switch (operation.charAt(0))
45          {
46          case '+':
47              return leftValue + rightValue;
48          case '-':
49              return leftValue - rightValue;
50          case '*':
51              return leftValue * rightValue;
52          case '/':
53              return leftValue / rightValue;
54          default:
55              return null;
56          }
57      }
58  }
```

Notice that the exception is now being caught by the `try` statement in `main` that spans lines 19-31. In this version of the program, a different error message is displayed for invalid numbers than for other syntax errors.

Another noteworthy observation is that it is not absolutely necessary to enclose only the statements that can throw the exception in the `try` block. In this case, it is only the call to `evaluate` that absolutely needs to be in the `try` block, but enclosing a large portion of the method is acceptable, which is what we do in this case.

Our primary purpose for creating this modified version is to illustrate the need for a `throws` clause when a method can throw a checked exception that it does not catch. Notice that, on line 35, we must now include that clause. Failure to include that clause results in a compilation error.

Exception Propagation

In our introduction to this discussion on exceptions, we used the term *exception propagation* to describe what happens when an exception is not caught by a method that throws it. The previous example illustrates this propagation. Because `parseInt` does not catch `NumberFormatException`, `evaluate` is examined to see whether it catches it. Because `evaluate` does not catch it, `main` is examined next. We see that `main` does catch it.

Having seen a specific example, let's now consider how the process proceeds in general. Although not used frequently, to fully understand exception propagation, we must begin with the possibility of nested `try` statements. If the innermost `try` statement does not catch an exception, any enclosing `try` statements must be examined from innermost to outermost. The first such `try` statement with a `catch` block matching the exception, assuming there is one, would be executed.

If the exception cannot be caught in the method in which it is thrown, the method that called it is checked at the point of the method call to see whether it can catch it. If the calling method cannot catch it, the method that called the calling method is checked, and so on. In Chapter 4, we introduced the structure chart diagram. As we mentioned then, UML diagrams have replaced such diagrams, but the structure chart is a diagram that is still helpful for understanding exception propagation. The propagation of exceptions means following the branch of the structure chart that leads to the root in search of a `catch` block that can catch the exception. If the root is reached without finding any such `catch` block, the program terminates.

In programs that do not involve any windows—excluding the windows created by the `InputOutput` class—the root of the structure chart is always the method `main`. In applets and applications that use the `Application` class, there may be more than one root. In that case, the structure chart is like a forest—a collection of trees, not just a single tree. In an applet, `init` might be at the root or `paint`. Regardless of what the method is at the top, if no method along the branch of calling methods can catch the exception, the program terminates.

Preconditions and Postconditions

Although it is a less common practice now, there was a period during which most introductory programming texts discussed preconditions and postconditions from the very beginning. These concepts have their origin in an advanced area of computer science that deals with proving that programs are correct. The preconditions and postconditions, written in formal mathematical logic, are taken to define the program meaning or requirements. Using formal proof techniques, proofs begin by assuming the precondition is true and show that after the program executes, the postcondition will be true.

When adopted by introductory texts, these pre- and postconditions became comments written in English. The postcondition for a method typically describes what a method does, which is certainly a good documentation style. Often there are no meaningful preconditions, however. But when preconditions do exist, what is better than stating a precondition as a comment is to enforce the precondition by using exceptions. When a precondition is stated, it really means that if this condition is not met, there is no guaranteed behavior for this program. When a significant precondition exists, the best practice is to throw an exception when the precondition is not met. We put this approach into practice when we discuss defining and throwing exceptions later in this chapter.

The `InputOutput` Class

Now that we understand how to catch exceptions, we can examine the code for the `InputOutput` class that we have been using since Chapter 4. Listing 11.3 contains that code.

LISTING 11.3   Our Predefined Package for Input and Output (found on the CD-ROM at
ON THE CD   common\InputOutput.java.)

```
 1 package common;
 2
 3 import java.awt.*;
 4 import java.util.*;
 5 import javax.swing.*;
 6
 7 public class InputOutput
 8 {
 9     public interface Validator
10     {
```

```
11          boolean validate(int value);
12      }
13
14      public static boolean getBoolean(String prompt)
15      {
16          int response;
17          response = JOptionPane.showConfirmDialog(null,prompt);
18          return response == JOptionPane.YES_OPTION;
19      }
20      public static char getCharacter(String prompt,
21          String validChars)
22      {
23          int selectedCharIndex = -1;
24          String inputString;
25          while (true)
26          {
27              inputString = JOptionPane.showInputDialog (prompt);
28              if (inputString.length() > 0)
29                  selectedCharIndex = validChars.indexOf
30                  (inputString.charAt(0));
31              if (selectedCharIndex < 0)
32                  JOptionPane.showMessageDialog(null,
33                  "Must Enter One Of The Following Characters "
34                  + validChars);
35              else
36                  return validChars.charAt (selectedCharIndex);
37          }
38      }
39      public static Color getColor(String prompt)
40      {
41          Color color = Color.WHITE;
42          color = JColorChooser.showDialog(null, prompt, color);
43          return color;
44      }
45      public static Enum getEnum(String prompt, Enum[] enums)
46      {
47          String[] choices = new String[enums.length];
48          int choice, i = 0;
49
50          for (Enum enumValue: enums)
51              choices[i++] = toTitleCase(enumValue.name());
52          choice= JOptionPane.showOptionDialog(null, prompt,
53              "Choice Selection", JOptionPane.DEFAULT_OPTION,
54              JOptionPane.QUESTION_MESSAGE, null, choices,
```

```
55                choices[0]);
56          return enums[choice];
57      }
58      public static int getInteger(String prompt)
59      {
60          int value;
61          String inputString;
62          while (true)
63          {
64              inputString = JOptionPane.showInputDialog (prompt);
65              try
66              {
67                  value = Integer.parseInt(inputString);
68              }
69              catch(NumberFormatException exception)
70              {
71                  JOptionPane.showMessageDialog(null,
72                      "You Must Enter an Integer");
73                  continue;
74              }
75              return value;
76          }
77      }
78      public static int getInteger(String prompt, int min, int max)
79      {
80          int value;
81
82          while (true)
83          {
84              value = getInteger(prompt + min + "-" + max + ": ");
85              if (value >= min && value <= max)
86                  return value;
87              JOptionPane.showMessageDialog(null,
88                  "You Must Enter an Integer in the Range "
89                  + min + "-" + max);
90          }
91      }
92      public static int getInteger(String prompt, String errorMessage,
93          Validator validator)
94      {
95          int value;
96          String inputString;
97          while (true)
98          {
```

```
99              inputString = JOptionPane.showInputDialog (prompt);
100             try
101             {
102                 value = Integer.parseInt(inputString);
103             }
104             catch(NumberFormatException exception)
105             {
106                 JOptionPane.showMessageDialog(null,
107                     "You Must Enter an Integer");
108                 continue;
109             }
110             if (!validator.validate(value))
111                 JOptionPane.showMessageDialog(null,
112                     errorMessage);
113             else
114                 return value;
115         }
116     }
117     public static String getString(String prompt)
118     {
119         String inputString;
120         inputString = JOptionPane.showInputDialog(prompt);
121         return inputString;
122
123     }
124     public static void putString(String string)
125     {
126         JOptionPane.showMessageDialog(null, string);
127     }
128     private static String toTitleCase(String string)
129     {
130         String result = "";
131         char previous = ' ', current;
132
133         for (int i = 0; i < string.length(); i++)
134         {
135             current = string.charAt(i);
136             if (previous != ' ')
137                 current = Character.toLowerCase(current);
138             if (current == '_')
139                 current = ' ';
140             result += current;
141             previous = current;
142         }
```

```
143              return result;
144       }
145 }
```

We begin with some overall observations about this class. First, as we know from having used it, it is a utility class. All its methods are class methods. The class has no instance variables, and none of our programs that used this class has ever created any objects of this class. The next general observation is that each of the methods in this class relies on methods from either of two predefined Java classes: JOptionPane and JColorChooser.

Let's examine the class in more detail. We begin with the interface named Validator spanning lines 9-12. This interface is used by the getInteger method whose signature is on lines 92 and 93. This method accepts an object as a parameter that implements the Validator interface. Our desire with this method is to supply three items to getInteger: a string that contains the prompt, a string that contains an error message, and a method that returns a Boolean value that determines whether the supplied input is valid. Although passing the two strings as parameters is not a problem, methods cannot be passed as parameters in Java. We should note that many other programming languages do allow some implementation of method parameters. To compensate for the absence of this language feature, we must instead pass an object that we know has a method, in this case validate, which can be invoked on such an object. When we come to that method, we will examine it in more detail.

Next, we consider the individual methods in turn, beginning with getBoolean, whose signature is on line 14. Our primary reason for creating this class was to enable us to defer exception handling, but you should notice that getBoolean requires no exception handling. It was included in this package for consistency. It uses the showConfirmDialog method of JOptionPane. That method has numerous overloaded versions. The signature of the one that we are using is shown below.

```
static int showConfirmDialog(Component parentComponent,
        Object message)
```

The first parameter is the parent component, which is required by many of the methods of JOptionPane, and, in each case, there is no parent, so we supply null. The second parameter is the prompt. We supply the prompt received from the caller of getBoolean. The method showOptionDialog returns either JOptionPane.YES_OPTION or JOptionPane.NO_OPTION. On line 18, we return true for JOptionPane.YES_OPTION and false otherwise.

The next method, getCharacter, again requires no exception handling, but was included for consistency. It uses the method showInputDialog from JOptionPane, which is used by several other methods in the InputOutput class. The signature of showInputDialog is shown below.

```
static String showInputDialog(Object message)
```

It accepts a prompt and returns the string supplied by the user. The method getCharacter ensures that the user has entered one of the allowable characters.

The next method, getColor, uses the method showDialog of the JColorChooser the class, whose signature is shown below.

```
static Color showDialog(Component component, String title,
    Color initialColor)
```

It provides a simpler signature, requiring only one parameter, rather than three.

The method getEnum uses the method showOptionDialog whose signature is shown below.

```
static int showOptionDialog(Component parentComponent,
    Object message, String title, int optionType, int messageType,
    Icon icon, Object[] options, Object initialValue)
```

Again the method getEnum requires no exception handling, but it does provide the user with a signature that allows an array of enumerated literals to be supplied as a parameter. Notice the type Enum, which is the type of the array parameter's components and also the return type. This type is a predefined class, which is the foundation of all enumerated types. Before calling showOptionDialog, on lines 52 and 53, getEnum creates an array of strings that correspond to the array of enumerated literals that was passed as a parameter. It uses the private method toTitleCase to capitalize only the first letters of each word when converting the enumerated literals to strings. Finally, it uses the value returned by showOptionDialog as the index into the array of enumerated literals to obtain the literal to be returned.

The getInteger method has three overloaded versions. The first one, whose signature is on line 58, is one that we began using in Chapter 6. It contains a try statement that spans lines 65-74 to catch any number format exceptions that are thrown by parseInt should the user enter characters that cannot be converted to an integer. It repeatedly prompts the user for a correct entry and does not return to the caller until a valid integer has been input. Like the getCharacter method, it uses the show-InputDialog method.

The second overloaded getInteger, whose signature is on line 78, allows the user to supply a lower and upper bound that specify the range of acceptable values. It calls the previous version of getInteger until a value within range is supplied.

The third version uses a parameter, whose type is the interface Validator that we discussed earlier. We have already explained the need for the interface, so let's now consider how the parameter is used. It is used on line 110 to call the method validate. Because the parameter object is of type `Validator`, this call will compile. The method `validate` is called to ensure the integer that was input meets some validation criteria, which is known only to the caller of `getInteger`. We have not yet used this method, but will use it in Chapter 13.

Finally, `getString` involves a direct call to `showInputDialog`, and `putString` uses the `showMessageDialog` method whose signature is shown below.

```
static void showMessageDialog(Component parentComponent,
        Object message)
```

Although we have now explained the `JOptionPane` class and some of its methods and could use it directly, we will continue to use our `InputOutput` class when needed. The reason for our decision to do so is that it will enable us to avoid the code duplication that would otherwise result when we need to input integers or enumerated values. For consistency, we will use it even in cases in which little duplication would be avoided.

FILE INPUT/OUTPUT

From the very beginning, our focus in this book has been on programs that perform input and output in windows, which is how most programs work today. It is not how most programs used to work before the advent of window operating systems, however. The interface provided by earlier operating systems was a textual interface, also referred to as a command-line interface. Interaction with the operating system and with programs was through commands entered at the command prompt. Most window operating systems still allow running programs in this mode. So for completeness, we now examine this other kind of interaction.

Programs with this kind of user interaction can be further subdivided into batch programs that deal with input from files and output to files, and interactive programs that allow the user to enter input and display output on the command line. We begin with the former kind of programs and consider the other kind later in this chapter.

Opening, Reading, and Closing Input Files

Before we examine an example of a program that receives its input from a file, we need to understand the mechanics of input file processing. First the file name must be obtained. Keep in mind that the file name must be qualified with a complete path unless the file is in same directory as the program. Once the file name has been obtained, a two-step process is needed. We must first open the file by creating a `FileReader` object using the constructor whose signature is shown below.

```
FileReader(File file) throws FileNotFoundException
```

Using that `FileReader` object, we must then create a `BufferedReader` using the following constructor.

```
BufferedReader(Reader in)
```

Once we have the `BufferedReader` object, we use the method `readLine`, whose signature is shown below, to extract the lines of the file one by one.

```
String readLine() throws IOException
```

It returns `null` when we have reached the end of the file. Finally, once we have finished with the file, we close it with the method `close` of the `BufferedReader` class, whose signature is the following.

```
void close() throws IOException
```

Opening, Writing, and Closing Output Files

We need to know similar details for working with output files. Like with input files, a two-step process is needed before we can write to an output file. The first step is to open the file by creating a `FileWriter` object with the following constructor:

```
FileWriter(String fileName) throws IOException
```

Next, we create a `PrintWriter` from the `FileWriter` with this constructor:

```
PrintWriter(Writer out)
```

Now we can write to that file with either of the following methods:

```
void print(String x)
void println(String x)
```

The second one outputs a new line character at the end, the first one does not. Actually there are many overloaded versions of both of these methods that allow parameters of a variety of different types.

As with input files, it is recommended that we close the file once we have finished using it, which is done by `close`, as before.

A Batch Processing Example

Having introduced the details of file input and output, we are now ready to consider an example that illustrates their use. The following program reads in a file and converts every word in that file to title case, meaning that the first letter of the word is capitalized, and writes the modified text to another file.

This program consists only of a single class named TitleCase, shown in Listing 11.4.

ON THE CD **LISTING 11.4** A Program that Converts the Words of a File to Title Case (found on the CD-ROM at chapter11\TitleCase.java.)

```
1   package chapter11;
2
3   import java.io.*;
4   import common.*;
5
6   public class TitleCase
7   {
8       public static void main(String[] args)
9           throws IOException
10      {
11          String line;
12          StringBuffer buffer;
13          BufferedReader input = null;
14          PrintWriter output = null;
15
16          try
17          {
18              input = openInputFile();
19              output = openOutputFile();
20              line = input.readLine();
21              while (line != null)
22              {
23                  buffer = new StringBuffer(line);
24                  convert(buffer);
25                  output.println(buffer);
26                  line = input.readLine();
27              }
28          }
29          catch (IOException exception)
30          {
31              InputOutput.putString(exception.getMessage());
32          }
33          finally
```

```
34              {
35                  input.close();
36                  output.close();
37              }
38          }
39          private static BufferedReader openInputFile()
40              throws IOException
41          {
42              String fileName =
43                  InputOutput.getString("Enter input file name: ");
44              FileReader reader = new FileReader(fileName);
45
46              return new BufferedReader(reader);
47          }
48          private static PrintWriter openOutputFile()
49              throws IOException
50          {
51              String fileName =
52                  InputOutput.getString("Enter output file name: ");
53              FileWriter writer = new FileWriter(fileName);
54
55              return new PrintWriter(writer);
56          }
57          private static void convert(StringBuffer buffer)
58          {
59              char previous = ' ';
60
61              for (int i = 0; i < buffer.length(); i++)
62              {
63                  if (Character.isWhitespace(previous))
64                      buffer.setCharAt(i,
65                          Character.toUpperCase(buffer.charAt(i)));
66                  previous = buffer.charAt(i);
67              }
68          }
69  }
```

Let's begin with the subordinate methods that open the files. The method open-
InputFile obtains the file name from the user and then performs the necessary steps
that we described earlier to create a BufferedReader, which it returns. It makes no effort to recover if the file does not open. The method openOutputFile similarly obtains the file name from the user and creates a PrintWriter from it, which it returns.

Next, let's examine main. After calling the two methods we just described to
open both files, it successively reads in lines from the file with the loop spanning

lines 21-27. Notice that a priming read is needed on line 20 to start this process, and another read is needed at the bottom of the loop on line 26 for subsequent lines. It is necessary to read in one line before the loop begins so we can properly check for end-of-file. In our example at the end of this chapter, we will show a technique that avoids this duplication. On line 23, we change the string to a mutable string buffer, which is then passed to the method convert, which performs the title case conversion. A call to println on line 25 writes the converted line to the output file.

Notice that the bulk of the code in main, including the calls to the methods to open the files, is embedded in a try statement. Any exceptions that are thrown throughout this process are caught on line 31 and the message associated with the exception is displayed, then the program terminates. Also noteworthy is the fact that this is our first example of the use of the finally clause, which spans lines 33-37. Placing the file close operations here ensures that the files are closed regardless of whether any exceptions are thrown.

Finally, we include just a few words about the remaining method convert. To determine whether a character is the first letter of a word, we check whether the previous letter is whitespace, using the method isWhitespace. Whitespace includes a space and other delimiting characters.

The InputFile Class

Now that we have discussed the details of file input, we can return to a class that we used first in Chapter 9. It is the class that we placed in the package common named InputFile. It allowed us to use an iterator to read in the lines of a file, ignoring all the file input details. Listing 11.5 contains its code.

LISTING 11.5 The Input File Class (found on the CD-ROM at common\InputFile.java.)

ON THE CD

```
 1  package common;
 2
 3  import java.io.*;
 4  import java.util.*;
 5
 6  public class InputFile implements Iterable<String>
 7  {
 8      private String fileName;
 9
10      private    class FileIterator implements Iterator<String>
11      {
12          private BufferedReader file;
13          private String nextLine;
14
```

```
15          public FileIterator()
16          {
17              try
18              {
19                  file = new BufferedReader(new FileReader(fileName));
20              }
21              catch (FileNotFoundException exception)
22              {
23                  InputOutput.putString("File did not open");
24              }
25              getNextLine();
26          }
27          public boolean hasNext()
28          {
29              return nextLine != null;
30          }
31          public String next()
32          {
33              String thisLine = nextLine;
34              getNextLine();
35              return thisLine;
36          }
37          public void remove()
38          {
39          }
40          private void getNextLine()
41          {
42              try
43              {
44                  nextLine = file.readLine();
45              }
46              catch (IOException exception)
47              {
48              }
49          }
50      }
51      public InputFile(String fileName)
52      {
53          this.fileName = fileName;
54      }
55      public Iterator<String> iterator()
56      {
57          return new FileIterator();
58      }
59 }
```

Because we have already studied classes that implement the `Iterable` interface, the overall structure of this class should be familiar. The constructor of the outer class initializes its one instance variable, `fileName`, to the string supplied as a parameter. Its constructor attempts to open the file and create the buffered reader `file` declared on line 12, which is an instance variable of the inner class. If the file fails to open, a message is displayed. Otherwise the constructor reads in the first line of the file by calling the private method `getNextLine`, which saves that string in `nextLine`—the other instance variable of the inner class.

The `hasNext` method of `FileIterator` checks whether the end-of-file has been reached by checking whether the last line of the file was read in `null`. The `next` method returns what was in the `nextLine` variable at the point of the call and reads in the next line by calling `getNextLine`.

DEFINING AND THROWING EXCEPTIONS

We are now ready to consider how to define our own exceptions and how to throw them. As we mentioned earlier in this chapter, exceptions are just objects of some class. User-defined checked exceptions should extend the predefined class `Exception`. User-defined unchecked exceptions should extend the class `RuntimeException`. When we define an exception class, it can consist of nothing more than a class name without any methods or data. We will see such an example later in this chapter. Exception classes can, however, contain methods or data like any class, as our next example will illustrate.

Although no special syntax is needed to declare an exception class, throwing an exception does require the use of a statement that we have not yet seen. It is the `throw` statement whose syntax is illustrated in Syntax Definition 11.2.

Syntax Definition 11.2 Syntax of a `throw` Statement.

```
throw_statement

    throw  exceptionObject ;
```

This statement is syntactically simple, consisting of one new reserved word throw and the name of the exception object that is to be thrown. Although it is not a requirement, it is customary that this exception object be anonymous—being created at the point that it is thrown. Consequently, we most often see the reserved word new following throw followed by a call to the constructor of some exception class. We explained the action of this statement earlier in this chapter in our discussion of exception propagation.

A Cryptography Example

Our next example illustrates declaring an exception class and throwing exceptions, but also provides another example of file input and output. This program either encodes or decodes the letters in a file using a cipher and produces a new file. Using ciphers is one of the first encoding techniques. It represents each letter with a different letter. It is a simple technique, and, consequently, one that is easy to crack. By computing the frequency of each letter in the encoded file—something we did in one of our examples in Chapter 9—and comparing those frequencies with the known frequencies of English letters, it is not difficult to crack a cipher. Nonetheless, it provides a suitable basis for our next example.

There is one utility class that we use in this example, and will use in several more examples in the remaining chapters, that we wish to present first. Recall that utility classes are ones that typically have only class methods, no instance data or constructors. This class, which we have named Permutation, provides a method to generate a random permutation and another to check whether a given array of values contains a permutation. A permutation is a reordering of a collection of numbers. In our case, arrays of length n are intended to contain permutations of the numbers from 0 to $n-1$. The code for this class is contained in Listing 11.6.

LISTING 11.6 The Utility Class for Permutations (found on the CD-ROM at
ON THE CD chapter11\Permutation.java.)

```
1   package chapter11;
2
3   public class Permutation
4   {
5       public static int[] randomize(int size)
6       {
7           int whichValue, lastValue;
8           int[] random = new int[size], allValues = new int[size];
9
10          for (int value = 0; value < size; value++)
11              allValues[value] = value;
12          for (int value = 0; value < size; value++)
13          {
14              whichValue = ((int) Math.floor(Math.random() *
15                  (size − value)));
16              random[value] = allValues[whichValue];
17              lastValue = size − value − 1;
```

```
18                      allValues[whichValue] = allValues[lastValue];
19              }
20          return random;
21      }
22      public static boolean check(int values[])
23      {
24          int[] frequencies = new int[values.length];
25
26          for (int i = 0; i < values.length; i++)
27              if (values[i] < 0 || values[i] >= values.length)
28                  return false;
29              else
30                  frequencies[values[i]]++;
31          for (int frequency: frequencies)
32              if (frequency != 1)
33                  return false;
34          return true;
35      }
36 }
```

The first method, randomize, produces an array containing a random permutation of the number of values specified by the parameter. It initializes each element in the array allValues to contain its index in the for loop on lines 10 and 11. It then randomly chooses an index among all the indices the first time on line 14 and moves the value in that index into the first position of the array random. It then moves the value in the last position of the array allValues to the chosen position with the assignment on line 18 so that it will not be selected again. The second time it chooses among all values except the last one, the third time from all but the last two, and so on.

The other method check is given an array, which presumably contains a permutation, and checks whether or not it does. It performs this check by computing the frequency of each value and then checking that each value occurs only once.

With that utility class now available, we can present the class that enciphers or deciphers a text file. Listing 11.7 contains the code for this class, which we have named Cipher.

LISTING 11.7 The Class Defining a Cipher for Encoding Letters (found on the CD-ROM at chapter11\Cipher.java.)

```
1  package chapter11;
2
3  import java.io.*;
4
```

```
 5  class Cipher
 6  {
 7      public enum Conversion{ENCODE, DECODE};
 8      public class InvalidCipher extends Exception
 9      {
10          public InvalidCipher(String message)
11          {
12              super(message);
13          }
14      }
15
16      private static final int LETTERS = 52;
17      private int[] encoder, decoder;
18
19      public Cipher(PrintWriter cipherFile)
20      {
21          encoder = Permutation.randomize(LETTERS);
22          for (int cipher: encoder)
23              cipherFile.println(cipher);
24      }
25      public Cipher(BufferedReader cipherFile) throws InvalidCipher,
26          IOException
27      {
28          String line;
29
30          encoder = new int[LETTERS];
31          for (int letter = 0; letter < LETTERS; letter++)
32          {
33              line = cipherFile.readLine();
34              if (line == null)
35                  throw new InvalidCipher("Too Few Values");
36              try
37              {
38                  encoder[letter] = Integer.parseInt(line);
39              }
40              catch (NumberFormatException exception)
41              {
42                  throw new InvalidCipher("NonNumeric Value");
43              }
44          }
45          if (cipherFile.readLine() != null)
46              throw new InvalidCipher("Too Many Values");
47          if (!Permutation.check(encoder))
48              throw new InvalidCipher("Not a Permutation");
```

```
49            decoder = new int[LETTERS];
50            for (int letter = 0; letter < LETTERS; letter++)
51                decoder[encoder[letter]] = letter;
52        }
53        public String convert(String text, Conversion conversion)
54        {
55            char nextChar;
56            String converted = "";
57
58            for (int i = 0; i < text.length(); i++)
59            {
60                nextChar = text.charAt(i);
61                if (Character.isLetter(nextChar))
62                {
63                    switch (conversion)
64                    {
65                        case ENCODE:
66                            converted += numberToLetter
67                                (encoder[letterToNumber(nextChar)]);
68                            break;
69                        case DECODE:
70                            converted += numberToLetter
71                                (decoder[letterToNumber(nextChar)]);
72                            break;
73                    }
74                }
75                else
76                    converted += nextChar;
77            }
78            return converted;
79        }
80        private int letterToNumber(char letter)
81        {
82            if (Character.isLowerCase(letter))
83                return letter - 'a';
84            else
85                return letter - 'A' + LETTERS / 2;
86        }
87        private char numberToLetter(int number)
88        {
89            if (number < LETTERS / 2)
90                return (char)(number + 'a');
91            else
92                return (char)(number - LETTERS / 2 + 'A');
```

```
93        }
94  }
```

The inner class `InvalidCipher`, spanning lines 8-14, is our first example of a user-defined exception class. Notice that it is a checked exception because it extends the predefined class `Exception`. It contains one method, a constructor, which accepts a string describing the error, which it passes on to the constructor of `Exception`, which contains a similar constructor.

Next, let's examine the instance data of the outer class. It contains a constant specifying the number of letters, including both upper- and lowercase, and two arrays, `encoder`, and `decoder`, which define the cipher in both directions.

The outer class has two constructors. The first one is only used when encoding is being done. It creates a random permutation of the numbers from 0 to 51, using the `randomize` method of the `Permutation` class on line 21, and then saves that permutation in the output file supplied as the parameter to the constructor. Notice that, although this class performs file input and output, it is the responsibility of the class that uses it to open and close the files.

The second constructor accepts an input file—the file containing the cipher—as a parameter. This constructor could be used for either encoding or decoding. It reads the values contained in the file into the array `encoder`. It verifies that the file contains the right number of lines, that each line contains a number and that the collection of numbers is a permutation of the number from 0 to 51. If any of these conditions fail, the exception `InvalidCipher` is thrown. Notice that it is thrown in four different places in this method. In each case, the exception object is anonymous and instantiated within the `throw` statement. A message is passed to the constructor indicating the cause of the error. In the case that a line contains a nonnumeric value, we are catching the `NumberFormatException` that is thrown by the call to `parseInt` on line 38 and throwing an `InvalidCipher` exception instead on line 42. Provided that the data in the file passes all the necessary tests, the array `decoder` is created from the array `encoder` in the `for` loop on lines 50 and 51.

Aside from the constructors, the outer class only contains one public method, `convert`, that is used for both encoding and decoding. This method provides the string to be converted and a parameter of the enumerated type `Conversion` defined on line 7, which specifies the direction of the conversion. It converts the string character by character—converting only the characters that are letters. The private method `letterToNumber` is used to map the lowercase letters to the numbers 0 to 25 and the uppercase letters to the numbers 26 to 51. The method `numberToLetter` performs the inverse mapping.

There is one more class needed to complete this program, but before we discuss that class, we introduce one additional topic—input and output from the command line.

COMMAND-LINE INPUT/OUTPUT

It is customary to use programs that contain output to the command line as the very first program examples in programming textbooks. We took a very different approach in this book, however, beginning with input and output in windows, in keeping with our overall approach that favors examples that use graphics. For completeness, you should be aware of how to perform input and output at the command line, although it is rarely an approach used by most real software.

Command-line Arguments

We begin this discussion by explaining the significance of the parameter args, which is the parameter that every main method must have. From its declaration, it is apparent that it is an array of strings. Specifically, it is the array of strings that follow the program name when a program is started from the command line. Let's return to the example that we have been working on—the program to encode or decode files. The name of the class that contains main, which will see shortly, is named EncodeDecode. Suppose we start this program on the command line using the following command.

```
java —classpath .. chapter11.EncodeDecode encode input.txt
```

The two strings that follow the name of the program are the command-line arguments. Inside main, args[0] will contain the string encode, and args[1] will contain input.txt. So, we can use these command-line arguments as a way of supplying input to a program. In this case, it would be the type of conversion and the name of the input file.

Command-line Output

Next we turn to explicit command-line input/output, beginning with the simpler of the two, which is output. There is a predefined PrintWriter object named out contained in the utility class System, which specifies the command-line as the output stream. The methods print and println that are used with file streams are the same ones used to output to the command line. To output "Hello World" to the command line, a favorite first program in many books, we would use the following method call.

```
System.out.println("Hello World");
```

Command-line Input

Performing input is only slightly more complicated because we must create the necessary BufferedReader from the predefined object in defined in the class System. The following instantiation accomplishes that task.

```
BufferedReader stdin = new BufferedReader
    (new InputStreamReader(System.in));
```

Once we have the object stdin, we use the readLine object, just as we do with buffered readers that are connected to input files. We will see such calls in our next example.

There is another class that can be used for command-line input, called Scanner, that was added to Java recently. It is commonly used in introductory books because it conceals the exception handling, parsing, and format conversion necessary with input. Because we have already discussed each of these concepts, the Scanner class offers little benefit at this point, so we have elected to forego its use.

The Cryptography Example Again

Having introduced the necessary details for command-line input and output, we are now ready to complete the example that we began earlier, which is intended to encipher and decipher text files. The last class, named EncodeDecode, necessary to complete this program is contained in Listing 11.8.

LISTING 11.8   The Class Containing the main Method for the Encoding and Decoding
ON THE CD   Program (found on the CD-ROM at chapter11\EncodeDecode.java.)

```
 1    package chapter11;
 2
 3    import java.io.*;
 4    import java.awt.*;
 5    import javax.swing.*;
 6
 7    public class EncodeDecode
 8    {
 9        private static BufferedReader stdin =
10            new BufferedReader(new InputStreamReader(System.in));
11
12        public static void main(String[] args) throws IOException
13        {
14            Cipher cipher;
15            String convertType, inputFileName, cipherFileName;
16            BufferedReader cipherInput, inputFile;
```

```
17              PrintWriter cipherOutput, outputFile;
18
19          convertType = getCommandLineArgument
20              (args, 0, "Enter e for encode, d for decode: ");
21          inputFileName = getCommandLineArgument
22              (args, 1, "Enter input file: ");
23          switch (convertType.charAt(0))
24              {
25              case 'e':
26                  cipherOutput = openOutputFile("cipher.txt");
27                  cipher = new Cipher(cipherOutput);
28                  cipherOutput.close();
29                  inputFile = openInputFile(inputFileName);
30                  outputFile = openOutputFile("coded.txt");
31                  convertFile(inputFile, outputFile, cipher,
32                      Cipher.Conversion.ENCODE);
33                  break;
34              case 'd':
35                  inputFile = openInputFile(inputFileName);
36                  outputFile = openOutputFile("output.txt");
37                  cipherFileName = getCommandLineArgument
38                      (args, 2, "Enter cipher file: ");
39                  cipherInput = openInputFile(cipherFileName);
40                  try
41                  {
42                      cipher = new Cipher(cipherInput);
43                  }
44                  catch (Cipher.InvalidCipher exception)
45                  {
46                      System.out.println(exception.getMessage());
47                      break;
48                  }
49                  finally
50                  {
51                      cipherInput.close();
52                  }
53                  convertFile(inputFile, outputFile, cipher,
54                      Cipher.Conversion.DECODE);
55                  break;
56              default:
57                  System.out.println("Invalid operation");
58                  return;
59              }
60          inputFile.close();
```

```
61                  outputFile.close();
62          }
63      public static void convertFile(BufferedReader inputFile,
64          PrintWriter outputFile, Cipher cipher,
65          Cipher.Conversion conversion) throws IOException
66      {
67          String line;
68
69          line = inputFile.readLine();
70          while (line != null)
71          {
72              outputFile.println(cipher.convert(line, conversion));
73              line = inputFile.readLine();
74          }
75      }
76      private static String getCommandLineArgument(String[] args,
77          int index, String prompt) throws IOException
78      {
79          if (args.length > index)
80              return args[index];
81          System.out.print(prompt);
82          return stdin.readLine();
83      }
84      private static BufferedReader openInputFile(String fileName)
85          throws IOException
86      {
87          FileReader reader = null;
88
89          while (true)
90              try
91              {
92                  reader = new FileReader(fileName);
93                  break;
94              }
95              catch (FileNotFoundException exception)
96              {
97                  System.out.println("File " + fileName + " Not Found");
98                  System.out.print("Re-enter file name: ");
99                  fileName = stdin.readLine();
100             }
101         return new BufferedReader(reader);
102     }
103     private static PrintWriter openOutputFile(String fileName)
104         throws IOException
```

```
105        {
106               FileWriter writer = new FileWriter(fileName);
107               BufferedWriter buffered = new BufferedWriter(writer);
108
109               return new PrintWriter(buffered);
110        }
111    }
```

This program is designed to allow the user to enter input on the command line, as we illustrated earlier. The first command-line argument is the type of the conversion, e for encoding, or d for decoding. The second command-line argument is the name of the input file. For decoding, there is a third command-line argument, which is the name of the cipher file. Notice that the output file names are hard-coded. We have also designed the program so that if any portion of the required command-line argument is not supplied, it is subsequently requested at the command line. A private class method named getCommandLineArgument is included for that purpose. It is called on lines 19-22 to get the first two arguments. If the command-line argument is not present, the user is prompted to enter it on line 81, using the prompt supplied by the caller, and on line 82, the string input by the user is returned. With interactive input and output of this kind, it is always necessary to prompt the user first so the user knows that input is expected and what kind.

Next the appropriate files are opened depending upon the type of conversion that is to be performed. With an encoding, the cipher file is opened as an output file, and with decoding, it is opened as an input file. Private methods are provided for opening both kinds of files. The method for opening input files reprompts the user for a different name if the input file cannot be opened. For an encoding, a Cipher object is instantiated that creates a new cipher file. With decoding, a Cipher object is created that is supplied the cipher file that was used for the encoding. The exception InvalidCipher is caught on line 46 and the message that was supplied when the exception object was instantiated is extracted by a call to the method getMessage, which InvalidCipher inherits from Exception. If no errors occur, the method convertFile is called for either kind of conversion. It reads the input file line by line, either encoding or decoding it with a call to convert on line 72, and writes the converted line to the output file.

When you run this program, create a text file named input.txt as your input, and then use the following pair of commands.

```
java -classpath .. chapter11.EncodeDecode e input.txt
java -classpath .. chapter11.EncodeDecode d coded.txt cipher.txt
```

The encoding should produce an output file named coded.txt and a cipher file named cipher.txt. The decoding will produce a file named output.txt, which should be identical to input.txt. Try omitting one or more of the command-line arguments to see whether it then prompts for them. You might also try supplying the name of an invalid input file to verify that the program prompts you for another name until you supply the name of a file that can be opened.

OTHER INPUT/OUTPUT TOPICS

There are two final topics that are related to input and output that we introduce in preparation for the final example of this chapter. They include the use of the stream tokenizer and object serialization.

The `StreamTokenizer` Class

In Chapter 9, we introduced the `StringTokenizer` class, which provides one technique for breaking apart a string into substrings by specifying the delimiting characters. We noted that, despite its name, it really returns lexemes, not tokens. The `StreamTokenizer` class, by contrast, does return tokens. The possible tokens include `TT_EOL`, `TT_EOF`, `TT_NUMBER` or `TT_WORD`, which represent end-of-line, end-of-file and a number or a word, respectively.

Another difference between `StringTokenizer` and `StreamTokenizer` is that the former subdivides a string, whereas the latter tokenizes an input stream, as their names suggest. The constructor for the `StreamTokenizer` is shown below:

```
StreamTokenizer(Reader r)
```

Once we have extracted the token from the stream, there are two public instance variables that enable us to obtain the lexeme. In the case of a numeric token, the variable named `nval` provides us the lexeme already converted to a `double`. When we know that the token is `TT_WORD`, the instance variable `sval` allows us to access the lexeme.

Object Serialization

The final topic that we introduce in this chapter is *object serialization*. To serialize an object means to create a representation of the state of that object, which can be either input or output.

There are one interface and two classes that are directly needed for object serialization. The interface is `Serializable`, which is a somewhat unusual interface in that it contains no method signatures, but any class whose objects are to be serialized must designate that they implement this interface. The two classes directly associated with object serialization are `ObjectInputStream` and `ObjectOutputStream`.

An object of those classes is necessary for inputting or outputting a serialized object. The constructors needed to create objects of those classes are shown below.

```
ObjectInputStream(InputStream in)
ObjectOutputStream(OutputStream out)
```

Assuming that we wish to perform file input or output, which is what we most often do, we need to supply objects of the classes `FileInputStream` and `FileOutput-Stream`, which will be coerced to `InputStream` and `OutputStream`, respectively. In the next chapter, we will explain the rules for coercion among objects in greater detail. The constructors for those classes are shown below.

```
FileInputStream(String name) throws FileNotFoundException
FileOutputStream(String name) throws IOException
```

Using the above constructors, we create these streams by providing them the names of the input or output files.

Once we have created an `ObjectInputStream` object, the method that performs the serialization and the input is `readObject`, whose signature is shown below.

```
Object readObject() throws OptionalDataException,
    ClassNotFoundException, IOException
```

The object then must be type cast to the appropriate type.

On the output side, the method `writeObject` that belongs to the `ObjectOutput-Stream` class is used to output a serialized object. Its signature is shown below.

```
void writeObject(Object obj) throws IOException
```

As is true with input and output in Java, in general, this process is rife with details. Seeing an example, like the one that follows, is especially helpful to see how these details fit together.

GRAPHICS SERIALIZATION EXAMPLE

Our final example for this chapter involves many of the topics that we introduced in this chapter, including declaring and throwing exceptions, file and command-line input and output, command-line arguments, stream tokenization, and object serialization. Like all of the final examples in each chapter, it involves graphics. This example is somewhat similar to the final example in Chapter 9, which allowed us to display a collection of shapes in a window, which were read in from an input text file. In this program, however, we allow both input and output of the shapes in two formats. The first format is similar to what we used in Chapter 9. It is a textual representation that we defined. The second format is the serialized format provided by default. Although the program might be more interesting had we allowed additional shapes to be created once a file was read in, we elected to omit that capability so as to not overly complicate the example and because our primary purpose with this program is to illustrate file input and output.

To begin we have created an interface named Shape is shown in Listing 11.9.

LISTING 11.9   The Shape Interface (found on the CD-ROM at chapter11\Shape.java.)

ON THE CD

```
 1  package chapter11;
 2
 3  import java.awt.*;
 4  import java.io.*;
 5
 6  interface Shape extends Serializable
 7  {
 8      void draw(Graphics graphics);
 9      String toString();
10  }
```

This is our first example of an interface that extends another interface. Any methods defined in the interface being extended would be incorporated in the new interface being defined. In this case, Serializable contains no methods. Nonetheless, this designation is essential because now any class that implements Shape will be also implementing Serializable. We have included a method, draw, that enables the shape to be drawn, and toString, which is a method that converts the object state into a string representation, which itself is a kind of serialization.

We have defined two classes that implement this interface—Line and Oval. The code for the former is shown in Listing 11.10.

LISTING 11.10   The Class Defining a Line Shape (found on the CD-ROM at

ON THE CD chapter11\Line.java.)

```
 1  package chapter11;
 2
 3  import java.awt.*;
 4
 5  class Line implements Shape
 6  {
 7      private int x1, y1, x2, y2;
 8
```

```
 9      public Line(int[] values)
10      {
11          this.x1 = values[0];
12          this.y1 = values[1];
13          this.x2 = values[2];
14          this.y2 = values[3];
15      }
16      public void draw(Graphics graphics)
17      {
18          graphics.drawLine(x1, y1, x2, y2);
19      }
20      public String toString()
21      {
22          return "L " + x1 + " " + y1 + " " + x2 + " " + y2;
23      }
24  }
```

There should be nothing in this class that requires explanation, but we do want to highlight how the toString method captures the object's state. The string returned by toString contains the letter L to designate the kind of shape, a line, and the values of the coordinates of the endpoints of the line, which correspond to the instance variables of the class.

To make the example interesting, we wanted at least two different classes implementing the Shape interface. The second one, Oval, is shown in Listing 11.11.

LISTING 11.11 The Class Defining an Oval Shape (found on the CD-ROM at
ON THE CD chapter11\Oval.java.)

```
 1  package chapter11;
 2
 3  import java.awt.*;
 4
 5  class Oval implements Shape
 6  {
 7      private int x, y, width, height;
 8
 9      public Oval(int[] values)
10      {
11          this.x = values[0];
12          this.y = values[1];
13          this.width = values[2];
14          this.height = values[3];
15      }
16
```

```
17      public void draw(Graphics graphics)
18      {
19          graphics.drawOval(x, y, width, height);
20      }
21      public String toString()
22      {
23          return "O " + x + " " + y + " " + width + " " + height;
24      }
25  }
```

There are two more classes needed to complete this program. The first of those is a class that defines a window onto which the shapes are to be drawn. This class also contains methods that input objects from a file and output the objects in the window to a file. The code for this class, named, ShapesWindow, is in Listing 11.12.

 LISTING 11.12   The Class a Window for Displaying the Shapes (found on the CD-ROM at
ON THE CD   chapter11\ShapesWindow.java.)

```
1  package chapter11;
2
3  import java.awt.*;
4  import java.io.*;
5  import java.util.*;
6  import common.*;
7  import static java.io.StreamTokenizer.*;
8
9  public class ShapesWindow extends Application
10 {
11     public class InputFileFormatError extends RuntimeException
12     {
13     }
14
15     private ArrayList<Shape> shapes =
16         new ArrayList<Shape>();
17
18     public void add(Shape shape)
19     {
20         shapes.add(shape);
21         repaint();
22     }
23     public void paintComponent(Graphics graphics)
24     {
25         super.paintComponent(graphics);
26         for (Shape shape: shapes)
```

```
27              shape.draw(graphics);
28      }
29      public void input(String fileName)
30          throws IOException
31      {
32          int token;
33          char shapeType;
34          int[] values = new int[4];
35          FileReader inputFile = new FileReader(fileName);
36          StreamTokenizer tokenizer =
37              new StreamTokenizer(inputFile);
38
39          shapes = new ArrayList<Shape>();
40          while ((token = tokenizer.nextToken())!= TT_EOF)
41          {
42              if (token != TT_WORD)
43                  throw new InputFileFormatError();
44              shapeType = tokenizer.sval.charAt(0);
45              for (int i = 0; i < values.length; i++)
46              {
47                  token = tokenizer.nextToken();
48                  if (token != TT_NUMBER)
49                      throw new InputFileFormatError();
50                  values[i] = (int)tokenizer.nval;
51              }
52              switch (shapeType)
53              {
54                  case 'L':
55                      shapes.add(new Line(values));
56                      break;
57                  case 'O':
58                      shapes.add(new Oval(values));
59                      break;
60                  default:
61                      throw new InputFileFormatError();
62              }
63          }
64          inputFile.close();
65      }
66      public void output(String fileName)
67          throws IOException, FileNotFoundException
68      {
69          PrintWriter outputFile = new PrintWriter
70              (new BufferedWriter(new FileWriter(fileName)));
71
```

```
72              for (Shape shape: shapes)
73                  outputFile.println(shape);
74              outputFile.close();
75          }
76      public void read(String fileName)
77              throws IOException, ClassNotFoundException
78          {
79              ObjectInputStream inputFile = new ObjectInputStream
80                  (new FileInputStream(fileName));
81
82              shapes = (ArrayList<Shape>)inputFile.readObject();
83              inputFile.close();
84          }
85      public void write(String fileName)
86              throws IOException, ClassNotFoundException
87          {
88              ObjectOutputStream outputFile = new ObjectOutputStream
89                  (new FileOutputStream(fileName));
90
91              outputFile.writeObject(shapes);
92              outputFile.close();
93          }
94  }
```

Notice, first, that this class contains an inner class `InputFileFormatError` that defines an unchecked exception. We know it is unchecked because it extends `RuntimeException`. We elected to make it unchecked because we do not anticipate file format errors to be recoverable.

Let's now consider the four methods provided by this class for inputting and outputting the shapes. The first pair—`input` and `output`—implement a user-defined serialization. We have provided them not only to show how much simpler it is to use the system-provided serialization, but also as a way to test this program. Let's begin with `input`, which is the more complicated of the two. It is provided the name of an input file as a parameter. On lines 35-37, it constructs the `StreamTokenizer` object `tokenizer` for that file in the two steps we discussed earlier. Then it extracts the tokens one by one in the loop that spans lines 40-63. By embedding the call to `nextToken` in the `while` condition, as we have done on line 40, we avoid having to do priming calls outside the loop and at the end of the loop. The required format of an input file is that each line contains a letter, which is a word token, followed by four number tokens. Notice that we throw an exception if that format is violated. Otherwise we access the token values and place the letter designating the kind of shape in `shapeType` on line 44 and the data needed for that shape in the array values in the loop spanning lines 45-51. Then, based on the shape type, we create an object of that type and add it to the array list shapes.

The method output is somewhat simpler than input because it makes use of the toString method to serialize each shape. It creates a PrintWriter object in the usual two steps from the file name passed as a parameter. It then iterates across the array list of shapes, outputting the serialization of each shape. The call to println on line 73 makes an implicit call to the appropriate toString method to serialize the object.

The next pair of methods, read and write, makes use of the system-supplied serialization. In the case of read, an ObjectInputStream is constructed from the file name passed as a parameter, using the steps we discussed earlier. Then a single call to readObject reads in the entire array list of shapes. An analogous and equally simple set of instructions is needed in the method write. Notice how much shorter the code is when we make use of the object serialization supplied for us.

To complete this program, we need a main method. The class ShapesFileMain shown in Listing 11.13 contains that method.

LISTING 11.13   The Class Containing main that Loads and Saves the Shapes to Files
ON THE CD   (found on the CD-ROM at chapter11\ShapesFileMain.java.)

```
1   package chapter11;
2
3   import java.awt.*;
4   import java.io.*;
5
6   public class ShapesFileMain
7   {
8       public static void main(String[] args)
9           throws IOException, ClassNotFoundException
10      {
11          ShapesWindow window = new ShapesWindow();
12
13          for (String argument: args)
14              switch (argument.charAt(0))
15              {
16                  case 'i':
17                      window.input(argument.substring(2));
18                      break;
19                  case 'o':
20                      window.output(argument.substring(2));
21                      break;
22                  case 'r':
23                      window.read(argument.substring(2));
24                      break;
```

```
25                    case 'w':
26                        window.write(argument.substring(2));
27                        break;
28                    default:
29                        System.out.println("Invalid command");
30                        return;
31            }
32         window.display();
33     }
34  }
```

Notice that the program does not catch any of the exceptions that might be thrown but, instead, just allows the program to terminate should any errors occur.

This program relies on command-line arguments for its input. It accepts a list of commands that instructs it to perform one of four input or output operations. The first letter of each command specifies the kind of operation, and the substring beginning at the third character specifies the file name. To help you better understand how it works, let's consider two runs of this program. First suppose that we have a file named input.txt that contains the following two lines of text.

```
L 20 30 70 80
O 60 90 45 56
```

For the first run of this program, assume we enter the following at the command line:

```
java -classpath .. chapter11.ShapesFileMain i-input.txt
     w-write.txt
```

We are indicating that we wish to read the shapes from the input.txt and save the system serialization in the file write.txt. When we give this command, the window will display the line and oval designated by the input file and will also create the output file write.txt. Examine the latter file to get a sense of what it contains. One way to verify that this process works is to perform a second run of the program with the following command:

```
java -classpath .. chapter11.ShapesFileMain r-write.txt
     o-output.txt
```

In this run, we test the other two operations. This program has worked correctly if the file output.txt matches our original file, input.txt.

SUMMARY

In this chapter, we introduced exceptions and explained how to declare classes whose objects are exceptions, how to throw exceptions and how to catch them. We also discussed several kinds of input and output that we had not yet studied, including file input and output and I/O from the command line. The key points to remember from this chapter are as follows:

- By catching an exception, which is an unexpected error, a program can attempt to recover from that error rather than abruptly terminating.
- Checked exceptions must either be caught or designated as thrown.
- Exceptions are propagated through the chain of method calls until a catch block is found that catches them, if one exists.
- Files provide an alternate way to supply input and create output for programs.
- The throw statement allows both predefined and user-defined exceptions to be thrown when an error condition that cannot be immediately resolved occurs.
- Command-line arguments are the values supplied when a program is started from the command line and become the parameter args accepted by main.
- Interactive programs that do not execute in a windows environment can be created using command-line input and output.
- Object serialization is a built-in facility of Java that allows the state of objects to be saved and retrieved.

Review Questions

1. Why are exceptions an important part of any modern programming language?
2. How can you determine whether an exception is checked or unchecked?
3. Explain the steps required to prepare an input or an output file for reading or writing, respectively.
4. When is the finally block executed in a try statement?
5. What is the difference between the use of the reserved word throw and the reserved word throws?
6. What is a batch program? How does it differ from an interactive program?
7. When requesting input at the command line, why is it important to always prompt the user first?
8. Can command-line arguments be used for applets?
9. Explain how the StreamTokenizer class differs from the StringTokenizer.
10. Why is object serialization a useful feature?

Programming Exercises

11. Write a method that accepts an array list of integers, an integer, and a subscript as parameters. It should try to put the integer into the array list at the specified subscript, catching the exception `IndexOutOfBoundsException`, should it be thrown. The method should return `true` if no exception is thrown and `false` otherwise.

12. Write a method, `computeQuotient`, that repeatedly prompts the user at the command line for two integers and computes their quotient as long as the computation generates an `ArithmeticException`. If no exception occurs, the quotient should be returned.

13. Write a method that accepts a `BufferedReader` designating an input file and a `PrintWriter` designating an output file as parameters. It should copy the input file to the output, converting all letters to upper case.

14. Write a method that repeatedly prompts the user to enter a number at the command line. It stops when a nonnumeric value is read in and returns the largest number that was entered.

15. Write a method that accepts a `StreamTokenizer` as a parameter. It should return an array list of type `Double` containing the numbers that were in the input stream supplied by the tokenizer. It should throw the predefined exception `NumberFormatError` if any of the tokens is not a number.

16. Define a class called `Empty` that is a checked exception. Include neither methods nor instance variables.

17. Define a class called `Full` that defines an unchecked exception. Include no methods or instance variables.

18. Write a class named `Container` that has private instance variables that maintain the number of elements currently in the container and the maximum number it can hold. The class should have a constructor and two other methods—`insert` and `remove`—that permit one element to be inserted or removed respectively. If the `insert` method is called when the container is full, it should throw the exception `Full`, defined in the previous exercise. If `remove` is called and the container is empty, it should throw the exception `Empty` that you defined in Programming Exercise 16.

19. Write a `main` method that examines its command-line arguments, computes the sum of all of them that are numbers and displays that sum on the command line.

20. Define a class called `Circle` that contains instance variables that define its center and radius and a method to draw the circle, given a graphics object. Objects of the class should be able to be serialized.

Programming Projects

21. Write a program that copies an input file to an output file, extracting only the numbers that are in the input file and placing them in the output file, one number on each line. Use the StreamTokenizer class to extract the tokens that are numbers.

22. Write a program that accept the names of input and output files as command-line arguments, and copies the input file to the output file, converting all letters to upper case, using the method from Programming Exercise 13.

23. Write an application that reads a file of numbers and displays their sum. The file name should be supplied at the command line. It should make use of the method from Programming Exercise 15. It should display an error message if the file contains nonnumeric values.

24. Write a program that uses interactive command-line input and output that allows the user to insert and remove elements from a Container object, as defined in Programming Exercise 18, by repeatedly displaying a menu of choices. The program should catch the Empty exception when thrown and display an appropriate message.

25. Write a program that reads in a file containing the specification for objects of class Circle, defined in Programming Exercise 20. Each line of the file should contain three integers that specify the characteristics of a circle. The program should add them to an array list as they are read in and output the serialization of that array list to a file once all the values have been read in.

12 Generalization and Aggregation Relationships

In this chapter

- Generalization Relationships
- Class-Interface Relationships
- Aggregation Relationships
- Polygonal Number Application

GENERALIZATION RELATIONSHIPS

In Chapter 10, we examined compositional relationships that are characterized by a *has a* predicate. At that time, we also contrasted *has a* relationships with *is a* relationships. Now we will more fully explore those class relationships defined by the *is a* predicate. When we first introduced these relationships, we observed that such relationships are generalization relationships. Let's return to our simplistic, yet helpful, technique involving the analysis of the requirements for uncovering classes and methods. We observed that nouns are candidates for classes, and verbs are most likely methods. Adjectives, too, play a role. An adjective modifying a noun creates a generalization relationship. As an example, consider the following sentence.

- A fast car is a car.

Car is a generalization of fast car or we might say fast car is a specialization of car. Such an *is a* relationship holds no matter what noun and adjective we choose.

In our discussion of compositional relationships, we learned that such relationships are realized through the use of instance variables. We now need to understand how generalization relationships translate into Java code. Inheritance is the language feature that allows us to implement such relationships.

Extending the `JApplet` and `Application` Classes

We have been using inheritance since our very first applet example. Although we did briefly mention that inheritance was used, we did not explain the significance of inheritance in much detail. So, let's return to the inheritance that we have used with every applet example that we have studied so far and discuss more of the details involving its use. First, let's observe the following relationship between every applet class that we have created and the predefined class `JApplet`.

- Every applet class we have created *is a* `JApplet`.

Recall that the reserved word `extends` is what denotes the use of inheritance. Let's consider exactly what it means when we say that one class extends another, which will help us understand why inheritance is used to characterize this language feature. First, the *derived class*, whose name precedes `extends`, inherits all of the methods of its *base class*, whose names follow `extends`. Second, it also inherits all of its instance data.

We have made use of inherited methods on numerous occasions in the applets that we have written. Frequently we have called the method `repaint`. It is a method that we did not write, but inherited from `JApplet`. To be precise, `JApplet` inherited that method from `java.applet.Applet`, which in turn inherited it from `java.awt.Panel`, which inherited it from `java.awt.Container`, which finally, inherited it from `java.awt.Component`. Each of the classes in that sequence extends the subsequent one. So a derived class not only inherits all the methods and instance data defined in its base or parent class, but from all its *ancestor classes*—parent, grandparent, and so on.

Although we did so less frequently, we did make use of inherited data on at least one occasion. We did not call your attention to it at the time, but in the threshold graph example in Listing 7.4 we made use of a constant, `WIDTH`, that was inherited from its base class `Application`. We also used the inherited constant `WIDTH` in Listing 10.9.

Inheritance Hierarchies and Type Compatibility

One important restriction in Java is that a class can only extend one other class. In other words, every derived class can have only one base or parent class. This restriction can also be expressed by stating that Java does not allow *multiple inheritance* of classes. We should add that some object-oriented languages do permit such multiple inheritance, and it introduces a number of complexities, so the Java designers were wise to avoid it. Because each derived class has only one base, inheritance relationships define a hierarchy of classes. In fact, every class is a derived class, even those that are not explicitly defined with an extends clause. Such classes implicitly extend the predefined class Object, which we first introduced in Chapter 8. As a result, all Java classes in any program form a single hierarchy with the class Object at the top. All classes are ultimately derived from Object, or, to state it in reverse, Object is the ancestor of all classes. When we see the UML representation for inheritance relationships, we will see how these hierarchies are illustrated.

In Chapter 2, we discussed type coercion and type casting in regard to the primitive types. In this chapter, we need to understand how those concepts apply to classes. The rules are as follows: 1) An object of any class can be coerced to any of its ancestor classes; 2) An object of any class can be type cast to any of its descendant classes; 3) No other type conversions are permitted. Let's illustrate these rules with some examples. The following declaration illustrates the first rule:

```
Object someObject = new String("some string");
```

To illustrate the second rule, consider the following declaration that assumes the previous one:

```
String someString = (String)someObject;
```

Notice that the syntax for these type casts is the same as with primitive types. The class name is placed in parentheses before the object to be type cast. Type casts of this kind are referred to as *downcasts*. The reason is that the type conversion is down the inheritance hierarchy—from some class to one of its descendants. Casts in the other direction are referred to as *upcasts*. Although we could have used an explicit upcast in our first example, because upcasts are always safe, they are not required. Coercion can be relied upon instead. By contrast, downcasts are potentially unsafe. Let's clarify what we mean by unsafe. We mean that an error can occur—not a compilation error because, in general, the compiler lacks the information necessary to make that determination. With downcasts, the potential exists for what is called a class cast exception—a runtime error. We will see an example of how this can occur later in this chapter.

Finally, let's consider an example that illustrates the third rule.

```
Integer someInteger = new Integer(5);
String someString = (String)someInteger;
```

The second declaration will result in a compilation error. It is neither an upcast nor a downcast, so it is always invalid.

One final point is that, just like with primitive types, these rules apply also in initialized declarations, and in assignments between arguments and parameters in method calls.

Extending the Representation

Recall that when Java classes are used to define new data types from which instances can be created, those classes contain a specification defined by the public methods, a representation defined by the private instance variables, and an implementation defined by the method bodies. Next we consider how inheritance can affect each of these three aspects of a data type definition.

We begin by considering how a derived class can be used to extend the representation of its base class. The class whose representation we extend is the Rectangle class that we introduced in Chapter 10. We extend the representation by adding another instance variable that contains the color of the rectangle. The name that we give to this derived class is ColoredRectangle. Notice how the name of the derived class uses the name of the base class prefaced by an adjective—a clear indicator of a generalization relationship, as we noted earlier. We are now ready to discuss the code necessary for this extension to the class Rectangle. The code is shown in Listing 12.1.

LISTING 12.1   A Colored Rectangle Class (found on the CD-ROM at

ON THE CD   chapter12\ColoredRectangle.java.)

```
1   package chapter12;
2
3   import java.awt.*;
4
5   class ColoredRectangle extends chapter10.Rectangle
6   {
7       private Color color = Color.BLACK;
8
9       public ColoredRectangle(int x, int y, int width, int height,
10          double angle, Color color)
11      {
12          super(x, y, width, height, angle);
13          this.color = color;
14      }
15      public void draw(Graphics graphics)
16      {
17          graphics.setColor(color);
18          super.draw(graphics);
19          graphics.setColor(Color.BLACK);
20      }
21  }
```

The class `ColoredRectangle` extends its base class rectangle by adding the additional instance variable `color`, which is declared on line 7. It inherits the five instance variables `x`, `y`, `length1`, `length2`, and `angle` from `chapter10.Rectangle`. Consequently the representation of a `ColoredRectangle` object consists of all six instance variables. As an aside, notice that in referring to the class `Rectangle`, we have qualified it with its package name `chapter10` to distinguish it from `java.awt.Rectangle`.

We mentioned earlier that derived classes inherit all the methods of their base class. There is one exception, however. Constructors are not inherited because of the requirement that the name of the constructor must be the same as the class name. Consequently we need a constructor in this class that calls the constructor of the base class to initialize the five instance variables it inherits from that class and then initializes its one additional instance variable. The call to the constructor of `Rectangle` is made on line 12, using the reserved word `super` that we introduced in Chapter 5. When present, this call must be the first statement of the constructor. If we omit a call to the constructor of the base class, the compiler automatically generates a call to the default constructor of the base class.

The only other method defined in `chapter10.Rectangle` is draw. The derived class would inherit this method, but if we allowed it to be inherited, we would be unable to achieve the goal of this class, which is to create colored rectangles. Consequently, we need to modify the implementation by *overriding* the method draw. To override means to redefine a method that would otherwise be inherited from the base class. Unlike overloaded methods, overridden methods have signatures identical to the ones they are overriding. When we extend the representation of a class, it is common to need to also modify the implementation by overriding some of the methods. In the overridden version of draw, we set the color on line 17 and then call the method that we are overriding to perform the actual drawing on line 18. The overridden method must be qualified by the reserved word `super` to distinguish it from the method performing the call.

Notice that both of these methods called the corresponding methods in the base class. This practice is a desirable one when appropriate because it avoids code duplication.

Extending the Specification

Next, we consider an example of a derived class that extends only the specification of its base class. The example that we have chosen is a class that allows us to incorporate the `ColoredRectangle` class that we have just discussed into a complete program. The class that we extend is the `RectanglesWindow` class introduced in Chapter 10 and shown in Listing 10.2. The name that we have given it is `MixedRectanglesWindow`. As before, we added an adjective as a prefix to the name of the base class to make clear that objects of the class are windows that contain mixed rectangles—

both regular ones that are black by default and others that are colored. The code for this class is shown in Listing 12.2.

LISTING 12.2 A Window Class Containing a Collection of Mixed Rectangles (found on the CD-ROM at chapter12\MixedRectanglesWindow.java.)

```
1  package chapter12;
2
3  import java.awt.*;
4  import chapter10.*;
5
6  class MixedRectanglesWindow extends RectanglesWindow
7  {
8      public void addColoredRectangle(ColoredRectangle rectangle)
9      {
10          rectangles.add(rectangle);
11          repaint();
12      }
13  }
```

This class inherits the representation from `RectanglesWindow`, which is the array list of rectangles. No extension is made to that representation.

As we indicated earlier, constructors are not inherited, but you should also recall that if we supply no constructor for a class, the compiler generates a default constructor. Because this is a derived class, the default constructor implicitly calls the default constructor of the base class.

This class inherits the method `addRectangle` from the base class and extends the specification, as we indicated this example would. This class allows one new operation—the ability to add colored rectangles to the window—which is accomplished by the method `addColoredRectangle`. The two methods are similar overall, but there is one important difference, which is that the type of the parameter is now `Colored Rectangle`, not `Rectangle`. This point requires some additional discussion. The type of the argument that we are passing into the `add` method of `ArrayList` is `Colored Rectangle`, but the type of that parameter is `Rectangle`. The reason that the parameter type is `Rectangle` is because we constrained the generic class `ArrayList` to be an array list of rectangles. The type conversion that occurs here is up the inheritance hierarchy. As we discussed earlier, such conversions are always safe, so no type cast is needed—automatic type coercion is performed.

Finally, the method `paintComponent` is inherited from the base class `Rectan-glesWindow`. When inherited, this method now exhibits a behavior that we have not yet discussed. Let's examine the `for` loop in that method, which is on lines 24-25 of Listing 10.2. We repeat that `for` loop below to facilitate this discussion.

```
for (Rectangle rectangle: rectangles)
    rectangle.draw(graphics);
```

The call to the method draw is now a *polymorphic method call.* What is meant by that statement is that by looking at the program, we cannot determine which method is being called, the method draw defined in the class Rectangle, or the method draw defined in ColoredRectangle. In fact, it is possible that during the execution of the program, sometimes it is the one in the base class being called; other times, it is the one in the derived class. What determines which method is called is the type of the individual rectangle object. You should realize that it is now possible that the array list rectangles contains some rectangles of type Rectangle and others of type ColoredRectangle.

Let's compare this polymorphic behavior, which results from overriding, with what occurs when methods are overloaded. Although we prefer to confine the use of the term polymorphism to what results from overriding, some books refer to overloaded methods as polymorphic methods also. The term polymorphism means many forms. With both overloading and overriding, we have more than one method with the same name. There is an important difference, however. With overloading, although the method names are the same, the signatures must be distinguishable. As a result, the determination of which method to call can be made at compile time by comparing the argument types with the parameter types of the various overloaded methods. When a method is overridden, we have multiple methods with identical signatures. It is the type of object that is needed to determine which method is being called. That determination, in general, can only be made at runtime, as our example illustrates.

To complete this example, we need the method main. Listing 12.3 contains the code for a class that contains this method.

LISTING 12.3 The Class Containing main for the Mixed Rectangles in a Window
ON THE CD Application (found on the CD-ROM at chapter12\MixedRectanglesMain.java.)

```
 1  package chapter12;
 2
 3  import java.awt.*;
 4  import common.*;
 5
 6  public class MixedRectanglesMain
 7  {
 8      private enum MenuChoices {REGULAR_RECTANGLE, COLORED_RECTANGLE,
 9          NO_MORE};
10
11      public static void main(String[] args)
```

```
12      {
13          final int MAX_POS = 250, MAX_LENGTH = 60;
14          int x, y, length1, length2;
15          double angle;
16          Color color;
17          MenuChoices choice;
18          MixedRectanglesWindow window = new MixedRectanglesWindow();
19
20          window.display();
21          while (true)
22          {
23              choice = (MenuChoices)InputOutput.getEnum(
24                  "Select rectangle type: ", MenuChoices.values());
25              if (choice == MenuChoices.NO_MORE)
26                  return;
27              x = (int)(Math.random() * MAX_POS);
28              y = (int)(Math.random() * MAX_POS);
29              length1 = (int)(Math.random() * MAX_LENGTH);
30              length2 = (int)(Math.random() * MAX_LENGTH);
31              angle = Math.random() * chapter10.Rectangle. RIGHT_ANGLE;
32              switch (choice)
33              {
34                  case REGULAR_RECTANGLE:
35                      window.addRectangle(new chapter10.Rectangle
36                          (x, y, length1, length2, angle));
37                      break;
38                  case COLORED_RECTANGLE:
39                      color = InputOutput.getColor(
40                          "Enter rectangle color: ");
41                      window.addColoredRectangle(new ColoredRectangle
42                          (x, y, length1,    length2, angle, color));
43                      break;
44              }
45          }
46      }
47  }
```

This method is similar to the one in Listing 10.3 and contains nothing new that should require explicit explanation, so we simply describe its overall behavior. Like the first version of this program, the user is permitted to repeatedly add rectangles with randomly chosen positions, sizes, and orientations to the window. The one important difference in this version is that the user is permitted to select whether a regular or a colored rectangle is added. For colored rectangles, the user is permitted to select the color. If you choose a mixture of rectangles when you run this program, each time the window is repainted, the call to draw will choose which method to call based on the type of the rectangle.

UML Diagrams Depicting Generalization Relationships

Now that we have a complete program consisting of five classes, let's consider the UML diagram that illustrates the class relationships, shown in Figure 12.1.

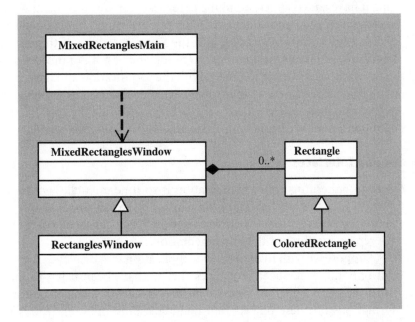

FIGURE 12.1   UML diagram for the window of mixed rectangles application.

This diagram contains both generalization and composition relationships. There are two generalization relationships that we implemented with inheritance, the ColoredRectangle class extending the representation of the Rectangle class and the MixedRectanglesWindow class extending the specification of the RectanglesWindow class. The UML symbol depicting inheritance relationships is the hollow arrowhead. Like composition, generalization is a directed relationship. Notice that the arrowheads are placed adjacent and pointing to the base classes. It is customary to place the base class above the derived class in inheritance diagrams.

One other feature to notice in this diagram is that we show the composition relationship between MixedRectangleWindow and Rectangle only. It is understood that by indicating that the window class contains rectangles, it can contain any kind of rectangle, including any derived class.

CLASS-INTERFACE RELATIONSHIPS

We have observed that a generalization relationship may extend either the specification or representation of its base class. Certainly, it can also extend both. We might have added a method to the ColoredRectangle class to allow the color of the rectangle to be changed once it is created. In that case, we would have been extending both the specification and the representation. With generalization relationships, whether or not we are extending one or both of those aspects of the base class, we typically desire to inherit both the specification and the representation, although, in some cases, we may totally override the inherited specification. Next we will consider situations where we wish to inherit only the specification or only the representation. We begin with an example illustrating the former.

Implementing Interfaces

Because inheriting only a specification is so fundamental, Java provides a special syntax—one that we introduced in Chapter 8. Recall that Java interfaces are similar to classes except that they define only the specification of a data type, but neither the representation nor the implementation.

Suppose we wish to create a Java application that displays a window containing not only the generalized rectangles that we have been using in this chapter, but other figures as well. Furthermore, we would like to be able to perform some transformations on these objects that include scaling them and translating them—a term commonly used to mean moving. Let's define an interface that includes these capabilities. Its code is shown in Listing 12.4.

LISTING 12.4 A Drawable, Translatable, and Scalable Interface (found on the CD-ROM
ON THE CD at chapter12\Transformable.java.)

```
1  package chapter12;
2
3  import java.awt.*;
4
5  public interface Transformable
6  {
7      void draw(Graphics graphics);
```

```
 8        void scale(double factor);
 9        void translate(int deltaX, int deltaY);
10  }
```

In addition to the ability to perform scaling and translating, we have also included drawing in this interface. We explain the reason for that capability shortly.

Throughout this chapter and previous ones, we have been emphasizing the role of English words in object-oriented design, so let's examine their role in naming interfaces. The word *transform* is a verb. In English, many verbs can be turned into adjectives by adding the suffix *able*, which is the case here. Such adjectives confer the ability to perform some actions, so any class that implements such an interface would have methods that would allow these operations to be performed on objects of that class. It is not uncommon for interface names to be adjectives of this kind. One example of a predefined interface that has such a name is the interface Comparable, which requires the ability of objects to be able to be compared. On the other hand, such names are not required. In the previous chapter, we encountered an interface named MouseListener. When the name of an interface is an adjective, it is not unusual for a class that implements it to contain that adjective—especially when that class is adding these new capabilities to an existing class. Such is the case with our modified version of the generalized rectangle class that we have been using in this chapter. The code for this modified version, which we name TransformableRectangle, is shown in Listing 12.5.

LISTING 12.5   A Transformable Rectangle Class (found on the CD-ROM at
ON THE CD   chapter12\TransformableRectangle.java.)

```
 1 package chapter12;
 2
 3 import java.awt.*;
 4
 5 public class TransformableRectangle extends chapter10.Rectangle
 6     implements Transformable
 7 {
 8     public TransformableRectangle(int x, int y, int length1,
 9         int length2, double angle)
10     {
11         super(x, y, length1, length2, angle);
12     }
13     public void scale(double factor)
14     {
15         length1 = (int)(length1 * factor + .5);
16         length2 = (int)(length2 * factor + .5);
17     }
```

```
18        public void translate(int deltaX, int deltaY)
19        {
20            x += deltaX;
21            y += deltaY;
22        }
23  }
```

On lines 5 and 6, notice that both the reserved words `extends` and `implements` are used. Although we first encountered a class that both extends a class and implements an interface in Chapter 8—the `DrawablePolygon1` class—this program is the first example in which we are both inheriting from a class that we wrote and implementing an interface that we wrote. Although Java prohibits multiple inheritance of classes, multiple implementation of interfaces is permitted, so a class can extend another class and implement any number of interfaces.

The next thing to notice is that this class contains no instance variables, so no extension is being made to the representation. Transformable rectangles and regular rectangles have the same representation because this class inherits all the instance variables defined in its base class. Although derived classes inherit all instance variables, if the instance variables are declared with the access modifier `private` in the base class, the methods of the derived class cannot access them. The methods that are a part of this extension need to access the representation for the rectangle, which is why we declared the instance variables with the access modifier `protected` on lines 9 and 10 of Listing 10.1, which contains the definition of the base class `Rectangle`.

Clearly our desire to hide the representation of objects of a class, an important software engineering principle that we encountered in Chapter 3, is at odds with the need of derived classes that rely on the representation defined in their base classes. This conflict is exacerbated by the fact that whenever we declare instance data as `protected`, that data becomes accessible to not only methods of all derived classes, but to all methods of every class in the same package. Although we have relied on the package structure to organize the programs in this book by chapter, we would need to carefully consider the design of the package structure in large programs to ensure that the principle of information hiding is not overly compromised. One technique would be to place the base class and all classes derived from it in a separate package, or perhaps subpackage. By so doing, we could limit access to the representation to only those classes that genuinely need it.

Now we consider each of the methods, beginning with the constructor. As before, it calls the constructor of its base class to initialize the instance variables inherited from the base class. We now realize that the instance data of the base class is accessible because it is labeled with the modifier `protected`. Consequently, instead of calling the constructor of the base class, the constructor of the derived class could directly initialize the instance variables inherited from the base class. Although possible, it is never a good practice to do so, because it results in unnecessary and undesirable code duplication.

Next, let's consider the two new methods `scale` and `translate`. The first method, `scale`, multiplies the lengths of the sides by the scale factor, either decreasing or increasing the size of the whole rectangle. The second method, `translate`, adds the supplied x-y increments to the first vertex, which results in the whole rectangle being moved by the specified increment. Both of these methods preserve the class invariant—the fact that the quadrilateral has four right angles.

Representation Relationships

We had indicated that our reason for defining the interface `Transformable` is that we wanted to be able to perform transformations on graphical objects other than just our generalized rectangles. Now we create a second class that also implements this interface. With our next example, we wish to illustrate another kind of relationship between classes. It is a relationship that might be expressed by the predicate *is represented by*. We plan to construct a graphical object, which is a square parallel to the axes from the predefined class `java.awt.Rectangle`. On the surface, the relationship may seem like a generalization relationship. The statement "a square *is a* rectangle" is indeed true. This case highlights why we must try other predicates beyond *is a* to really be certain that we have generalization. What is not true is that a square is not an extension of a rectangle; it is really a restriction of one. The relationship that we are relying upon is that a square *can be represented as* a rectangle. Identifying class relationships can be somewhat subtle and does require practice. In any case, let's examine the code for this class before elaborating upon the significance of this relationship any further. Listing 12.6 contains the code for this class.

LISTING 12.6 A Class Defining a Square Parallel to the Axes Derived from `java.awt.Rectangle` (found on the CD-ROM at `chapter12\InheritedSquare.java.`)

```
 1  package chapter12;
 2
 3  import java.awt.*;
 4
 5  class InheritedSquare extends Rectangle
 6      implements Transformable
 7  {
 8      public InheritedSquare(int x, int y, int size)
 9      {
10          super(x, y, size, size);
11      }
```

```
12      public void draw(Graphics graphics)
13      {
14          graphics.drawRect(x, y, width, height);
15      }
16      public void scale(double factor)
17      {
18          width = (int)(width * factor + .5);
19          height = (int)(height * factor + .5);
20      }
21      public void translate(int deltaX, int deltaY)
22      {
23          x += deltaX;
24          y += deltaY;
25      }
26  }
```

We named this class InheritedSquare to emphasize the fact that we have used inheritance to realize the *is represented by* relationship. Like the previous example, this class both extends a class and implements an interface. One thing that is worth noting on line 5 is that the name Rectangle refers to java.awt.Rectangle because we imported the package java.awt, but not chapter10.

Next, let's consider the methods of this class. The constructor of this class, whose signature is on line 8, allows the user to supply the *x-y* coordinates of the upper-left corner and the length of a side—since all sides are equal. On line 10, a call is made to the constructor of java.awt.Rectangle. The same length is passed as both the height and width. The methods scale and translate are quite similar to the ones in the TransformableRectangle class that we just examined.

Next we need a class that defines a window onto which these transformable objects can be drawn. It will be similar to the class RectanglesWindow that we used earlier, but not similar enough that we can reuse or extend it. This new class TransformablesWindow is shown in Listing 12.7.

LISTING 12.7   A Window Class Containing a Collection of Transformable Objects
(found on the CD-ROM at chapter12\TransformablesWindow.java.)

```
1  package chapter12;
2
3  import java.awt.*;
4  import java.util.*;
5  import common.*;
6
7  public class TransformablesWindow extends Application
8  {
```

```
 9      private ArrayList<Transformable> objects =
10          new ArrayList<Transformable>();
11
12      public void add(Transformable object)
13      {
14          objects.add(object);
15          repaint();
16      }
17      public void paintComponent(Graphics graphics)
18      {
19          super.paintComponent(graphics);
20          for (Transformable object: objects)
21              object.draw(graphics);
22      }
23      public void scale(double factor)
24      {
25          for (Transformable object: objects)
26              object.scale(factor);
27          repaint();
28      }
29      public void translate(int deltaX, int deltaY)
30      {
31          for (Transformable object: objects)
32              object.translate(deltaX, deltaY);
33          repaint();
34      }
35  }
```

There are some similarities between `RectanglesWindow` and `TransformablesWindow`. On lines 9 and 10, we are declaring and instantiating an array list of type `Transformable` rather than `Rectangle`. The `paintComponent` methods also differ only in the type of the loop control variable. On line 20, we use the type `Transformable` in place of `Rectangle`. Finally, we consider the additional methods, `scale` and `translate`. Both of these methods behave in a similar way. They iterate across the array list and apply the corresponding method to each of the objects.

Finally, to complete this program, we need, as always, a class that contains `main`. That class, which we have named `TransformablesMain`, is shown in Listing 12.8.

LISTING 12.8 The Class Containing `main` for Transformable Objects in a Window *ONTHECD* Application (found on the CD-ROM at `chapter12\TransformablesMain.java`.)

```
1  package chapter12;
2
```

```
3  import java.awt.*;
4  import common.*;
5
6  public class TransformablesMain
7  {
8      private enum ObjectChoices {SQUARE, RECTANGLE, NO_MORE};
9      private enum ActionChoices {SCALE, TRANSLATE, QUIT};
10
11     public static void main(String[] args)
12     {
13         final int MAX_POS = 250, MAX_LENGTH = 60, MAX_TRANS = 50;
14         int x, y, length1, length2;
15         double angle, scaleFactor;
16         char response;
17         ObjectChoices objectChoice;
18         ActionChoices actionChoice;
19         TransformablesWindow window = new TransformablesWindow();
20
21         window.display();
22         while (true)
23         {
24             objectChoice = (ObjectChoices)InputOutput.getEnum
25                 ("Select an object: ", ObjectChoices.values());
26             if (objectChoice == ObjectChoices.NO_MORE)
27                 break;
28             x = (int)(Math.random() * MAX_POS);
29             y = (int)(Math.random() * MAX_POS);
30             length1 = (int)(Math.random() * MAX_LENGTH);
31             switch (objectChoice)
32             {
33                 case SQUARE:
34                     window.add(new InheritedSquare(x, y, length1));
35                     break;
36                 case RECTANGLE:
37                     length2 = (int)(Math.random() * MAX_LENGTH);
38                     angle = Math.random() *
39                         chapter10.Rectangle.RIGHT_ANGLE;
40                     window.add(new TransformableRectangle(x, y,
41                         length1, length2, angle));
42                     break;
43             }
44         }
45         while (true)
46         {
```

```
47              actionChoice = (ActionChoices)InputOutput.getEnum
48                  ("Select an action: ", ActionChoices.values());
49              if (actionChoice == ActionChoices.QUIT)
50                  return;
51              switch (actionChoice)
52              {
53                  case SCALE:
54                      scaleFactor = Math.random() * 2;
55                      window.scale(scaleFactor);
56                      break;
57                  case TRANSLATE:
58                      x = (int)(Math.random() * MAX_TRANS);
59                      y = (int)(Math.random() * MAX_TRANS);
60                      window.translate(x, y);
61                      break;
62              }
63          }
64      }
65  }
```

There is not much in this method that requires explanation, so, instead, we give an overview of its behavior. It first allows the user to add as many objects to the window as desired. The user is given a choice between squares and rectangles. Once the desired number of objects has been added, the user is permitted to repeatedly choose between scaling and translating the objects. As always, we recommend running this program to be sure you understand its behavior.

There is one aspect of this program that warrants additional explanation, however. Notice that in the call to the method add on line 34, an object of type InheritedSquare is passed in as the argument. On lines 40 and 41, the same method is called but the type of the argument is TransformableRectangle. The type of the parameter object of the method add, which is declared on line 12 of Listing 12.7, is the interface type Transformable. Type coercion is occurring in both calls. So next let's consider type compatibility rules for objects of an interface type and objects of any class type that implement that interface. If we regard the interface as the base type, the same rules apply as with derived and base classes. An object of an implemented type is automatically coerced to its interface type, which is what is happening in both of these method calls.

UML Diagrams Depicting Implementation Relationships

With the TransformableMain class, our program is now complete. It consists of six classes and one interface that we have written. The UML diagram that illustrates the class and interface relationships is shown in Figure 12.2.

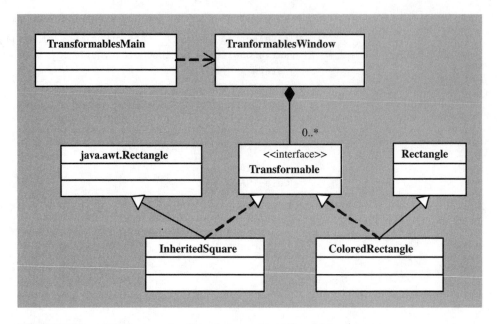

FIGURE 12.2   UML diagram for the window of transformable objects.

This diagram contains dependency, generalization, composition, and implementation relationships. There are two generalization relationships: the InheritedSquare class extending the java.awt.Rectangle class and the Transformable Rectangle class extending the specification of the RectanglesWindow class. Normally, we do not include predefined classes in our diagrams, but we wanted to emphasize the fact that InheritedSquare was a derived class. There are two implementation relationships, the InheritedSquare and TransformableRectangle, both implementing the Transformable interface.

The UML symbol depicting implementation relationships is a dotted line with a hollow arrowhead pointing to the interface. The other UML symbolism that is new is how interfaces are designated. Remember that UML is intended to be programming language independent. Not all languages syntactically distinguish classes from interfaces like Java does. In UML, we designate an interface by using a class diagram, adding what UML calls a stereotype above the interface name. The stereotype is the word interface enclosed in guillemets—double corner brackets. We have mentioned throughout that Java classes play different roles, such as role of the utility class played by the Math class. In UML, that role would be designated with the stereotype utility.

Problems with Using Inheritance for Representation Relationships

Now we return to the InheritedSquare class that we used in the previous example. Using inheritance as we did has an undesirable consequence. We derived InheritedSquare from Rectangle because we wished to inherit its representation, but we also inherited its complete specification and corresponding implementation. In Java, there is no way to prevent inheriting everything. In particular, we inherited a method setSize, whose signature is shown below:

```
void setSize(int width, int height)
```

As a result, the following code fragment could be used:

```
InheritedSquare square = new InheritedSquare(10, 10, 50):
square.setSize(25, 75);
```

We create a square whose sides are initially 50 pixels, but then change the width to 25 and the height to 75, so we no longer have a square. We really did not even need to call the method because the instance variables x and y are public in Rectangle, which means they are public in InheritedSquare, so we could have broken the invariant with direct assignments to those instance variables.

For this reason, using inheritance to realize an *is represented by* relationship is a design error in Java. Some object-oriented languages provide a mechanism that allows inheritance to be used for this purpose without creating such problems. Many software engineers, however, believe such uses of inheritance are improper, regardless. We should note that the designers of Java made this error with the predefined Stack class, which is derived from the class Vector—a class similar to ArrayList but one that predates it.

Let's consider an alternate design that prevents this problem. Listing 12.9 contains the class ComposedSquare, which implements the *is represented by* relationship with composition.

LISTING 12.9 A Class Defining a Square Parallel to the Axes Composed of a
ON THE CD java.awt.Rectangle (found on the CD-ROM at chapter12\ComposedSquare.java.)

```
1  package chapter12;
2
3  import java.awt.*;
4
5  public class ComposedSquare implements Transformable
6  {
7      private Rectangle square;
```

```
 8
 9      public ComposedSquare(int x, int y, int size)
10      {
11          square = new java.awt.Rectangle(x, y, size, size);
12      }
13      public void draw(Graphics graphics)
14      {
15          graphics.drawRect(square.x, square.y, square.width,
16              square.height);
17      }
18      public void scale(double factor)
19      {
20          square.width = (int)(square.width * factor + .5);
21          square.height = (int)(square.height * factor + .5);
22      }
23      public void translate(int deltaX, int deltaY)
24      {
25          square.x += deltaX;
26          square.y += deltaY;
27      }
28  }
```

Let's examine the differences between this implementation and the one that used inheritance. First, the extends clause is omitted on line 5 and, instead, an instance variable of type java.awt.Rectangle named square is declared on line 7. Finally, wherever we were able to reference the instance variables x, y, width, and height, we must now qualify them with the object square. Lines 15 and 16 contain one such example.

We could now replace InheritedSquare with ComposedSquare in our previous example by making one simple change in the TransformablesMain class on line 34 in Listing 12.8. The advantage of this change would be that the class invariant of our squares would now be unbreakable.

Downcasts and Class Cast Exceptions

In our discussion of type compatibility at the beginning of this chapter, we mentioned that type conversions up an inheritance hierarchy are safe, but conversions downward, which require type casts, are potentially unsafe. Our next example is designed to illustrate this point. We plan to reuse some of the classes that we have developed so far in this chapter in this example, but we need two new classes. First, we need a new window class for displaying rectangles. This class, which we name TransformableRectanglesWindow, is a variation of ones we have already discussed. Its code is contained in Listing 12.10.

LISTING 12.10   A Window Class Containing a Collection of Transformable Rectangles
ON THE CD   (found on the CD-ROM at chapter12\TransformableRectanglesWindow.java.)

```
 1  package chapter12;
 2
 3  import chapter10.*;
 4
 5  class TransformableRectanglesWindow extends RectanglesWindow
 6  {
 7      public void addTransformableRectangle(TransformableRectangle
 8          rectangle)
 9      {
10          rectangles.add(rectangle);
11          repaint();
12      }
13      public void scale(double factor)
14      {
15          for (Rectangle rectangle: rectangles)
16              ((TransformableRectangle)rectangle).scale(factor);
17          repaint();
18      }
19      public void translate(int deltaX, int deltaY)
20      {
21          for (Rectangle rectangle: rectangles)
22              ((TransformableRectangle)rectangle).
23                      translate(deltaX, deltaY);
24          repaint();
25      }
26  }
```

It is similar to the MixedRectanglesWindow class in that it inherits the representation of RectanglesWindow, but instead of adding a new method to add colored rectangles, it adds a new method to add transformable rectangles. It is similar to the TransformablesWindow class because it contains both the methods scale and translate, but there is an important difference in these methods. Notice that on lines 16 and 22 the object rectangle, whose type is Rectangle, must be downcast to type TransformableRectangle. The downcast is necessary because the methods rotate and scale are not defined on the general rectangles defined by class Rectangle. Without that downcast, this program would not compile.

We are now ready to illustrate why downcasts are considered unsafe. We need a short class containing a method main for this purpose. That class is shown in Listing 12.11.

LISTING 12.11   A Class Illustrating a Class Cast Exception (found on the CD-ROM at *ON THE CD* chapter12\ClassCastExample.java.)

```
1   package chapter12;
2
3   import java.awt.*;
4   import common.*;
5
6   public class ClassCastExample
7   {
8       public static void main(String[] args)
9       {
10          final int MAX_POS = 250, MAX_LENGTH = 60, RECTANGLES = 4;
11          int x, y, length1, length2;
12          double angle;
13          TransformableRectanglesWindow window =
14              new TransformableRectanglesWindow();
15
16          window.display();
17          for (int count = 0; count < RECTANGLES; count++)
18          {
19              x = (int)(Math.random() * MAX_POS);
20              y = (int)(Math.random() * MAX_POS);
21              length1 = (int)(Math.random() * MAX_LENGTH);
22              length2 = (int)(Math.random() * MAX_LENGTH);
23              angle = Math.random() *
24                  chapter10.Rectangle.RIGHT_ANGLE;
25              if (count < RECTANGLES / 2)
26                  window.addTransformableRectangle(
27                      new TransformableRectangle(x, y, length1,
28                      length2, angle));
29              else
30                  window.addRectangle(new chapter10.Rectangle
31                      (x, y, length1, length2, angle));
32          }
33          angle = Math.random() * chapter10.Rectangle.RIGHT_ANGLE;
34          window.scale(angle);
35      }
36  }
```

In the `for` loop that spans lines 17-32, four rectangles with random positions, sizes, and angles are created and added to the window. The first two are transformable rectangles. The second two are generalized rectangles that are not transformable. There is no problem with adding both kinds of rectangles to the window.

The problem arises on line 34, when we call the method `scale` to scale all the rectangles. It will be able to scale the first two, but when it attempts to scale the third one, the program will terminate with a runtime error, called a *class cast exception*. When the downcast is performed on the first two objects it succeeds because they are `TransformableRectangle` objects, but it fails on the third object, because its type is `Rectangle`.

Because downcasts are potentially unsafe, they should be regarded as red flags for possible design errors. In this case, one could argue that the design error is using inheritance for what is really an *is represented by* relationship. We really want the class `TransformableRectanglesWindow` to inherit the representation of `RectanglesWindow` only, but we cannot prevent it from inheriting the method `addRectangle`, which was the source of the problem. In this case, one alternative would have been to override `addRectangle` rather than extend the specification with `addTransformableRectangle`. We are not suggesting that downcasts are always design errors. There are some instances where they are unavoidable, but they should be used with caution.

Recall our discussion in Chapter 8 on generic classes. We mentioned that the advantage that generic classes provide is avoiding the need for downcasts. Had we not constrained all our array lists in all the examples throughout this chapter, each time we removed one from the list, a downcast would have been needed.

AGGREGATION RELATIONSHIPS

The final kind of class relationship that we discuss in this chapter is the aggregation relationship. Composition and aggregation are similar relationships, but there is one important difference. In a compositional relationship, the containing object has exclusive ownership of the component object. In an aggregation relationship, the component object may be shared among objects.

Let's consider an example in general terms before examining how these relationships are implemented in Java. Suppose that we were developing an object-oriented database for a university. Such a system would need classes for students, courses, instructors, and so on. One class relationship would be that a student was enrolled in a particular course. Such a relationship is aggregation, not composition, because that student might be a part of many courses. By contrast, one of the components of each student is that student's grade point average. Every student has exclusive ownership of that value.

Both aggregation and composition relationships must be implemented by having the component be an instance variable of its containing class. To properly distinguish between these two kinds of relationships, ideally, we would like the component and its container to have identical lifetimes with composition and independent lifetimes with aggregation. When instance variables are primitives, they always have the lifetime of their containing object, but when instance variables are objects themselves, they only have the lifetime of the containing object if there are no other references to that object. To ensure that there are no other references, we must create the component objects inside the class and never export those references.

Insisting upon identical lifetimes to properly represent composition is really a somewhat excessive requirement in many cases. If you look back at our previous examples of composition, in no case have we done that. We typically created the object in main and passed it to the constructor of the containing class. The reason was that all the component objects that we used were immutable. Again we return to this important distinction between mutable and immutable objects. When a class contains an instance variable that is an immutable object, the containing class behaves as though it is the exclusive owner. With mutable objects, if we really want to properly capture the exclusive ownership characteristic of composition, insisting upon identical lifetimes is necessary.

The example that we use to illustrate the aggregation relationship involves a class that defines strings that have styles. The relationship is aggregation because many strings can have the same style. The first class necessary for this example is the one that defines styles. The code for that class is contained in Listing 12.12.

LISTING 12.12 A Class Defining a Style Consisting of a Font and Color (found on the CD-ROM at chapter12\Style.java.)

```
1   package chapter12;
2
3   import java.awt.*;
4
5   class Style
6   {
7       private Font font;
8       private Color color;
9
10      public Style(Font font, Color color)
11      {
12          this.font = font;
13          this.color = color;
14      }
15      public void recolor(Color color)
16      {
17          this.color = color;
18      }
19      public void resize(int size)
20      {
21          font = new Font(font.getName(), font.getStyle(), size);
```

```
22        }
23        public void setStyle(Graphics graphics)
24        {
25            graphics.setFont(font);
26            graphics.setColor(color);
27        }
28 }
```

The representation for a style consists of the two instance variables font and color, declared on lines 7 and 8. The initial creation of the fonts in this example will be done in main. One thing to note here is that there is a compositional relationship between the font and color and style. In other words, a style is composed of a font and a color. By allowing the font and color to be created outside the class, these objects may actually have longer lifetimes than the objects in which they are contained but, as with our previous examples, both are immutable objects.

It should be apparent to you that objects of the class Style are mutable objects because of the presence of the methods recolor and resize that allow the representation of these objects to be changed after they are created. The constructor of Font is called on line 21 in the resize method when the font size needs to be changed. The fact that we must create a new font object to accomplish this resizing is evidence of the immutability of font objects. We must extract the name and style of the existing font with the method getName and getStyle and use that information to create the new font. The style returned by getStyle is whether the font is plain, bold, or italic.

Finally, the method setStyle is provided so objects of this style can call this method to set the font and color before they paint themselves.

The next class that is required for this example is the class that defines strings that have defined positions and styles. The code for this class, StyledString, is shown in Listing 12.13.

LISTING 12.13 A Class Defining a String that has a Position and Style (found on the CD-ROM at chapter12\StyledString.java.)

```
1  package chapter12;
2
3  import java.awt.*;
4
5  class StyledString implements Transformable
6  {
7      private int x, y;
8      private String string;
9      private Style style;
10
```

```
11        public StyledString(int x, int y, String string,
12            Style style)
13        {
14            this.x = x;
15            this.y = y;
16            this.string = string;
17            this.style = style;
18        }
19        public void draw(Graphics graphics)
20        {
21            style.setStyle(graphics);
22            graphics.drawString(string, x, y);
23        }
24        public void scale(double factor)
25        {
26        }
27        public void translate(int deltaX, int deltaY)
28        {
29            x += deltaX;
30            y += deltaY;
31        }
32   }
```

In the class declaration on line 5, we elected to have this class implement the Transformable interface. Implementing that interface allows us to reuse the Trans-formablesWindow class to display the strings and saves us from having to create another class for that purpose.

Because we just completed the discussion of situations where composition should be used rather than inheritance, we should revisit that question in the design of this class. Our name, StyledString, suggests that a styled string *is a* string, but let's consider whether we really have a generalization relationship here. We suggest that it is not. Perhaps using the name "string with a style" might have been a more accurate, although awkward, name. What ultimately should convince us that inheritance would be the wrong choice is the fact that we do not wish to inherit all of the methods of the String class.

The representation of objects of this class consists of the four instance variables defined on lines 7-9. It consists of the position of the string defined by the coordinates, the string, and its style. As constructors so often do, the constructor of this class accepts four parameters and copies them to their corresponding instance variables. We claim that the relationship between style and styled strings is an aggregation relationship. Styled strings do not have exclusive ownership of their style, although they do exclusively "own" their positions and strings. Styles are mutable objects, so the fact that they are created outside the class, and therefore have separate lifetimes, is significant. By contrast, although the string component is created outside the class, string objects are immutable.

Now let's consider the methods of this class, beginning with draw. It sets the style to the proper font and color with a call to setStyle on line 21 and then draws the string on line 22. To implement the Transformable interface, we needed to implement scale, but as is apparent from the code, we chose to have it do nothing. It would be inappropriate to allow this class to change any part of its style, since it does not have exclusive ownership of its style. It does "own" its position, so allowing translate to change its position is acceptable.

We are now ready to consider the final class necessary to complete this example, which is, of course, the class containing main. The code for that class is shown in Listing 12.14.

LISTING 12.14 The Class Containing main for the Styled Strings Example (found on the CD-ROM at chapter12\StyledStringsMain.java.)

```
1   package chapter12;
2
3   import java.awt.*;
4   import common.*;
5
6   public class StyledStringsMain
7   {
8       public static void main(String[] args)
9       {
10          final int STRINGS = 6, MAX_POS = 200, DELTA_X = 20,
11              DELTA_Y = 30, NEW_POINT_SIZE = 24;
12          int x, y;
13          String string;
14          StyledString styledString;
15          Font text = new Font("Serif", Font.PLAIN, 12),
16              heading = new Font("Sans Serif", Font.BOLD, 16);
17          Style styles[] = {new Style(heading, Color.BLACK),
18              new Style(text, Color.RED), new Style(text, Color.BLUE)};
19          TransformablesWindow window = new TransformablesWindow();
20
21          window.display();
22          for (int i = 0; i < STRINGS; i++)
23          {
24              x = (int)(Math.random() * MAX_POS);
25              y = (int)(Math.random() * MAX_POS);
```

```
26              string = InputOutput.getString("Enter a string: ");
27              styledString = new StyledString(x, y, string,
28                  styles[i % styles.length]);
29              window.add(styledString);
30          }
31          InputOutput.putString("About to do translation");
32          window.translate(DELTA_X, DELTA_Y);
33          InputOutput.putString("About to change first style");
34          styles[0].recolor(Color.GREEN);
35          styles[0].resize(NEW_POINT_SIZE);
36          window.repaint();
37      }
38  }
```

On lines 15 and 16, we create two fonts named `text` and `heading`. The font `text` is a font with serifs that is neither bold nor italic whose point size is 12 points, while `heading` is a 16 point bold font without serifs. The three choices for font names are `Serif`, which typically produces Times Roman, `SansSerif`, typically giving an Arial or Helvetica font and `Monospaced` for Courier New. On lines 17 and 18, we create an array, `styles`, containing two anonymous style objects.

Next, let's discuss the executable statements in this method. The `for` loop spanning lines 22-30 creates six objects of class `StyledString` and adds them to the window. It allows the user to supply the actual strings. The positions are randomly generated and the two styles are alternated. On line 31, it displays a message and waits for an acknowledgement. Once received, it calls `translate`, which moves all the strings in the window 20 pixels to the right and down 30 pixels. Next, another message is displayed that awaits acknowledgment. Finally, and most importantly, the first style is recolored on line 34 and resized on line 35 and the window is repainted. If you ran this program, you know that all three of the strings that have this style were affected by this change. We should expect such behavior with aggregation relationships.

UML Diagrams Depicting Aggregation Relationships

We are now ready to see how aggregation relationships are depicted in a UML diagram. The UML diagram for the styled strings example is shown in Figure 12.3.

Although this diagram contains a variety of relationships, the one that we are most interested in is the relationship between `StyledString` and `Styles`. The UML symbol depicting this aggregation relationship is a line with a hollow diamond adjacent to the containing class, which, in this case, is `StyledStyle`. There is one other difference besides whether the diamond is solid or hollow in distinguishing between

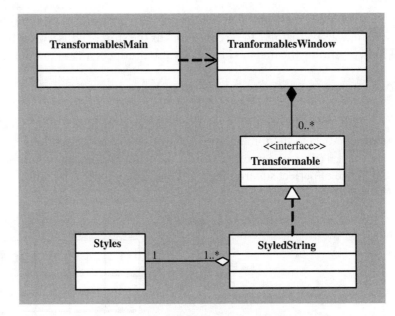

FIGURE 12.3   UML diagram for the window of styled strings.

composition and aggregation. Notice that with an aggregation relationship, the multiplicity markers are on both ends of the relationship. In this case, a styled string contains one style, but zero or more styled strings can contain a style.

POLYGONAL NUMBER APPLICATION

We are now ready to begin our final example for this chapter. It builds on one of the classes that we developed in Chapter 10 and illustrates a number of the concepts that we have studied in this chapter. This example deals with a collection of number sequences similar to the triangular number sequence that we studied earlier. These sequences are called the sequences of polygonal numbers. Actually the triangular number sequence is the first sequence in this collection. Let's consider the next such sequence—the sequence of square numbers. Rather than each term being the sum of the first n integers, each term of the sequence of square numbers is the sum of the first n odd numbers. Computing each term as the sum of the first n odd integers is expressed in Equation 12.1.

$$\square\,(n) = \sum_{i=1}^{n} 2i - 1 \tag{12.1}$$

It should be evident that the formula $2i - 1$ produces odd numbers. In Chapter 10, we saw that n^2 can be computed as the sum of consecutive triangular numbers. Summing the first n odd integers also produces n^2, as Equation 12.2 illustrates.

$$n^2 = \sum_{i=1}^{n} 2i - 1 \tag{12.2}$$

Equation 12.2 is another popular summation whose validity is easy to prove by mathematical induction. In any case, putting together Equations 12.1 and 12.2, we see that $\square (n) = n^2$—in other words, the sequence of square numbers is really the sequence of perfect squares. Figure 12.4 is a geometric illustration of this fact.

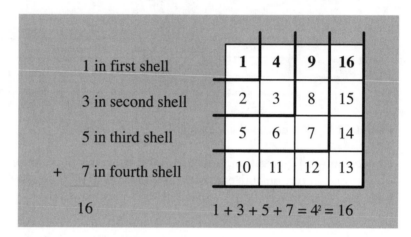

FIGURE 12.4   Perfect squares as the sum of odd integers.

Having seen the triangular number sequence and the square number sequence, we generalize a definition of the collection of polygonal number sequences defined by Equation 12.3.

$$P(n, s) = \sum_{i=1}^{n} (s - 2)i - (s - 3) \tag{12.3}$$

The variable s in Equation 12.3 represents the number of sides of the polygon. If you substitute 3 for s in this equation, you get the sequence of triangular numbers. When s is 4, it produces the square number sequence, and so on.

With that introduction, we are ready to describe the program that we are about to see. It will produce a drawing akin to the ones in Figures 10.4 and 12.4. Figure 12.5 shows the output of this program for the sequence of pentagonal numbers—the sequence produced when s is 5.

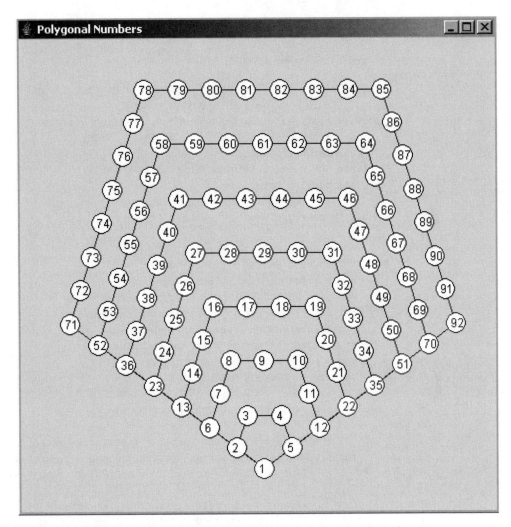

FIGURE 12.5 Output of polygonal number program for pentagonal numbers.

This program consists of several classes. The first of these is a class, Numbered-Polygon, that is derived from the RegularPolygon class, which we used in the previous example. Its code is contained in Listing 12.15.

LISTING 12.15 A Class that Draws Polygons with Numbers Along the Sides (found on the CD-ROM at chapter12\NumberedPolygon.java.)

```
1  package chapter12;
2
3  import java.awt.*;
4  import chapter10.*;
```

```
 5  import common.*;
 6
 7  class NumberedPolygon extends RegularPolygon
 8  {
 9      public static final int WIDTH = 500, POLYGON_RADIUS = 30,
10          X_ORIGIN = WIDTH / 2, Y_ORIGIN = 400;
11      private static int polygonNumber = 1, nextStartingVertex = 1,
12          startingVertexIncrement = 1, xCenter = X_ORIGIN,
13          yCenter = Y_ORIGIN;
14      private int numberOfPoints, firstVertexNumber;
15      private double theta, radius;
16
17      public NumberedPolygon(int numberOfSides)
18      {
19          super(numberOfSides, xCenter, yCenter,
20              POLYGON_RADIUS * polygonNumber);
21          numberOfPoints = polygonNumber;
22          radius = POLYGON_RADIUS * polygonNumber++;
23          nextStartingVertex += startingVertexIncrement;
24          firstVertexNumber = nextStartingVertex;
25          startingVertexIncrement += numberOfSides - 2;
26          theta = 2 * Math.PI / numberOfSides;
27          yCenter -= POLYGON_RADIUS;
28      }
29      public void paintNumbers(Graphics graphics)
30      {
31          int xPoint, yPoint, vertexNumber = firstVertexNumber;
32          for (int vertex = 1; vertex < numberOfSides - 1; vertex++)
33              for (int point = 0; point < numberOfPoints; point++)
34                  {
35                      xPoint = interpolate(x[vertex], x[vertex + 1],
36                          point, numberOfPoints);
37                      yPoint = interpolate(y[vertex], y[vertex + 1],
38                          point, numberOfPoints);
39                      paintOneNumber(graphics, Color.BLACK, xPoint,
40                          yPoint, vertexNumber++);
41                  }
42          paintOneNumber(graphics, Color.RED, x[numberOfSides - 1],
43              y[numberOfSides - 1], vertexNumber);
44      }
45      public static void paintOneNumber(Graphics graphics,
46          Color color, int xPoint, int yPoint, int vertexNumber)
47      {
48          final int RADIUS = 10;
49          graphics.setColor(Color.WHITE);
```

```
50          graphics.fillOval(xPoint — RADIUS, yPoint — RADIUS,
51              RADIUS * 2, RADIUS * 2);
52          graphics.setColor(color);
53          graphics.drawOval(xPoint — RADIUS, yPoint — RADIUS,
54              RADIUS * 2, RADIUS * 2);
55          graphics.drawString("" + vertexNumber, xPoint — RADIUS / 2,
56              yPoint + RADIUS / 2);
57          graphics.setColor(Color.BLACK);
58      }
59      private int interpolate(int coordinate1, int coordinate2,
60          int point, int numberOfPoints)
61      {
62          return (point * coordinate2 + (numberOfPoints — point) *
63              coordinate1) / numberOfPoints;
64      }
65  }
```

Algorithmically, this class is somewhat complicated, but it does not use any features that we have not already discussed, so our focus will be on the general behavior of this class.

Class variables allow objects to be created based on the history of the objects already created. One of the simplest examples is numbering window objects as they are created. A class variable is needed to accomplish that task, as we will see when we discuss our predefined class Application in Chapter 13. These numbered polygons are created based on the history of what was created before. The class variables on lines 11-13 maintain this history. Notice that the constructor for the class both accesses and updates these class variables. It uses their values to establish the values for most of the instance variables of the object being created. Because this class is derived from RegularPolygon, it calls the constructor of that base class to create the polygon itself.

The method paintNumbers paints numbers along all but two sides—the first and last—of the polygon, which should be apparent from the bounds of the outer for loop on line 32. The inner loop paints the numbers along the side. Notice that the number of numerals painted along a side is determined by the instance variable numberOfPoints, which depends upon the class variable polygonNumber. Consequently each time another one of these numbered polygon objects is created, it paints more numbers along each side than the previous one did. The position of these numbers is determined by the private method interpolate, which calculates the position of the number based on the coordinates of the endpoints of the side and the number of numbers along that side. It is called once to compute the x ordinate and once for the y ordinate. The actual painting of the number is done by the class method paintOneNumber. Notice that the last number painted in paintNumbers, on lines 42 and 43, is painted in red, to indicate that it is a number in the polygonal number sequence.

The next class needed for this program is one that creates the window in which the numbered polygons are drawn. The code for that class, named `PolygonShells`, is shown in Listing 12.16.

LISTING 12.16 The Polygon Shells Window Class (found on the CD-ROM at *ON THE CD* chapter12\PolygonShells.java.)

```
1  package chapter12;
2
3  import java.awt.*;
4  import common.*;
5
6  class PolygonShells extends Application
7  {
8      private NumberedPolygon[] polygons;
9
10     public PolygonShells(int numberOfSides, int numberOfPolygons)
11     {
12         super("Polygonal Numbers", NumberedPolygon.WIDTH,
13             NumberedPolygon.WIDTH);
14         polygons = new NumberedPolygon[numberOfPolygons];
15         for (int polygonIndex = 0; polygonIndex < polygons.length;
16             polygonIndex++)
17             polygons[polygonIndex] =
18                 new NumberedPolygon(numberOfSides);
19     }
20     public void paintComponent(Graphics graphics)
21     {
22         super.paintComponent(graphics);
23         for (NumberedPolygon polygon: polygons)
24             polygon.paintPolygon(graphics);
25         NumberedPolygon.paintOneNumber(graphics, Color.RED,
26             NumberedPolygon.X_ORIGIN, NumberedPolygon.Y_ORIGIN +
27             NumberedPolygon.POLYGON_RADIUS, 1);
28         for (NumberedPolygon polygon : polygons)
29             polygon.paintNumbers(graphics);
30     }
31 }
```

This class contains a single instance variable, which is the array `polygons` declared on line 8. It is instantiated by the constructor on line 14 to contain the number of polygons specified by the parameter `numberOfPolygons`. Once the array is instantiated, each of the individual numbered polygons is instantiated in the `for` loop that spans lines 15-18.

The other method in this class is the customary method `paintComponent`. It performs the painting in three steps. It first paints the polygons themselves with a call to `paintPolygon`, which is defined in the base class `Polygon`. Next, it calls the class method `paintOneNumber` to paint the number 1 in red at that the base of the polygons. Finally, it calls `paintNumbers` to paint the remaining numbers on each of the polygons.

As always, we need one final class to complete this program, which is the class `ShellsMain` that contains `main`. Its code is provided in Listing 12.17.

LISTING 12.17 The Class Containing `main` for the Polygonal Numbers Application

ON THE CD (found on the CD-ROM at `chapter12\ShellsMain.java`.)

```
1   package chapter12;
2
3   import common.*;
4
5   public class ShellsMain
6   {
7       public static void main(String[] args)
8       {
9           final int MIN_SIDES = 3, MAX_SIDES = 10, MIN_SHELLS = 2,
10              MAX_SHELLS = 7;
11          int numberOfSides = InputOutput.getInteger
12              ("Number of Sides in Polygon ", MIN_SIDES, MAX_SIDES);
13          int numberOfShells = InputOutput.getInteger
14              ("Number of Polygons ", MIN_SHELLS, MAX_SHELLS);
15          PolygonShells polygons = new PolygonShells(numberOfSides,
16              numberOfShells);
17          polygons.display();
18      }
19  }
```

This method prompts the user for the number of sides of the polygons and the number of polygons to draw. It then creates a `PolygonShells` object and displays the window.

Finally, we provide the UML diagram for this program in Figure 12.6.

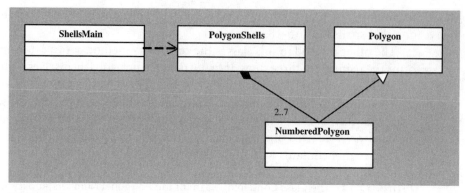

FIGURE 12.6   UML diagram for the polygonal numbers application.

SUMMARY

In this chapter, we examined the various relationships between classes. We discussed how to identify the various kinds of relationships and how to represent those relationships with UML notation. The key points to remember from this chapter are as follows:

- Generalization relationships exist when one object is a special kind of another object.
- Inheritance should be used to implement generalization relationships.
- Derived classes can extend the specification, the representation, or both.
- Type casts up the inheritance hierarchy are always safe, so automatic type conversion is performed. Type casts down the hierarchy, called downcasts, can potentially generate class cast exceptions.
- A polymorphic method call is a call to a method that has been overridden in at least one derived class. The determination of which method is actually being called must be made at runtime.
- When a class inherits only a specification, it should do so by implementing an interface.
- Inheriting only a representation in Java is problematic because there is no way to prevent the inheritance of the specification. Composition is best used in these situations.
- A class can only inherit from one other class, but it can implement any number of interfaces.
- Aggregation relationships exist when one object is a component of more than one other object.

Review Questions

1. Can derived classes access the instance variables of their base classes?
2. What causes a class cast exception to occur?
3. Explain why Java cannot determine some improper type casts until run-time.
4. Explain the difference between overloading and overriding.
5. Why is it sometimes appropriate to override a method that would otherwise be inherited?
6. In what ways can a derived class extend its base?
7. Why does Java prohibit multiple inheritance of classes?
8. Why is it a problem to attempt to inherit only a representation but not a specification in Java?
9. Explain how the implementation of composition and aggregation relationships should differ.
10. Why are multiplicity markers generally placed on one end of a composition relationship, but on both ends of an aggregation relationship?

Programming Exercises

11. Indicate whether each of the following is an appropriate or inappropriate use of inheritance:
    a. Vehicle derived from car
    b. Man derived from person
    c. Apple derived from fruit
    d. Window derived from house

12. Write a class named `Circle` that defines the characteristics of a circle, including its position and its radius. Include a constructor that initializes the instance variable to values supplied by the parameters. Make all the instance variables protected.

13. Define an interface, `Drawable`, that requires the presence of a method named `draw` that is supplied a graphics object upon which to draw.

14. Extend the class `Circle`, defined in Programming Exercise 12, to implement the interface defined in Programming Exercise 13. Name this class `DrawableCircle`.

15. Write a derived class named `LabeledCircle` that extends the class in the previous exercise. It should override `draw` so that it displays a message above the circle indicating its area.

16. Write a derived class named `FilledCircle` that extends the class `DrawableCircle`. A color should be added to its representation that represents the color of the inside of the circle. The method `draw` should be overridden to fill the circle with the fill color, but also draw the outline in black.

17. Write a program that declares a `Drawable` object as defined in Programming Exercise 13. Instantiate it to be a `LabeledCircle` object. Perform a type cast that will compile, but will cause a class cast exception to be thrown when the program runs.

Refer to the following class for the next three exercises:

```
public class NumberedObject
{
    private static int nextNumber = 1;
    private int number;

    public NumberedObject()
    {
        number = nextNumber++;
    }
}
```

18. Add an instance method to the class `NumberedObject` that returns the number of the object and a class method than returns the number of the last created object.

19. Write an interface called `Valued` that has two methods: `namedValue` that returns a `String` and `numericValue` that returns an integer.

20. Extend the `NumberedObject` class so that it implements the `Valued` interface.

Programming Projects

21. Create a class that extends `Application` that draws a circle inside a square. Its objects should be composed of an object of class `ComposedSquare` defined in Listing 12.9 and an object of class `DrawableCircle` defined in Programming Exercise 14. The size and position of these objects should be randomly generated.

22. Write a class that extends `Application` that draws three concentric circles. Its objects should be composed of an array of three objects of class `DrawableCircle` defined in Programming Exercise 14. The radii of the circles should be 30, 60, and 90 pixels. Their position should be randomly generated.

23. Write an application that allows the user to add any number of circles to a window. Their sizes and positions should be randomly generated. The user should be able to choose between regular circles, labeled circles, and filled circles. Use the classes defined in Programming Exercises 14-16 to accomplish this task.

24. Modify the circle classes defined in Programming Exercises 14-16 so that they implement the `Transformable` interface defined in Listing 12.4. Modify the `TransformablesMain` class so that it allows circles to be added to the window also.

25. Write a class called `NumberedString` that extends the class `StyledString` defined in Listing 12.13 so each string that is created is numbered consecutively. When `draw` paints these strings, it should prefix each string with its number. Modify `StyledStringsMain`, defined in Listing 12.14, so that it creates these numbered strings instead.

13 Multidimensional Arrays and GUIs

In this chapter

- Multidimensional Arrays
- Introduction to Developing GUIs
- Nonmodal Input
- Wrapper Classes that Wrap Methods
- Magic Square Application

MULTIDIMENSIONAL ARRAYS

In Chapter 7, we introduced one-dimensional arrays—collections of data elements that are identified by a single subscript. We now consider multidimensional arrays—those that have more than one subscript. Although it is possible to have arrays that have any number of dimensions, it is uncommon to have arrays with more than three dimensions. The syntax for declaring and accessing multidimensional arrays does not differ much from the one-dimensional case. Consider the declaration and instantiation of a two-dimensional array of integers shown below:

```
int[][] matrix = new int[10][10];
```

The placement of the brackets can be either after the type name or after the array object name, just as was true for one-dimensional arrays. To access one element of a multidimensional array, we must specify a subscript value for each of the dimensions. The assignment below assigns a value to the first row and first column of the previously declared array.

```
matrix[0][0] = 5;
```

Note that it is customary with two-dimensional arrays to refer to the first dimension as the row and the second dimension as the column.

It is possible to initialize multidimensional arrays to constant values in their declaration, just as was true for one-dimensional arrays. The only difference now is that the array constants must contain nested braces. An example will best illustrate this syntax. Consider the following example.

```
int[][] identity = {{1, 0, 0}, {0, 1, 0}, {0, 0, 1}};
```

The array identity is initialized to a three-by-three array with ones down the main diagonal and zeroes elsewhere.

One other reminder is in order regarding arrays of objects. Just as was true with one-dimensional arrays, when we instantiate an array of objects, we have only created object references. We must subsequently instantiate the objects themselves.

In Chapter 4, our final example was an applet that drew a checkerboard consisting of alternating red and black squares. A checkerboard is a visual depiction of a two-dimensional array. Because we only drew the checkerboard, but did not need to save any data corresponding to each square, we did not need a two-dimensional array in our code. Let's return to that example with one added feature, which is to allow the user to toggle the color of any square by clicking on it. Adding that requirement makes it now necessary to keep track of the color of each square. A two-dimensional array is ideal for this purpose. Unlike the version in Chapter 4, this program is an application, not an applet. Listing 13.1 contains the class that defines the window containing the checkerboard.

LISTING 13.1 A Window Containing a Checkerboard that Allows the Square Colors to
ON THE CD be Changed (found on the CD-ROM at chapter13\ColoredSquares.java.)

```
1  package chapter13;
2
3  import java.awt.*;
4  import java.awt.event.*;
5  import common.*;
6
```

```
 7  class ColoredSquares extends GraphicsApplication
 8  {
 9      private static final int UP = 20, LEFT = 20, SIZE = 30,
10          SQUARES = 8, COLORED_SQUARES =
11          new ColoredSquares().display();
12      private SquareColors[][] squareColors =
13          new SquareColors[SQUARES][SQUARES];
14
15      private class SquareMouseAdapter extends MouseAdapter
16      {
17          public void mouseClicked(MouseEvent event)
18          {
19              Point clickPoint = event.getPoint();
20              int row = (clickPoint.y — UP) / SIZE;
21              int col = (clickPoint.x — LEFT) / SIZE;
22
23              if (row >= 0 && row < SQUARES && col >=0 && col < SQUARES)
24                  if (squareColors[row][col] == SquareColors.RED)
25                      squareColors[row][col] = SquareColors.BLACK;
26                  else
27                      squareColors[row][col] = SquareColors.RED;
28              repaint();
29          }
30      }
31
32      public ColoredSquares()
33      {
34          addMouseListener(new SquareMouseAdapter());
35          for (int row = 0; row < SQUARES; row++)
36              for (int col = 0; col < SQUARES; col++)
37                  switch ((row + col) % 2)
38                  {
39                      case 0:
40                          squareColors[row][col] = SquareColors.RED;
41                          break;
42                      case 1:
43                          squareColors[row][col] = SquareColors. BLACK;
44                          break;
45                  }
46      }
47      public void paintComponent(Graphics graphics)
48      {
49          super.paintComponent(graphics);
50          for (int row = 0; row < SQUARES; row++)
```

```
51                    for (int col = 0; col < SQUARES; col++)
52                    {
53                        graphics.setColor(squareColors[row][col].getColor());
54                        graphics.fillRect(LEFT + col * SIZE,
55                            UP + row * SIZE, SIZE, SIZE);
56                    }
57        }
58  }
```

Let's begin with the two-dimensional array that is now required as an instance variable of this class. That array, named squareColors, is declared on line 12 and is instantiated on line 13. It consists of eight rows and columns. Its components are an enumerated type, SquareColors, that we will examine shortly.

We chose this example for another reason, which is to review how mouse events are handled—a topic that we first encountered in Chapter 8. Later in this chapter, we will encounter handling of additional kinds of user-generated events, so this review will prepare you for that discussion. Recall that we have the option of making this class implement the MouseListener interface or we can create an inner class that extends the class MouseAdapter. We have chosen the second option because the first option requires us to provide numerous empty methods. Our inner class is SquareMouseAdapter that begins on line 15. It provides the method, mouseClicked, whose signature is on line 17, for the only mouse event that we plan to respond to—mouse click events. On lines 20 and 21, the method computes the row and column of the checkerboard that was clicked on. Because it is possible that the user could click outside the checkerboard, we must check to be sure the subscripts are in bounds, which is accomplished with the if statement on line 23. For valid mouse clicks the color of the square is toggled and the window is repainted. The nested if statements in this method, which have an if statement nested in the if part of another if statement, provide an opportunity to review a topic from Chapter 6—the dangling else. In such situations, we need to be certain that the else clause matches the proper if. Our desire is that it match the second if, which is the default, so our code is correct as written. Whenever you encounter such situations, you should confirm whether the statement will be interpreted as you want it to be.

The constructor of the outer class must first register this class as a listener for mouse events, which it does by the call to addMouseListener on line 34, passing it an anonymous object of the class SquareMouseAdapter. It is easy to forget to include this registration. The consequence of forgetting is that mouse clicks will be ignored. Next, the constructor sets the colors in the array squareColors to the usual checkerboard pattern. The paintComponent method accesses that two-dimensional array to determine which color each square should be painted, because now the square colors can change. It is noteworthy that both methods contain nested for loops. Nested for loops are as commonplace in code that processes multidimensional arrays, as single for loops are with code acting on one-dimensional arrays.

Next, let's examine the enumerated type SquareColors, which was not a part of our original checkerboard applet. Its code is shown in Listing 13.2.

LISTING 13.2 Enumerated Type for Checkerboard Square Colors (found on the CD-ROM at chapter13\SquareColors.java.)

```
 1  package chapter13;
 2
 3  import java.awt.*;
 4
 5  enum SquareColors
 6    {
 7      RED(Color.RED),
 8      BLACK(Color.BLACK);
 9
10      private Color color;
11
12      private SquareColors(Color color)
13      {
14          this.color = color;
15      }
16      public Color getColor()
17      {
18          return color;
19      }
20  }
```

This enumerated type couples a java.awt.Color with each square color so that it can be accessed by the getColor method—a technique that we began using in Chapter 5 with our RainbowColors type.

Two-Dimensional Array Iterations

When a two-dimensional array is rectangular—every column has the same number of elements—there are numerous orders that one might choose to iterate across a two-dimensional array. We add the stipulation about being rectangular because we will see shortly that, unlike many programming languages, rectangular arrays are not required in Java. Recall that, in our original checkerboard applet from Chapter 4, we numbered the squares in a variety of different orders. One order is what we called horizontal, numbering them row-by-row. With two-dimensional arrays, this order is referred to as *row-major*. Another order we used with the checkerboard applet was one was called vertical, numbering them column-by-column. That order is called *column-major* in the context of two-dimensional arrays. Other orders exist as well. We might choose to follow the diagonals or number them in shells, as illustrated in Figure 12.4.

To illustrate two of the possible iteration orders for two-dimensional arrays, we have chosen an example that creates a ten-by-ten integer array consisting of randomly chosen one-digit integers, which are displayed in a window. The user is asked to select a search order, either row-major or column-major, and an integer to search for. It finds the first instance of that integer in the designated order and highlights it. The code for the class that defines such an array, together with iterator classes that define these orders, is shown in Listing 13.3.

LISTING 13.3 A Class Defining a Two-Dimensional Integer Array with Iterators (found
ON THE CD on the CD-ROM at `chapter13\Matrix.java`).

```
1    package chapter13;
2
3    import java.awt.*;
4    import java.util.*;
5    import common.*;
6    import static java.lang.Math.*;
7
8    class Matrix extends Application
9    {
10       private static final int SIZE = 20, LEFT_MARGIN = 20,
11          TOP_MARGIN = 20, X_OFFSET = 2, Y_OFFSET = 16;
12       private int maxValue, rows, cols, highlightedRow,
13          highlightedCol;
14       private int[][] matrix;
15
16       public interface MatrixIterator extends Iterator<Integer>
17       {
18          void highlight();
19       }
20       private class Major
21       {
22          protected int currentRow, currentCol, nextRow = 0,
23             nextCol = 0;
24
25          public Major()
26          {
27             highlightedRow = rows;
```

```
28                  highlightedCol = cols;
29              }
30          public boolean hasNext()
31          {
32                  return nextRow < rows && nextCol < cols;
33          }
34          public void highlight()
35          {
36                  highlightedRow = currentRow;
37                  highlightedCol = currentCol;
38          }
39          public void remove()
40          {
41          }
42      }
43      public class RowMajor extends Major implements MatrixIterator
44      {
45          public Integer next()
46          {
47                  currentRow = nextRow;
48                  currentCol = nextCol;
49                  if (++nextCol == cols)
50                  {
51                      nextRow++;
52                      nextCol = 0;
53                  }
54                  return matrix[currentRow][currentCol];
55          }
56      }
57      public class ColumnMajor extends Major implements MatrixIterator
58      {
59          public Integer next()
60          {
61                  currentRow = nextRow;
62                  currentCol = nextCol;
63                  if (++nextRow == rows)
64                  {
65                      nextCol++;
66                      nextRow = 0;
67                  }
68                  return matrix[currentRow][currentCol];
69          }
70      }
71
```

```
72      public Matrix(int maxValue, int rows, int cols)
73      {
74          this.maxValue = maxValue;
75          this.rows = rows;
76          this.cols = cols;
77          highlightedRow = rows;
78          highlightedCol = cols;
79          matrix = new int[rows][cols];
80          for (int row = 0; row < rows; row++)
81              for (int col = 0; col < cols; col++)
82                  matrix[row][col] = (int) (random() * maxValue);
83      }
84      public ColumnMajor makeColumnMajorIterator()
85      {
86          return new ColumnMajor();
87      }
88      public RowMajor makeRowMajorIterator()
89      {
90          return new RowMajor();
91      }
92      public void paintComponent(Graphics graphics)
93      {
94          int x, y = TOP_MARGIN;
95          for (int[] rows: matrix)
96          {
97              x = LEFT_MARGIN;
98              for (int value: rows)
99              {
100                 graphics.drawRect(x, y, SIZE, SIZE);
101                 graphics.drawString("" + value, x + X_OFFSET,
102                     y + Y_OFFSET);
103                 x += SIZE;
104             }
105             y += SIZE;
106         }
107         if (highlightedRow < rows && highlightedCol < cols)
108             for (int box = 1; box <= 2; box++)
109                 graphics.drawRect(LEFT_MARGIN + highlightedCol
110                     * SIZE + box, TOP_MARGIN + highlightedRow *
111                     SIZE + box, SIZE - box * 2,    SIZE - box * 2);
112     }
113 }
```

This class, `Matrix`, whose definition begins on line 8, will display the two-dimensional integer array in a window, hence its extension of the class `Application`. Because we plan to include two different iterators in this class, we elected to not make it implement the `Iterable` interface as we had done when we defined iterators in the previous examples.

The instance variables `rows` and `cols` that are declared on line 12 represent the number of rows and columns in the two-dimensional array, respectively. The two-dimensional array itself, `matrix`, is declared on line 14, but is instantiated in the constructor once the number of rows and columns has been established. By declaring the array internal to the class and allowing the client to supply the number of rows and columns, we guarantee that the array is rectangular.

Next, let's consider the iterator classes, which are inner classes, as before. Beyond providing the customary methods common to all iterators, they both provide the ability to highlight the current element. For that reason, we have defined a new interface, `MatrixIterator`, beginning on line 16. Notice that we have created an interface that extends another interface—something we first encountered in Chapter 11. You should recognize that, like classes, interfaces can form hierarchies. So the interface `MatrixIterator` includes all the method signatures of `Iterator<Integer>` plus the added method signature for the method `highlight`, declared on line 18.

Because both iterator classes have common instance variables and some common methods, we elected to create a common base class called `Major` that begins on line 20. Creating this class allows us to avoid duplicating code—a goal that we have stressed from the beginning. This process of moving common code into a common base class is sometimes referred to as "factoring code up the inheritance hierarchy." The instance variables of `Major` are declared on line 22 and 23. They include `currentRow`, `currentCol`, `nextRow`, and `nextCol`. The first pair represents the row and column of the current element—the one last returned by the iterator. The second pair represents the row and column of the element that will be returned on the next call to `next`. For emphasis, we initialized the latter pair to zero. Although this class has a constructor, which begins on line 25, that constructor is called only by the default constructors of its derived classes. The constructor initializes the variables `highlightedRow` and `highlightedCol` to indicate that no array element is initially highlighted. The `hasNext` method, whose signature is on line 30, indicates that a next element is available as long as both subscripts are within the bounds of the array. The method `highlight` sets the highlighted element to the current element.

Both iterator classes extend the base class `Major` and implement the interface `MatrixIterator`. Because they differ on how the next element is computed, it is necessary to define the `next` method for each of them. They inherit all the other methods required to satisfy the `MatrixIterator` from `Major`. The `next` method for `RowMajor`, beginning on line 45, moves to the next element on the same row, whereas the next method for ColumnMajor, beginning on line 59, moves to the next element in the same column.

In the next chapter, we will introduce abstract classes. At that time, we will return to this example and see how the interface MatrixIterator and the base class Major can be folded into a single class and discuss the advantage in doing so.

Now we turn to the methods of the outer class, beginning with the constructor whose signature appears on line 72. The constructor begins by copying the supplied parameters to their corresponding instance variables, as is customary for a constructor. On line 79, it instantiates the two-dimensional array instance variable matrix and then initializes it to random values.

As we have done whenever we defined inner iterator classes, we provide methods, makeColumnMajorIterator and makeRowMajorIterator, to allow clients outside the class to create their corresponding iterators.

Finally, let's consider the method paintComponent that paints the two-dimensional integer matrix and possibly highlights one of its elements. Like all code that processes all the elements of a two-dimensional array, this code contains nested for loops. These loops help us understand what iterators are implicitly provided for two-dimensional arrays. Examine the for loop that begins on line 95. Notice that when a two-dimensional integer array appears on the right side of the colon in a *for-each* style for loop, the type of the elements on the left side is a one-dimensional integer array. This underscores an important characteristic of multidimensional arrays in Java. They are really arrays of arrays. We will elaborate on the significance of this characteristic in the next section. The inner for loop that begins on line 98 iterates across the resulting one-dimensional arrays. In the nested loop body that spans lines 99-104, we draw a square and, inside it, the value contained in the corresponding array element.

Finally, the if statement on line 107 checks whether there is an element to highlight. If there is, it is highlighted by painting two additional rectangles inside the original one with the for loop that spans lines 108-111. The first one is one pixel smaller on all sides than the original and the second one is two pixels smaller.

To complete this program, like all applications, we need the method main. Because that method for this program requires more than just a few lines, we have placed it in a separate class. That class, named MatrixMain, is shown in Listing 13.4.

LISTING 13.4 The Class Containing the main Method for the Matrix Search Program (found on the CD-ROM at chapter13\MatrixMain.java.)

```
1   package chapter13;
2
3   import static common.InputOutput.*;
4
5   public class MatrixMain
```

```
6  {
7      public static enum MenuChoices {ROW_MAJOR, COLUMN_MAJOR, QUIT};
8
9      public static void main(String[] args)
10     {
11         final int ROWS = 10, COLS = 10, MAX_VALUE = 10;
12         int value, matrixValue;
13         MenuChoices choice;
14         Matrix matrix = new Matrix(ROWS, COLS, MAX_VALUE);
15         Matrix.MatrixIterator iterator = null;
16
17         matrix.display();
18         while(true)
19         {
20             choice = (MenuChoices)getEnum("Select Choice",
21                 MenuChoices.values());
22             if (choice == MenuChoices.QUIT)
23                 break;
24             value = getInteger("Enter an integer to find: ");
25             switch (choice)
26             {
27                 case ROW_MAJOR:
28                     iterator = matrix.makeRowMajorIterator();
29                     break;
30                 case COLUMN_MAJOR:
31                     iterator = matrix.makeColumnMajorIterator();
32                     break;
33             }
34             while (iterator.hasNext())
35             {
36                 matrixValue = iterator.next();
37                 if (value == matrixValue)
38                 {
39                     iterator.highlight();
40                     break;
41                 }
42             }
43             matrix.repaint();
44         }
45     }
46 }
```

This class contains no new concepts, so we will focus only on its overall behavior. It allows the user to repeatedly select an iteration order and enter a number. It searches for that number, using the appropriate iterator in the Matrix class, and then highlights the cell in which it was first found.

Ragged Arrays

We now elaborate on a comment made earlier regarding the implementation of multidimensional arrays in Java—that they are really arrays of arrays. In many programming languages, multidimensional arrays are implemented differently, using one contiguous linear block of memory, since all memory is really only one-dimensional, and establishing a correspondence between the physical one-dimensional memory and the logical multidimensional array. In such cases, the language must elect some ordering. Typically either the row-major or column-major ordering just discussed is used. Then the compiler must calculate the actual address of a particular element based on the row and column and type of ordering. Figure 13.1 illustrates the difference between these two implementations.

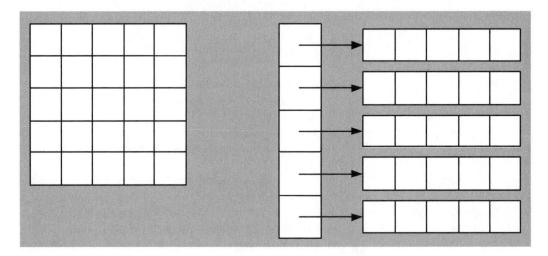

FIGURE 13.1   Comparing contiguous multidimensional arrays with arrays of arrays.

As with most differing implementations, there are some tradeoffs. With a contiguous block of memory, only a single memory access is needed once the position of the element is computed. With arrays of arrays, two or more accesses are required. For two-dimensional arrays, one is needed to extract the one-dimensional array of rows and then one to extract elements from the specified column. Keep in mind that the compiler handles these details, so they are transparent to the programmer. One important difference, which is apparent to the programmer, is whether the multidimensional arrays must be rectangular. When a contiguous block of memory is used, rectangular arrays are required. Arrays of arrays can be *ragged*, however. A ragged array is one in which different rows have a different number of columns. Figure 13.2 illustrates a ragged two-dimensional array.

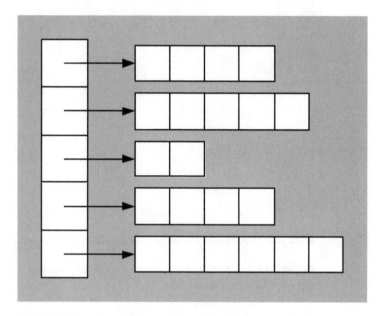

FIGURE 13.2   A ragged two-dimensional array.

This capability can be a useful one. Next, we illustrate an example that uses a triangular two-dimensional array. A mileage chart that often accompanies a map is an example of a triangular two-dimensional array. Our example will be a similar one. It involves a randomly generated collection of points and a two-dimensional triangular array is used to maintain a record of the distance between each pair of points. Like the distance between cities, the distance between points is a symmetric relationship; the distance between points *a* and *b* is the same as the distance between points *b* and *a*. Consequently a triangular array suffices. In this program, the user is permitted to click on any pair of points. A line is then drawn connecting them and the distance between the points is displayed. The output of this program is shown in Figure 13.3.

This program consists of two classes. The first of those two is the class Distance. It defines the triangular array that maintains the distance between pairs of points. The code for that class is shown in Listing 13.5.

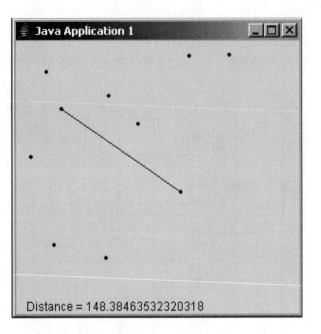

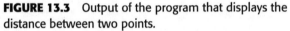

FIGURE 13.3   Output of the program that displays the distance between two points.

LISTING 13.5   A Class that Uses a Triangular Array to Maintain the Distance Between
ON THE CD   Points (found on the CD-ROM at `chapter13\Distance.java.`)

```
1  package chapter13;
2
3  import java.awt.*;
4  import static java.lang.Math.*;
5
6  public class Distance
7  {
8      private double[][] distance;
9
10     public Distance(Point[] points)
11     {
12         int length = points.length;
13
14         distance = new double[length][];
15         for (int i = 0; i < length; i++)
16             distance[i] = new double[i + 1];
17         for (int from = 0; from < distance.length; from++)
```

```
18                  for (int to = 0; to < distance[from].length; to++)
19                      distance[from][to] =
20                          computeDistance(points[from], points[to]);
21          }
22          public static double computeDistance(Point from, Point to)
23          {
24              int deltaX = from.x - to.x, deltaY = from.y - to.y;
25              return sqrt(pow(deltaX, 2) + pow(deltaY, 2));
26          }
27          public double getDistance(int from, int to)
28          {
29              if (from <= to)
30                  return distance[to][from];
31              return distance[from][to];
32          }
33  }
```

The two-dimensional array distance of type double, declared on line 8, is the triangular array that contains the distances between pairs of points. Notice that the length of the first dimension is the same as the length of the array points, which is supplied as a parameter. That array is instantiated in the constructor on line 14. Notice how it is instantiated. Unlike the instantiation of all the two-dimensional arrays that we have seen thus far, no value is given for the size of the second dimension. Consequently, this instantiation only creates a one-dimensional array of null references to one-dimensional arrays of type double. We must explicitly instantiate each individual row, which is exactly what is done by the for loop on lines 15 and 16. Notice that the rows are different lengths. The first row contains one element, the second row contains two elements, and so on. Finally, the constructor initializes each element of the array in the nested for loops that span lines 17-20. What is characteristic of nested loops examining each element of a ragged array is that although distance.length can be used for the number rows, which is the upper bound of the outer loop on line 17, distance[from].length must be used for the number of columns in each row, which is the upper bound of the inner loop on line 18. The distance between the points is computed by a call to the class method computeDistance supplying it the coordinates of a pair of points.

The class method computeDistance computes the *x* and *y* differentials on line 24 and then uses the Pythagorean Theorem to compute and return the distance on line 25. Finally the method getDistance returns the distance between a pair of points, given their subscripts in the array points. Because the array is triangular, a check must be made to determine whether the subscripts are specified in ascending order, which is done by the if statement on line 29. If they are in the proper order, it uses them as the subscripts of the triangular array. Otherwise it uses them in reverse order. Failing to make this check could result in subscripts outside the bounds of the array.

The second class of this program is the class Points. It creates the window that displays the points, draws the lines, and displays the distance. The code for that class is shown in Listing 13.6.

LISTING 13.6 A Class that Displays Random Points and the Distance Between any Pair
ON THE CD (found on the CD-ROM at chapter13\Points.java.)

```
1  package chapter13;
2
3  import java.awt.*;
4  import java.awt.event.*;
5  import common.*;
6  import static java.lang.Math.*;
7
8  public class Points extends GraphicsApplication
9  {
10     private static final int RADIUS = 2, DIAMETER = RADIUS * 2,
11         TEXT_HEIGHT = 30, NUMBER_OF_POINTS = 10,
12         POINTS = new Points().display();
13     private int from, to, pointsClicked;
14     private Point[] points;
15     private Distance distance;
16
17     private class PointsMouseAdapter extends MouseAdapter
18     {
19         public void mouseClicked(MouseEvent event)
20         {
21             int point;
22             Point clickPoint = event.getPoint();
23
24             for (point = 0; point < points.length; point++)
25                 if (Distance.computeDistance(clickPoint,
26                     points[point]) < DIAMETER)
27                         break;
28             if (point == points.length)
29                 return;
30             if (++pointsClicked % 2== 1)
31                 from = point;
32             else
33             {
34                 to = point;
35                 repaint();
```

```
36                 }
37             }
38         }
39
40     public Points()
41     {
42         int x, y;
43
44         addMouseListener(new PointsMouseAdapter());
45         points = new Point[NUMBER_OF_POINTS];
46         for (int point = 0; point < points.length; point++)
47         {
48             x = (int)(random() * WIDTH + .5);
49             y = (int)(random() * (HEIGHT - TEXT_HEIGHT * 2) + .5);
50             points[point] = new Point(x, y);
51         }
52         distance = new Distance(points);
53     }
54     public void paintComponent(Graphics graphics)
55     {
56         super.paintComponent(graphics);
57         for(Point point: points)
58             graphics.fillOval(point.x - RADIUS, point.y -
59                 RADIUS, DIAMETER, DIAMETER);
60         graphics.drawLine(points[from].x, points[from].y,
61             points[to].x, points[to].y);
62         graphics.drawString("Distance = " +
63             distance.getDistance(from, to), 10,
64             HEIGHT - TEXT_HEIGHT);
65     }
66 }
```

Let's begin with the instance variables of this class. The variables from and to are declared on line 13. They represent the subscripts in the array of points of the two endpoints of the currently selected line segment. The variable pointsClicked contains a total of the number of valid points clicked, which is used to determine when a new line segment needs to be drawn. The array points, declared on line 14, contains the coordinates of the points drawn in the window. The object distance, declared on line 15, is the object that contains the triangular array of distances between pairs of points. It is an object of class Distance, whose code we just discussed.

Like the first example in this chapter, we are again using mouse clicks as the input to this program. The user must click on two points. The program will then draw a line connecting those points and display its length. Consequently, we again need an inner class, which we have named `PointsMouseAdapter`, that contains the method `mouseClicked` that responds to these events. Let's examine the method `mouseClicked`. In the `for` loop that spans lines 24-27, it computes the distance between the position of the mouse click, contained in the object `clickPoint`, with the position of the points in the array `points`. If it finds one close enough, it breaks out the loop on line 27. The distance is computed using the class method `computeDistance` of the `Distance` class, which used it to compute the distances between points. In this case, we have elected to use an allowable syntax for `for` loops that we have never used before. We declared the loop control variable `point` on line 21 as a local variable of the method, not in the `for` loop itself. We chose this approach because we need the value of `point` after the loop completes. Had we declared it in the `for` loop as we have always done in the past, we would have been unable to access its value outside the loop. On line 28, we check whether `point` equals `points.length`. If it does, it means that we did not find a match after examining every point. In that case, we ignore the mouse click and exit the method with the `return` statement on line 29. If the mouse was clicked on a valid point, we assign it to either the variable `from` or `to`. When the incremented value of `pointsClicked` is an odd number, the assignment to `from` is made. When it is even, `point` is assigned to `to`, and the window is repainted so that the new line segment will be drawn.

Next, we consider the constructor of the outer class whose signature is on line 40. This constructor instantiates the array `points` to be an array of the length specified by the constant `NUMBER_OF_PRIMES`, on line 45. In the `for` loop that spans line 46-51, it generates random coordinates for those points and initializes the array `points` with those coordinate values. On line 52, the instance variable `distance` is instantiated, supplying the array `points` as the argument.

Finally, we consider the last method in the outer class, `paintComponent`. It draws all the points with the `for` loop spanning lines 57-59. It then draws a line segment connecting the points in the array `points` whose subscripts are `from` and `to`. Lastly, it displays the length of that line segment by calling the method `getDistance`.

INTRODUCTION TO DEVELOPING GUIs

Although we have been using graphics from our very first program, we have not yet created any graphical user interfaces (GUIs) that contain any GUI components such as labels, text fields, buttons, and so on. All computer users are familiar with such interfaces because they have become the predominate kind of interface due to their ease of use.

Before we explore the various components, it is useful to discuss the containers into which such components must be placed. These containers include frames, which we normally call windows, and panels. Although we have used these containers from the beginning, we have not yet studied how to create them. In the first four chapters, we used applets exclusively and relied upon the Web browser to provide the window in which we did our painting. In Chapter 5, we began to write applications, but relied upon a predefined class that we provided called Application to supply the window. We are now ready to discuss how to create these frames and panels.

Frames and Panels

Before discussing the mechanics of creating GUIs, there is a more general issue that pertains to frames and panels and all GUI components that warrant discussion. As an evolving language, Java originally introduced a set of classes in the package java.awt named Frame, Panel, Button, and so on. The subsequent introduction of the package swing provided a comparable but lighter weight set of components with similar names JFrame, JPanel, JButton, and so on. Because using the components in the swing package is the preferred approach, we plan to use them exclusively.

Now let's consider the class JFrame. For every window that we need in our program, aside from the ones created by the JOptionPane class, we need a JFrame object. This class has two constructors whose signatures are shown below.

```
JFrame()
JFrame(String title)
```

The first is a default constructor, of course. The second allows the caller to supply a title that will typically appear in the border along the top of the window.

There are several other methods in the JFrame class that are needed. The first of them is getContentPane, whose signature is shown below.

```
Container getContentPane()
```

Typically, we have a panel associated with every frame. We need to add that panel to the container returned by getContentPane to make that association. Another method in JFrame that is frequently used is setDefaultCloseOperation that specifies what to do when the frame is closed.

```
void setDefaultCloseOperation(int operation)
```

The option that we will always specify is JFrame.EXIT_ON_CLOSE, which indicates that the window is to be closed when the program exits. See the JFrame class definition at the Sun Website at http://java.sun.com/2se/1.5.0/docs/api/ for more of the other possible values.

Inheritance is used extensively in the definition of the classes that define the GUI components. The class JFrame, along with all the GUI components, is derived

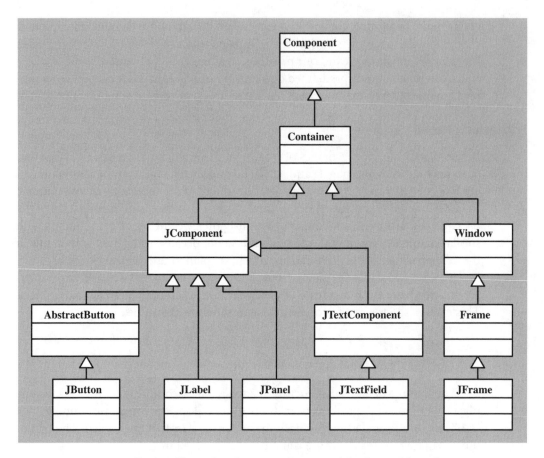

FIGURE 13.4 A UML diagram illustrating the GUI component inheritance hierarchy.

from the class java.awt.Component. Figure 13.4 contains a UML diagram that illustrates a portion of this inheritance hierarchy that pertains to our discussion.

We mention this fact because there are a number of methods defined in Component that JFrame inherits and that we plan to use. So, let's examine the signatures of those methods and discuss their behavior beginning with setBackground, whose signature is show below.

```
void setBackground(Color c)
```

As the name suggests, this method sets the background color of the component to the color supplied as a parameter.

The next method we consider is setLocation, which specifies the location for the component. Its signature is as follows.

```
void setLocation(int x, int y)
```

The parameters x and y specifies the upper-left corner of the location.

The method setSize is used to specify the size of a component by providing its width and height. Shown below is its signature.

```
void setSize(int width, int height)
```

A frequently used method with frames is the method setVisible, whose signature follows.

```
void setVisible(boolean b)
```

It causes the component to be shown or hidden depending on the value of parameter b.

We now turn to the class JPanel, the necessary companion class to JFrame. We already indicated that we must add some panel to the content pane of every frame. It is the panel that we are then able to paint onto and add GUI components to. Since Chapter 5, we have been using the method paintComponent in the Application class. We will see shortly that Application is derived from JPanel, so the method paintComponent is inherited by Application from JPanel, which actually inherits it from JComponent. Similarly, the method repaint that we have used so often with Application inherits this method ultimately from java.awt.Component.

To construct any GUI, we must add components to some panel. It is common for complex GUIs to consist of multiple panels. We often add panels to other panels. There is one important heavily overloaded method that is used frequently in defining the object composition relationships of every GUI. It is the method add. One overloaded version of this method is defined in java.awt.Container. Its signature is shown below.

```
Component add(Component comp)
```

It allows a component to be added to some container.

The Application and GraphicsApplication Classes

Let's now examine the code for the class Application—the class that we predefined and placed in our package common so we could defer discussion of frames and panels until now. Its code is shown in Listing 13.7.

LISTING 13.7   The `Application` Class from the Package `common` (found on the CD-ROM at `common\Application.java`.)

```
1  package common;
2
3  import java.awt.*;
4  import javax.swing.*;
5
6  public class Application extends JPanel
7  {
8      public static final int WIDTH = 300, HEIGHT = 300;
9      private static final int GAP = 20, SPACING = WIDTH + GAP;
10     private static int windowNumber = 0;
11     private JFrame window;
12
13     public Application()
14     {
15         window = new JFrame("Java Application " + (windowNumber + 1));
16         initialize();
17     }
18     public Application(String windowName)
19     {
20         window = new JFrame(windowName);
21         initialize();
22     }
23     public Application(String windowName, int width, int height)
24     {
25         window = new JFrame(windowName);
26         window.setDefaultCloseOperation(JFrame.EXIT_ON_CLOSE);
27         window.setBackground(Color.WHITE);
28         window.getContentPane().add(this);
29         window.setSize(width, height);
30     }
31     public int display()
32     {
33         window.setVisible(true);
34         return 0;
35     }
36     private void initialize()
37     {
38         window.setDefaultCloseOperation(JFrame.EXIT_ON_CLOSE);
39         window.setBackground(Color.white);
40         window.getContentPane().add(this);
41         window.setLocation(windowNumber % 2 * SPACING + GAP,
```

```
42                    windowNumber / 2 * SPACING);
43              window.setSize(WIDTH, HEIGHT);
44              windowNumber++;
45        }
46  }
```

The first important thing to notice on line 6 is that the Application class extends JPanel and thus inherits the methods paintComponent, repaint, and others, as we mentioned earlier. This class provides a nice illustration of the use of class variables. The class variable windowNumber, declared on line 10, enables each new instance of this class to be assigned a distinct number. It is also used to determine the location of the frame.

Because we have already used this class extensively, we are familiar with the signatures of its various constructors, but now we can examine what each one does. The default constructor sets the name "Java Application" followed by the window number as the frame title on line 15. As an aside, notice the use of parentheses around (windowNumber + 1). Because the plus operator is overloaded to mean both string concatenation and integer addition, we need those parentheses to ensure that plus operation is interpreted as the latter. We have factored out code common to the first two constructors, so after the default constructor creates the frame object, it relies upon the method initialize to finish the remaining tasks.

Like the first constructor, the second one calls the private method initialize to complete the initialization after creating a frame containing a title supplied by the caller. Either of the first two constructors can be used to create multiple nonoverlapping windows.

The third constructor also creates a frame with the title supplied by the caller. Unlike the previous two constructors, it creates a frame of the size specified by the parameters width and height. This constructor is intended for programs that create only a single instance of this class.

We know from our use of the Application class that we must call display after the Application object has been created. We now see that it displays the frame by a call to setVisible. Although it may be tempting to do so, the call to setVisible must not be done in the constructors. It is important that the frame be fully created before it is made visible. There is one other feature of this class that is noteworthy, which is the fact that it returns the value 0 on line 34. We will see shortly that this method is inherited by the class GraphicsApplication. The reason that we made this method return a value is so that calls to this method could be made in the initialization of class constants, which we have done each time we created a class that extended GraphicsApplication. Refer back to line 12 of Listing 13.6 for an example of what we just described. The value returned by this method is just a "dummy" value, which is never referenced.

The private method `initialize` is called by the first two constructors. After setting the default action to perform on frame closing and setting the background color of the frame, the method `initialize` makes the association between the panel and frame. The call to `add` on line 40 adds the panel object referred to by `this` to the container returned by the call to `getContentPane`. It then sets the size of the frame and computes its location based on the current frame number so that the frames will not overlap. In preparation for the next object instantiation, it then increments the class variable `windowNumber`.

Next we consider the class `GraphicsApplication`, which is derived from `Application`. Recall that we have used this class for each graphics application that needed an empty `main`. Its code is provided in Listing 13.8.

LISTING 13.8 The `GraphicsApplication` Class from the Package `common` (found on the CD-ROM at `common\GraphicsApplication.java`.)

```
 1  package common;
 2
 3  public class GraphicsApplication extends Application
 4  {
 5      public GraphicsApplication()
 6      {
 7      }
 8      public GraphicsApplication(String windowName)
 9      {
10          super(windowName);
11      }
12      public GraphicsApplication(String windowName, int width,
13          int height)
14      {
15          super(windowName, width, height);
16      }
17      public static void main(String[] args)
18      {
18      }
19  }
```

Remember that constructors are not inherited, so this class must provide a constructor that matches each one in its base class. Each does nothing but call the constructor of the base class passing along the parameters.

The most interesting aspect of this class is the presence of the empty `main`. Including `main` here enabled us to omit it from a number of our previous examples. This example is our first and only example that illustrates the fact that class methods are inherited.

Now that we have explained the construction of frames and panels, because creating a frame and its panel involves relatively few lines of code, we will refrain from using the `Application` and `GraphicsApplication` classes in our subsequent examples that involve creating a single window.

Labels and Borders

We are now ready to examine our first primary GUI component—primary in the sense that it is not intended to contain other components. We begin with one of the simplest GUI components—the label. As its name suggests, a label is a component that contains some text.

As with most classes, this one has numerous constructors, but let's consider one of them that is commonly used and the one we plan to use in our next example. Its signature is shown below.

```
public JLabel(String text, int horizontalAlignment)
```

It requires us to specify the text contained in the label and its alignment, which is usually one of the following: LEFT, CENTER, or RIGHT.

Because the text contained in a label is its fundamental property, there are two methods provided for accessing a label's text. Their signatures are shown below.

```
void setText(String t)
String getText()
```

As we mentioned earlier, all the GUI components belong to a large inheritance hierarchy and, consequently, inherit many methods from their ancestors. The class that `JLabel` is immediately derived from is `JComponent`, which contains two methods that we plan to use with labels. Their signatures follow.

```
void setFont(Font font)
void setForeground(Color fg)
```

They set the font or foreground color of the label and override these settings in `Component`.

There is one other GUI component that we plan to use in conjunction with our labels—the line border. It allows us to place borders around our labels. The signature of one constructor of the class `LineBorder` is shown below.

```
LineBorder(Color color)
```

It creates a line border with the specified color and a default thickness of one. As you might imagine, other constructors are available if we desire wider borders.

Because we are planning to use the line borders with labels, there is one more method that we wish to introduce, which is one that allows us to change the border around labels. Like some of the earlier methods we discussed, the JLabel class inherits this method from its immediate ancestor JComponent. Consider its signature, which is self-explanatory.

```
void setBorder(Border border)
```

Layout Managers

When developing a GUI, the spatial arrangement of its components needs to be specified. One alternative is to hard code the location and size of every component. If one elects to use that approach, then using a GUI builder that accompanies most Java IDEs is the best strategy. Such GUI builders allow the user to drag and drop the components in their desired locations. The builders then generate the necessary Java code.

There is one important disadvantage to hard coding the sizes and locations, which is that the windows that contain the GUI components can usually be resized. Such resizing can result in the disappearance of some of the components. Layout managers provide an alternative. With a layout manager, you specify certain constraints that define the relative location of the GUI components, rather than absolute locations. In that way, when a window is resized, the layout manager will attempt to rearrange the components, still adhering to the constraints in a way that they fit in the resized window. If the window is made too small, it is still possible for some components to disappear, but the likelihood of it happening is reduced.

Java provides a variety of different layout managers. Each allows the relative location of components to be specified in a different way. We explore several of the simplest ones in this chapter, beginning with the grid layout. The grid layout allows us to specify a two-dimensional collection of components. Because several of our examples will involve the visual representation of two-dimensional arrays, we will have occasion to use this one several times. The signature of the constructor of the GridLayout class that we will use exclusively is shown below.

```
GridLayout(int rows, int cols, int hgap, int vgap)
```

As with a rectangular two-dimensional array, the number of rows and columns must be provided. We have selected a constructor for each of the layout managers that allows us to specify horizontal and vertical gaps in pixels, which is what the third and fourth parameters represent. Specifying gaps makes the GUI more attractive. Without them, the components are all immediately adjacent to one another. When we use the add method, which we discussed earlier, it is important to know that the components are added to the grid in row-major order.

Another simple layout manager is the one that specifies a flow layout. With flow layout, the components flow from left to right and top to bottom, like text flows on a page. Reducing the width of a window might cause the top rightmost component to move to "the next line." The signature of the constructor of the FlowLayout class that we plan to use is shown below.

```
FlowLayout(int align, int hgap, int vgap)
```

The common choices for the first parameter that specifies the alignment are LEFT, CENTER, or RIGHT. The other two parameters specify gaps, as with the grid layout. Although we plan to use the flow layout manager in some of our examples, in each case we will do so primarily to specify the gaps. When we add components to a container that uses the flow layout, they are added in the order of the flow.

The final layout manager that we plan to use in this chapter is the border layout. It allows us to attach components to a specified side or in the center of its container. The constructor of the BorderLayout class that we intend to use is the one shown below that allows gaps to be specified.

```
BorderLayout(int hgap, int vgap)
```

A special overloaded version of the add method defined in the class Container is needed when adding to a container with a border layout. We must specify a constraint, as shown by the method signature.

```
void add(Component comp, Object constraints)
```

The second parameter indicates the relative location of the object. The possible values for that parameter are the constants NORTH, EAST, SOUTH, WEST, or CENTER, defined in BorderLayout. In practice, this layout manager is most useful when we wish to align, at most, three objects either horizontally or vertically.

There is one last issue to consider, which is how we specify the layout managers. We generally designate a layout manager for every panel that we create. The method used to make that designation is setLayout, which is inherited by the JPanel class from Container, where it is defined. Its signature, shown below, tells us that we invoke that method on the panel whose layout manager we wish to designate and supply it an instance of that layout manager as a parameter.

```
void setLayout(LayoutManager manager)
```

The 14-15 Puzzle

For our first example of a program with a GUI, we have chosen to implement a puzzle called the 14-15 puzzle that was developed by the American puzzle maker Sam Loyd, whose life spanned the later part of the eighteenth and early part of the nineteenth centuries. It is a puzzle you may have seen because mechanical versions of this puzzle are still sold today. Figure 13.5 illustrates this puzzle as generated by our program.

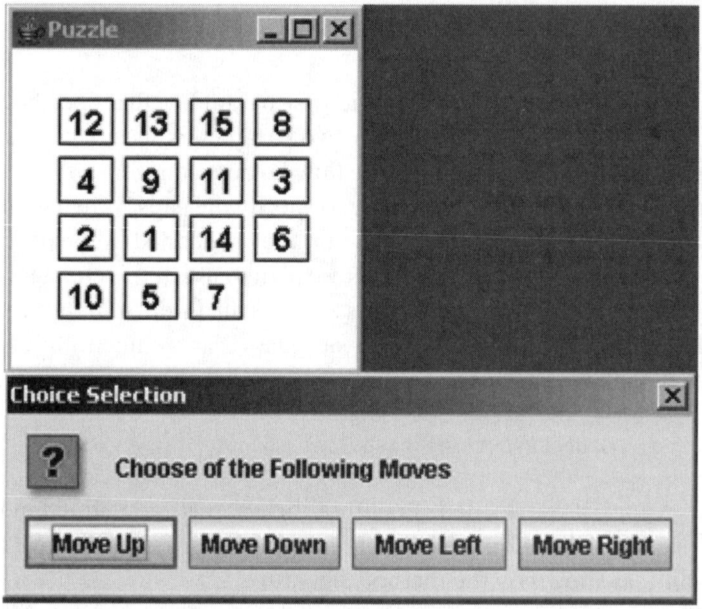

FIGURE 13.5   The 14-15 puzzle GUI.

The goal of this puzzle is to rearrange the squares so that the numbers 1 through 15 fill the two-dimensional array in row-major order, with the lower-right corner empty. This puzzle has an invariant property that concerns the count of the pairs of numbers that are out of order. If that count is initially even, it will remain even no matter how many moves are made. The same is true if it is initially odd. Consequently, if the numbers are initially arranged so that the count is initially odd, the puzzle cannot be solved. If you are interested in more details about the history of this puzzle and its invariant property, we suggest consulting Simon Singh's recent book, *Fermat's Enigma*, which contains an interesting discussion of this puzzle.

We chose this puzzle because it provides an interesting example that requires a simple GUI, so let's consider the code required for implementing the puzzle and its GUI. The class `Puzzle`, in Listing 13.9, contains that code.

LISTING 13.9 A Class Implementing the 14-15 Puzzle (found on the CD-ROM at chapter13\Puzzle.java.)

```java
1     package chapter13;
2
3     import java.awt.*;
4     import javax.swing.*;
5     import javax.swing.border.*;
6     import chapter11.*;
7
8     class Puzzle
9     {
10        private static final int GRID_GAP = 6, FRAME_GAP = 25,
11            TEXT_WIDTH = 3, SIZE = 4;
12        private static final Font squareFont =
13            new Font("Sans Serif", Font.BOLD, 16);
14        private static final LineBorder
15            blackBorder = new LineBorder(Color.BLACK),
16            whiteBorder = new LineBorder(Color.WHITE);
17        private int emptyRow, emptyCol;
18        private boolean isSolvable;
19        private JFrame frame = new JFrame("Puzzle");
20        private JLabel squares[][];
21
22        public class InvalidMove extends Exception
23        {
24        }
25
26        public Puzzle()
27        {
28            int[] values = Permutation.randomize(SIZE * SIZE - 1);
29            JPanel squaresPanel = new JPanel();
30
31            isSolvable = solvable(values);
32            emptyRow = emptyCol = SIZE - 1;
33            squares = new JLabel[SIZE][SIZE];
34            squaresPanel.setLayout(new GridLayout(SIZE, SIZE,
35                GRID_GAP, GRID_GAP));
36            squaresPanel.setBackground(Color.WHITE);
37            for (int index = 0; index < values.length; index++)
38                addSquare(squaresPanel, index / SIZE, index % SIZE,
39                    " " + (values[index] + 1) + " ", blackBorder);
40            addSquare(squaresPanel, SIZE - 1, SIZE - 1, " ",
41                whiteBorder);
42            frame.setDefaultCloseOperation(JFrame.EXIT_ON_CLOSE);
```

```
43              frame.getContentPane().setLayout(
44                  new FlowLayout(FlowLayout.CENTER, FRAME_GAP,
45                  FRAME_GAP));
46              frame.getContentPane().setBackground(Color.WHITE);
47              frame.getContentPane().add(squaresPanel);
48          }
49          public void display()
50          {
51              frame.pack();
52              frame.setVisible(true);
53          }
54          public boolean getSolvable()
55          {
56              return isSolvable;
57          }
58          public void moveDown() throws InvalidMove
59          {
60              if (emptyRow == 0)
61                  throw new InvalidMove();
62              move(emptyRow - 1, emptyCol);
63          }
64          public void moveLeft() throws InvalidMove
65          {
66              if (emptyCol == SIZE - 1)
67                  throw new InvalidMove();
68              move(emptyRow, emptyCol + 1);
69          }
70          public void moveRight() throws InvalidMove
71          {
72              if (emptyCol == 0)
73                  throw new InvalidMove();
74              move(emptyRow, emptyCol - 1);
75          }
76          public void moveUp() throws InvalidMove
77          {
78              if (emptyRow == SIZE - 1)
79                  throw new InvalidMove();
80              move(emptyRow + 1, emptyCol);
81          }
82          public boolean solved()
83          {
84              if (squares[SIZE - 1][SIZE - 1].getText() != "")
85                  return false;
86              for (int value = 1; value < SIZE * SIZE; value++)
```

```
87                  if (!squares[(value − 1) / SIZE][(value − 1) % SIZE].
88                      getText().equals(" " + value + " "))
89                      return false;
90              return true;
91          }
92      private boolean solvable(int[] values)
93      {
94          int outOfOrderCount = 0;
95
96          for (int i = 0; i < values.length; i++)
97              for (int j = i + 1; j < values.length; j++)
98                  if (values[i] > values[j])
99                      outOfOrderCount++;
100         return outOfOrderCount % 2 == 0;
101     }
102     private void addSquare(JPanel panel, int row, int col,
103         String labelString, LineBorder border)
104     {
105         squares[row][col] = new JLabel(labelString, JLabel. CENTER);
106         squares[row][col].setFont(squareFont);
107         squares[row][col].setForeground(Color.BLACK);
108         squares[row][col].setBorder(border);
109         panel.add(squares[row][col]);
110     }
111     private void move(int newEmptyRow, int newEmptyCol)
112     {
113         String value = squares[newEmptyRow][newEmptyCol]. getText();
114         squares[emptyRow][emptyCol].setText(value);
115         squares[emptyRow][emptyCol].setBorder(blackBorder);
116         squares[newEmptyRow][newEmptyCol].setText("");
117         squares[newEmptyRow][newEmptyCol].setBorder (whiteBorder);
118         emptyRow = newEmptyRow;
119         emptyCol = newEmptyCol;
120     }
121 }
```

This is our first example of an application that uses a window without using the predefined class Application, which we have used until now for such applications. You should notice that this class incorporates much of what the Application class contains. One difference, however, is that there was no need in this case to have this class extend JPanel as Application did. Creating a local JPanel object in the constructor suffices.

On line 22, we define an exception InvalidMove as an inner class. It extends Exception because we want it to be a checked exception. This exception is thrown when a move is requested that is not possible in the current state.

Let's examine the constructor, whose primary task is to build the GUI for the puzzle. To create a random initial state for the puzzle, we used the Permutation class that we introduced in Chapter 11. We generate a random permutation of the numbers from 0 to 14 and save it into the one-dimensional integer array values. On line 31, we check whether the puzzle is solvable by calling the private method isSolvable that computes the number of pairs that are out of order in the array values and we save the result in the variable isSolvable. We are now ready to construct the GUI, which consists of a two-dimensional array of labels. On line 33, we instantiate the array and we construct the panel, squaresPanel, on lines 34-41. The grid layout manager is used for this panel because it is the ideal layout manager for displaying two-dimensional collections. The remainder of the constructor sets up the frame itself. It contains many of the same statements that the Application class contains.

The invariant property of this puzzle that we discussed earlier is preserved because we allow the user to modify the puzzle using one of four moves captured by the four public methods moveDown, moveLeft, moveRight, and moveUp. Each of those methods verifies that the move is valid given the current state of the puzzle and throws the InvalidMove exception if it is not. Otherwise it uses the private method move, which we consider shortly, to accomplish the move.

The method solved determines whether the puzzle has been solved. It checks that the empty square is at the lower-right and that the numbers 1 to 15 are in row-major order. We will see that main calls this method after each move to see whether the puzzle has been solved.

Next, we consider the three private methods of this class. We already noted that the constructor calls the first one, solvable, to initialize the instance variable isSolvable. The method solvable computes a count of pairs of numbers in the puzzle that are out of order. It considers only pairs in which the first value is to the left of the second, which explains why the lower bound of the inner loop, defining the index j, begins at a value 1 greater than the index i. Line 97 contains the inner loop to which we just referred. The puzzle is solvable when the count is even. Its solvability is determined on line 100 and returned to the caller.

The constructor also calls the next private method, addSquare. That method instantiates a label object, attaches a border to it and adds it to the panel of squares.

The third private method, move, is the one called by the four public methods that initiate the four kinds of moves. It accomplishes the move by changing the text and border colors of the two squares that are involved in the move.

Now we are ready to consider the second class needed to implement the 14-15 puzzle—the class that contains `main`. Its code is contained in Listing 13.10.

LISTING 13.10 The `main` Method for the 14-15 Puzzle Example (found on the CD-ROM
ON THE CD at chapter13\PuzzleMain.java.)

```java
1   package chapter13;
2
3   import common.*;
4
5   public class PuzzleMain
6   {
7       private enum Moves {MOVE_UP, MOVE_DOWN, MOVE_LEFT, MOVE_RIGHT};
8
9       public static void main(String[] args)
10      {
11          final int UNSOLVABLE_LIMIT = 100;
12          int tries = 0;
13          Moves move;
14          Puzzle puzzle = new Puzzle();
15          boolean solvable = puzzle.getSolvable();
16
17          puzzle.display();
18          do
19          {
20              if (!solvable && tries++ >= UNSOLVABLE_LIMIT)
21              {
22                  InputOutput.putString(
23                      "Give up, This puzzle can't be solved");
24                  return;
25              }
26              move = (Moves)InputOutput.getEnum(
27                  "Choose one of the Following Moves", Moves.values());
28              try
29              {
30                  switch (move)
31                  {
32                      case MOVE_UP:
33                          puzzle.moveUp();
34                          break;
35                      case MOVE_DOWN:
36                          puzzle.moveDown();
37                          break;
38                      case MOVE_LEFT:
```

```
39                        puzzle.moveLeft();
40                        break;
41                    case MOVE_RIGHT:
42                        puzzle.moveRight();
43                        break;
44                }
45            }
46            catch (Puzzle.InvalidMove exception)
47            {
48                InputOutput.putString("Invalid Move");
49            }
50        }
51        while (!puzzle.solved());
52        InputOutput.putString(
53            "Congratulations, You solved the puzzle!");
54    }
55 }
```

The method main repeatedly prompts the user for one of four moves in each of the four possible directions. It calls the corresponding method to accomplish that move. If the exception InvalidMove is thrown, an error message is displayed on line 48. After each move, a check is made on line 51 to determine whether the puzzle was solved. If solved, the program terminates with a congratulatory message on lines 52 and 53. The other way the program can terminate is if the puzzle is unsolvable and 100 moves were attempted. The if statement on line 20 makes this check—one that can only succeed for unsolvable puzzles, which is determined by the call to the getSolvable method of the Puzzle class on line 15.

NONMODAL INPUT

Although our implementation of the 14-15 puzzle allowed us to introduce building a simple GUI using labels as the components, we could have written that program by painting strings and rectangles—something we have done extensively. One of the inherent benefits of building a GUI, which our 14-15 puzzle program lacked, is allowing the user to interact with its components. The user interaction in the 14-15 puzzle was strictly *modal*. Modal interaction permits the user to do only one thing at any time during the execution of the program. The methods of the JOptionPane class, which our InputOutput class uses, allow the user to supply input in a window. Nonetheless, it is still modal input. To better understand this idea, run the 14-15 puzzle program again and when you are prompted to select a move, try resizing the window that contains the puzzle. You will find that you are unable to do so. Such behavior is indicative of modal interaction. Another indication that the user interaction in that program is modal is the fact that the input and output is in main. The flow of control of main dictates what the user can do next.

As an alternative, we might have used a similar GUI, but with buttons—a component we will discuss shortly—instead of labels, and allowed the user to press the button to be moved. In such an implementation, main would contain only a few lines of code—something we will now begin to notice often. Instead the input would be handled with event handling code similar to what we have already seen with mouse clicks. With such user interaction, the user has much more freedom. The window could be resized, any button could be pressed, and so on.

We now introduce two more GUI components—the text field and the button. Both naturally move us toward a nonmodal user interface.

Text Fields

We begin with the text field. Like a label, it contains text, but unlike a label, the user can edit it, if we choose to make it editable. The constructor of the JTextField class that we plan to use is the one whose signature is shown below.

```
JTextField(int columns)
```

By specifying the number of columns, we are designating the width of the field.

There are several other methods that we plan to use with these text fields. Each of them is inherited from JTextComponent, which is the class from which JTextField is immediately derived. Their signatures are shown below.

```
String getText()
void setText(String t)
void setEditable(boolean b)
```

The getText and setText methods are like the methods of the same name in JLabel. The method setEditable allows us to decide if we wish to allow the user to edit this field. Supplying the value true enables the editing.

It is possible to respond to events associated with text fields, such as whenever the user performs an edit. However, in the examples that follow, we never plan to do so.

Buttons

The GUI component, whose events we plan to respond to, is the button. The constructor of the class JButton that we plan to use exclusively is the one whose signature follows.

```
JButton(String text)
```

It allows us to specify a string that will become the label on the button.

We have already encountered the need for registering some object as a listener for mouse events. We must do the same for button events. Each button must have its own listener specified. The method for designating this registration is a method in the JButton class, whose signature is shown below.

```
void addActionListener(ActionListener l)
```

This method specifies the action listener object that will respond to button events. The parameter to this method is the interface ActionListener, whose definition is the following:

```
interface ActionListener
{
    public void actionPerformed(ActionEvent e)
}
```

Because it requires only a single method, unlike MouseListener, it is easy for the listener class to implement the interface. It is often the case that an action listener will respond to many different buttons. Consequently, there is a method, getSource, that we need in such cases, which ActionEvent inherits from its ancestor class EventObject. Its signature follows.

```
Object getSource()
```

It returns the object that caused actionPerformed to be called.

A Calculator Program

One classic example of a Java program that makes use of buttons and a text field is a program that implements a simple calculator. Calculators typically have one button for each of the ten digits and one button for each possible operation. In addition, there is typically a button with an equal sign to force a calculation and another to clear the value. There is also a text field that contains the current input value. Figure 13.6 illustrates the calculator that will be displayed by our calculator program.

Our program to implement this calculator consists of four classes and one enumerated type. Let's begin with the class that builds the GUI and handles the events associated with pressing the buttons. The code for that class is shown in Listing 13.11.

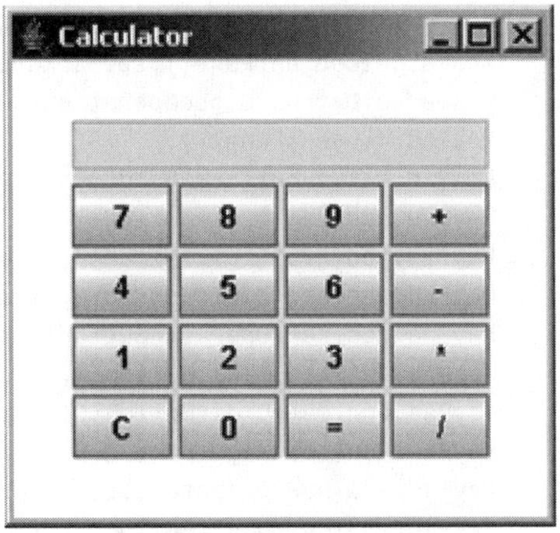

FIGURE 13.6 The calculator GUI.

LISTING 13.11 A Simple Calculator Implemented with Buttons (found on the CD-ROM
ON THE CD at chapter13\Calculator.java.)

```
 1  package chapter13;
 2
 3  import java.awt.*;
 4  import java.awt.event.*;
 5  import javax.swing.*;
 6
 7  class Calculator implements ActionListener
 8  {
 9      private static final int ROWS = 4, COLS = 4, GAP = 3,
10          FLOW_GAP = 25, TEXT_WIDTH = 10, HEIGHT = 200, WIDTH = 200;
11      private JFrame frame = new JFrame("Calculator");
12      private JButton clear = new JButton("C"),
13          enter = new JButton("=");
14      private JTextField display = new JTextField(TEXT_WIDTH);
15      private int result;
16      private String displayText = "";
17      private OperatorButton lastOperator;
18
19      public Calculator()
20      {
21          JPanel keyPad, calculator;
22
23          frame.setSize(WIDTH, HEIGHT);
24          frame.getContentPane().setLayout(
```

```
25              new FlowLayout(FlowLayout.CENTER, FLOW_GAP, FLOW_GAP));
26          frame.getContentPane().setBackground(Color.WHITE);
27          frame.setDefaultCloseOperation(JFrame.EXIT_ON_CLOSE);
28          keyPad = new JPanel();
29          keyPad.setLayout(new GridLayout(ROWS, COLS, GAP, GAP));
30          keyPad.add(new DigitButton(7, this));
31          keyPad.add(new DigitButton(8, this));
32          keyPad.add(new DigitButton(9, this));
33          keyPad.add(new OperatorButton(Operation.ADD, this));
34          keyPad.add(new DigitButton(4, this));
35          keyPad.add(new DigitButton(5, this));
36          keyPad.add(new DigitButton(6, this));
37          keyPad.add(new OperatorButton(Operation.SUBTRACT, this));
38          keyPad.add(new DigitButton(1, this));
39          keyPad.add(new DigitButton(2, this));
40          keyPad.add(new DigitButton(3, this));
41          keyPad.add(new OperatorButton(Operation.MULTIPLY, this));
42          keyPad.add(clear);
43          keyPad.add(new DigitButton(0, this));
44          keyPad.add(enter);
45          keyPad.add(new OperatorButton(Operation.DIVIDE, this));
46          clear.addActionListener(this);
47          enter.addActionListener(this);
48          calculator = new JPanel(new BorderLayout(GAP, GAP));
49          calculator.add(display, BorderLayout.NORTH);
50          calculator.add(keyPad, BorderLayout.SOUTH);
51          frame.add(calculator);
52          display.setEditable(false);
53      }
54      public void actionPerformed(ActionEvent event)
55      {
56          Object object = event.getSource();
57
58          if (object instanceof OperatorButton || object == enter)
59          {
60              if (lastOperator != null)
61              {
62                  result = lastOperator.evaluate(result,
63                      Integer.parseInt(display.getText())));
64                  display.setText("" + result);
65              }
66              else
67                  result = Integer.parseInt(display.getText());
68              displayText = "";
```

```
69              if (object == enter)
70                  lastOperator = null;
71              else
72                  lastOperator = (OperatorButton) object;
73          }
74          else if (object instanceof DigitButton)
75          {
76              displayText += ((DigitButton)object).getDigit();
77              display.setText(displayText);
78          }
79          else if (object == clear)
80          {
81              lastOperator = null;
82              displayText = "";
83              display.setText(displayText);
84          }
85      }
86      public void display()
87      {
88          frame.pack();
89          frame.setVisible(true);
90      }
91      public static void main(String[] args)
92      {
93          Calculator calculator = new Calculator();
94
95          calculator.display();
96      }
97  }
```

We begin with the instance variables of this class. As was true in the Application and Puzzle classes that we just studied, this class also needs a window object
as an instance variable, which we again named frame. Most of the buttons are
anonymous objects, but we need names for two of them—clear and enter—
which are declared and instantiated on lines 12 and 13. The text field display, declared and instantiated on line 14, is the text field that will contain the currently
input number or the result if an operator button has been pushed. The integer result contains the result of the last operation performed. It is necessary to maintain
this value to enable subsequent operations to be performed. One point to mention
about our calculator is that all arithmetic is integer arithmetic, so division loses
any remainder. The string displayText is what is currently displayed in the text
field. It is not absolutely necessary to maintain this string, as we could extract it
from the text field, but we do so for convenience. Finally, we must keep track of

the operator button that was pushed last, which is the role of the object `lastOper-`
`ator`. It is an object of the class `OperatorButton`, which is one of the classes of this
program that we will discuss shortly. The reason that it is necessary to keep track
of this button is that when an operator button is pushed on a typical calculator, it
does not perform that operation, but the one that was entered previously. If you
have doubts about this behavior, try any typical calculator and you will see how
they operate.

This class has two important parts—the constructor that builds the GUI and the
event handling method that responds to button events. We begin with the constructor. By using a flow layout manager with gaps on the main panel of the window,
which we create on lines 24 and 25, we ensure a margin between the calculator and
the edges of the window. The bulk of the code in the constructor builds the keypad.
On line 28, we instantiate the panel that holds the keypad and on line 29, we give it
a grid layout with four rows and four columns, similar to what we did in our previous 14-15 puzzle example. Lines 30-45 add the 16 buttons to the keypad. Notice that
most of the buttons that are created are anonymous objects. You will see that it is not
necessary to refer to them by name in the event handling code. Note also that the
digit buttons belong to a class, `DigitButton`, that we will examine shortly. On lines 46
and 47, the instance of this class is registered as the listener for button events on the
two buttons named `clear` and `enter`. You will see that this registration is done for all
the other buttons in the constructor of `OperatorButton` or `DigitButton`, which is why
the instance of this class, `this`, must be passed into the constructors of both of those
classes. On line 48, another panel named `calculator` is created. It is given a border
layout, which allows objects to be added according to a position aligned with one of
the borders. The display window is then added at the north end and the keypad at
the south end, and then the panel `calculator` is added to the panel frame itself. Figure 13.7 illustrates a UML object diagram showing the object relationships of the objects belonging to this GUI.

Next we consider the code to handle the events of this program. Unlike the
`MouseListener` interface, the `ActionListener` interface requires that we provide only
a single method, `actionPerformed`, so there is no need for creating an inner class.
The class `Calculator` implements the `ActionListener` interface directly, which is indicated on line 7. Recall that an instance of this class has been registered as the listener for the button events of all the buttons. Consequently, what we must do first
in this method is determine which button was pressed. We make that determination on line 56, by invoking the method `getSource` on the action event that we received as the parameter to this method. Once we know which button object was
pressed, we must determine what kind of a button it is.

The `if` statement on line 58 determines whether either an operator button or
the enter button was pressed. Notice that to determine whether a button is an operator button, we need to use an operator we have not encountered before—

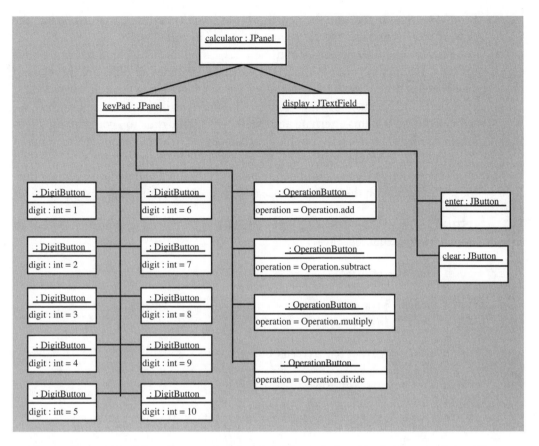

FIGURE 13.7 A UML object diagram showing the object relationships in the calculator GUI.

`instanceof`. It determines whether the object on its left is an instance of the class on its right. Overuse of this operator can indicate a failure to do good object-oriented design. Recall what we mentioned earlier—that when an operator button is pressed, the operation performed is the previous operation. So we must first check that there was a previous operation, which is accomplished by the `if` statement on line 60. If there was, we perform that previous operation by calling the `evaluate` method of the `OperatorButton` class, passing in the previous result saved in `result` as the left operand and the current value displayed as the right operand. The result of the calculation becomes the value of `result`. If there was no previous operation, `result` becomes what was currently in the text field `display`. If it was the enter button that was pressed, there is no longer a previous operation. Otherwise, the operator button that was pressed becomes `lastOperator`.

When digit buttons are pressed, the integer that corresponds to that digit, which is obtained by calling the `getDigit` method of the `DigitButton` class, is appended to displayText and the new text is put into the text field display. When the button clear is pressed, the calculator is reset to its initial state.

There is one final necessary comment regarding this class. Notice that we have included the method main in this class, which instantiates an object of this class as a local object of that method. Because we are no longer using the GraphicsApplication class, and because main is so short, as it often is with graphics applications, we have elected to use this alternate approach, which allows us to avoid having a separate class for main. We will use this approach again, when appropriate, in some of the remaining examples in this chapter and following chapters.

Now we are ready to examine the classes that define the digit and operator buttons. We begin with the former whose code is provided in Listing 13.12.

LISTING 13.12 A Class Extending Buttons to be Digit Buttons (found on the CD-ROM at ON THE CD chapter13\DigitButton.java.)

```
 1  package chapter13;
 2
 3  import java.awt.event.*;
 4  import javax.swing.*;
 5
 6  class DigitButton extends JButton
 7      {
 8      private int digit;
 9
10      public DigitButton(int digit, ActionListener listener)
11      {
12          super("" + digit);
13          this.digit = digit;
14          addActionListener(listener);
15      }
16      public int getDigit()
17      {
18          return digit;
19      }
20  }
```

The first observation that we make is that on line 6, we see that the DigitButton class extends the predefined JButton class. A digit button *is a* button, so the relationship passes our primary test to determine whether inheritance is appropriate. This example is not our first extension of a predefined class. In fact, we have been doing this very thing since our first applet class, which extended JApplet. This class has one instance variable, digit, which contains the digit that this button represents. It is initialized by the constructor and returned by `getDigit`, which we just saw called on line 76 of Listing 13.11. Notice also that the object to be registered as the listener for events generated by this button is supplied to the constructor as the parameter `listener`, and that registration takes place on line 14.

Next, we consider the class that defines the operator buttons, which is shown in Listing 13.13.

LISTING 13.13 A Class Extending Buttons to be Operator Buttons (found on the CD-ROM at `chapter13\OperatorButton.java`.)

```java
 1  package chapter13;
 2
 3  import java.awt.event.*;
 4  import javax.swing.*;
 5
 6  class OperatorButton extends JButton
 7  {
 8      private Operation operation;
 9
10      public OperatorButton(Operation operation, ActionListener
    listener)
11      {
12          super(operation.getSymbol());
13          this.operation = operation;
14          addActionListener(listener);
15      }
16      public int evaluate(int left, int right)
17      {
18          switch (operation)
19          {
20              case ADD:
21                  return left + right;
22              case SUBTRACT:
23                  return left − right;
24              case MULTIPLY:
25                  return left * right;
26              case DIVIDE:
27                  return left / right;
28          }
29          throw new Error();
30      }
31  }
```

Like the `DigitButton` class, `OperatorButton` also extends the predefined class `JButton`. This class has one private instance variable, `operation`, which specifies the operation that this button represents. The type of `operation` is the enumerated type `Operation` that we will examine next. The constructor for this class calls the `getSymbol` method of that enumerated type on line 12 to obtain the string that contains the symbol for this operation that must be placed on the button. Like the constructor of the `DigitButton` class, the constructor for this class also registers the listener supplied as a parameter as the listener for the events of this button.

The other method in this class is `evaluate`, which is called on line 62 of Listing 13.11—in the event handling code for this program. The `switch` statement that spans lines 18-28 computes the result based on the type of the operator. The design approach that we have taken here warrants comment. The presence of `switch` statements of this kind should be a red flag that we may not have done the best job of creating a truly object-oriented design. In the next chapter, which discusses abstract classes, we return to this problem and consider a design alternative that eliminates the `switch` statement. One final comment about this method concerns the exception thrown on line 29. It is impossible for this statement to ever be executed. We know that, but the compiler does not, so that statement is included to satisfy the compiler, which would have generated a compilation error had this statement been omitted. We have elected to throw the generic unchecked exception `Error`, recognizing that it would be pointless to require catching an exception that could never be thrown. We could have satisfied the compiler with a "dummy" return statement as well, but throwing this exception makes it clear that this path is one that we recognize can never be taken.

Next we consider the definition of the enumerated type `Operation` that we just made use of in the `OperatorButton` class. Its code is shown in Listing 13.14.

ON THE CD **LISTING 13.14**   The `Operation` Enumerated Type (found on the CD-ROM at chapter13\Operation.java.)

```
1   package chapter13;
2
3   enum Operation
4   {
5       ADD("+"),
6       SUBTRACT("-"),
7       MULTIPLY("*"),
8       DIVIDE("/");
9
10      private String symbol;
11
12      private Operation(String symbol)
```

```
13      {
14          this.symbol = symbol;
15      }
16      public String getSymbol()
17      {
18          return symbol;
19      }
20  }
```

The enumerated literals have one instance variable associated with them, which is symbol, declared on line 10. It is a string that contains the operator symbol associated with this operation. That string is returned by the method getSymbol, whose signature is on line 16. Recall that getSymbol is called by the constructor of OperationButton to place the symbol on the button.

WRAPPER CLASSES THAT WRAP METHODS

Throughout this book, we have been emphasizing the fact that classes can play many different roles in Java. Let's summarize the various roles that we have discussed so far:

- Classes containing instance variables and instance methods that have objects created, which are instances of such classes.
- Classes containing main, which contains the main thread of control of the program.
- Utility classes that have only class methods, no instance variables, and have no objects that are instances of such classes.

We actually have been using classes that play one additional role that we wish to explore in more detail. The classes that define the event listeners are playing a role different from any of the above three roles. The role of event listener classes is primarily to wrap methods, because Java does not permit method parameters. Classes that play this role typically have instance methods, but no instance variables. The objects of such classes are stateless objects because they have associated methods but no data.

Recall that whenever we extended the MouseAdapter class, we made it an inner class because its methods needed access to the instance variables of the outer class. Java uses the term inner class rather than nested class, because it not only allows classes to be nested inside another class, but it also allows inner classes to be nested inside the methods of other classes. When classes are created for the sole purpose of wrapping methods so they can be passed as parameters, it is not unusual to see such classes declared within the methods of other classes. We explore this deep nesting of classes in two steps, beginning first with named classes declared inside the methods of another class.

Named Local Inner Classes

The example that we have chosen to illustrate, named local inner classes, is a simple program that will repeatedly display the next perfect square each time a button is pressed. The code for this application is shown in Listing 13.15.

LISTING 13.15   An Application that Repeatedly Displays the Next Perfect Square (found on the CD-ROM at `chapter13\PerfectSquares.java`.)

```
1   package chapter13;
2
3   import java.awt.*;
4   import java.awt.event.*;
5   import javax.swing.*;
6
7   public class PerfectSquares
8   {
9       private static final int GAP = 75, WIDTH = 400, HEIGHT = 200;
10      private int square = 0, odd = 1;
11      private JFrame frame = new JFrame("Perfect Squares");
12      private JPanel panel = new JPanel();
13      private JTextField display = new JTextField(10);
14      private JButton button = new JButton("Next Square");
15
16      public PerfectSquares()
17      {
18          display.setEditable(false);
19          panel.setLayout(new FlowLayout(FlowLayout.CENTER, GAP,GAP));
20          panel.setBackground(Color.WHITE);
21          panel.add(button);
22          panel.add(display);
23          frame.setSize(WIDTH, HEIGHT);
24          frame.setDefaultCloseOperation(JFrame.EXIT_ON_CLOSE);
25          frame.getContentPane().add(panel);
26      }
27      public void initialize()
28      {
29          class ButtonListener implements ActionListener
30          {
```

```
31              public void actionPerformed(ActionEvent event)
32              {
33                  square += odd;
34                  odd += 2;
35                  display.setText("" + square);
36              }
37          }
38
39      button.addActionListener(new ButtonListener());
40      frame.pack();
41      frame.setVisible(true);
42      }
43      public static void main(String[] args)
44      {
45          PerfectSquares squares = new PerfectSquares();
46
47          squares.initialize();
48      }
49  }
```

Notice the placement of the class `ButtonListener`. It is inside the method `initialize`. As a class local to a method, there is one difference in its syntax. Labeling such a class as `public` would be meaningless, so it is not permitted, because clearly the scope of the class name extends only to the end of the method. On line 39, we create an anonymous instance of the `ButtonListener` class, which is passed to `addActionListener`, as we did with our mouse listener objects. There is really no need to give that object a name because it will never be referenced again in this method.

There is one important thing to understand about classes declared inside methods, which is that they cannot access the local variables of that class. Notice that on line 35, the method `actionPerformed` must reference the text field `display`. From the perspective of scope, it would be sufficient to declare `display` as a local object inside `initialize`, as we did with `button`. Neither is referenced in any other method of `PerfectSquares`, since it has only one method—`initialize`. The reason `actionPerformed` is not given access to the local variables of `initialize` has to do with its lifetime. The method `actionPerformed` will be called long after the method `initialize` terminates and its local objects disappear, so we are required to make `display` an instance variable of `PerfectSquares` to ensure it exists whenever `actionPerformed` is called.

You may be wondering why we would want to nest a class inside a method, as we have done here. Why not just nest it inside the class `PerfectSquares`, as we did for the mouse listeners or better yet, just make `PerfectSquares` implement `ActionListener` and make `actionPerformed` a method of `PerfectSquares`, as we have been doing? In fact, there is no real advantage to this approach. Our reason for presenting it is to help you make the transition to anonymous local inner classes, which we consider next.

Anonymous Local Inner Classes

So that you realize that method wrapper classes have uses other than for event handlers, we have chosen a different kind of example. It is an example where our underlying desire to pass a method as a parameter may be more apparent than with the listeners. The program that we have chosen for this purpose is one that graphs various mathematical functions. To write such a program, we would like to have a common method that graphs every function. One of the parameters supplied to that method is the mathematical function, implemented as a Java method that is to be graphed. We cannot pass methods as parameters, however. So what we must do is define an interface, like the listener interfaces MouseListener and ActionListener. The interface defines the method signature, and then we must define classes that implement that interface and pass objects of those classes as parameters. Let's begin with the interface Function, shown in Listing 13.16, which contains the signature of the method compute.

LISTING 13.16   The Interface Defining a Mathematical Function (found on the CD-ROM at chapter13\Function.java.)

```
1   package chapter13;
2
3   interface Function
4   {
5       int compute(int n);
6   }
```

Any class implementing this interface must contain the method compute, which accepts an integer parameter and returns an integer result. Next, let's examine the program that graphs a variety of mathematical functions. The code for that program is shown in Listing 13.17.

LISTING 13.17   The Function Graphing Application (found on the CD-ROM at chapter13\FunctionGraphs.java.)

```
1   package chapter13;
2
3   import java.awt.*;
4   import javax.swing.*;
5
```

```
6  public class FunctionGraphs extends JPanel
7  {
8      private static final int WIDTH = 300, HEIGHT = 300;
9      private JFrame frame = new JFrame("Function Graphs");
10
11     public FunctionGraphs()
12     {
13         setBackground(Color.WHITE);
14         frame.setSize(WIDTH, HEIGHT);
15         frame.setDefaultCloseOperation(JFrame.EXIT_ON_CLOSE);
16         frame.getContentPane().add(this);
17     }
18     public void display()
19     {
20         frame.setVisible(true);
21     }
22     public void paintComponent(Graphics graphics)
23     {
24         super.paintComponent(graphics);
25         plot(graphics, Color.RED,
26             new Function(){public int compute(int n)
27                 {return 1;}});
28         plot(graphics, Color.ORANGE,
29             new Function() {public int compute(int n)
30                 {return (int) Math.log(n);}});
31         plot(graphics, Color.YELLOW,
32             new Function() {public int compute(int n)
33                 {return n;}});
34         plot(graphics, Color.GREEN,
35             new Function() {public int compute(int n)
36                 {return (int)(n * Math.log(n));}});
37         plot(graphics, Color.BLUE,
38             new Function() {public int compute(int n)
39                 {return (int)Math.pow(n, 2);}});
40         plot(graphics, Color.MAGENTA.darker(),
41             new Function() {public int compute(int n)
42                 {return (int)Math.pow(n, 3);}});
43         plot(graphics, Color.MAGENTA,
44             new Function() {public int compute(int n)
45                 {return (int)Math.pow(2, n);}});
46     }
47     public void plot(Graphics graphics, Color color,
48         Function function)
49     {
```

```
50              final int INCREMENT = 10, MAX_Y = HEIGHT - 30;
51              int x, y, a = 0, b = MAX_Y;
52
53              graphics.setColor(color);
54              for (x = INCREMENT; x < WIDTH; x += INCREMENT)
55              {
56                  y = MAX_Y - function.compute(x / INCREMENT);
57                  graphics.drawLine(x, y, a, b);
58                  if (y < 0)
59                      break;
60                  a = x;
61                  b = y;
62              }
63          }
64      public static void main(String[] args)
65      {
66          FunctionGraphs graphs = new FunctionGraphs();
67
68          graphs.display();
69      }
70  }
```

In our examples, the objects of classes designed to wrap methods were made anonymous because after being passed as parameters, the objects were never again referenced. In this program we go one step further. Not only are the objects anonymous, but the wrapper classes are also anonymous. The reason is that we really never use the class again after creating a single instance of it to pass as the argument to some method.

Let's examine this program more closely to see how these anonymous classes are used. Let's begin with the method that receives the mathematical functions that are to be graphed, which is plot. The method plot has three parameters: the graphics object onto which the drawing is to be done, the color of the graph, and the mathematical function to be graphed. The third parameter is the one that really represents a method parameter with an object wrapped around it. The method plot graphs the function by drawing line segments connecting the successive points on the graph. The y ordinate of each point is computed by calling the method compute, which is called on line 56. It is important to understand that compute represents a different method on each call to plot.

So, let's now consider the calls to plot, which are contained in paintComponent. Notice the third argument in each call to plot is an anonymous object of an anonymous class. We really have no need of a name for either the object or the class. Our real goal here is passing a new implementation of compute to plot. Let's examine the syntax of these anonymous classes. At first, it may seem that an object of the interface `Function` is being created, but in fact it is an object of an anonymous class that implements `Function` that is being created, whose class definition follows the clause `new Function()`. To help you understand what is happening on lines 25-27, we have rewritten those lines using a named local class, as we had done in the perfect squares example earlier. The code segment shown below is equivalent to and could be substituted for lines 25-27.

```
class Anonymous implements Function
{
    public int compute(int n)
    {
        return 1;
    }
}
plot(graphics, Color.RED, new Anonymous());
```

As in the previous two examples, we placed `main` in this class. To set it apart from the instance methods, we departed from our usual alphabetical ordering of public methods and placed it last.

The output of this program is shown in Figure 13.8.

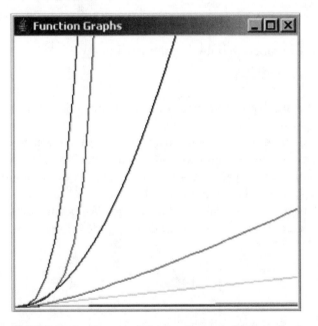

FIGURE 13.8 Output of the function graphing application.

Understanding the relative growth rates of the functions graphed by this program is necessary in order to fully understand algorithm efficiency—an important topic in computer science, but one that we only explore informally in this book.

MAGIC SQUARE APPLICATION

Our final example of this chapter will illustrate all the new topics we encountered in this chapter—multidimensional arrays, event handling connected with GUI components, and anonymous classes that wrap methods.

This example involves a mathematical idea that has intrigued those interested in number patterns for several millennia—magic squares. A magic square is a two-dimensional array with the n rows and n columns that satisfy the following properties.

- The numbers 1 to n^2 each appear once in some cell of the magic square.

- The numbers in every row add to $\dfrac{n(n^2+1)}{2}$.

- The numbers in every column add to $\dfrac{n(n^2+1)}{2}$.

- The numbers in both diagonals add to $\dfrac{n(n^2+1)}{2}$.

- The number of rows and columns, n, must be at least three.

This program allows the user to try to make a magic square and then tests whether the square submitted is magic or not. Upon request, a solution is provided. The output of this program after the user has requested a solution for a five-by-five magic square is shown in Figure 13.9.

This program consists of three classes. We begin with the class that defines the magic square. Listing 13.18 contains the code for that class.

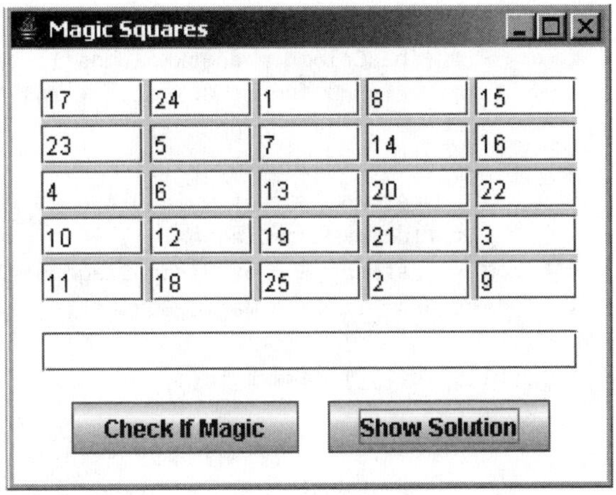

FIGURE 13.9 A magic square with five rows and five columns.

LISTING 13.18 A Class Defining a Magic Square (found on the CD-ROM at chapter13\MagicSquare.java.)

```java
1    package chapter13;
2
3    import chapter11.*;
4
5    public class MagicSquare
6    {
7        private int size, numberOfSquares, expectedSum;
8        private int[][] square;
9
10       public MagicSquare(int size)
11       {
12           this.size = size;
13           numberOfSquares = size * size;
14           expectedSum = (size * (numberOfSquares + 1)) / 2;
15           square = new int[size][size];
16       }
17       public String checkMagic()
18       {
19           int badRow, badColumn;
20
21           if (!checkPermutation())
22               return "Not a Permutation of 1-" + numberOfSquares;
23           if ((badRow = checkRows()) != size)
```

```
24              return "Sum of Row " + (badRow + 1) + " Is Incorrect";
25          if ((badColumn = checkColumns()) != size)
26              return "Sum of Column " + (badColumn + 1) +
27                  " Is Incorrect";
28          if (!checkMainDiagonal())
29              return "Sum of Main Diagonal Is Incorrect";
30          if (!checkMinorDiagonal())
31              return "Sum of Minor Diagonal Is Incorrect";
32          return "It Is a Magic Square";
33      }
34      public int[][] makeMagic()
35      {
36          int row, col, nextRow, nextCol;
37
38          for (row = 0; row < size; row++)
39              for (col = 0; col < size; col++)
40                  square[row][col] = 0;
41          row = 0;
42          col = size / 2;
43          for (int value = 1; value <= numberOfSquares; value++)
44          {
45              square[row][col] = value;
46              nextRow = (row + size − 1) % size;
47              nextCol = (col + 1) % size;
48              if (square[nextRow][nextCol] != 0)
49              {
50                  nextRow = row + 1;
51                  nextCol = col;
52              }
53              row = nextRow;
54              col = nextCol;
55          }
56          return square;
57      }
58      public void set(int row, int col, int value)
59      {
60          square[row][col] = value;
61      }
62      private boolean checkPermutation()
63      {
64          int i = 0;
65          int[] linearEnumeration = new int [numberOfSquares];
66
67          for (int row = 0; row < size; row++)
```

```
68                    for (int col = 0; col < size; col++)
69                        linearEnumeration[i++] = square[row][col] − 1;
70                return Permutation.check(linearEnumeration);
71            }
72            private int checkRows()
73            {
74                int sum;
75
76                for (int row = 0; row < size; row++)
77                {
78                    sum = 0;
79                    for (int col = 0; col < size; col++)
80                        sum += square[row][col];
81                    if (sum != expectedSum)
82                        return row;
83                }
84                return size;
85            }
86            private int checkColumns()
87            {
88                int sum;
89
90                for (int col = 0; col < size; col++)
91                {
92                    sum = 0;
93                    for (int row = 0; row < size; row++)
94                        sum += square[row][col];
95                    if (sum != expectedSum)
96                        return col;
97                }
98                return size;
99            }
100           private boolean checkMainDiagonal()
101           {
102               int sum = 0;
103
104               for (int rowCol = 0; rowCol < size; rowCol++)
105                   sum += square[rowCol][rowCol];
106               return sum == expectedSum;
107           }
108           private boolean checkMinorDiagonal()
109           {
110               int sum = 0;
111
```

```
112              for (int row = 0; row < size; row++)
113                  sum += square[row][size - row - 1];
114              return sum == expectedSum;
115          }
116      }
```

Because this program is intended to work for magic squares of different sizes, the number of the rows and columns, the total number of squares, and the sum are instance variables of the class, which are named size, numberOfSquares, and expectedSum, respectively and are declared on line 7. The magic square is also an instance variable, a two-dimensional array, which is declared on line 8. The instance variables size, numberOfSquare and expectedSum are initialized by the constructor on lines 12-14. The sum is initialized using the formula discussed earlier, $\frac{n(n^2+1)}{2}$, where n is the number of rows and columns. The magic square—the instance variable named square, is instantiated in the constructor also.

The method checkMagic, whose signature is on line 17, determines whether the values that are currently in the array square constitute a magic square. It makes this determination by calling a sequence of private methods that check each of the requirements specified earlier that are necessary to satisfy the definition of a magic square. The method checkMagic returns a string to its caller containing either an error message indicating what part of the definition failed or a message confirming that all requirements were satisfied. We have elected not to use an exception in this case because failing to be a magic square is not really an unexpected occurrence.

The method makeMagic supplies a solution for the magic square. The algorithm that it uses assumes that the number of rows and columns is an odd number. Because no check is made, that requirement is a precondition—a term we introduced in Chapter 11—of this method. This algorithm needs to be able to distinguish filled squares from empty ones, so all the squares are initialized to zero in the nested for loops that span lines 38-40 to designate them as empty initially. The first element of the array that is filled is the one in the center column of the first row. The assignments of row and col on lines 41 and 42 accomplish this initial setting. Filling the magic square is accomplished by the for loop that spans lines 43-55. The assignment on line 45 places the loop control variable value into the proper element of the array. The values are placed into the magic square in sequential order, so understanding the order in which the array is filled is the key to understanding this algorithm. The order is to follow diagonals that move in the direction toward the upper-right. To move to the element one up and one to the right, we must decrement the row and increment the column. The assignments on line 46 and 47 accomplish that movement. If we encounter a filled square, we then move down one row. The if statement on line 48 makes this check and the assignment on line 50 adjusts the row downward. Figure 13.10 traces the order in which a five-by-five magic square is filled.

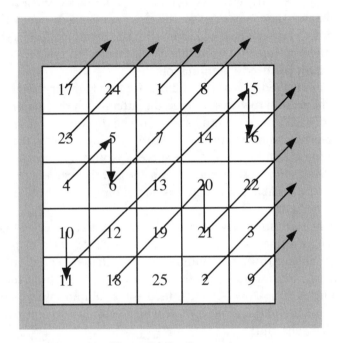

FIGURE 13.10   Filling a five-by-five magic square.

We have glossed over one aspect of moving along the diagonals that should be apparent from the diagram in Figure 13.10, which is what to do when we go above the first row or to the right of the last column. Notice that we use modular arithmetic when decrementing the row and incrementing the column on lines 46 and 47. In Chapter 4, we used a similar technique when numbering the checkerboard in row-major or column-major orders. What we have done conceptually is taken the two-dimensional square and turned it into a cylinder by joining the top and bottom edges, similar to what Figure 4.7 illustrates, except now each column at the bottom matches the same column on the top. Then the two ends of the cylinder are connected to form a torus—a shape that we more commonly refer to as a donut.

Next, one brief comment is warranted regarding the method set. It allows an element of the array, specified by row and column, to be set to a particular value. Because we have separated the magic square from the GUI that displays the square, we need to provide this capability.

The remaining methods of this class are all private methods that are called by checkMagic. Each one checks to determine whether one of the requirements for being a magic square is satisfied. The first such method, `checkPermutation`, determines whether the array contains each number in the range from 1 to the number of squares, exactly once. We again rely on the `Permutation` class that we developed in Chapter 11 to help us make this determination. We copy the values of the matrix into a one-dimensional array with the nested `for` loops spanning lines 67-69, and then on line 70 we use the `check` method of the `Permutation` class to verify whether it is indeed a permutation.

The methods `checkRows` and `checkColumns` are very similar. The former examines the array in row-major order, the latter in column-major. Each verifies that the sum of each row or column is correct. The row or column number of one that has an improper sum is returned. A sentinel value equal to the number of rows and columns is returned to indicate success. Notice that because we are computing a sum for just one row or one column and not the whole array, it is necessary to initialize the variable `sum` to zero inside the outer loop, but before the inner loop in both methods.

The remaining private methods are `checkMajorDiagonal` and `checkMinorDiagonal`. The former is the easier of the two because all the elements along the major diagonal have row and column subscripts that are equal. In `checkMinorDiagonal`, we need a formula to compute the column subscript from the row subscript. That formula is `size - row - 1` and is used as the column subscript on line 113. This formula is a useful one whenever we wish to compute the mirror image subscript of another subscript.

We are now ready to examine the second class required for this program, which is the class that defines the GUI for the magic square. We already noted that we have elected to separate the magic square from the GUI that displays it. Such a separation is generally a wise design choice. It keeps each part simpler and allows the class that implements the magic square to be used in other programs independent of the GUI. The code for this class is provided in Listing 13.19.

LISTING 13.19   A Class Defining the GUI for the Magic Square (found on the CD-ROM at

ON THE CD   chapter13\MagicSquareGUI.java.)

```
1  package chapter13;
2
3  import java.awt.*;
4  import java.awt.event.*;
5  import javax.swing.*;
6
7  public class MagicSquareGUI implements ActionListener
8  {
9      private static final int GRID_GAP = 3, MAIN_GAP = 15,
```

```
10              TEXT_WIDTH = 3, MESSAGE_WIDTH = 15;
11      private int size;
12      private JFrame frame = new JFrame("Magic Squares");
13      private JTextField squares[][];
14      private JButton check = new JButton("Check If Magic"),
15          show = new JButton("Show Solution");
16      private JTextField message = new JTextField(MESSAGE_WIDTH);
17      private MagicSquare magicSquare;
18
19      public MagicSquareGUI(int size)
20      {
21          JPanel squaresPanel = new JPanel(),    buttonPanel =
22              new JPanel(), mainPanel = new JPanel();
23
24          this.size = size;
25          magicSquare = new MagicSquare(size);
26          squares = new JTextField[size][size];
27          squaresPanel.setLayout(
28              new GridLayout(size, size, GRID_GAP, GRID_GAP));
29          for (int row = 0; row < size; row++)
30              for (int col = 0; col < size; col++)
31              {
32                  squares[row][col] = new JTextField(TEXT_WIDTH);
33                  squaresPanel.add(squares[row][col]);
34              }
35          buttonPanel.setLayout(
36              new FlowLayout(FlowLayout.CENTER, MAIN_GAP, 0));
37          buttonPanel.setBackground(Color.WHITE);
38          buttonPanel.add(check);
39          buttonPanel.add(show);
40          mainPanel.setLayout(
41              new BorderLayout(MAIN_GAP, MAIN_GAP));
42          mainPanel.setBackground(Color.WHITE);
43          mainPanel.add(squaresPanel, BorderLayout.NORTH);
44          mainPanel.add(message, BorderLayout.CENTER);
45          mainPanel.add(buttonPanel, BorderLayout.SOUTH);
46          frame.setDefaultCloseOperation(JFrame.EXIT_ON_CLOSE);
47          frame.getContentPane().setLayout(new FlowLayout
48              (FlowLayout.CENTER, MAIN_GAP, MAIN_GAP));
49          frame.getContentPane().setBackground(Color.WHITE);
50          frame.getContentPane().add(mainPanel);
51          check.addActionListener(this);
52          show.addActionListener(this);
53      }
```

```
54        public void actionPerformed(ActionEvent event)
55        {
56            if (event.getSource() == check)
57                checkMagic();
58            else
59                makeMagic();
60        }
61        public void display()
62        {
63            frame.pack();
64            frame.setVisible(true);
65        }
66        private void checkMagic()
67        {
68            int badRow, badColumn;
69            for (int row = 0; row < size; row++)
70                for(int col = 0; col < size; col++)
71                    try
72                    {
73                        magicSquare.set(row, col, Integer.parseInt
74                            (squares[row][col].getText()));
75                    }
76                    catch(NumberFormatException exception)
77                    {
78                        message.setText( "Row " + (row + 1) + " Column "
79                            + (col + 1) + " Not an Integer");
80                    }
81            message.setText(magicSquare.checkMagic());
82        }
83        private void makeMagic()
84        {
85            int[][] solution = magicSquare.makeMagic();
86            for (int row = 0; row < size; row++)
87                for(int col = 0; col < size; col++)
88                    squares[row][col].setText("" + solution[row][col]);
89        }
90  }
```

The instance variables of this class consist of the GUI components that need to be referenced after their creation, and an instance of the MagicSquare class, declared on line 17, together with the integer variable size that contains the number of rows and columns that the magic square contains.

As we have seen in several earlier programs that build GUIs, the constructor of the class MagicSquareGUI creates the GUI. For this GUI, we have three panels:

squaresPanel, the one that contains the text fields corresponding to each element of the magic square, buttonPanel, the one panel for the two buttons, and a third panel, mainPanel that contains the other two panels. Lines 26-34 construct the panel squaresPanel. The grid layout is the obvious choice for this panel given that it contains a two-dimensional array of text fields. Lines 35-39 construct the panel buttonPanel. The two buttons, one for checking whether the user-supplied values constitute a magic square and the other one for requesting that a solution be provided, are added to this panel, which is laid out with the flow layout manager. The main panel is constructed with lines 40-45 by adding three components to it: the squarePanel, a text field for displaying a message, and the buttonPanel. The border layout is ideal for this purpose. Finally the frame itself is set up with lines 46-50. A layout manager is specified here primarily to specify gaps. The last two lines of the constructor register the instance of this class as the listener for button events.

Because the instances of this class listen for button events, we need the method actionPerformed. That method checks which button was pressed with the if statement on line 56 and calls checkMagic when the button check is pressed and method makeMagic when the button show is pressed.

The method checkMagic ensures that all the squares contain integers and displays an error message if not. If so, it calls the checkMagic method of the MagicSquare class to determine whether the square is a magic square and displays the message returned by that call. The method makeMagic calls the makeMagic method of the MagicSquare class to construct a magic square. It fills the array of text fields with the values returned by that call.

Finally, we consider the third class of this program—MagicSquareMain—which, as the name suggests, contains main. Listing 13.20 contains the code for that class.

LISTING 13.20 The Class Containing main for the Magic Square Program (found on the CD-ROM at chapter13\MagicSquareMain.java.)

```
1   package chapter13;
2
3   import common.*;
4
5   public class MagicSquareMain
6   {
7       public static void main(String[] args)
8       {
9           final int MIN_SIZE = 3, MAX_SIZE = 15;
10          String range = "" + MIN_SIZE + "- " + MAX_SIZE,
11              prompt = "Enter Square Size, An Odd Integer from " + range,
12              errorMessage = "Must Be Odd Integer from " + range;
13          int size = InputOutput.getInteger(prompt, errorMessage,
```

```
14                  new InputOutput.Validator()
15                  {
16                      public boolean validate(int value)
17                          {
18                              return value % 2 == 1 &&
19                                  value >= MIN_SIZE && value <= MAX_SIZE;
20                          }
21                  });
22          MagicSquareGUI gui = new MagicSquareGUI(size);
23
24          gui.display();
25      }
26  }
```

The method main prompts the user for the size of the magic square before creating the object gui on line 22. It uses the version of the method getInteger in the InputOutput class that allows us to provide a validation method. Although we discussed this version of getInteger in Chapter 11, we have not used it until now. As we have mentioned throughout this chapter, Java does not allow method parameters, so it is necessary to wrap the method in an object and pass the object. On lines 14-21, we create an anonymous object of an anonymous class that implements the interface InputOut.Validator. It wraps the method validate, which verifies that the integer passed to it as a parameter is an odd number between 3 and 15. This validation is what we wish to perform on the size of the magic square input by the user.

SUMMARY

In this chapter, we introduced multidimensional arrays and saw a variety of examples that used them. Although we have used graphic output from the first chapter, this chapter illustrated our first programs that contained a GUI built with labels, text fields, and buttons. The key points to remember from this chapter are as follows:

- Java allows arrays of any number of dimensions to be created.
- Unlike a one-dimensional array, which has only one forward order, multidimensional arrays can be enumerated in a variety of different orders.
- A ragged two-dimensional array is one in which different rows have different numbers of columns.
- A frame object creates a window that is needed by any Java application that uses GUI components. Panels are used to organize the components in the interface.
- Labels, text fields, and buttons are among the primary components used in creating a GUI.

- Layout managers allow the relative positions of GUI components to be specified using a variety of constraints, rather than specifying absolute locations.
- With nonmodal user interaction, input is handled by responding to events.
- Methods cannot be passed as parameters. They must be wrapped into objects and the objects must be passed instead.

Review Questions

1. What is the maximum number of dimensions permitted for an array?
2. Explain the advantage and disadvantage of implementing multidimensional arrays as arrays of arrays rather than using a block of contiguous memory.
3. Give an example of when a ragged array would be useful.
4. What role do frames play in developing a GUI?
5. Explain how panels are used when creating a GUI.
6. Explain the benefit of using layout managers to specify the location of the components of a GUI.
7. What kinds of user interactions are possible on labels, text fields, and buttons?
8. Describe the characteristics of a modal user interface. How does it differ from a nonmodal interface?
9. Is the prohibition of method parameters universal among programming languages?
10. What is an anonymous inner class? When are such classes useful?

Programming Exercises

11. Given the following two-dimensional array definition:

    ```
    int[][] matrix = new int[5][3];
    ```

    write the necessary statements to accomplish each of the following:
    a. Set all the elements to 1.
    b. Set the element in the first row, last column to 10.
    c. Set all elements of the second row to 8.
    d. Set all elements of the last column to 7.

12. Write a method that accepts a two-dimensional array of integers as a parameter and returns whether the array is a square array—a rectangular array with the same number of rows as columns.

13. Write a method that accepts a two-dimensional array of integers as a parameter and returns whether the array is a triangular array. In a triangular array, the first row has one column, the second has two, and so on.

14. Write a method that accepts an integer size n as a parameter and returns a square array of integers filled with the numbers from 1 to n^2. The elements should be filled diagonally, as shown in Figure 13.11, for a four-by-four array.

15. Write a method that accepts an integer size n as a parameter and returns a square array of integers filled with the numbers from 1 to n^2 by filling it in shells, as shown in Figure 13.12, for a four-by-four array.

1	3	6	10
2	5	9	13
4	8	12	15
7	11	14	16

FIGURE 13.11   A four-by-four array filled diagonally.

16. Write a method that creates a panel laid out with the grid layout manager that contains 16 buttons in a four-by-four configuration that is labeled with the hexadecimal digits.

17. Write a method that creates a panel laid out with the flow layout that contains a label containing "Name" and a text field wide enough to accommodate 20 characters.

18. Write a method that creates a frame whose content pane contains a panel laid out with the border layout in which two text fields and one button are arranged vertically.

19. Write a method that accepts three text fields as parameters. It should place the concatenation of the strings in the first two text fields into the third one.

FIGURE 13.12   A four-by-four array filled in shells.

20. Write a method that accepts a text field as a parameter and determines whether the string contained in that text field is an integer.

Programming Projects

21. Write a program that prompts the user for a size n, and then displays a two-dimensional array of labels containing the numbers 1 to n^2, arranged diagonally. Use the method developed in Programming Exercise 14 as a part of this program.

22. Write a program that prompts the user for a size n, and then displays a two-dimensional array of uneditable text fields containing the numbers 1 to n^2, arranged in shells. Use the method developed in Programming Exercise 15 as a part of this program.

23. Write a program that displays a window containing two text fields and a button, arranged vertically with the button in the middle. The top text field should be editable; the bottom should not. When the button is pressed, the square root of the value in the top text field should be displayed in the bottom one. Use the method developed in Programming Exercise 20 to verify that the top text field contains an integer.

24. Write a program that implements a tic-tac-toe game. The interface should consist of a three-by-three grid of buttons, initially without labels. When an unlabeled button is pressed it is labeled alternately with an X label or an O label. Pressing already labeled buttons, has no effect. The program terminates when

any row, column, or diagonal contains all X's or O's. In that case, the winner is announced. It also terminates when all buttons are labeled. A tie is announced in that case.

25. Write a program that displays a ten-by-ten grid of editable text fields. To the right of each row and below each column is an uneditable text field. Below the text field is a button labeled "Compute." When the button is pressed, the sum of each row is displayed in the uneditable text field to the right of that row. Similarly the sum of each column is displayed in the uneditable text field below each column. Empty text fields are treated as though they contain zero. An error message is displayed if any text field contains nonnumeric text.

14 | Abstract Enumerated Types and Classes

In this chapter

- Abstract Enumerated Types
- Abstract Classes and Methods
- Choosing Between Abstract Enumerated Types and Classes
- More GUI Features
- Card Game of War Application

ABSTRACT ENUMERATED TYPES

Abstract enumerated types and abstract classes are similar in many ways, which is why we have elected to introduce them in the same chapter. Among their similarities is the fact that they both contain *abstract methods*. Although we have not used this term before, we have been using the concept. The method signatures in every interface are really abstract methods, because an abstract method is a method declaration that has no defined body and therefore must be defined elsewhere. In the case of interfaces, any class that implements an interface must define all of the abstract methods declared in the interface. Both the absence of a method body and the presence of the reserved word abstract characterize abstract methods. Although we are permitted to label the abstract methods of an interface with the modifier abstract, we elected not to do so because all methods defined inside an interface are understood to be both public and abstract.

Another Implementation of the Colored-Circles Application

Our first use of enumerated types was in Chapter 4, where we presented them in their simplest form, which also happens to be the form that they take in most other programming languages. Although enumerated types were introduced late in Java, their implementation is far richer in Java than in other languages. In Chapter 5, we saw how data and methods can be associated with enumerated types, and now we will explore their remaining feature—the fact that some of these methods can be abstract. Abstract enumerated types are also sometimes referred to as *polymorphic enumerated types* because of the polymorphic behavior of the abstract methods.

When an enumerated type contains an abstract method, that method must be defined separately for each enumerated literal of the type. The definition of those methods must follow each literal. Syntactically, the definition of those methods looks exactly like the syntax for the anonymous classes that we encountered in Chapter 13.

We begin with an example that we have implemented twice already to help you compare the possible implementations and to help you understand the advantages of the use of abstract methods. This example is the colored-circles program that we first encountered as an applet in Chapter 4. In that implementation, we needed a switch statement to determine the java.awt.Color that was associated with each Rainbow-Color. In the second implementation in Chapter 5, we provided a method getColor as a part of the enumerated type. In that way we were able to eliminate the need for a switch statement. We noted that the disappearance of switch statements was something that we would encounter again. The use of polymorphic methods, abstract methods in particular, achieves this same goal. Whenever a call is made to an overridden method or an abstract method, the compiler must determine which method should be called. The compiler, in effect, generates the switch statement for us.

Now let's consider how the enumerated type RainbowColors can be implemented as an abstract enumerated type. Listing 14.1 contains the code for that implementation.

LISTING 14.1   The Rainbow Colors Enumerated Type Implemented as an Abstract
ON THE CD Enumerated Type (found on the CD-ROM at chapter14\RainbowColors.java.)

```
1   package chapter14;
2
3   import java.awt.*;
4
5   public enum RainbowColors
6   {
7       RED
8       {
```

```
 9          Color getColor()
10          {
11              return Color.RED;
12          }
13      },
14      ORANGE
15      {
16          Color getColor()
17          {
18              return Color.ORANGE;
19          }
20      },
21      YELLOW
22      {
23          Color getColor()
24          {
25              return Color.YELLOW;
26          }
27      },
28      GREEN
29      {
30          Color getColor()
31          {
32              return Color.GREEN;
33          }
34      },
35      BLUE
36      {
37          Color getColor()
38          {
39              return Color.BLUE;
40          }
41      },
42      INDIGO
43      {
44          Color getColor()
45          {
46              return Color.MAGENTA;
47          }
48      },
49      VIOLET
50      {
51          Color getColor()
52          {
```

```
53                return Color.MAGENTA.darker();
54            }
55        };
56
57        abstract Color getColor();
58  }
```

Let's examine what is different about this implementation. First, we have eliminated the variable color and the explicit constructor, so when we declare an enumeration literal like RED, which is declared on line 7, the color is not supplied to the constructor. Instead what follows each of the literals, and RED in particular on lines 8–13, is what we described earlier as syntactically similar to an anonymous class definition. In this case, it contains only one method—getColor. Finally, after all the enumeration literals is the abstract method declaration on line 57. The reserved word abstract is required now because enumerated types can contain both abstract and fully defined methods. Notice that, as with the method declarations in an interface, a semicolon replaces the method body. We have omitted the access modifier public on this method because all abstract methods in an enumerated type are implicitly public methods.

The class that defines the window for this version of the colored circles application that must be used with this implementation of RainbowColors illustrates nothing new, so we chose not to include the code here, but you will find that class at chapter14\ColoredCircles.java on the CD-ROM that accompanies this book.

ON THE CD

You are no doubt wondering what is better about this version compared to the one that we saw last in Chapter 5. In fact, using an abstract enumerated type for this program is more than what the problem warrants. We began with it to make the transition to abstract enumerated types.

Another Implementation of the Calculator

So let's consider a different problem where an abstract enumerated type is essential to eliminate the switch statement. We return to the example of the calculator that we presented in Chapter 13. Recall that we used an enumerated type to define the kind of operation that was associated with each operator button. In the class OperatorButton that contained a method evaluate, we needed a switch statement to determine what operation was to be performed. By using an abstract enumerated type, we can replace the method evaluate in OperatorButton with an abstract method in the enumerated type Operation. Consider the code for this new implementation, which is shown in Listing 14.2.

LISTING 14.2   An Abstract Enumerated Type for Calculator Button Operations (found on
ON THE CD the CD-ROM at chapter14\Operation.java.)

```
1  package chapter14;
2
3  public enum Operation
4  {
5      ADD("+")
6      {
7          public int evaluate(int left, int right)
8          {
9              return left + right;
10         }
11     },
12     SUBTRACT("-")
13     {
14         public int evaluate(int left, int right)
15         {
16             return left - right;
17         }
18     },
19     MULTIPLY("*")
20     {
21         public int evaluate(int left, int right)
22         {
23             return left * right;
24         }
25     },
26     DIVIDE("/")
27         {
28         public int evaluate(int left, int right)
29         {
30             return left / right;
31         }
32     };
33
34     private String symbol;
35
36     private Operation(String symbol)
37     {
38         this.symbol = symbol;
39     }
40     public static Operation anOperation(String symbol)
```

```
41      {
42          for (Operation operation: Operation.values())
43              if (symbol.equals(operation.getSymbol()))
44                  return operation;
45          return null;
46      }
47      abstract public int evaluate(int left, int right);
48      public String getSymbol()
49      {
50          return symbol;
51      }
52  }
```

Notice that this abstract enumerated type contains both abstract and ordinary methods. It also still has the variable symbol that was defined in the previous version, the constructor, and the ordinary method getSymbol. What has been added is the abstract method evaluate, declared on line 47. Each enumerated literal must now implement this method, as ADD does on lines 7–10.

The new version of the class OperatorButton is shown in Listing 14.3.

LISTING 14.3   The Revised Class for Operator Buttons (found on the CD-ROM at chapter14\OperatorButton.java.)

```
1  package chapter14;
2
3  import java.awt.event.*;
4  import javax.swing.*;
5
6  class OperatorButton extends JButton
7  {
8      private Operation operation;
9
10     public OperatorButton(Operation operation, ActionListener listener)
11     {
12         super(operation.getSymbol());
13         this.operation = operation;
14         addActionListener(listener);
15     }
16     public int evaluate(int left, int right)
17     {
18         return operation.evaluate(left, right);
19     }
20 }
```

Although this class still has the method `evaluate`, its `switch` statement is gone. In its place is the call to the abstract method `evaluate` of the enumerated type `Operation` on line 18. Let's review the significance of polymorphic method calls, because all calls to abstract methods are polymorphic. What we mean when we say that the method call on line 18 is polymorphic is that we cannot determine by looking at the code which `evaluate` method will be called. That determination must be made at runtime by examining what kind of operation is contained in the enumerated variable `operation`.

Because the remaining classes that comprise the calculator example, `Calculator` and `DigitButton`, are unchanged, we have not repeated the code here. You will, however, find another copy of each of those classes in package `chapter14` on the CD-ROM that accompanies this book so that you can run this new version of the program.

ON THE CD

ABSTRACT CLASSES AND METHODS

Next, let's begin our discussion of abstract classes by comparing abstract classes with abstract enumerated types. A similarity between the two is that, like an abstract enumerated type, an abstract class can contain abstract methods and also ordinary methods. A difference is that abstract classes must have some derived classes to be useful. Clearly that does not apply to enumerated types.

Next, let's compare abstract classes with interfaces. Both have abstract methods, but recall that interfaces must contain only abstract methods. Interfaces cannot contain instance variables. By contrast, abstract class can have instance variables. Another difference between interfaces and abstract classes is that interfaces cannot contain constructors. Although abstract classes can contain constructors, only the constructors of derived classes can call them. As with interfaces, the reserved word `new` can never appear before the name of an abstract class.

An Application Containing Radial Shapes

As always, an example will help amplify some of these similarities and differences. The example that we have chosen is a collection of shapes that we call radial shapes, which encompass circles, squares, and equilateral triangles. They are "radial" in the sense that each can be defined by its center point and a radius—which, for the latter two shapes, is the radius of the inscribed circle. The code for the abstract class `RadialShapes` is provided in Listing 14.4.

LISTING 14.4 An Abstract Class Defining Shapes having a Center and a Radius (found on the CD-ROM at chapter14\RadialShapes.java.)

```java
1  package chapter14;
2
3  import java.awt.*;
4  import static java.lang.Math.*;
5
6  abstract class RadialShapes
7  {
8      protected int x, y, radius;
9
10     public RadialShapes(int x, int y, int radius)
11     {
12         this.x = x;
13         this.y = y;
14         this.radius = radius;
15     }
16     public static RadialShapes aRandomShape(int x, int y,
17         int radius)
18     {
19         int choice = (int)(random() * 3);
20         switch (choice)
21         {
22             case 0:
23                 return new Square(x, y, radius);
24             case 1:
25                 return new Circle(x, y, radius);
26             case 2:
27                 return new Triangle(x, y, radius);
28         }
29         return null;
30     }
31     abstract public double area();
32     public void compute()
33     {
34     }
35     abstract public void draw(Graphics graphics);
36     public void translate(int deltaX, int deltaY)
37     {
38         x += deltaX;
39         y += deltaY;
40         compute();
41     }
42  }
```

Notice first, on line 6, that unlike abstract enumerated types, classes with abstract methods must be designated as abstract by labeling them with the reserved word abstract. Next observe that line 8 contains the instance variable that we described as characteristic of all radial shapes, the center's coordinates and the radius. Notice that we have applied the modifier protected to these variables. To be useful, every abstract class must have at least one derived class—usually more. In this case, there will be three derived classes, and each of them will need to access these variables.

This class does have a constructor, whose signature begins on line 10. As we mentioned earlier, abstract classes, unlike interfaces, can have constructors, but such constructors can only be called by the constructors of the derived classes. Because the constructors of abstract classes cannot be called by classes outside the inheritance hierarchy, class methods, such as aRandomShape, whose signature is on lines 16 and 17, are often provided with abstract classes. Such class methods are often referred to as *factories*. A factory is a *design pattern*—a commonly occurring technique for solving a particular kind of problem. The factory design pattern is sometimes implemented as a separate class. For simplicity, we prefer simply using a class method. The method aRandomShape returns a shape randomly chosen with the center and radius values, which are supplied as parameters. Notice that such methods are one place that the switch statement is not eliminated.

This abstract class has two abstract methods. The method area is the first of the two. Every shape has an area, so it is appropriate to have such a method that can be applied to any shape, but each of the various shapes has a different formula for computing its area. The characteristics described in the previous sentence typify those that suggest the need for an abstract method.

We might call the next method, compute, a quasi-abstract method. It has a body, so it is technically not abstract, but it is an empty one. Notice that compute is called by translate on line 40. Looking at this class alone, there may seem to be no purpose to having such a method. Although the compiler will not force this method to be overridden as it does an abstract method, nonetheless, it should be apparent that this method can only serve some useful purpose if it is overridden in at least one derived class. We could have made compute an abstract method, but then it would have been necessary for each derived class that did not need it to provide a method with an empty body. Implementing in the way that we have, those derived classes that do not need this method can simply inherit the empty method. Another way we might describe methods of this kind is as abstract methods with default empty bodies.

The second abstract method is draw. Every shape can be drawn, but each of the various shapes requires a different algorithm to do the drawing, which is, again, exactly the characteristic of an operation that needs to be made abstract.

The final method in this class is the method translate, which is an ordinary method. Recall that, unlike interfaces, abstract classes can contain both abstract and ordinary methods. The translation process is largely independent of what kind of shape is being translated. Translation means moving the center point, which is exactly what is being done on lines 38 and 39. Once we see the code for the derived classes, we will see that the call to compute on line 40 will only do something for one of the three radial shapes—the triangle.

We are now ready to examine the three derived classes. We begin with Square, whose code is shown in Listing 14.5.

LISTING 14.5   The Class Defining the Radial Shape that is a Square (found on the CD-ROM at chapter14\Square.java.)

ON THE CD

```
 1  package chapter14;
 2
 3  import java.awt.*;
 4  import static java.lang.Math.*;
 5
 6  class Square extends RadialShapes
 7  {
 8      private int diameter;
 9
10      public Square(int x, int y, int radius)
11      {
12          super(x, y, radius);
13          diameter = radius * 2;
14      }
15      public double area()
16      {
17          return pow(diameter, 2);
18      }
19      public void draw(Graphics graphics)
20      {
21          graphics.drawRect(x - radius, y - radius,
22              diameter, diameter);
23      }
24  }
```

To avoid computing the diameter from the radius more than once, we made diameter the only instance variable of this class. It is computed on line 13 of the constructor. Before that computation, the constructor of the abstract base class RadialShapes is called on line 12, passing it each of the three parameters received by the constructor of the derived class. Providing a constructor in an abstract class enables us to eliminate the duplication of the initialization of the instance variables that are common to all derived classes and therefore defined in the base class.

The methods to compute the area and draw the square need no explanation, but one final observation is that this class does not override `compute`, and so inherits the empty method defined in the base class.

The second of the derived classes is `Circle`. The code for that class is contained in Listing 14.6.

LISTING 14.6 The Class Defining the Radial Shape that is a Circle (found on the CD-ROM at `chapter14\Circle.java`.)

```
 1  package chapter14;
 2
 3  import java.awt.*;
 4  import static java.lang.Math.*;
 5
 6  class Circle extends RadialShapes
 7  {
 8      private int diameter;
 9
10      public Circle(int x, int y, int radius)
11      {
12          super(x, y, radius);
13          diameter = radius * 2;
14      }
15      public double area()
16      {
17          return PI * pow(radius, 2);
18      }
19      public void draw(Graphics graphics)
20      {
21          graphics.drawOval(x - radius, y - radius,
22              diameter, diameter);
23      }
24  }
```

Aside from a different formula for area and the need to call a different method to do the drawing, this class is quite similar to the class `Square`, which should not be surprising.

Now let's examine the third of the three derived classes, `Triangle`. Its code is in Listing 14.7.

LISTING 14.7   The Class Defining the Radial Shape that is a Triangle (found on the CD-ROM at chapter14\Triangle.java.)

```
1  package chapter14;
2
3  import java.awt.*;
4  import static common.Geometry.*;
5  import static java.lang.Math.*;
6
7  class Triangle extends RadialShapes
8  {
9      private static final double ONE_THIRD_CIRCLE =
10         2 * PI / 3;
11     private int circumRadius, x1, y1, x2, y2, x3, y3;
12
13     public Triangle(int x, int y, int radius)
14     {
15         super(x, y, radius);
16         circumRadius = 2 * radius;
17         compute();
18     }
19     public double area()
20     {
21         double side = 3 * circumRadius / sqrt(3);
22         double height = side / 2 * sqrt(3);
23         return side * height / 2;
24     }
25     public void compute()
26     {
27         double theta = -(PI / 2);
28
29         x1 = computeX(x, circumRadius, theta);
30         y1 = computeY(y, circumRadius, theta);
31         theta += ONE_THIRD_CIRCLE;
32         x2 = computeX(x, circumRadius, theta);
33         y2 = computeY(y, circumRadius, theta);
34         theta += ONE_THIRD_CIRCLE;
35         x3 = computeX(x, circumRadius, theta);
36         y3 = computeY(y, circumRadius, theta);
37     }
38     public void draw(Graphics graphics)
39     {
40         graphics.drawLine(x1, y1, x2, y2);
41         graphics.drawLine(x2, y2, x3, y3);
```

```
42              graphics.drawLine(x3, y3, x1, y1);
43      }
44  }
```

We will now examine how this class is different from the previous two. We have been drawing triangles since Chapter 3, so the fact that we need the coordinates of the three vertices is no surprise. They are the instance variables declared on line 11 together with the radius of the circumscribed circle circumRadius. We know from geometry that the radius of a circle that circumscribes a triangle is twice that of the inscribed triangle. The assignment on line 16 performs that calculation. Perhaps the most significant difference between this class and the other two is that this class overrides the method compute defined in the base class. The method compute calculates the three coordinates using what should now be familiar calculations. It is called by the constructor on line 17 and must also be called to recompute the coordinates when triangles are translated. Refer back to line 40 of Listing 14.4 to see the latter call.

One other new aspect of this class is the computation of the area of an equilateral triangle. It requires three formulas. Equation 14.1 contains the formula for computing the length of a side s from the radius r.

$$s = \frac{3r}{\sqrt{3}} \tag{14.1}$$

The second formula, shown in Equation 14.2, computes the height of the triangle h from the side s.

$$h = \frac{\sqrt{3s}}{2} \tag{14.2}$$

Finally, Equation 14.3 gives the formula for computing the area A from the height h and the side s. This formula applies to all triangles.

$$A = s \, \frac{h}{2} \tag{14.2}$$

We are now ready to consider the class that defines the windows that contain these radial shapes. The approach we are using is similar to what we had done originally in Chapter 5. To avoid repeating the code to generate multiple windows contained in our predefined Application class, the class ShapesWindow is derived from Application. Listing 14.8 contains the code for the class ShapesWindow.

LISTING 14.8 The Class Defining a Window Containing a Radial Shape (found on the
ON THE CD CD-ROM at `chapter14\ShapesWindow.java`.)

```
1  package chapter14;
2
3  import java.awt.*;
4  import java.text.*;
5  import common.*;
6
7  public class ShapesWindow extends Application
8  {
9      private static DecimalFormat decimal =
10         new DecimalFormat("0.###");
11     private int AREA_X = 100, AREA_Y = 250;
12     private RadialShapes shape;
13
14     public ShapesWindow(RadialShapes shape)
15     {
16         this.shape = shape;
17     }
18     public void paintComponent(Graphics graphics)
19     {
20         double area = 0;
21
22         super.paintComponent(graphics);
23         shape.draw(graphics);
24         graphics.drawString("Area =" +
25             decimal.format(shape.area()), AREA_X, AREA_Y);
26     }
27     public void translate(int x, int y)
28     {
29         shape.translate(x, y);
30         repaint();
31     }
32 }
```

Most of what is in this class should be familiar, with one exception. We have
made use of a predefined class that formats floating point numbers—Decimal
Format—which we have never needed before because our examples have focused on
graphics with limited use of numeric output. We declare an object of this class called
decimal on line 9 and instantiate it on line 10, supplying the constructor the string
"0.###", which means that the value should be rounded so that there are at most
three digits to the right of the decimal. The zero to the left of the decimal signifies

that at least one digit should be displayed to the left of the decimal point. On line 25, we invoke the method format on the object decimal, passing to it the number that we wish to format. It returns a string containing the number formatted to our specifications.

To complete this program, we need a class that contains main, which is the class RandomShapes shown in Listing 14.9.

LISTING 14.9 The Class Containing the Method main for the Random Shapes Application (found on the CD-ROM at chapter14\RandomShapes.java.)

```
1  package chapter14;
2
3  import java.awt.*;
4  import javax.swing.*;
5  import common.*;
6
7  public class RandomShapes
8  {
9      public static void main(String[] args)
10     {
11         final int XY = 150, RADIUS = 50, DELTA = 30;
12         ShapesWindow[] shapes = new ShapesWindow[4];
13
14         for (int i = 0; i < shapes.length; i++)
15             shapes[i] = new ShapesWindow(
16                 RadialShapes.aRandomShape(XY, XY, RADIUS));
17         for (ShapesWindow window: shapes)
18             window.display();
19         InputOutput.putString("Ready to Translate");
20         for (ShapesWindow window: shapes)
21             window.translate(DELTA, DELTA);
22
23     }
24 }
```

The method main creates four windows, each containing a randomly generated shape. It then displays the windows and after the user acknowledges a prompt, it translates the shapes. Figure 14.1 shows the output of this program.

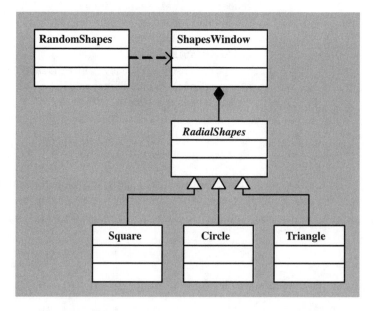

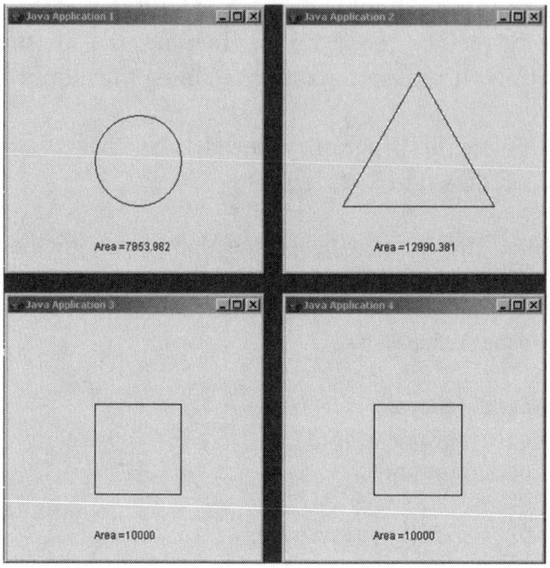

FIGURE 14.1 Output of the random shapes application.

Because this example is our first to contain an abstract class, we provide a UML diagram to illustrate how abstract classes are shown in these diagrams. Figure 14.2 contains the UML diagram for this program.

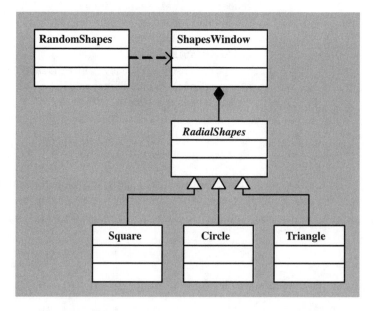

FIGURE 14.2 UML diagram for the random shapes application.

From the diagram, you should observe that when a class is abstract, its name is italicized.

The Matrix Iterator Implemented as an Abstract Class

Next we return to an example that we introduced in Chapter 13—the program that searched for a number in a matrix in either row major or column major order. The parts of the program that we are particularly interested in are the inner interface and classes that defined the iterators. Recall that we declared an interface, MatrixIterator and a base class, Major. From the base class, we derived two classes, RowMajor and ColumnMajor, that implemented the MatrixIterator interface. An abstract class in many ways combines the features of a base class with those of an interface. We have chosen this example to illustrate that point. Instead of needing both the interface MatrixIterator and the base class Major, we can create an abstract base class by moving the abstract method highlight, which was defined in MatrixIterator, into the base class Major. We have named the new abstract base class MatrixIterator. The code for that inner class and its two derived classes is shown in Listing 14.10.

LISTING 14.10 The Abstract Base Matrix Iterator Class and its Derived Classes (found on ON THE CD the CD-ROM at chapter14\Matrix.java.)

```
1   abstract public class MatrixIterator
2       implements Iterator<Integer>
3   {
4       protected int currentRow, currentCol, nextRow = 0,
5           nextCol = 0;
6           public MatrixIterator()
7       {
8           highlightedRow = rows;
9           highlightedCol = cols;
10      }
11      public boolean hasNext()
12      {
13          return nextRow < rows && nextCol < cols;
14      }
15      public void highlight()
16      {
17          highlightedRow = currentRow;
18          highlightedCol = currentCol;
19      }
20      abstract public Integer next();
21      public void remove()
22      {
```

```
23        }
24  }
25  public class RowMajor extends MatrixIterator
26  {
27        public Integer next()
28        {
29            currentRow = nextRow;
30            currentCol = nextCol;
31            if (++nextCol == cols)
32            {
33                nextRow++;
34                nextCol = 0;
35            }
36            return matrix[currentRow][currentCol];
37        }
38  }
39  public class ColumnMajor extends MatrixIterator
40  {
41        public Integer next()
42        {
43            currentRow = nextRow;
44            currentCol = nextCol;
45            if (++nextRow == rows)
46            {
47                nextCol++;
48                nextRow = 0;
49            }
50            return matrix[currentRow][currentCol];
51        }
52  }
```

ON THE CD   Because the outer class is unchanged from the original, as is the class Matrix-Main, we have not repeated the code here. You will, however, find the complete class at chapter14\Matrix.java, containing the modified inner classes, and another copy of MatrixMain at chapter14\MatrixMain.java on the CD-ROM that accompanies this book, so that you can run this new version of the program.

CHOOSING BETWEEN ABSTRACT ENUMERATED TYPES AND CLASSES

Now that we have seen examples of both abstract enumerated types and abstract classes, let's consider what criteria we should use to decide which of the two to implement. First, let's consider one important similarity. The *is a* predicate that we use as a test for the proper use of inheritance also fits the relationship between enumerated literals and their types. Using two of the examples that we discussed earlier, we can express the following relationships:

- Red *is a* rainbow color.
- A square *is a* radial shape.

In our previous discussion of object-oriented design, we have suggested that the English parts of speech can give us clues to identifying objects, their methods and inheritance relationships. We again rely on these distinctions to help us here. Notice that we say "a square" but not "a red." The reason for this difference is that red is a proper noun and square is a common noun. There is only one color red but many squares. This difference is exactly the distinction between enumerated types and classes. There can be only one instance of every enumeration literal. Recall that although enumerated types have constructors, those constructors cannot be called from outside the type definition. We can never use the reserved word new before an enumerated type constructor. By contrast, the very purpose of having a class is so that we can create multiple instances of that class.

The explanation that we have just given should be the primary consideration in deciding whether to use an enumerated type or a class, but in some situations the decision may not be so clear-cut. For example, it may be that in a particular program, we never need more than a single instance of certain objects, but used in a different program, we may have reason to create multiple instances. In such situations, we must exercise judgment in making our decisions—assessing the likelihood of whether this code will be reused.

There are other considerations. It may be that we only want single instances of some derived classes, but the base class from which they are derived is itself derived from some other class. In such a case, an enumerated type is not an option. In the main example at the end of the chapter, we will encounter this situation and reiterate this point.

One last reason we may opt to use classes rather than an enumerated type is if we wish to have some intermediate abstract classes. Enumerated types cannot be extended, so we cannot have any intermediate abstract enumerated types.

Singleton Objects

Although it is a slight digression from the main topic of this chapter, we wish to discuss a topic related to the distinction we have been making between when to use an abstract enumerated type and when to use a class. It is not uncommon in the design of programs to need single instance objects that are not part of some collection of objects.

Although nothing prevents us from creating an enumerated type with a single enumeration literal, we contend that doing so would be a misuse of the enumerated type.

So let's consider some other alternatives for implementing single instance objects. The first possibility, the one we chose in the previous example, is to simply create a class, but only to instantiate a single instance within the program. That approach is acceptable, especially when we anticipate that if this class were reused in some other program, there might be a need for multiple instances. In other situations, we might wish to emphasize that there should only ever be one instance of this class and prevent the creation of multiple instances. Creating single instance objects is another frequently occurring design problem for which a design pattern has been identified. This design pattern is called the singleton design pattern. So let's consider how we might implement this pattern in Java.

An Example Containing a Singleton

To illustrate the way a singleton object can be created, we have chosen a simple example. This program will read in a file of words, add them to a set of words, which excludes duplicates, and allow the user to make queries whether a particular word is in the set. This problem requires only a single word set object. The class WordSet, shown in Listing 14.11, defines a singleton word set object.

LISTING 14.11   The Class that Defines a Singleton Word Set Object (found on the CD-ROM at chapter14\WordSet.java.)

```
1   package chapter14;
2
3   import java.util.*;
4
5   class WordSet
6   {
7       private static ArrayList<String> words =
8           new ArrayList<String>();
9
10      private WordSet()
11      {
12      }
13      public static void add(String word)
14      {
15          if (!contains(word))
16              words.add(word);
17      }
18      public static boolean contains(String word)
19      {
```

```
20              for (String wordInSet: words)
21                  if (word.equals(wordInSet))
22                      return true;
23              return false;
24      }
25  }
```

What makes this class define a singleton object is the fact that it contains only class variables and class methods. Using a class to create a singleton object is yet another role that classes can play in Java. To ensure that no ordinary instances of this class can be created, we have defined a private default constructor on line 10, which prevents the creation of such objects.

We should mention that the singleton design pattern is more often implemented by providing a constructor that prevents more than one object from being created by the use of a class variable. That approach is just another technique for implementing a common design goal.

Next, let's consider the class that contains the main method that uses this class. Its code is shown in Listing 14.12.

LISTING 14.12 The Class that Defines a Singleton Word Set Object (found on the CD-ROM at chapter14\WordSetMain.java.)

```
1  package chapter14;
2
3  import common.*;
4
5  public class WordSetMain
6  {
7      public static void main(String[] args)
8      {
9          boolean found;
10         String wordToCheck;
11         String[] words;
12         InputFile file = new InputFile("input.txt");
13
14         for (String line: file)
15         {
16             words = line.split("[.,:;!\\s]+");
17             for (String word: words)
18                 WordSet.add(word);
19         }
20         while (true)
21         {
```

```
22              wordToCheck = InputOutput.getString(
23                  "Enter a word, empty string to quit: ");
24              if (wordToCheck.equals(""))
25                  break;
26              found = WordSet.contains(wordToCheck);
27              if (found)
28                  InputOutput.putString(wordToCheck +
29                      " is in the file");
30              else
31                  InputOutput.putString(wordToCheck +
32                      " is not in the file");
33          }
34      }
35  }
```

The main method of this program is similar to the main method of the word frequency example from Chapter 9, so you may want to review that one first, if there are any parts of this program that seem unfamiliar. You should notice one difference between the two programs, however. In this program, we never declare, and so never instantiate, any object of the class WordSet. The class is the object. In effect, the class name is the object name. So when the methods of the class are invoked—the method add on line 18, and contains on line 26—they are invoked on the class name. Those methods are class methods, so there should really be nothing surprising about the fact that they are invoked on the class name.

When we create a singleton object using the technique that we have just illustrated, we elevate the object name, which is really the class name, to package-wide scope. It is not unusual for programs to require a collection of singleton objects. Elevating the object names to package-wide scope makes it simpler for them to communicate with one another.

The technique that we just discussed will not work when the class that is being defined is derived from some other class. In such situations, we can not enforce preventing multiple instances from being created, but we can use another technique for effectively elevating singleton objects to package-wide scope. We will illustrate this technique for creating singleton objects with package-wide scope in our final example of this chapter.

MORE GUI FEATURES

Java provides a wide array of GUI components. These components allow the user to select among a collection of choices and possibly to initiate actions. It is not our intent to discuss the details of all such components, but we instead encourage you to consult the Sun Website at *http://java.sun.com/2se/1.5.0/docs/api/* and other references for a more complete list. Instead we focus on what we will use in our primary example at the end of this chapter. For that example, we use radio buttons, which allow a selection among choices and menus on frames that are used to initiate actions. We also describe how to create a GUI component that can be painted on that can be mixed with other predefined GUI components.

Radio Buttons

Radio buttons are one of a number of GUI components that allow the user to choose from a discrete selection of choices. The term radio button has its origin in the mechanical buttons on car radios that were used until electronic buttons were introduced some time in the 1980s. These buttons allowed the listener to select a radio station. What was most significant about their behavior was that only one could be pushed in at a time. When a different one was pushed in, the one currently pushed in would pop out. To capture the fact that only one can be pushed in and to enable these buttons to be used to select more than one feature—radio station and volume, for example—radio buttons must be grouped. In that way, only one can be selected in each group. Consequently we need to create button groups and radio buttons. The constructors that we will use for each are shown below.

```
ButtonGroup()
JRadioButton(String text, boolean selected)
```

With this constructor for creating radio buttons, we specify the label and whether this button is initially selected.

To make the association between buttons and groups, we add a button to a group using the method add of the ButtonGroup class, whose signature is shown below.

```
void add(AbstractButton b)
```

The last thing we need to know about radio buttons is how to respond to their events. Normally, they are not used to initiate an action but to set some value to the selected choice. To register an object as a listener, the method addItemListener must be invoked on the radio button. Its signature is shown below.

```
void addItemListener(ItemListener l)
```

The interface that must be implemented to listen for radio button events is ItemListener, which requires that we provide the method ItemStateChanged, whose signature is shown below.

```
void itemStateChanged(ItemEvent e)
```

Frame Menus

Anyone who has used a program with a GUI is familiar with the menus that are usually along the top of the window. Menu selections frequently are used to initiate actions in much the same way buttons are used, but they can also be used simply for selecting among choices.

To create menus, we need three kinds of objects: menu items, menus, and menu bars. The constructors for each of the three are shown below.

```
JMenuItem(String text)
JMenu(String s)
JMenuBar()
```

The text in a menu item is what appears when the menu is opened up. The text in a menu is the text that appears at the top of the list of items.

The menu items must be added to a menu. The menus must be added to a menu bar. The add method we have used repeatedly is used to accomplish these additions. Finally the menu bar must be associated with the frame. The setJMenuBar method whose signature is shown below is used for that purpose. It is invoked on the frame to which the menu is to be attached.

```
void setJMenuBar(JMenuBar menubar)
```

Event handling on menu items is done using the same method that is used for buttons. The addActionListener method is used to register a listener and action-Performed is executed when an event occurs.

Mixing Painted Components with Other GUI Components

Although we have been drawing graphics since Chapter 1, we have not mixed drawn graphic objects with predefined GUI components in the same user interface. To create objects that can be mixed with other components, we need to define a class that extends JPanel and overrides the method paintComponent. Objects of such a class can then be added to another panel together with other GUI components. To ensure that the objects are of the proper size, we must override two methods of JPanel whose signatures are shown below.

```
void setMinimumSize(Dimension minimumSize)
void setPreferredSize(Dimension preferredSize)
```

We supply both methods a `Dimension` object, which we create with the constructor, whose signature is shown below.

```
Dimension(int width, int height)
```

Failing to provide these methods will cause the panel to be reduced to nothing by the layout manager that lays out the panel to which they were added.

CARD GAME OF WAR APPLICATION

We are now ready to present our final example for this chapter. This program will be one of the largest ones that we have encountered so far and will incorporate all of the topics that we introduced in this chapter—abstract enumerated types and classes, singleton objects, and some GUI components that we have not used before

We begin by explaining the requirements for this program. The program should implement the simple card game of war, in which the dealer and player each draw a card from the deck. The one with the highest card wins. The rank is considered when comparing cards, but the suit is unimportant, so two cards with the same rank produce a tie. The dealer wins on ties. The opponent is to be given $1000 at the beginning of the game and should be allowed to select bets in one of three amounts: $50, $100, or $150. Upon command, a card should be dealt to both the dealer and the opponent. When the cards are dealt, they should appear face-down. Upon command they should be turned face-up and the winner announced. The opponent's winnings should updated based on who won and the amount of the bet. The deck should be reshuffled once the last card has been drawn and also at the opponent's request. Upon the appropriate request, the game should be restarted or terminated.

Because this problem is more involved than most of the previous examples, it provides a good opportunity to apply some the techniques of object-oriented design that we have discussed earlier. In that discussion, we mentioned that the first step is identifying the necessary classes or possibly enumerated types, which likely will have appeared as nouns in the requirements. Some obvious choices are the following: card, deck, suits, rank, dealer, opponent, player, game, and bet. Next, let's identify some of the relationships between them.

- A deck *has* 52 cards.
- A card *has a* rank.
- A card *has a* suit.
- A dealer *is a* player.
- An opponent *is a* player.
- A game *has* two players.

We have managed to identify at least one relationship for every noun we selected except bet. You should never expect to uncover the final design on the first try, but let's work with what we have identified so far.

Clearly a card object should consist of its rank and suit. Let's explore rank and suit a bit further, because it is advisable to begin with one of the smallest identified objects. We need to determine whether there are any more elementary nouns than rank or suit—especially those that are related to them. The specification assumes the software designer is familiar with playing cards, so there are some nouns in the problem domain that we must uncover through our own knowledge. Those who are familiar with playing cards know that there are clubs, aces, and so on. Let's see what relationships we can uncover pursuing that direction. Below is a small subset of the relationships we should know if we have ever played cards.

- Clubs *is a* suit.
- Ace *is a* rank.

Based upon what we have learned from the examples earlier in this chapter, these relationships should suggest that we likely need either abstract classes or enumerated types. If you look at how we stated these relationships and recall the guidance provided by distinguishing between common and proper nouns, you should conclude that enumerated types are needed. Perhaps you are thinking that we have made the wrong choice. There are four aces in a deck of cards, so ace is not a proper noun, but a common one. To that, we respond that words in English are often used very loosely. More carefully stated, a deck contains four cards with the rank of ace, but there is only one rank of ace. Whether you have been persuaded by this careful reframing of the statement or not, at least we have highlighted that selecting the right choice in these cases can sometimes be subtle. Furthermore, let's make clear that there is never a perfect or correct design. What design is best is often subjective. Experienced designers can disagree.

So, let's continue with the choice we have selected and assume that rank should become an enumerated type. Our knowledge of playing cards tells us what the literals should be, so let's consider next what operations would be needed for this type. The requirements tell us that we need to compare cards based on their rank, so we need the ability to compare ranks. One capability that we must infer is the need to be able to draw the cards when they are face-up. Furthermore we know that how we draw them depends upon their rank. Taking these considerations into account, our enumerated type definition for rank appears in Listing 14.13.

LISTING 14.13 The Enumerated Type that Defines the Rank of a Playing Card (found on the CD-ROM at chapter14\Rank.java.)

```
1  package chapter14;
2
3  enum Rank implements Comparable<Rank>
4  {
5      TWO("2"),
6      THREE("3"),
7      FOUR("4"),
8      FIVE("5"),
9      SIX("6"),
10     SEVEN("7"),
11     EIGHT("8"),
12     NINE("9"),
13     TEN("10"),
14     JACK("J"),
15     QUEEN("Q"),
16     KING("K"),
17     ACE("A");
18
19     private String symbol;
20
21     private Rank(String symbol)
22     {
23         this.symbol = symbol;
24     }
25     public static Rank aRank(int ordinal)
26     {
27         return Rank.values()[ordinal];
28     }
29     public String getSymbol()
30     {
31         return symbol;
32     }
33  }
```

On line 3, there are two features of this type that you should notice. The first is that although Rank is an enumerated type, it is not an abstract enumerated type. Regardless of whether an enumerated type is abstract or not, the enumeration literals still have an *is a* relationship with the type to which they belong. Furthermore, we only make an enumerated type abstract if necessary. In this case, it is not. The second feature to notice is that the type Rank implements the interface Comparable<Rank>. Normally, you would expect to find the method compareTo, but with enumerated types this method is inherited from the predefined class Enum, the class from which enumerated types are implicitly derived. Consequently all enumerated types have a compareTo method. We added the implements clause for emphasis. For proper comparisons, it is essential that we order the literals from smallest to largest, which we have done.

Next, observe that we have included one string variable symbol, declared on line 19, as part of this type definition. It is initialized by the constructor and can be retrieved from outside the type definition by the getSymbol method. We have elected to not get too fancy in how we draw the face of the cards. The requirements are not specific, so we opted to simply draw a number or letter to represent the rank. Our expectation is that the card class will actually draw the card and call upon this method to facilitate that drawing.

On line 25, the class method aRank is a factory method that creates a Rank literal object given its ordinal value. We saw factory methods used with abstract classes earlier in this chapter. They are also useful with enumerated types—whether or not they are abstract. Notice that with an enumerated type we have the luxury of avoiding a switch statement. We can simply extract the literal from the array returned by the method values. We have repeatedly opted to eliminate switch statements whenever possible. In this case, clearly the advantage of that choice is that if we were to add additional literals, no change would be needed to this method. Had we used a switch statement, we would have had to add a case to it.

Next, we present the enumerated type Suits. Our choice of an enumerated type rather than an abstract class is for the same reason we explained for Rank. Like the Rank class, we need to modify the ability to draw some symbol to represent each suit as shown in Listing 14.14.

LISTING 14.14 The Enumerated Type that Defines the Suits of a Playing Card (found on the CD-ROM at chapter14\Suits.java.)

```
1   package chapter14;
2
3   import java.awt.*;
4
5   enum Suits
6   {
7       CLUB
8       {
9           void drawSymbol(Graphics graphics)
10          {
11              int x1[] = {38, 33, 43};
12              int y1[] = {38, 45, 45};
13
```

```
14                   graphics.setColor(Color.BLACK);
15                   graphics.fillOval(33, 25, 9, 9);
16                   graphics.fillOval(30, 31, 9, 9);
17                   graphics.fillOval(36, 31, 9, 9);
18                   graphics.fillPolygon(x1, y1, 3);
19              }
20          },
21          DIAMOND
22          {
23              void drawSymbol(Graphics graphics)
24              {
25                  int x1[] = {38, 31, 38, 45};
26                  int y1[] = {23, 33, 43, 33};
27
28                  graphics.setColor(Color.RED);
29                  graphics.fillPolygon(x1, y1, 4);
30              }
31          },
32          HEART
33          {
34              void drawSymbol(Graphics graphics)
35              {
36                  int x1[] = {31, 38, 45};
37                  int y1[] = {33, 43, 33};
38
39                  graphics.setColor(Color.RED);
40                  graphics.fillOval(30, 25, 9, 9);
41                  graphics.fillOval(36, 25, 9, 9);
42                  graphics.fillPolygon(x1, y1, 3);
43              }
44          },
45          SPADE
46          {
47              void drawSymbol(Graphics graphics)
48              {
49                  int x1[] = {38, 31, 45};
50                  int y1[] = {23, 33, 33};
51                  int x2[] = {38, 31, 43};
52                  int y2[] = {38, 45, 45};
53
54                  graphics.setColor(Color.BLACK);
55                  graphics.fillOval(30, 31, 9, 9);
56                  graphics.fillOval(36, 31, 9, 9);
57                  graphics.fillPolygon(x1, y1, 3);
```

```
58                  graphics.fillPolygon(x2, y2, 3);
59          }
60      };
61
62      public static Suits aSuit(int ordinal)
63      {
64          return Suits.values()[ordinal];
65      }
66      abstract void drawSymbol(Graphics graphics);
67  }
```

Unlike the enumerated type Rank, Suits is an abstract enumerated type, because rather than just returning a string that represents the symbol for each suit, we have elected to provide a method that draws the symbol. Clearly the symbol for each suit requires different code for drawing it, hence the need for an abstract method drawSymbol. We have chosen this approach primarily to again illustrate the need for an abstract method. Using icons, already drawn symbols, would be another, perhaps simpler approach. Until now, we have almost always named every numeric constant—a practice that we dispense with for this class because there are so many numeric values associated with drawing each symbol, which is perhaps also a clue that another technique might be suitable here.

One final comment about this type definition is that like Rank, Suits also contains a factory method aSuit, whose signature appears on line 62. It works in much the same way that aRank does. We will see how it is used when we examine the code for the Card class.

Before we present the Card class, there is another enumerated type that we wish to examine. In our initial list of nouns, there were two nouns in the requirements that we overlooked, perhaps because they are less obvious—being two-word nouns. They are face-up and face-down. They represent the orientation of each card and so together with its suit and rank comprise the three values that represent the state of a card. Now that we have identified them, we need to consider the relationship between card orientation and face-down. The relationship is as follows:

■ Face-up *is a* card orientation.

For reasons much the same as with Suits and Rank, an enumerated type rather than an abstract class is the proper choice. The code for this enumerated type is shown in Listing 14.15.

LISTING 14.15 The Enumerated Type that Defines the Orientation of a Playing Card (found on the CD-ROM at chapter14\CardOrientation.java.)

ON THE CD

```
1  package chapter14;
```

```
2
3   import java.awt.*;
4
5   enum CardOrientation
6   {
7       FACE_UP
8       {
9           void draw(Graphics graphics, Suits suit,
10              Rank rank)
11          {
12              drawBorder(graphics);
13              suit.drawSymbol(graphics);
14              graphics.setFont(rankFont);
15              graphics.drawString("" + rank.getSymbol(), 12, 43);
16          }
17      },
18      FACE_DOWN
19      {
20          void draw(Graphics graphics, Suits suit,
21              Rank rank)
22          {
23              graphics.setColor(GameOfWar.lightYellow);
24              graphics.fillRect(0, 0, Card.WIDTH, Card.HEIGHT);
25              graphics.setColor(GameOfWar.darkGreen);
26              for (int y = 10; y < Card.HEIGHT; y += 10)
27                  graphics.drawLine(0, y, Card.WIDTH, y);
28              for (int x = 10; x < Card.WIDTH; x += 10)
29                  graphics.drawLine(x, 0, x, Card.HEIGHT);
30              drawBorder(graphics);
31              graphics.setFont(backFont);
32              graphics.drawString("D", 20, 22);
33              graphics.drawString("J", 20, 44);
34              graphics.drawString("J", 20, 66);
35          }
36      };
37
38      private static final Font
39          rankFont = new Font("Serif", Font.BOLD, 24),
40          backFont = new Font("Serif", Font.ITALIC, 24);
41
42      abstract void draw(Graphics graphics, Suits suit,
43          Rank rank);
44      private static void drawBorder(Graphics graphics)
45      {
```

```
46          graphics.setColor(Color.BLACK);
47          graphics.drawRect(0, 0, Card.WIDTH - 1, Card.HEIGHT - 1);
48          graphics.drawRect(1, 1, Card.WIDTH - 3, Card.HEIGHT - 3);
49      }
50  }
```

This enumerated type must be abstract because the key difference between whether a card is face-up or face-down is whether the face or the back of the card is drawn. So the method `draw` is abstract. The `draw` method for the literal `faceUp` calls upon methods in both the `Suits` type and the `Rank` type. It calls the method `drawSymbol` of `Suits` on line 13 to draw the symbol that corresponds to the suit and the method `getSymbol` of `Rank` on line 15 to get the string that represents the rank of the card. We have factored out code common to the drawing of the card, regardless of its orientation, into a private method, `drawBorder`, that is called on lines 12 and 30.

The `draw` method for the literal `faceDown` simply draws a pattern on the card that is independent of the card's suit or rank. Figure 14.3 shows an example of a card drawn both face-down and face-up.

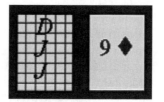

FIGURE 14.3 A playing card drawn face-down (left) and face-up (right).

We are now ready to consider the class that defines the actual card objects themselves. This example is our first in which we have mixed components that we draw on with other GUI components. We discussed earlier that when we wish to create such painted objects we must define a class that extends `JPanel` and paint onto the panel. The code for this class is shown in Listing 14.16.

LISTING 14.16 The Class that Defines a Playing Card (found on the CD-ROM at
ON THE CD chapter14\Card.java.)

```
1   package chapter14;
2
3   import java.awt.*;
4   import javax.swing.*;
5
```

```
 6   class Card extends JPanel implements Comparable<Card>
 7   {
 8       public static final int WIDTH = 60, HEIGHT = 80;
 9       private Rank rank;
10       private Suits suit;
11       private CardOrientation orientation;
12
13       public Card(int cardOrdinal)
14       {
15           setCard(cardOrdinal);
16       }
17       public int compareTo(Card otherCard)
18       {
19           return rank.compareTo(otherCard.rank);
20       }
21       public Dimension getMinimumSize()
22       {
23           return getPreferredSize();
24       }
25       public Dimension getPreferredSize()
26       {
27           return new Dimension(WIDTH, HEIGHT);
28       }
29       public void paintComponent(Graphics graphics)
30       {
31           super.paintComponent(graphics);
32           orientation.draw(graphics, suit, rank);
33       }
34       public void setCard(int cardOrdinal)
35       {
36           int suitOrdinal = cardOrdinal / Rank.values().length;
37           int rankOrdinal = cardOrdinal % Rank.values().length;
38
39           this.rank = Rank.aRank(rankOrdinal);
40           this.suit = Suits.aSuit(suitOrdinal);;
41           orientation = CardOrientation.FACE_DOWN;
42       }
43       public void turnFaceUp()
44       {
45           orientation = CardOrientation.FACE_UP;
46           repaint();
47       }
48   }
```

We begin our explanation with two comments about the class declaration on line 6. First, note that this class extends `JPane`, as we indicated was necessary to be able to paint on this object. The other feature that you should notice is that this class implements `Comparable<Card>`. Remember that we need to be able to compare cards according to their rank to determine which player has won, each time the cards are turned face-up. Consequently, we should expect this class to contain the method `compareTo`.

Next, let's consider the instance variables of this class. A card has a suit, a rank, and an orientation. So this class has instance variables for each of those attributes, which are declared on lines 9–11. Their types correspond to each of the three enumerated types that we have already discussed.

This class has one constructor, whose signature is on line 13. It accepts an ordinal value from 0 to 51. Each of those values corresponds to one suit-rank combination. The determination of the suit and rank is made by the `setCard` method that we discuss shortly. We allow the rank and suit of a card to change after it has been created, which suggests that objects of this class really do not represent the individual cards in a deck of cards, but a current card on the board.

As noted earlier, we must provide the method `compareTo`. In the requirements, we stated that card comparison would be based on rank only. We compare the rank of two cards—the card object on which the method was invoked and the other card that was passed as a parameter. That comparison is achieved by a call to the `compareTo` method of the enumerated type `Rank` on line 19. If we were implementing a different card game, the suit might also enter the comparison.

Recall that when we use a panel for painting, we must provide two methods, `getMinimumSize` and `getPreferredSize`, which are accessed by the layout manager. These methods are defined on lines 21–28. In this case, they return the same size, so the former simply calls the latter.

When the purpose of a panel is to serve as a container for GUI components, we simply inherit the method `paintComponent` from `JPanel`. In this case, the panel is serving as a canvas for our painting, so it is essential that we override `paintComponent`. Drawing the card is accomplished by the method `draw` of `CardOrientation`, which we have already seen. The call to that method appears on line 32.

Next, let's consider the method `setCard` that is called by the constructor but is also called from outside the class. As we mentioned when we discussed the constructor, it is supplied an ordinal value from 0–51. On lines 36 and 37, it then determines the ordinal value for both the suit and rank, using integer division and remainder, respectively. We have used a similar technique frequently when computing a row and column from a linear numbering of a two-dimensional object. Because the class method `values` returns an array of the literals of an enumerated type, we can use the length of that array to determine the number of literals in any enumerated type. Once the ordinal values have been computed, it obtains the enumerated literal values of both the suit and rank by calling the factory methods on lines 39 and 40. Whenever a card is created or a new suit and rank are set, the orientation of the card is always initialized to be face-down.

There is one final method that is needed, based on our requirements. Those requirements state that after cards are dealt, upon command, they should be turned face-up. The method turnFaceUp fulfills that need. After changing the card orientation instance variable, it causes the panel to be repainted on line 46.

A closely related class, Deck, is the one we consider next. In our initial list of class relationships, we suggested that a compositional relationship exists between cards and decks. A deck has 52 cards. But recall that we said that the class Card, as we developed it, really represents the current card on the board for one of the players, not an actual card whose identity never changes. This deviation illustrates that as we further develop any design, our initial ideas may need to be modified. The proper characterization of the relationships now is that a deck consists of card ordinals and a card can be set to such an ordinal. Because these ordinals are just integers, they are not objects of any class. Having clarified these relationships, let's examine the code for the class Deck, which is contained in Listing 14.17.

LISTING 14.17   The Class for a Deck of Cards (found on the CD-ROM at *ON THE CD* chapter14\Deck.java.)

```
 1  package chapter14;
 2
 3  import chapter11.*;
 4
 5  class Deck
 6  {
 7      private static final int CARDS_IN_DECK = 52;
 8      private int cards[];
 9      private int nextCard;
10
11      public Deck()
12      {
13          shuffle();
14      }
15      public boolean isEmpty()
16      {
17          return nextCard == CARDS_IN_DECK;
18      }
19      public int deal()
20      {
21          return cards[nextCard++];
22      }
```

```
23      public void shuffle()
24      {
25          cards = Permutation.randomize(CARDS_IN_DECK);
26          nextCard = 0;
27      }
28  }
```

The instance variables include the integer array `cards`, which contains the array of card ordinals, and `nextCard`, which is the subscript of the next card to be drawn from the deck.

This class contains a default constructor, which shuffles the deck—one of the primary operations that we perform on a deck of cards. Once we recognize that shuffling the ordinal values of 52 cards involves creating a random permutation of the numbers from 0–51, the possibility of reusing the `Permutation` class that we created in Chapter 11 should seem like a possibility—one that would avoid rewriting some code. So we have elected to reuse that class, which should be apparent looking at line 25 of the method `shuffle`, which relies upon the `randomize` method of the `Permutation` class to perform the shuffling. The deck is shuffled initially and upon any call to the method `shuffle`. This class also provides a mechanism for checking whether the deck is empty, using the `isEmpty` method, which should be called before calling the method `deal`, which deals a card from the top of the deck. The method `deal` returns the card ordinal value of the card at the top.

We are now ready to move to another group of classes that this card game requires. We identified these classes in our initial list. They are the dealer and opponent, which are both players. We again have a situation where we must choose between an enumerated type and a hierarchy of classes. Let's apply the chief factor that we have been using to make this determination, whether or not the objects are singletons. In this program, there is only one opponent and one dealer, suggesting an enumerated type. There is another factor that we must consider in this case. We intend to implement these objects as panels—derived from `JPanel`. That design choice immediately excludes the possibility of using an enumerated type, because an enumerated type cannot be derived from a class. So, let's now examine the class `Player` shown in Listing 14.18.

LISTING 14.18   The Class that Defines Card Game Players (found on the CD-ROM at
ON THE CD   chapter14\Players.java.)

```
1 package chapter14;
2
3 import java.awt.*;
4 import javax.swing.*;
5 import static chapter14.GameOfWar.*;
```

```
6
7   abstract class Players extends JPanel
8       implements Comparable<Players>
9   {
10      public static final Font cardFont =
11          new Font("Helvetica", Font.BOLD, 16);
12      private static final int GAP = 10;
13      private JPanel innerPanel = new JPanel();
14      private Label label;
15      private Card card;
16      private String name;
17
18      public Players(String name, Deck deck)
19      {
20          this.name = name;
21          card = new Card(deck.deal());
22          setLayout(new BorderLayout(GAP, GAP));
23          setBackground(darkGreen);
24          label = new Label(name, Label.CENTER);
25          label.setBackground(Color.white);
26          label.setFont(cardFont);
27          add(label, BorderLayout.NORTH);
28          innerPanel.setLayout(new FlowLayout(FlowLayout.CENTER));
29          innerPanel.setBackground(darkGreen);
30          innerPanel.add(card);
31          add(innerPanel, BorderLayout.SOUTH);
32      }
33      public int compareTo(Players otherPlayer)
34      {
35          return card.compareTo(otherPlayer.card);
36      }
37      public void deal(Deck deck)
38      {
39          if (deck.isEmpty())
40              deck.shuffle();
41          card.setCard(deck.deal());
42          repaint();
43      }
44      abstract public int pay(int winnings, int bet);
45      public String toString()
46      {
47          return name;
48      }
49      public void turnFaceUp()
```

```
50        {
51              card.turnFaceUp();
52        }
53  }
```

Looking at the class declaration on lines 7 and 8, you should notice what we mentioned earlier—the fact that this class extends JPanel—but what you should also notice is that it implements Comparable<Player>. Let's examine what frequently occurs with the kind of compositional relationships that exist in this program. In our design, a player has a card and a card has a rank. All three classes, Players, Card, and Rank, have a method, compareTo. The compareTo of Players calls the compareTo of Card and as we have seen, the compareTo of Card calls the compareTo of Rank. The methods deal and turnFaceUp behave in a similar way. They just call the corresponding methods in Card. One other observation to make about the class declaration is that the class Players is abstract. The abstract method is pay, which updates the winnings.

The panel that comprises objects of this class contains a label, which contains the player's name and current card. The card object is placed in an inner panel so that the card can be horizontally centered.

We now need two derived classes, one for the dealer and the other for the opponent. Both must override the method pay. The first of these two derived classes, Dealer, is shown in Listing 14.19.

LISTING 14.19   The Class for the Card Game Player Who is the Dealer (found on the CD-ROM at chapter14\Dealer.java.)

```
1  package chapter14;
2
3  class Dealer extends Players
4  {
5      public Dealer(Deck deck)
6      {
7          super ("Dealer", deck);
8      }
9      public int pay(int winnings, int bet)
10     {
11         return winnings - bet;
12     }
13  }
```

This class contains a constructor, which initializes the player's name when calling the constructor of the base class and passes through the deck, which the players need access to. The method pay decreases the overall winnings, which is what happens when the dealer wins.

Listing 14.20 contains the code for the other derived class—Opponent.

LISTING 14.20 The Class for the Card Game Player Who is the Opponent (found on the CD-ROM at chapter14\Opponent.java.)

```
1  package chapter14;
2
3  class Opponent extends Players
4  {
5      public Opponent(Deck deck)
6      {
7          super ("Opponent", deck);
8      }
9      public int pay(int winnings, int bet)
10     {
11         return winnings + bet;
12     }
13 }
```

In this case, the method pay increases the winnings by the amount of the bet.

The only remaining potential class in our original list is game. There will be more classes in our final design; however, the next collection of classes arises, not from examining the requirements, but from laying out how the interface for this program should look. Figure 14.4 shows the complete GUI.

Clearly we will need a class to define the window. If we were so inclined, we could build the entire GUI in that class, but if we did so that class would be very large. Consequently we have elected to subdivide it into three classes—a class for the window, another for the panel containing the players, and one more for the panel containing the winners.

We begin with the panel containing the cards for both players. We named the class that contains this panel BoardPanel. Its code is contained in Listing 14.21.

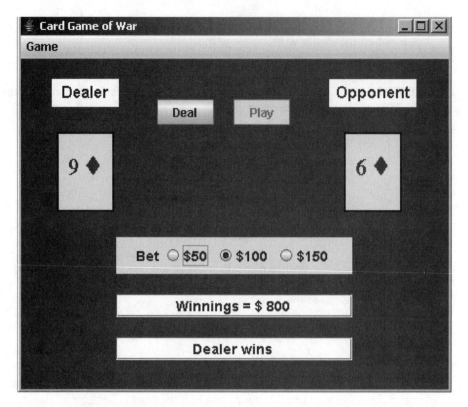

FIGURE 14.4 GUI for the card game of war.

LISTING 14.21 The Class Defining the Panel Containing the Player's Cards (found on the CD-ROM at chapter14\BoardPanel.java.)

```
1  package chapter14;
2
3  import java.awt.*;
4  import java.awt.event.*;
5  import javax.swing.*;
6  import static chapter14.GameOfWar.*;
7
8  class BoardPanel extends JPanel implements ActionListener
9  {
10     private static final int GAP = 20;
11     private Deck deck = new Deck();
12     private JPanel controls = new JPanel();
13     private Players dealer = new Dealer(deck),
14         opponent = new Opponent(deck);
```

```
15      private JButton deal = new JButton("Deal"),
16          play = new JButton("Play");
17
18      public BoardPanel()
19      {
20          setBackground(GameOfWar.darkGreen);
21          setLayout(new BorderLayout(GAP, GAP));
22          controls.setLayout(new FlowLayout(FlowLayout.CENTER, GAP,
23          GAP));
24          controls.setBackground(GameOfWar.darkGreen);
25          controls.add(deal);
26          controls.add(play);
27          add(dealer, BorderLayout.WEST);
28          add(controls, BorderLayout.CENTER);
29          add(opponent, BorderLayout.EAST);
30          deal.addActionListener(this);
31          play.addActionListener(this);
32          deal.setEnabled(false);
33      }
34      public void actionPerformed(ActionEvent event)
35      {
36          Object object = event.getSource();
37
38          if (object == deal)
39          {
40              dealer.deal(deck);
41              opponent.deal(deck);
42              deal.setEnabled(false);
43              play.setEnabled(true);
44              winningsPanel.clearMessage();
45              repaint();
46          }
47          else if (object == play)
48          {
49              dealer.turnFaceUp();
50              opponent.turnFaceUp();
51              if (dealer.compareTo(opponent) >= 0)
52                  winningsPanel.updateWinnings(dealer);
53              else
54                  winningsPanel.updateWinnings(opponent);
55              deal.setEnabled(true);
56              play.setEnabled(false);
57          }
58      }
```

```
59      public void shuffle()
60      {
61          deck.shuffle();
62          dealer.deal(deck);
63          opponent.deal(deck);
64          deal.setEnabled(false);
65          play.setEnabled(true);
66      }
67  }
```

This class builds the GUI in the constructor. In addition to containing the cards for both players, it also contains two buttons—one to deal each player a new card and a second one to turn those cards face-up. To assist in the layout, the two buttons are placed in an inner panel named controls. As with any GUI, we must decide who will handle which events. By subdividing the GUI into three classes, we distribute the event handling also. In this case, the panel object will handle the button click events. We registered the object as the listener for both buttons on lines 30 and 31. We wish these two buttons to be alternatively active, so initially the button that causes new cards to be dealt is set to be inactive. In addition to containing the cards and buttons, this class also contains the deck, which is declared and instantiated on line 11. It is then passed to both player objects when they are instantiated on lines 13 and 14.

As is always the case, the button click events are handled by the method actionPerformed. When the button deal is clicked, lines 40–45 are executed. A new card is dealt to each player, the active status of the buttons is reversed, and the message text field is cleared. Both this panel and the winnings panel are singleton objects. Being derived from JPanel, they cannot be made singletons by making all variables class variables and all methods class methods. Instead these objects are declared in the class GameOfWar, which is the class containing main—the class we will examine last. Because they are public class variables, and because we have imported the static members of GameOfWar on line 6, we can refer to the object winningsPanel, which we do on line 44, as though it were an object with package-wide scope.

When the button play is clicked, lines 49–56 are executed. Both cards are turned face-up. The winner is determined and the winnings panel is updated accordingly. Finally, the active status of the buttons is reversed.

This class has one other public method—shuffle, whose signature appears on line 59. It is called when the shuffle option is selected on the menu that belongs to the window. When we examine the code for the window, we will see the call to this method. This method shuffles the deck, deals a card to each player, and initializes the active settings of both buttons.

The other panel contained in the game window is the winnings panel. The code for the class that creates that panel is in Listing 14.22.

LISTING 14.22 The Class Defining the Panel Containing the Winnings Total and the
ON THE CD Current Bet (found on the CD-ROM at chapter14\WinningsPanel.java.)

```
 1  package chapter14;
 2
 3  import java.awt.*;
 4  import java.awt.event.*;
 5  import javax.swing.*;
 6  import static chapter14.GameOfWar.*;
 7
 8  class WinningsPanel extends JPanel implements ItemListener
 9  {
10      private static final int GAP = 20, TEXT_WIDTH = 20;
11      private static final Font winningsFont =
12          new Font("Sans Serif", Font.BOLD, 14);
13      private JTextField winnings = new JTextField(TEXT_WIDTH),
14          message = new JTextField(TEXT_WIDTH);
15      private JPanel betPanel = new JPanel();
16      private JRadioButton bet50 = new JRadioButton("$50", false),
17          bet100 = new JRadioButton("$100", true),
18          bet150 = new JRadioButton("$150", false);
19      private ButtonGroup betGroup = new ButtonGroup();
20      private int bet = 100, winningsAmount = 1000;
21
22      public WinningsPanel()
23      {
24          JLabel betLabel = new JLabel("Bet");
25
26          setBackground(darkGreen);
27          setLayout(new BorderLayout(GAP, GAP));
28          winnings.setFont(winningsFont);
29          winnings.setHorizontalAlignment(JTextField.CENTER);
30          winnings.setText("Winnings = $ " + winningsAmount);
31          message.setFont(winningsFont);
32          message.setHorizontalAlignment(JTextField.CENTER);
33          betGroup.add(bet50);
34          betGroup.add(bet100);
35          betGroup.add(bet150);
36          betLabel.setFont(winningsFont);
37          bet50.setFont(winningsFont);
38          bet100.setFont(winningsFont);
39          bet150.setFont(winningsFont);
40          bet50.addItemListener(this);
41          bet100.addItemListener(this);
```

```
42          bet150.addItemListener(this);
43          betPanel.add(betLabel);
44          betPanel.add(bet50);
45          betPanel.add(bet100);
46          betPanel.add(bet150);
47          add(betPanel, BorderLayout.NORTH);
48          add(winnings, BorderLayout.CENTER);
49          add(message, BorderLayout.SOUTH);
50      }
51      public void clearMessage()
52      {
53          message.setText("");
54      }
55      public void init()
56      {
57          bet = 100;
58          bet100.setSelected(true);
59          winningsAmount = 1000;
60          winnings.setText("Winnings = $ " + winningsAmount);
61          message.setText("");
62      }
63       public void itemStateChanged(ItemEvent event)
64      {
65          Object object = event.getSource();
66
67          if (object == bet50)
68              bet = 50;
69          else if (object == bet100)
70              bet = 100;
71          else if (object == bet150)
72              bet = 150;
73      }
74      public void updateWinnings(Players winner)
75      {
76          winningsAmount = winner.pay(winningsAmount, bet);
77          winnings.setText("Winnings = $ " + winningsAmount);
78          message.setText(winner.toString() + " wins");
79      }
80  }
81  }
```

This panel consists of two text fields, one used to display the current winnings and another to display who won each time the cards are played. Between those two text fields is an inner panel containing the label "Bet" followed by three radio buttons, which allow the current bet to be selected among three choices: $50, $100, or $150. The GUI is built in the constructor. Recall from our earlier discussion in this chapter that radio buttons must be added to a group, because only one button in any group can be selected at a time. On lines 33–35, the three radio buttons are added to the group betGroup. To handle the events for radio buttons, a class must implement the ItemHandler interface, which this class does on line 8. Objects of this class are registered as the listeners for each of the radio buttons on lines 40–42.

The method clearMessage clears the text field message. We saw that this method is called in the actionPerformed method of the BoardPanel class when the deal button is clicked. The method init is called when the menu item "New Game" is selected. We will see this call when we examine the GameFrame class next.

The next method in this class is itemStateChanged. This method must be provided when a class implements the itemListener interface. This method is called when any of the radio buttons is selected. It updates the instance variable bet to reflect the bet selected by the radio button.

The final method in this class is updateWinnings. We saw that this method is called in the actionPerformed method of the BoardPanel class when the play button is clicked to update the displayed winnings amount and to display a message indicating which player won.

An object of each of the two classes that we just discussed forms the two panels contained in the window for this game. The class that defines this window is GameFrame. The code for that class is in Listing 14.23.

LISTING 14.23 The Class Defining the Window for the Card Game of War (found on the CD-ROM at chapter14\GameFrame.java.)

```
1  package chapter14;
2
3  import java.awt.*;
4  import java.awt.event.*;
5  import javax.swing.*;
6  import static chapter14.GameOfWar.*;
7
8  class GameFrame implements ActionListener
9  {
10     private static final int GAP = 20, WIDTH = 450, HEIGHT = 380;
11     private JFrame frame;
12     private JMenuItem newGameItem = new JMenuItem("New Game"),
13         shuffleItem = new JMenuItem("Shuffle"),
14         exitItem = new JMenuItem("Exit");
15     private BoardPanel boardPanel;
16     private WinningsPanel winningsPanel;
17
```

```
18      public GameFrame(String name, BoardPanel boardPanel,
19          WinningsPanel winningsPanel)
20      {
21          JMenu gameMenu = new JMenu("Game");
22          JMenuBar menuBar = new JMenuBar();;
23
24          this.boardPanel = boardPanel;
25          this.winningsPanel = winningsPanel;
26          frame = new JFrame(name);
27              frame.setSize(HEIGHT, WIDTH);
28          frame.getContentPane().setLayout(
29              new FlowLayout(FlowLayout.CENTER, GAP, GAP));
30          frame.getContentPane().setBackground(darkGreen);
31          frame.setDefaultCloseOperation(JFrame.EXIT_ON_CLOSE);
32          gameMenu.add(newGameItem);
33          gameMenu.add(shuffleItem);
34          gameMenu.add(exitItem);
35          menuBar.add(gameMenu);
36          newGameItem.addActionListener(this);
37          shuffleItem.addActionListener(this);
38          exitItem.addActionListener(this);
39          frame.setJMenuBar(menuBar);
40          frame.setSize(WIDTH, HEIGHT);
41          frame.add(boardPanel, BorderLayout.NORTH);
42          frame.add(winningsPanel, BorderLayout.SOUTH);
43      }
44       public void actionPerformed(ActionEvent event)
45      {
46          Object object = event.getSource();
47
48          if (object == newGameItem)
49          {
50              boardPanel.shuffle();
51              winningsPanel.init();
52              frame.repaint();
53          }
54          else if (object == shuffleItem)
55          {
56              boardPanel.shuffle();
57              frame.repaint();
58          }
59          else if (object == exitItem)
```

```
60              frame.setVisible(false);
61      }
62      public void display()
63      {
64          frame.setVisible(true);
65      }
66  }
```

The two panels belonging to the window are supplied to the constructor by the main method and are copied to instance variables on lines 24 and 25. The constructor sets up the menu for the window on lines 32–35. On lines 36–38, objects of this class are registered as listeners for the selection of any of the three menu items. Finally, the two panels are added to the window on lines 41 and 42.

To handle menu selection events, it is necessary to implement the ActionListener interface, which this class does. The method actionPerformed handles the three menu items. When "New Game" is selected, the deck is shuffled and the init method of the BoardPanel class is called. When "Shuffle" is selected, the deck is shuffled without completely reinitializing the game. Selecting "Exit" closes the game window.

To complete this program, we need the class that contains main, which we have named GameOfWar. Its code is in Listing 14.24.

LISTING 14.24 The Class Containing the main Method for the Card Game of War (found *ON THE CD* on the CD-ROM at chapter14\GameOfWar.java).

```
1  package chapter14;
2
3  import java.awt.*;
4
5  public class GameOfWar
6  {
7      public static final Color darkGreen = new Color(0, 128, 0),
8          lightYellow = new Color(255, 255, 128);
9      public static WinningsPanel winningsPanel =
10          new WinningsPanel();
11      public static BoardPanel boardPanel =
12          new BoardPanel();;
13
14      public static void main(String[] args)
15      {
16          GameFrame frame = new GameFrame("Card Game of War",
17              boardPanel, winningsPanel);
18
```

```
19          frame.display();
20      }
21  }
```

The main method creates the window and displays it. There is one aspect of this class that is different from anything we have done before. The class variables winningsPanel and boardPanel have been declared public. They are singleton objects. Making them public facilitates communication between these two objects. This is a rare instance when we compromise the information hiding principle that we first introduced in Chapter 3.

This program is the largest one that we have studied thus far. It contains 12 classes or enumerated types. Figure 14.5 contains the UML diagram for this program.

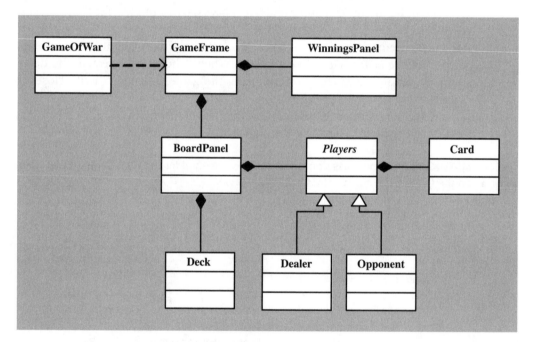

FIGURE 14.5 UML diagram for the card game of war.

SUMMARY

In this chapter, we studied abstract enumerated types and classes. We learned when to use them and how to choose between them. We encountered several more GUI components, radio buttons and menus, and learned how to create painting objects that can be mixed with other GUI components. The key points to remember from this chapter are as follows:

- An abstract method is a method that has a signature but no method body.
- Abstract enumerated types are enumerated types that contain abstract methods that must be defined for each literal.
- Abstract classes are classes that contain an abstract method. Such classes must have derived classes in which the abstract methods are overridden.
- Although abstract classes can have constructors, they can only be called by the constructors of derived classes. A class method called a factory method acts as a constructor outside the class hierarchy.
- Singletons are one-of-a-kind objects. There are several techniques for creating singleton objects.
- There is a variety of factors that must be considered when choosing between an abstract enumerated type and an abstract class.
- To create an object that can be painted on, which can be mixed with other GUI components, panels must be used.
- Radio buttons provide an ideal user interface for selecting among a discrete number of choices, when only one among those choices can be selected.
- Frame menus provide an alternative to buttons that allows the user to trigger specific events.

Review Questions

1. Besides abstract classes and enumerated types, where else can abstract methods appear?

2. Explain why some class on each branch of the inheritance hierarchy must override every abstract method in an abstract class.

3. Explain why objects of abstract classes cannot be created.

4. Are factory methods class methods or instance methods? Explain. What is their return type?

5. What is the primary consideration when choosing between an abstract enumerated type and an abstract class?

6. Explain why using abstract enumerated types and classes tends to eliminate `switch` statements.

7. When a class is used to create both singleton classes and utility classes, the methods are class methods. How do the two kinds of classes differ?

8. What will occur if we fail to provide methods that specify the minimum size of panels that are used for painting objects?

9. What interface must be implemented to handle events associated with radio buttons?

10. Provide one advantage of using menus compared to using a collection of buttons.

Programming Exercises

11. Write an abstract enumerated type for the days of the week that includes an abstract method, computePay, that accepts an hourly rate and a number of hours worked and returns an amount paid. Saturdays should be paid at time and a half and Sundays at double time.

12. Write an abstract enumerated type for coins that contains an abstract method that draws coins on a graphic object at a specified location. Both the graphic object and the location should be supplied as parameters. Make the coins the appropriate size and color.

13. Write an abstract enumerated type for a die, one of a pair of dice, that has an abstract method that draws the die on a graphic object supplied as a parameter. Provide a factory method that creates such an object from its ordinal value and make the literals comparable.

14. Write an abstract enumerated type for directions that has the four directions of a compass as its literals. It should contain an abstract method that is given a Point object and a distance as parameters and returns the point that results from moving the specified distance in that direction.

15. Write an abstract class for gender that extends JPanel. It should have an abstract method that draws a stick figure. That method should be called by paintComponent. Write two derived classes, one for a man and one for a woman, that override the abstract method and draw an appropriate stick figure representing the gender.

16. Write an abstract class for colored shapes that has an abstract method that draws the shape. Provide a factory method that returns a random shape. Create three derived classes; one for a red circle, one for a blue square, and a third one for a green rectangle twice as wide as it is high.

17. Create a class that extends JPanel that paints a pair of dice. This class should contain a method that allows the values on each die to be set to a specific value.

18. Create a class that extends JPanel that paints a small solid circle centered at a specific point. This class should contain a method that allows the circle's center to be moved and then repaints itself.

19. Create a radio button panel that contains four radio buttons, one for each of the four directions on a compass. Have the panel handle the events associated with these buttons and provide a method that returns the currently selected direction.

20. Create a class that defines a window that has a menu that has two choices: "Roll" and "Exit."

Programming Projects

21. Write an application that contains a window with one text field for each day of the week and one for an hourly rate and a button to cause the pay to be computed and displayed. Use the enumerated type defined in Programming Exercise 11 to compute the pay.

22. Write an application that randomly generates an amount of change less than one dollar. Display the coins required to make that amount of change using the fewest coins. Incorporate the enumerated type defined in Programming Exercise 12 in your program.

23. Write an application that uses the window defined in Programming Exercise 20 that displays the result of a roll of a pair of dice whenever the "Roll" choice is selected from the menu. Use the panel class from Programming Exercise 17 and the enumerated type definition from Programming Exercise 13 as a part of your solution.

24. Write an application that contains a panel that displays a small solid circle at a specified location, using the class created by Programming Exercise 18, and a radio panel that allows the user to select a direction using a radio button panel using the class defined for Programming Exercise 19. Also include a button that, when pressed, causes the circle to be moved some fixed distance in the direction selected by the radio buttons. Use the abstract enumerated type defined in Programming Exercise 14 to compute the location of the center of the circle after each move.

25. Write an application that draws five randomly generated shapes of the kind defined by the hierarchy of classes from Programming Exercise 16.

15 Recursive Control Structures

COMPARING ITERATION AND RECURSION

We begin our discussion by defining the term *recursion*. Recursion means self-referential. Both control structures and data structures can be recursive. Our focus in this chapter will be on recursive control structures—specifically, recursive methods. A recursive method is a method that calls itself. To be more precise, recursive methods call another activation of themselves. This distinction is important because we will see that each activation of a recursive method has its own copy of all its local variables.

Recursion and iteration are alternative techniques for solving the same class of problems, but there are tradeoffs between the two approaches. To help you better understand both the advantages and potential disadvantages of recursion, we present both iterative and recursive solutions with our first examples.

A Framework for Displaying the Terms of a Number Sequence

These initial examples involve methods that compute the *n*th term of some number sequence given *n*. We have elected to develop a common framework to use in each of these examples to minimize the duplication of code. The first component of this framework is an abstract class that we call Sequence, which contains an abstract method computeTerm, which will vary in each of our examples. The definition of Sequence is shown in Listing 15.1.

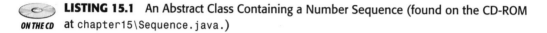

LISTING 15.1 An Abstract Class Containing a Number Sequence (found on the CD-ROM **ON THE CD** at chapter15\Sequence.java.)

```
 1  package chapter15;
 2
 3  abstract class Sequence
 4  {
 5      protected int counter;
 6
 7      abstract public int computeTerm(int n);
 8      public int getCounter()
 9      {
10          return counter;
11      }
12      public void startCounter()
13      {
14          counter = 0;
15      }
16  }
```

Notice that in addition to the abstract method, this class includes an instance variable counter with the access modifier protected, so that it can be updated by its derived classes. It also includes a method startCounter, which initializes this counter, and a method getCounter, which retrieves its value. The purpose of this counter is so that we can compare the number of operations performed by the method that computes a particular term of the sequence.

The second class in our common framework is one that defines a window that allows the user to display a selected term of the sequence. This code for this class, named SequenceWindow, is shown in Listing 15.2.

LISTING 15.2   A Class that Allows the User to Display a Selected Term of Some
ON THE CD Numbers Sequence (found on the CD-ROM at chapter15\SequenceWindow.java.)

```java
1   package chapter15;
2
3   import java.awt.*;
4   import java.awt.event.*;
5   import javax.swing.*;
6
7   public class SequenceWindow implements ActionListener
8   {
9       private static final int MAIN_GAP = 15,    TEXT_WIDTH = 5;
10      private JFrame frame;
11      private JLabel nLabel = new JLabel("Enter n: "),
12          nthTermLabel = new JLabel("nth Term"),
13          counterLabel = new JLabel("Counter");
14      private JTextField index = new JTextField(TEXT_WIDTH),
15          value = new JTextField(TEXT_WIDTH),
16          counter = new JTextField(TEXT_WIDTH);
17      private JButton compute = new JButton("Compute nth Term");
18      private Sequence sequence;
19
20      public SequenceWindow(String title, Sequence sequence)
21      {
22          JPanel mainPanel = new JPanel();
23
24          this.sequence = sequence;
25          frame = new JFrame(title);
26          mainPanel.setLayout(
27              new FlowLayout(FlowLayout.CENTER, MAIN_GAP, MAIN_GAP));
28          mainPanel.setBackground(Color.WHITE);
29          value.setEditable(false);
30          counter.setEditable(false);
31          mainPanel.add(nLabel);
32          mainPanel.add(index);
33          mainPanel.add(compute);
34          mainPanel.add(nthTermLabel);
35          mainPanel.add(value);
36          mainPanel.add(counterLabel);
37          mainPanel.add(counter);
38          frame.setDefaultCloseOperation(JFrame.EXIT_ON_CLOSE);
39          frame.getContentPane().setLayout(new FlowLayout
40              (FlowLayout.CENTER, MAIN_GAP, MAIN_GAP));
41          frame.getContentPane().setBackground(Color.WHITE);
```

```
42              frame.getContentPane().add(mainPanel);
43              compute.addActionListener(this);
44          }
45      public void actionPerformed(ActionEvent event)
46      {
47          int n, nthTerm;
48
48          sequence.startCounter();
49          n = Integer.parseInt(index.getText());
50          nthTerm = sequence.computeTerm(n);
51          value.setText("" + nthTerm);
52          counter.setText("" + sequence.getCounter());
53      }
54      public void display()
55      {
56          frame.pack();
57          frame.setVisible(true);
58      }
59
```

The window defined by this class contains three text fields. The first is an editable field called index that allows the user to enter which term to compute. The second is an uneditable text field, value, which is used to display the value of the nth term of the sequence. The third text field, counter, also uneditable, is used to display the value of the counter after the computation is performed.

The window also contains a button called compute. The object of the SequenceWindow class is the listener for the events of this button. When pressed, the method actionPerformed first initializes the counter defined in Sequence by calling startCounter on line 49. Next it extracts the value of n from the text field index. Then it calls the method computeTerm to compute the nth term of the sequence and displays that value in the text field value on line 51. Finally it displays the value of the counter in the text field named counter. This window is illustrated in Figure 15.1.

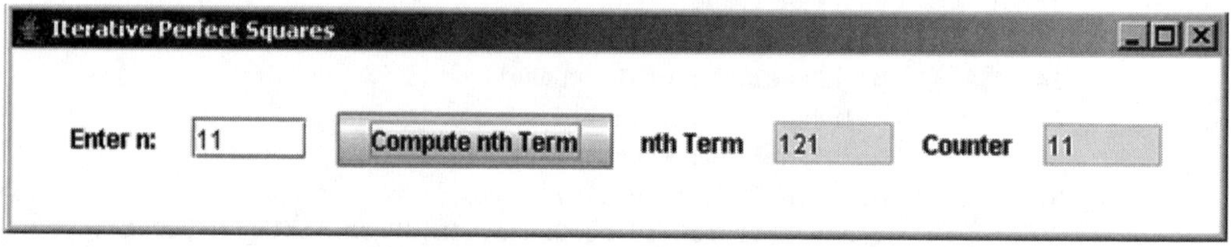

FIGURE 15.1   The window for computing the terms of an arbitrary number sequence.

The Sequence of Perfect Squares

Next, let's consider our first number sequence. It is the sequence of perfect squares, computed as the sum of the first n odd numbers, a sequence that we have discussed previously. Let's review the formula that we first encountered in Chapter 9, shown again in Equation 15.1.

$$n^2 = \sum_{i=1}^{n} 2i - 1 \qquad (15.1)$$

We begin with the iterative implementation defined in a class called IterativeSquares, derived from our abstract class Sequence, that overrides the method computeTerm so that it computes the nth perfect square iteratively, using the definition that we just discussed. That class is an inner class in the class IterativeSquaresMain, which also contains the method main. The code for IterativeSquaresMain is shown in Listing 15.3.

LISTING 15.3 A Class Containing an Iterative Method for Computing Perfect Squares
ON THE CD (found on the CD-ROM at chapter15\IterativeSquaresMain.java.)

```
1  package chapter15;
2
3  public class IterativeSquaresMain
4  {
5      private static class IterativeSquares extends Sequence
6      {
7          public int computeTerm(int n)
8          {
9              int sum = 0;
10
11             for (int i = 1; i <= n; i++)
12             {
13                 counter++;
14                 sum += 2 * i - 1;
15             }
16             return sum;
17         }
18     }
19
20     public static void main(String[] args)
21     {
22         SequenceWindow window = new SequenceWindow
23             ("Iterative Perfect Squares", new IterativeSquares());
24
```

```
25            window.display();
26      }
27  }
```

Notice that the inner class `IterativeSquares` must be declared as `static`. This example is our first encounter with an inner class requiring that modifier. It is necessary to label it `static` because we are creating an instance of this class inside the class method `main`.

The method `computeTerm` computes the nth perfect square using an algorithm that implements the definition in Equations 15.1. Notice the strong correspondence between the mathematical symbol for summation and the `for` loop of Java. In addition to performing that computation, it also increments the variable `counter`, which this class inherits from `Sequence`. After the computation is complete, `counter` will contain the required number of iterations.

Next, we consider the same number sequence implemented with recursion. Before we examine the code for that implementation, we begin with a recursive definition for this sequence.

$$n^2 = 1, \text{ if } n = 1 \tag{15.2}$$

$$n^2 = 2n - 1 + (n-1)^2, \text{ if } n > 1 \tag{15.3}$$

Because this is our first recursive definition, there are several characteristics about recursive definitions that warrant discussion. Recursive definitions must have at least one base case and one recursive case. The first part of this definition, in Equation 15.2, applies when n is 1 is the base case. A base case is not recursive. It does not use the sequence being defined as part of the definition. Clearly the second part of the definition, in Equation 15.3, is recursive. It uses $(n-1)^2$ to define n^2.

When defining English words, we are often warned against using the word that we are attempting to define as a part of the definition. Such definitions are considered circular and, therefore, not meaningful. If we did not understand what the word meant in the first place, how could a definition using the word be meaningful? Yet recursive definitions do this very thing—almost. Had we defined n^2 using n^2, we would indeed have a meaningless definition. With recursive definitions of number sequences, we do not use the very term of the sequence we are defining, but the previous term, or sometimes several previous terms. That difference is all-important. Equally important is the presence of a base case. Applying this definition for a specific value of n should help you understand the importance of the base case. Equations 15.4-15.6 show the computation of 3^2 by repetitive application of this definition.

$$3^2 = 2 \times 3 - 1 + 2^2 = 5 + 2^2 = \tag{15.4}$$

$$5 + 2 \times 2 - 1 + 1^2 = 5 + 3 + 1^2 \qquad (15.5)$$

$$5 + 3 + 1 = 5 + 4 = 9 \qquad (15.6)$$

In the first two equations, we apply the recursive part of the definition. In the third equation, we apply the base case.

Without a base case, this definition would be unending. Given that iteration and recursion solve the same class of problems, you should expect some analog to an infinite loop. That analog is infinite recursion. Notice that we have carefully avoided defining this sequence for nonpositive values because for such values the repeated application of the recursive part of the definition would never lead to the base case and therefore would be infinitely recursive.

Let's now consider the recursive implementation of this number sequence using a Java method. Listing 15.4 contains that implementation.

ON THE CD

LISTING 15.4   A Class Containing a Recursive Method for Computing Perfect Squares (found on the CD-ROM at `chapter15\RecursiveSquaresMain.java`.)

```
1  package chapter15;
2
3  public class RecursiveSquaresMain
4  {
5      private static class RecursiveSquares extends Sequence
6      {
7          public int computeTerm(int n)
8          {
9              counter++;
10             if (n == 1)
11                 return 1;
12             return 2 * n - 1 + computeTerm(n - 1);
13         }
14     }
15
16     public static void main(String[] args)
17     {
18         SequenceWindow window = new SequenceWindow
19             ("Recursive Perfect Squares", new RecursiveSquares());
20
21         window.display();
22     }
23 }
```

The code for recursive methods directly mirrors their corresponding recursive definitions. On line 9, we are using the counter to count the number of times this method is called. Notice that lines 10 and 11 implement the base case and line 12 implements the recursive case. There is one minor difference, however, which is that we did not check whether n is positive in the recursive case. Supplying this method a negative value for n will cause the infinite recursion that we discussed earlier. In Chapter 11, we introduced preconditions. Stating that the n must be positive, as a precondition, would be appropriate in this case if we elect not to make an explicit check.

Let's now compare the iterative and recursive methods. There are two differences that should be readily apparent. The recursive method requires fewer lines of code and fewer local variables. In fact, the recursive method has no local variables at all. The ability to solve problems with less code and fewer variables is clearly an advantage of the recursive approach.

Although understanding the mechanics of recursion generally does not help those new to recursion develop recursive solutions, anyone unfamiliar with recursion has a desire to better understand how it works—what makes recursive methods shorter and simpler. You must realize that during the execution of a recursive method, some of the code is executed on the way into the recursion. Other parts of the code are executed on the way out. The code executed on the way in is the code prior to the recursive call. During the execution of a recursive method the code prior to the recursive call is repeatedly executed until the base case is reached. Then the code after the recursive call is repeatedly executed in the reverse order. In our recursive implementation of the perfect squares sequence, the code for computing the odd number is placed before the recursive call, whereas the code for summing those odd numbers is placed after the recursive call. Let's return to Equations 15.4-15.6, which should help us understand this process. Notice that in the first two equations the odd numbers 5 and 3 are computed on the way in. In the third equation the odd number 1 is generated as the base case. The addition of these numbers happens on the way out and in reverse order. The numbers 3 and 1 are added first, then that sum is added to 5. We will perform a similar analysis of the code in each of our recursive implementations to ensure this distinction becomes clear.

If you are still unclear about the mechanics of recursion, studying Figure 15.2 should help you better understand how recursive methods execute. It illustrates the computation of 4^2. Each circle represents one activation of the method `computeTerm` in the `RecursiveSquares` class. The number inside the circle represents the value of the parameter n. The computation to the right of each circle is the computation performed on line 12 of Listing 15.4. This computation happens on the way out of the recursion using the value returned by the previous activation in the computation and the current value of n.

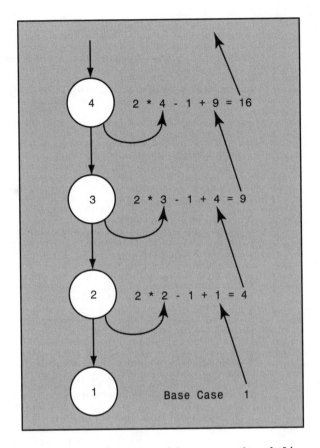

FIGURE 15.2 Illustration of the computation of 4^2 by the recursive method.

The Sequence of Fibonacci Numbers

We are now ready to consider a second number sequence, which illustrates one of the primary drawbacks of recursion—inefficiency. This sequence is the famous Fibonacci number sequence that we first encountered in Chapter 4. Recall that the 0th term of this sequence is 0. The 1st term is first and every subsequent term is the sum of the two previous terms. This definition is a recursive one. First, let's consider the iterative solution, which is shown in Listing 15.5.

LISTING 15.5 A Class Containing an Iterative Method for Computing Fibonacci Numbers
ON THE CD (found on the CD-ROM at chapter15\IterativeFibonacciMain.java.)

```
1  package chapter15;
2
```

```
 3  public class IterativeFibonacciMain
 4  {
 5      private static class IterativeFibonacci extends Sequence
 6      {
 7          public int computeTerm(int n)
 8          {
 9              int previous = 0, current = 0, next = 1;
10
11              for (int i = 1; i <= n; i++)
12              {
13                  counter++;
14                  previous = current;
15                  current = next;
16                  next = previous + current;
17              }
18              return current;
19          }
20      }
21
22      public static void main(String[] args)
23      {
24          SequenceWindow window = new SequenceWindow
25              ("Iterative Fibonacci Squares",
26              new IterativeFibonacci());
27
28          window.display();
29      }
30  }
```

Because we have dealt with this sequence before, the algorithm that we have used, which requires a window across the sequence containing three successive terms, should be familiar. Worth noting now, however, is how the initializations on line 9 account for the base cases in the definition and the computation on line 16 is used to satisfy the recursive case. Nonetheless, this solution uses a `for` loop, and is therefore iterative.

Next, let's consider the implementation that is recursive. The code for the class containing the recursive implementation is shown in Listing 15.6.

LISTING 15.6 A Class Containing a Recursive Method for Computing Fibonacci Numbers
ON THE CD (found on the CD-ROM at `chapter15\RecursiveFibonacciMain.java`.)

```
 1  package chapter15;
 2
```

```
 3  public class RecursiveFibonacciMain
 4  {
 5      private static class RecursiveFibonacci extends Sequence
 6      {
 7          public int computeTerm(int n)
 8          {
 9              counter++;
10              if (n <= 1)
11                  return n;
12              return computeTerm(n - 1) + computeTerm(n - 2);
13          }
14      }
15
16      public static void main(String[] args)
17      {
18          SequenceWindow window = new SequenceWindow
19              ("Recursive Fibonacci Squares",
20              new RecursiveFibonacci());
21
22          window.display();
23      }
24  }
```

Lines 10 and 11 implement the two base cases. Although we should still have a precondition that states that the parameter n should not be negative, supplying it negative values will not result in infinite recursion as before. The recursive case is implemented on line 12. One important observation to make about this method is that it is doubly recursive because it contains two recursive calls. With doubly recursive methods, code can appear in three different places. The first place is before both calls. The second place is in between calls, and the third is after both calls. In this method, checking for the base case is done before both calls. The addition of the two numbers is performed after both calls.

Figure 15.3 illustrates each of the recursive calls that are made when this method is passed a value of 5 for the parameter n. Each circle represents one activation of the method. The number inside the circle represents the value of n that is passed into the method.

Although the recursive implementation of the method to compute the terms of the Fibonacci sequence has fewer lines of code and fewer local variables, it has one important disadvantage, which is that it takes much more time to compute than its iterative counterpart. The inefficiency should be somewhat apparent from Figure 15.3. Notice that the method is called five separate times to compute the first term of the sequence.

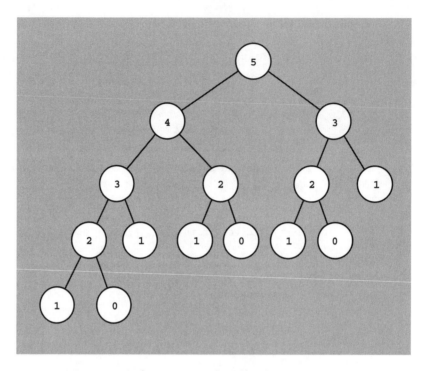

FIGURE 15.3 Recursively computing the fifth Fibonacci number.

We have provided another mechanism to help you understand the extent of this inefficiency, which is the counter variable. Like we had done with the perfect square sequence, we increment the counter once for every iteration in the iterative version and once for each activation of the method in the recursive implementation. The value of this counter gives us a way to compare the amount of time required in each case. Table 15.1 shows the resulting value of the variable counter for various values of n.

TABLE 15.1 Comparing the Efficiency of the Iterative and Recursive Fibonacci Methods

N	Iterative counter	Recursive counter
5	5	15
10	10	177
15	15	1973
20	20	21,891
25	25	242,785

The dramatic inefficiency of the recursive solution is readily apparent from this table. Although the value of counter increases linearly as n increases in the iterative version, it increases exponentially with the recursive solution. Programs that exhibit this level of inefficiency are unusable in practice because the exponential function grows so rapidly that n does not have to become too large before the amount of time required is inordinate. We encourage you to construct a similar table for the perfect square example to see whether the same problem exists in that case.

To become skilled at developing recursive solutions, you must learn to "think recursively." Recursive thinking means identifying the base case and recursive case for a particular problem, which really means finding a recursive definition. Iterative thinking can actually be an obstacle to developing the ability to think recursively because the approaches are so different.

Although we were able to provide an iterative definition for the perfect square sequence using a summation, finding an equivalent iterative definition for Fibonacci numbers, although possible, is not at all straightforward. Algorithms, not iterative definitions, are really what we need in general when searching for iterative solutions.

PROBLEMS REQUIRING UNBOUNDED MEMORY

After the discussion of the inefficiency of the recursive implementation of the Fibonacci sequence, you may be wondering whether the advantage of recursion—shorter programs with fewer variables—outweighs the disadvantage, which is the potential inefficiency. Understanding this tradeoff is really essential in knowing when to use recursion.

Before we address this issue directly, let's return to the first example that we discussed—the sequence of perfect squares. If you took our suggestion and compiled a table of the values of the counter variable for various values of n for each of the two implementations, you observed that there was no difference between the two. In both cases the value of counter increased linearly as n increased. Nonetheless the iterative solution would still likely be faster by a constant factor because a method call takes more time than one iteration through a loop. There is another factor to consider—the efficient use of memory. Although the iterative version has more local variables, it only uses a constant amount of memory, which is the memory required for each of those variables. Recursive methods always require more than constant memory because each recursive call requires another activation record to be created. For the recursive squares example, the memory required increases linearly as n increases.

Recursive solutions are never more efficient than their iterative counterparts. The best that we can hope for is that they are no less efficient in their use of both time and memory in general terms—excluding constant factors. What is really necessary is to identify the class of problems for which the previous statement is true. For such problems we gain the simplicity offered by recursion without the potential inefficiency that can result. This class of problems can be best characterized as those problems that cannot be solved without an unbounded amount of memory.

To help you better understand this characterization, we have selected perhaps the simplest example of such a problem—the reversal problem—reading in a sequence of data elements and outputting them in reverse order. Because we must save all the lines as they are read in and because we do not know in general how many there will be, a fixed amount of memory, such as a fixed sized array, will not suffice. Done iteratively, we need an array list that can grow to the extent needed as the program executes.

Specifically, we consider a program that reads in the lines of a file and outputs them in reverse order. We forgo the iterative implementation and present only the recursive version, which is contained in Listing 15.7.

LISTING 15.7 A Program that Outputs the Lines of a File in Reverse Order (found on the **ON THE CD** CD-ROM at chapter15\ReverseLines.java.)

```
1   package chapter15;
2
3   import java.io.*;
4
5   public class ReverseLines
6   {
7       public static void main(String[] args)
8           throws IOException
9       {
10          BufferedReader input = new BufferedReader(
11              new FileReader("input.txt"));
12
13          reverse(input);
14      }
15      private static void reverse(BufferedReader input)
16          throws IOException
17      {
18          String line;
19
20          line = input.readLine();
21          if (line != null)
22          {
23              reverse(input);
24              System.out.println(line);
```

```
25          }
26      }
27  }
```

The recursive method reverse is very short but, as is often the case with recursive programs, how it accomplishes its task may be initially elusive. To help you understand how it works, let's return to the analysis of which code is placed before the recursive call and which code is placed after it. The lines are input before the recursive call and output after the call, in the reverse order. All the lines are input before any line is output. One idea that is sometimes difficult to grasp for those new to recursion is how the code after the recursive call executes. It may seem that after the null line is read in, reverse returns to main and nothing is output, but that is not what happens. Once the null line is read in, reverse returns to its previous activation of itself at the point after the call. So it returns to the previous activation on line 24, which performs the output. Then that activation returns to the previous one, and so on.

In both of our previous examples of recursive methods, those methods had no local variables. Although recursive methods tend to have fewer local variables than their iterative counterparts, they still can have some, as this example illustrates. Realizing that there is a separate copy of the local variable line, declared on line 18, is essential to understanding the behavior of this method also.

Let's now consider the efficiency issues. The amount of time and the amount of memory needed increase linearly as the number of lines in the file increases, regardless of how we implement this problem, with iteration or recursion. So this problem is one of the simplest examples of one where the recursive version is no less efficient in general terms than its iterative counterpart.

RECURSION AND NESTED STRUCTURES

Next, we consider a class of problems that cannot be solved with a constant amount of memory—problems that deal with any kind of nested structure. Programs themselves are nested structures because statements can be nested inside other statements, and so on. The task performed by the part of a compiler known as the *parser*, which determines whether a program is syntactically correct, is an example of such a problem. Recursion is one technique that can be used to parse programs. The example that we wish to consider is a simpler one that involves, not whole programs, but just expressions. Let's examine the syntax rules for expressions that can contain only literal values, shown in Syntax Definition 15.1.

Syntax Definition 15.1 Syntax choices of an Expression.

```
expression

    expression operator expression    |
    literal
```

One important thing to notice about the definition of the syntax of nested structures is that the rules themselves are recursive. The first part of the rule is the recursive case; the second part is the base case. Consequently, it should not be surprising that recursion is a helpful technique when processing such nested structures.

Prefix Expressions

The specific example that we have chosen is one that involves prefix expressions—expressions in which the operator is placed before rather than between the two operands. Some programming languages, like LISP, use this syntax rather than the more traditional infix notation. Prefix expressions have the advantage that no parentheses, no precedence rules, and no associativity rules are needed. Equation 15.7 contains an example of a prefix expression showing the steps of the evaluation.

$$+ - 8\ 3\ *\ 3\ 2 = + 5\ 6 = 11 \tag{15.7}$$

Like all expressions, prefix expressions are evaluated from the inside out, from the most deeply nested to the most shallowly nested.

A Program That Evaluates Prefix Expressions

Now that we have given an example of a prefix expression and the steps involved in its evaluation, we are ready to study a program that recursively evaluates an expression that is entered in prefix form. Figure 15.4 illustrates the output of this program for the prefix expression in Equation 15.7.

This program consists of the enumerated type Operation from the previous chapter, a class that defines the GUI, and one additional class that defines an exception. The class that defines the GUI is shown in Listing 15.8.

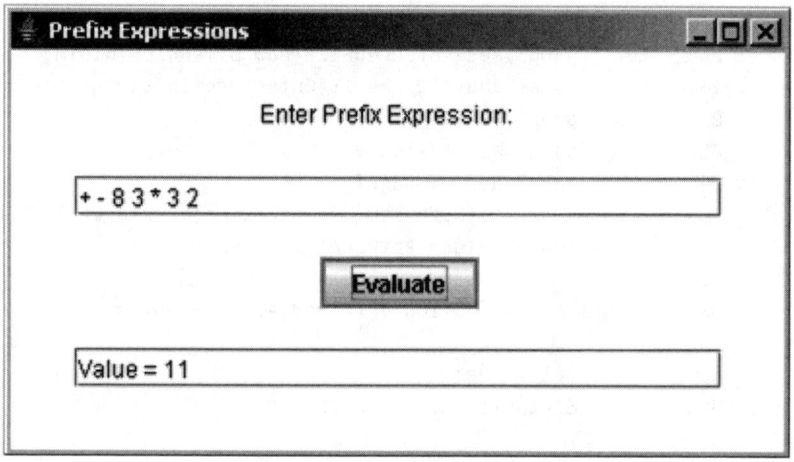

FIGURE 15.4 Output of the prefix expression evaluation application.

LISTING 15.8 A Program that Evaluates Prefix Expressions (found on the CD-ROM at
ON THE CD chapter15\PrefixExpression.java.)

```
1  package chapter15;
2
3  import java.awt.*;
4  import java.awt.event.*;
5  import java.util.*;
6  import javax.swing.*;
7
8  import chapter14.*;
9
10 public class PrefixExpression implements ActionListener
11 {
12     private static final int GAP = 20, WIDTH = 400,
13         HEIGHT = 200, TEXT_WIDTH = 30;
14     private JFrame frame = new JFrame("Prefix Expressions");
15     private JPanel panel = new JPanel();
16     private JTextField input = new JTextField(TEXT_WIDTH),
17         message = new JTextField(TEXT_WIDTH);
18     private JButton evaluate = new JButton("Evaluate");
19
20     public PrefixExpression()
21     {
22         panel.setLayout
23             (new FlowLayout(FlowLayout.CENTER, GAP, GAP));
```

```
24              panel.setBackground(Color.WHITE);
25              panel.setPreferredSize(new Dimension(WIDTH, HEIGHT));
26              panel.add(new Label("Enter Prefix Expression: "));
27              panel.add(input);
28              panel.add(evaluate);
29              panel.add(message);
30              frame.setDefaultCloseOperation(JFrame.EXIT_ON_CLOSE);
31              frame.getContentPane().add(panel);
32          }
33      public void actionPerformed(ActionEvent event)
34      {
35          int value;
36          StringTokenizer tokenizer;
37
38          try
39          {
40              tokenizer = new StringTokenizer(input.getText(),
41                  "+-*/ ", true);
42              value = doEvaluation(tokenizer);
43              if (tokenizer.hasMoreTokens())
44                  throw new SyntaxException("Extra Tokens");
45              message.setText("Value = " + value);
46          }
47          catch (SyntaxException exception)
48          {
49              message.setText(exception.getMessage());
50          }
51      }
52      public int doEvaluation(StringTokenizer tokenizer)
53          throws SyntaxException
54      {
55          int left, right;
56          String token;
57          Operation operation;
58
59          do
60          {
61              if (tokenizer.hasMoreTokens())
62                  token = tokenizer.nextToken();
63              else
64                  throw new SyntaxException("Missing Tokens");
65          }
66          while (token.equals(" "));
67          operation = Operation.anOperation(token);
```

```
68          if (operation == null)
69              try
70              {
71                  return Integer.parseInt(token);
72              }
73              catch (NumberFormatException exception)
74              {
75                  throw new SyntaxException("Invalid Token");
76              }
77          left = doEvaluation(tokenizer);
78          right = doEvaluation(tokenizer);
79          return operation.evaluate(left, right);
80      }
81      public void initialize()
82      {
83          evaluate.addActionListener(this);
84          frame.pack();
85          frame.setVisible(true);
86      }
87      public static void main(String[] args)
88      {
89          PrefixExpression expression = new PrefixExpression();
90
91          expression.initialize();
92      }
93  }
```

In addition to the usual frame and panel, the GUI for this application consists of two text fields, input and message, declared on lines 16 and 17, and one button, evaluate, declared on line 18. When the user enters the prefix expression in the text field input and presses the button evaluate, the result is displayed in message. If a syntax error occurs, an appropriate error message is displayed in the text field message instead.

Next, let's examine the sequence of events that occurs when the button evaluate is pressed. As with all button events, actionPerformed will be called. In this program there is only one button, so we need not check to see what caused the event. On lines 40 and 41, we instantiate a StringTokenizer object that we will use to break the input into tokens. Notice that we have specified the four operations and a space as delimiters. The third argument, true, indicates that the delimiters should also be returned as tokens. On line 42, we call doEvaluation, which is the recursive method that will evaluate this expression. If no syntax error occurred during the evaluation, it will return the value of the expression, which we store in the integer variable value. At this point all the tokens should have been consumed. If any remain, the expression is not syntactically correct, so we throw an expression. We catch that exception and any that were thrown by the call to doEvaluation in the catch block that spans lines 47-50. If the expression was syntactically correct, we display the result on line 45.

The method doEvaluation is the only recursive method in this program, and so it is the one of greatest interest to us. Because we have configured the tokenizer to return the delimiters as tokens, it is necessary to skip over any spaces. The loop that spans lines 59-66 accomplishes that task. Should the supply of tokens be exhausted at this point, we have a syntax error and so throw an exception on line 64. Once we have a token that is not a space, we pass it to the factory method anOperation to check whether it is an operator. If it is not an operator, presumably we have an operand, which is the base case. Operands must be integer literals, so we attempt to convert this string to an integer by calling parseInt on line 71. If that operation succeeds, we return the integer value as the value of the subexpression. Otherwise we throw an exception because we have encountered a token, which is neither a valid operator nor a valid operand. If the token was a valid operator, we have the recursive case. This method is doubly recursive. It calls itself on line 77 and again on line 78 to obtain the values of the left and right subexpressions, respectively. Once it has those values, it uses the method evaluate of the Operation type to calculate the value of this subexpression.

The other class needed to complete this program is the class that defines the exception that is thrown when a syntactically incorrect prefix expression is input. Listing 15.9 contains the code for that class, which is named SyntaxException.

LISTING 15.9 The Class Defining a Syntax Exception (found on the CD-ROM at
ON THE CD chapter15\SyntaxException.java.)

```
1 package chapter15;
2
3 public class SyntaxException extends Exception
4 {
5     public SyntaxException(String message)
6     {
7         super(message);
8     }
9 }
```

These exceptions are checked exceptions, which should be apparent from the base class. There is only constructor. It requires a message to be supplied as a parameter. That message can subsequently be accessed by the getMessage method this class inherits from Exception.

There is one important final observation to be made about this program. It is not significantly less efficient than its iterative counterpart. That point is worth emphasizing in case you have mistakenly concluded from the Fibonacci number example that double recursion was responsible for inefficiency.

BACKTRACKING

There is a class of problems for which it is difficult to devise algorithms that can find the solution in a direct fashion. For such problems it is often necessary to search a decision tree of possible solutions because there may be no simple way to know which path to follow at every juncture. With such an approach, it becomes necessary to *backtrack*, when it is discovered that a particular path does not lead to a solution.

Both our next example and the final example of this chapter will illustrate how helpful recursion can be in solving problems that require such backtracking. For our next example, we have chosen a problem that will enable us to use some of the classes that we developed in an earlier problem related to triangular numbers. Having a fascination for the curious patterns of number theory will be an asset to understanding this example because you will need patience to follow the details involved. This example pertains to one of Fermat's many theorems—one far less famous than his so-called "last theorem." This theorem states that any positive integer can be expressed as the sum of at most three triangular numbers. To illustrate what is meant by this theorem, let's choose an example. Equation 15.8 gives the decomposition of the number 25 into three triangular numbers.

$$25 = 1 + 3 + 21 = \Delta(1) + \Delta(2) + \Delta(6) \tag{15.8}$$

You may want to refer back to Chapter 10 to review triangular numbers if you do not recall how this number sequence is defined and what some of its properties are. One of those properties that we employ for the purpose of illustrating the output is that the number of lines connecting all vertices of a regular polygon with n sides is the $(n-1)^{st}$ triangular number. So for output, we will display the three triangular numbers but also the regular polygons with that number of lines as shown in Figure 15.5.

The question remains as to how to find this three number decomposition. Let's outline the approach that we plan to use. It is to begin with the largest triangular number less than the number that we are trying to decompose. If it is a triangular number, then we are done. Otherwise we apply this process recursively to the difference between the original number and the largest triangular number less than it. First we must determine how to find the largest triangular number less than a particular number. We accomplish that by solving Equation 15.9, which gives the formula for the nth triangular number, for n in terms of the number t.

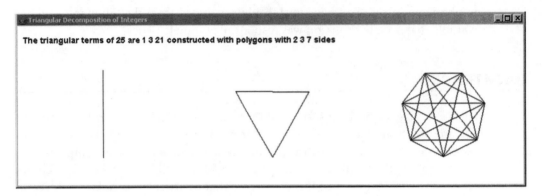

FIGURE 15.5   Output of triangular decomposition of the number 25.

$$t = \frac{n(n+1)}{2} = \frac{1}{2}n^2 + \frac{1}{2}n \tag{15.9}$$

Equation 15.9 is a quadratic equation, so we use the formula for solving quadratic equations, giving us the result in Equation 15.10.

$$n = \frac{-\frac{1}{2} \pm \sqrt{\left(\frac{1}{2}\right)^2 + 2t}}{2 - \frac{1}{2}} = \frac{\pm\sqrt{1+8t}-1}{2} \tag{15.10}$$

Quadratic equations have two roots, of course. We are only interested in the positive one. Furthermore, we are interested in the integer part of the result. Incorporating those two features gives us our final formula in Equation 15.11.

$$n = \left\lfloor \frac{\sqrt{1+8t}-1}{2} \right\rfloor \tag{15.11}$$

Let's apply this technique to the number 25 to see how it works. We substitute 25 for t in Equation 15.11 giving Equation 15.12.

$$n = \left\lfloor \frac{\sqrt{1+8\times25}-1}{2} \right\rfloor = \lfloor 6.5887 = 6 \rfloor \tag{15.12}$$

The value of n, which is 6, is the index of the triangular number, so the triangular number is $\Delta(6) = 1 + 2 + 3 + 4 + 5 + 6 = 21$. Now we apply recursion and say that the triangular decomposition of 25 is 21 plus the triangular decomposition of 4, which is the difference $25 - 21$. To find the triangular decomposition of 4, we use the same technique, applying the formula in Equation 15.10 with t as 4, which gives us $\lfloor 2.372 \rfloor = 2$. $\Delta(2)$ is 3, so 3 is the next triangular term. We compute the difference $4 - 3$, which is 1. 1 is a triangular number, so that is a base case. Consequently the three triangular terms of 25 are 21, 3, and 1.

Although we have offered no proof, this technique does appear to work, but there is one problem. Although it will always give us a decomposition of the number into triangular terms, there is no guarantee that the decomposition will consist of only three terms as Fermat's theorem claims is possible. Let's consider what happens when we apply this technique to the number 20. Applying Equation 15.10 with t as 20, n is $\lfloor 5.844 \rfloor = 5$. $\Delta(5)$ is 15, so 15 is the first triangular term. Next, we apply this technique to $20 - 15$, which is 5. With t as 5, n is $\lfloor 2.702 \rfloor = 2$. $\Delta(2)$ is 3. We apply the technique to $5 - 3$, which is 2. With t as 2, n is $\lfloor 1.562 \rfloor = 1$. $\Delta(1)$ is 1. Finally the difference $2 - 1$ is 1, which is a triangular number, so we have reached the base case. We have decomposed 20 as the sum $15 + 3 + 1 + 1$. There is only one problem. Our decomposition has four, terms not three, as Fermat's theorem claims is possible. Starting with the largest triangular number less than 20, which is 15, was the wrong choice. The problem is that until we proceeded further down the path of decomposition, we did not realize it. Once we realize it, we must backtrack. Instead, we must begin with the next smaller triangular number than 15, which is easy to compute. With a slight rearrangement of the recursive definition of triangular numbers, we have Equation 15.13.

$$\Delta(n - 1) = \Delta(n) - n \tag{15.13}$$

So 15, being the fifth triangular number, is preceded by $15 - 5$, which is 10—the fourth triangular number. Instead of beginning with 15, we begin with 10 as our first term. Next, we recursively apply our technique to the difference $20 - 10$, which is 10—a triangular number, and so a base case. Consequently, taking this path we have decomposed 20 into $10 + 10$, the sum of two triangular numbers, which satisfies Fermat's theorem.

Clearly this example has taken more explanation than most, but we should now be ready to examine the code for this program. It consists of two new classes and two classes that we introduced in Chapter 10—PolygonNTuple and Regular-Polygon. We begin with the class that contains main, which also contains the recursive method. Listing 15.10 contains this class, which is named TriangularMain.

LISTING 15.10   The main Class for the Triangular Decomposition Application (found on the CD-ROM at chapter15\TriangularMain.java.)

```
1  package chapter15;
2
```

```
 3  import javax.swing.*;
 4  import common.*;
 5
 6  public class TriangularMain
 7  {
 8      public static void main(String[] args)
 9      {
10          int number;
11          TriangularTerms terms;
12
13          while (true)
14          {
15              number = InputOutput.getInteger("A Positive Integer");
16              if (number <= 0)
17                  return;
18              terms = termDecomposition(number);
19              terms.show();
20          }
21      }
22      private static TriangularTerms termDecomposition(int number)
23      {
24          int index, term;
25          TriangularTerms terms;
26
27          index = TriangularTerms.numberToIndex(number);
28          term = (index * (index + 1)) / 2;
29          if (term == number)
30          {
31              terms = new TriangularTerms();
32              terms.add(term);
33              return terms;
34          }
35          while (true)
36          {
37              terms = termDecomposition(number - term);
38              if (terms.length() < TriangularTerms.MAXIMUM_TERMS)
39              {
40                  terms.add(term);
41                  return terms;
42              }
43              term -= index-;
44          }
45      }
46  }
```

The method `main` requires little explanation. It repeatedly allows the user to enter a positive integer and calls `termDecomposition` to form the triangular decomposition of the number input and then it displays the result.

It is the recursive method `termDecomposition` which is of greatest interest. The parameter `number` is the integer to be decomposed. On line 27 the class method `numberToIndex` is called. It performs the calculation defined in Equation 15.11. It returns the index of the largest triangular number less than or equal to `number`. Line 28 computes the triangular number `term` from its index using Equation 15.9. The `if` statement on line 29 checks whether `number` is a triangular number, which is the base case. If so, that number is the first one that is added to `term`, by calling the method `add` of `TriangleTerms`. The method `termDecomposition` then returns the object `term`, which contains that first term.

The remainder of this method is the recursive case. This code is different from anything we have seen until now. It is a loop containing a recursive call. This loop will only iterate more than once if backtracking is needed—meaning the largest triangular number, and possibly subsequent ones, led us down wrong paths. Line 37 contains the recursive call to which we supply the difference of the number we are decomposing and what we have selected as its first triangular term. On line 38 we check whether this path was a fruitful one, which we do by checking whether the number of terms in the recursive decomposition is less than three. If so, we have a solution. In that case we add the integer in `term` to the others and return that collection. If the number of terms in the recursive decomposition is three, we have taken a wrong turn, because adding an additional one would give us a decomposition with four terms, which is unacceptable. In this case, we must backtrack. If we ever execute line 43, we are backtracking. The calculation on that line is computing the next smaller triangular number using the formula in Equation 15.13.

Now we consider the other new class needed for this program, named `TriangularTerms`, whose code is contained in Listing 15.11.

LISTING 15.11 A Class that Defines a Graphic Depiction of a Collection of Triangular
ON THE CD Terms (found on the CD-ROM at `chapter15\TriangularTerms.java`.)

```
 1  package chapter15;
 2
 3  import chapter10.*;
 4
 5  public class TriangularTerms
 6  {
 7      public static final int MAXIMUM_TERMS = 3;
 8      private int[] terms = new int[MAXIMUM_TERMS];
 9      private int termCount = 0;
10
```

```
11      public void add(int term)
12      {
13          terms[termCount++] = term;
14      }
15      public int length()
16      {
17          return termCount;
18      }
19      public static int numberToIndex(int number)
20      {
21          return (int)((Math.sqrt(1 + 8 * number) - 1) / 2);
22      }
23      public void show()
24      {
25          int theNumber = 0;
26          PolygonNTuple polygons;
27          int[] numberOfSides = new int[terms.length];
28          String termString = "", sidesString = "";
29
30          for (int i = 0; i < termCount; i++)
31          {
32              theNumber += terms[i];
33              termString += terms[i];
34              termString += " ";
35              numberOfSides[i] = numberToIndex(terms[i]) + 1;
36              sidesString += numberOfSides[i];
37              sidesString += " ";
38          }
39          polygons = new PolygonNTuple(
40              "Triangular Decomposition of Integers",
41              "The triangular terms of " + theNumber + " are "
42              + termString + "constructed with polygons with "
43              + sidesString + "sides", numberOfSides);
44          polygons.display();
45      }
46  }
```

The code in this class is far more straightforward than the previous one and re-quires less explanation. The instance variables of this class consist of an array of at most three integers, the array terms, declared and instantiated on line 8, and a counter of how many integers are currently in the array, which is the instance variable termCount.

The instance method add adds a term to the collection and length returns how many terms the collection currently contains. The class method numberToIndex implements the formula contained in Equation 15.11, which we mentioned when first encountered a call to it.

Finally, the method `show` constructs a `PolygonNTuple` object containing one regular polygon for each term. The number of sides for a polygon is determined on line 35 using the fact that a polygon with n sides has $\Delta(n-1)$ lines connecting pairs of vertices. On line 44, the window containing these polygons and an appropriate message is displayed.

MAZE SEARCH APPLICATION

Our final example for this chapter again illustrates the concept of backtracking, but in a more visual way, so if you did not fully grasp the idea from the last example, you may have an easier time understanding it after this one.

This example involves a maze consisting of an eight-by-eight matrix of squares. Those squares can be open or blocked. The pattern is to be selected at random. One square is to be randomly selected as the starting point and another as the goal. The program must search for the goal square beginning at the starting point. It stops when one of two things happens—either the goal square has been found or all accessible squares have been examined. Finally, the search process is to be animated. Figure 15.6 shows how the maze should look before the search begins.

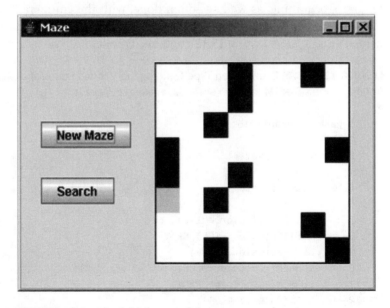

FIGURE 15.6   The initial state of the maze search program.

We have added a requirement that no program we have presented so far has had—animating the search process. So before we proceed to the implementation of this example, we discuss a technique for implementing an animation, which uses an object of the class Timer defined in javax.swing. Let's consider the methods of this class that we need, beginning with the constructor whose signature is shown below.

```
Timer(int delay, ActionListener listener)
```

This constructor allows us to specify a delay in milliseconds and which object will listen for the timer events. Once we have created a timer, we can start it generating events by calling start and we can stop the timer events by calling stop. The signatures of both methods follow.

```
void start()
void stop()
```

When a timer event is generated, the actionPerformed method of the timer's listener will be called. We create an animation by making whatever changes are appropriate for the next frame of our animation and then call repaint to cause that new frame to be painted. We will elaborate on the details required for this particular animation when we explain the class that contains the timer.

Now, let's examine the one enumerated type and five classes that comprise this program, beginning, as we have often done, with the enumerated type. We have elected to define the various states that a square can be in using an enumerated type named SquareState. Listing 15.12 contains its code.

LISTING 15.12 An Enumerated Type Defining the Various States of a Maze Square
ON THE CD (found on the CD-ROM at chapter15\SquareState.java.)

```
 1 package chapter15;
 2
 3 import java.awt.*;
 4
 5 enum SquareState
 6 {
 7     UNVISITED(Color.WHITE),
 8     VISITED(Color.LIGHT_GRAY),
 9     BLOCKED(Color.BLACK),
10     CURRENT_IN(Color.BLUE),
11     CURRENT_OUT(Color.RED),
12     GOAL(Color.YELLOW);
13
14     private Color color;
```

```
15
16      private SquareState(Color color)
17      {
18          this.color = color;
19      }
20      public Color getColor()
21      {
22          return color;
23      }
24  }
```

We are using this enumerated type to create an association between the state of a square and the color that we plan to use to represent that state. Using an enumerated type in this fashion is something that by now should be very familiar to you. Among the list of square states, there are two that require further discussion—CURRENT_IN and CURRENT_OUT. As we animate the search for the goal square, we plan to color the current square with one of these two colors. The difference between the "in" and "out" states indicates when the search is moving "into" the recursion or, when it is backtracking, that the search is "backing out" of the recursion. As we had mentioned earlier, this program provides a visual depiction of backtracking, which you will see when you run it.

The first class we present is one that represents a square location. To accomplish the animation, we will capture a list of square locations that contain the location of the current square. These locations represent the various frames of our animation. Listing 15.13 contains the code for this class.

LISTING 15.13 The Class Defining the Location of a Maze Square (found on the CD-ROM at chapter15\SquareLocation.java.)

```
1 package chapter15;
2
3  class SquareLocation
4  {
5      private int row, col;
6
7      public SquareLocation(int row, int col)
8      {
9          this.row = row;
10         this.col = col;
11         }
12     public int getRow()
13     {
14         return row;
```

```
15        }
16        public int getCol()
17        {
18            return col;
19        }
20        public SquareLocation moveDown()
21        {
22            return new SquareLocation(row + 1, col);
23        }
24        public SquareLocation moveLeft()
25        {
26            return new SquareLocation(row, col - 1);
27        }
28        public SquareLocation moveRight()
29        {
30            return new SquareLocation(row, col + 1);
31        }
32        public SquareLocation moveUp()
33        {
34            return new SquareLocation(row - 1, col);
35        }
36 }
```

A location is defined by the two instance variables, which specify the row and column. In addition to the two methods that allow the row and column to be retrieved, there are four methods that define moving the current square in one of four directions. Each of these methods returns the new square location after the specified kind of move.

Next, we consider the classes necessary to represent the maze itself. We have elected to separate the code related to the searching from the code that defines the current state of the maze. We begin with the latter class, named Maze, shown in Listing 15.14.

LISTING 15.14 The Class Defining the Internal State of the Maze (found on the CD-ROM at chapter15\Maze.java.)

```
1 package chapter15;
2
3 import java.awt.*;
4
5 class Maze
6 {
7        private static final int UP = 20, LEFT = 20, SIZE = 25,
```

```
8           SQUARES = 8;
9      private static final double RATIO = .2;
10     private SquareState[][] squares =
11         new SquareState[SQUARES][SQUARES];
12     private int currentRow, currentCol, goalRow, goalCol;
13
14     public Maze()
15     {
16         for (int row = 0; row < SQUARES; row++)
17             for (int col = 0; col < SQUARES; col++)
18                 if (Math.random() >= RATIO)
19                     squares[row][col] = SquareState.UNVISITED;
20                 else
21                     squares[row][col] = SquareState.BLOCKED;
22         squares[0][0] = SquareState.UNVISITED;
23         goalRow = (int)(Math.random() * SQUARES);
24         goalCol = (int)(Math.random() * SQUARES);
25         squares[goalRow][goalCol] = SquareState.GOAL;
26     }
27     public void clearVisits()
28     {
29         for (int row = 0; row < SQUARES; row++)
30             for (int col = 0; col < SQUARES; col++)
31                 if (squares[row][col] != SquareState.BLOCKED)
32                     squares[row][col] = SquareState.UNVISITED;
33         currentRow = currentCol = −1;
34         squares[goalRow][goalCol] = SquareState.GOAL;
35     }
36     public static Dimension getSize()
37     {
38         return new Dimension(LEFT * 2 + SIZE * SQUARES,
39             UP * 2 + SIZE * SQUARES);
40     }
41     public boolean isVisitable(SquareLocation location)
42         throws GoalReached
43     {
44         int row = location.getRow(), col = location.getCol();
45
46         if (row == goalRow && col == goalCol)
47             throw new GoalReached(location);
48         if (row < 0 || row >= SQUARES || col < 0 || col >= SQUARES
49             || squares[row][col] != SquareState.UNVISITED)
50             return false;
51         squares[row][col] =    SquareState.VISITED;
```

```
52          return true;
53      }
54      public void moveTo(SquareLocation location)
55      {
56          int row = location.getRow(), col = location.getCol();
57
58          if (squares[row][col] == SquareState.VISITED)
59              squares[row][col] = SquareState.CURRENT_OUT;
60          else
61              squares[row][col] = SquareState.CURRENT_IN;
62          if (currentRow >= 0 && currentCol >= 0)
63              squares[currentRow][currentCol] =
64                  SquareState.VISITED;
65          currentRow = row;
66          currentCol = col;
67      }
68      public void paint(Graphics graphics)
69      {
70          for (int row = 0; row < SQUARES; row++)
71              for (int col = 0; col < SQUARES; col++)
72              {
73                  graphics.setColor(squares[row][col].getColor());
74                  graphics.fillRect(LEFT + col * SIZE,
75                      UP + row * SIZE, SIZE, SIZE);
76                  graphics.drawRect(LEFT, UP,
77                      SIZE * SQUARES,    SIZE * SQUARES);
78              }
79      }
80  }
```

We begin with a discussion of the data defined in this class, starting with the class constants. The constants UP and LEFT represent the coordinates of the upper-left corner of the maze. Each square in the maze is SIZE pixels wide and SIZE pixels high. The maze itself has SQUARES rows and columns. The value RATIO defines the average ratio of blocked squares to the number of total squares. The two-dimensional array squares represents the state of the entire maze because it contains the state of each of the individual squares. The pair of instance variables currentRow and currentCol identifies the one square that represents the currently selected square during a search. Although technically redundant, maintaining this information is useful in the method moveTo that is called to move the current square to a new square. Similarly, the pair goalRow and goalCol maintain which square is the goal square—information needed by the method isVisitable.

Now let's consider the constructor, which generates a random maze by randomly selecting which squares will be blocked and which will be free. The nested for loops that span lines 16-21 accomplish this task. The assignment on line 22 ensures that the upper-left square is always designated as free because it is always the starting point. Finally a goal square is chosen at random.

In addition to the constructor, this class has four instance methods and one class method. The first instance method, clearVisits, sets the state of the maze back to the state it was in prior to a search. This method must be called before an animation of the search is begun.

The next instance method, isVisitable, is used during the search process when the list of moves that comprise the search is being generated. The first check that is made by this method is checking whether the goal square has been reached. If so, an exception is thrown. We have deviated somewhat from the traditional use of an exception as an anomalous condition. We hope that this condition will occur. We have taken advantage of the behavior of throwing an exception for another reason. By throwing an exception, we avoid "backing out" of the recursion, which would otherwise occur. Once we find the goal square, we wish for the search process to stop. Your ability to understand how throwing an exception nicely accomplishes this objective is a measure of your understanding of both recursion and exceptions. If the square that we are attempting to visit is not the goal square, we check whether it is able to be visited. If it is within the eight-by-eight grid and is currently in the state unvisited, it can be visited. In that case, it is changed to the state visited to prevent it from being visited again.

The next instance method, moveTo, is called during the animation of the search. It is supplied the square location that is to become the new current location. Because we wish to distinguish between the forward movement and the backward movement—the backtracking—a check is made on line 58 to determine whether the square that it is being moved to has already been visited. It will become clear that this situation is possible when we see the code that generates the list of moves. If the square we are moving to has never been visited, we are moving forward. Otherwise we are backtracking. Finally, the state of the square that was designated as the current square must now be marked as visited and a new current square must be established.

The last instance method is the method paint. It paints each square of the maze the proper color according to the current state of each square.

The one class method, getSize, returns the dimensions of the maze based on the number of squares and the size of each square. It allows for a border around the maze. The class MazePanel, which we examine next, needs this method. That class, whose code is shown in Listing 15.15, defines the panel onto which the maze is painted and contains the code that performs the search and animates it.

LISTING 15.15 The Class Defining the Panel that Contains the Maze (found on the CD-ROM at chapter15\MazePanel.java.)

```
1  package chapter15;
2
3  import java.awt.*;
4  import java.awt.event.*;
5  import java.util.*;
6  import javax.swing.Timer;
7  import javax.swing.JPanel;
8
9  class MazePanel extends JPanel implements ActionListener
10 {
11     public static final int DELAY = 200;
12     private Maze maze;
13     private SquareLocation previousLocation = null;
14     private ArrayList<SquareLocation> moves;
15     private Iterator<SquareLocation> iterator;
16     private Timer timer;
17
18     public MazePanel()
19     {
20         maze = new Maze();
21         timer = new Timer(DELAY, this);
22     }
23     public void actionPerformed(ActionEvent event)
24     {
25         SquareLocation location;
26
27         if (iterator.hasNext())
28         {
29             location = iterator.next();
30             maze.moveTo(location);
31             repaint();
32         }
33         else
34             timer.stop();
35     }
36     public Dimension getMinimumSize()
37     {
38         return getPreferredSize();
39     }
40     public Dimension getPreferredSize()
41     {
```

```
42            return Maze.getSize();
43        }
44        public void newMaze()
45        {
46            maze = new Maze();
47            repaint();
48        }
49        public void paintComponent(Graphics graphics)
50        {
51            super.paintComponent(graphics);
52            maze.paint(graphics);
53        }
54        public void startSearch()
55        {
56            moves = new ArrayList<SquareLocation>();
57            try
58            {
59                search(new SquareLocation(0, 0));
60            }
61            catch (GoalReached goal)
62            {
63                addMove(goal.getLocation());
64            }
65            maze.clearVisits();
66            iterator = moves.iterator();
67            timer.start();
68        }
69        private void search(SquareLocation location)
70            throws GoalReached
71        {
72            if (maze.isVisitable(location))
73            {
74                addMove(location);
75                search(location.moveDown());
76                addMove(location);
77                search(location.moveRight());
78                addMove(location);
79                search(location.moveUp());
80                addMove(location);
81                search(location.moveLeft());
82                addMove(location);
83            }
84        }
85        private void addMove(SquareLocation location)
```

```
86      {
87          if (!location.equals(previousLocation))
88          {
89              moves.add(location);
90              previousLocation = location;
91          }
92      }
93  }
```

The most fundamental component of this class is the object maze, declared on line 12. Other instance variables include an array list of square locations called moves, which is created when the search is performed and used when the search is animated, an iterator to iterate across that list of moves during the animation, and a timer used to pace the animation of the search. We will explain the role of the remaining instance variable, previousLocation, when we discuss the method addMove, which uses it.

The constructor for this class instantiates the objects maze and timer. Notice that when timer is instantiated, the instance of the class MazePanel is registered as the listener for the timer events.

Rather than discussing the remaining methods in the order they appear, as has been our custom, in this case we prefer to discuss them in the order that they will be executed. The method that will be called from the GUI when the button "Search" is pressed is startSearch. It creates an empty array list of moves that will be used by the animation. Then the private method search is called, passing it the square in the upper-left corner, which we always take as the starting square. It is a recursive method and the one of greatest interest to us in this program.

Before finishing startSearch, let's examine how search works. It first makes a call to isVisitable. The base case for this recursive method is reaching a square that cannot be visited, either because it is blocked, it is already visited, or it is the goal square. Notice that this method can throw GoalReached, which is thrown by isVisitable when the goal square is reached. Also noteworthy is the fact that this method calls itself four times—once for each of the four possible directions in which a move can be made. The order of these four calls is unimportant with regard to whether the goal square can be found, although the order may affect how quickly the goal is found in a particular case. No order will find the goal fastest in all cases, however. Another important feature of this method is the presence of the five calls to the private method addMove. The last four calls add backtracking moves. As an exercise that should help you better understand their significance, we recommend commenting out the last four calls to addMove and running this program to see how it behaves differently.

The method addMove adds a move, which consists of the location to which the move was made, to the array list moves. It is possible for addMove to be called with the same square location twice in a row. This can happen when an attempt is made to visit an adjacent square, which is immediately determined to not be able to be visited. By maintaining the previousLocation as an instance variable, we are able to filter out these consecutive moves.

Let's return to the startSearch method. If the goal was reached, the Goal-Reached exception will have been thrown by isVisitable and caught by start-Search. In that case, on line 63, the goal location is retrieved from the exception and added to the list of moves as the final move. We will examine the code for the Goal-Reached exception once we have completed our discussion of the MazePanel class.

Once the search has been completed, either because the goal square was found or because it was not found after visiting all squares reachable from the start square, the search is animated. The method clearVisits must be called first to reset all the squares that were marked visited when the list of moves was being compiled. Next an iterator is created for the list of moves. Finally the timer is started. By starting the timer, we are causing the method actionPerformed to be called at 200 millisecond intervals, which is the value of the class constant DELAY.

The repeated execution of actionPerformed causes the animation to be displayed —one frame of the animation for each move. On each call to actionPerformed, a check is made to see whether the iterator has more elements. If so, the next move is extracted from the array list, and a call is made to the method moveTo of Maze to update the state of the maze to reflect the new current square. Then repaint is called, which causes paintComponent to be called. When the iteration of the list of moves is complete, the timer is stopped.

Finally, when actionPerformed causes paintComponent to be called, it calls the method paint of Maze, which we discussed earlier, to paint the squares the proper colors to reflect their current states.

Next, let's examine the exception class GoalReached, whose objects are thrown by the isVisitable method of Maze and caught by the startSearch method of MazePanel. Listing 15.16 contains its code.

LISTING 15.16 The Exception Class to Define the Goal Reached Event (found on the *ON THE CD* CD-ROM at chapter15\GoalReached.java.)

```
1 package chapter15;
2
3 class GoalReached extends Exception
4 {
5     private SquareLocation location;
6
```

```
 7        public GoalReached(SquareLocation location)
 8        {
 9            this.location = location;
10        }
11        SquareLocation getLocation()
12        {
13            return location;
14        }
15   }
```

Because we want these exceptions to be checked exceptions, this class extends the predefined class Exception. It has one instance variable, which is the location of the square where the goal was reached. The constructor initializes this variable when the exception is thrown and it is retrieved by the method getLocation when the exception is caught.

There is one final class required for this program, which is the class that defines the method main and the GUI. That class is named MazeGUI and its code is shown in Listing 15.17.

LISTING 15.17   The Class that Defines the GUI for the Maze Search Program (found on the CD-ROM at chapter15\MazeGUI.java.)

```
 1 package chapter15;
 2
 3 import java.awt.*;
 4 import java.awt.event.*;
 5 import javax.swing.*;
 6
 7 public class MazeGUI implements ActionListener
 8 {
 9     private static final int GAP = 30, WIDTH = 400, HEIGHT = 300;
10     private JFrame frame = new JFrame("Maze");
11     private JPanel panel = new JPanel(), controls = new JPanel();
12     private MazePanel mazePanel = new MazePanel();
13     private JButton newMaze = new JButton("New Maze"),
14         search = new JButton("Search");
15
16     public MazeGUI()
17     {
18         controls.setLayout(
19             new BoxLayout(controls, BoxLayout.Y_AXIS));
20         controls.add(newMaze);
21         controls.add(Box.createRigidArea(new Dimension(GAP, GAP)));
```

```
22              controls.add(search);
23              panel.add(controls);
24              panel.add(mazePanel);
25              frame.setDefaultCloseOperation(JFrame.EXIT_ON_CLOSE);
26              frame.getContentPane().add(panel);
27          }
28      public void actionPerformed(ActionEvent event)
29          {
30              Object object = event.getSource();
31
32              if (object == newMaze)
33                  mazePanel.newMaze();
34              else if (object == search)
35                  mazePanel.startSearch();
36          }
37      public void initialize()
38          {
39              newMaze.addActionListener(this);
40              search.addActionListener(this);
41              frame.setVisible(true);
42              frame.pack();
43          }
44      public static void main(String[] args)
45          {
46              MazeGUI gui = new MazeGUI();
47
48              gui.initialize();
49          }
50  }
```

This class should require little explanation. The constructor builds the GUI consisting of two buttons and an instance of the MazePanel class. The actionPerformed method responds to the button events. We have used one feature that we have not used before, which is the layout manager BoxLayout. It allows vertical or horizontal layouts. In this case, we chose vertical, which the parameter to the constructor BoxLayout.Y_AXIS indicates. Unlike all the previous layout managers that we have used, gaps are not specified when the layout manager is created. Instead, rigid area objects are placed between objects to create spacing as we did on line 21.

Because this program contains many classes, we provide a UML diagram in Figure 15.7 to be sure you see how each of these classes is related to the others.

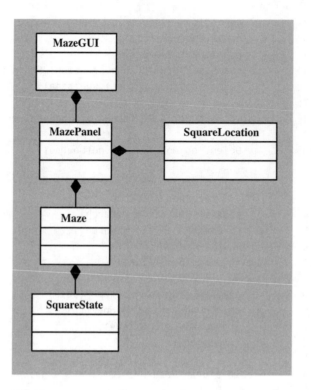

FIGURE 15.7   UML diagram for the maze search program.

SUMMARY

In this chapter, we introduced recursive control structures, specifically recursive methods, which are methods that call themselves. We also encountered our first example of a program that implements an animation. The key points to remember from this chapter are as follows:

- Recursion can be used to solve any problem that can be solved using iteration.
- Recursive methods contain fewer lines of codes and fewer local variables than their iterative counterparts.
- Recursive thinking involves finding a recursive definition rather than an algorithm, which is characteristic of iterative thinking.
- Recursive solutions can be dramatically less efficient in their use of time and memory compared to their iterative counterparts when used for some problems.

- Recursion is most effective and involves the least efficiency penalty when used for problems that cannot be solved with constant memory.
- Recursion is effective when processing nested structures, which are defined by recursive definitions.
- Backtracking, which is needed when searching for a solution to some problems, can be accomplished easily with recursion.
- The Timer class can be used to create animations, where each frame of the animation is painted when successive timer events are fired.

Review Questions

1. What two kinds of cases must every recursive method have?

2. Explain how infinite recursion can occur and describe how recursive methods must be written to prevent it.

3. When you write a recursive method that computes the terms of a numeric sequence, what is normally the base case?

4. What causes some recursive methods to be far more inefficient than their iterative counterparts?

5. In a singly recursive method, what portion of the method is executed on the way into the recursion? What portion is executed on the way out?

6. How can you determine whether a method is singly recursive or doubly recursive?

7. Is it true that doubly recursive methods are always significantly more inefficient than their iterative counterparts?

8. Explain why arithmetic expressions are considered nested structures.

9. What are the characteristics of problems that require backtracking?

10. What method is called when a timer is fired?

Programming Exercises

11. Write a recursive method that computes the nth term of the following arithmetic progression: 1 4 7 11 ..., where each term is 3 more than the previous term.

12. Referring to the nth term of the arithmetic progression defined in the previous exercise as $p(n)$, write a recursive method that computes another sequence defined by the formula:

$$P(n) = \sum_{i=1}^{n} p(i)$$

What sequence of numbers is produced by P?

13. Write a recursive method that computes the *n*th term of the following geometric progression. 1 2 4 8 16 ..., where each term is 2 times the previous term.

14. Write a recursive method that is passed a string as a parameter. It should determine and return a Boolean value indicating whether the string is a palindrome—the same spelled backward as forward.

15. Write a recursive method that accepts a string as a parameter and returns a string containing the same letters in reverse order.

16. Write a recursive method that computes *n*!—*n* factorial. The factorial function is defined as follows:

$$n! = \prod_{i=1}^{n} i$$

17. Write a recursive method that performs a search of an array of integers. It should be provided the array and the integer value to search for. It should return the subscript of the element that contains that value and a −1 if it was not found.

18. Write the insertion sort that was presented in Chapter 7 using recursion instead of iteration.

19. Write a recursive method that returns the smallest value in an array of integers.

20. Use the method in the previous exercise to implement the selection sort, which was discussed in Chapter 7.

Programming Projects

21. Write a program that displays the *n*th term of the function *P* defined in Programming Exercise 12. Incorporate the methods you wrote for the first two programming exercises into a class that implements the Sequence interface defined in this chapter. Increment the counter of Sequence each time either method is called. Make use of the SequenceWindow class presented in this chapter in your solution.

22. Replace the recursive methods in project 1 with an iterative method that computes the function *P*. Determine whether the iterative solution is significantly more efficient than the recursive one by running both programs for a series of different values of *n* and examining the value of the counter.

23. Write a program that displays the *n*th term of the geometric progression using the method you wrote for Programming Exercise 13. Incorporate the Sequence Window class presented in this chapter into your solution as was done in the first several examples in this chapter.

24. Modify the program presented earlier in this chapter that evaluates prefix expressions so that, instead, it evaluates fully parenthesized infix expressions. A fully parenthesized expression has one pair of parentheses for each operator.

25. Using the program that evaluates prefix expressions as a model, write a program that determines whether a string consisting of pairs of delimiters including parentheses, square brackets, and braces are properly matched. An example of a string in which they are properly matched is the following: {()[]({})}. An example of an improper string is]}{.

16 Recursive Data Structures

In this chapter

- Singly Recursive Graphic Images
- Linked Lists
- Doubly Recursive Graphic Images
- Arithmetic Expression Tree Application

SINGLY RECURSIVE GRAPHIC IMAGES

When we first defined recursion at the beginning of the previous chapter, we noted that both control structures and data structures can be recursive. In this chapter, we explore what it means for a data structure to be recursive.

As has been our focus throughout this book, most of the examples that we will examine in this chapter involve graphics—this time recursive graphic objects. Recursive graphic images, which are the images produced by such objects, may be more familiar to you than you realize. If you have ever been in a room that has mirrors on opposite walls, you have seen a recursive graphic image. When you look at either mirror you see that it contains a smaller reflection of itself, which in turn contains a smaller reflection of itself and so on. So recursive objects do not contain themselves exactly, but another object of the same kind.

You may be familiar with *fractals*, which are infinitively recursive graphic images. Recursive objects that can be drawn however, must eventually contain a non-recursive object, just as recursive methods must reach a base case. Keep in mind that our goal will be to draw these objects and that every physical drawing mechanism has finite resolution. So once the size of the object becomes too small to draw with the available resolution, we have reached our base case.

For our first example, we return to one of the first examples that we examined in this book—a triangle in a circle, or stating it in reverse, a circle circumscribed around a triangle. But now, inscribed within that triangle is another circle circumscribed around another triangle, and so on. As is often the case, a picture conveys this idea far better than words. Figure 16.1 shows the output of our first example.

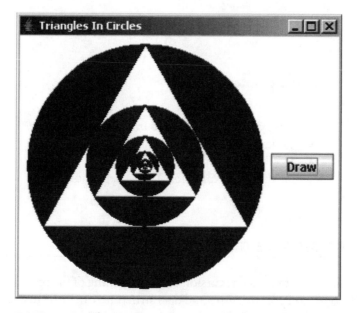

FIGURE 16.1 The output of the recursive triangle in circle application.

This program contains three classes. We begin with the class that defines the recursive object named TriangleInCircle. The code for that class is contained in Listing 16.1.

LISTING 16.1 Class Defining a Recursive Triangle in Circle Object (found on the CD-ROM at chapter16\TriangleInCircle.java.)

```
1  package chapter16;
2
3  import java.awt.*;
```

```
4   import common.*;
5
6   public class TriangleInCircle
7   {
8       private final int VERTICES = 3;
9       private int radius, diameter, center;
10      private Polygon triangle;
11      private TriangleInCircle next;
12
13      public TriangleInCircle(int diameter, int center)
14      {
15          final double ONE_THIRD_CIRCLE = 2 * Math.PI / 3;
16          int[] x = new int[VERTICES + 1], y =
17              new int[VERTICES + 1];
18          double theta = -(Math.PI / 2);
19
20          this.diameter = diameter;
21          this.center = center;
22          radius = diameter / 2;
23          for (int vertex = 0; vertex < VERTICES; vertex++)
24          {
25              x[vertex] =
26                  Geometry.computeX(center, radius, theta);
27              y[vertex] =
28                  Geometry.computeY(center, radius, theta);
29              theta += ONE_THIRD_CIRCLE;
30          }
31          x[VERTICES] = x[0];
32          y[VERTICES] = y[0];
33          triangle = new Polygon(x, y, VERTICES + 1);
34          if (radius > 1)
35              next = new TriangleInCircle(radius, center);
36      }
37      public TriangleInCircle getNext()
38      {
39          return next;
40      }
41      public void paint(Graphics graphics, TriangleInCircle last)
42      {
43          if (triangle == null)
44              return;
45          graphics.setColor(Color.BLACK);
46          graphics.fillOval(center - radius, center - radius,
47              diameter, diameter);
```

```
48              graphics.setColor(Color.WHITE);
49              graphics.fillPolygon(triangle);
50              if (next != null && next != last)
51                  next.paint(graphics, last);
52      }
53  }
```

Most of the instance variables of this class—the radius of the circle and the polygon object, should be familiar. The one instance variable that is especially note-worthy is the instance variable next declared on line 11. Notice that its type is TriangleInCircle, which is the name of the class being defined. It is this instance variable that makes this object a recursive object. In some object-oriented languages, object declarations are not implicit references like they are in Java. In such a language, a declaration of this kind would be improper because an object cannot contain itself. Such a definition would be truly circular and not well-defined. Because object declarations represent references in Java, a declaration of this kind means we are defining a class for objects that do not contain themselves, but a reference to another object of the same class.

Next, let's examine the constructor. None of the code in the constructor should require any explanation aside from final if statement on lines 34 and 35. Let's begin with the call to the constructor on line 35. This call is recursive. It should not be surprising that creating a recursive object requires a recursive call in the constructor. Note that the object being created is being supplied the radius—half the diameter—of the outer circle as the diameter of the inner circle that is being created. The reason the inner circle should have a diameter half the outer circle is because of a geometric property that the diameter of a circle inscribed in a triangle is half that of the circumscribed circle. Fortunately there is a base case; otherwise we would have infinite recursion. When the radius of the inner circle is reduced to one pixel, the circle has degenerated to a point with the resolution of our drawing system. This case is our base case and ends the recursion. It leaves the object next as a null reference.

The method getNext returns the inner object. The need for this method will become clear when we examine the rest of this program. The final method is paint, which draws this recursive object. The caller supplies a parameter, which designates the last inner object to draw. The reason that we supply this parameter is that we wish to animate the drawing of this object showing one new inner object on each frame of the animation. The parameter last enables us to specify how far inward to go with this particular drawing. The last if statement of this method, on lines 50 and 51, is the only part that warrants discussion. Line 51 contains a recursive call to cause the inner object to be painted. The base case is when either the inner object is null or it matches the parameter last.

The second class of this program is the one that defines the panel onto which this recursive object is painted. It also is responsible for animating the painting so that one triangle inside a circle is painted at a time. Listing 16.2 contains the code for this class, which is named TriangleInCircleDrawing.

LISTING 16.2   Class that Animates the Drawing of a Recursive Triangle in Circle Object
(found on the CD-ROM at chapter16\TriangleInCircleDrawing.java.)

```
1 package chapter16;
2
3 import java.awt.*;
4 import java.awt.event.*;
5 import javax.swing.*;
6
7 class TriangleInCircleDrawing extends JPanel
8      implements ActionListener
9 {
10     private static final int DELAY = 400, BORDER = 25;
11     private int size;
12     private TriangleInCircle head, last = null;
13     private Timer timer = new Timer(DELAY, this);
14
15     public TriangleInCircleDrawing(int size)
16     {
17         head = new TriangleInCircle(size - BORDER, size / 2);
18         setBackground(Color.WHITE);
19         this.size = size;
20     }
21     public void actionPerformed(ActionEvent event)
22     {
23         if (last != null)
24         {
25             repaint();
26             last = last.getNext();
27         }
28         else
29             timer.stop();
30     }
31     public void draw()
32     {
33         last = head;
34         timer.start();
35     }
36     public Dimension getMinimumSize()
```

```
37      {
38          return getPreferredSize();
39      }
40      public Dimension getPreferredSize()
41      {
42          return new Dimension(size, size);
43      }
44      public void paintComponent(Graphics graphics)
45      {
46          super.paintComponent(graphics);
47
48          head.paint(graphics, last);
49      }
50  }
```

The instance variable head is a reference to the outermost circle-triangle pair. Because each one refers to the next one inside it, we only need a reference to the first one. What we have is a *linked list* of these circle-triangle pairs. In our next example we more fully explore the significance of being a linked list. The instance variable last is used to keep track of how many circle-triangle pairs to paint.

To help you understand the behavior of this class, we elect to explain it in the order in which the events occur when the animation is initiated—an approach we took with the animation example in the previous chapter. It is a call to the method draw that begins this process. By initializing last to head on line 33, only the outermost pair is painted during the first frame of the animation. Starting the timer begins the animation. Recall that when a timer is started it fires action events at regular intervals, specified by the delay supplied when the timer was created. In this case, the class constant DELAY was provided, which specifies 400 millisecond intervals. Each time actionPerformed is called one frame of the animation is painted. The animation is complete when we have painted the entire linked list of circle-triangle pairs. We know that the entire list has been painted when last has become null, because the next reference of the last element of a linked list is always null. If the entire list has been painted, the timer is stopped. Otherwise, repaint is called, causing paintComponent to be called, and last is advanced to include one more circle-triangle pair the next time by calling the getNext method on line 26. Finally paintComponent needs to invoke the method paint only on the outermost circle-triangle pair referred to by head., because the paint method of the TriangleInCircle class is recursive. It continues to call itself until it reaches the circle-triangle pair referred to by last.

The third and final class of this program is the one that defines the GUI. Listing 16.3 contains the code for that class, named TriangleInCircleGUI.

LISTING 16.3 The Class that Defines the GUI for a Recursive Triangle in Circle Object **ON THE CD** (found on the CD-ROM at chapter16\TriangleInCircleGUI.java.)

```
 1 package chapter16;
 2
 3 import java.awt.*;
 4 import java.awt.event.*;
 5 import javax.swing.*;
 6
 7 public class TriangleInCircleGUI implements ActionListener
 8 {
 9     private static final int SIZE = 250;
10     private JFrame frame = new JFrame("Triangles In Circles");
11     private JPanel panel = new JPanel();
12     private TriangleInCircleDrawing drawing =
13         new TriangleInCircleDrawing(SIZE);
14     private JButton draw = new JButton("Draw");
15
16     public TriangleInCircleGUI()
17     {
18         panel.setBackground(Color.WHITE);
19         panel.add(drawing);
20         panel.add(draw);
21         frame.setDefaultCloseOperation(JFrame.EXIT_ON_CLOSE);
22         frame.getContentPane().add(panel);
23     }
24     public void actionPerformed(ActionEvent event)
25     {
26         Object object = event.getSource();
27
28         if (object == draw)
29             drawing.draw();
30     }
31     public void initialize()
32     {
33         draw.addActionListener(this);
34         frame.pack();
35         frame.setVisible(true);
36     }
37     public static void main(String[] args)
38     {
39         TriangleInCircleGUI gui = new TriangleInCircleGUI();
40
41         gui.initialize();
```

```
42      }
43  }
```

This class contains a `TriangleInCircleDrawing` object and a button named `draw`, which, when pressed, causes the animation of the drawing of the recursive triangle inside the circle.

LINKED LISTS

In our previous example, we mentioned that what we had created was a linked list of circle-triangle pairs—each one containing a reference to the smaller one inside it. Now we will elaborate on linked lists by examining an example in which the presence of the linked list is more apparent, and then create a generic class that can be used for linked lists—regardless of the type of elements that they contain.

Before we study these examples, there are some broader issues that warrant discussion. Linked lists and arrays are two different ways to represent what we might refer to generally as lists—collections of elements that are linearly ordered. Being linearly ordered means each element but the first has exactly one predecessor and each element but the last has one successor. Each representation has its advantages. Using an array allows us to access each element by its subscript. This capability makes it possible to do a binary search of arrays of elements that are sorted by some key. With a binary search the array is repeatedly cut in half until the element is found or there are no elements left. Linked lists have the advantage that elements can be inserted into sorted lists without having to shift all the elements. Linked lists also have the advantage that their size need not be fixed upon instantiation and so they can grow to whatever size is needed. We were also able to achieve this flexibility with arrays, however, by using an `ArrayList` object in place of an array.

Diagrams are especially helpful for understanding both the algorithms associated with linked lists, and they are equally important in simply understanding the basic structure of a linked list. Figure 16.2 contains such as illustration.

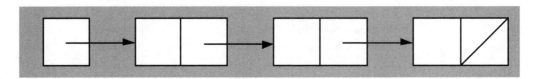

FIGURE 16.2   The diagram of a singly linked list.

Each of the rectangles in the diagram represents a *node* of the linked list. Each node contains some data, which is represented by the left half of each node. In a generic linked list class, we leave the type of this data unspecified. The right half contains a reference to the next node in the list. The diagonal line in the last node symbolizes a null reference. Although we have drawn the linked list showing each node appearing adjacent to the next, they do not need to be adjacent to one another in memory.

Reversing Lines with a Linked List

In the last chapter, we mentioned that problems that require an unbounded amount of memory are well suited to recursive control because they are not substantially less efficient than their iterative counterparts. When these problems are solved iteratively, using a recursive data structure like a linked list is one natural choice. So, let's return to such a problem—the problem of reversing the lines of a file—that we solved in the previous chapter using a recursive method, and examine how it could be solved with iteration using a linked list. The code for this solution is contained in Listing 16.4.

LISTING 16.4 A Program to Reverse Lines Using a Linked List (found on the CD-ROM at chapter16\ReverseLines.java.)

```
1 package chapter16;
2
3  import java.io.*;
4
5  public class ReverseLines
6  {
7      private static class Node
8      {
9          private String data;
10          private Node next;
11      }
12
13      public static void main(String[] args)
14          throws IOException
15      {
16          BufferedReader input = new BufferedReader
17              (new FileReader("input.txt"));
18          String line;
19          Node head = null, node;
20
21          line = input.readLine();
22          while (line != null)
23              {
```

```
24                    node = new Node();
25                    node.data = line;
26                    node.next = head;
27                    head = node;
28                    line = input.readLine();
29                }
30            while (head != null)
31            {
32                    System.out.println(head.data);
33                    head = head.next;
34            }
35        }
36    }
```

The presence of a linked list is more apparent in this example than it was in the first example of this chapter because it contains an explicit inner class named Node that defines the node of the linked list. Notice that in this case, the data portion of the node consists of a string defined by the instance variable data on line 9.

Recall the recursive implementation of this problem for a moment. In that implementation the lines were read in on the way into the recursion and displayed in reverse on the way out. When using iteration to solve such problems, there is often a need for two loops—one to accomplish what happened on the way into the recursion, the other to accomplish what had been done on the way out of the recursion. In this program, we have exactly that scenario.

The loop that spans lines 22-29 reads in the lines of the file and adds them to the head of the list. The new node is created on line 24, the line is copied into the instance variable data on line 25, and the next reference of the new node is set to point the node that was first node until now. The newly created node then becomes the new first node by assigning it to the reference head on line 27. We are constructing this linked list so that the elements are in the reverse order of that in which they are read. Figure 16.3 illustrates this insertion process.

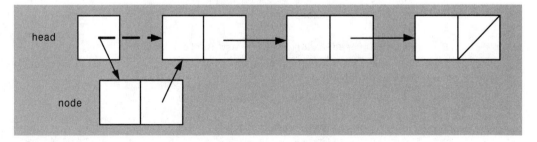

FIGURE 16.3   Inserting a node at the beginning of a linked list.

The loop that spans lines 30-34 displays the lines. It performs a *traversal* of the linked list. Traversing a list means visiting each node of the list in sequence beginning with the first node. Linked list traversals have several common features regardless of what kind of processing is done during the traversal. The first feature is that the while condition checks whether the reference, in this case head, has become null. When it has, we must stop because we have reached the end of the list. The second common feature is the statement, which is typically the last statement in the loop, involves advancing to the next node of the list. In this program, that task is performed on line 33, which sets the reference head to be the next reference of the current node.

A Generic Linked List Class

In Chapter 8, we implemented a generic class for an array list. We are now going to implement a similar generic class for a linked list. Like we did with the array list, we make use of the Java 5.0 feature that allows us to create generic classes. Also similar is the fact that this class allows its users to add new elements to the end of the list and traverse the list using an iterator. The code for this class is shown in Listing 16.5.

LISTING 16.5   A Generic Linked List Class (found on the CD-ROM at
chapter16\LinkedList.java.)

```
 1  package chapter16;
 2
 3  import java.util.*;
 4
 5  class LinkedList<Element> implements Iterable<Element>
 6  {
 7      private class Node
 8      {
 9          private Element data;
10          private Node next;
11      }
12      public class ListIterator implements Iterator<Element>
13      {
14          private Node current;
15
16          public boolean hasNext()
17          {
18              if (current == null)
19                  return head != null;
20              else
21                  return current.next != null;
22          }
```

```
23              public Element next()
24              {
25                  if (current == null)
26                      current = head;
27                  else
28                      current = current.next;
29                  return current.data;
30              }
31              public void remove()
32              {
33              }
34          }
35
36      private Node head, tail;
37      private int nodeCount = 0;
38
39      public void add(Element data)
40      {
41          Node newNode = new Node();
42
43          newNode.data = data;
44          if (tail != null)
45              tail.next = newNode;
46          else
47              head = newNode;
48          tail = newNode;
49          nodeCount++;
50      }
51      public Iterator<Element> iterator()
52      {
53          return new ListIterator();
54      }
55      public int size()
56      {
57          return nodeCount;
58      }
59  }
```

On line 5, notice the parameterized type, Element, which is enclosed in corner brackets. The name Element represents the type of the elements of the linked list. The name Element is just a placeholder, a type parameter, which is replaced by an actual type when a linked list object is declared. On that same line, we specify that this class will provide a method iterator that produces an iterator for these lists.

Like the previous example, this class contains an inner class named Node. The only difference is that the type of the instance variable data is now Element. There is now also a second inner class ListIterator, which is the class that enables us to create iterator objects of the linked list. This iterator class maintains the current position of the iterator in the instance variable current declared on line 14. This variable refers to the node, whose data was last returned by the method next. Consequently, it is initially left set to null. We have made a deliberate choice to have current refer to the last node processed rather than the node about to be processed on the next call to next. By designing the iterator in this way, if nodes are added to the end of the list during a traversal, they will be included in that traversal. This behavior is essential for this linked list class to be useful in our next example.

Now let's examine the two fundamental methods of this iterator. The hasNext method determines whether there is another node to process. Two cases are needed. The first case is when no nodes have been processed, which is when current is null. In this case we must check whether the list has any nodes at all—that is whether head is null. If at least one node has been processed, we then check whether there is a node after the one last processed. The next method uses the same two cases to decide how to advance to the next node. After advancing, it returns the data element contained in what is now the current node.

Next, we consider the instance variables of the outer class—the class that defines the linked list. Because we wish to be able to add elements to the end of the list, we need a reference to the last element of the list, which is what is contained in tail. Because our iterator traverses the list from the beginning, we still also need a reference to the first node, which is what head contains. Finally, because we also provide a method size, which returns a count of how many elements are in the list, we have included the instance variable nodeCount. Maintaining a count of how many nodes are in the list as we add them saves us from having to traverse the whole list and count them when the method size is called requesting that count.

The method add adds a node to the end of the list. As we did in the previous example, which added a node at the beginning of the list, we must first allocate a new node and copy the data into it, which is done on lines 41 and 43 respectively. Because the newly allocated node will be the last in the list, we leave its next reference set to the default, which is null. We must, however, create a lasting reference to this node. We must consider two cases. The first is that this node is actually the first node in the list. In that case the reference head must refer to that node. Otherwise the next reference of what was previously the last node must refer to it. The assignment on line 45 accomplishes the second case. Regardless of whether or not the new node is the first node, it is always the new last node, so the reference tail must be set to refer to it, as shown on line 48. Finally we increment the counter nodeCount. Figure 16.4 illustrates this insertion process in the case that the list already contained some nodes.

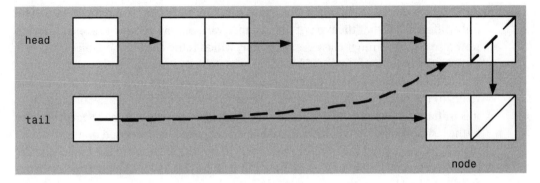

FIGURE 16.4   Inserting a node at the end of a linked list.

We plan to make use of this class in both of the remaining examples in this chapter.

DOUBLY RECURSIVE GRAPHIC IMAGES

A data structure can be singly or doubly recursive in much the same way that methods can. Our final two examples in this chapter will involve such doubly recursive structures. The first of those two involves a doubly recursive graphic image—an image that contains two images like itself. The images that we have selected we call Fibonacci rectangles. These rectangles approximate golden rectangles, which we will explain first. Golden rectangles are rectangles with the property that the ratio of the width to the height is the golden ratio. The golden ratio is defined as the ratio achieved by dividing a line into two parts so that the ratio of the longer part to the shorter part is the same as the ratio of the whole to the longer part. Representing the shorter part as *a* and the longer part as *b*, Equation 16.1 expresses this definition.

$$\frac{b}{a} = \frac{a+b}{b} \tag{16.1}$$

Setting the smaller part *a* to 1, gives us the quadratic equation in Equation 16.2.

$$b^2 - b + 1 = 0 \tag{16.2}$$

Solving that equation gives us Equation 16.3.

$$b = \frac{\sqrt{5} \pm 1}{2} \tag{16.3}$$

So the values for $b \approx 1.618$ and .618. These two roots are reciprocals. What is important about a golden rectangle is that if we divide the width by the golden ratio and the height by the golden ratio, we divide the rectangle into four smaller rectangles. The upper-left and lower-right rectangles are golden rectangles.

The golden ratio is related to the sequence of Fibonacci numbers. The ratio of successive Fibonacci numbers approaches the golden ratio as the numbers get larger. Because the Java drawing system involves integral values for the coordinates, we have elected to draw rectangles we call Fibonacci rectangles, which approximate golden rectangles. A Fibonacci rectangle is one whose height and width are successive Fibonacci numbers. We know each Fibonacci number can be expressed as the sum of the two previous Fibonacci numbers. So by subdividing the width and height into two parts whose lengths are equal to the previous two Fibonacci numbers, we subdivide the Fibonacci rectangle into four rectangles. The upper-left and lower-right rectangles are Fibonacci rectangles, just as was true with the golden rectangles. Figures 16.5 illustrates this subdivision.

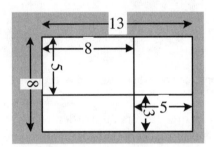

FIGURE 16.5 Dividing a Fibonacci rectangle into two Fibonacci rectangles.

In this program we plan to animate the construction of a recursive Fibonacci rectangle. Because this image is doubly recursive, there is more than one order in which we can animate it. To better understand why, it is helpful to understand that doubly recursive images have a corresponding doubly recursive data structure called a binary tree. The binary tree that corresponds to the recursive Fibonacci rectangle that begins with a width of 13 is illustrated in Figure 16.6.

Each node in this tree corresponds to a Fibonacci rectangle. The number inside the node represents its width.

Unlike a linked list, a binary tree is not a linear structure, so there are a variety of ways that we might enumerate the nodes of such a tree, and so different orders in which we might animate the painting of the rectangles that correspond to each of the nodes. In this example, we choose two different orders—breadth-first and

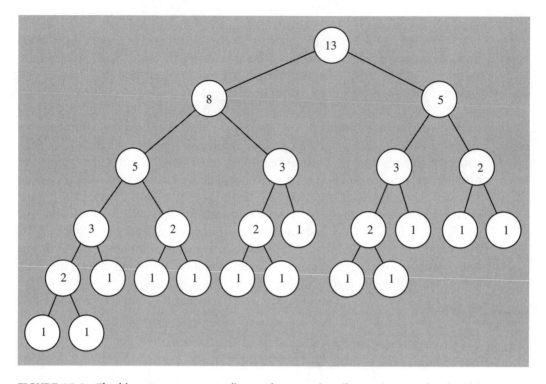

FIGURE 16.6 The binary tree corresponding to the recursive Fibonacci rectangle of width 13.

depth-first. With breadth-first, the order begins at the top of the tree and proceeds level-by-level—visiting every node at that level moving left to right before going to the next level. With depth-first, we travel all the way down the left-most branch first and then back up moving down the right-most branches.

Although we have encouraged you to run all the programs before studying the code, it is especially helpful with this program so you can see the difference between this recursive object being constructed in these two different orders. Regardless of the order in which it is run, the final result is shown in Figure 16.7.

One other characteristic to note about the output is that we have colored the rectangles using different shades of gray. The smaller the rectangle is, the darker its color.

With that introduction, we are now ready to begin to examine the code required for this program. Like the triangle in circle program, we have subdivided this program into three classes. The first of these classes defines the recursive Fibonacci rectangle object. Listing 16.6 contains its code.

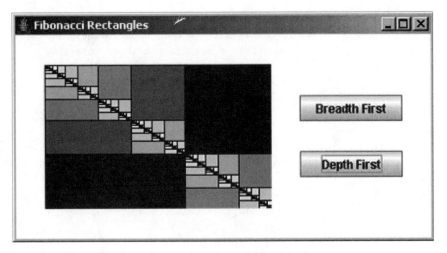

FIGURE 16.7   Output of the recursive Fibonacci rectangle program.

LISTING 16.6   A Class Defining a Doubly Recursive Fibonacci Rectangle (found on the CD-ROM at chapter16\FibonacciRectangle.java.)

```
1   package chapter16;
2
3   import java.awt.*;
4   import java.util.*;
5
6   class FibonacciRectangle
7   {
8       private static final int LIGHTEST = 255;
9       private int x, y, width, height;
10      private FibonacciRectangle upperLeft, lowerRight;
11
12      public FibonacciRectangle(int x, int y, int width,
13          int height)
14      {
15          int upperLeftWidth = height,
16              upperLeftHeight = width - height,
17              lowerRightWidth = upperLeftHeight,
18              lowerRightHeight = upperLeftWidth - upperLeftHeight;
19
20          this.x = x;
21          this.y = y;
22          this.width = width;
```

```
23              this.height = height;
24              if (upperLeftWidth > 0 && upperLeftHeight > 0)
25                  upperLeft = new FibonacciRectangle(x, y,
26                      upperLeftWidth,    upperLeftHeight);
27              if (lowerRightWidth > 0 && lowerRightHeight > 0)
28                  lowerRight = new FibonacciRectangle(
29                      x + upperLeftWidth, y + upperLeftHeight,
30                      lowerRightWidth, lowerRightHeight);
31          }
32          public void breadthFirst(LinkedList<FibonacciRectangle> list)
33          {
34              if (upperLeft != null)
35                  list.add(upperLeft);
36              if (lowerRight != null)
37                  list.add(lowerRight);
38          }
39          public void depthFirst(LinkedList<FibonacciRectangle> list)
40          {
41              list.add(this);
42              if (upperLeft != null)
43                  upperLeft.depthFirst(list);
44              if (lowerRight != null)
45                  lowerRight.depthFirst(list);
46          }
47          public void paint(Graphics graphics)
48          {
49              graphics.setColor(new Color(LIGHTEST - width,
50                  LIGHTEST - width, LIGHTEST - width));
51              graphics.fillRect(x, y, width, height);
52              graphics.setColor(Color.BLACK);
53              graphics.drawRect(x, y, width, height);
54          }
55  }
```

The instance variables for this class consist of the usual four variables needed for any rectangle, which are declared on line 9, and the two recursive instance variables upperLeft and lowerRight declared on line 10. So every Fibonacci rectangle has two Fibonacci rectangles inside it.

The constructor is provided the usual four variables that define the rectangle. It then must subdivide that rectangle into its two component Fibonacci rectangles. The widths and heights of the two components are calculated on lines 15-18. These calculations make use of the fact that when we subtract two successive Fibonacci numbers, the result is the Fibonacci number that preceded the smaller of the two.

This property follows directly from the definition of Fibonacci numbers. Not surprisingly, the constructor is doubly recursive. The base cases are when the sizes of the component rectangles are too small to draw. The two base cases are not reached at the same time, so each must be checked individually.

Before we examine the next two methods, it is necessary to explain how we plan to accomplish the animation. Depending upon the order selected by the user, a list will be compiled that will enumerate the order in which the rectangles will be painted. We are making use of the LinkedList class that we just developed for this purpose. Notice that the parameters supplied to both breadthFirst and depthFirst are linked lists of objects of type FibonacciRectangle. The method breadthFirst simply adds both component rectangles to the list provided that they exist. This method needs to be called many times to accomplish its task. We will see the remainder of the algorithm in the next class. By contrast the method depthFirst needs to be called only once on the outermost rectangle. It is doubly recursive and will add each component rectangle to the list in a depth-first order before returning to its caller. There is a natural correspondence between recursion and depth-first enumerations.

The final method in the class is paint. It is not recursive. It paints only the one rectangle specified by the instance variables on line 9. The color set on lines 49 and 50 is a shade of gray, which is lightest for the largest rectangles. For every rectangle a black hollow rectangle is also painted.

Next we consider the second of the three classes of this program, which defines the panel for the drawing of the rectangle and animates the drawing. Listing 16.7 contains its code.

LISTING 16.7 A Class Defining the Animation of a Doubly Recursive Fibonacci Rectangle (found on the CD-ROM at chapter16\FibonacciRectangleDrawing.java.)

```
1  package chapter16;
2
3  import java.awt.*;
4  import java.awt.event.*;
5  import java.util.ArrayList;
6  import javax.swing.*;
7  import java.util.Iterator;
8
9  class FibonacciRectangleDrawing extends JPanel
10      implements ActionListener
11  {
12      private static final int DELAY = 100, WIDTH = 233,
13          HEIGHT = 144;
14      private FibonacciRectangle rectangle =
```

```
15              new FibonacciRectangle(0, 0, WIDTH, HEIGHT);
16          private LinkedList<FibonacciRectangle> rectangles =
17              new LinkedList<FibonacciRectangle>();
18          private Timer timer = new Timer(DELAY, this);
19          private int rectangleCount;
20
21          public void actionPerformed(ActionEvent event)
22          {
23
24              if (rectangleCount++ < rectangles.size())
25                  repaint();
26              else
27                  timer.stop();
28          }
29          public void drawBreadthFirst()
30          {
31              FibonacciRectangle current;
32              Iterator<FibonacciRectangle> iterator;
33
34              rectangles = new LinkedList<FibonacciRectangle>();
35              rectangles.add(rectangle);
36              iterator = rectangles.iterator();
37              while (iterator.hasNext())
38              {
39                  current = iterator.next();
40                  current.breadthFirst(rectangles);
41              }
42              rectangleCount = 0;
43              timer.start();
44          }
45          public void drawDepthFirst()
46          {
47              rectangles = new LinkedList<FibonacciRectangle>();
48              rectangle.depthFirst(rectangles);
49              rectangleCount = 0;
50              timer.start();
51          }
52          public Dimension getMinimumSize()
53          {
54              return getPreferredSize();
55          }
56          public Dimension getPreferredSize()
57          {
58              return new Dimension(WIDTH, HEIGHT);
```

```
59        }
60        public void paintComponent(Graphics graphics)
61        {
62            int count = rectangleCount;
63
64            super.paintComponent(graphics);
65            for (FibonacciRectangle rectangle: rectangles)
66            {
67                if (count-- == 0)
68                    break;
69                rectangle.paint(graphics);
70            }
71        }
72  }
```

Among the instance variables of this class is rectangle, declared on line 14. It represents the recursive Fibonacci rectangle that is painted on the panel associated with objects of this class. When instantiated on line 15, it's given a width of 233 and a height of 144—two successive Fibonacci numbers. The other instance variables facilitate the animation process. The linked list rectangles contains the linear enumeration of the rectangles that are used during the animation. As with the previous animations, a timer is needed and also a counter, in this case rectangleCount, which contains the number of rectangles within the linked list that are to be painted during the current frame of the animation.

Next let's examine the two methods that initiate the painting of the recursive Fibonacci rectangle in one of the two different orders. We begin with the method drawBreadthFirst. This method adds the individual rectangles to the linked list rectangles in breadth-first order. It starts the process by adding the outermost rectangle on line 35. It then traverses the linked list at the same time it adds new elements. Recall that in our design of the iterator for the linked list class, we designed the methods hasNext and next so that elements added during a traversal would be included in that traversal. That design decision was essential for the correct operation of the drawBreadthFirst method. The loop that spans lines 37-41 creates the breadth-first enumeration. On each iteration, it accesses the next rectangle in the list and then calls the method breadthFirst in the FibonacciRectangle class, which adds its two component Fibonacci rectangles to the list. Once the list is created, the timer is started, as has become customary, to begin the animation.

Next we consider the method drawDepthFirst. Like drawBreadthFirst, it constructs a linked list of rectangles in the order in which they are to be animated during the drawing. Unlike drawBreadthFirst, it relies entirely upon a single call to the method depthFirst in the FibonacciRectangle class, on line 48, to create this list. Then it too starts the timer to begin the animation.

The last method in this class that requires some explanation is `paintComponent`. It is the responsibility of this method to traverse the list of rectangles painting each one with a call to `paint` on line 69. It only traverses the list until the required number of rectangles has been painted. That number is incremented by `actionPerformed` each time a timer event is fired so that one more rectangle will be painted on the subsequent frame of the animation.

The third and final class of this program is the one that defines the GUI. The code for that class is shown in Listing 16.8.

LISTING 16.8 A Class Defining the GUI Containing a Doubly Recursive Fibonacci Rectangle (found on the CD-ROM at `chapter16\FibonacciRectangleGUI.java`.)

```
1   package chapter16;
2
3   import java.awt.*;
4   import java.awt.event.*;
5   import javax.swing.*;
6
7   public class FibonacciRectangleGUI implements ActionListener
8   {
9       private static final int GAP = 30, ROWS = 1, COLS = 2;
10      private JFrame frame = new JFrame("Fibonacci Rectangles");
11      private JPanel panel = new JPanel(), buttons = new JPanel();
12      private FibonacciRectangleDrawing drawing =
13          new FibonacciRectangleDrawing();
14      private JButton breadth = new JButton("Breadth First"),
15          depth = new JButton("Depth First");
16
17      public FibonacciRectangleGUI()
18      {
19          buttons.setLayout(new GridLayout(COLS, ROWS, GAP, GAP));
20          buttons.setBackground(Color.WHITE);
21          buttons.add(breadth);
22          buttons.add(depth);
23          panel.setLayout(new FlowLayout
24              (FlowLayout.CENTER, GAP, GAP));
25          panel.setBackground(Color.WHITE);
26          panel.add(drawing);
27          panel.add(buttons);
28          frame.setDefaultCloseOperation(JFrame.EXIT_ON_CLOSE);
29          frame.getContentPane().add(panel);
30      }
31      public void actionPerformed(ActionEvent event)
32      {
```

```
33              Object object = event.getSource();
34
35              if (object == breadth)
36                  drawing.drawBreadthFirst();
37              else if (object == depth)
38                  drawing.drawDepthFirst();
39          }
40      public void initialize()
41      {
42          breadth.addActionListener(this);
43          depth.addActionListener(this);
44          frame.pack();
45          frame.setVisible(true);
46      }
47      public static void main(String[] args)
48      {
49          FibonacciRectangleGUI gui = new FibonacciRectangleGUI();
50
51          gui.initialize();
52      }
53  }
```

The constructor builds the GUI, which consists of the drawing and two buttons. The method `actionPerformed` responds to the buttons events as we have seen in many other previous examples.

ARITHMETIC EXPRESSION TREE APPLICATION

Our final program for this chapter deals with arithmetic expressions—a topic of one of our examples in the previous chapter. Recall that expressions are nested structures and therefore recursive objects—expressions can contain other subexpressions. This program is an application that allows the user to enter a prefix expression, and then allows the user to perform one of two operations. The user can choose to have the expression evaluated or choose to draw the arithmetic expression tree for the expression animating the ordering of the nodes in one of three traversal orders—preorder, inorder, or postorder. Figure 16.8 shows the output of this program when supplied the same prefix expression after the "Traverse" button is pressed and the "Inorder" radio button is selected.

Because we now allow both an action that draws the tree animating various enumerations and an action which evaluates the expression, we have elected to keep an internal representation of the expression. Being a recursive structure, an expres-

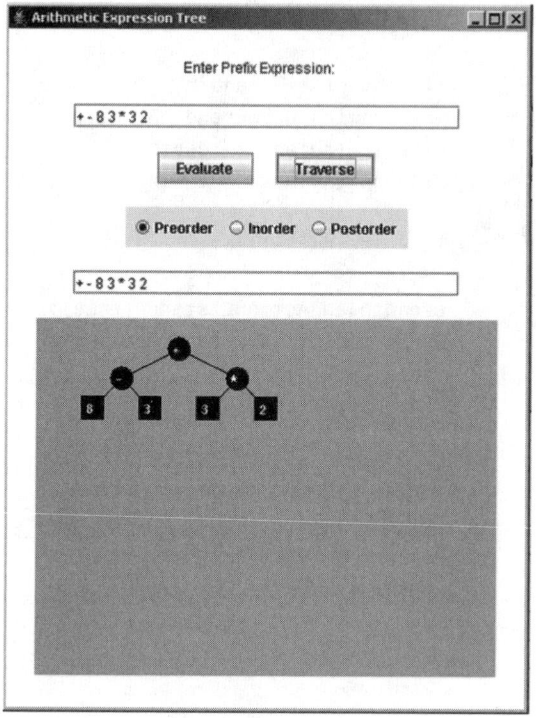

FIGURE 16.8 Output of the expression tree program after requesting and inorder traversal.

sion can be in either of two forms: either an expression containing an operator and two subexpressions, which is the recursive case, or an expression consisting of just a literal value, which is the base case. Consequently, we need a class to define each of those two possibilities and an abstract class from which both of those classes are derived. We begin with that abstract class. Its code is shown in Listing 16.9.

LISTING 16.9 The Abstract Class Defining a Token of an Expression (found on the CD-ROM at chapter16\Token.java.)

```
1  package chapter16;
2
3  import java.awt.*;
4  import java.util.*;
5  import chapter14.*;
6  import chapter15.*;
7
8  abstract public class Token
```

```
 9  {
10      protected static final int SIZE = 20, SPACING = 25;
11      protected static int x;
12      protected Point center;
13
14      public static Token aToken(StringTokenizer tokenizer,
15          int depth) throws SyntaxException
16      {
17          String token;
18          Operation operation;
19
20          do
21          {
22              if (tokenizer.hasMoreTokens())
23                  token = tokenizer.nextToken();
24              else
25                  throw new SyntaxException("Missing Tokens");
26          }
27          while (token.equals(" "));
28          operation = Operation.anOperation(token);
29          if (operation != null)
30              return new Operator(operation, tokenizer, depth);
31          return new Literal(token, depth);
32      }
33      abstract public Point drawTree(Graphics graphics);
34      abstract public void drawToken(Graphics graphics);
35      abstract public int evaluate();
36      public static void init()
37      {
38          x = SPACING;
39      }
40      abstract public String label(LinkedList<Token> tokens,
41          Order order);
42  }
```

This class contains a combination of class data and methods and instance data together with several abstract instance methods. We begin with the class data and methods. On line 11 is the one class variable x. It represents the horizontal position of each node in the arithmetic expression tree. As the internal representation of the expression is constructed, the value of x is incremented by the constant value SPAC-ING. The class method init initializes x and must be called prior to calling the factory method aToken. The variable x cannot be initialized in aToken because it must be done only once for each expression. The factory method aToken and the constructor Operator are *mutually recursive*, so placing the initialization of x in anExpression would cause it to be done more than once. These methods are mutually recursive because aToken calls Operator and Operator calls aToken. Mutual recursion is a special case of the more general *indirect recursion* in which there is a circular chain of method calls of some length.

In Chapter 14, we saw numerous examples of abstract classes that contained a factory method like the method aToken. Its job is to call the constructor of one of the two derived classes based on the next token. The loop on lines 20-27 skips any whitespace tokens. If no more tokens are available while looking for the next non-space token, a syntax error exists, so the exception SyntaxException, whose definition we saw in the previous chapter, is thrown. Because the input to this program comes from the user, there is no guarantee that the expression input will be syntactically correct, so such checks are needed. Next a call is made to the factory method of the abstract enumerated type Operation that we encountered in Chapter 14. If the next token is a valid operator, we call the constructor of the derived class Operator on line 30. Otherwise we call the constructor of the derived class Literal on line 31.

Finally, we consider the instance data and methods. This class has only one instance object, center, which contains the coordinates of the center of either an operator or operand node of the arithmetic expression tree. This object is initialized in the constructors of the derived classes. All four instance methods of this class are abstract. The first one, drawTree, draws the nodes of the arithmetic expression without placing any tokens in the nodes. The method drawToken paints the token, either operator or operand, on its node in the arithmetic expression tree. The method evaluate evaluates the expression and displays the value in one of the text fields of the GUI. Finally, the method label returns a linked list of the nodes of the arithmetic expression tree ordered according to one of the three depth-first enumerations.

Next we consider the two derived classes beginning with the class Operator, whose code is provided in Listing 16.10.

LISTING 16.10 The Class Defining an Operator Token (found on the CD-ROM at chapter16\Operator.java.)

```
1   package chapter16;
2
3   import java.awt.*;
4   import java.util.*;
5   import chapter14.*;
6   import chapter15.*;
7
8   class Operator extends Token
```

```
 9  {
10      private Token left, right;
11      private Operation operation;
12
13      public Operator(Operation operation, StringTokenizer
14          tokenizer, int depth) throws SyntaxException
15      {
16          this.operation = operation;
17          left = Token.aToken(tokenizer, depth + 1);
18          x += SPACING;
19          center = new Point(x, depth * SPACING);
20          right = Token.aToken(tokenizer, depth + 1);
21      }
22      public Point drawTree(java.awt.Graphics graphics)
23      {
24          Point leftCenter = left.drawTree(graphics),
25              rightCenter = right.drawTree(graphics);
26
27          graphics.fillOval(center.x - SIZE / 2,
28              center.y - SIZE / 2, SIZE, SIZE);
29          graphics.drawLine(leftCenter.x, leftCenter.y,
30              center.x, center.y);
31          graphics.drawLine(rightCenter.x, rightCenter.y,
32              center.x, center.y);
33          return center;
34      }
35      public void drawToken(Graphics graphics)
36      {
37          graphics.drawString(operation.getSymbol(),
38              center.x - SIZE / 3, center.y + SIZE / 4);
39      }
40      public int evaluate()
41      {
42          int value = operation.evaluate(left.evaluate(),
43              right.evaluate());
44
45          return value;
46      }
47      public String label(LinkedList<Token> tokens,
48          Order order)
49      {
50          return order.traverse(tokens, left, this, right,
51              operation);
52      }
53  }
```

Objects of this class correspond to an operator token, which sits on a node at the root of a subtree of the arithmetic expression tree that has two subexpressions. The instance variable operation, declared on line 11, represents that operator token. The instance variables left and right, declared on line 10, represent the tokens that correspond to the two subexpressions.

As we have already noted, the factory method aToken of the Token class and the constructor of this class are mutually recursive. Actually this constructor makes two calls, which are indirectly recursive on lines 17 and 20. Although we saw an example of double recursion with Fibonacci numbers, no code was placed between the two recursive calls. This method does have code in that position. On line 18, we advance the class variable x, which then becomes the *x* ordinate of this node of the expression tree. The *y* ordinate is based on depth, which reflects the depth of the recursive calls. Notice that when depth is passed to the factory method on lines 17 and 20, a value one more than the current value is supplied. Increasing its value indicates that we are going one level deeper into the recursion.

Next, we consider the four abstract methods defined in the base class that this class must define beginning with drawTree. Looking at lines 24 and 25, this method appears to be doubly directly recursive. The actual behavior here is a bit more subtle. Because these method calls are polymorphic, we can only say that these may be recursive calls. That determination can really only be made at runtime. If the type of left or right is Operator, then the call is recursive. If the type is Literal, the call is not recursive. Your ability to understand this point is a measure of the degree to which you have mastered the concepts of polymorphism and recursion and how they interact. After the left and right subtrees are drawn by these two calls, a circle is drawn at the center point for this subexpression by the call to fillOval on lines 27 and 28. Next, a line is drawn from the center point of this expression down to the center of the left subexpression on lines 29 and 30. Finally, a similar line is drawn down to the center of the right subexpression on lines 31 and 32. This method then returns the center point to its caller to enable a line to be drawn down to it.

The method drawToken paints the operator symbol on the node of the tree that corresponds to that token.

The method evaluate again exhibits a similar behavior to drawTree. The calls on lines 42 and 43 are potentially recursive. This method computes the value of this subexpression using the values returned by those two calls. It also uses the abstract method evaluate of the enumerated type Operation to perform the actual computation.

Finally, the method label generates a linked list of the tokens in one of three depth-first orders by making a call to the method traverse of the enumerated type Order. We consider the code for that enumerated type, shown in Listing 16.11 next.

LISTING 16.11 The Enumerated Type Defining the Traversal Orders (found on the CD-
ON THE CD ROM at chapter16\Order.java.)

```
1   package chapter16;
2
3   import chapter14.*;
4
5   enum Order
6   {
7       PREORDER
8       {
9           String traverse(LinkedList<Token> tokens, Token left,
10              Token current, Token right, Operation operation)
11          {
12              String leftString, rightString;
13
14              tokens.add(current);
15              leftString = left.label(tokens, Order.PREORDER);
16              rightString = right.label(tokens, Order.PREORDER);
17              return operation.getSymbol() + " " + leftString + " "
18                  + rightString;
19          }
20      },
21      INORDER
22      {
23          String traverse(LinkedList<Token> tokens, Token left,
24              Token current, Token right, Operation operation)
25          {
26              String leftString, rightString;
27
28              leftString = left.label(tokens, Order.INORDER);
29              tokens.add(current);
30              rightString = right.label(tokens, Order.INORDER);
31              return "(" + leftString + " " + operation.getSymbol()
32                  + " " + rightString + ")";
33          }
34      },
35      POSTORDER
36      {
37          String traverse(LinkedList<Token> tokens, Token left,
38              Token current, Token right, Operation operation)
39          {
40              String leftString, rightString;
41
```

```
42              leftString = left.label(tokens, Order.POSTORDER);
43              rightString = right.label(tokens, Order.POSTORDER);
44              tokens.add(current);
45              return leftString + " "     + rightString +
46                  operation.getSymbol();
47          }
48      };
49
50      abstract String traverse(LinkedList<Token> tokens, Token left,
51          Token current, Token right, Operation operation);
52  }
```

In our previous example involving the recursive Fibonacci rectangle, we investigated the difference between a breadth-first and depth-first traversal. In fact there are a variety of different depth-first traversals. Recall from the previous chapter when we first encountered doubly recursive methods we observed that code could be placed in three different places in such methods: before both calls, between the two calls, or after both calls. These three possibilities give rise to the three fundamental depth-first binary tree traversals. If the processing is done before both recursive calls, the result is a preorder traversal. If it is done between them, an inorder traversal is produced. Finally, processing after both calls produces a postorder traversal. The depth-first traversal that we used in the recursive Fibonacci rectangle example was a preorder traversal.

With the preceding explanation, it should now be easy to identify the differences between the code for each of the three traverse methods in the enumerated type Order. But first, let's examine the similarity. Each of the three methods is doubly indirectly recursive. They each call the method label twice, which is an abstract method in Token. The method label in Operator, derived from Token, calls traverse. The first difference between the three is where the call to the method add, which adds the token to the linked list of tokens, is done. In the traverse method of PRE-ORDER, it is done before both calls to label. In the traverse method of INORDER, it is done between calls, and in the traverse method of POSTORDER, it is done after both calls. The other difference between these three methods concerns the string that is returned. Notice first that the two calls to label produce a pair of strings, left-String and rightString. The traverse method in preorder concatenates the operator in front of the concatenation of those two strings, inserting the necessary spaces. So it will return a string for the expression in prefix form—the same form in which it was input. The traverse method in INORDER performs a similar concatenation, except the operator is placed between them, and a left parenthesis is included at the beginning and a right one at the end. The syntax of infix expressions should be familiar because that syntax is what most programming languages, including Java, use. Unlike the prefix expression, an infix expression must be fully parenthesized so that the precedence and associativity rules do not alter its meaning. Finally, you should notice that the traverse method of postorder concatenates the operator after both strings, producing a postfix expression. To help you see the difference between these three forms, the expression from Equation 15.7 is shown in all three forms in Table 16.1.

TABLE 16.1 An Expression in Prefix, Infix, and Postfix Forms.

Expression Form	Expression String
Prefix	$+-8\,3*3\,2$
Infix	$((8-3)+(3*2))$
Postfix	$8\,3-3\,2*+$

If you still do not see the difference between these three orders, be sure to run this program again and watch the how the nodes of the tree are labeled with the tokens using each traversal order and study the form in which the expression string is displayed.

Next, we consider the other derived class of Token, which is Literal. The code for that class is shown in Listing 16.12.

LISTING 16.12 The Class Defining a Literal Token of an Expression (found on the CD-
ON THE CD ROM at chapter16\Literal.java.)

```
1  package chapter16;
2
3  import java.awt.*;
4  import chapter15.*;
5
6  class Literal extends Token
7  {
8      private int value;
9
10      public Literal(String literal, int depth)
11          throws SyntaxException
12      {
13          x += SPACING;
14          center = new Point(x, depth * SPACING);
15          try
```

```
16              {
17                  value = Integer.parseInt(literal);
18              }
19          catch (NumberFormatException exception)
20          {
21              throw new SyntaxException("Invalid Token");
22          }
23      }
24      public Point drawTree(java.awt.Graphics graphics)
25      {
26          graphics.fillRect(center.x - SIZE / 2,
27              center.y - SIZE / 2, SIZE, SIZE);
28          return center;
29      }
30      public void drawToken(Graphics graphics)
31      {
32          graphics.drawString("" + value, center.x - SIZE / 3,
33              center.y + SIZE / 4);
34      }
35      public int evaluate()
36      {
37          return value;
38      }
39      public String label(LinkedList<Token> tokens,
40          Order order)
41      {
42          tokens.add(this);
43          return "" + value;
44      }
45  }
```

Because objects of this class represent the base case of the definition of an expression, we should expect neither the instance data nor the methods to be recursive. Beginning with the one instance variable value, declared on line 8, which is simply an integer value, we confirm the first half of our expectation.

Next, we examine the methods, beginning with the constructor. Just as the constructor of the other derived class Operator, this method must compute the center point for this subexpression, which it does on line 14. This constructor is called by the factory method of Token when the token is not one of the valid operators. The factory method did not establish that the token was an integer. If the call to parseInt on line 17 fails, we catch the NumberFormatException and throw an exception of the class SyntaxException indicating that this token is neither a valid operator nor an integer literal operand.

The remaining four methods behave similar to their counterparts in Operator, except none of them is recursive as we anticipated. One slight difference in drawTree is that we draw the node as a square to distinguish operand nodes from operator nodes.

We have elected to define one additional class for the expressions, which is the class that performs the initialization necessary to start the recursive expression creation. We named this class Expression and have provided its code in Listing 16.13.

LISTING 16.13 The Class Defining an Arithmetic Expression Tree (found on the CD-ROM at chapter16\Expression.java.)

```
1  package chapter16;
2
3  import java.util.*;
4  import chapter15.*;
5
6  class Expression
7  {
8      private Token root;
9
10     public Expression(String expression)
11         throws SyntaxException
12     {
13         StringTokenizer tokenizer =
14             new StringTokenizer(expression, "+-*/ ", true);
15         Token.init();
16         root = Token.aToken(tokenizer, 1);
17         if (tokenizer.hasMoreTokens())
18             throw new SyntaxException("Extra Tokens");
19     }
20     public Token getRoot()
21     {
22         return root;
23     }
24 }
```

This class has one instance variable, which we named root, since it is the top of the expression tree. It contains the first token of the prefix expression. It is created by the constructor and returned by the method getRoot.

The constructor of this class performs those tasks that must be done only once when an expression is created, which include creating the tokenizer from the actual expression string, which it does on lines 13 and 14, and calling the method init, which initializes the horizontal position of the nodes. On line 16, it calls the factory method aToken to construct the internal representation of the expression. If the tokenizer is not empty after the return from that call, the expression has extraneous tokens, so an exception is thrown on line 18.

Now we consider the two classes that construct the GUI for this program. The first of those is the class that defines a panel onto which the expression tree is drawn. The code for that class, named ExpressionDrawing is shown in Listing 16.14.

LISTING 16.14 The Class Defining the Expression Drawing (found on the CD-ROM at chapter16\ExpressionDrawing.java.)

```
 1  package chapter16;
 2
 3  import java.awt.*;
 4  import java.awt.event.*;
 5  import javax.swing.*;
 6
 7  import chapter15.*;
 8
 9  class ExpressionDrawing extends JPanel
10      implements ActionListener
11  {
12      private static final int DELAY = 400, WIDTH = 400,
13          HEIGHT = 300;
14      private static Font expressionFont =
15          new Font("Monospaced", Font.BOLD, 12);
16      private Expression expression;
17      private LinkedList<Token> tokens =
18          new LinkedList<Token>();
19      private Timer timer = new Timer(DELAY, this);
20      private int tokenCount;
21
22      public ExpressionDrawing()
23      {
24          setBackground(Color.LIGHT_GRAY);
25      }
26      public void actionPerformed(ActionEvent event)
27      {
28          if (tokenCount++ < tokens.size())
29              repaint();
30          else
31              timer.stop();
32      }
33      public String draw(String input, Order order)
34          throws SyntaxException
35      {
```

```
36          String expressionString;
37
38          expression = new Expression(input);
39          tokens = new LinkedList<Token>();
40          expressionString = expression.getRoot().
41              label(tokens, order);
42          tokenCount = 0;
43          timer.start();
44          return expressionString;
45      }
46      public int evaluate(String input)
47          throws SyntaxException
48      {
49          expression = new Expression(input);
50          return expression.getRoot().evaluate();
51      }
52      public Dimension getMinimumSize()
53      {
54          return getPreferredSize();
55      }
56      public Dimension getPreferredSize()
57      {
58          return new Dimension(WIDTH, HEIGHT);
59      }
60      public void paintComponent(Graphics graphics)
61      {
62          int count = tokenCount;
63
64          super.paintComponent(graphics);
65          graphics.setColor(Color.BLACK);
66          if (expression != null)
67              expression.getRoot().drawTree(graphics);
68          graphics.setColor(Color.WHITE);
69          graphics.setFont(expressionFont);
70          for (Token token: tokens)
71          {
72              if (count- == 0)
73                  break;
74              token.drawToken(graphics);
75          }
76      }
77  }
```

This class has several instance variables. The first one, `expression`, is the arithmetic expression that is drawn on the panel that this class creates. That variable is declared on line 16 and instantiated in the method `draw` on line 38 and in the method `evaluate` on line 49. The remaining three instance variables are needed to perform the animation. Having done a number of these kinds of animations, the role of those three variables should be familiar.

Calling `draw` initiates the expression drawing and the animation of painting the tokens onto the nodes in the prescribed order, which was supplied as a parameter. It calls the `label` method on line 41 to fill the linked list with the nodes enumerated in that order and to obtain the corresponding expression string. It starts the timer to begin the animation.

As always, `paintComponent` paints one frame of the animation as the timer runs. It first draws the skeleton of the tree by the call to `drawTree` on line 67. Then the loop that spans lines 70-75 paints the tokens onto their corresponding nodes with successive calls to `drawToken` until it reaches the number of nodes that are to be painted in the current animation frame.

The final class for this program is the one that defines the overall GUI and contains the method `main`. Listing 16.15 contains the code for this class, which is named `ArithmeticExpressionTree`.

LISTING 16.15 The Class Defining the Arithmetic Expression GUI (found on the CD-ROM at chapter16\ArithmeticExpressionTree.java.)

```
 1 package chapter16;
 2
 3 import java.awt.*;
 4 import java.awt.event.*;
 5 import javax.swing.*;
 6
 7 import chapter14.*;
 8 import chapter15.*;
 9
10 public class ArithmeticExpressionTree
11     implements ActionListener, ItemListener
12 {
13     private static final int GAP = 20, WIDTH = 450,
14         HEIGHT = 570, TEXT_WIDTH = 30;
15     private JFrame frame =
16         new JFrame("Arithmetic Expression Tree");
17     private JPanel panel = new JPanel(),
18         orderPanel = new JPanel();
19     private JTextField input = new JTextField(TEXT_WIDTH),
20         message = new JTextField(TEXT_WIDTH);
```

```
21      private JButton evaluate = new JButton("Evaluate"),
22          traverse = new JButton("Traverse");
23      private JRadioButton
24          preorder = new JRadioButton("Preorder", true),
25          inorder = new JRadioButton("Inorder", false),
26          postorder = new JRadioButton("Postorder", false);
27      private ButtonGroup orderGroup = new ButtonGroup();
28      private ExpressionDrawing drawing = new ExpressionDrawing();
29      private Order order = Order.PREORDER;
30
31      public ArithmeticExpressionTree()
32      {
33          orderGroup.add(preorder);
34          orderGroup.add(inorder);
35          orderGroup.add(postorder);
36          orderPanel.add(preorder);
37          orderPanel.add(inorder);
38          orderPanel.add(postorder);
39          panel.setLayout
40              (new FlowLayout(FlowLayout.CENTER, GAP, GAP));
41          panel.setBackground(Color.WHITE);
42          panel.setPreferredSize(new Dimension(WIDTH, HEIGHT));
43          panel.add(new Label("Enter Prefix Expression: "));
44          panel.add(input);
45          panel.add(evaluate);
46          panel.add(traverse);
47          panel.add(orderPanel);
48          panel.add(message);
49          panel.add(drawing);
50          frame.setDefaultCloseOperation (JFrame.EXIT_ON_CLOSE);
51          frame.getContentPane().add(panel);
52      }
53      public void actionPerformed(ActionEvent event)
54      {
55          Object source = event.getSource();
56
57          try
58          {
59              if (source == evaluate)
60                  message.setText("Value = " +
61                      drawing.evaluate(input.getText()));
62              else if (source == traverse)
63                  message.setText(
64                      drawing.draw(input.getText(), order));
```

```
65            }
66            catch (SyntaxException exception)
67            {
68                message.setText(exception.getMessage());
69            }
70        }
71        public void itemStateChanged(ItemEvent event)
72        {
73            Object object = event.getSource();
74
75            if (object == preorder)
76                order = Order.PREORDER;
77            else if (object == inorder)
78                order = Order.INORDER;
79            else if (object == postorder)
80                order = Order.POSTORDER;
81        }
82        public void initialize()
83        {
84            evaluate.addActionListener(this);
85            traverse.addActionListener(this);
86            preorder.addItemListener(this);
87            inorder.addItemListener(this);
88            postorder.addItemListener(this);
89            frame.pack();
90            frame.setVisible(true);
91        }
92        public static void main(String[] args)
93        {
94            ArithmeticExpressionTree tree =
95                new ArithmeticExpressionTree();
96
97            tree.initialize();
98        }
99 }
```

There should be little in this class that is unfamiliar. The constructor builds the GUI and actionPerformed responds to the button events. The latter displays the value of the expression when the button labeled "Evaluate" is pressed, and draws the tree and animates the traversal in the order contained in the instance variable order when the button labeled "Traverse" is pressed. That instance variable is up-dated in the method itemStateChanged whenever one of the radio buttons is selected. If a syntax error is generated when either button is pressed, the exception is caught and its message displayed on line 68.

To help you see how the various classes in this program interact, examine its UML diagram in Figure 16.9.

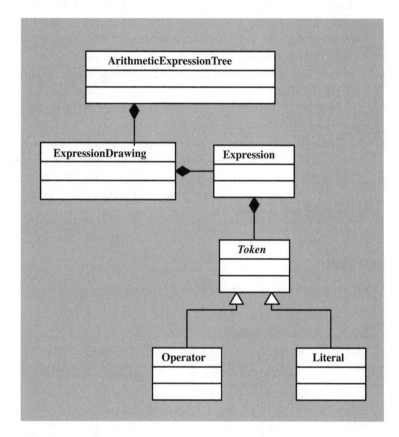

FIGURE 16.9 UML diagram for the arithmetic expression tree application.

SUMMARY

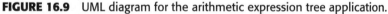

In this chapter, we encountered recursive data structures, which are objects that contain references to other objects of the same kind. Like recursive control structures, recursive data structures must contain some base, nonrecursive objects, so that the definition is not endless. The key points to remember from this chapter are as follows:

- The methods of classes that define recursive data structures are often recursive methods.
- Problems that require unbounded memory to solve can be solved with a recursive data structure and iteration in place of recursive control.
- A linked list is a data structure that consists of nodes that are singly recursive objects. Each node contains a reference to another such node.
- Graphic images are recursive when an image contains one or more smaller images of the same kind.
- A binary tree is a data structure that consists of nodes, which contain two references to other nodes of that kind.
- The two fundamental traversals of binary trees are the breadth-first and depth-first traversals.
- All depth first traversals are naturally implemented with recursion. Preorder, inorder and postorder are the three kinds of depth-first traversals.
- Enumerating the tokens on the nodes of an arithmetic expression tree in pre-order, inorder, and postorder produces an expression written in prefix, infix, and postfix respectively.

Review Questions

1. What is the base case when drawing recursive images?
2. How is a singly recursive image similar to a linked list?
3. When a problem is solved iteratively, using a recursive data structure in place of recursive control, why are two loops often needed?
4. What advantages are there to using a linked list of objects rather than an array list?
5. When traversing a linked list, how do we know that we have reached the end of the list?
6. Explain how a doubly recursive image is similar to a binary tree.
7. Describe the difference between drawing a doubly recursive image using a breadth-first traversal compared with a depth-first one.
8. Explain why the arithmetic expression that is represented by an arithmetic expression tree must be parenthesized when written in infix.
9. In a prefix expression, where is the operator that is evaluated last located? Where is it located in the corresponding arithmetic expression tree?
10. In a postorder binary tree traversal, which node of the tree is enumerated last?

Programming Exercises

11. Write a class defining a recursive image of a circle inscribed inside a square, which contains another square inscribed within the circle, and so on until the image size is too small to draw. Provide a constructor and a method that is supplied a graphics object and draws the image. Figure 16.10 illustrates this recursive image.

FIGURE 16.10   Recursive circle inside a square image.

12. Write class defining a recursive image of a diamond inscribed inside a square, which contains another diamond inscribed within a square. Provide a constructor and a method that draws this image, which is illustrated in Figure 16.11.

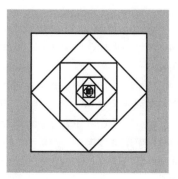

FIGURE 16.11   Recursive diamond inside a square image.

13. Write class defining a doubly recursive image of two rectangles inside a rectangle. The outer rectangle is twice as wide as high. The inner rectangles are twice as high as wide. One is aligned with the left side of the outer rectangle and the other with the right side. Provide a constructor and a method that draws this image illustrated in Figure 16.12.

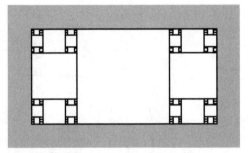

FIGURE 16.12 Doubly recursive rectangles inside rectangle.

Assume the following inner class definition of a linked list of integers for the next four exercises.

```
class ListNode
{
    int data;
    ListNode next;
}
```

14. Write a recursive method that accepts a reference to the head of a linked list as a parameter and displays the values in the list, one per line, on the command line.

15. Write a recursive method that accepts a reference to the head of a linked list and an integer as parameters and returns a count of how many nodes in that list contain that integer.

16. Write a recursive method that accepts a reference to the head of a linked list as a parameter and returns the largest integer in that list.

17. Write a recursive method that accepts a reference to the head of a linked list as a parameter and returns a reference to a copy, which it makes, of the linked list.

    Assume the following inner class definition of a binary tree of integers for the next three exercises.

```
class TreeNode
{
    int data;
    TreeNode next;
}
```

18. Write a recursive method that accepts a reference to the root of a binary tree as a parameter and returns a count of how many nodes are in that tree.

19. Given the following recursive definition of the height of a binary tree, use that definition to write a method that computes the height of a tree given a reference to the root as a parameter.

   ■ Base case: The height of an empty tree is 0.
   ■ Recursive case: The height of a nonempty tree is one more than the height of the larger of the left and right subtrees.

20. Given the following recursive definition of a balanced binary tree, use that definition and the method from the previous exercise to write a method that determines whether a binary tree is balanced.

   ■ Base case: Every empty tree is balanced.
   ■ Recursive case: A nonempty tree is balanced if the absolute difference of the height of the two subtrees is no more than one and both subtrees are balanced.

Programming Projects

21. Modify the program presented earlier in this chapter that animated the recursive triangle in a circle so that it instead draws a recursive circle inside a square. Use the class written in the Programming Exercise 11 in your solution.

22. Modify the program in this chapter that reversed the lines of a file iteratively using a linked list so that it uses the linked list recursively.

23. Modify the program that draws and evaluates arithmetic expressions presented earlier in this chapter so that it displays the height of the tree when a button is pressed. Adapt the method written in the Programming Exercise 19 in your solution.

24. Modify the arithmetic expression application so that it displays whether the arithmetic expression tree is balanced when a button is pressed using the method you wrote for Programming Exercise 20 as a basis for your solution.

25. Modify the arithmetic expression application so that fully parenthesized infix expressions are input instead of infix expressions.

A Answers to the Review Questions

Chapter 1

1. An applet is a program that is embedded in a Web page. It must be executed using a Web browser or an appletviewer.
3. Naming constants can make programs easier to read if well-chosen names are used. Furthermore, it simplifies program maintenance because a change to the value of a constant need only be made in one place.
5. A lexical convention is a standard style that makes programs easier to read. Violating lexical conventions does not result in a compilation error. Syntax rules are rules of the language. Failing to adhere to a syntax rule will produce a compilation error.
7. The method `paint` is called by the Web browser whenever the window that contains the applet needs to be repainted..
9. The programmer must detect any logic errors by comparing the behavior of the program with its expected behavior. Making any change to a program, including fixing a logic error, can always generate new compilation errors.

Chapter 2

1. Randomly generated values make programs produce different output on different executions of the program.
3. Java expressions are written in plain text, so there is no way to graphically depict the implied parentheses. Division lines and root lines imply parentheses.

5. If i and j are integer variables, it would be necessary to type cast one of them to be double so as to not lose the remainder in a division. For example (double)i / j.

7. A void method call cannot be placed inside a compound expression because a call to a void method does not return a value.

9. Java requires explicit type casting on narrowing conversions to force the programmer to acknowledge that a loss of data can occur in such assignments.

Chapter 3

1. Declarations that are inside a method are local declarations. Declarations inside the class but outside any method are instance declarations.

3. The scope of a private instance variable includes all methods of that class and any instance declarations that follow it. Its lifetime is the lifetime of the object to which it belongs.

5. A method of a class should be made private when other methods of the same class are the only ones who need to call it.

7. Making all instance variables private hides the representation of objects of that class and ensures loose coupling with other classes.

9. A value-returning method is required to return a value to its caller, which is accomplished by a return statement. Because the return statement also returns control to the caller, the return statement must be the last statement executed.

Chapter 4

1. The tab character is an example of a character that has no corresponding glyph. Such characters are written using an escape sequence that begins with the backslash character. The tab character is written as '\t'.

3. The symbol used to specify string concatenation is the + operator. Any kind of data can be concatenated onto strings using this operator.

5. Programs that do not allow user input are uninteresting because they behave the same each time they are run.

7. The restriction that is placed on the case expressions is that they must be constant expressions—ones able to be evaluated at compile time.

9. A for statement iterates across all the values of an enumerated type in the order that they are defined in the enumerated type definition.

Chapter 5

1. A Java application is a complete program that can be run independently. A Java applet must be run from a Web browser or from an applet viewer.

3. The reserved word new signifies a request for dynamic allocation of memory.

5. The compiler examines the type and number of the arguments in a method call and matches the call to the signature of all the overloaded methods with that name. It chooses the one whose signature most closely matches to the method call.

7. A shallow copy copies only references. A deep copy copies values. Assignments of primitives are deep copies. Assignments of objects are shallow copies.

9. Automatic garbage collection reclaims the memory allocated to garbage so that memory is available to be allocated to other objects.

Chapter 6

1. The result of an inclusive *or* is true when both operands are true. An exclusive *or* is false in that case. The logical operator || is inclusive.

3. Because strings are object references comparing them using the == operator compares their addresses, not their values. The method equals should be used instead.

5. Logical operators short-circuit when the result can be determined by the left operand alone. In that case, the right operand is not evaluated. A conjunction short-circuits when the left operand is false. A disjunction short-circuits when the left operand is true.

7. The if statement is more general. An if condition can involve data of any type. A switch condition can only involve discrete type data.

9. The words *while* and *until* are logical opposites.

Chapter 7

1. Using the traditional for statement to iterate across the elements of an array requires a loop control variable and a reference to .length to determine the number of elements in the array. The *for-each* syntax requires neither a loop control variable nor a reference to .length, but its use is restricted to loops in which the elements are referenced only and not modified.

3. When a prefix increment or decrement operator is placed on a variable that is an array subscript, the variable is incremented or decremented, respectively, before it is used as the subscript. When it is in postfix position, the variable is incremented or decremented after it is used as a subscript.

5. After an array of objects is declared and instantiated, it is still necessary to instantiate each of the objects in the array.

7. Meaningful data in an array can be sent out of a method by either changing the values of the array parameter or by returning a new array using a return statement.

9. A class constant must be used when a constant must be shared by several class methods of a class that has no instantiated objects.

Chapter 8

1. Generic classes define classes that are type independent and can therefore be used for a range of different types. They avoid having to make a separate copy of the class for every particular type for which it will be used.
3. In languages that allow method parameters, the method to be called back when an event occurs can be passed to the method that registers the event handler.
5. An inner class is appropriate when some method of an outer class needs to create an object whose methods need to access the private instance variables of the outer class.
7. Generic arguments must be class types and cannot be primitive types. When a primitive type is required, its corresponding wrapper class must be used instead.
9. The method `hasNext` returns whether there are more elements remaining in the iteration and `next` returns the next element.

Chapter 9

1. The `String` class does not provide a method for modifying particular characters within a string because `String` objects are immutable.
3. A −1 is a reasonable sentinel value for the method `indexOf` to return when the specified character is not in the string, because −1 cannot be a valid subscript.
5. In regular expressions, parentheses are used as a grouping mechanism, whereas square brackets are used to define a collection of characters from which one can be chosen.
7. The reason that we can conclude that the class `InputFile` implements the interface `Iterable` is because we are able to use the *for-each* style `for` loop to iterate across the lines in the file.
9. It is more efficient to use the `StringBuffer` class than the `String` class when we wish to modify individual characters within a string.

Chapter 10

1. Composition relationships are implemented by making the component objects instance objects of the containing class.
3. The constructor of the containing class generally calls the constructor of the component class to create the component objects.
5. The reserved word `static` is used to distinguish class variables from instance variables.
7. When a class variable is initialized in its declaration, that initialization is performed when the class is created.

9. When a static import is used, the names of the imported data and methods can be used without qualification.

Chapter 11

1. Exceptions provide a technique for handling unexpected errors without the need for every method to return an error flag.
3. To read from an input file, it is necessary to open the file by creating a `File Reader` object, which must then be used to create a `BufferedReader`. To write to an output file, it is necessary to open the file by creating a `FileWriter` object, which must then be used to create a `PrintWriter`.
5. The reserved word `throw` is used in the `throw` statement to cause an exception to be thrown. The reserved word `throws` is used in a method signature to indicate that the method may throw particular exceptions.
7. When requesting input at the command line, it is necessary to always prompt the user first; otherwise the user may not realize that input is expected.
9. The `StreamTokenizer` accepts input from an input stream and actually returns tokens when the method to extract the next token is called. The `StringTokenizer` accepts its input from a string and it returns only lexemes when the method to extract the next token is called.

Chapter 12

1. A derived class can access the public and protected instance variables of their base classes, but not the private ones.
3. The reason that Java cannot determine whether some type casts are improper until runtime is that the actual type of the object may not be able to be determined until runtime.
5. Inherited methods typically need to be overridden when the method must access data that was added to the derived class.
7. Multiple inheritance of classes causes ambiguity when a class is derived from two classes that have a common ancestor.
9. With a composition relationship, the object and its component object have the same lifetime. With an aggregation relationship, the component object typically has a longer lifetime than the object in which it is contained.

Chapter 13

1. There is no maximum number of dimensions permitted for an array.
3. A ragged array is useful for implementing a triangular matrix.
5. Panels are used to group GUI components. Each panel has its own layout manager.

7. No interaction is available with labels. They provide a display of constant text. Text fields can be used for input and output of text. Buttons are used to trigger events.
9. Many programming languages permit methods to be passed as parameters, but Java does not.

Chapter 14

1. Besides abstract classes and enumerated types, abstract methods can also appear in interfaces.
3. Objects of abstract classes cannot be created because the constructors of an abstract class can only be called by the constructors of its derived classes.
5. An abstract enumerated type should be used when the objects that have an *is a* relationship with the type are singleton objects, not collections of objects.
7. Utility classes have no data associated with them. Singleton classes generally have class variables that define the state of the singleton object.
9. The ItemListener interface must be implemented to handle events associated with radio buttons.

Chapter 15

1. Every recursive method must have at least one base case and at least one recursive case.
3. The base case for recursive methods that compute the terms of a numeric sequence is usually the first term of the sequence or the first several terms.
5. In a singly recursive method, the code before the recursive call is executed on the way into the recursion and the code after the recursive call is executed on the way out.
7. It is not true that doubly recursive methods are always more inefficient than their iterative counterparts. The inefficiency of recursion is unrelated to the number of recursive calls that are contained with the method.
9. Problems for which it is difficult to decide which path in a decision tree to take typically require backtracking.

Chapter 16

1. The base case when drawing recursive images is when the image becomes too small to draw.
3. When a problem is solved iteratively using a recursive data structure, one loop is often needed to replace the actions that were performed on the way into the recursion and a second loop is needed to duplicate what was performed on the way out.

5. When traversing a linked list, we know that we have reached the end of the list when the `next` reference is `null`.

7. When drawing a doubly recursive image using a breadth-first traversal, the larger images are drawn first. When drawn depth-first, all the images inside a particular image are drawn before the adjacent ones.

9. In a prefix expression, the first operator is the one that is evaluated last. It is located at the root of the corresponding arithmetic expression tree.

B | About the CD-ROM

The CD-ROM contains all the Java source code, HTML files for applets, and sample input files for all the programs contained in this book. The directories are organized according to the package structure used throughout the book. In addition, there is a directory named `figures`, which contains all the figures in the book. That directory contains a subdirectory for each chapter.

More detailed information about the files on the CD-ROM can be found on the disc in the "About the CD-ROM" document.

SYSTEM REQUIREMENTS

- Windows XP, 2000, 98 Second Edition, ME, Server 2003
- Mozilla 1.4+, Netscape, or IE 5.5
- 35 MB hard drive space (this includes room to copy the figures)

All Java programs contained on this CD-ROM must be compiled with the Java 2 Platform Standard Edition 5.0 (J2SE 5.0) compiler. Note that this CD-ROM contains only source code. All programs, including the applets, must be compiled before they can be run.

Index